THE
COMMUNICATION
PLAYBOOK

We dedicate this book to our children, Matthew, a scientist, and Lindsay, an attorney, and their partners Tong and Daniel. We also write it in the memory of our parents, Martha and Marcel Kwal, and Nan and Wesley Gamble, and for our grandchild, Beckham Myles, who came into our lives last year, joyously reminding us of the magic of the cycle of life. Every day in Beckham's life is an adventure, as it should be for us all.

Sara Miller McCune founded SAGE Publishing in 1965 to support the dissemination of usable knowledge and educate a global community. SAGE publishes more than 1000 journals and over 800 new books each year, spanning a wide range of subject areas. Our growing selection of library products includes archives, data, case studies and video. SAGE remains majority owned by our founder and after her lifetime will become owned by a charitable trust that secures the company's continued independence.

Los Angeles | London | New Delhi | Singapore | Washington DC | Melbourne

THE
COMMUNICATION
PLAYBOOK

TERI KWAL
GAMBLE
*College of
New Rochelle*

MICHAEL W.
GAMBLE
*New York Institute
of Technology*

Los Angeles | London | New Delhi
Singapore | Washington DC | Melbourne

FOR INFORMATION:

SAGE Publications, Inc.
2455 Teller Road
Thousand Oaks, California 91320
E-mail: order@sagepub.com

SAGE Publications Ltd.
1 Oliver's Yard
55 City Road
London EC1Y 1SP
United Kingdom

SAGE Publications India Pvt. Ltd.
B 1/I 1 Mohan Cooperative Industrial Area
Mathura Road, New Delhi 110 044
India

SAGE Publications Asia-Pacific Pte. Ltd.
3 Church Street
#10-04 Samsung Hub
Singapore 049483

Acquisitions Editor: Terri Accomazzo
Editorial Assistant: Sarah Wilson
Content Development Editors: Sarah Calabi and
                               Jennifer Jovin
Production Editor: Andrew Olson
Copy Editor: Colleen Brennan
Typesetter: C&M Digitals (P) Ltd
Proofreader: Dennis W. Webb
Indexer: Sheila Bodell
Cover Designer: Scott Van Atta
Marketing Manager: Staci Wittek

Copyright © 2019 by SAGE Publications, Inc.

All rights reserved. No part of this book may be reproduced or utilized in any form or by any means, electronic or mechanical, including photocopying, recording, or by any information storage and retrieval system, without permission in writing from the publisher.

Printed in the United States of America

Library of Congress Cataloging-in-Publication Data

Names: Gamble, Teri Kwal, author. | Gamble, Michael, author.

Title: The communication playbook / Teri Kwal Gamble, Michael W. Gamble.

Description: Los Angeles : Sage, [2019] | Includes bibliographical references and index.

Identifiers: LCCN 2018021124 | ISBN 9781544337807 (spiral)

Subjects: LCSH: Communication—Textbooks.

Classification: LCC P90 .G2986 2019 | DDC 302.23—dc23
LC record available at https://lccn.loc.gov/2018021124

This book is printed on acid-free paper.

21 22 10 9 8 7 6 5 4 3

Brief Contents

Detailed Contents

iStock/DMEPhotography

iStock/mapodile

Chapter 4: Communicating With Words: Helping Minds Meet 80

iStock/shapecharge

Maria Symchych/
Shutterstock.com

iStock/MangoStar_Studio

Iryna Inshyna/
Shutterstock.com

Jacob Lund/
Shutterstock.com

**Chapter 8: Person to Person:
Handling Emotions and Conflict 196**

iStock/Jacob
Ammentorp Lund

iStock/Tinpixels

iStock/recep-bg

iStock/Jacob
Ammentorp Lund

Chapter 12: Researching, Supporting, and Outlining Your Speech 314

iStock/gilaxia

**Chapter 13: Using Presentation
Aids and Delivering Your Speech 350**

iStock/monkey business images

Preface

The Communication Playbook is *the* text for the hybrid communication course designed to meet the complex needs of 21st-century communicators—those concerned with how to present themselves to others across the communication spectrum, whether face-to-face, using social media, in workspaces and workplaces, or in public.

How might those who matter in your life describe for others what it's like to interact with you? Might they describe you as being present or distracted, empathetic or distant? How might they describe your behavior as coworker or team member? Might they assess you as cooperative and collaborative or instead report that you come off as self-concerned and a blocker? What words might people listening to you use to describe your presentation skills? Might they find you to be prepared and persuasive or ill-prepared and uninspiring? And were you to switch roles with them, how might those individuals describe you as a member of their audience? Might they report you to be attentive and encouraging or bored and disengaged? In each case, the adjectives others attribute to you is how you come across to them.

We 21st-century communicators face complex challenges. Each of us bears personal and social responsibility for developing, sharing, and managing a unique identity—the composite of characteristics we place on display in both physical and online worlds. Effectively, we create both a real-world or face-to-face identity and a digital-world or virtual identity for others to consume. It is as we navigate between these two spaces—the physical and the digital—that we shape our unique and personal communication presence, influencing the nature and course of our relationships and perceived communication effectiveness both online and offline.

Our goal in writing *The Communication Playbook*, of course, is for the communication presence you become known for in your personal life, in the workplace, and in your community to be positive and success enhancing. Becoming adept at connecting with others, whether you actually are in their presence or digitally dispersed, is a skill to be mastered. As such, this text seeks to help you present yourself as competently and confidently as possible in the communication arenas you frequent. Although various means of communication may become more popular than others at different times in our lives, for better or worse, they all evolve. *The Communication Playbook* shows you how to make communication work across the spectrum of available communication channels. Ultimately, because the communication presence you present and share in social, civic, and professional arenas and personal, group, and public settings affects your relationships and life satisfaction, we believe that you never can become too effective at communicating.

THE STRATEGY OF THE COMMUNICATION PLAYBOOK

The Communication Playbook coaches you to personal and career success, guiding you in learning to use and manage an authentic and effective communication toolset that will serve you today and in the future. How skillful you are at communicating as you navigate different life arenas influences how others in your social, professional, and civic spheres perceive and respond to you.

What are the competencies you need to master for others to perceive you as having value? What are the skills you need to hone to be considered an effective communicator? What are the understandings you need to develop as you navigate from one life arena to another? These are the questions we answer in this new outcomes- and skills-based hybrid text for the introductory communication course.

The Communication Playbook explores communication basics and key life arenas, highlighting the outcomes you need to achieve to become proficient in the essentials of communication; interpersonal communication and interviewing; group communication, leadership/teambuilding, and problem solving; and the preparation, practice, and delivery of public presentations. To accomplish this, *The Communication Playbook* investigates the communication domains and practices of 21st-century communicators and identifies steps to take, skills to master, and understandings to apply to build and manage a unique and value-laden communication presence, one that is authentic and approachable and that enables you to develop and maintain meaningfully effective personal, community, and work relationships.

TO THE INSTRUCTOR: WHAT DIFFERENTIATES *THE COMMUNICATION PLAYBOOK* FROM OTHER HYBRID TEXTS ON THE MARKET?

The Communication Playbook incorporates some of the successful material that our best-selling textbook *Communication Works* was known for. However, we also have given *The Communication Playbook* a renewed focus and fresh content, making it a particularly useful and relevant text for the hybrid course.

A prime differentiator of *The Communication Playbook* is our highlighting the importance of both the physical and the digital domains in students' lives. We coach students in conceptualizing, creating, cultivating, and communicating an authentic communication presence to foster success not only in their personal relationships online and offline but in their careers and civic lives as well. Although other texts may cover similar topics, none place students in personal control of how others value and perceive them—even though that is what happens as they engage others in both the physical and digital worlds. As Amazon founder Jeff Bezos has said, "Branding is what people say about you when you're not in the room." We wrote this text so individuals with whom students interact in any life arena will have good things to say about them both to their faces and in their absence. We wrote this text so that those with whom our students interact are able to perceive their value and open doors and opportunities for them. We want our students to learn more about themselves as communicators—to develop empathy and perspective-taking so that they may envision how they affect others, to tap into existing talents and build communication skills that facilitate goal achievement, and to chart a course that nurtures the continual improvement of their authentic and unique communication presence.

In addition, woven through *The Communication Playbook* are the following proven pedagogical techniques:

- A series of objectives and desired outcomes designed to facilitate personal development in communication
- A selection of individual and group activities and self-assessments built to foster engagement
- A series of personal goals for students to realize as they build their communication presence and develop communication skills and competence
- End-of-chapter checklists and word-mastery lists that guide students in reviewing and demonstrating learning.

Four thematic threads are woven through *The Communication Playbook*:

1. A concern for communicating ethically
2. A focus on multiculturalism and global and gender self-awareness, particularly what it takes to be comfortable engaging with people who are culturally and ideologically diverse
3. A consideration of how technology and social networks impact every communication arena
4. An exploration of how to build bridges of understanding among those with whom we engage socially, professionally, and civically

To this end, *The Communication Playbook* also contains a series of highlighted boxes within its chapters.

Skill Builders: Learning activities for use inside or outside of class. Skill Builders encourage students to observe and consider their own and others' face-to-face and digital communication practices, to assess their effects, and to experience the insights and practice they need to become more skillful communicators.

Career Builders: Exercises and checklists exploring the relationship between communication skills and career success.

Exploring Diversity: Activities designed to help students explore the connections between culture, gender, and communication.

Ethics and Communication: Experiential vehicles designed to help students work their way through ethical quandaries and define for themselves the meaning of "ethical communication."

Each boxed series is designed to promote critical inquiry and reflection as it challenges students to complete and analyze self-inventories, assess how advances in technology are reshaping communication, and become actively involved in meeting 21st-century communication challenges and designing a "future me"—envisioning and demonstrating how improving communication skills paves a path to personal and professional success.

We hope students and instructors enjoy using *The Communication Playbook* as much as we enjoyed working on it!

All our best,

Teri and Michael Gamble

Acknowledgments

It is such a pleasure to work with the professionals at SAGE that it makes it difficult to single out who to thank because the work that all the folks at SAGE do is seamless. From the firm commitment given this project by Matthew Byrnie; to the unyielding support and fresh ideas provided by acquisitions editor Terri Accomazzo, who believed in this project from the get-go; to the understanding, creativity, and insights provided by content developmental editors Sarah Calabi and Jennifer Jovin; the team behind *The Communication Playbook* has been phenomenal. We also want to offer a shout-out to the painstaking efforts of production editor Andrew Olson and copy editor Colleen Brennan, who asked all the right questions and helped to ensure the book's readability and accuracy. But what would a text be without its design team? We would like to offer a very special thanks to them: C&M Digitals and cover designer Scott Van Atta.

We are also grateful to the many talented faculty who read our book, offering their suggestions and making this edition a better one. These individuals include:

Chantele Carr, *Estrella Mountain Community College*

Yvonne M. Fielder, *Des Moines Area Community College*

Sean McPherson, *Massachusetts Maritime Academy*

Emily Richardson, *University of Pikeville*

David Scales, *Naugatuck Valley Community College*

About the Authors

Teri Kwal Gamble, a full professor of communication at the College of New Rochelle in New Rochelle, New York (PhD, New York University; MA and BA, Lehman College CUNY), and **Michael W. Gamble**, a full professor of communication at the New York Institute of Technology in New York City (PhD, New York University; BA and MFA, University of Oklahoma) are long-time partners in life and work.

Professional writers of education and training materials, the Gambles are the coauthors of numerous text and trade books. Their most recent publication was the second edition of the *Public Speaking Playbook* (2018). Among some of the other books the Gambles have written are *Nonverbal Messages Tell More: A Practical Guide to Nonverbal Communication* (2017), *The Gender Communication Connection* (2nd ed., 2014), and *Leading With Communication* (2013).

Prior to Michael's career as a college professor, he served as an officer and taught leadership skills for the U.S. Army Infantry School. Together, Teri and Mike founded Interact Training Systems, a communication consulting firm. They love living and working together!

iordani/Shutterstock.com

1

Start Right Here

**AFTER COMPLETING THIS CHAPTER,
YOU SHOULD BE ABLE TO:**

1.1 Discuss the nature of "communication presence."

1.2 Define communication.

1.3 Explain the essential elements of communication and their interaction.

1.4 Use a transactional model of communication to visualize the communication process in action.

1.5 Describe the core principles of good communication.

1.6 Evaluate the benefits of communicating effectively.

1.7 Apply skills for improving your communication effectiveness.

Communication—the human connection, is the key to personal and career success.

Paul J. Meyer

Be brutally honest. Do you spend any of your free time thinking about communication? More specifically, have you ever imagined the words others might choose to describe you as a communicator? Take a moment and do that now. After engaging in conversation with you, might others say that you were present or distracted, authentic or fake, empathetic or distant? How are they likely to describe your behavior as a coworker or team member? Might they see you as cooperative and collaborative, or would they instead judge you to be self-concerned and a blocker? What words might those in an audience you were speaking to use to describe your speech-making abilities? Would they find you prepared and persuasive or ill prepared and uninspiring? And when roles were switched, how might other speakers describe you as a member of their audience? Might they report that you were attentive and encouraging, or would they perceive you to be bored or "out-to-lunch"? In each case, the adjectives others attribute to you, how you come across to them, are your communication presence.

Our goal is to help you make communication work as effectively as you can in all the social and professional settings you frequent, whether you are engaging with others online or face-to-face. With this in mind, welcome to *The Communication Playbook*, your resource for communication skills for life and career success. ■

WHAT IS COMMUNICATION PRESENCE?

We 21st-century communicators face complex challenges. Each of us bears personal and social responsibility for developing, sharing, and then managing a unique identity or

communication presence—the composite of characteristics we present both in the physical and online world. Effectively, we each create a real-world or face-to-face identity and a digital-world or virtual identity for others to consume. It is as we navigate between these two spaces—the physical and the digital—that the unique personal communication presence that others attribute to us when we interact with them, both online and offline takes shape, and it speaks volumes.

How others in both the physical and digital world perceive our communication presence affects their opinions of us and our relationships with them. The objective, of course, is for our communication presence to be positive, authentic, and serve as a success catalyst.

Becoming adept at connecting with others, whether they are actually present or digitally dispersed, is one skill we all should want to master. We should want to present ourselves as competently and confidently as possible in the communication arenas we frequent daily, regardless of whether we happen to be physically in the same space or are using social media.

SKILL BUILDER

Wi-Fi Me (It's Not a Question)

Based solely on the name of your Wi-Fi network, what impressions might others form of you?

In an effort to influence others' reactions, Wi-Fi network names have morphed from boring series of digits to personalized monikers much like vanity license plates.

Choose a Wi-Fi name that you believe will reveal to others something they may not know about you. For example, one ballet dance instructor branded her Wi-Fi network "PointToMe."[1] What will you brand yours? What do you think your brand communicates about you?

COMMUNICATION CHOICES ARE ABUNDANT

We have an abundance of communication options today. To be sure, various means of communicating become more popular than others at different times in our lives. For example, for many of us texting is the dominant form of interaction.[2] But for better or worse, our communication choices evolve. The question is: *Do we make sound decisions about how to communicate most effectively and appropriately with others?*

Once we understand what makes communication work across the spectrum of communication channels available to us, we will know how to make it work for us. Ultimately, because the communication presence we present and share in social, civic, and professional arenas and personal, group, organizational, and public settings affects our relationships, our ability to engage with others, and our life satisfaction, we can never become too effective at communicating.

COMMUNICATION PRESENCE AND TECHNOLOGY

What is your personal "go-to" means of communicating? If you're like many 21st-century students, your smartphone serves as your prime personal connector. You likely use it to check Facebook, text, tweet, or post on Instagram—but rarely make a phone call. For some people, actually talking to another person causes discomfort. Such individuals find technology freeing, because they don't have to be in the physical presence of others. They feel able to say what they want without fear of being interrupted or even having to listen to another's response.

Are We Addicted?

Although we sometimes discount communicating face-to-face or forget it altogether, doing so effectively is equally, if not more, important than connecting through technology. Despite this, in a 2015 Pew Research Center study, 89% of smartphone owners reported using their phones during the last social gathering they attended. They also reported that they were not happy about it because it impeded conversation.[3]

A few years back, a YouTube video titled "I Forgot My Phone" went viral. By now, the video has been viewed more than 50 million times. At the video's start, we see a couple in bed. The woman stares into space while her boyfriend focuses on his smartphone. The scenes that follow show the woman in the midst of a series of dystopian situations. Her friends ignore her and stare at their phones during lunch. Concertgoers are too busy recording the performance to enjoy it. The guest of honor at a birthday party takes selfies while his friends sing. The last scene finds the couple back in bed. Her boyfriend is still phone obsessed.

Are we addicted to smartphones and social media? According to research, we well might be captives of our devices. Many of us use our phones more than we even imagine we do. In fact, when asked to estimate their smartphone usage, participants estimated an average of 37 uses daily. The actual number was about 85 times daily, or once every 11 minutes of your typical waking day. The duration of use was 5.05 hours, including phone calls and listening to music.[4]

Facebook, Instagram, and Twitter are hypnotically compelling for many of us, in part because they deliver unscheduled "variable rewards"—much like slot machines do. Messages, alerts, notifications, photos, and "likes" are sent to us randomly, making it virtually impossible for us not to react to them. They induce large numbers of us to become compulsive site checkers looking for a dopamine boost—almost as if we were seeking a fix.

The Upshot

What is the future of person-to-person conversation as texting replaces talking? We have to be able to connect both remotely and in-person, in a social or professional network, or in a social or professional circle. Whenever and wherever we connect, the goal is to make communication work—and that is the primary goal of this book.

HUMAN AND SOCIAL CAPITAL

What will it take to make communication work for you?

Neither job-specific talent, nor technical expertise, nor graduating from college alone will guarantee you upward mobility or the attainment of goals. In fact, many of us get our jobs because of our **social capital**, rather than our **human capital**—the people we know, not what we know.[5] This might be because, although our communities and workplaces are prime environments for connecting with others, the Internet makes it relatively easy today to find out anything we don't know.

THE COMMUNICATION–SUCCESS CONNECTION

What differentiates people who ascend both personal and professional ladders of success from those who do not? The answer is superior communication skills.

Among the top 10 skills employers seek when hiring college graduates is the ability to communicate with others both inside and outside of the organization.[6] Although not guaranteed, people with good communication skills are more likely to be promoted rapidly, be happy in relationships, and believe their lives are rich and fulfilling. Whatever your age, sex, marital status, or employment history, it is never too late to learn skills that will enrich and improve your career and life.

We are not born knowing how to make communication work. We learn and develop communication skills. If you want to improve your ability to relate to people in your social life, job, or academic life, now is the time to start making communication work better for you!

WHAT IS COMMUNICATION?

We are all communicators. We engage in intrapersonal (with ourselves), dyadic (one-to-one), small-group (one to a few), public (one to many), and mass communication (communicating messages that are shared across great distances with potentially large audiences through a technological device or mass medium). We also engage in computer-assisted or online communication.

DEFINING COMMUNICATION

Every time we knowingly or unknowingly send a verbal or nonverbal message to anyone, communication takes place. We define **communication** as the deliberate or accidental transfer of meaning. It is the process that occurs whenever someone observes or experiences behavior and attributes meaning to that behavior. As long as what someone does or says is interpreted as a message—as long as the behavior of one person affects or influences that behavior of another—communication is occurring. Communication is our link to the rest of humanity and serves a number of purposes.

Which of the following quotations, if any, do you find most applicable to your own communication experiences?

India Picture/Shutterstock.com

- Talk and change the world. (Slogan of a group of U.S. senators who happened to be female)

- Whatever words we utter should be chosen with care for people will hear them and be influenced by them for good or ill. (Buddha)

- We all need people who will give us feedback. That's how we improve. (Bill Gates)

- The best way to solve problems and fight against war is through dialogue. (Malala Yousafzai)

- Two monologues do not make a dialogue. (Jeff Daly)

What would you say?

TYPES OF COMMUNICATION

Because our focus is communication, we need to distinguish among the types of communication we use.

- During **intrapersonal communication**, we think about, talk with, learn about, reason with, and evaluate ourselves. We listen and interact with the voice in our head.

- When we engage in **interpersonal** (or dyadic) **communication**, we interact with another, learn about him or her, and act in ways that help sustain or terminate our relationship.

- When we participate in **group communication**, we interact with a limited number of others, work to share information, develop ideas, make decisions, solve problems, offer support, or have fun. Every person in a group can actively participate with others in the group.

- **Organizational communication** is conducted with larger, more stable collections of people who work together to achieve the organization's goals. Organizations include corporations, nonprofits, entertainment, sports, health operations, and political, religious, and charitable groups.

- Through **public communication**, we inform others. We also persuade the members of various audiences to hold certain attitudes, values, or beliefs so that they will think, believe, or act in a particular way. We also function as members of different audiences, in which case another person will do the same for us.

- During **mass communication**, the media entertain, inform, and persuade us. Messages are sent to large dispersed audiences using electronic and print media. We, in turn, have the ability to use our viewing and buying habits to influence the media.

- When engaged with **digital and social media**, we navigate cyberspace as we converse, research, exchange ideas, and build relationships with others using computers and the Internet. Social media are more personal than the mass media. The size of the intended audience in social media varies, and the communication itself can be more interactive.

SKILL BUILDER

Communication Self-Assessment and Future Me

Identify five individuals with whom you shared a sustained conversation during the past 7 days. For each person you name, indicate the *nature of your relationship* (e.g., was the person your instructor, parent, boss, friend, or significant other?), the *context* in which the interaction occurred (was it a classroom, office, home, or restaurant?), the *channel(s)* used to communicate the messages that were sent and received (did you communicate face-to face, e-mail, phone, text, or via social media?), and the *outcome* of the exchange (what happened as a result of your communicating?).

Finally, and this is most important, evaluate your communication effectiveness in each interaction by rating it on a scale of 1 to 5, where 1 represents extremely ineffective and 5 represents extremely effective, giving your reasons for each rating.

Person	Context	Channel	Outcome	Rating With Reasons
1.				
2.				
3.				
4.				
5.				

After reviewing your self-evaluations, how would you replay any of the preceding interactions if given the opportunity? Be specific. For example, might you opt not to text while walking down a street with a friend? Would you decide not to answer your phone when dining with a coworker?

If it were up to you, would you opt to increase or decrease the number of online versus face-to-face interactions that you shared? Why?

ESSENTIALS OF COMMUNICATION

Whatever the nature or type of communication in which we are involved, the communication act itself is characterized by the interplay of seven elements. All communication interactions have these common elements that together help define the communication process. The better you understand these components, the easier it becomes for you to develop your own communicative abilities. Let's begin by examining the **essentials of communication**, those elements present during every communication event.

PEOPLE

Obviously, human communication involves people. Interpersonal, small-group, and public communication encounters take place between and among all types of **senders** (people who encode and send out messages) and **receivers** (people who take in messages and decode). Although it is easy to picture a communication experience beginning with a sender and ending with a receiver, it is important to understand that during communication the role of sender does not belong exclusively to one person and role of receiver to another. Instead, the processes of sending and receiving occur simultaneously. Even if only one person is speaking, others can communicate through facial expression, attentiveness, or raising a hand to ask a question.

MESSAGES

A **message** is the content of a communicative act. During every communication act, we all send and receive verbal and nonverbal messages. What you talk about, the words you use to express your thoughts and feelings, the sounds you make, the way you sit and gesture, your facial expressions, and perhaps even your touch or your smell all communicate information.

Some messages we send are private (a kiss accompanied by "I love you"); others are public and may be directed at hundreds or thousands of people. We send some messages purposefully ("I want you to know. . .") and others accidentally ("I had no clue you were watching . . . or 'lurking'").

Everything a sender or receiver does or says is a potential message as long as someone is there to interpret it.

CHANNELS

Channels are the media we use to carry messages. We classify channels according to which of our senses carries or receives the message, whether the message is being delivered verbally, nonverbally,

or both, and the primary means of communication we use to deliver the message, that is, whether we use face-to-face interaction, text messaging, or a mass medium such as television or a podcast.

We are multichanneled communicators. We receive sound messages (we hear noises from the street), sight messages (we size up how someone looks), taste messages (we enjoy the flavor of a particular food), smell messages (we like the scent of a friend's perfume), and touch messages (we feel the roughness of a fabric).

Which channel are you most attuned to? To what extent do you rely on one or more channels while excluding or ignoring others? Effective communicators are adept channel switchers. They recognize that communication is a multichannel experience. The following dialogue between a husband and wife illustrates the multichannel nature of communication:

Wife: Jim, you're late again. Is that a drink I smell on your breath? Now, we'll never get to the Adams' on time.

Husband: No, I didn't stop for a drink. You must be smelling what's left of my cologne. I tried my best to be on time (places a consoling hand on her shoulder).

Wife: (Sarcastically) Sure, you tried your best. (Drawing away and shaking her finger) I'm not going to put up with this much longer. My job is every bit as demanding as yours, you know.

Husband: (Lowering his voice) Ok. Ok. I know you work hard, too. I don't question that. Listen, I really did get stuck in a conference. (Smiles at her) Let's not blow this up. I'll tell you about it on the way to Bill and Ellen's.

What message is the wife (the initial source-encoder) sending to her husband (the receiver-decoder)? She is letting him know with her words, her voice, and her physical actions that she is upset and angry. Her husband responds in kind, using words, vocal cues, and gestures in an effort to explain his behavior. Both are affected by the nature of the situation (they are late for an appointment), by their attitudes (how they feel about what's happened), and by their past experiences.

NOISE

In the context of communication, **noise** is anything that interferes with or distorts our ability to send or receive messages. Although we are accustomed to thinking of noise as particular sound or group of sounds, noise can have both internal and external causes. Internal noise is attributed to a communicator's psychological makeup, intellectual ability, or physical condition. External noise is attributed to the environment. Thus, noise includes distractions such as a loud siren, a disturbing odor, and a hot room; personal factors such as prejudices, daydreaming, and feelings of inadequacy; and semantic factors such as uncertainty about what another person's words are supposed to mean.

CONTEXT

Communication always takes place in a **context**, or setting. Sometimes a context is so natural that we barely notice it. At other times, however, the context exerts considerable control over our behavior. Would your behavior be the same at a friend's 21st birthday party and at a baby shower? Both are parties, but the context is different. Consider how your present environment affects the way you act toward others. Also, consider the extent to which certain environments might cause you to alter your posture, manner of speaking, attire, or means of interacting.

FEEDBACK

Whenever we communicate, we receive feedback in return. The verbal and nonverbal cues that we perceive in reaction to our communication function as **feedback**. Feedback tells us how we are coming across. A smile, a frown, a chuckle, a sarcastic remark, a muttered thought, or simply silence in response to something we do or say can cause us to change, continue, or end a communication exchange.

Feedback that encourages us to continue behaving as we are is **positive feedback**; it enhances behavior in progress. In contrast, **negative feedback** extinguishes a behavior; it serves a corrective rather than a reinforcing function. Note that the terms *positive* and *negative* should not be interpreted as "good" and "bad"; these labels simply reflect the way the responses affect behavior.

Both positive and negative feedback can emanate from internal or external sources. **Internal feedback** is feedback you give yourself as you monitor your own communicative behavior. **External feedback** is feedback from others who are involved in the communication event. To be an effective communicator, you must be sensitive to both types of feedback.

EFFECT

As we communicate, we are changed in some way by the interaction. Communication has an effect and can be viewed as an exchange of influences.

An **effect** can be emotional, physical, cognitive, or any combination of the three. Communication can elicit feelings of joy, anger, or sadness (emotional); it can cause you to fight, argue, become apathetic, or evade an issue (physical); or it can lead to new insights, increased knowledge, the formulation or reconsideration of opinions, silence, or confusion (cognitive). Some effects are not always visible or immediately observable. Effects can be delayed.

VISUALIZING THE COMMUNICATION PROCESS IN ACTION

Through communication, we share meaning with others by sending and receiving messages—sometimes intentionally and sometimes unintentionally. Thus, communication includes every element that could affect two or more people as they knowingly or unwittingly relate to one another. At this point, we need to reiterate that communication occurs whenever one person assigns significance or meaning to another's behavior. But, you might ask, will knowing this enable you to understand or establish better and more satisfying relationships with your friends, significant other, employer, parents? The answer is yes! If you understand the processes that permit people to contact and influence each other, if you understand the forces that can impede or foster the development of every kind of effective communication, then you stand a better chance of communicating effectively yourself.

A TRANSACTIONAL MODEL OF COMMUNICATION

Now that we have examined the basic elements of communication, we are ready to see how we can use a picture, or transactional model, of the communication process to reflect our understanding of communication in action. A model is a useful tool in discovering how communication operates and in examining your own communication encounters.

The model of communication in Figure 1.1 is a transactional one. A **transactional communication model** depicts communication as a continuous circle with sending and receiving as simultaneous rather than separate acts. Such a model enables us to visualize the vital complexity and dynamic nature of communication. Each person in the model is pictured sending and receiving messages (including feedback) through one or more channels at the same time as the other, because they both have sending and receiving responsibilities and their messages will build upon and affect one another.

Each person's field of experience—their culture, past experiences, education, biases, and heredity—influences the interaction. Of consequence is the extent to which their fields of experience overlap. In theory, the more individuals communicate with each other, the more overlap they create.

FIGURE 1.1
Gamble and Gamble's Model of Communication

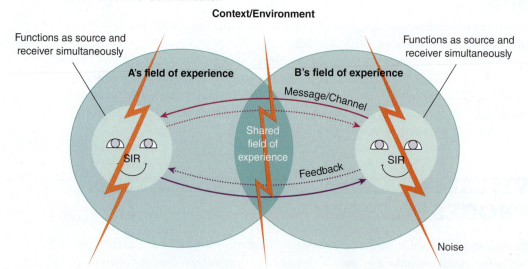

In addition, we see that noise can enter the interaction at any point—it can pop up in the message, be present in the channel, come from one's field of experience, or derive from the context. Such noise can affect the sending and/or the receiving abilities and effectiveness of the communicators.

Every interaction we have with another has an impact on our future interactions with that person and potentially with others.

HOW GOOD A COMMUNICATOR ARE YOU?

Simply communicating frequently does not mean that you are as effective a communicator as you could be. Too often, we neglect problems with our communicative relationships. When we either lack empathy or fail to consider the feelings of others, our relationships suffer.

There is no such thing as being too effective at establishing maintaining and controlling personal and public contacts with others. Being mindful of the principles discussed in this section can help you to improve your communication skills.

COMMUNICATION IS DYNAMIC

When we call communication a dynamic process, we mean that all its elements constantly interact with and affect each other. Because we are interconnected, whatever happens to one person determines in part what happens to others.

Relationships evolve. Nothing about communication is static. Everything is accumulative. We communicate as long as we are alive. Thus, every interaction we engage in is part of a series of connected happenings. Present communication experiences can be thought of as points of arrival from past encounters and as points of departure for future ones. Do your experiences support this?

COMMUNICATION IS UNREPEATABLE AND IRREVERSIBLE

Every human contact we experience is unique. It has never happened before and will never again happen in just the same way. Our interpretation of the adage "You can never step into the same river twice" is that the experience changes both you and the river forever. A communication encounter similarly affects and changes people so that one encounter can never occur exactly in the same way a second time.

In addition to being unrepeatable, communication is also irreversible. We cannot take back something we have said or tweeted any more than we can erase the effects of something we have done. Just as toothpaste cannot be squeezed back into a tube, the e-mails, texts, and tweets we send are going to be out there forever.

When has the unrepeatable and irreversible nature of communication caused you a problem?

COMMUNICATION HAS NO OPPOSITE

We often assume that communication is purposeful and that we communicate only because we want to. Although this sometimes is true, it is also true that sometimes we communicate without any awareness of doing so—and just as often, even without wanting to.

Whenever we are involved in an interaction, we respond in some way. Even if we choose not to respond verbally, even if we maintain absolute silence and attempt not to move a muscle, our lack of response is itself a response; it constitutes a message, influences others, and communicates. We can never stop behavior—because behavior has no opposite. No matter how hard we try, we cannot not communicate, because all behavior is communication and therefore is a message.

EXPLORING DIVERSITY

Focus on Hate

Years ago, researcher Gordon Allport wrote the following in his now classic *The Nature of Prejudice*:

See that man over there?

Yes.

Well, I hate him.

But you don't know him.

That's why I hate him.

Although Allport wrote this long ago, his observations remain true today and are being magnified by social media. To what extent do you believe that enhanced understanding can help resolve this? Why does a lack of knowledge or familiarity help breed hate? Why might some people experience "hate" when encountering individuals from a new or unfamiliar culture or group?

CULTURE INFLUENCES COMMUNICATION

As we will learn in Chapter 2, how we formulate and interpret messages depends on our culture. Cultural diversity, including race, ethnicity, gender, and age, influences the meanings we attribute to communication. Cultural differences exist not only between people who speak different languages but also between people who speak the same language. Every cultural group has its own rules or preferences for interaction. When these are unknown or ignored, we are apt to misinterpret the meaning of messages received and miscalculate the impact of messages sent.

iStock/FamVeld

GENDER INFLUENCES COMMUNICATION

"To be an 'I' at all means to be gendered."[7] Our culture shapes our conceptions of gender, and conceptions of gender shape our communication.[8] We learn socially accepted variations in the definitions of gender differences as we grow up. Girls, for example, learn to "play nice." Boys learn to act tough. Gender is a relational construct with individuals promoting the gender ideologies they accept.

To what extent do you believe that your communication has been influenced by gender constructions or restrictions and what society considers "normal"?

PERSONAL ETHICS INFLUENCE COMMUNICATION

Every time we communicate, we decide implicitly or explicitly if we will do so ethically. Ethics are the moral principles, values, and beliefs that members of society use to guide behavior. Since communication has consequences, it involves judgments of right and wrong. When the agreed-upon standards of behavior are violated, the behavior is judged unethical. For example, most of us expect those with whom we interact to be honest, play fair, respect our rights, and accept responsibility for their actions.

COMMUNICATION IS COMPETENCE BASED

A communication scholar once said that if communication can fail, it will.[9] Our challenge is determining how we can prevent communication from failing. One solution is to make wise choices. In certain situations, some messages are appropriate and okay to say to particular receivers, whereas others are not.

Even though we all have different communication strengths and weaknesses, we can all benefit from getting better at communicating. When we add to our knowledge and make a commitment to develop the skills to apply that knowledge across an array of communication situations or contexts, we gain communication competence. For example, included among the skills necessary for effective communication is the ability to think critically. When we think critically, we have the ability to examine ideas reflectively and to decide what we should and should not believe, think, or do, given a specific set of circumstances.[10]

DIGITAL AND SOCIAL MEDIA ARE TRANSFORMING COMMUNICATION

Decades ago, media critic Marshall McLuhan cautioned, "The medium is the message."[11] In McLuhan's view, different channels of communication affected both how a sender encoded a message and how a receiver responded to it. This means that the same words delivered face-to-face, on paper, via text, or with a tweet do not constitute the same message. The channel of communication changes things. What channel would you use to say good-bye to someone who was moving away? Which channel would you use to tell someone "I'm sorry?" What about "I love you?"

New communication forms—new channels—alter our communication experiences. Technology and social media are game changers. Using them speeds up communication. Instead of valuing sequential understanding and careful logic, we seek immediate gratification and emotional involvement with people near and distant, close to home and around the world. As our real and virtual communication repertoires expand, we exist simultaneously both in the physical world and online.

Living Brands

Do you know anyone whose life has become a brand? A 2017 film, *Ingrid Goes West,* satirized the sometimes very painful ways in which social media impact lives.[12] In the film Ingrid goes into a rage after seeing photos online of a wedding to which she wasn't invited. A loner, she turns her life on its head by traveling to Los Angeles and reinventing herself into the image of her Instagram obsession, Taylor, a person who posts perfectly posed photos of herself along with inspirational quotes and has gazillions of followers.

Now, who would you rather be: Ingrid or Taylor? The devoted follower or the influencer? Has a filtered life that you have observed ever made you green with envy?

Changes Have Upsides and Downsides

The changes in how we communicate affect our social, emotional, and professional lives. On the upside, they influence our cultural sensibilities, making it easier for many among us to identify like-minded people who share our interests. On the downside, they make it less likely that we will expose ourselves to different points of view. Also on the downside, they make it possible for us to remain anonymous or to disguise ourselves. But on the upside, if

iStock/hocus-focus

we do remain anonymous, our online communication will be evaluated more for what we write than for how we look. On the downside, again, social media allow us to present our lives through filters—delivering a carefully curated image of ourselves to the world—but then again, those filters can be humorous too.[13]

Social media reshape human consciousness and relationships. Because there are only so many hours in a day, the time we spend using social media takes time away from other activities. Social media impede our living "in the moment." Rather than enjoying the company of others or an event or celebration, we tweet, use Snapchat, or check Facebook. They also foster our dependency on others—we wait anxiously to see if our post will receive approval and affirmation.[14] On the other hand, they do make it more possible for marginalized groups to find support. They have upsides and downsides, downsides and upsides.

Being a communicator in a digital age adds multiple layers to our communication experiences. For one thing, our messages become more permanent. For another, ethically challenged individuals can troll our pages, hack into our files, make our private messages public, and forward to other people something that we had no intention of communicating to them. What happens online influences offline realities.

WHY DO WE COMMUNICATE?

Every communication experience serves one or more functions. For example, communication can help us discover who we are, help us establish more meaningful personal and professional relationships, or prompt us to examine and try to change either our own attitudes and behaviors or the attitudes and behaviors of others.

TO GAIN SELF-UNDERSTANDING AND INSIGHT INTO OTHERS

One key function of communication is self–other understanding: insight into ourselves and others. When we get to know another person, we also get to know ourselves and when we get to know ourselves, we learn how others affect us. We depend on communication to develop self-awareness.

We need feedback from others all the time, and others are constantly in need of feedback from us. Interpersonal, small-group, public, and mediated and digital communication offer us numerous opportunities for self–other discovery. Through communication encounters we are able to learn why we are trusting or untrusting, whether we can make our thoughts and feelings clear, under what conditions we have the power to influence others, and whether we can effectively make decisions and resolve conflicts and problems.

Modern communicators need to be able to interact with people culturally different from themselves. Although it might be feasible in the virtual world to seek comfort in similarity, insulating ourselves from intercultural contact in our social networks, communities, and workplaces is neither possible nor desirable. It is through communication that we reveal to others what is important to us and what we stand for.

TO FORM MEANINGFUL RELATIONSHIPS

In building relationships, we cannot be overly concerned with ourselves but must consider the needs and wants of others. It is through effective communication that our basic physical and social needs are met.

Psychologists tell us that we need other people just as we need water, food, and shelter. When we are cut off from human contact, we become disoriented and maladjusted, and our life itself

may be placed in jeopardy. People who are isolated from others—people who lack satisfying social relationships—are more likely to experience health problems and to die earlier than those who have an abundance of satisfying relationships.

Communication offers each of us the chance to satisfy what psychologist William Schutz calls our "needs for inclusion, control, and affection."[15] The **need for inclusion** is our need to be with others, our need for social contact. We like to feel that others accept and value us, and we want to feel like a full partner in a relationship. The **need for control** is our need to feel that we are capable and responsible, that we are able to deal with and manage our environment. We also like to feel that we can influence others. The **need for affection** is our need to express and receive love. Because communication allows each of these needs to be met, we are less likely to feel unwanted, unloved, or incapable if we are able to communicate meaningfully with others.

Communication also gives us the chance to share our personal reality with people from our own and different cultures. Whether we live in an East Coast urban area, a southern city, a desert community, a home in sunny California, a village in Asia, a plain in Africa, or a town in the Middle East, we all engage in similar activities when we communicate. We may use different symbols, rely on different strategies, and desire different outcomes, but the processes we use and the motivations we have are strikingly alike. Equally significant is the fact that insensitivity to another's needs and preferred ways of interacting can hamper our ability to relate effectively.

TO INFLUENCE OTHERS

During all kinds of communication, we have ample opportunities to influence each other subtly or overtly. We spend a great deal of time trying to persuade others to think as we think, do what we do, like what we like. Sometimes our efforts meet with success. In any case our experiences with persuasion afford each of us the chance to influence others so that we may try to realize our personal and professional goals.

FOR CAREER DEVELOPMENT

Employers are concerned about the lack of communication skills in new hires. In fact, most are less concerned about technical skills and more concerned with the abilities of potential employees to relate to and engage with others in the workplace.[16] Among the perennial complaints of employers are the poor written communication and presentation abilities of applicants, along with their lack of interpersonal skills. Employers report that recent college graduates tend to ramble when asked to explain something, have difficulty making a point, and are prone to sending e-mails and texts that are far too casual for the professional world.[17]

As we noted earlier in this chapter, a positive relationship exists between the ability to communicate and career success. Employers seek to hire those who know how to make communication work. If you develop the ability to speak so that others listen, listen when others speak, critically evaluate what you read and hear, adapt to differences in cultural perspectives, handle conflicts and solve problems, and make sound decisions, then you will exhibit skills valued by employers.[18]

CAREER BUILDER: PROFESSIONAL CHALLENGES AND FUTURE ME

1. Using what you have learned to this point, explain what you think distinguishes an effective communicator in the workplace from a poor one.

2. Elaborate on how improving a specific communication skill could benefit you professionally in the future.

3. Identify the pros and cons of virtual versus face-to-face workplace interactions.

4. Explain how improving communication skills will enable you to make a difference in your workplace.

COMMUNICATION SKILLS
Practice Effective Communication

The primary purpose of this book is to help you gain an understanding of communication and to assist you in developing your interpersonal, small-group, public, and digital and social media skills. Engaging with the following tasks will give you a great start.

Become actively involved in studying communication.

Once you commit to putting the principles we discuss into practice, you are on your way to becoming a better communicator. Use the learning objectives in this text to clarify your personal communication objectives. Use the embedded self-assessments and boxed features to further explore what you must know and do to become a more effective communicator.

Make the effort to increase both your self-awareness and your awareness of others by developing the following assets.

- An appreciation of the extent to which gender, culture, and digital and social media affect communication
- The capacity to listen to and process information

(Continued)

(Continued)

- Sensitivity to silent messages that you and others send
- Knowledge of how words affect us
- An understanding of how relationships develop
- A realization of how feelings and emotions affect relationships
- The ability to disagree without being disagreeable
- An understanding of how beliefs, values, and attitudes affect the formulation and reception of messages and the development of speaker-audience relationships

Believe in yourself.

Above all else, you need to believe that you are worth the time and effort required to develop your communication skills. You also need to believe that developing these skills will improve the quality of your life immeasurably.

> "Communication is a skill that you can learn. It's like riding a bicycle or typing. If you're willing to work at it, you can rapidly improve the quality of every part of your life.
>
> Brian Tracy

COMPLETE THIS CHAPTER 1 CHECKLIST

1.1 I can discuss the nature of *communication presence*. ☐

Communication presence is the composite of characteristics we present both in the physical and online world. Effectively, we each create a real-world or face-to-face identity and a digital-world or virtual identity for others to consume.

1.2 I can define *communication*. ☐

Communication is the deliberate or accidental transfer of meaning. Human communication takes place interpersonally (one-to-one), in small groups (one to a few), in public forums (one to many), and via digital and social media.

1.3 I can explain the essential elements of communication and their interaction. ☐

The essential elements of communication are people, messages, channels, noise, context, feedback, and effects. A transactional model of communication illustrates the communication process in action.

1.4 I can use a transactional communication model to visualize the communication process in action. ☐

A transactional communication model depicts communication as a continuous circle with sending and receiving as simultaneous rather than separate acts, helping us to visualize the vital complexity and dynamic nature of communication.

1.5 I can describe the core principles of good communication. ☐

Communication reflects a number of general principles. First, because communication is a dynamic process, each interaction is part of a series of interconnected communication events. Second, every communication experience is unique, unrepeatable, and irreversible. Third, behavior has no opposite. Fourth, culture influences communication. Fifth, ethics influence communication. Sixth, communication is competence based.

1.6 I can evaluate the benefits of communicating effectively. ☐

Effective communication promotes self–other understanding, helps us establish meaningful relationships, enables us to examine and attempt to change the attitudes and behaviors of others, and enhances career development. Developing communication skills is a lifelong process. This book explains the strategies you can use to assess your communication abilities, improve the effectiveness of your communication relationships, and enhance the quality of your life.

1.7 I can apply skills for improving my communication effectiveness. ☐

Once you become involved in the study of communication, commit to setting and tracking personal goals, and demonstrate belief in yourself, you are on the road to mastering communication skills to last a lifetime.

BECOME A WORD MASTER

channels 7

communication 4

communication presence 2

context 9

digital and social media 6

effect 9

essentials of communication 7

ethics 13

external feedback 9

feedback 9

group communication 5

human capital 4

internal feedback 9

interpersonal communication 5

intrapersonal communication 5

mass communication 6

message 7

need for affection 16

need for control 16

need for inclusion 16

negative feedback 9

noise 8

organizational communication 5

positive feedback 9

public communication 5

receivers 7

senders 7

social capital 4

transactional communication model 10

iordani/Shutterstock.com

iStock/DMEPhotography

2

Having Communication Presence in a Multicultural Society and World

2.1 Explain the significance of intercultural communication in the global community.

2.2 Explain how U.S. society evolved from a melting pot philosophy to a philosophy of cultural pluralism.

2.3 Analyze attitudes toward diversity.

2.4 Explain influences on cultural identity, distinguishing the difference between cultures and co-cultures.

2.5 Illustrate the five main dimensions of cultural variability.

2.6 Explain how technology brings diversity into our lives.

2.7 Apply communication skills to reduce the strangeness of strangers.

A lot of different flowers make a bouquet.

Anonymous

Have you ever decided that you liked or disliked someone without really knowing him or her? Has anyone ever done the same to you—forming a positive or negative opinion of you—judging you, without really knowing you? If your answer to either of these questions is yes, it is likely that *stereotypes*, the mental images that guide our reactions to others, played a role.

A stereotype expresses the knowledge, beliefs, and expectations we have of the members of a particular group.[1] Whereas some of the stereotypes we hold of cultural groups are positive, others are astoundingly negative and overly generalized. Some contain kernels of truth, whereas others prevent us from recognizing our misconceptions.

What groups of people do you stereotype positively and/or negatively? What stereotypes might others hold of you? And how do our evaluations of one another affect our communication?

Some years back, Representative Peter King, chair of the House Committee on Homeland Security, convened a series of controversial hearings on the radicalization of Muslims in the United States. Critics of the hearings objected to the broad-stroke inquiry, arguing that we should view the Muslim community more objectively and stop treating Muslims with automatic suspicion. Furthermore, they asserted that individuals should be able to distinguish between mainstream Muslims and those belonging to the radical fringe.[2] Representative Keith Ellison, the first Muslim elected to Congress, observed that individuals, not communities, commit terrorist acts. He said, "When you assign their violent actions to the entire community, you assign collective blame to the whole group. This is the very heart of stereotyping and scapegoating."[3]

It's not just Muslims who face stereotypes. Relations between all groups are complicated by stereotypes. Yet we all share a common desire—and a need—to get along better with one another.[4] Stereotyping is just one of the topics we address in this chapter as we explore a host of factors that influence our ability to communicate in a multicultural society and world. ■

CULTURES' MANY FACES

Globalization is the increasing economic, political, and cultural integration and interdependence of diverse cultures—the worldwide integration of humanity. Diversity, a related concept, is the recognition and valuing of difference, encompassing such factors as age, gender, race, ethnicity, ability, religion, education, marital status, sexual orientation, and income. Because the likelihood of our working and living with people from all over the world is increasing, the time is right to embrace diversity and learn about other cultures so that we refrain from unfairly stereotyping them.

An early observer of how technology affects behavior and thinking, Marshall McLuhan, predicted many years ago that our world would become a global village.[5] He was right. We now are linked physically and electronically to people around the globe. Digital technology is playing its part in erasing the notion of territorial boundaries between countries, gradually eroding the idea of the term *nation*.

People we once considered strangers are now friends and coworkers, highlighting the importance of multiculturalism—engagement with and respect toward people from distinctly different cultures. In addition to using the Internet with increasing frequency, many of us move a number of times during our lives for personal or professional reasons.[6] We also travel abroad regularly, some of us to visit relatives (one in five Americans was born abroad or has at least one parent who was), others to represent an employer, and still others to vacation. Each of these provides us with opportunities to improve cultural understanding. We don't have to be in the diplomatic corps to assume an active role.

ATTITUDES TOWARD DIVERSITY

Some people do not embrace diversity eagerly. In the book *Bowling Alone*, written at the turn of this millennium, author Robert Putnam reported that reciprocal and trustworthy social networks were on the decline. Aware that people were doing more and more things alone, Putnam asked why? After studying 30,000 people across the United States, Putnam found a correlation between ethnically mixed environments and withdrawal from public life. He reported that the people living in diverse communities tended to "hunker down." Sadly, they were more likely to distrust their neighbors—whether they were of the same or a different race, a similar or different background.[7] Do you find this to be true today?

Is It Different in the Working World?

Happily, the working world reveals a different story. In organizations, people with *identity diversity* (people who come from different races and religions) and *cognitive diversity* (people who come from different outlooks and training) come together to do the organization's work.

Thus, the challenge facing us is to follow the lead of diverse organizations by working to create a new and broader sense of "us." In effect, we need to harness community out of diversity.[8]

The Many Faces of Intercultural Communication

The remainder of this chapter will explore the ways cultural values and habits influence interaction. We'll introduce you to **intercultural communication**, the process of interpreting and sharing meanings with individuals from different cultures,[9] to help you better understand how cultural variability influences communication. In reality, we practice intercultural communication in our own backyards as well as with people around the world.

Among intercultural communication's many aspects are **interracial communication** (which occurs between people of different races), **interethnic communication** (which occurs when the communicating parties have different ethnic origins), **international communication** (which occurs between people representing different political structures), and **intracultural communication** (which includes all forms of communication among members of the same racial, ethnic, or other co-culture groups). By sensitizing yourself to the many faces of culture, you will become better able to respond appropriately to varied communication styles, expand your choices as a communicator, and increase your effectiveness in interacting with people from diverse cultural groups.

WHAT HAPPENED TO THE MELTING POT?

To what extent has the amount of contact you have with people of diverse cultural backgrounds changed since you were a child? Changes in demography and technology have made it more likely that you will interact with people unlike yourself. For most of us, intercultural communication is now the norm. In fact, living in the United States gives us an incredible opportunity to engage with intercultural communication without having to pay for international travel. But it hasn't always been that way.

iStock/RoosterHD

THE MELTING POT PHILOSOPHY

Years ago, the United States embraced a **melting pot philosophy**. According to that theory, when individuals immigrated to the United States, they lost or gave up their original heritage and became Americans. The national motto, *E pluribus unum* (a Latin phrase meaning "one out of many"), reflected this way of thinking. It was believed that diverse cultural groups should be assimilated into the parent or dominant culture.

THE PHILOSOPHY OF CULTURAL PLURALISM

Over time, the philosophy of **cultural pluralism**, allowing for cultures to maintain differences while coexisting in broader society, replaced the melting pot philosophy. Cultural pluralists believe in respect for uniqueness and tolerance for difference. In a multicultural society, every group will do things differently, and that's OK.

DIVERSITY IS RESHAPING THE FUTURE

Demographers tell us that diversity will shape our country's future. According to U.S. Census Bureau statistics, the five largest ethnic groups currently are composed of people who identify themselves as White (223.6 million), African American (38.9 million), Hispanic (50.5 million), Asian American (14.7 million), and Native American (American Indian and Alaska Native) (3.8 million).[10] Hispanics are now the largest minority group. Within one generation, minorities are forecast to become the majority (Figure 2.1). Recent projections, however, assert that Asian immigration will make Asians the largest immigrant group by 2065 at 38%, surpassing Hispanics who are estimated to then comprise 31% of the population.[11]

Additionally, acknowledging the blurring of racial lines and the evolution of racial identity, the 2010 U.S. Census let the nation's more than 308 million people define their racial makeup as one race or more. Results revealed that multiracial Americans are among the fastest growing demographic groups.[12]

The United States is the most demographically diverse country in the world, making it very probable that the number of contacts we have with people of other cultures will continue to increase in the future. This alone makes it important for us to be able to understand and communicate with those whose backgrounds, nationalities, and lifestyles differ from our own.

FIGURE 2.1

Projected U.S. Population by Race and Hispanic Origins

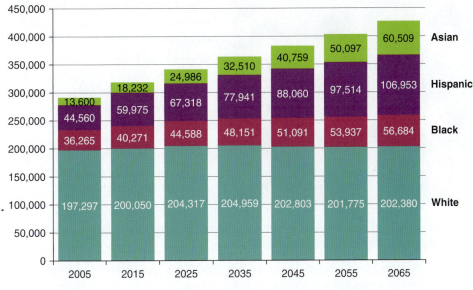

(in thousands)

Source: Pew Research Center, "Modern Immigration Wave Brings 59 Million to the U.S., Driving Population Growth and Change Through 2065," September 28, 2015, http://www.pewhispanic.org/2015/09/28/modern-immigration-wave-brings-59-million-to-u-s-driving-population-growth-and-change-through-2065.

CULTURE AND COMMUNICATION

As cultural anthropologist Edward T. Hall put it, "Culture is communication and communication is culture."[13] Culture is the lens through which we view the world. It is the mirror we use to reflect and interpret reality.[14] It teaches us how to think and what to think about. It reveals to us what is beautiful or ugly, helpful or harmful, appropriate or out of place.

CULTURE IS A TEACHER

In effect, every culture provides its members with a series of lessons. Among the lessons we learn are how to say "hello" and "good-bye," when to speak or remain silent, how to act when angry or upset, where to focus our eyes when functioning as a source and receiver, how much to gesture, how close to stand to another, and how to display emotions such as happiness or rage. By instructing its members, culture guides behavior and communication, revealing to members how to act, think, talk, and listen.[15]

WHAT WE *KNOW* ABOUT DIFFERENCE MATTERS

Cultures outside of our own are operating with their own expectations for behavior and communication. If we fail to realize that people from different cultures may not look, think, or act as we

AP Photo/ASSOCIATED PRESS

do, we risk appearing insensitive, ignorant, or **culturally confused** (lacking knowledge of cultural difference). The culturally confused pay a high price. The following examples demonstrate the cost of cultural ignorance and its effect on communication.

- Showing the sole of a shoe (while crossing one's legs, e.g.) means nothing to observers in the United States or Europe. In Muslim cultures, the gesture is perceived as insulting.[16] Similarly, crossing your legs in the United States indicates you are relaxed, whereas in Korea it is a social faux pas.

- Blinking while another person talks is considered normal to North Americans; to Taiwanese it is considered impolite.[17]

- McDonald's fast-food chain unintentionally offended thousands of Muslims when it printed an excerpt from the Koran on its throwaway hamburger bags.[18] Muslims saw this as sacrilegious.

- The Japanese view business cards as an extension of a person, handling them with great care, whereas North Americans view them as a business formality and a convenience. Consequently, Americans often end up insulting the Japanese by treating a business card too casually.[19]

- Arabs typically adopt a direct body orientation when communicating, which can seem aggressive and unnerving to North Americans, who employ a stance that is somewhat less direct. Arabs and South Americans also tend to gesture vigorously when speaking to others, which the less physical North Americans construe as inappropriate and unmannerly. It is common in Middle Eastern cultures for both males and females to physically exaggerate responses, whereas in the United States emotions are more likely to be less public. In Japan, individuals may try to hide or mask certain emotions. It is common among Asian cultures to exhibit reserve and emotional restraint.

- North Americans place a high value on looking someone in the eye and tend to distrust those who fail to do so. The Japanese, in contrast, believe eye contact over a sustained period of time shows disrespect. Among Asian cultures, too much eye contact is deemed intrusive. Arabs, on the other hand, maintain direct eye contact for prolonged periods.

The Effects of Cultural Imperialism

Cultural imperialism is the expansion or dominion of one culture over another culture. When one culture presents itself as superior to others, relationships between members of the diverse cultures suffer. Not taking cultural practices into account impedes relationship building, whereas recognizing, respecting, and responding to differences among cultures allows for more meaningful relationships.

We need to be mindful not to rely on stereotypes. Everyone from a particular culture does not necessarily exhibit the same characteristics and communication traits. Failing to develop insights into cultural nuances can lead to lost opportunities and increased levels of tensions between people.

Being unaware of how others outside a culture view that culture's members can be equally costly. Deficient self- and cultural-awareness takes a toll on individuals and society. A survey was conducted of 1,259 teenagers from 12 countries whose main contact with Americans was through popular culture, including television programs and movies they watched and the music they listened to. Based on these experiences, in their judgment, Americans were violent, materialistic, sexually promiscuous, disrespectful of people unlike them, unconcerned about the poor, and prone to criminal activity. The study concluded that the export of American popular culture contributed to impressions of cultural imperialism. Because the way of life in the United Stated was promoted as superior to other ways of life, feelings of anti-Americanism had been fostered inadvertently.[20]

iStock/tanukiphoto

According to critics of cultural imperialism, the news, entertainment, and products of industrialized countries such as the United States tend to overwhelm the national cultures of other countries. There are signs, however, that the reign of American pop culture is beginning to erode. Increasing numbers of foreign films have been successes in the United States. U.S. music charts also regularly feature vocalists from the United States or other countries who sing in foreign languages, often Spanish. Foreign news services are increasingly influencing news coverage. Such exposure contributes to learning about diverse cultures and ourselves.

HOW WE *FEEL* ABOUT DIFFERENCE MATTERS

When we interact with people whose values or behavioral norms are different from ours, we need to be able to accept that diversity. Being culturally flexible enables us to communicate more effectively.

The Dangers of Ethnocentrism

When we reject diversity, we exhibit **ethnocentrism**, the tendency to see our own culture as superior to all others. This also is a key characteristic of failed intercultural communication. People who are ethnocentric experience great anxiety when engaging with people outside their culture. They may say things like, "They take our jobs," "They're everywhere," or "They're just not like us." The more ethnocentric individuals are, the greater their tendency to view groups other than their own as inferior. As a result, they blame others for problems they face and often turn the facts inside out, making unsupported accusations.[21] When we develop sets of "alternative facts," we close ourselves to learning the truth.

In an effort to combat revisionist histories, some decide to take action. Theo Wilson was one such person. Wilson was a Black man who had posted YouTube videos about culture and race. Wilson soon found himself being trolled by people who attacked him with racial slurs and cited twisted facts. Wilson decided to go undercover online by presenting himself as a White supremacist in an effort to figure out the reasons for their hatred of him. He created a ghost profile, and an avatar named John Carter, and passed himself off as a digital White supremacist. Through the 8 months he communicated with other White supremacists, he came to appreciate how their existence in an alt-right bubble contributed to their ability to generate an endless stream of non-White and non-Christian groups to blame for their problems as they struggled to maintain their cultural traditions; yet they were unable to offer any viable solutions.[22]

The Promise of Cultural Relativism

The opposite of ethnocentrism is **cultural relativism**. When you practice cultural relativism, instead of viewing the group to which you belong as superior to all others, you work to understand the behavior of other groups based on the context in which the behavior occurs, not just from your own frame of reference.

On the Look Out for Stereotypes and Prejudice

Two other factors, stereotypes and prejudice, also influence our reactions to people whose cultures differ from our own. Stereotypes, again, are mental images we carry around in our heads. They are shortcuts, both positive and negative, that we use to guide our reactions to others.[23] Stereotypes can generate unrealistic pictures of others and prevent us from distinguishing an individual from a group. Racial profiling is just one example of how stereotyping affects us.

Why do we engage in racial profiling? Consider these facts: The human brain categorizes people by race in the first one-fifth of a second after seeing a face. Brain scans suggest that, even when asked to categorize others by gender, people also categorize them by race.[24] Could this be a factor in racial profiling? Racial profiling is indicative of prejudice. Prejudice describes how we feel about a group of people whom, more likely than not, we don't know personally. A negative or positive prejudgment, prejudice arises either because we want to feel more positively about our own group or because we feel others present a threat, real or not.[25] Thus, prejudice leads to the creation of in- and out-groups with out-group members becoming easy targets for discrimination.

Because of the negative expectations that stereotypes and prejudice produce, we may try to avoid interacting with people who are the objects of our prejudice (perhaps those of another race) or attack them when we do. (We discuss stereotypes and prejudice again in Chapter 3.)

CULTURES WITHIN CULTURES

To become more adept at communicating with people who differ culturally from us, we need to learn not only about their cultures but also about our own.

INFLUENCES ON CULTURAL IDENTITY AND COMMUNICATION PRESENCE

We all belong to a number of groups, including those defined by gender, age, racial and ethnic, religious, socioeconomic, and national identities. Our cultural identity, based on these group memberships, influences our behavior, including our personal, community, and professional relationships.

Gender Roles

How we define gender roles affects the ways males and females present themselves, socialize, work, perceive their futures, and communicate. U.S. men tend to adopt a problem-solving orientation, while women tend to be relationship oriented.[26]

Age

We also have ideas regarding the meaning and significance of age, including how people our age should look and behave. In the United States, large numbers of people place great value on appearing youthful and younger than their actual ages. In contrast, in Muslim, Asian, and Latin American cultures, people respect rather than deny aging.

Racial and Ethnic Identities

Our racial and ethnic identities are similarly socially constructed. Some racial and ethnic groups, for example, share experiences of oppression. Their attitudes and behaviors may reflect

ETHICS AND COMMUNICATION

Through Others' Eyes

Imagine you arrive in the United States from another country. Perhaps unlikely, also imagine that you are totally unfamiliar with what life in the United States is like. In fact, until now you have never viewed American television, watched American films, or listened to American music. You do, however, read and understand English. You find TVGuide.com on the Internet. Based on your perusal of the titles and descriptions of prime-time network and cable programming, what characteristics would you attribute to Americans? How many of your listed characteristics would you consider positive? Negative?

If asked to summarize your discoveries, what conclusions would you draw about what Americans value? What subjects would you identify as of great interest to them? How would you assess their attitudes toward people from other cultures? Finally, what suggestions would you like to offer them?

their struggles, influencing their attitudes toward contemporary issues such as affirmative action.

Religious Identity

Religious identity is at the root of countless contemporary conflicts occurring in numerous areas, including the Middle East, India, Pakistan, and the United States, with anti-Muslim sentiment becoming a factor in the 2016 U.S. presidential election.[27] The least religiously diverse states in the United States are in the South.[28]

Socioeconomic Identity

Similarly, socioeconomic identity frames how we respond to issues of our day. The significant gap between the ultra-wealthy and the middle and working classes in the United States is contributing to their developing different attitudes on a wide array of issues. National identity refers to our legal status or citizenship. People whose ancestors were from other countries may have been U.S. citizens for generations, yet some still perceive them as foreigners. Do you?

Generational Differences

In addition to recognizing how gender, racial and ethnic, religious, socioeconomic, and national differences affect cultural identity, we also need to acknowledge the role generational differences play in our communication with one another.

Demographers usually classify people into the following generations: matures, boomers, Gen X, Gen Y (the millennial generation), and iGen.

The Greatest Generation. Called "the greatest generation," matures were born between 1900 and 1945. World War II and the Cold War were two of their defining experiences. Matures are known for respecting authority, following the rules, being loyal to their employing organizations, and respecting timeliness.

The Baby Boom. Boomers, born between 1946 and 1964, came of age during the space race, the civil rights movement, the Vietnam War, and Watergate. They are famous for questioning authority, displaying a "can do" attitude, and focusing on how to get their way. The first TV generation, boomers actually had to get off the couch to change channels.

Generation X. Gen X-ers, who were born between 1965 and 1982, saw traditional gender roles bend and flex. The Web emerged during their formative years. They are known for seeking a work–life balance and being loyal to people, not organizations.

Generation Y: The Millennials. Gen Y members, born between 1983 and 1995, are referred to as the millennial generation or as digital natives. They are known for being technologically savvy. They also have exceedingly high expectations and think they are proficient multitaskers. They are apt to spend more time with the Internet and media than they do face-to-face with others. One out of three Gen Y members is a minority.

iGeneration. The postmillennial generation (born after 1995) is the most digitally savvy among us and the first generation to grow up with smartphones. Also called Generation Z or the App Generation, the iGeneration has no memory of a time without social media. Although still forming their identities, they nonetheless are expected to present a crystallized and idealized online identity.[29] Described as conscientious, somewhat anxious, and predisposed to "play it safe," they are looked to as prime influencers of tomorrow and mindful of the future. They tend to embrace anonymous media platforms where incriminating images disappear virtually instantly. Sometimes referred as "millennials on steroids," they are concerned with their personal brands but believe that the generation before them posted too openly.[30]

CAREER BUILDER: GEN-YOU AND FUTURE ME

Culture influences many of our work orientations, including the ability to work in a team, conceptions of leadership, ideas of rewards, attitudes toward gender, ideas about power, the amount of uncertainty one can tolerate, and the topics discussed with coworkers. Of course, culture also impacts ability to work with the members of diverse generations.

1. First, explain how your cultural identification influences you on each of the variables identified in the previous paragraph.

2. Next, discuss the behaviors that you and others of your generation should adopt in order to work successfully in organizations alongside members of earlier and/or later generations. What would you explain to members of these other generations regarding how to work successfully with you?

3. Finally, indicate how you would determine if an organization's culture reflected your values and was a good fit for you.

CULTURES AND CO-CULTURES

A **culture** is the system of knowledge, beliefs, values, customs, behaviors, and artifacts that are acquired, shared, and used by its members during daily living.[31] Within a culture as a whole are co-cultures. **Co-cultures** are composed of members of the same general culture who differ in some ethnic or sociological way from the parent culture. In our society, African Americans, Hispanic Americans, Japanese Americans, the disabled, gays and lesbians, and the elderly are just some of the co-cultures belonging to the same general culture[32] (Figure 2.2).

FIGURE 2.2

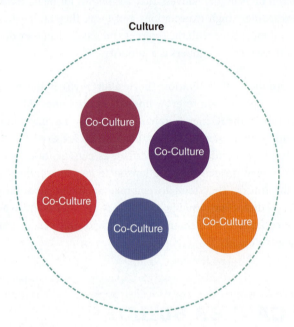

Co-Cultures and Communication Strategies

Have you ever identified as an outsider? People who believe they belong to a marginalized group—that is, a group whose members feel like outsiders—have a number of options to choose from regarding how they want to interact with members of the dominant culture or even if they want to interact with them at all. Have you, or has anyone you know, used any of the strategies that follow?

Assimilation. Co-culture members who use the strategy of **assimilation** attempt to fit in or join with members of the dominant culture. They converse about subjects that members of the dominant talk about, such as cars or sports, or they dress as members of the dominant culture dress. They give up their own ways in an effort to assume the modes of behavior of the dominant culture.

Accommodation. In comparison, co-culture members who use the strategy of **accommodation** attempt to maintain their cultural identity even while they strive to establish relationships with members of the dominant culture. A gay man or lesbian who takes his or her partner to an occasion at which members of the dominant culture will be present, such as a company or family celebration, is using the strategy of accommodation.

Separation. On the other hand, when members of a co-culture resist interacting with members of the dominant culture, they employ the strategy of resistance, or **separation**. Because these people, such as Hasidic Jews, prefer to interact with each other rather than have contact with people they perceive to be outsiders, they tend to keep to themselves.

Co-Cultures and Communication Approaches

Members of co-cultures can use passive, assertive, aggressive, or confrontational communication approaches in their efforts to accomplish their objectives relative to the dominant culture.

Passive Communication. Co-culture members who use a passive communication approach seek to avoid the limelight. They accept their position in the cultural hierarchy. Rather than defend their ways and oppose others, they embrace the cultural beliefs and practices of the dominant culture. Recent immigrants to the United States who desire to attain citizenship may choose this path, hoping to blend in so that they do not disturb the status quo.

Assertive Communication. Co-culture members who use an assertive communication approach may seek to communicate a shared cultural identity with members of the dominant group. They want others to accommodate their diversity. They are receptive to rethinking a number of their ideas and may give up or modify some while holding on to others. After the September 11, 2001, terrorist attacks, for example, many Arab Americans spoke openly of their patriotism, their support for the war against terror, and their desire for others to allow them to live according to their values and beliefs.

More Aggressive Communication. Co-culture members who use a more aggressive communication approach defend their own beliefs and traditions with intensity and may be perceived by members of the dominant culture as "hurtfully expressive" or "self-promoting." They make it difficult for members of the dominant culture to ignore their presence or pretend they do not exist.[33] They adopt this strategy to demarginalize themselves and actively participate in the world known to members of the dominant culture. In the early years of Act Up, a gay rights organization, members employed this approach (Table 2.1).

TABLE 2.1 PREFERRED STRATEGIES AND COMMUNICATION APPROACHES OF MARGINALIZED GROUPS

STRATEGY	COMMUNICATION APPROACH	EXAMPLE
Separation	Passive	Lunching alone, living in an area with similar people
Accommodation	Assertive	Wearing a yarmulke to work, wearing a sari to a party
Assimilation	Aggressive, confrontational	Staging a protest

SKILL BUILDER

Assessing Ethnocentrism Versus Cultural Relativism

Evaluate your culturally ethnocentric or relativistic tendencies. Label the following statements as true or false, providing an example of a behavior you used when either interacting with or avoiding interacting with a member of another culture.

1. I go out of my way to be with people who are like me.

2. I can cooperate with people like me, but I find it difficult to cooperate with people unlike me.

3. I trust those who are like me more freely than I trust those who are different from me.

4. I am less fearful when I am around people like me than when I am around people unlike me.

5. I am much more apt to blame people unlike me for causing trouble than I am to blame people like me.

6. I believe that people unlike me should make an effort to become more like me.

What do your answers and examples reveal? Are there some cultures different from your own that you are more comfortable with than others? What steps are you willing to take, if any, to minimize the potentially negative effects of ethnocentrism?

Understanding both the general culture and its co-cultures is essential for effective communication. Merely knowing another's language is not enough. It also is necessary to become aware of the norms and rules of the culture or co-cultures that might influence the nature of interactions you have with its members. It is important to understand the ways culture shapes interaction.

> Visit the interactive e-Book to access the Exploring Diversity feature "Understanding Other Cultures," which will help you reflect on the different cultures you encounter in your everyday life.

DIMENSIONS OF CULTURE IN ACTION

By exploring five dimensions used to distinguish cultures, we can increase our ability to understand our own and other cultures. These five dimensions are (1) individualistic versus collectivistic, (2) high-context versus low-context communication, (3) high power distance versus low power distance, (4) monochronic versus polychronic, and (5) masculine or feminine culture.

INDIVIDUALISM VERSUS COLLECTIVISM

The cultural dimension of individualism versus collectivism reveals how people define themselves in their relationships with others.

Individualistic cultures, such as those of Great Britain, the United States, Canada, France, and Germany, stress individual goals, whereas collectivistic cultures, represented by many Arab, African, Asian, and Latin American countries, give precedence to group goals. Individualistic cultures cultivate individual initiative and achievement, while collectivistic cultures tend to nurture group influences. This means that, whereas the "I" may be most important in individualistic cultures, the "we" is the dominant force in collectivistic ones. In collectivistic cultures, the individual is expected to fit into the group; in individualistic cultures, emphasis is placed on developing the sense of self.

HIGH CONTEXT VERSUS LOW CONTEXT

A second way that cultures vary in communication style is in their preference for high-context or low-context communication.

Cultures with high-context communication systems are tradition bound. Their cultural traditions shape the behavior and lifestyle of group members, causing them to appear to members of low-context cultures to be overly polite and indirect in relating to others. In contrast, cultures with low-context communication systems generally encourage members to exhibit a more direct communication style

Members of low-context cultures tend to gather background information when meeting someone for the first time. Thus, they will ask people they have just met where they went to college, where they live, and who they work for. People from high-context cultures are much less likely to ask such questions up front.[34] In addition, people from low-context cultures are apt to feel that they have to explain everything rather than rely on nonverbal, contextual information. In contrast, people who believe that most messages can be understood without direct verbal interaction reveal their preference for high-context communication. Asian cultures typically emphasize high-context communication, whereas Western cultures typically represent low-context systems. For example, the Japanese traditionally value silence, believing that a person of few words is thoughtful, trustworthy, and respectable. Thus, the Japanese spend considerably less time talking than do people in the United States. This orientation also helps explain why the Japanese often perceive self-disclosures during interaction as socially inappropriate.

HIGH POWER DISTANCE VERSUS LOW POWER DISTANCE

Power distance measures the extent to which individuals are willing to accept power differences.

Individuals from **high power distance cultures** such as Saudi Arabia, India, and Malaysia, view power as a fact of life and are apt to stress its coercive or referent nature. Superiors and subordinates in these countries are likely to view each other differently; subordinates are quick to defer to superiors. In contrast, individuals from **low power distance cultures**, such as Israel, Sweden, and the United States, believe power should be used only when it is legitimate; thus, they are apt to employ expert or legitimate power. Superiors and subordinates from low power distance countries emphasize their interdependence by displaying a preference for consultation; subordinates will even contradict their bosses when necessary.[35]

MONOCHRONIC VERSUS POLYCHRONIC CULTURE

Life in some places around the globe is not as fast paced as it is in most of Europe and North America. In Kenya, Argentina, and southern U.S. states, activities are often conducted at

iStock/Paul Bradbury

a slower rhythm and without the same sense of urgency. According to Hall, cultures approach time in one of two ways: as **monochronic** or **polychronic**.[36]

People attuned to monochronic time schedule time carefully, one event at a time, preferring to complete an activity before beginning another. In contrast, people brought up using polychronic time are not obsessed with time and refuse to be its slaves. Rather than rigidly scheduling or segmenting their time, they readily give in to distractions and interruptions, even choosing to tackle several different problems or hold several different conversations at the same time. Additionally, rather than trying to be on time, like monochronic people, polychronic people may be late for an appointment, change an appointment right up to the last minute, or opt not to arrive for their appointment at all.[37]

MASCULINE VERSUS FEMININE CULTURE

Cultures differ in their attitudes toward gender roles.[38] In highly **masculine cultures**, members value aggressiveness, strength, and material symbols of success. In highly **feminine cultures**, members value relationships, tenderness in members of both sexes, and a high quality of life. Among highly masculine cultures are Japan, Italy, Germany, Mexico, and Great Britain. Among highly feminine cultures are Sweden, Norway, the Netherlands, Thailand, and Chile. Masculine cultures socialize members to be dominant and competitive. They tend to confront conflicts head-on and are likely to use a win–lose conflict resolution strategy. In contrast, the members of feminine cultures are more apt to compromise and negotiate to resolve conflicts, seeking win–win solutions.

INTERPRETING CULTURAL DIFFERENCES

Where a culture falls on the individualistic–collectivistic, low-context versus high-context communication, and power distance scales affects the interactional preferences of its members. Developing a fuller comprehension of these dimensions can improve communication between the members of diverse cultures. For example, knowing whether individuals tend to understate their accomplishments or take credit for personal achievements can keep you from passing judgments that may be ill-founded.

When people from diverse cultures interact, unless their differences in orientation are acknowledged, interactions may well result in misunderstandings.

TECHNOLOGY AND COMMUNITY

Like communication, technology and culture shape one another. Technology and computers are changing the traditional definition of a community.

NEIGHBORHOODS NEED NOT BE REAL

When we speak of community today, we no longer are limited to real neighborhoods. We have widened the concept of community to include those existing in cyberspace, and the number of virtual communities in cyberspace continues to rise. Because the Internet permeates national boundaries, it erodes the connection between location and experience, enabling us to interact more easily with people who have different worldviews than we do.[39] At the same time, it enables us to find groups of people who think the same way we do and who resemble us in every conceivable way.

WE CONSCIOUSLY CAN CHOOSE OUR NEIGHBORS

We can choose our "online neighbors" just as we choose a real neighborhood.

The fear in this development is that communicating solely with like-minded people may lead to the polarization of opinions, whereas communicating with mixed-minded people tends to bring about a moderation of viewpoints.[40] A preference for likeness and an intolerance for difference often leads to the development of online in-groups (composed of people whom we perceive to be like us) and out-groups (composed of those we view as different from us) whom we may block or "unfriend."

On the bright side, sites such as Facebook do let us stay in touch with friends as well as provide opportunities to reacquaint us with those with whom we have lost touch. They also let us friend people we barely know.

OTHER REASONS WE SEEK VIRTUAL COMMUNITIES

Many virtual communities are social networking sites in which users create profiles or avatars—alternate selves or images of characters—that they use to interact with others online. Why are people seeking multiple lives? Could it be because the neighborhoods they live in are not delivering the person-to-person contacts they seek? Millions of people go online in search of surrogate neighborhoods and relationships. This has led some critics to assert that rather than bringing people together, computer networks are isolating us. They contend that online communities are missing the essence of real neighborhoods, including a sense of location and a feeling of permanence and belonging.

THE POWER OF DIALOGUE

The ability to reach so many different people from so many different places so quickly gives communicators a new sense of power. Wherever we live, we can use the Internet to help bring diversity and new cultures into our lives, changing our social, political, and business lives. Some worry that the culture of computing, especially participating in the Internet's message boards, attracts extreme political positions and contributes to long-standing international conflicts. In contrast, advocates believe it facilitates international dialogue.[41]

Are all voices really being heard? Are we becoming more or less tolerant of each other? Are we aware that words posted to global online groups have consequences, just as they do when delivered in person? If we use the Internet wisely, we will find ways to increase the scope and diversity of our knowledge and develop our abilities to work together in diverse teams to solve personal, professional, and societal problems.[42]

FOR GOOD AND BAD

The Internet can be used for good and for evil. Those in control of governments during periods of unrest in such places such as Egypt and China have censored the Web, even suspending access to YouTube and Twitter in the effort to preserve their power by controlling what the people in their countries were able to say and see over the Internet. However, tech-savvy activists usually find ways to circumvent such Internet controls. In fact, the Arab Spring uprisings across the Middle East played out on a global digital stage.[43] The numbers of people going online to follow world events or for social networking continues to grow.

The **digital divide**, which refers to inequality in access to technology and the Internet, is shrinking. Minorities, the elderly, and the poor are going online in greater numbers, democratizing access. Still, gaining access to computers remains a problem in many places around the world because of high poverty levels and the absence or unreliability of electricity.

Photographee.eu/Shutterstock.com

Let us close this section with some questions for you to think about. When you go online, do you seek to interact in communities based on difference or likeness? In other words, how many of the sites you visit online are visited by people who think and behave similarly to you, and how many are frequented by people who think and behave differently from you? Do you think the Internet is better at creating more insular communities, or does it foster interest in diversity?

COMMUNICATION SKILLS
Practice Communicating Interculturally

Despite technology's inroads, there are too many of "us" who do not work as hard as we should at communicating with people from different cultures, simply because we do not wish to live or interact with "them."[44] To counter this, we need to make reducing the strangeness of strangers a priority in our lives. How can we do this?

Focus on mastering and maintaining these skills as you work to eliminate ineffective behaviors.

Refrain from formulating expectations based solely on your culture.

When those you interact with have diverse communication styles, it is critical that you acknowledge the differences and accept their validity. By not isolating yourself within your own group or culture, you allow yourself to be more fully a part of a multicultural society and thus a better communicator.

Recognize how faulty education can impede understanding.

It is important to identify and work to eliminate any personal biases and prejudices you have developed over the years. Determine, for example, the extent to which your family and friends have influenced your feelings about people from other cultural groups. Do those you have grown up with appear comfortable or uncomfortable relating to people of different cultural origins? To what extent have their attitudes affected your intercultural communication competence?

(Continued)

(Continued)

Make a commitment to develop intercultural communication skills for life in a multicultural world.

Although culture is a tie that binds, the creation of a global village makes it essential that you leave the comfort of your cultural niche, become more knowledgeable of other cultures, and strive to be culturally aware.

Familiarize yourself with the communication rules and preferences of members of different cultures so that you can increase the effectiveness of your interactions. Act on these suggestions.

- Seek information from people whose cultures are different from your own.
- Try to understand how the experiences of people from different cultures lead them to develop different perspectives.
- Pay attention to the situation and context of any intercultural communication.
- Make efforts to become a more flexible communicator; don't insist that people from other cultures communicate on your terms.

> Diversity is about all of us, and about how to figure out how to walk through this world together.

Jacqueline Woodson

COMPLETE THIS CHAPTER 2 CHECKLIST

2.1 I can explain the significance of intercultural communication in the global community. □

Globalization is the increasing economic, political, and cultural integration and interdependence of diverse cultures. Diversity is the recognition and valuing of difference. Multiculturalism is the practice of respecting and engaging with people from different cultures. Through intercultural communication, we interpret and share meanings with individuals from different cultures.

2.2 I can explain how and why U.S. society has moved away from a melting pot philosophy, which advocates the assimilation of different cultures into the dominant culture. □

As demographics changed and minorities gained visibility in all areas of society, cultural pluralism, or acknowledging that other cultural groups are equal in value to one's own, has gained prominence. Respect and appreciation for difference are key in today's society.

2.3 I can analyze various attitudes toward diversity. □

Ethnocentrism is the tendency to see one's own culture as superior to all others. Cultural relativism is the opposite of ethnocentrism. Stereotypes are mental images or pictures we carry around in our heads; they are shortcuts we use to guide our reactions to others. A prejudice is a negative or positive prejudgment that leads to the creation of in- and out-groups.

2.4 I can explain influences on cultural identity, distinguishing the difference between cultures and co-cultures. □

Among the groups that influence cultural identity, and on which cultural identity is based, are those defined by gender, age racial, ethnic, religious, socioeconomic, national, and generational identities. A culture is a system of knowledge; beliefs, values, customs, behaviors, and artifacts that are acquired, shared, and used by members. A co-culture is a group of people who differ in some ethnic or sociological way from the parent culture.

2.5 I can illustrate the five main dimensions of cultural variability. □

Cultures vary in five general ways: (1) individualism versus collectivism, (2) high versus low context, (3) high versus low power distance, (4) monochronic versus polychronic, and (5) masculine versus feminine. Individual cultures stress individual goals. Collectivistic cultures stress group goals. High-context communication cultures are bound to tradition and value indirectness. Low-context communication cultures encourage directness in communication. High power distance cultures view power as a fact of life with subordinates deferring to superiors. Low power distance cultures believe power should be used only if legitimate. Monochronic cultures schedule time carefully. Polychronic cultures refuse to be time's slaves. Masculine cultures value aggressiveness, strength, and material success. Feminine cultures value relationships, tenderness, and high quality of life.

· ·

2.6 I can discuss how technology brings diversity into our lives. □

For many of us, the Internet facilitates this task. By enabling us to join a wide range of online communities and interact with people who hold different worldviews, the Internet enhances our ability to communicate within and across cultural boundaries. We also risk becoming more isolated or insulated from other viewpoints if we are not careful.

· ·

2.7 I can apply communication skills to reduce the strangeness of strangers. □

Although the lessons taught by culture influence our communication style preferences, there are techniques we can use to reduce the strangeness of strangers. By adding to the storehouse of knowledge that underscores our communication competence, we increase our ability to handle communication challenges.

· ·

BECOME A WORD MASTER

accommodation 34

assimilation 34

co-cultures 34

collectivistic cultures 37

cultural imperialism 28

cultural pluralism 26

cultural relativism 30

culturally confused 28

culture 34

digital divide 41

diversity 24

ethnocentrism 29

feminine cultures 39

globalization 24

high-context communication 37

high power distance cultures 38

individualistic cultures 37

intercultural communication 25

interethnic communication 25

international communication 25

interracial communication 25

intracultural communication 25

low-context communication 37

low power distance cultures 38

masculine cultures 39

melting pot philosophy 26

monochronic 38

multiculturalism 24

polychronic 38

separation 35

iStock/DMEPhotography

iStock/mapodile

3

The "I" Behind the Eye: Perception and the Self

3.1 Define and explain the process of *perception*.

3.2 Describe the nature of self-concept.

3.3 Describe the various ways self-concept affects behavior.

3.4 Describe the factors affecting self-concept and outlook.

3.5 Explain how to use life scripts, the Johari window, and impression management to develop self-awareness.

3.6 Identify common barriers to perception.

3.7 Explain how gender impacts perception of the self and others.

3.8 Explain how culture impacts perception of the self and others.

3.9 Analyze how media, including digital and social media, influence perception of the self and others.

3.10 Use communication skills to improve the accuracy of self-perception, perception of others, and perceptions of events.

> As I am, so I see.
>
> Ralph Waldo Emerson

Can we believe our eyes? Do we actually see what's there? Are you aware that the testimony given by eyewitnesses during trials is wrong about one third of the time?[1] How can we account for differences in how we perceive ourselves, other people, objects, and events? What do our contrasting reports tell us about how we think and feel about ourselves, and our relationship to others and society? And if we do not see the same thing and cannot agree on what we see, how are we able to communicate with one another about anything? These are some of the questions we address in this chapter. ■

PERCEPTION OF THE SELF, OTHERS, AND EXPERIENCE

How we perceive ourselves, others, and experience influences all we say and do. Perception, self-concept, and communication are intertwined, interacting with and influencing one another. Two or more people will not necessarily perceive you similarly. In fact, many of them may not see you as you see yourself. For example, when one consultant asked a group of college students to select a word representing how employers perceived them, she told the students that the word she was looking for began with the letter *e*. What word would you have selected? Students, believing that employers viewed them positively, suggested answers such as *enthusiastic* and *energetic*. The correct answer was *entitled*.[2]

The meanings we form, and the messages we send to others about what we see and how we think, shape their understanding of us. Similarly, how you perceive yourself affects your relationship with yourself. What words would you select to describe that relationship? Do your chosen words suggest you feel good about yourself? If not, what is it about your perception of you that keeps you from doing so?

People living in different countries, the members of different generations, and the members of different genders, races, religions, or classes (just to name a few demographic categories) also tend to perceive things differently. They have different opinions about many things, including the alt-right, same-sex marriage, transgender people, immigration, human rights, and the news media. By exploring the "I" behind the eye, we will come to better understand why each of us is much more than a camera and why the "I" of the perceiver makes such a big difference.

WHAT IS PERCEPTION?

Perception is the complex process we use to make experience our own. Thus, what actually occurs in the "real world" may be quite different from what we perceive. We define **perception** as the process of selecting, organizing, subjectively interpreting, retrieving, and responding to sensory data in a way that enables us to make sense or meaning of our world. Our physical location, interests, personal desires, attitudes, values, personal experiences, physical condition, and psychological states interact to influence our perceptions.

PERCEPTION OCCURS IN STAGES

Perception involves a series of stages: (1) the selecting stage, during which we attend to only some stimuli from all those to which we are exposed; (2) the organizing stage, during which we give order to the selected stimuli; (3) the interpreting/evaluating stage, during which we make sense of or give meaning to the stimuli we have selected and organized based on our life experiences; (4) the retrieving stage, during which we use our memory to recall related information; and (5) the responding stage, during which we decide what to think, say, or do as a result of what we have perceived (Figure 3.1).

FIGURE 3.1

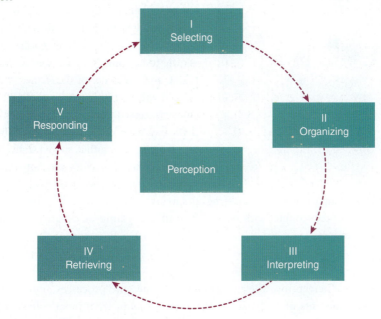

PERCEPTION IS SELECTIVE AND PERSONAL

Our senses function as perceptual antennae gathering information at all times, which makes it impossible for us to process every stimulus available to us. Without realizing it, we take steps to select or limit what we perceive. According to information theorists, the eye processes about 5 million bits of data per second. The brain, however, is able to use only some 500 bits per second. Therefore, we are forced to select those stimuli that we will attend to or experience. We combat data overload by simply not assimilating large amounts of data, focusing instead on the data we want for closer and more careful viewing. Effectively, attention helps us focus. We shift our searchlight of attention from one person, place, or thing to another, until one catches our interest, transforming our perceptual searchlight into a perceptual spotlight that we now focus on a selected stimulus.[3]

As we saw in Figure 3.1, selection is a key part of the perception process. We use **selective perception**—an aspect of the perceptual process that includes **selective exposure** (the tendency to expose oneself to information that reaffirms existing attitudes, beliefs, and values; the tendency to close oneself to new experiences), **selective attention** (the tendency to focus on certain cues or stimuli and ignore others), and **selective retention** (the tendency to remember those things that reinforce one's way of thinking and forget those that do not).

EFFECTS OF SELECTIVITY

Selective perception enables us to create a more limited and also a more coherent and personally meaningful picture of the world, one that conforms to the beliefs, expectations, and convictions we hold. For example, in a famous experiment, subjects were shown a short video of two teams, one wearing white shirts and the other in black shirts, moving around and passing basketballs

© 1999, Daniel J. Simons. Video screenshot taken at http://www.theinvisiblegorilla.com/videos.html

to one another. The subjects were asked to count the number of passes made by members of the white team. Halfway through the video, a person wearing a full-body gorilla-suit walks slowly to the middle of the screen, pounds its chest, and walks out of the frame. While consumed with counting passes, about 50% of the subjects missed the gorilla. Their mental spotlight had been directed elsewhere. They were not looking for a gorilla, so they didn't see one.[4]

Perceptual processes are not only highly selective, they also are personally based. As a result, different people experience the same cues in very different ways. In essence, we never really come into direct contact with reality.[5] Instead, everything we experience is mediated by the nervous system.

Age and Memory Influence Perception

Age can influence perception. The aging brain consumes and processes more data, sifting through larger amounts of information than the brains of traditional college-aged students. Students this age are more able to ignore distractions, whereas older people, because of their reduced ability to filter, exhibit more inclusive attention. As a result, older people tend not to make snap judgments regarding what is or could become important. This frees them to learn more about situations and people—giving them a potential perceptual advantage.[6]

Memory and perception are also linked. Earlier perceptions influence future ones.[7] How we interpret and respond to selected stimuli determines if a particular person or experience enters our memory. If a perception does enter our memory, we are able to retrieve and use it again and again.

A reliable memory, however, depends on whether our reconstruction of experience is accurate and clear.[8] Our perceptual abilities, distorted by our beliefs, desires, and interests, affect how we interpret and remember events.[9] For example, although it occurred in 2001, many of us still have vivid memories of 9/11. In interviews, when asked to recall those memories, people spoke of having watched television all morning, riveted by images of the two planes striking the twin towers. This memory was, in fact, false. There was no video of the first plane hitting the North Tower of the World Trade Center on 9/11. Despite this reality, 73% of Americans surveyed said they saw this happen. What's more, they felt confident about their memories.

Memories of events that did not actually happen the way we remember them are the cause of countless disputes. Memory is a human construct, an amalgam of what we experience, read, piece together, and want to be true. A number of reasons account for our misremembering events: Memories are transient and tend to fade over time; we remember aspects of an event but are likely to misattribute them; and our biases distort our recollections.

When has memory influenced your perception of an event? Our memories, like perception, are fallible, something we need to remember.[10]

WE ORGANIZE OUR PERCEPTIONS

How do we make sense of our world? How do we process the stimuli that compete for our attention? Just as we use an array of strategies to select those impressions we notice, so we employ a number of strategies to facilitate meaningful organization of these impressions.

The Figure–Ground Principle

During the perception process, we are active participants. We do not simply sit back and absorb the stimuli available to us the way a sponge absorbs liquid. We select, organize, and evaluate the multitude of stimuli that bombard us, so that what we are focusing on becomes *figure* and the rest of what we experience becomes *ground*.[11] This is how the **figure–ground principle** functions.

To experience the concept of figure and ground, examine Figure 3.2. What do you see? At first glance, you likely see a vase—or you may see two people facing each other. When stimuli compete for our attention, we can focus only on one, because it is simply impossible to perceive something in two ways at once. Although we may be able to switch our focus rapidly, we still will perceive only one stimulus at any given time.

FIGURE 3.2

Face Vase Illusion

Perceptual Constancy

Perceptual constancy is the tendency we have to maintain the same perception of something or someone over time. As a consequence of perceptual constancy, we see people not as they are, but as we have been conditioned to see them. This helps explain why it is hard for us to alter a perception once we form it.

Perceptual Schemata

We also use *perceptual schemata* to organize our perceptions. For example, we'll categorize people using *physical constructs*, which describe people's appearance to classify them, such as whether one is overweight or slender, beautiful or ugly; *role constructs*, which describe social position, including wife, daughter, teacher; *interaction constructs*, which are descriptive of people's social behavior, like caring, ingratiating, or approachable; and *psychological constructs*, which emphasize people's state of mind, such as whether one is secure, sad, or self-obsessed.[12]

FIGURE 3.3

Closure

The tendency to fill in missing perceptual pieces is called **closure**. Look at the stimuli pictured in Figure 3.3. What do you see? Most see a dog rather than a collection of inkblots, and a rectangle, triangle, and circle rather than some lines and an arc. Because we seek to fill in gaps, we mentally complete the incomplete figures. We fill them in on the basis of our previous experiences and our needs. We make sense of ourselves, people, and events in much the same way. We fill in what is not there by making assumptions or inferences, some of which are more accurate and valid than others. We should remember this when we explore how we perceive the self.

PERCEIVING THE "I" AFFECTS PERCEPTION OF YOU

How we perceive and communicate with ourselves, and how others perceive and communicate with us, builds in us a sense of self. Our sense of self evolves as we interact with different people, experience new situations, and form new relationships.

LOOKING AT THE SELF

It is important to spend time considering who you think you are.

If someone asked you to answer the question "Who are you?" 10 separate times—and if each time you had to supply a fresh response—what responses would you offer? Would you

be able to group your answers into categories? For example, do you see yourself in reference to your gender (male, female, trans), your religion (Buddhist, Jewish, Muslim, Christian), your race (African, Hispanic, Caucasian, Asian), your nationality (U.S. citizen, Turkish, German), your physical attributes (heavy, slim), your roles (wife, son, student, employee), your attitudes and emotions (hopeful, pessimistic, personable), your mental abilities (sharp, slow), and your talents (musically or artistically gifted)? The words you use to describe yourself are revealing both to yourself and to others.

THE IMPORTANCE OF SELF-AWARENESS

The self is a social product—a composite of who we think we are, who other people think we are, and who we think others think we are. Some of us are more self-aware than others; this developed **self-awareness** (the ability to reflect on and monitor one's own behavior) facilitates a fuller understanding of the self, including our attitudes, beliefs, and values, as well as our strengths and weaknesses.[13]

THE NATURE OF SELF-CONCEPT

How we think about ourselves, or our **self-concept** (the consistent and organized image you form of yourself) is composed of two parts—self-image and self-esteem.

Self-image is your mental picture of yourself. It is the kind of person you perceive yourself to be. Self-image includes the roles you see yourself performing, the categories you place yourself within, the words you use to describe or identify yourself, and your understanding of how others see you.

Self-esteem, on the other hand, is a self-assessment of yourself. It is your evaluation of your ability and worth and indicates how well you like and value yourself. Self-esteem usually derives from your successes and failures, coloring your self-image with a predominantly positive or negative hue. By age 5, many of us already have developed a sense of our self-worth.[14]

According to researcher Chris Mruk, self-esteem has five dimensions that affect your feelings about yourself and your communication with others:

- Competence (your beliefs about your ability to be effective)

- Worthiness (your beliefs about the degree to which others value you)

- Cognition (your beliefs about your character and personality)

- Affect (your evaluation of yourself and the feelings generated by your evaluation)

- Stability (your assessment of how much beliefs about yourself change)[15]

Self-concept significantly affects behavior, including what we think is possible, whom we choose to communicate with, and even whether we desire to communicate with anyone.

HOW SELF-CONCEPT DEVELOPS

How did your self-concept form? The day you recognized yourself as separate from your surroundings, life for you began to change. At that moment, your concept of self—that relatively stable set of perceptions you attribute to yourself—became your most important possession.

Although you are not born with a self-concept, you definitely play a role in its construction.[16] Even though you are constantly undergoing change, once built, the theory or picture you have of yourself is fairly stable and difficult to alter. Have you ever tried to revise your parents' or friends' opinions about themselves? Did you have any luck? Over time, our opinions about ourselves grow more and more resistant to change.

A number of forces converge to create your self-concept. Among them are the ways in which others relate to you; how you experience and evaluate yourself; the roles you enact; the messages you absorb from popular and social media; the expectations you and others have for you; and the gender, cultural, and technological messages you internalize.

To a large extent, your self-concept is shaped by your environment and by the people around you, including your parents, relatives, teachers, supervisors, friends, and coworkers. If those important to you have a good image of you, they probably make you feel accepted, valued, worthwhile, lovable, and significant. As a result, you are likely to develop a positive self-concept. In comparison, if those important to you have a poor image of you, it can make you feel left out, small, worthless, unloved, or insignificant. You, more than likely, will develop a negative self-concept as a consequence.

THE CONNECTION BETWEEN SELF-CONCEPT AND BEHAVIOR

We are both cause and the controlling force of our perceptions. But what leads us to respond to what we experience as we do?

ATTRIBUTION THEORY

According to **attribution theory**, we like to be able to explain why things happen. We assign meaning to behavior, coming up with possible motives and causes. When we attribute behavior to something in the disposition of others, we assume their behavior to have an internal cause—it is caused by something about them and their characteristics. When we attribute it to something about the situation or environment, we identify an external cause—and ascribe it as being the result of something outside of the person.

When we assume too often that the primary motivation for another's behavior is in the person, and not the situation, we commit a *fundamental attribution error*. We overemphasize factors internal to the individual and discount the role played by the situation. For example, a friend disappoints us by failing to show up on time to a study group. We're more likely to decide it's because our friend is inconsiderate rather than to believe that external factors, like the bus running late, are the cause.

It's different, however, when we ascribe reasons for our own behavior. When offering reasons for why we behave as we do, we are more likely to overemphasize external factors and downplay internal ones. This tendency, known as the *self-serving bias*, functions to raise our own self-esteem. We take credit for the positive while denying culpability for the negative. When it comes to ourselves, we attribute any negatives to factors beyond our control.

We also are prone to committing *over-attribution errors*—the attributing of everything a person does to a single or a few specific factors. For example, we might ascribe a person's alcohol use, poor grades, lackluster job performance, and lack of interest in close relationships to a broken romance.[17]

Quite simply, when it comes to interpreting the behavior of others and ourselves, we find behavior's causes where we look for them.

SELF-ESTEEM

A teacher praises a student for a job that wasn't done very well, observing that "I didn't want to hurt the student's self-esteem."[18] Others challenge the merit of a "feel-good curriculum" bemoaning the fact that we walk around on eggshells not to hurt another's self-esteem.[19] Why is self-esteem so critical? How does it impact us?

The Dark Side of Self-Esteem

Might an overemphasis on reinforcing self-esteem, especially in individuals whose self-esteem is already high, lead to an increase in bullying and narcissism?

Bullies are often among the most popular people.[20] This popularity can lead to self-appraisals that are unrealistically inflated.[21] Typically, high self-esteem combined with a sense of arrogance and narcissistic tendencies contributes to bullying.[22]

iStock/PeopleImages

Next, consider the adulation given to professional athletes, musicians, movie stars, and trendsetters on social networks. Our behavior toward them helps precipitate the self-centered, egomaniacal characteristics that they too often exhibit.

Do you think that we should balance the amount of praise we give to public figures, lest we feed their sense of self-importance to outsized proportions? When self-esteem is undeservedly high, people tend to ignore their own weaknesses. They suffer from an inflated sense of their worth, displaying an inappropriate overconfidence in their abilities. Unprepared for criticism, however, they quickly fall apart if told that they are wrong or lacking in some ability.[23]

Unlike those with high self-esteem, people with low self-esteem primarily define themselves by their limitations and can be negative about a lot of things. Those who possess either extremely high or low self-esteem do share something in common, however: self-absorption.

The Bright Side of Self-Esteem

People with normally high self-esteem tend to be happier[24] and less affected by peer pressure than those who have low self-esteem.[25] Individuals with healthy self-esteem are not self-absorbed. Rather than filling themselves with "unwarranted self-regard," they have a realistic sense of their abilities.[26] In touch with both their strengths and their weaknesses, they display grit—a combination of passion and perseverance for a singularly important goal, together with resilience and a tolerance for feeling frustrated.[27] Expecting a positive outcome, they persist in spite of failure. They are both confident and resilient, traits necessary for success.[28]

Researchers assert that high self-esteem is an effect of good performance, rather than its cause. According to J. D. Hawkins, president of the National Self-Esteem Association (NSEA), "Self-esteem is more than just feeling good about yourself. It's about being socially and individually responsible."[29]

SKILL BUILDER

Me, You, and Popular and Social Media

1. Choose an adjective or color to describe how you felt when interacting with every person you came into contact with yesterday, either face-to-face or online. Evaluate why some people made you feel more positive or negative about yourself.

2. Consider how celebrities affect your picture of yourself. For example, how is your self-evaluation influenced by exposure to the lifestyles and standards of living experienced by pop-culture icons such as the Kardashians? To what extent do programs like *theirs* create expectations in you that are likely unattainable?

3. When texting or messaging friends, many of us now use a personal emoji, often a caricature or somewhat goofy cartoon of ourselves. Typically, while the one each of us creates may resemble us, and we may even make it lightly mocking, we also usually make it more physically pleasing—as if it represents our "better self."

If you haven't done so, download the Bitmoji app and create one to represent you. Explain the ways in which this selected public image represents an extension of yourself and what you hope it communicates to others.[30]

4. Consider how you feel after spending time on social media. Do you ever suffer from FOMO (fear of missing out) after seeing your friends failed to include you at a party? In general, do you feel better or worse once you log off? To what do you attribute these feelings?

FACTORS AFFECTING SELF-CONCEPT AND OUTLOOK

People we value influence the picture we have of ourselves and the way we behave. How you see yourself is affected by how you look at others, how others actually look at you, and how you imagine or perceive that others look at you. We become different selves as we move from one set of conditions to another. The words we use, the attitudes we display, and the appearances we present change as we vary the people we interact with, the masks we wear, and the roles we perform.

RESILIENCE AND GRIT

Are you an optimist or a pessimist? When it comes to thinking about the self and who we want to be today, some of us categorize ourselves as optimists and others as pessimists.

If we are an optimist and suffer a defeat, we view it as a temporary setback brought about by circumstances, bad luck, or other people. Optimists are resilient and gritty; they do not view defeat as a result of some insurmountable innate inability. Psychologist Albert Bandura tells us that an optimistic belief in our own possibilities and competence endows us with feelings of *self-efficacy*. (Note: We are speaking about optimism, not unrealistic optimism based on overconfidence.) When we have strong feelings of self-efficacy, we are more persistent, less anxious, and less depressed. We don't dwell on our inadequacy when something goes wrong; instead, we seek a solution. If we are persistent, we are apt to accomplish more. And as we do so, our belief in ourselves grows.[31]

Unlike optimists, pessimists lack resilience and believe that bad events are their own fault, will last, and will undermine whatever they do. Rather than believe they can control their own destiny, pessimists believe that outside forces determine their fate. In effect, pessimists "can't because they think they can't," while optimists "can because they think they can." Psychologist Martin Seligman tells this story:

> We tested the swim team at the University of California at Berkeley to find out which swimmers were optimists and which were pessimists. To test the effects of attitude, we had the coach "defeat" each one: After a swimmer finished a heat, the coach told him his time—but it wasn't his real time. The coach had falsified it, making it significantly slower. The optimists responded by swimming their next heat faster; the pessimists went slower on their next heat.[32]

DEVELOPING SELF-UNDERSTANDING

Clues to self-understanding come to you continually as you engage with others in physical and digital environments. To understand yourself, you need to be open to information that others give you. Just as we tend to categorize ourselves and others, they do the same for us. For better or worse, the categorization process is a basic part of interpersonal communication.

We classify people according to their roles, their status, their material possessions, their personality traits, their physical and vocal qualities, their skills and accomplishments, the number of "likes" they receive, and the number of followers they have. Which of these are most important to you? Which do you imagine are most important to the significant people in your life? How do others help shape your image of yourself? How do they enhance or belittle your sense of self?

Combatting Stigma, Stereotypes, and Prejudice

We define stigma as extreme disapproval resulting from prejudice and stereotypes that leads to discrimination and the promotion of shame in those targeted.

How might stigma attached to the elderly, the physically disabled, and those suffering from mental illnesses affect them? What messages do we send older, physically challenged, and mentally ill individuals regarding assessments of their worth and abilities? Stigma and negative preconceptions are among the significant barriers people in these groups have to combat.

Our society is both age-conscious (people classify us and treat us certain ways because of how old or young we appear to be) and age-obsessed (many people fixate on looking and acting youthful).

The Chinese, in contrast, respect age. As part of a cultural exchange program, the Chinese sent experienced scholars in their 50s and 60s to the United States and expressed offense when the United States, in return, sent young adults to China.[33] In Arab cultures, the proverb "A house without an elderly person is like an orchard without a well" expresses their view of aging. Contrast this with the U.S. practice of segregating elderly people from the rest of society by encouraging them to live in retirement communities and nursing homes. Because the elderly often assimilate society's devalued appraisals of them, unfortunately, many suffer from lower self-esteem.[34]

We also have stereotyped and discriminated against those who are physically challenged or mentally ill. Although there has been some improvement, many persist in predicting negative outcomes when relating to people believed to be disabled, partly because they are seen as dependent, potentially unstable, and more easily offended than the able-bodied. Employers also worry about the costs of accommodating them.[35]

To combat discrimination and change the way people respond, develop a checklist of suggestions for combatting ageism and stigmas attached to being physically or mentally challenged.[36]

EXPECTATIONS MATTER: THE SELF-FULFILLING PROPHECY

A self-fulfilling prophecy occurs when an individual's expectation of an event helps create the very conditions that permit the event to happen (Figure 3.4). In other words, your predictions can cause you to behave in ways that increase the likelihood of an occurrence. For

FIGURE 3.4

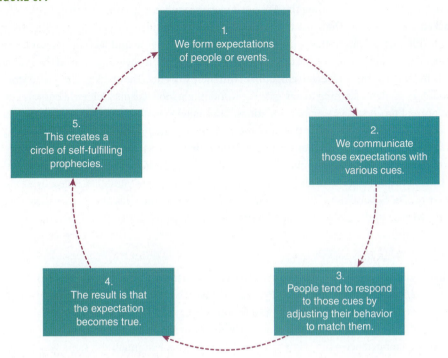

example, have you ever anticipated botching a job interview and then did so? Have you ever assumed that you wouldn't like someone, and you turned out to be right? Did it occur to you that you might have acted in a way that caused your prediction to come true?

The Pygmalion Effect

Perhaps the most widely known example of the self-fulfilling prophecy is the **Pygmalion effect**. The term comes from the Greek myth of Pygmalion, a sculptor, who falls in love with a beautiful statue of his own creation. The goddess Aphrodite, moved by Pygmalion's obsession with the statue, comes to his rescue and brings it to life. The playwright George Bernard Shaw adapted the story to a more modern setting and Shaw's version, in turn, served as the basis for the stage and film musical *My Fair Lady*. In this version, Henry Higgins (Pygmalion) seeks to transform an unsophisticated flower seller, Eliza Doolittle, into a refined, well-spoken lady. The play illustrates the principle that we live up to labels.

We, like Eliza Doolittle, learn to act like the people others perceive us to be. If, for example, a parent tells a child that he or she cannot do anything right, the child will soon incorporate this idea into his or her self-concept and fail at most of the tasks he or she attempts. In contrast, if a parent repeatedly demonstrates to a child that he or she is lovable or capable, the child will probably live up to the expectation.[37]

Real-Life Examples

A real-life example of the startling effects of self-fulfilling prophecies can be seen in a recent study involving students and their teachers. Research revealed that African American students were more than three times as likely to be suspended or receive detention for bad behavior as were their White peers, leading the African American students to conclude that the deck was stacked against them. They lost trust in their teachers, and their negative attitudes became a self-fulfilling prophecy that continued to fuel their falling behind, acting out, and being suspended. Experimenters instituted an intervention to see if they might break the vicious cycle by teaching the teachers to empathize with their students. They had teachers read stories about how students learning to navigate the world might look like disobedience but was really the normal process of testing new identities. They taught the teachers how to build rapport. They also let them know what they and their students shared in common—even something as simple as a birthday—so that stronger relationships between teachers and students might form. They did. The change in the teachers' understanding and knowledge led them to listen to their students rather than rush to suspend or discipline them. Students ended up earning better grades because they felt more respected and valued. They discovered that their voices mattered. The students also developed more respect for their teachers.[38]

The Galatea Effect

What about the messages you send yourself? A variation of the Pygmalion effect is the *Galatea effect* (Galatea is the name Pygmalion gave his statue once it was brought to life), which refers to the expectations we have for ourselves, rather than the ones others have for us. We react to the internal messages that we continually send to ourselves. Our feelings about our competence and abilities influence our behavior in much the same way that our performance can be influenced by others' high or low expectations for us. Thus, our answer to the question "Who are you?" affects how we behave.

HOW TO ENHANCE SELF-AWARENESS

To enhance our communication abilities, we need to use ourselves as a resource. By becoming more aware of how we perceive ourselves, and more sensitive to our own thoughts and feelings, we also become more adept at presenting ourselves to others.

IDENTIFY LIFE SCRIPTS

Self-understanding is the basis of self-concept. To understand yourself, you must understand how you operate in the world. Psychiatrist Eric Berne believes that we enact identity scripts—the rules for living we learned while growing up that spell out our roles and how to play them.[39] Berne finds that we are apt to pattern our interactions in such a way that we repeatedly enact the same script but with different sets of players. We might, for example, repeatedly enact life scenes in which we express the belief that others are out to get us, or that they are jealous of us. This urge to repeat these scripts becomes a problem when doing so causes us to fail.

The remedy is to become aware of the scripts we enact, identify those that are unproductive, and rewrite them. Once we are in control of the scripts we use, taking part as an active player, we put ourselves in a better position to script our own lives.

USE THE JOHARI WINDOW

At one time or another, we all wish that we knew ourselves and others better. The concept of self-awareness, so basic to all functions and forms of communication, can be explored through a psychological testing device known as the **Johari window**. Joseph Luft and Harrington Ingham developed an illustration of a paned window to help us examine both how we view ourselves and how others view us (Figure 3.5).[40]

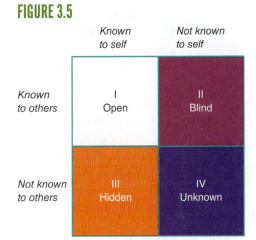

FIGURE 3.5

Pane I, the *open area*, represents information about yourself that is known to you and another. For example, your name, age, religious affiliation, and food preferences might all be found in this window pane. The size and contents of this quadrant vary from one relationship to another, depending on the degree of closeness you share with the other person. Which people do you allow to know more about you than others?

Pane II, the *blind area*, contains information about you that others, but not you, are aware of. Some people have very large blind areas, because they are oblivious to their own faults or virtues. At times, people may feel it necessary to seek outside help or therapy to reduce the size of their blind areas. Do you know something about a friend that he or she does not know?

Pane III, the *hidden area*, represents your hidden self. It contains information you know about yourself but do not want others to find out for fear they will reject you. Sometimes, it takes a great deal of effort to conceal aspects of yourself from others. At one time or another, each of us probably feels a need to have people important to us know and accept us for who we are.

When we move information from Pane III to Pane I, we engage in the process of self-disclosure. **Self-disclosure** occurs when we purposely reveal to another something about ourselves that he or she would not otherwise know about us. This does not suggest that the hidden area should not be allowed to exist within each of us. It is up to each of us to decide when it is appropriate for us to share our innermost thoughts, feelings, and intentions with others. It is also up to each of us to decide when complete openness or transparency is not in our best interest.

Pane IV of the Johari window is the *unknown area* in your makeup. It contains information of which neither you nor others are aware. Eventually, education and life experience may help bring some of the mysteries of this pane to the surface. Only then will its contents be available for examination. Have you ever done something that surprised both you and those close to you? Did you and a friend ever exclaim together, "Wow! I didn't know I felt that way!" or "I didn't know you could do that!"?

Interpersonal Styles in the Johari Window

People become known for their interpersonal style—a consistent and preferred way of behaving. Figure 3.6 illustrates four representative interpersonal styles. Style A is characteristic of those of us who adopt a fairly impersonal approach to interpersonal relationships. Dominated by their unknown areas, these individuals usually withdraw from contacts, avoid personal disclosures or involvements, and thus project an image that is rigid, aloof, and uncommunicative. In Style B, the hidden area is the dominant pane. Here we find people who desire relationships but also greatly fear exposure and generally mistrust others. Once others become aware of the façade such people erect, they are likely to lose trust in them. Style C is dominated by the blind area. People with this style are overly confident of their own opinions and painfully unaware of how they affect or are perceived by others. Those who communicate with them often feel that their own ideas or beliefs are of little concern. In Style D, the open area is dominant. Relationships involve candor, openness, and sensitivity to the needs and insights of others.

Communication of any depth or significance is difficult if those involved have little open area in common. In any relationship you hope to sustain, your goal should be to increase the size of the open area while decreasing the size of the hidden, blind, and unknown areas. As human beings, we think about others and what they think about us. The question is whether we are able and willing to share what we are thinking.

FIGURE 3.6

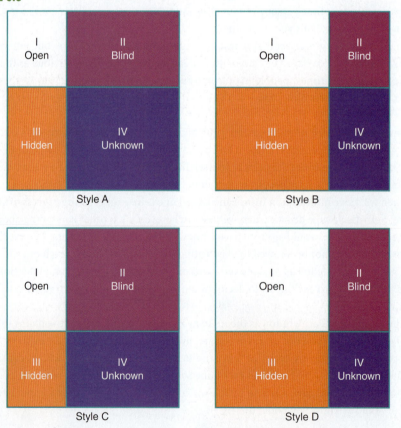

SKILL BUILDER

Symbolizing the Self

This exercise requires the selection of four objects. The first object you choose should reveal something about the way you see yourself, something you believe everyone recognizes about you. In other words, this object should represent an aspect of your open area. The second object you select should reveal something about you that up until now has resided in your hidden area. It could represent an attitude, feeling, desire, or fear that you were keeping from others but are now ready to move into the open area. Your third object choice should represent how you believe another person sees you. The last object is one you need to ask that other person to choose. This object should represent the person's actual perception of you.

Assess the extent to which your perceptions of yourself and the other person's perceptions either conflicted or coincided. How has each phase of this experience altered the appearance of your Johari window? Was any information moved from your blind area into the open area?

MANAGE IMPRESSIONS

It is normal to want to present ourselves in ways that cause others to perceive us positively. This reality, however, leads us to ask some questions: When we say something publicly, should we always feel it privately? Should we ever present a different self to others than the ones we know to be authentic?

Identify Your Multiple Identities

We do not possess a single identity. Rather we have multiple ones. In the course of a normal day, we perform different roles. In school, we are a student. At home, we may be a child, a sibling, or a parent. On a date, we are a romantic partner. We act differently with different people and when in different settings. We may even act differently with the same person—switching how we behave when we feel it necessary.

Competent communicators naturally display role versatility. They also possess the know-how to construct multiple identities that match the culture of the person they are communicating with and the context. To do this, they engage in *frame switching*, adopting different perspectives based on the culture and specific situations in which they find themselves. By making conscious choices about how to construct their identity, choosing to act appropriately and not offend others, they create a positive impression.[41]

Life Is Like a Performance

When we create a positive image of ourselves to influence positively what others think of us and how they feel about us, we are practicing **impression management**.

According to sociologist Erving Goffman, all of life is a performance. In effect, we act out a role in every interaction, based on the shared relationship. While the *perceived self* is the self we believe ourselves to really be, Goffman asserts that we use **facework** to present a public image to others. That self, our *presenting self*, is a favorable self-image. Often, we adjust the presenting self to accommodate different people. Sometimes this choice is conscious and our communication is designed to accomplish a specific purpose. Other times, this choice is unconscious. What matters most is that the side we show is an authentic reflection of our self-concept. If it is not, then Goffman suggests our front-stage, or public, behavior may contrast with our back-stage, or private, behavior.[42] Do your experiences support this?[43]

iStock/m-gucci

Human beings are unique in their ability to observe their behavior. **High self-monitors** are people who are highly attuned to their impression management efforts. **Low self-monitors** pay little attention to how others respond to their messages. Some contend that it is unethical to attempt to artificially control a communication by trying to present to others a version of you that is idealized; they believe it is disingenuous to treat relating to others like a performance. What do you think?

CAREER BUILDER: WORK PLACES AND FACES

1. Give an example of when you have used *facework* to make a good impression during a job interview.

2. Google yourself. Based on what you find, how do you imagine that a potential employer would perceive you? Did you come across anything online that you would rather a potential employer not know or see?

3. Interpret the following statement with a supervisor in mind: *I may not be what I think I am. I may not be what you think I am. I may well be what I think you think I am.* What does it suggest about the relationship between employer and employee?

4. Analyze the different impressions that specific coworkers and your boss might have of you. Which person's view would you evaluate to be most positive, the most negative, and the most accurate? Explain your reasons and what you can do to combat the negative and inaccurate perceptions.

BARRIERS TO PERCEIVING YOURSELF AND OTHERS CLEARLY

Many variables affect perception, a number of which function as barriers, preventing us from perceiving ourselves, others, and situations accurately.

PAST EXPERIENCES FOLLOW US

Past experiences can create expectations that produce in us a readiness to process experience in predetermined ways. If, for example, we had a bad experience working on a group project with another student, we likely would become upset if asked to work on a subsequent project with that same student. These **perceptual sets** affect our interpretation of ourselves, others, and experience.

To better understand how a perceptual set affects us, quickly read the statements written in the triangles in Figure 3.7. Then examine the individual words more carefully. During your first reading, did you miss anything that you now perceive? Many of us fail to see the second *the* or *a* in the statements in their first reading. Did you? Why? We are so accustomed to seeing words in familiar groups, or clusters, that often we simply fail to perceive extra words when we see them in such phrases.

FIGURE 3.7

Motivations such as hunger and poverty also can alter interpretations of experience. In one study, researchers showed sailors some ambiguous pictures and asked them to describe what they saw. Hungry sailors "saw with the stomach"—to them, an elongated smudge looked like a fork, and a swirl looked like a fried onion. In a second study, rich and poor children were shown circles of various sizes and asked which ones were the same sizes as some coins. The poor children consistently chose circles that were much too large. Why? A quarter looks bigger to the poor than to the rich.[44]

Perceptual sets are the product of our unique life experiences. The lessons life has taught you necessarily differ from those life has taught others. As a result, we may perceive the same stimulus differently.

WE CLOSE OUR MIND

A key factor in how we view our world is the extent to which we open ourselves to new experiences. We select what we will perceive by deciding whether to expose ourselves to a variety of types and sources of information. How difficult is it for you to expose yourself to new ideas, people, places, or experiences?

For example, when driving through a poverty-stricken area on a nice cool day, some people immediately roll up their car windows and keep their eyes focused straight ahead, looking neither to their right nor to their left. They tell themselves that they are doing this for self-protection, but rolling up the windows and not looking out of them is also a means of avoiding contact with some of the depressing sights and sounds of a blighted area.

Whenever we close our eyes or minds, we bias the selection process, ending up with a distorted view of society and others' lives. When it comes to selective attention, for example, you are more likely to overhear someone talking about buying a home if you are a real estate agent than if you are a computer engineer. When in a crowd, most people actively filter what doesn't interest them and respond selectively to their preferred conversations, exhibiting what psychologists call "the cocktail party effect."

Now, think about a relationship that you recently terminated or are planning to end. Since making the decision, have you become more aware of the negative qualities of the person you broke up or are breaking up with? When we like or love someone, we tend to perceive primarily their positive qualities. This is called the *halo effect*. However, when our perception of another person changes for the worse, we are more likely to perceive only their negative qualities. We call this the *horn effect*.

WE FREEZE OUR FIRST IMPRESSION

How important are *first impressions*—initial judgments of others? Do the snap judgments we make about others matter?

Research suggests that assessments we make during the first few minutes of meeting someone strongly influence the relationship's course. Study results reveal that students who reported that another person made a positive first impression on them were more likely to develop a friendly relationship with that person, even if given only 3 minutes to make their initial evaluation. The results support the **predicted outcome value theory** developed by Mike Sunnafrank, which says that when we first meet another person, based on our first impression of the person, we are able to predict the probable outcome of our relationship.[45]

How do you form a first impression of someone? What makes you decide if you like or dislike someone? It turns out that people judge one another on two main qualities: *warmth* (whether they come across as friendly and well-intentioned) and *competence* (whether we think they have the ability to deliver on their intentions). We view positively those people we believe to possess both qualities, but develop negative perceptions toward other blends. For example, we tend to envy and even may wish harm to those we judge to be competent but cold, while people we see as warm but incompetent elicit pity.[46]

Because sometimes we rely on inaccurate mental shortcuts such as stereotypes, first impressions can dramatically affect perception. A first impression—or *primacy effect*, as it is sometimes called—even can affect the course or outcome of an event or relationship. And even if our first impressions are wrong, we tend to hold on to them—although doing so may be illogical. We may cling to an inaccurate first impression and reshape the conflicting information available to us until it conforms to the image we hold. As a consequence, we may never come to experience the real person—only our erroneous perception of him or her—and will base our responses to that person on that faulty conception.

Suppose, for example, a new employee, Kevin, is hired at work. You tell a good friend and coworker this, and your friend says, "Yeah, I know him. He worked in my unit 2 years back. He's nothing but trouble—always looking to use people. He'll bleed you of your ideas, pass them off as his own, and leave you behind as he builds a name for himself." Your friend's evaluation may be unfair, biased, or simply wrong. Kevin might have changed during the past

2 years, or your friend's initial assessment of Kevin might be incomplete. But your friend's words will likely influence how you interact with Kevin, and you'll probably find reasons to substantiate your first impressions of him because you closed your mind once you formed it.

WE EXHIBIT THE BEHAVIORS OF A LAZY PERCEIVER

A **stereotype** is a generalization about people, places, or events that many members of a society hold. The term *stereotype* is derived from an old printing practice, a shortcut in which the typesetter repeatedly used the same type to print a text. Metaphorically, when we stereotype, we repeatedly use the same thoughts or fixed mental images to "print" the same judgment about someone over and over again. We apply the judgment to all members of a group, failing to acknowledge the uniqueness of any one individual in the group.

Stereotypes affect how we process stimuli. For one thing, we remember more favorable information about in-groups and retain more unfavorable information about out-groups. Our stereotypes also cause us to disregard any distinguishing characteristics that individuals may have that set them apart from the stereotyped group. Instead of responding to an individual, we respond to our expectations, assume they are valid, and behave as if they had occurred. When we stereotype, we judge people on the basis of what we believe about the group that we have placed them in. We emphasize similarities and overlook differences. We oversimplify, overgeneralize, and grossly exaggerate our observations.

Lazy perceivers develop **prejudice**, which is a biased, negative attitude or prejudgment toward particular groups or social categories of people. Because lazy perceivers also rely on stereotyping as their "go-to" or default perceptual process, they fail to engage in careful observation or note differences among people. Such behavior leads to the pigeonholing and rigid categorization of others.

Even when we believe that we are prejudice free, we can harbor **unconscious bias**, stereotypes, both positive and negative, that exist in our subconscious and influence our behavior. Unwittingly, people rely on unconscious mental shortcuts that are rooted in stereotypes. These mental shortcuts creep into our personal and professional lives.[47] Unconscious bias, for example, promotes racial profiling. For many years, police have stopped and frisked people on the basic of their skin color rather than their behavior. Some individuals have been placed on "no fly" or "watch" lists simply because of their Muslim names. Although most Caucasian Americans perceive themselves to be unbiased, when unconscious biases are measured, a majority link African Americans with negative traits. In fact, job applicants with "Black-sounding" names are less likely to get call-backs than those with "White-sounding" names—and applicants called Jennifer are likely to be offered a lower salary than applicants called John.[48] Thus, unconscious bias contributes to a lack of diversity. (To test your own unconscious bias go to https://implicit.harvard.edu/implicit.)

A stereotype of any group is based on incomplete information. As we noted earlier, although stereotypes may be partly true, they are never completely true. To improve our perceptual capabilities, we must make an effort to see differences as well as similarities among people. When we make a conscious attempt to see someone as an individual, race- and gender-based stereotypes diminish.[49] To paraphrase communication expert Irving J. Lee, the more we are able to discriminate among individuals, the less we will actively discriminate against individuals.[50] We can be aware of stereotypes but reject them.

Visit the interactive e-Book to access the Skill Builder feature "Can Future Me Be Stereotype Free?" which will help you contemplate the impact of stereotyping people of different backgrounds.

WE THINK WE KNOW IT ALL

Even with the Internet, knowledge of everything about anything is impossible. In the now classic work *Science and Sanity,* Alfred Korzybski coined the term *allness* to refer to the erroneous belief that any one person possibly can know all there is to know about everything.[51]

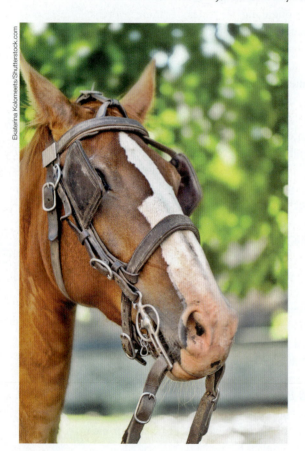

Ekaterina Kolomeets/Shutterstock.com

To avoid allness, we begin by recognizing that, because we can focus on only a portion of available stimuli, we necessarily neglect other portions. Another safeguard is to refrain from thinking of ourselves as the center of the world. Allness can impede the development of effective relationships. To counter it, try ending every assessment you make with the words *et cetera* (and the rest). You can never know everything there is to know about anything, and those words remind you that you should never pretend to know it all.

WE BLINDER OURSELVES

Blinders on a horse reduce the number of visual stimuli it receives. Similarly, we put figurative blinders on ourselves. The following exercise illustrates the concept of *blindering* as a perceptual hindrance: Attempt to draw four straight lines that will connect each of the dots in Figure 3.8. Do this without lifting your pencil or pen from the page or retracing a line.

Did you find the exercise challenging? Most do, but why? The problem imposes only one restriction—that you connect the dots with four straight lines without lifting your pencil or pen from the page or backtracking over a line. Most of us, however, add another restriction. After examining the dots, we assume that the figure to be formed must be a square. Actually, no such restriction exists, and once you realize this, the solution becomes clear. (Check the answer in the Answer Key at the back of the book.) In effect, you were "blindered" by the image of a square as you tried to solve the problem. Wearing blinders may help horses, but they dramatically limit humans. Blindering is a habit that forces us to see in limited ways. It often leads to undesirable actions or prevents us from finding solutions outside of our narrow viewpoints.

FIGURE 3.8

WE CONFUSE FACTS AND INFERENCES

Another factor affecting our perception and evaluation of people and events is the failure to distinguish what we think, wish, or infer to be true from what we observe.

It is important to distinguish inferences from facts. A **fact** is something that we know is true on the basis of observation. You see a woman walking down the street, carrying a briefcase. The statement "That woman is carrying a briefcase" is a fact. If the woman with the briefcase has a frown on her face, you may state, "That woman is unhappy." The second statement is an **inference**, because it cannot be verified by observation. Failure to recognize the difference between a fact and an inference can be embarrassing or dangerous. For example, if an actor begins flubbing lines and walking unevenly, he might be accused of coming to work drunk, when the truth could be that he has a neurological illness.

When we confuse an inference with a fact, we are likely to jump to a conclusion—which just might be wrong. This is not to discourage you from making inferences. After all, we live our lives on an inferential level. We do, however, want to caution you against making inferences unconsciously. What is consequential is to stop operating as if inferences were facts.

The following lists summarize the essential differences between facts and inferences:

FACTS

- May be made only after observation or experience
- Are limited to what has been observed
- Can be offered by the observer only
- May refer to the past or to the present
- Approach certainty

INFERENCES

- May be made at any time
- Extend beyond observation
- Can be offered by anyone

- May refer to any time—past, present, or future
- Represent varying degrees of probability

WE EXHIBIT DEFICIENT EMPATHY SKILLS

Differing perceptions lie at the heart of many of our personal and societal challenges. If we can exhibit empathy, that is, experience the world from a perspective other than our own, we can do our part to foster mutual understanding.

Both cognitive and emotional behaviors are integral to empathy. The cognitive component, *perspective taking* (the ability to assume the viewpoint of another person), requires that we take on the point of view of another, setting our own point of view away until we understand theirs. The second component of empathy, *emotional understanding*, requires that we step into the shoes of the other person and feel what they are feeling. The third component is *caring*.

When you genuinely care about the welfare of another person and you combine this with the personal realization of what that person's situation is like, you gain a greater appreciation of what you and the world look like through that person's eyes. The reflection or mirroring response reveals that we have the capacity to understand more fully what others are doing, feeling, and saying. Empathizing frees us to take action, feel emotions, and perceive situations in different ways.

Unfortunately, research reveals that since 2000, the ability of college students to empathize has declined. Researchers believe that social media bears some of the blame because it encourages self-promotion at the expense of self-awareness. It also reduces the amount of time we spend face-to-face during which we ordinarily would learn to make eye contact and develop skills to interpret the other person's posture and tone.[52]

> Visit the interactive e-Book to access the Skill Builder feature "Assessing the Nature of Fact–Inference Confusions," which will test your ability to distinguish facts from inferences.

GENDER, SELF-CONCEPT, AND PERCEPTION

Do you think you might feel differently and look at things differently were you to identify with a gender other than the one you currently identify with? If your answer is yes, is it because you believe a change in your gender-identification would cause you to perceive things differently, or because you imagine that others would treat you differently?

STANDPOINTS: LESSONS FRAME PERCEPTIONS

Men, women, and gender-nonconforming people adopt different standpoints, perceive different realities, have different expectations set for them, and exhibit different communication preferences. Through interaction with parents, teachers, peers, and others, we internalize the lessons of appropriate male and female behavior. These lessons frame our perceptions and teach us how society expects us to behave. These constructs, however, can limit the way gender is perceived and may contribute to our being judged on the basis of gender expectations rather than observed cues or how we define our gender.

BELIEFS CAN BLIND US

Beliefs regarding gender-appropriate behavior not only influence how we see ourselves but also how we relate to others. Some people treat others differently simply because of their gender. In fact, many people persist in dressing boy and girl babies in different colors and styles. Our experiences during our formative years influence our later views of gender, affecting our identity and self-perceptions. For this reason, when asked to describe their characteristics, men mention qualities such as initiative, control, and ambition. Women, in contrast, lead with qualities such as creativity, concern for others, and consideration. Generally, men in the United States derive their self-esteem from their achievements, status, and income, while women derive their self-esteem based on appearance and relationships.[53]

Unfortunately, many women develop less positive self-concepts than do men. Our society expects those who identify as female to be nurturing, unaggressive, deferential, and emotionally expressive. Because of this expectation, women with female identities are rewarded for having pleasing appearances, revealing their feelings, and being forgiving and helpful to others. Starting at a young age, girls are more likely to be self-critical and self-doubting than boys. Although women of all ages tend to value relationships, adolescent girls in particular can become so preoccupied with pleasing others that they metaphorically "bend themselves into pretzels."[54] Do you find this true?

Men are more apt to develop an independent sense of self. Because men are expected to be strong, resilient, ambitious, in control of their emotions, and successful, they experience positive reinforcement for displaying these characteristics. Independence is central to their lives and often leads to those with masculine identities feeling better about themselves than do those with feminine identities.[55]

Although appearance traditionally has played little role in the self-image of men, in recent years this has changed. More emphasis is now placed on the looks and builds of men, with extreme muscularity or thinness often the goal. For the most part, media present and reinforce prevalent conceptions of masculinity and femininity although they also can pave the way for societal acceptance of alternative conceptions.

All too frequently, rigid categorization creates communication problems. For example, beginning with the war in Iraq, we witnessed an evolution in the Pentagon's and public's perceptions of the positions in which women and men could serve in the military. Women and men, including trans women and men, have served in combat roles, come under attack, and been injured and killed. Whereas many are able to reconcile the traditional feminine role with that of a soldier in combat, others find it difficult to juxtapose contrasting perceptions. In fact, in 2017, the president of the United States ordered the military to reevaluate the presence of transgender soldiers in the military. Is this based on fact or prejudice? Where do you stand?

CULTURE, SELF-CONCEPT, AND PERCEPTION

Culture is a powerful teacher. Whether we are judging beauty or evaluating a child's behavior, the cultural lens we look through influences our assessments of reality. Many years back, researchers seeking to demonstrate this used a binocular-like device to compare the perceptual preferences of Americans and Mexicans. They showed each subject 10 pairs of photographs. In each pair, one photo displayed a picture from U.S. culture and the other photo a picture from Mexican culture. After viewing the paired images through the binoculars, the subjects reported their observations. Both the Americans and the Mexicans were more likely to report having seen a picture from their own culture—the other image visible through the viewfinder was not perceived.[56] Similarly, we tend to be more perceptually accurate in recognizing and interpreting expressions of emotion sent by members of our own culture.[57]

BARRIERS TO UNDERSTANDING

In an effort to blunt "the culture effect," educators in some conflict-ridden societies use textbooks that encourage students to synthesize conflicting versions of events rather than choose one side. For example, the Peace Research Institute in the Middle East published a booklet that divided pages into three columns, one for the Israeli version of history, one for the Palestinian version, and one left blank for the student to fill in.[58]

Misunderstandings may result, however, when the cultures of interacting parties cause them to operate according to different assumptions and rules. For example, North Americans perceive talk as desirable. They value directness and are apt to perceive someone who fails to "tell it like it is" either as vague or cowardly. In contrast, members of Asian cultures place more value on silence, believing that one who understands need not speak. From the Asian standpoint, a person who states the obvious is a show-off. When we fail to realize that we have not all absorbed the same cultural lessons, *cultural nearsightedness*—the failure to understand that not all of us attribute the same meanings to behavioral cues—can cause us to misread signs and miss opportunities to use the differences between us to perceive one another more clearly.

NOTIONS OF THE SELF ARE CULTURALLY BASED

Like perception, identity does not develop identically in every society. At least in part, who we are, or our whole notion of self, emerges from participation in a culture. In North American and Western European cultures, the self is considered paramount. Members of these cultures tend to reflect the importance placed on individuals as they first set and then work toward personal goals. In comparison, people from Asia, Africa, and Central and South America (where collectivistic cultures are dominant) are more likely to downplay their own goals, emphasizing instead goals set or valued by the group as a whole.[59] For example, Japanese parents typically do not lavish praise on their children out of concern that if they did the children would think too much of themselves and not enough about the group.[60]

DISTINCTNESS STANDS OUT

Your self-concept is influenced by unique personal experiences as well as by membership in one or more groups. Together with culture, these influences help you formulate your sense of self. According to **distinctiveness theory**, a person's distinctive traits (e.g., red-headed, minority group member, or left-handed) are more salient to him or her than are more prevalent traits (e.g., brunette, Caucasian, or right-handed) possessed by other people in the immediate environment. For

example, belonging to a group that is a numeric minority makes you more mindful of your ethnicity. For this reason, a White person is much less apt than a minority group member to mention his or her ethnicity when asked to define himself or herself, whereas an African American woman in a large group of Caucasian women will likely be more aware of her race. When the same woman is with a large group of African American men, she will be more conscious of her gender and less aware of her race.[61]

SELF-CONCEPT, PERCEPTION, AND TECHNOLOGY

Technology also influence our perceptions of experience—influencing our views of ourselves, others, and events.

EXPLORING DIVERSITY

Assessing Your Preference for "I" Versus "We"

You can assess the extent to which you exhibit an individualistic or collectivistic orientation by evaluating the following statements. If the statement is very important to you, rate it 5; somewhat important, 4; neither important nor unimportant, 3; somewhat unimportant, 2, and very unimportant, 1.

I Matter

_____1. I desire to prove my personal competency.

_____2. I've got to be me.

_____3. I want others to perceive me as having stature.

_____4. I need to achieve personal fulfillment.

_____Total

We Matter

_____1. If I hurt you, I hurt myself.

_____2. I desire harmony at all costs in my relations with others.

_____3. My goal is to preserve the welfare of others even if it is at my expense.

_____4. I am loyal to tradition.

_____Total

To determine your score, total the numbers you entered for each category. Which of your scores is higher? A higher "I Matter" score indicates greater individualistic tendencies. A higher "We Matter" score indicates greater collectivistic tendencies. What do your results suggest about your concern for self and others?

TECHNOLOGY INFLUENCES INFORMATION PROCESSING

Where does most of your news and information come from? For many of us, the answer is from the media, particularly social media. By age 18, 88% get their news from Facebook and other social media.[62] Unfortunately, online it is easy to find support for any prejudices and false premises we may have. As stories (true and false) are circulated via Facebook, Google, and Twitter, it becomes easy to believe biased or inaccurate information and challenging to distinguish what is true from what is false.[63]

Pop culture also is a perceptual influencer. Many of the ads presented to us today, for example, contain images of multicultural socializing. The repetition of these ads is bound to have an impact on perceptions of multiculturalism. Although American pop culture may be depicted as increasingly transracial, the portrayals are not necessarily complimentary. When it comes to how Muslims are portrayed, for example, the Council on American-Islamic Relations is concerned that they have become the new media "bad guys," because they often are shown as neighbors who are terrorists.[64] If most of our knowledge about Muslims comes from the media, what messages do such portrayals send?

Unfortunately, the more television we view, the more accepting we become of social stereotypes, and the more likely we are to develop unrealistic and limited perceptions of those depicted. According to **cultivation theory**, because of the media's ability to influence users' attitudes and perceptions of reality, the more time we spend watching such offerings, the greater is our chance of developing perceptions that are inconsistent with facts. Heavy viewers are more likely to view the world as a mean and dangerous place and to develop fears that are out of proportion with actual dangers.[65]

TECHNOLOGY INFLUENCES OUR ONLINE PRESENCE

According to a 2016 Nielsen report, Americans spend almost 11 hours a day in front of a screen—a PC, a tablet, a smartphone, a TV, or other.[66] According to the Pew Research Center, 21% of us are online seemingly constantly.[67] But what are we really learning? And how is all that time devoted to "screens" affecting how we look at ourselves? What kind of online presences are we building? After all, in many ways, building a social media presence is akin to building a brand.[68] Focused on self-promotion, research reveals that we try to put our best digital foot forward when using social media.

For example, we use our Facebook and Instagram accounts to create and present others with the most positive version or persona of ourselves possible. Selfies, often digitally enhanced, help us accomplish this. Our posts imply that our lives are more fun-filled and exciting than they actually are. Whereas for some individuals this offers a psychological ego boost, for others it actually becomes anxiety producing. According to theorists, instead of allowing the self to develop internally, it is now being externally manufactured and virtually packaged in our effort to influence others' views of us.

Effectively, we play to audiences when using social media, working to create a self that others will respond to positively.[69] We also tend to perceive and interact differently when we relate to people online and not face to face. In effect, the Internet allows us to facilitate perceptual revisions of ourselves.[70] If others approve of the way we present ourselves, they will encourage its continuation. If, however, they believe we are trying to present ourselves as someone whom we are not, then they will judge us to be untrustworthy and not credible.[71]

THE INTERNET AND SOCIAL NETWORKS PROMOTE SELF–OTHER COMPARISONS

Of course, what we see in the media and what others present online often compel us to perceive ourselves, our relationships, and our lives as inferior in comparison to the lives of others. This takes an emotional toll and may be responsible for increases in the number of people suffering from depression and loneliness.[72]

The media frequently present the human body in perfect form, which makes many of us think that no one could love us the way we are. Even with "body-positive" movements on the rise, a bias for skinny women persists.[73]

When it comes to social networks, others may have more contacts or friends than we do. They may possess significantly greater online influence than we do. Those who spend considerable time viewing and commenting on posts and pictures of peers are likely to experience greater dissatisfaction with their own appearance and social lives.[74]

Kotin/Shutterstock.com

TECHNOLOGY ALTERS PERCEPTIONS OF REALITY

Digital media make it hard to discern what is real or true. In entertainment, sports, and news magazines, for example, men's biceps are enlarged, birthmarks are removed, and weight is redistributed. In general, appearances are "improved." Of course, it's not just the approved, curated image that is available for our inspection.

What is even worse, however, is that false information is too frequently put forth as factual. Conspiracies and false news sites abound. When repeated and replicated, the barrage of fake stories creates an echo-chamber effect. As a result, we need to develop the ability to look critically at what we find online rather than simply accept what is before our eyes as being true.

COMMUNICATION SKILLS
Practice Improving Perception of the Self and Others

Although our effectiveness as communicators is determined in part by our perceptual abilities, we rarely consider how to increase the accuracy of our perceptions. Focus on mastering and maintaining these skills as you work to eliminate ineffective behaviors.

Understand perception is personally based.

Become aware of your role in perception, recognize that you have biases, and acknowledge that you don't have a corner on the truth market. Doing this increases the probability that your perceptions will provide you with accurate information. It also is important to be willing to review, revise, and update your perceptions.

Watch yourself in action.

You can increase your self-awareness by continuing to explore your self-image and your relationship to others. Developing a clear sense of who you are is one of the most worthwhile goals you can set in life. Periodically examine your own self-perceptions—and your self-misconceptions.

Ask how others perceive you.

How others perceive you may be very different from how you perceive yourself. Obtaining information from others can help you assess how realistic your self-concept is. Others who know you well may see strengths in you that you have overlooked, traits you undervalue, or weaknesses you choose to ignore. You don't need to accept others' views of you, but keep yourself open to them.

Take your time.

It takes time to process information about yourself, others, or events fairly and objectively. When we act too quickly, we are likely to make careless decisions based on poor judgment. This often is a result of overlooking important clues, making inappropriate or unjustified inferences, and jumping to conclusions. Delaying a response gives you an opportunity to check or verify your perceptions.

Commit to self-growth.

As you move from yesterday through today and into tomorrow, your self is in constant transition. Try not to let your view of yourself today prevent you from adapting to meet the demands of changing circumstances and conditions. Uncover the vibrant, flexible, and dynamic qualities of you.

> **Thought is the talk which the soul has with itself.**
>
> Plato

COMPLETE THIS CHAPTER 3 CHECKLIST

3.1 I can define and explain the process of perception. ☐

Perception is the process of selecting, organizing, subjectively interpreting, remembering, and responding to sensory data in a way that enables us to make sense of ourselves and our world.

3.2 I can describe the nature of self-concept. ☐

Self-concept is the entire collection of attitudes and beliefs you hold about who you are. It is the mental picture you have of yourself. Self-concept, which influences all aspects of behavior, can be positive or negative, accurate or inaccurate. You are not born with a self-concept. Rather, it is shaped by your environment and those around you.

3.3 I can describe the various ways self-concept affects behavior. ☐

Based on our self-concept, we ascribe reasons for behavior. Excessive self-esteem can lead to unrealistically high self-appraisals and problematic behavior, but people with normally high self-esteem tend to be happier and less influenced by their peers.

3.4 I can describe the factors affecting self-concept and outlook. ☐

We become different selves as we move from one set of conditions to another. Resilience and grit, self-understanding, and expectations (including self-fulfilling prophecies) affect our self-concept and outlook.

3.5 I can explain how to use life scripts, the Johari window, and impression management to develop self-awareness. ☐

Self-concept changes and improves with self-awareness. Understanding the life scripts you employ that lead to success or failure and using the Johari window can facilitate improved self-concept. The Johari window helps to identify the open, blind, hidden, and unknown areas of yourself. When we create a positive image of ourselves to influence what others think of us and how they perceive us, we are practicing impression management.

3.6 I can identify common perceptual barriers. ☐

By becoming aware of your role in perception, by recognizing that you have biases, and acknowledging the limiting effects of first impressions and stereotypes, you can increase perceptual accuracy. Perception also is improved by not taking perceptual shortcuts, including being careful not to stereotype others in ways that promote prejudice and prevent you from seeing the uniqueness in every individual. Also of import is that we not act with too much certainty or too quickly, not think we know it all, not place unnecessary restrictions on problem solving, and not make unjustified inferences. On the other hand, being able to empathize increases our capacity to perceive accurately.

. . . .

3.7 I can explain how gender affects perceptions of me and others. ☐

Gender preferences contribute to our adopting different standpoints, perceiving different realities, and having different expectations set for us. They also lead to our exhibiting different communication behaviors.

. . . .

3.8 I can explain how culture affects perceptions of me and others. ☐

We view reality through a cultural lens that biases us toward our own culture. This can precipitate cultural nearsightedness and serve as a barrier to self–other understanding.

. . . .

3.9 I can analyze how media and technology influence perceptions of me and others. ☐

According to critics, we learn the stereotypes and skewed images of reality that media, including social media, present to us. Digital and social media raise a host of perception-based issues about the nature of our identity and our ability to identify what is truthful.

. . . .

3.10 I can use communication skills to improve the accuracy of self-perception, perception of others, and perception of events. ☐

We increase our perceptual abilities when we recognize that perceptual processes are personally based, take the time we need to process information about ourselves, others, and events fairly and objectively; and try to become more open to change. By watching ourselves in action, learning how others perceive us, and committing to self-growth, we improve our self-awareness.

. . . .

BECOME A WORD MASTER

attribution theory 54

closure 51

cultivation theory 75

distinctiveness theory 73

empathy 70

facework 64

fact 69

figure–ground principle 51

grit 55

high self-monitors 64

impression management 63

inference 69

Johari window 61

low self-monitors 64

perception 48

perceptual sets 65

predicted outcome value theory 66

prejudice 67

Pygmalion effect 59

selective attention 49

selective exposure 49

selective perception 49

selective retention 49

self-awareness 52

self-concept 53

self-disclosure 61

self-esteem 53

self-fulfilling prophecy 58

self-image 53

stereotype 67

stigma 58

unconscious bias 67

iStock/shapecharge

4

Communicating With Words: Helping Minds Meet

4.1 Define language, and explain the triangle of meaning.

4.2 Explain the factors at work in the communication of meaning.

4.3 Identify problems experienced when attempting to share meaning, including patterns of miscommunication.

4.4 Discuss the relationship between culture and language.

4.5 Discuss the relationship between gender and language.

4.6 Explain how power affects language use.

4.7 Explain how incivility affects language use.

4.8 Analyze how technology influences language use.

4.9 Apply techniques for improving language skills.

> Whatever we call a thing, whatever we say it is, it is not. For whatever we *say* is words, and words are words and not things. The words are maps, and the map is not the territory.
>
> Harry L. Weinberg

In the film *Arrival*, a linguist stands inside a spaceship separated from two aliens by a glass-like partition. She approaches the aliens, placing her palm against the partition. Her plan to save Earth from presumed annihilation is to communicate with them. Their language, she realizes, is unlike ours. It is based on a nonlinear perception of time, a perception she was able to gather by listening, empathizing, and talking. The linguist used words—not weapons—to save the world.[1] ■

LANGUAGE IS ALIVE: WE USE WORDS TO SHARE MEANING

The English language contains over 1 million words, and a new word enters the vocabulary about every 98 minutes. In 2015, the Oxford Dictionaries named as its "word of the year" an emoji titled "face with tears of joy." They say that for the first time they recognized a pictograph as word of the year because of the symbol's ability to transcend linguistic borders.[2] In 2016, their new word of the year was *post-truth*—a term signifying that appeals to emotion and personal belief are more important than objective facts when it comes to being able to influence us. A contender, but not the winner, was *chatbot*—a computer program that engages in conversation with human users.[3] What do these choices say about the value we place on words or verbal language?

We depend on words to help us share meaning. By understanding how language works, we can improve our ability to do that. In this chapter, we define language and explore the roots of miscommunication. We consider how aspects of our society affect our word choices and conclude with guidelines for developing our ability to make word choices that help others understand us. Although most Americans know about 20,000 words, each of us actually uses only about 7,500 of them on any given day.[4] On what basis do we choose our words? And what happens when we select the wrong ones?

WORDS, THINGS, AND THOUGHTS

Language is a unified system of symbols that permits the sharing of meaning. A **symbol** stands for, or represents, something else. Words are symbols, and thus words represent things. Notice that words *represent* and *stand for* rather than *are*. This is an essential distinction. Words are spoken sounds or the written representations of sounds that we have agreed will stand for something else. By mutual consent, we can make anything stand for anything.

The process of communication involves using words to help create meanings and expectations. However, as important as words are in representing and describing objects and ideas, meaning is not stamped on them. Meanings are in people, not in words. The goal when communicating is to have our meanings overlap, so that we can make sense out of and understand each other's messages.

The Triangle of Meaning

Language fulfills its potential only when we use it correctly. The **triangle of meaning** developed by two communication theorists—C. K. Ogden and I. A. Richards—helps explain how language works (Figure 4.1).[5]

FIGURE 4.1

The Triangle of Meaning

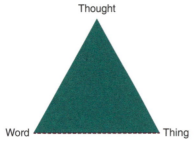

In Ogden and Richards's triangle of meaning, the three points are *thought*, *word*, and *thing*. The broken line connecting *word* (a symbol) and *thing* (a referent or stimulus) indicates that the word is not the thing and that there is no direct connection between the two. Thus, when we use words, we need to remind ourselves that the only relationships between the words we use and the things they represent are those that exist in people's thoughts (including, of course, our own).

Frequently, even the existence of an image or a physical object does not establish meaning. Some time ago, a public service commercial depicting a rat and a child living in a tenement was shown on television. The child was seen beckoning to the rat as she repeated, "Here, kitty, kitty, kitty." Although this example may seem bizarre, its meaning is clear: It is possible for us to look at the very same object but give it very different meanings. This is because the meaning of anything is inside each person who experiences it.[6] If we are to be successful at communicating, we should understand the relationships that exist between words and people's thoughts and their reactions.[7]

PROBLEMS WITH THE COMMUNICATION OF MEANING

The communication of meaning is a key function of language. The factors identified in this section relate to problems we may have when attempting to share meaning.

Visit the interactive e-Book to access the Ethics and Communication feature "Looking at Language," in which you will consider the consequences of indirect language and the benefits of learning a second language.

UNDERSTANDING MEANING'S MEANING

In talking to others, we often assume too quickly that they understand what we mean. There are many reasons, however, we may not be understood as we want to be. Simply put, the words we use can create barriers to understanding. In Lewis Carroll's *Through the Looking Glass*, Humpty Dumpty and Alice have the following conversation:

> "I don't know what you mean by 'glory,'" Alice said.
>
> Humpty Dumpty smiles contemptuously, "Of course you don't—till I tell you. I meant, 'There's a nice knock-down argument for you!'"
>
> "But 'glory' doesn't mean 'A nice knock-down argument,'" Alice objected.
>
> "When I use a word," Humpty Dumpty said in a rather scornful tone, "it means just what I choose it to mean—neither more nor less."

We can make words mean whatever we want them to mean. Nothing stops us—except our desire to share meaning with others.

When presented with the word "bark," are you more likely to picture a dog or a tree?

MEANINGS ARE BOTH DENOTATIVE AND CONNOTATIVE

We may experience a problem in communication if we consider only our own meaning for a word. Although *we* know what *we* mean, the crucial question is: What do our words bring to mind for those with whom we are communicating?

When we think about what language means, we must think in terms of both **denotative** (objective or dictionary) **meaning** and **connotative** (subjective or personal) **meaning**. Although each word has a dictionary definition, your own experiences influence the meanings you assign to words. That is, your connotative meanings vary according to your own feelings for the object or concept you are considering.

MEANING IS DATED

Every noteworthy event, particularly catastrophes, catapults words into everyday speech and dictionaries. September 11, 2001, was no exception. When the American Dialect Society met to decide the top or newly reconditioned words of the year, "9/11" was voted the expression most likely to last.

Not all words' meanings persist, however. For example, in the 1940s, if you were well dressed, people might say you looked *spiffy*. In the 1960s, they might say you looked *swell*. A few years ago, they might say, "You're on fleek." What we used to refer to as *awesome* now is termed *dope*.[8] Words lose their luster for other reasons too. For example, at Princeton University, the term for the leaders of residential colleges was changed from *master* to *head*, at least in part because of the former term's associations with slavery.[9]

Words come and go from dictionaries. Now that many Internet-inspired expressions have crossed over into everyday use, the *Oxford English Dictionary* approved the addition of the following acronyms to its latest edition: *OMG* (oh, my God!), *LOL* (laughing out loud), and *BFF* (best friends forever). Also added was *ego-surfing* (the practice of searching for your own name on the Internet).[10]

SKILL BUILDER

A Time Capsule for Words

1. Briefly define each of the following terms:

    Net

    Hooking up

    Cougar

    Rap

    Colbert Bump

    Spam

    McJob

    Straight

    Crack

2. Show the list without definitions to your parents, older relatives, or older friends, and ask them to provide definitions for the words.

3. Compare your meaning for each term with the meanings given by others. Why do you suppose their meanings differed from yours?

4. Pretend it is now the year 2030. On a separate sheet of paper, create a new meaning for each word listed.

Many "old" words acquire vivid new meanings every decade or so. Viruses today are not just germs spread from person to person, but malicious software that can spread instantaneously from one computer to computers globally.[11] Consequently, when we use a word that referred to a particular object at a particular time, we should attempt to determine if it still means the same thing now.

MEANING IS LOCATIONAL

Words' meanings also change from one region of the country to another. For example, what would you envision having if you were to stop for a soda? For an egg cream? What each word brings to mind probably depends on the region of the country you grew up in.

In some parts of the United States, soda refers to a soft drink, but in others it refers to a concoction of ice cream and a soft drink. In some sections of the country, egg cream refers to a mixture of seltzer, syrup, and milk, but elsewhere it conjures up the image of an egg mixed with cream.

Do you have examples of situations where place influences the meaning of words?

EXPERIENCE INFLUENCES MEANING

We assign meanings to words based on our past experiences with the words and the things they represent. Consider the word *cancer*, for example. If you were dealing with three people in a hospital—a surgeon, a patient, and a statistician—how do you imagine each would react to this word? The surgeon might think about operating procedures or diagnostic techniques, or about how to tell a patient that he or she has cancer. The patient might think about the odds for recovery and might well be frightened. The statistician might see cancer as an important factor in life expectancy tables.

Experience also influences whether it is appropriate for us to use jargon or slang.

Jargon

A specialized vocabulary of technical terms that is shared by a community of users, such as the members of a profession, is called <mark>jargon</mark>. For example, whereas physicians commonly use medical terminology when communicating with other doctors, it is probably inappropriate for them to assume that their patients would understand such terms. In fact, 9 out of 10 adults report finding the medical advice that their physicians provided to them incomprehensible. As a result, federal and state officials advise public health professionals to simplify the language they use to communicate with the public. Instead of warning a patient of hyperpyrexia after a procedure, the physician should instead tell the patient that she might have an abnormally high fever.[12] Similarly, when teachers use jargon without defining the terms being used, it can hamper students' understanding.

Slang

In contrast to jargon, **slang** is a much more informal vocabulary that bonds its users together while excluding others who do not share an understanding of the terminology. Usually popular with young people, members of marginalized groups, and users of online social networks, examples of slang include "My bad" (I made a mistake), and "lol" (laughing out loud).

WHETHER LANGUAGE IS CONCRETE OR ABSTRACT INFLUENCES MEANING

The language we use varies in specificity. Consider the family pet. We could call it:

A domesticated animal

A dog

A poodle

A standard poodle

My standard poodle Lucy

In each instance, our description becomes somewhat more specific. Alfred Korzybski and S. I. Hayakawa designed an abstraction ladder to describe this process.[13] The ladder is composed of a number of descriptions of the same thing. Items lower on the ladder focus specifically on the person, object, or event, while items higher on it are generalizations that include the subject as part of a larger class. As our words move from abstract (less specific) to concrete (more specific), they become more precise in meaning and are more likely to appeal to the senses and conjure up a picture. Specific words, such as *Lucy*, clarify meaning by narrowing the number of possible images that we imagine.

Using high-level abstractions serves a number of functions. First, because high-level abstractions function like verbal shorthand, they let us generalize, making communication easier and faster. Second, because they also let us be deliberately unclear, high-level abstractions allow us to avoid confrontations when we believe it is necessary. If, for example, your boss asks you what you think of a new corporate strategy and telling the truth appears too risky to you, you can offer an abstract answer to the question and avoid being put on the line. On the other hand, relying on high-level abstractions can also cause meaning to become fuzzy—primarily because the words you use can be misunderstood. The goal is to use the level of abstraction that meets the needs of your communication objectives and the situation.

BARRIERS TO UNDERSTANDING: PATTERNS OF MISCOMMUNICATION

If we fail to consider how people's backgrounds influence them in assigning meaning, we may have trouble communicating with them. Words often have more than a single meaning. In fact, a commonly used word can frequently have more than 20 definitions.

For example, a strike in bowling is different from a strike in baseball. Striking a match is not the same as striking up the band. Thus, we must pay careful attention to a message's context. Unfortunately, we sometimes forget that words are rarely used in one and only one sense, assuming that others will understand our words in only the way we intend them to be understood. Our receivers, however, may assume that their interpretation of our words is the meaning we intended. Let's explore what happens when this occurs.

BYPASSING: CONFUSING MEANINGS

All someone said was "Hi, Jack!" But at a suburban Detroit airport those two words precipitated a crisis. A microphone happened to be on when an individual aboard a corporate jet greeted the co-pilot. Air traffic controllers on the airport's control tower heard the word *hijack*. The police, the SWAT team, and the FBI were alerted. The plane was ordered to return to the tower.[14]

People often think they understand each other, when, in fact, they miss each other's meaning. This pattern of miscommunication is called **bypassing**, because meanings pass by each other.

There are two main kinds of bypassing.[15] The first occurs when people use different words to represent the same thing but are unaware that they are both talking about the same thing. Imagine two politicians arguing vehemently over welfare policies. One holds that their city's welfare program should be "overhauled," whereas the other believes that "minor changes" should be made. Eventually they realize the first politician's overhaul is actually equivalent to the second politician's minor changes.

The second and more common type of bypassing occurs when people give different meanings to the same word or phrase. In such cases people appear to be agreeing when they substantially disagree. For example, imagine you are on a hike in the woods with a friend when your friend suddenly says, "Bear to the right." You run to the left, hoping to avoid an encounter with what you believe is a big brown bear, when all your friend was actually doing was telling you to turn right.

Developing an awareness that bypassing can occur when you communicate is a first step in preventing it from needlessly complicating your relationships. If you believe it is possible for your listener to misunderstand you, then take the time you need to ensure that your meanings for words overlap. To avoid bypassing, you must be "person-minded" instead of "word-minded." Remind yourself that your words may generate unpredictable or unexpected reactions in others. Trying to anticipate those reactions will help you prevent communication problems.

LABELING: MIXING UP WORDS AND THINGS

Sometimes we forget that people, not words, make meanings. When this happens, we pay too much attention to labels and too little attention to reality. We can approach this phase of our study of meaning by considering the problem of labels and how strongly they influence us.

How important are labels in our culture? Consider this: A judge ruled that an individual could not change his name to a number because doing so would be totalitarian and an offense to human dignity. What does a number, as opposed to a name, signify? Would we change if our names were changed?[16]

We display an *intensional orientation* when we let words or labels fool or blind us. When we focus on what a label really represents, we display an *extensional orientation*.

Our name-brand society is a testament to the power of labels to alter perceptions of value. Recent tests, demonstrating how advertising can trick the taste buds of young children, revealed that anything tastes better to them—even carrots, milk, and apple juice—if wrapped in paper with the McDonald's label. Labeling is known in marketing jargon as *branding* and appears to have the ability to physically alter perceptions of taste.[17]

CAREER BUILDER: "THE NAME GAME"

In your opinion, could your name have anything to do with your chances of succeeding in your chosen career? Could the appellation used to represent a group function similarly?

What does a name do? Your name identifies you. It also distinguishes you from others. Your name is part of your identity. The question is: Does a name reveal any other pertinent information? The fact is that others will make assumptions about us based solely on our names.

Names have been shown to influence whether or not an employer chooses to interview or hire a potential employee. Such implicit bias is particularly harmful to people with unusual sounding names, especially non-Whites.[18] Passing judgment on someone's potential to succeed based solely on her or his name is one harmful name-game effect.[19]

Another harmful name-game effect involves having a name that stereotypically matches the gender of the job for which you are applying. Some first names, for example, suggest your sex and ethnicity and even perhaps your age and personality. College students demonstrated their own implicit bias when asked to predict what careers job applicants with feminine- and masculine-sounding names were most likely to succeed in, indicating that those with masculine-sounding names would most likely be successful in stereotypically masculine occupations such as plumbing and construction, as compared to

predicting success in the nursing or child-care field for those who had feminine-sounding names.[20]

1. Why do we place such a premium on names?

2. To what extent, if any, have you found your reaction to a person shaped by his or her name?

3. What if your own name is an unusual one? How do you imagine it will affect your career opportunities and success?

4. What if you're not applying for a position that is associated closely with your gender? Would you change your name or use just your first and middle initials in lieu of your whole name on your application?

5. Do you believe that if you altered your name and it was discovered by others that they would view you as competing fairly or cheating? Why?

6. What do you see as a viable solution to the name game?

In the effort to avoid such gender effects, genderless words are increasingly substituted for gendered ones, including Latinx (representing anyone in North America with roots in Latin America—male, female, or gender-nonconforming) and Chicanx (representing anyone of Mexican descent). Some prefer using these words in place of the masculine Latino and Chicano because they see them as a means of removing the machismo in the culture and the language, as well as a means of empowering others.[21]

POLARIZATION: THE MISSING MIDDLE

Polarization is the use of *either–or* language that causes us to perceive and speak about the world in extremes. If you think about it, the English language encourages these false dichotomies, or choices. Even though most people are not beautiful or ugly, tall or short, fat or thin, for you or against you, the English language has few words descriptive of the middle positions. How does polarized language affect your ability to express yourself clearly?

Can you fill in the opposites for each of the following words?

Conservative

Fat

Happy

Bold

Brave

Tall

Next, try filling in two or more words between each pair of opposites. That's more difficult, isn't it? It's harder for us to find words that express all possibilities, rather than the extremes. Because polarizing words fail to reflect the vast middle, they do not represent reality. Instead, they emphasize artificial divisions.

EVASIVE AND EMOTIVE LANGUAGE

Frequently, our reaction to a person or event is totally changed by words. If we are not vigilant, we can easily be manipulated or conned by language.

Analyze the following sets of words to see how your reactions may change as the words used change:

1. coffin   casket   slumber chamber
2. girl   woman   broad
3. backward   developing   underdeveloped
4. correction   price drop   loss

Words Announce Our Attitudes

If we like an old piece of furniture, we might refer to it as an antique. If we don't like it, we'd probably call it a piece of junk. Words broadcast attitudes. For example, a few years ago, PETA (People for the Ethical Treatment of Animals) asked the Federal Trade Commission to revise the fur label phrase "animal producing the fur" to read "animal slaughtered for the fur."[22]

The word **euphemism** is derived from the Greek term meaning "to use words of good omen." When we use a euphemism, we substitute a pleasant term for a less pleasant one.

Euphemisms help conceal a communicator's meaning by making the message delivered appear more congenial than it actually is. Employees who lose their jobs are "de-hired," undergo a "vocational relocation," are left "indefinitely idling," experience a "realignment" or "constructive dismissal," or are "freed up for the future." It seems that only on *The Apprentice* did someone actually utter the phrase "You're fired!"

When the environment became a political issue, political strategist Frank Luntz advised using the term *climate change* in place of *global warming* because "while global warming has catastrophic implications attached to it, climate change sounds like a more controllable and less emotional challenge."[23] He also suggested using the word *conservationist* instead of *environmentalist* because the former conveys a "moderate, reasoned, common sense position," while the latter has the "connotation of extremism."[24] Of late, some have identified the term *alt-right* as dangerous, believing that it is a euphemism for an extremist group that is racist, anti-Semitic, and antifeminist, with roots in White nationalism and White supremacy.[25] Do you agree?

Do You Talk Doublespeak?

William Lutz, the coiner of the term *doublespeak,* equates the evasive use of language with linguistic fraud and deception.[26] Lutz lists the following as prime examples of doublespeak: calling the invasion of another country a "predawn vertical insertion," naming a missile the "Peacemaker," and referring to taxes as "revenue enhancement." Do euphemisms reveal changes in attitude? What do you think?

POLITICALLY CORRECT LANGUAGE

The following definitions appear in Henry Beard and Christopher Cerf's tongue-in-cheek guide, the *Official Politically Correct Dictionary and Handbook:*

Lazy: motivationally deficient

Wrong: differently logical

Ugly: cosmetically different

Prostitute: sex-care provider

Fat: horizontally challenged[27]

Are your connotations for the term *politically correct language* positive or negative? Do you define it as speech that is sensitive or speech that is censored?

According to Diane Ravitch, author of *The Language Police,* words that might offend feminists, religious conservatives, multiculturalists, minority activists, or members of other groups are routinely deleted from the textbooks used in U.S. schools because they are believed to be politically incorrect. For example, one textbook author rewrote Bob Dylan's folk song "Blowin' in the Wind" which had asked, "How many roads must a man walk down before you call him a man?" to read: "How many roads must an individual walk down before you can call them an adult?"[28]

Yet, like so many other words, politically correct language means different things to different groups of people. For some of us, being politically correct means making the effort not to offend by selecting words that show our respect for and sensitivity to the needs and interest of others. Politically correct language can help take the sting out of confrontations by blunting the sharpness of our words. For example, in the United States, over a period of time the word *slow* was replaced by the word *retarded,* which was then changed to *challenged,* next to *special,* and then to *an individual with an intellectual disability.* Similarly, over a half century ago, the defining term for persons of African ancestry has shifted from *colored* to *Negro* to *Black,* to *Afro-American,* to *people of color* or *African American.*[29] When we use politically correct language, we reveal our sensitivity to the preferences of those with whom we are conversing.

For others, however, political correctness means that we feel compelled by societal pressures not to use some words—referred to as taboo words—because we believe that using them might cause others to label us as racist, sexist, homophobic, or ageist. For example, some years ago, a student in one Ivy League university was thought to be a racist when he yelled, "Shut up, you water buffalo" out a window at a noisy group of African American women. Still others view political correctness and sensitivity training as dangers to free speech. Which position comes closest to the one you hold?

SKILL BUILDER

Political Correctness and Free Speech

The iGeneration (also referred to as Generation Z) includes those of us born after 1995. If you belong to this cohort, chances are you grew up in an era of protective parenting. You probably prioritize safety, both physical and emotional.[30] Might a relationship exist between the desire for political correctness, the safety emphasis of iGen members, and the "safe-space" movement on our college campuses?

Some students today assert that it is their right to be protected from the expression of ideas with which they disagree, even campaigning for the firing of faculty members who offend their sensibilities and disinviting speakers whose points of view they disagree with.

Here's the challenge: How do you balance this belief with the beliefs of others who say that the purpose of a college education is to experience diverse ideas and to encourage conversation among people whose perspectives differ? How can we have discussions about ideas if everything needs to feel "emotionally safe"? How can we change the perception that merely being exposed to and talking about ideas we don't like can harm us?

CULTURE AND LANGUAGE

Because culture influences language use, communication between members of diverse cultures presents its own challenges. The more diverse our life experiences are, the more difficult it can be for us to achieve mutual understanding.

CULTURE INFLUENCES THE WORDS USED

If a concept is important to a culture, there will be a number of terms used to describe it. For example, in our culture, the word *money* is very important, and we have many words to describe it, including *wealth, capital, assets, backing, resources,* and *finance.* Inuktitut, the Inuit language, has different words for snow that is falling (*quanniq*), snow on the ground (*aput*), snow that is blowing (*pirsiriug*), snow that is drifting (*natiruvaaq*), wet snow (*masak*), wet and compact snow (*kiniraq*), fresh, wet soggy snow (*aquilluqaaq*), the first snowfall of autumn (*apigiannagaut*), encrusted snow that gives way underfoot (*katakarktariaq*), and snow causing crunchy sounds when you walk (*qiqergranaartoq*), to name just a few.[31] In contrast to the Inuit, Arabs have only one word for snow—*talg*—and it refers to either ice or snow. Similarly, there are at least 19 Chinese words for silk and 8 for rice. And because the Chinese care deeply for their families, there are many words of relations. The Chinese have five words they can use for uncle, depending on whose brother he is.[32]

The Sapir–Whorf Hypothesis

The world we experience helps shape the language we speak, and the language we speak helps sustain our perception of reality and our view of our world. According to the **Sapir–Whorf hypothesis**, people from different cultures perceive stimuli and communicate differently, at least in part, because of their language differences. The Sapir–Whorf hypothesis has two threads: linguistic determinism and linguistic relativity. **Linguistic determinism** suggests that language determines our range of cognitive processes, effectually limiting how we see things by impeding us from seeing them any other way. Linguistic determinism has largely been discounted. **Linguistic relativity** suggests that languages divide up and name the world differently; it posits that since language affects thought, people who speak different languages will perceive the world differently. This helps to explain why the Inuit have many words for snow while Arabs use a single word only.

Benjamin Whorf claimed that if a language had no word for a concept, then speakers of the language would be unable to understand the concept. On the other hand, not having a word for something doesn't mean we can't have the experience. Thus, language may not limit ways of thinking as much as Whorf claimed.

Whorf never put forth hard evidence to support his claims, so over time his views have lost favor. Newer research on the subject reveals that as we learn our mother tongue, we acquire certain habits of thought that help shape our experience. For example, suppose someone told you, "I spent yesterday afternoon with my friend." If the person were speaking French or Spanish, he or she also would inform you about the friend's gender, as those languages have separate words for a male friend and a female friend. In contrast, an English speaker's words would not necessarily reveal that information.

Similarly, because Chinese speakers can use the same verb to refer to action in the past and present, they do not have to reveal the nature of the time they spent with their friend. English verbs require us to state that. Because we learn these options very early in life, they become habits of mind. Such habits influence our thoughts, feelings, and the way we look at things.[33]

CULTURAL DIFFERENCES CAN LEAD TO CONFUSED TRANSLATIONS

Translating ideas from one language to another can lead to problems. Sometimes the situation produced by a bungled translation can be amusing (though occasionally costly in a business context). For example, an English-speaking representative of an American soft drink company could not understand why Mexican customers laughed when she offered them free samples of Fresca soda. In Mexican slang, the word *fresa* can mean "lesbian." Similarly, Beck's beer has been translated into Chinese as *Bie Ke*, which means "shellfish overcome."[34] Along the same lines, Dr. Pepper no longer runs its "I'm a Pepper" ads in the United Kingdom, because *pepper* is British slang for "prostitute."

Other times, however, a poor translation can insult and confuse recipients. For example, one Spanish-language letter sent to welfare recipients about changes in New Jersey's welfare program contained numerous grammatical errors, suggesting a lack of multicultural competency. One section's translation of "parole violator" really meant "rapist under oath."[35]

CULTURE AFFECTS COMMUNICATION STYLE

Because members of Asian cultures practice the principles of *omoiyari* (listeners need to understand the speaker without the speaker's being specific or direct) and *sassuru* (listeners need to use subtle cues to infer a speaker's meaning), they are apt to keep their feelings to themselves and use language more sparingly and carefully than do Westerners.[36] Because Westerners value straight talk, prefer to speak explicitly, and use inductive and deductive reasoning to make points, they may interpret the roundabout expressions of Asians as evasive, manipulative, or misleading. Japanese girls and boys are likely to end their sentences differently. For example, whereas a boy might say, "*Samui yo*" to declare "It's cold, I say!" a girl would say, "*Samuiwa*," expressing the comment as a gentle question: "It's cold, don't you think?" Boys and girls also refer to themselves in different ways with boys often using the word *boku*, which means "I," while girls say *watashi*, which is a politer pronoun that either sex can use. Parents will also tell girls, "*Onnanoko nono ni*," which means, "You're a girl, don't forget."

The way parents in Western and Asian cultures handle a request they do not want to grant from a child provides a prime example of the cultural differences in directness. When confronted with such a situation, most U.S. parents would simply say *no*. In Japan, however, the parent would give reasons for denying the child's request but will not say no directly.[37] Every culture reaches its members using its preferred style. Whereas in the United States we prefer to be upfront and tell it like it is, many Asian cultures stand by the value of indirectness because it helps people save face and avoid being criticized or contradicted in public.

CULTURE INFLUENCES SYMBOLISM AND VAGUENESS

In some cultures, symbolism and vagueness are embedded in language, and people intuitively understand that words do not necessarily mean what they say. According to social scientist Kian Tajbakhsh, 80% of language in the West is denotative, whereas in countries such as Iran, 80% is connotative. In the West, *yes* generally means yes; in Iran, *yes* can mean yes, but it often also means maybe or no. In Iran, people use a social principle called *taarof* (insincerity) to avoid conflict. According to this principle, people will tell you what they think you want to hear. They will praise you, but they won't necessarily mean it.[38]

What kinds of problems can result when people from different cultures use words so differently?

PREJUDICED TALK

Both the **dominant culture** (the culture in power, the mainstream culture composed of people who share the same values, beliefs, and ways of behaving and communicating and who pass them on from one generation to another) and co-cultures (groups of people such as African Americans, Hispanics, Asians, musicians, athletes, environmentalists, and drug users, who have a culture of their own outside the dominant culture) have different languages. Hence, usages vary between these cultures.

Linguistic Prejudice

Sometimes members of a dominant culture use derogatory terms or racist language to label members of a co-culture, disparage them as inferior or undesirable, and set them apart from the mainstream group. **Linguistic prejudice**, or the use of prejudiced language, reflects the dominant group's desire to exert its power over less dominant groups. Such language stresses the differences between people of different groups, downplays any similarities, implies that the people who are different do not make an effort to adapt, and suggests that they are involved in negative acts and that they threaten the interest of the in-group members.[39]

Racial Code Words

The courts have ruled that managers who use **racial code words** (words that are discriminatory but not literally racist), such as "you people" and "one of them," help create a racially hostile environment. As a result of such rulings, many businesses are banning the use of such phrases.[40]

miker/Shutterstock.com

Additionally, corporate advertisers and educational institutions have long used Native American names such as "redskins," "braves," and "Seminoles," along with logos and images including severed heads and tomahawks to "play Indian" and sell products and events.[41] The National Collegiate Athletic Association (NCAA) has banned them as exploitative unless the named American Indian tribe explicitly approves the use. In your opinion, is the use of representations like these racist?

GLOBALIZATION'S EFFECTS ON LANGUAGE

Because of free trade, and the popularity of Hollywood and the Internet, the use of English around the world is growing. With globalization, more and more companies use English as their internal language.[42] This side effect of globalization does not please everyone. The fear among non-English-speaking nations is that their native languages will disappear, threatening national identity. For example, so many young Germans mix their language with English so freely that their speech is called Denglish, a blend of *Deutsch* (meaning "German") and English.[43] Similarly, many Chinese speak what is known as "Chinglish"[44] and the Hispanic community in New York has produced "Spanglish."

GENDER AND LANGUAGE

Too many of us persist in sex-role stereotyping. For example, if you refer to a surgeon as a "he" and a nurse as a "she" when you have no knowledge of the person's sex, or if you highlight the sex of a professional by alluding to a "male nurse" or a "female lawyer" instead of keeping language gender-free, sexism is present.

SEXIST LANGUAGE

michaeljung/Shutterstock.com

Sexist language perpetuates negative stereotypes and negatively affects communication. Past use of male generics, such as *mankind*, *chairman*, *spokesman*, *manpower*, and *Man of the Year*, share blame for causing men to be perceived as more important or significant than women. To counter this perception, many companies and individuals stopped using male generics and other kinds of sexist language and use gender-neutral language instead.

Another way that language use may be sexist is the way words are used to address women. Women, much more than men, are addressed through terms of endearment such as *honey, cutie*, and *sweetie*, which function to devalue women by depriving them of their name while renaming them with trivial terms.[45]

NAMING PRACTICES

Psychologist Albert Mehrabian has studied reactions to unisex names. He notes that when a boy's name catches on with girls, it usually loses favor as a name for boys. Historically, U.S. parents have felt free to choose androgynous names for girls. In contrast, some countries, like Finland, have official lists of boys' names and girls' names that parents must select from.[46] Names often reflect fashion, taste, and culture. In Venezuela, for example, legislators introduced a bill that prohibited Venezuelan parents from giving their children names that exposed them to ridicule or were hard to pronounce in Spanish.[47] In Thailand, children are given English nicknames like Pig, Money, Fat, and Seven because they are easier for foreigners to pronounce.[48] In southern Africa, parents choose the names of children to convey a special meaning, rather than participate in the latest fad, as is common in the West. Names that translate as God Knows, Enough, Wind, and Rain are common in southern Africa.[49] Alfred Mehrabian reports that people in the United States respond differently to different names, exhibiting more positive reactions to more common names.[50]

ETHICS AND COMMUNICATION

The Words We Choose

Phrases we recall readily and words chosen to highlight reveal a lot about the words' users. Consider the following:

The study "Sex Bias in the Newspaper Treatment of Male-Centered and Female-Centered News Stories" by K. G. Foreit and colleagues, published in 1980, revealed that a woman's marital status was mentioned in 64% of the newspaper stories examined, whereas a man's marital status was mentioned in only 12%. Have things changed today?

Pick up a copy of a current English-language newspaper or magazine or check online. Identify and count the number of male-centered and female-centered news stories in it. Also count the number of times the marital status of each person is referred to in each story. Have we made any progress?

> Visit the interactive e-Book to access the Ethics and Communication feature "More Words We Choose," which will help you reflect on the endurance of language and popular phrases.

GENDER AND SPEECH STYLE

Sometimes the sex of communicators affects not only the meaning we give to their utterances, but also the very structure of those utterances. Women, for example, tend to use more tentative phrases or **qualifiers**, in their speech than men do. Phrases like "I guess," "I think," and "I wonder if," abound in the speech of women but not in that of men.

This pattern of speaking also is passed on to the very young through their favorite cartoon characters. Past studies revealed that female cartoon characters, more than male characters, used verbs indicating a lack of certainty, such as "I suppose," and words judged to be polite.[51] When students were shown cartoon characters and asked to identify a character's sex based on the words the character spoke, students assigned the logical, concise, and controlling captions to male characters and the emotional, vague, and verbose captions to female characters.[52] Do cartoon characters continue to perpetuate such stereotypes? Have recent films with strong female characters started to break down this stereotype?

CONVERSATIONAL STRATEGIES

Men and women rely on different conversational strategies. Women, for example, tend to turn statements into questions more than men do, saying something like, "Don't you think it would be better to send them that report first?" Men typically respond with a more definitive, "Yes, it would be better to send them that report first." According to Robin Lakoff, a researcher on language and gender, women do not "lay claim to" their statements as frequently as men do.

In addition, women use more **tag questions** than men do. A tag is midway between an outright statement and a yes–no question. For instance, women often pose questions such as "Joan is here, isn't she?" or "It's hot in here, isn't it?" By seeking verbal confirmation for their perceptions, women acquire a reputation for tentativeness.

Similarly, women use more **disclaimers** than men do, prefacing their remarks with statements such as "This probably isn't important, but . . ." While male speech tends to be dominant, straightforward, and attention commanding, female speech tends to be gentle, friendly, and accommodating.[53] Such practices weaken the messages women send to others.

According to communications researcher Patricia Hayes Bradley, even if men use tag questions, the perceptual damage done to them by this weaker verbal form is not as great as the damage done to women. Bradley found that when women used tag questions and disclaimers or failed to support their arguments, they were judged to be less intelligent and knowledgeable—but men were not. Simply talking "like a woman" causes a woman to be judged negatively.[54] Researchers Nancy Henley and Cheris Kramarae believe that women face a disadvantage when interacting with men: "Females are required to develop special sensitivity to interpret males' silence, lack of emotional expression, or brutality, and to help men express themselves. Yet it is women's communication style that is often labeled as inadequate and maladaptive."[55] How can this be changed?

GENDER-LECTS

Gender affects how men and women use and process language in a number of other ways, too. According to linguist Deborah Tannen, men and women speak different **gender-lects**. Tannen finds that women speak and hear a language of connection and intimacy, whereas men speak and hear a language of status and independence.[56]

As a result, when conversing with men, women tend to listen attentively rather than interrupt or challenge what a man is saying. Why? Tannen holds that it is because challenging the man could damage the established connection that most women believe must be preserved at all costs.

In addition, men and women tend to speak about different topics. Monica Hiller and Fern Johnson conducted a topic analysis of conversations held in two coffee shops, one frequented by young adults and the other by middle-aged and older customers. Their research revealed that, whereas both men and women talked about work and social issues, women talked about personal issues and the older men virtually never discussed personal issues.[57] Although men and women frequently talk to each other, their cross-gender talk differs topically from man-to-man or woman-to-woman talk. Women talk to other women about their doubts and fears, personal and family problems, and intimate relationships, whereas, in general, men talk more about work and sports.

WORDS AND POWER

Although we may not realize it, some of us announce our powerlessness through our word choices. If we speak more indirectly than is expected, people could perceive that we lack self-confidence and power. In contrast, those of us perceived to be "powertalkers" make more definite statements, such as "Let's go out to dinner tonight." Powertalkers direct the action. They assume control.

Typically, powertalkers hesitate less in their speech, enhancing their sense of self-worth by projecting their opinions with more confidence. They eliminate fillers, such as "er," "um," "you know," "like," and "well," which serve as verbal hiccups, making the speaker appear weak.

Powerful talk comes directly to the point. It does not contain disclaimers ("I probably shouldn't mention this, but . . .") or tag questions (like those described in the section "Gender and Speech Style"). When you speak powertalk, your credibility and ability to influence others usually increase. Changing the power balance may be as simple as changing the words you use.

Talking powerfully is also less risky. According to Deborah Tannen, speaking indirectly in some situations actually causes problems. She cites the following conversation about de-icing between a pilot and co-pilot as an example of its dangers:

Co-pilot:	Look how the ice is just hanging on his, ah, back, back there, see that? . . .
Co-pilot:	See all those icicles on the back there and everything?
Pilot:	Yeah . . .
Co-pilot:	Boy, this is a, this is a losing battle here on trying to de-ice those things . . .
Co-pilot:	Let's check these tops again since we've been here a while.
Captain:	I think we get to go here in a minute.[58]

Less than a minute later, the plane crashed. While the co-pilot, probably because of his lower status, had tried to warn the pilot indirectly, the pilot failed to act on the cues. Indirectness, it seems is easier for higher-status persons to ignore. As a result, flight crews are trained to express themselves in more direct ways, and pilots are taught to pick up on indirect hints.

Language influences power in another way as well. According to Cheris Kramarae, because language is invented, it does not offer an adequate vocabulary to describe the unique experiences of all members of all groups. In other words, language does not serve all speakers equally well, usually meeting the needs of the powerful and wealthy more than the needs of women or members of less powerful groups, such as the poor, persons of color, or the physically challenged.[59] Kramarae contends that because men created words and established norms for their use, it is more difficult for the members of other groups to express their experiences.

In effect, the lack of appropriate means of expression mutes members of nondominant groups. Although this is not to suggest that the members of a muted group will always be silent, they may need to find new ways to encode their thoughts so that others understand them. As new words enter our vocabulary, however, it becomes increasingly possible for experiences, once difficult to give voice to, to enter the public sphere. Thus, terms such as *date rape*, *sexual harassment*, and *glass ceiling* helped change the nature of our discussions. In contrast to Kramarae, sociolinguist Deborah Tannen believes that men were not necessarily trying to control women. Rather, Tannen feels that the different communication style preferences of men and women may have contributed to resulting power imbalances.[60] What do you think?

PROFANITY AND OBSCENITY

The use of profane words comprises about half a percent of a typical person's vocabulary.[61] Virtually every language contains its share of profane words. Why? Researchers say it's because by using profanities, we are able to express what ordinary words don't enable us to express on their own. Also, hurling profanities enables us to convey our emotions symbolically rather than physically. When accepting an award on live television, rock singer Bono commented, "This is really, really f—king brilliant." An NBC news broadcaster, not realizing they were still on the air, yelled at the cohost. "What the f—k are you doing?" Students at one college screamed obscenities at a recent college basketball game, targeting a player who had chosen not to play for their school, yelling vulgarities at him and calling his relatives whores.[62] Has it become acceptable to utter obscenities in public, including in the media?

According to Timothy Jay, a leading scholar on cursing in the United States, contemporary teenagers are more likely to use expletives casually, uttering swear words 80 to 90 times each day. Because the lines between public and private language are blurred, today's teens have more difficulty than teens in previous generations adjusting their conversation to fit their audience.[63]

PROFANITY IN THE WORKPLACE

Profanity has also sought a home in the workplace. A female employee of a major construction company felt compelled to complain to the director of human resources about the cursing used in the company's facilities. The company responded by publishing "A Language Code of Ethics." It defined inappropriate language as "unwanted deliberate, repeated, unsolicited profanity, cussing, swearing, vulgar, insulting, abusive or crude language. The company is now a cuss-free workplace and workers who violate the policy can be disciplined."[64]

Profanity has become common, especially in high-stress jobs. Some policies differentiate between "casual" and "causal" swearing. Casual swearing is bad language we use for the fun of it, because we are too lazy to use other words when we think we can get away with it. Causal swearing is profanity produced by the inability to control an aroused emotion, such as anger, frustration, or impatience.[65]

Why are we so comfortable using profanity? Might it be because profanity and speech that degrades have become so much a part of our mediated language landscape, used in virtually every crime-adventure television, cable program, or film? Commonplace profanities now function as fillers—they slide off the tongue much as the words *you know* and *like*.

RECLAMATION OF PROFANITY AND SLURS

The use of insults, vulgar expressions, and speech that degrades and encourages hostility in others is on the rise. How are those against whom these words are used responding? In some cases, pejorative words that are used to stigmatize or demonstrate contempt for the members of a group are reclaimed by the group and redefined by group members as positive in nature.

For example, gays and lesbians adopted the terms *queer* (denoting a refusal of traditional sexual identity categories) and *genderqueer* (to reject conventional gender distinctions) as labels for new ways of experiencing sexuality and gender and to make positive statements about who they are.[66] Some women proudly refer to themselves as *girls*. While the "n-word" was coined by slave traders over 400 years ago to degrade Blacks, some African Americans, in an effort to invalidate the meaning that bigots attached to it, use the epithet among themselves.[67]

On the other hand, websites like abolishthenword.com and college and public forums have explored the n-word's usage, with some critics attempting to encourage the elimination of casual use of the word. Lawmakers have even sponsored resolutions to ban the word's use totally. Contrastingly, the website niggaspace.com draws a distinction between differently spelled versions of the n-word. According to the site's founder, "nigga" embodies brotherhood and fraternity, not ignorance and hate.[68]

In your opinion, can we solve the problem of racism by banning or respelling a word? For example, when advertisers criticized radio talk show host Dr. Laura Schlessinger for using this racial epithet on the air, she resigned because she did not want to have to prune her words, noting that African Americans use the word themselves.[69] Words, as we see, however, can take on different meanings depending on who uses them. A book publisher decided to issue a new version of Mark Twain's *Huckleberry Finn* replacing every use of the n-word in the novel with the word "slave." In your opinion, does taking the n-word out change the novel substantially? Do you think keeping the n-word in Twain's book promotes racism, or does it reflect the period of history accurately?[70]

TECHNOLOGY AND LANGUAGE USE

In excess of one trillion text messages are sent and received in the United States annually.[71] We frequently use text-messaging shorthand in our e-mails, posts, texts, and tweets. Some believe that our text-based culture is a key cause of the trend toward speaking in extremely short sentences. Additionally, some suggest that the excessive use of texting is contributing to our devaluing instantaneous or improvisational conversation—and eventually could cause face-to-face conversation to become obsolete, replaced by virtual and online options.

GIFS FRONT AND CENTER

Consider the smartphone-propelled use of GIFs, 3-second video loops prominent on sites like Twitter. These constitute a visual language all their own, absent facts and context but rife with emotion. We might add they are also often absent words, leading some to wonder if visual culture will become so dominant globally that we won't need words.[72] Whether in time GIFs will replace complex thought or not, right now online speak is proving to be pervasive.

ONLINE SPEAK

If you're like many students, you may lapse into <mark>online speak</mark> even when writing offline. When writing a paper for his economics class, one student wrote, "Surplus is an excess. But surplus can also b 2 much." His instructor deducted 10 points. The protocol of informality that marks digital communication finds us now debating whether the Internet invigorates language or strips it of its expressive power.[73]

When linguists talk of dialects, by tradition they are referring to the spoken word. Online speak and texting, however, have spawned a new written dialect, one in between speech and writing. In online speak, punctuation is abandoned, capital letters are used primarily to represent shouting, and an array of acronyms substitute for phrases. Knowing and using the dialect allows us to develop a sense of belonging to the group—a group that exists in cyberspace.

As we see, texting has its own private language or code. In fact, some young adults use acronyms to keep their parents from discovering their involvement with drugs, alcohol, or casual sex. It is not uncommon to find people together in one room, but they text rather than speak to one another. Why? They want to share but don't want others to hear what they are saying. Have you ever been part of or privy to such behavior, perhaps when in a car, a classroom, or your own living room? We use texting as a means of creating a social circle apart from others.

pecaphoto77/Shutterstock.com

Misunderstanding texting lingo can be embarrassing. For example, a woman had a friend whose mother had recently died. The woman texted her friend, "I'm really sorry to hear about your mom's passing. LOL. Let me know how I can help." She thought LOL meant "lots of love."

Users report talking much more enthusiastically online than in the real world: "Like if I see something remotely funny, I might say HAHAHAHAHAHAHAHAH, when really there is no expression on my face." Speech on Facebook is often breathless and emphatic, filled with words like "Okkkkkayyy" and "OMY!" It is as if some users feel the need to jump up and down to get the reader's attention.[74] Other observers believe that texting is popular because people long to share private conversations. The ability to send silent

iStock/izusek

text messages in public spaces is so appealing that many people send texts during movies, sports events, on public transportation, or when dining. Are you among the many? In your opinion, where should we draw the line indicating when texting becomes inappropriate?

INFORMALITY, ANONYMITY, AND INFLAMMATORY LANGUAGE

The informality of the Internet, together with its potential for anonymity, also affects language use in other ways. When online, people sometimes share their thoughts without displaying any concern for the feelings of others. Instead of conversing honestly and openly with one another, they comment *about* one another. Whereas gossip used to be whispered from person to person, racist, sexist, and homophobic remarks are now plastered across the Web for anyone to read. Comments like "*so-and-so* is a slut" and "*blank* has herpes" pop up on anonymous gossip sites.

Trash-talk has gone digital, and it encourages some to go to extremes in their voicing of distasteful and dubious comments. How would you suggest this issue be handled?

Online language also can be inflammatory. What you text or tweet in haste or in anger may reach a wide audience and have unimagined serious consequences. For example, when one teacher posted on her Facebook page that she was "a warden for future criminals," the district's school board scheduled a hearing to determine whether to revoke her tenure.[75] Do you think they should? Why?

COMMUNICATION SKILLS
Practice Thinking Critically About Language Use

Throughout this chapter, we have stressed that mastery of certain language skills will improve your ability to communicate effectively with others. Use the following advice to ensure that your words work for you rather than against you.

Identify how labels impact behavior.

Remember that words are nothing more than symbols. No connection necessarily exists between a symbol and what people have agreed that symbol represents.

All of us, at times, respond as if words and things were one and the same. Think of how often you buy a product because of what the label seems to promise. Examine your behavior with people. How many times have your judged a person—positively or negatively—because he or she was liberal, conservative, feminist, chauvinist, intellectual, or athletic? Make certain that you react to people, not to the categories in which you or others have placed them.

Analyze how words affect feelings and attitudes.

Few of the words you select to describe things are neutral. We all use snarl words (words that have highly negative connotations) and purr words (words that have highly positive connotations). These words do not describe the people or things we are talking about. Rather, they describe our personal feelings and attitudes. When we make statements like "He's a great American," "She's a dirty politician," "He's a bore," "She's a radical," we should not delude ourselves into thinking that we are talking about anything but our own preferences.

Identify how experience can affect meaning.

Because we assign meaning on the basis of our experience, and because no two people have had exactly the same set of experiences, it follows that no two people have exactly the same meanings for the same word.

Too frequently, we let our words lead us away from where we want to go; we unwittingly antagonize our families, friends, or coworkers. We are infuriated, for example when an important business deal collapses because our position has not been understood, or we are terrified when the leaders of government miscommunicate and put their countries on a collision course.[76] To avoid such problems, we must remember that meanings can change as the people who use words change.

Determine if meanings are shared.

Since intended meanings are not necessarily the same as perceived meanings, you may need to ask people with whom you are speaking questions such as "What do you think about what I've just said?" and "What do my words mean to you?"

Their answers serve two important purposes: They help you determine whether you have been understood, and they permit the other people to become involved in the encounter by expressing their interpretations of your message. If differences in the assignment of meaning surface during this feedback process, you will be able immediately to clarify your meanings by substituting different symbols or by relating your thoughts more closely to the background, state of knowledge, and experience of your listeners.

> Each of us has learned to see the world not as it is, but through the distorting glass of our words. It is through words that we are made human, and it is through words that we are dehumanized.
>
> Ashley Montagu

COMPLETE THE CHAPTER 4 CHECKLIST

4.1 I can define language and explain the triangle of meaning. ☐

Language is a unified system of symbols that permits a sharing of meaning. Language allows minds to meet, merge, and mesh. When we make sense out of people's messages, we learn to understand people. As Ogden and Richards's triangle of meaning illustrates, there is no direct relationship between words and things. Words do not "mean"; people give meaning to words.

4.2 I can explain factors at work in the communication of meaning. ☐

Among factors influencing the communication of meaning are differences between denotative and connotative meaning, the relationship between meaning and time, meaning and place, and meaning and experience, and whether language is concrete or abstract.

4.3 I can identify barriers to meaning, including patterns of miscommunication. ☐

Among factors contributing to confusion are the propensity for bypassing, labeling, evasive and emotive language use, and disagreements over politically correct language.

4.4 I can discuss the relationship between culture and language. ☐

Culture influences how we experience, process, and use language. In part,

because language and perception are intertwined, language use varies from culture to culture. We see this in how culture influences the words we use, contributes to confused translations, and affects communication style.

4.5 I can discuss the relationship between gender and culture. ☐

Gender influences the experiencing, processing, and use of language. Language also influences the attitudes we hold about males and females, as well as how males and females perceive each other.

4.6 I can explain how power affects language use. ☐

Some people talk more powerfully than others, coming directly to the point, projecting opinions with confidence, and eliminating nonfluencies and fillers from their speech.

4.7 I can explain how incivility affects language use. ☐

Incivility in language use is on the rise. It is increasingly common for individuals to use profane language in their daily lives, including when at work, neglecting their responsibility to control impulses and adapt to their audience.

4.8 I can analyze technology's effect on language use. ☐

How we communicate online frequently differs from how we communicate in person. Some people believe that the Internet is invigorating language, whereas others believe it is stripping language of its expressiveness.

4.9 I can apply techniques for improving language skills. ☐

We need to use common sense to recognize that certain styles of language are appropriate at certain times and in certain places. We also need to make ourselves as clear as possible by selecting words with meaning for our listeners and by taking into account their education level and the sublanguages they understand.

BECOME A WORD MASTER

bypassing 87

connotative
  meaning 83

denotative
  meaning 83

disclaimers 97

dominant culture 94

euphemism 89

gender-lects 97

jargon 85

language 82

linguistic
  determinism 92

linguistic
  prejudice 94

linguistic relativity 92

online speak 100

polarization 89

qualifiers 96

racial code
  words 94

Sapir–Whorf
  hypothesis 92

slang 86

symbol 82

tag questions 97

triangle
  of meaning 82

Maria Symchych/Shutterstock.com

5

Nonverbal Messages Speak

AFTER COMPLETING THIS CHAPTER, YOU SHOULD BE ABLE TO:

5.1 Define *nonverbal communication* and explain its characteristics.

5.2 Describe the functions of nonverbal communication.

5.3 Explain the following types of nonverbal messages: body language, voice, space and distance, appearance, color, clothing and artifacts, time, touch, and smell.

5.4 Describe how nonverbal cues help distinguish truth telling from lying.

5.5 Identify the influences of gender on nonverbal behavior.

5.6 Identify the influences of culture on nonverbal behavior.

5.7 Discuss technology's influence on nonverbal communication.

5.8 Apply skills in interpreting nonverbal cues to make valid judgments and decisions.

> He that has eyes to see and ears to hear may convince himself that no mortal can keep a secret. If his lips are silent, he chatters with his fingertips; betrayal oozes out of him at every pore.
>
> Sigmund Freud

Learning to interpret and send nonverbal messages effectively benefits us personally as well as professionally. Frequently more powerful than words, nonverbal communication provides reasons for how we respond to one another.

Do you know anyone who has experienced difficulty in establishing and maintaining good personal or professional relationships but can't figure out why? The answer may be that the person is lacking in nonverbal communication skills essential for social success.[1] Some of us find it harder to pick up on others' social cues. The nonverbally skill-less are, for all practical purposes, also communicationally clueless. ■

CHARACTERISTICS OF NONVERBAL COMMUNICATION

Nonverbal communication designates all messages not expressed in words:

The twinkle in your eye. The edge in her voice. The knowing look of his smile. The rigidness of their postures. The confidence in his walk. Her sophisticated dress. His open shirt. Where you sit. How closely he stands in relation to you. Her eagerness to arrive to work early. The modern design of your room. The cool colors the walls are painted. Her necklace. His lapel flag-pin.

Each of these cues offers clues regarding the attitudes, feelings, and personality of the displayer. What we do with our body, our voice, or the space around us has message value.

> Visit the interactive e-Book to access the Skill Builder feature "Nonverbal Self-Assessment," which will ask you to reflect on your ability to perceive, conceal, and express feelings through body language, facial expressions, and voice inflection.

WE ALL DO IT

We all communicate nonverbally. We cannot avoid doing it. In a normal two-person conversation, the verbal channel carries less than 35% of a message's social meaning. More than 65% of that meaning is communicated nonverbally (Figure 5.1).[2] By analyzing nonverbal cues, we improve our understanding of what *really* is being communicated. The nonverbal dimension also helps us define the nature of our relationships. With practice, we can use nonverbal cues to acquire information that we, otherwise, would not know.

FIGURE 5.1
Communication of Social Meaning

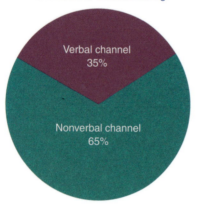

Verbal channel
35%

Nonverbal channel
65%

NONVERBAL COMMUNICATION CAN BE CONSCIOUS OR UNCONSCIOUS

Sometimes, we consciously use nonverbal cues to send specific messages. Our use of nonverbal cues is then purposeful. For example, we may smile when meeting someone for the first time, shake hands firmly when greeting the person about to interview us for a job, or wear a flag lapel pin as a sign of our patriotism. On the other hand, frequently we send nonverbal messages to others unconsciously. If, at this very moment, someone were to photograph you without you knowing it, what might others surmise by examining the photograph? Were you aware of how you are sitting? What messages might the clothing you were wearing in the photo suggest to others about you? What would your facial expression reveal about your reactions to this chapter?

Like verbal communication, nonverbal communication is ambiguous. Think again about a photograph taken of you reading this chapter. Would different people interpret it similarly? Similar to words, nonverbal messages may not mean to others what we think they will. Thus, we have to be careful not to misinterpret them. Don't be surprised if you find that the real reason a person left a meeting abruptly is quite different from what you assumed. All nonverbal communication must be evaluated or interpreted within the context in which it occurs.

FUNCTIONS OF NONVERBAL COMMUNICATION

Nonverbal communication serves an array of communicative functions that work both independently of and in conjunction with verbal messages to clarify meaning.[3]

MESSAGE REINFORCEMENT OR COMPLEMENTATION

Nonverbal cues reinforce the verbal message by adding redundancy. A woman says, "I love you," to her fiancé and covers her partner's face with kisses. An instructor asks, "Did you complete the assignment?" and you reply, "Sure did," and make an OK sign with your fingers. Message reinforcement occurs when the nonverbal and verbal messages complement or support each other.

MESSAGE NEGATION

Nonverbal cues also can contradict or negate a verbal message—such as a man who says to his lover, "I need us to spend more time apart," as he moves closer with each word spoken. The verbal message is contradicted or canceled by the communicator's nonverbal cues. Such an interaction represents a double or mixed message—the nonverbal cues and the words spoken are at odds with each other. Whenever you detect an incongruity between nonverbal and verbal messages, you will probably benefit by paying greater attention to the nonverbal messages. They are more difficult to fake than verbal cues—hence the importance of understanding the nonverbal dimension.

MESSAGE SUBSTITUTION

Nonverbal cues can replace or substitute for verbal cues. A hand gesture lets everyone know you're OK. A shrug of the shoulders lets others know when you don't care about something. Placing your finger over your lips can indicate that you'd like everyone in the room to stop talking. In each case, in lieu of words being spoken, an action is performed.

MESSAGE ACCENTUATION OR INTENSIFICATION

Nonverbal cues also can underscore or intensify parts of a verbal message. Slowing down speech to emphasize the meaning and importance of key words, smiling when you say, "It's nice to meet you," and clutching your hair when you say, "I'm so angry I could pull my hair out!" are nonverbal cues that accent or emphasize the verbal messages sent.

MESSAGE REGULATION

Nonverbal cues help regulate the back-and-forth flow of person-to-person interaction. We direct conversational turn taking with nonverbal cues. With eye contact, posture, gestures, and voice, we signal that we have finished speaking or indicate who should talk next. Nonverbal cues help us manage and control communication. They provide the traffic signals for verbal exchanges.

TYPES OF NONVERBAL COMMUNICATION

Let's look at the types of nonverbal messages we send and receive. The nonverbal message categories identified in this section are separated so we can examine them. However, they don't actually occur in isolation. Instead, they interact with one another and often occur simultaneously.

BODY LANGUAGE: KINESICS

Kinesics is the study of the relationship between body motion, or body language, and communication. Body language includes facial expression (particularly eyebrows, forehead, eyes, and mouth), posture, and gestures and helps to shape how you feel about yourself and how others perceive you.[4] Thus, hand movements, a surprised stare, dropping shoulders, a knowing smile,

and a tilt of the head are all part of kinesics. The role of signing and gestures in learning garnered attention when it was reported that infants and toddlers who learn to use and read gestures may learn to read faster and do better on future IQ tests.[5]

Facial Expressions

Of all the nonverbal channels, the face is the single most important broadcaster of emotions. Although many of us are able to decipher facial cues with great accuracy, others lack such ability. Unpopularity, poor grades, and a variety of other problems that plague school-aged children may be attributed to their inability to read the nonverbal messages of their teachers and peers. Because they don't realize the cues they're sending, or they misinterpret how others are feeling, unpopular children likely are unaware that they are missing many of the negative reactions that their peers are sending to them.[6] Our ability to read another's face increases when we know the person, understand the context of the interaction, and are able to compare and contrast the individual's facial expressions with other expressions we have seen him or her make.

pixabay/TeroVesalainen

iStock/stock_colors

Promoting Communication Presence Using Facial Management Techniques. Because we cannot put our faces away, we take great pains to control the expressions that we reveal to others. How do we do this? We use **facial management techniques**: intensifying, de-intensifying, neutralizing, and masking.

When we *intensify* an emotion, we exaggerate our facial expressiveness. Have you ever pretended you loved a gift when you really couldn't stand it? When we *de-intensify* an emotion, we de-emphasize our facial expressions so that others will evaluate them as more appropriate. Were you ever very angry with a professor but felt compelled to restrain yourself because you feared the professor's reaction if you let your anger show? When we *neutralize* an emotion, we do not display it at all. Sometimes neutralization is an attempt to display strength, as when we're saddened by the death of a relative but want to appear brave. In U.S. culture, men neutralize fear and sadness more often than women do. Finally, when we *mask* an emotion, we replace it with another expression to which we believe others will respond more favorably. Sometimes we conceal feelings of jealousy, disappointment, or rage.

Using Facial Appearance to Interpret and Evaluate Communication Presence. Our face reveals our identity. It is our primary means of identifying each other.[7] Our face's appearance influences judgments of our attractiveness with symmetry (similarity between the left and right sides of the face) and proportionality (the relative size of facial features) as key factors in that assessment.[8]

Facial appearance also affects others' beliefs about how emotional, dominant, or submissive we are.[9] We speak of a baby face, a face as cold as ice, a face as strong as a bulldog's, and so on. What words would you use to describe your own face?

Facial Areas

By now you are probably beginning to realize the importance of observing facial cues. But what should you watch for? For purposes of analysis, we can divide a person's face into three general areas: the eyebrows and forehead, the eyes, and the mouth.

The Eyebrows and Forehead. If you raise your eyebrows, what emotion are you showing? Surprise is probably most common, but fear can also be expressed by raised eyebrows. When you are experiencing fear, the duration of the movement will likely be longer.

The brows help express other emotions, too. Right now, move your brows into as many configurations as you can. With each movement, analyze your emotional response.

The forehead also helps communicate physical and emotional state. A furrowed brow suggests tension, worry, or deep thought. A sweating forehead suggests nervousness or great effort.

The Eyes. Many expressions refer to the eyes—"shifty eyes," "the look of love," "the evil eye," and "look me in the eye." Various eye movements are associated with the communication of emotion: a downward glance suggests modesty; staring suggests coldness; wide eyes suggest wonder, naiveté, honesty, or fright; and excessive blinking suggest nervousness or insecurity.[10] Once we start to take an interest in something, our blinking rate decreases and our pupils dilate.

How long we gaze or stare at a person or thing also communicates. In U.S. culture, it is acceptable to stare at animals and inanimate objects such as paintings or sculpture, but it is considered rude to stare at people. Instead, when it comes to people we don't know, we're supposed to practice **civil inattention**. This requires us to avoid sustained eye contact by letting our eyes rest only momentarily on people. Although it is permissible to look at someone we don't know for one or two seconds, after that we are expected to move our eyes along.

Other cultures have different norms around eye contact. Arabs engage in more direct eye contact and the Japanese in less eye contact than is typical of Americans. The Japanese, in fact, believe that prolonged eye contact is a sign of disrespect. Japanese children learn at an early age to avoid direct eye contact and to direct their gaze to the area of the Adam's apple instead.[11]

In the United States, despite the civil inattention rule, in any gathering, the first thing most people do is eye one another. Eye contact reveals whether the communication channel is open. It is much easier to avoid interacting if we have not made eye contact.

Eye contact also offers clues to the kind of relationship we share with another. For one thing, it can signal a need for inclusion or affiliation. People who have a high need for affiliation are likely to return the glances of others. There also is a high degree of eye contact between people who like each other. We also increase eye contact when communicating with others if the physical distance between us is increased. Increased eye contact psychologically helps to reduce distance.[12]

The Mouth. The area of the mouth has much to communicate. Smiles are so significant that even the curved lines on a jug of orange juice or an Amazon box are people pleasers. They draw us in.[13] Smile intensity influences assessments of warmth and competence. Approachability is also related to mouth shape and the presence of a smile.[14]

Those of us who smile rarely are more likely to be perceived as unfriendly, uninterested in others, or bored. We respond more favorably to people who smile.[15] When you smile, how do others react? We often find that others will return our smile but look away from us if our lips are pursed in a frown.

What impression does the "natural" expression of your face send to others? Some faces have a neutral expression; others have a frown, a snarl, or a habitual content expression, with the corners of the mouth seeming to turn up naturally. How is communication affected by how others respond to the appearance of your "resting face"?

Both men and women tend to smile when seeking approval, but in general, women smile more often than men. Women tend to smile even when receiving negative messages.[16] Why do you think this is so?

POSTURE

How many times have you been the target of statements like "Stand up straight!" or "Why are you all hunched over?" Our posture sends messages. The way we hold ourselves is a nonverbal broadcast, giving others information they then can use to assess our thoughts and feelings.

Slouching, for example, hampers social standing and feelings of emotional well-being. When you slouch, you literally take up less space, weakening your appearance and making yourself look less prepared. (Because it puts extra strain on your back, slouching also is not physically good for you.[17]) While depression can lead to slouching (mind over body), slouching alone can precipitate negative thoughts and feelings in us (body over mind).[18] In contrast, an erect posture has the opposite effect, energizing us and making us look more powerful.[19] When subjects looked at photos on an online dating site, they judged those with expansive postures as more romantically interesting.[20]

Media portrayals often contrast the upright bearing of a wealthy person with the submissive shuffle of a servant or the slumped demeanor of someone down on their luck. This reflects research suggesting that when people assume inferior roles, they reflect this by lowering their heads. In contrast, when they take on superior roles, people often raise their heads.[21] We have certain expectations regarding the postures we expect others to display. For example, we likely expect a high-ranking military officer to adopt an extremely straight and official posture.

Another aspect of posture is how we lean or orient ourselves when we are face-to-face with others. If you were speaking to someone who suddenly turned or leaned away from you, would you consider that a positive sign? Probably not. We usually associate liking and other positive attitudes with leaning forward rather than withdrawing. A slight forward tilt of your upper body suggests to others that you are interested in what they have to say. Interestingly, we lean either left or right when communicating with a person of lower status than ourselves. The right or left leaning is a part of our more relaxed demeanor.[22] Posture, similarly, suggests how much congruence exists between us and another person. The more we mirror the other's posture and behavior, the greater is our congruence.

CAREER BUILDER:
THE ETHICS OF ACHIEVING STATUS

Why do we assess those who are taller and speak louder as being more dominant? Before responding, consider these examples: One female CEO admits to wearing stiletto heels even though she is 5 feet, 9 inches tall, because she thinks they make her appear more intimidating.[23] A male CEO, 6 feet, 3 inches tall, in the midst of heated negotiations, puts his hand on the shoulder of those shorter than him, crowding into their personal space, in an attempt to demonstrate decisiveness and dominance. Another male CEO says that he would rather be bald than short.[24] According to Malcolm Gladwell, the author of *Blink*, 30% of Fortune 500 CEOs are at least 6 feet 2 inches tall, versus just 4% of all men.[25] How should those of us

who are shorter and more soft-spoken respond in light of these examples?

How do business people acquire status? Some do it by looking directly at others, using an open stance and vigorous gestures, speaking loudly in a deep voice, demonstrating their power by interrupting others at will, and by leaning in close to reduce the space of others while expanding their own. Some think that to advance, you need to try to be seen as taller and louder—perhaps even somewhat rude.[26] Others disagree, noting that chest beating and shouting matches are old-school, akin to bullying, and should be avoided at all costs.

Where do you stand? What nonverbal cues might you use to be perceived as having more status and being more dominant?

Gestures

We learn to gesture before we learn to speak. If you've ever watched a young child perform the arms-raised "pick me up" request, you know this. The movements of our arms, legs, hands, and feet carry important nonverbal data. For example, how you position your arms sends information about your attitudes. Cross your arms in front of you. Do you feel closed off from the world? Stand up and put your hands on your hips in a self-assured manner. Then, hold your arms stiffly at your sides, as if you were nervous. Finally, dangle your arms at your sides. Become aware of the arm positions that you use habitually. What message does each of the positions you just assumed communicate?

Our legs also convey information. Try standing as a model would. Next, sit down and put your feet up on a desk or table. Then stand with your feet wide apart. Does this last stance make you feel more powerful? Depending on the distribution of body weight and the placement of the legs and feet, we can communicate stability, femininity, masculinity, anger, happiness, or any number of other qualities. We need to choose the stance that most accurately reflects our goals.

Gestures don't have universal meanings. Consider the "OK" gesture made by forming a circle with our thumb and foreman. To most Americans this gesture signifies that all is positive, but in Japan, it is a symbol for money, whereas the French and Belgians interpret it as meaning "you're worth zero."[27]

VOICE: PARALANGUAGE

A friend asks you a question, and you matter-of-factly reply, "Mmmhmm." Another person shares a revealing piece of gossip with you, and you shout, "Huh!" Reading about the ethical lapses of some politicians, you click your tongue, making the sound, "Tsk, tsk, tsk." Elements of speech that are not standard words are a part of **paralanguage**. How good you are at using paralanguage determines how effectively you'll be able to convey a message's meaning to others.[28]

Are you happy with the sound of your voice? If a new haircut and a new outfit are part of the job search, why aren't we similarly concerned with the sound of our voice? Depth of knowledge and impact of voice are equally important in who gets hired and who succeeds in business.[29] It is estimated that 38% of a message's social meaning is communicated by voice or vocal cues.[30] *How* something is said often is *what* is said. Among the elements of paralanguage are pitch, volume, rate, and silence.

Pitch

The highness or lowness of the voice is called **pitch**. We tend to associate higher pitches with female voices and lower pitches with male voices. We also develop vocal stereotypes. We associate low-pitched voices with strength, sexiness, and maturity and high-pitched voices with helplessness, tenseness, and nervousness. Although we all have what is termed a characteristic pitch, or **habitual pitch**, we also have learned to vary our pitch to reflect our mood and promote listener interest.

Some people tend to overuse one tone to the exclusion of others. Those who do this have monotonous voices. Others speak at or near the upper end of their pitch scale, producing very fragile, unsupported tones. One way to discover a pitch that is not overly high is simply to yawn. Try that now. Permit yourself to experience a good stretch; extend your arms to shoulder level and let out a vocalized yawn. Do it again. Now count to 10 out loud. To what extent does the pitch of your voice appear to have changed? Is it more resonant? It should be. If you indulge yourself and yawn once or twice before a stressful meeting or occasion, you will be able to pitch your voice at a more pleasing level.

Volume

Degree of loudness, or **volume**, is a second paralinguistic factor affecting perceived meaning. Some people cannot seem to muster enough energy for others to hear them. Others blast through person-to-person encounters. Have you ever sat in a restaurant and heard more of the conversation at a table several feet away than of the discussion at your own table? Volume frequently reflects emotional intensity. Loud people are often perceived as aggressive or over-bearing. Soft-spoken people are often perceived as timid or polite.

Rate

The speed at which we speak, or **rate**, also is important. Do you, for example, expect high-pressure salespeople to talk rapidly or slowly? Most often, they speak very quickly. Similarly, those who pitch gadgets on the Home Shopping Network tend to speak at a quick clip to retain the audience's interest and involvement. Increased rate also tends to improve credibility judgments.[31]

Of course, more stately or formal occasions require more deliberate speaking rates, punctuated with planned pauses or silences. Politicians at rallies typically punctuate their speeches with pauses that function like applause signs. Two thirds of spoken language comes to us in chunks of fewer than six words.[32] Consequently, knowing when to pause is an essential skill.

Pauses slow the rate of speech and give both speaker and receiver a chance to gather their thoughts. Unfortunately, many of us feel pauses need to be filled and consciously or unconsciously seek ways to do so. We might fill a pause with meaningless sounds or phrases: "Er-huhn-uh—"; "You know?"; "Right! Right!"; or "OK, OK!" Such **nonfluencies** disrupt the natural flow of speech. Because pauses are a natural part of communication, we should stop trying to eliminate them. Instead, we should give pauses a chance to function.

Silence

Silence, the absence of both paralinguistic and verbal cues, also serves important communication functions. Silence, for example, can allow you time to organize your thoughts. It also can be used to alert receivers that the words you are about to share are consequential. In addition, choosing not to speak to someone at all can be a forceful demonstration of the indifference one person feels toward another and can be a very powerful message of disconfirmation. Silence also can be used as a form of punishment after an argument to indicate that one person is still angry with the other.

As we see, silence can communicate a number of meanings. It can indicate that two people are so comfortable with each other that they do not feel a need to talk, or, in a different context, it can reveal a person's shyness, by suggesting discomfort or the inability to keep a conversation moving. On the other hand, silence simply may indicate that you, at the moment, agree with what is being said or simply have nothing to say.[33]

Personal Characteristics

Besides communicating emotional content, the voice also communicates personal characteristics. Listening to a voice sometimes can help you identify the speaker's individual characteristics. For instance, when speaking on the phone, we often are able to determine an unfamiliar speaker's sex, age, vocation, and place of origin. We also tend to associate particular voice types with specific body or personality types. For example, what type of appearance would you expect in a person who has a breathy, high-pitched voice? How do you imagine a person who has a throaty, raspy voice would look? As a communicator, you should be aware that your voice suggests certain qualities about you to others.

Sometimes others not only distrust, but also lose confidence in, a person when a foreign accent makes it difficult for them to understand him or her. This distrust could be attributed to incomprehension as well as prejudice.[34] Whatever its source, unfortunately, the presence of a foreign accent can cause some people to judge nonnative speakers as less credible than they actually are.

SPACE AND DISTANCE: PROXEMIC AND ENVIRONMENTAL FACTORS

Office space is shrinking, affecting both workers' "me space" and their sense of privacy.[35] How much space do you carry around with you? Are there times when you feel that others are encroaching on your space?

In his book *The Hidden Dimension,* Edward Hall uses the term **proxemics** to represent our "use of space."[36] Proxemics is the study of the space that exists between us as we talk and relate to each other, as well as the way we organize the space around us in our homes, offices, and communities.

Architects and interior designers, for example, are using proxemics to humanize hospitals. In hospitals with soft lighting, single rooms, relaxing gardens, and artwork, patients heal more quickly, nurses remain more loyal to employers, and doctors perform better. By adding therapeutic design to a typically sterile environment, such as providing patients with views of trees from their windows and more accessibility for family and friends to visit, patients experience quicker and fuller recoveries.[37] How might another environment, such as a school, use an understanding of proxemics to encourage learning?

The Distance Between Us

Hall identified four distances that we keep between ourselves and others, depending on the type of interaction and the nature of our relationship.

Intimate Distance. The range from the point of touch to 18 inches from the other person is considered **intimate distance.** At this distance, physical contact is natural. We can wrestle and we can make love. Our senses are in full operation. They are easily stimulated but also easily offended if we find ourselves in an uncomfortable situation. Have you ever had someone come too close to you and wanted that person to back off? Did you, yourself, back away? Sometimes we are forced to endure intimate distance between ourselves and strangers in crowded buses, trains, and elevators.

Personal Distance. Hall's **personal distance** ranges from 18 inches to 4 feet. When communicating at this distance, you can still hold or shake hands. This is the most common distance between people talking informally in class, at work, or at parties, and we are apt to conduct most of our conversations within this range. If you reduce personal distance to intimate distance, you are likely to make the other person feel uncomfortable. If you increase the distance, the other person is likely to begin to feel rejected.

Social Distance. Hall's **social distance** ranges from 4 feet to 12 feet. At the social distance—in contrast to the personal distance—we are not likely to share personal concerns. By using social distance, we can keep people at more than arm's length. As a result, this is a safer distance, one at which we would communicate information and feelings that are not particularly private or revealing. Many of our conversations at business conferences or meetings occur within this space. In business, the primary protector of social space is the desk. Of course, the greater the distance is between people, the more formal their encounters will be. (At a social gathering, for example, we normally can tell how well people know each other by examining how closely they stand to one another.)

Public Distance. Beyond 12 feet is **public distance**, commonly reserved for strangers with whom we don't wish to have an interaction. People waiting in an uncrowded lobby for an elevator frequently use public distance. We can assume that if a person opts for public distance when she or he could have chosen otherwise, that person does not care to converse.

What happens when we violate distance norms? Interestingly, the outcomes of such violations are not necessarily negative. For example, if we perceive the approaching person to be attractive or view her or him as potentially a high-reward source, our evaluation may become more favorable, especially if the distance violation is accompanied by other behaviors, such as compliments.[38]

Spaces

The nature of the environment affects the amount of space we maintain between ourselves and others. We can divide environmental spaces into three classifications: informal, semi-fixed-feature, and fixed-feature. These categories are based on the perceived permanence of any physical space.

Informal Space. **Informal space** is highly mobile, quickly changing space that ranges from intimate to public (from no space between us and others to 25 feet or more). Informal space functions as a personal bubble that we can enlarge to keep people at a distance or decrease to permit them to get closer.

Semi-Fixed-Feature Space. In contrast to the high mobility of informal space, **semi-fixed-feature space** uses objects to create distance. Semi-fixed features include chairs, benches, sofas, plants, and other movable items. Some office walls and partitions can be classified as semi-fixed features, since they are designed to be relocated as spatial requirements change. Barriers such as desks

reduce interaction. One study of doctor–patient relationships, for example, found that patients were more at ease speaking with a physician seated in a chair across from them than they were when the physician was seated behind a desk.[39]

In many public places, if interaction is desired, the space usually will contain chairs facing each other. Such arrangements are found in bars, restaurants, and lounges. In contrast, the chairs in waiting rooms are often bolted together in long parallel rows.

Fixed-Feature Space. The relatively permanent objects that define the environment around us constitute **fixed-feature space**. Fixed features include immovable walls, doors, trees, sidewalks, roads, and highways. Such features help guide and control our actions. For example, some classrooms are rectangular with windows along one side, often to the student's left. The window location also determines the room's front. Shopping malls and department stores rely on fixed features to help route pedestrian traffic in certain directions to increase sales. The next time you shop in a carefully designed store, examine its fixed features. Can you walk, unimpeded to any department, or are you "directed" through the perfumes, lingerie, and knickknacks?

Territoriality and Personal Space. Another aspect of proxemics is our need for a defined territory. Some animals mark their territory by urinating around its perimeter and will defend the area against invaders. Human beings also stake out space or territory, and **territoriality**—the need to demonstrate a possessive or ownership relationship in space—is an important variable in interpersonal communication. What examples of territoriality can you recall encountering? Are you familiar with "Dad's chair"? "How do you feel when someone invades your room—your territory? What happens when someone stands too close to you? During the 2016 presidential debates, then-Republican candidate for president, Donald J. Trump, repeatedly invaded the space of Democratic candidate Hillary Rodham Clinton. Trump loomed behind Clinton—perhaps in an effort to demonstrate his power, literally breathing down her neck, and, according to her, making her skin crawl. Instead of confronting Trump's invasion and telling

him to withdraw from her space and go back into his place, Clinton carried on as if Trump weren't invading her space. She since has said that she wished she had confronted him.[40]

To establish our territory, we can use **markers**, items that reserve our space, set boundaries that help distinguish space, or identify a space as ours. At the library, for example, you may spread your things out across a table, so that others will not find it easy to enter your territory. In large corporations, a person's status is often reflected by the size of her or his space. Thus, the president may be accorded a large top-floor territory, while a clerk is given a desk in a second-floor room amid a number of other desks and office equipment. Regardless of the size and location, however, we identify with it and frequently act as if we own it.

ETHICS AND COMMUNCIATION

Security and Guarded Territory

For a while now, a majority of people living in the United States have desired to live in gated communities.[41] Access to gated communities is restricted to residents and their guests. They frequently are protected by security officers, gates, walls, or fences. Security measures in gated communities keep their members feeling safe by keeping out those whom the community does not want let in.

A prime motivator for living in gated communities is the desire for personal safety. On the other hand, because gated communities signal that outsiders should stay out, their critics contend that social fragmentation is the cost society pays to allow those living inside gated communities to feel secure. The fear is that gated communities precipitate the formation of in-groups and out-groups composed of those in and out of the community.

Where do you stand? Are gated communities a good idea? Are there other models of living arrangements that could be secure without closing off a community to the outside world?

APPEARANCE

Are we living in a "looks-based" world? Would it surprise you to know that in the first three months that he was in office, French President Emmanuel Macron spent over $30,000 on makeup services for public appearances?[42] Why does appearance matter? Why are some people discriminated against because of how they look?

In a culture that is image-obsessed, those seen as unattractive can be at a disadvantage. People perceived as unattractive earn lower salaries and receive longer prison sentences than their more attractive counterparts. Do you think such "beauty premiums" should exist?[43]

The Height Factor

How does height contribute to appearance judgments? When it comes to height, tall people tend to come out on top, whether in an election or a job interview.[44] In South Korea, thanks to the proliferation of Western models of beauty and success, parents spend large sums of money for treatments that are supposed to make their children taller because short kids are ostracized.[45]

The Weight Factor

Obese people are stigmatized, routinely given a cold shoulder and brusque treatment.[46] Many condemn fat-shaming as wrong, but it persists.[47] Obese women earn lower wages than do women of average weight.[48] Even physicians are influenced by the appearance of obese patients. The higher a patient's body mass is, the less respect doctors express for the patient.[49]

Other Appearance Effects

Appearance affects us in other ways too. Those of us judged to be attractive date more, earn higher grades, and are rated as more persuasive and likable.[50] Obsessing over attractiveness may cause men to engage in bodybuilding, women to diet, and both to turn to plastic surgery as a solution to feeling unattractive.[51]

Judgments of race also are based on clues that the face and body provide. For many marketers, ethnic ambiguity—the multiracial face of youth—represents the new American beauty ideal. Advertisers judge a face whose heritage is hard to discern as desirable. Ethnic mixing is changing the face of attractiveness and influencing casting choices in advertisements and entertainment.[52]

CLOTHING AND ARTIFACTS

What messages do your choice of personal adornments send to others? **Artifactual communication**, the use of clothing and personal adornments, such as jewelry, makeup, hairstyles, tattoos, and beards, provides others with important nonverbal cues. Wearing nice things can help you socially and enable you to achieve more professionally. Besides increasing your confidence level, dressing well may boost effective thinking and influence others to view you more positively and give you more respect.[53]

Ga Fullner / Shutterstock.com

Artifacts help us to create an image and register a first impression. How we dress influences both ourselves and others. Consider singer Rihanna, for example. Does her dress support her image? Given the kind of music she performs, could she just as easily have chosen to wear more prim and proper attire? While Rihanna purposefully wears clothing to make an impression and seek an effect, you probably would not opt to wear similar clothing to your job.

The clothing we choose to wear typically supports the roles and functions we perform. It also may project a political or social position, as the "Make America Great Again" hats do for Donald Trump and his supporters. In fact, although he claimed that he had worn it as a joke, one Canadian judge was required to appear before a disciplinary panel for wearing the cap. More than 90 complaints from law schools and individual lawyers demanded that the judge be sanctioned so public trust in the judiciary could be restored.[54] Clothing and artifacts can attract others or repel them. We also can use clothing, however, to protect ourselves and keep others at bay. One artist, for example, created a dress that would expand to reclaim the wearer's personal space whenever others stood too close.[55]

Because we react to others based, at least in part, on their clothing choices, it stands to reason that in the early stages of a relationship, clothing worn affects our impression of another person and exerts influences on us that lead to acceptance or rejection. Additionally, we make judgments regarding success, character, dominance, and competence on the basis of the type of clothing and jewelry worn.[56]

We tend to respond more positively to those whom we perceive to be well dressed and tastefully adorned. We are more likely to respond to requests or follow the lead of well-dressed individuals (including people wearing uniforms) than we are to listen to or emulate people whose dress suggests lower status or their lack of authority.[57]

Kathleen McDermott, 2014

Kathleen McDermott, 2014

COLORS: MEANINGS AND ASSOCIATIONS

Every year, the Pantone Color Institute names a color of the year. In 2017, that color was called "greenery"—nature's hue, a life-affirming shade symbolic of new beginnings.[58]

Color affects people emotionally and physiologically.[59] What is your favorite color and why? Many connect red, for example, with authority and self-confidence,[60] and the color may increase memory and make people's work more accurate. The color blue, meanwhile, actually helps to make us more creative[61] (Figure 5.2). Red excites the nervous system, whereas blue has a calming effect, lowering blood pressure, heart, and respiration rates. Orange is also a high-energy color in contrast to white, which, for Westerners, evokes feelings of serenity.

Marketers emphasize colors in product packaging to spur sales. Detergent sold in a solid yellow container was perceived as weak, whereas detergent in a red container was seen as strong. Detergent sold in a red or blue container with yellow specks, however, was "just right."[62] The color of a container similarly affects perceptions of coffee, with the same coffee offered for sale in a yellow container not considered strong enough, when offered in a brown container considered too bold, in a red container perceived as rich, and in a blue container evaluated as mild. Do you think we make

FIGURE 5.2
Seeing Red, Seeing Blue

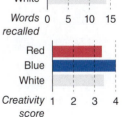

John Stillwell/PA Images via Getty Images

similar judgments about people based on the colors that others surround themselves with or wear?

Attitudes toward color vary within and across cultures. In the United States, green signifies capitalism, jealousy, and nature. Traffic lights that are green tell us to proceed. In China, the colors red and yellow are associated with prosperity, whereas in African countries the color red is associated with death and in Japan it connotes danger. In the United States, the color yellow is associated with cowardice or warmth. In Asian cultures, white is associated with death and mourning. Accordingly, brides in China do not wear white; instead, they wear red. Understanding cultural attitudes toward color can also foster diplomacy. When the British royal family travel abroad, they often wear the national colors of the host country.[63]

TIME: CHRONEMICS

Chronemics is the study of how we use time to communicate. The meanings we attribute to time differ not only around the United States, but also around the world.[64] Some of us are preoccupied with time; others habitually waste it. Whereas some of us typically arrive for appointments either early or on time, others of us are chronically late. While some of us travel through life with a sense of urgency, others amble through it at a more leisurely pace. Some of us are "early birds"; others are "night owls." Which are you? Whatever your answer, clock addiction is hard to break.

Do you feel like you have enough time for most of your activities? Are you usually prepared to take exams or turn in assignments on their due dates? Do you arrive for appointments on time, early, or late?

Wait Time

How long we are willing to wait for something to happen or someone to arrive is related to two factors: the value we place on whatever or whoever we are waiting for and our own status.

We are taught to value what we have to wait for. In fact, if something is too readily available, we may decide that we don't want it. Status also determines who waits for whom. If a person is "important," others usually have access to her or him only by appointment. Thus, it is easier for those who possess status to make others wait. High-status people simply feel more in control of time. Thus, time is both psychological and social, but it also is cultural. Every culture views time through a different frame, establishing norms and instructing members on time-appropriate responses. Some cultures, for example, are monochronic, with members believing that one activity should be scheduled at a time. Other cultures are polychronic, with members doing many things simultaneously or in the same time segment.

SKILL BUILDER

Assessing Your Use of Time

1. How well do you structure time?[65] Give an example of an occasion when you failed to use your time effectively because of each of the following barriers:

   - Attempting too much (taking on too many projects or commitments at once)
   - Estimating time unrealistically (not realizing how long a task will take to complete)
   - Procrastinating (putting it off, and off, and off)
   - Allowing too many interruptions (letting yourself be distracted)

2. Suggest strategies you could use to prevent each barrier from turning you into a time waster.

3. Consider the following situations. How quickly do you expect a response in each case?

   a. You text a friend with a question.
   b. You e-mail a professor to request an extension on an assignment.
   c. You invite a peer to connect on LinkedIn.
   d. You post a photo on Instagram and tag several friends.

   What do your time expectations reveal? Do others share the same expectations? Ask them.

Rush Time

Our sense of time is reflected in our use of and expectations for technology. Consider this: Rarely do we use commas when texting, which some attribute to the frenetic pace of our lives.[66] The comma, after all, signals a pause—the need to slow down before moving on—and slowing down is not what we seem to be doing. Instead, we often choose to multitask.

TOUCH: HAPTICS

Another category of nonverbal communication is touch, also referred to as **haptics**.

Touch Effects

A world without touch is unimaginable. Human beings need to touch and be touched. Touch lowers stress hormones and protects us throughout the day.[67] It is also good for our hearts—even if the touch lasts only 5 seconds. A hug and 10 minutes of hand holding with a romantic partner greatly reduce the harmful physical effects of stress. Touch, a significant means of emotional expression, also can be a relationship strengthener.[68]

Accessibility to Touch

Our accessibility to touch varies. In general, women are more accessible to touch than are men. Generally, men touch women more than women touch men.[69] Touch also correlates positively with openness, comfort with relationships, and the ability to express feelings.[70] The kind of touch we find appropriate depends on the nature of a relationship and the situation we find ourselves in. Review the following touch categories:

- Functional-professional touch is impersonal or businesslike, such as a doctor's examination.
- Social-polite touch is used to acknowledge another person, such as a handshake.
- Friendship-warmth touch expresses appreciation or warm feelings for another person, such as a pat on the back.
- Love-intimacy touch occurs in romantic relationships and includes a hug and kiss.
- Sexual arousal touch is the most intimate kind of personal contact and is used to express love and physical attraction.

Which of the preceding categories of touch do you use most frequently? *Marasmus*, which comes from a Greek word meaning "wasting away," was used in the 19th and early 20th centuries to describe how some babies placed in orphanages or hospitals failed to thrive because of a lack of touch and physical contact. Today, in part because of a fear of being accused of sexual harassment, including touching someone inappropriately, educators tend to avoid touching students, counselors are advised not to touch campers, and employers avoid touching employees.[71] To what extent might such fear contribute to impressions that schools and workplaces are cold and uncaring places?

Touch and Status

Touch and status also are related. High-status people touch others and invade their space more than do individuals with lower status.[72] The person who initiates touch usually is the one with the higher status. We are unlikely to go to our boss and put our hand on his or her shoulder.[73] The initiator of touch usually is the one who also controls the conversation.

SMELL: OLFACTICS

What do happiness and contentment smell like? **Olfactics**, the study of the sense of smell, can help us find the answer. Whole industries are based around our preoccupation with smells and odors.[74] We wear perfume or cologne. We use deodorant, scented soaps, mouthwash, scented sprays, fragrances and room fresheners, and aromatic candles—all in the effort to increase the desirability of how we and our surroundings smell.

Emotional Triggers and Recall

Smells are associated with attraction, often triggering emotional or romantic feelings. Pheromones, chemicals emitted by one individual to evoke a response in another individual, contribute to sexual arousal. Women, interestingly, prefer men whose smell resembles their own.[75] Gay men and straight women respond to men's scents in similar ways.[76]

The scents that serve as emotional triggers for us depend on our associations, memories, and, to some extent, our culture. For example, in the United Kingdom, the smell of root beer is reviled, whereas many in the United States think it smells good. In England, sarsaparilla and wintergreen, ingredients in root beer, are used in medicine.[77]

Smells both good and bad also aid memory recall. Our sense of smell sharpens when something bad happens, alerting us to the odor, and helping us steer clear of similar danger in the future.[78] On the other hand, the smell of vanilla and apple pie might trigger associations of home.

> Visit the interactive e-Book to access the Skill Builder feature "Assess
> Your General Knowledge of Nonverbal Cues," which will quiz you on your
> knowledge of various nonverbal cues used when communicating with others.

TRUTH, DECEPTION, AND NONVERBAL CUES

Actors use their understanding of nonverbal communication to persuade us to suspend our disbelief and accept them as someone they are not. They carefully rehearse their parts down to the smallest gestures and artifacts. As we watch them perform, we come to accept them as their characters.

What about the rest of us? Do we use nonverbal messages to create impressions in others that may not be real or true? Whereas the aim of some deceptive communication is to help save face (we try to appear relaxed when we're a nervous wreck) or to protect ourselves from the embarrassment that bluntness can cause ("Yes, I love your haircut," we say, smiling, when we think it's absolutely horrific), the goal of many who seek to deceive is to take advantage of others.

Most of us do not rehearse for every person-to-person encounter. Our lives are not that well plotted. We don't typically map out the nonverbal cues we will use when interacting with others. But what if we could and did? Would those we were with be able to discern our intentions? Would they know that we really weren't feeling what we were expressing?

Consider this: It is suspected that the terrorists who, in August 2017, drove a van into a crowd in Barcelona, killing 14 and maiming at least 130 others, had been recruited and trained by Abdelbaki Essati, a local imam. It is believed that Essati had used his charm and guile to carry on a double life for years. A master of deception, he often wore jeans, sported only a short beard, and appeared to be nice and friendly to those who knew him.[79]

In general, we pay closer attention to the nonverbal messages of people whom we don't trust or whom we suspect may be lying than to the rest of the people with whom we interact.[80] Those who plan and rehearse the sending of deceptive messages tend to be self-confident and experience no guilt about their deception. They are least likely to be suspected by others and, therefore, least likely to be uncovered as liars—which is not a good thing for those of us trying to detect deceptiveness in others.

WHO'S BEST AT DECEPTION?

Some of us are better at deception than others. People whose occupations require that they sometimes act differently than they actually feel are most successful at deception. Included in this group are lawyers, diplomats, and sales representatives.[81] As we age, we also become better liars.[82] Those among us who are high self-monitors are also usually better dissemblers than those who have less self-awareness. High self-monitors are more watchful.

Individuals who try to fake the nonverbal messages they send to others can fail because of leakage—deception clues that careful observers pick up. Sometimes the giveaway is a microfacial expression (a fleeting change in facial expression), asymmetrical expressions such as one-sided smiles, an ill-timed gesture, hand fidgeting, a posture shift, a rising pitch, a deep or shallow breath, a long pause, a higher than normal blink rate, expressions that look fixed or painted on, the making of speech errors, or a slip of the tongue.[83] Keep in mind that the context of the behavior must always be considered before assuming that someone is lying.

GENDER AND NONVERBAL BEHAVIOR

Gender influences the use of nonverbal cues, which are reflective of societal practices.

DOMINANCE AND AFFILIATION

Men tend to be more visually dominant than women. We measure **visual dominance** by comparing the percentage of looking while speaking with the percentage of looking while listening. When compared with women, men spend more time looking at others while speaking and less time when listening to others speak to them. This also reinforces perceptions of men as having more social power.[84]

Men also use space and touch to assert their dominance over others. Men tend to claim more personal space. This is seen as a power move and frequently is perceived as space infringing. When they sit in public spaces, for example, some men sit with their legs spread wide in a V shape rather than parallel, effectively taking up two or three seats. This has come to be known as "manspreading," a power move that others often find offensive.[85]

Men also more frequently walk in front of women than behind them. Remember, they also are the initiators of touch. In general, men are the touchers not the touchees, and the leaders not the followers.

Women smile and show emotion more often than do men. Women also stand closer to one another than men and use nonverbal signals to draw others into conversations more than men do. Women show more of an interest in affiliation, while men are more interested in demonstrating the strength of their ideas and agendas.[86] Women outperform men in decoding nonverbal cues, including the ability to read another's feelings.[87]

DRESS CODES

When it comes to clothing practices, sometimes dress codes rule. For example, the Montana Legislature passed a dress code that specified that its members may not wear jeans and then singled out women, noting that women "should be sensitive to skirt lengths and necklines." Congress's dress code prohibits women from wearing sleeveless attire on the floor of the House.[88] What do dress codes tell us about communication norms? What do they suggest about who is and who is not trusted to dress appropriately?

WHOSE VOICE?

Voice tends to be gendered. We usually can tell if a speaker is a male or a female. Having a gendered neutral voice is rare. Generally, studies of voices of chatbots and digital assistants reveal that both men and women judge a female voice to be warmer and more welcoming than a male voice. Female voices are also sex-typed as more helpful, supportive, and trustworthy. In contrast, a male voice is the default preference for the delivery of instructional material. Are the designers of digital chatbots and assistants such as Siri, Alexa, and Cortana playing to our stereotypes by giving them female voices?[89]

CULTURE AND NONVERBAL BEHAVIOR

Throughout the world, people use nonverbal cues both to help them express themselves and to interpret others' behavior.

Members of **contact cultures**—cultures that promote interaction and encourage displays of warmth, closeness, and availability—tend to stand close to each other when conversing, seek maximum sensory experiences, and touch each other naturally. This is not so for members of **low-contact cultures**, where such behaviors are discouraged. Saudi Arabia, France, and Italy are countries with contact cultures whose members relish the intimacy of contact when conversing. Middle Easterners do a significant amount of touching; for example, it is not uncommon to see Middle Eastern men walking with their arms around each other. In contrast, Scandinavia, Germany, England, and Japan are low- or lower-contact cultures, whose members value privacy, maintain more distance from each other when interacting, and touch each other less frequently.[90]

YAKOBCHUK VIACHESLAV/Shutterstock.com

EXPRESSING EMOTION AND INTIMACY

People from diverse cultures also may not display emotion or express intimacy similarly.

Among the members of Mediterranean cultures, for example, it is normal for emotive reactions to be uninhibited. These cultures' members share feelings like grief or happiness openly, together with expressive facial displays, magnified gestures, and vocal cues that reflect their feelings. In contrast, neither the Chinese nor the Japanese readily reveal their inner feelings in public. They prefer to display less emotion, maintain more self-control, and keep their feelings to themselves. As a result, to observers they often appear to remain expressionless.[91] In the United States, as in Mediterranean cultures, individuals are likely to be emotionally expressive.

JUDGMENTS OF BEAUTY

Beauty communicates around the world. Diverse cultures, despite their differences, are incredibly consistent in their judgments of beauty. People judged attractive in one culture are apt also to be perceived as attractive by the members of other cultures.[92]

ATTITUDES TOWARD DISTANCE AND TOUCH

Attitudes toward distance and touch also differ across cultures. Americans stand farther apart when conversing than do people from Middle Eastern cultures. Whereas in the United States we expect our neighbors to be friendly and to interact with us, Asian cultures don't share this expectation. Members of Asian cultures may view people in the United States as overly friendly, whereas people from the Middle East may conclude that Americans are distant.

BE CAREFUL MAKING MEANING

Even when the nonverbal cues displayed across cultures are the same, they don't necessarily convey the same meanings. In the United States, for example, a head nod symbolizes agreement or consent, whereas in Japan it means only that a message was received.

Members of different cultures also have dissimilar attitudes toward silence. In the United States, we are likely to perceive another's silence as a negative and indicative of self-absorption or disinterest. In contrast, in Asian cultures, silence is often preferred to speech.

To experience more effective communication with people from different cultures, we must make the effort to identify and understand how their cultures shape their use of nonverbal messages. Acknowledging that our communication style is not intrinsically better than others will contribute to more successful multicultural exchanges.

TECHNOLOGY AND NONVERBAL COMMUNICATION

Getty Images is a library of stock photography. In fact, many of the photos in this textbook were licensed from Getty Images. Back in 2007, the top-selling Getty image for the search term "woman" was one of a naked woman with a towel strategically placed over her lower half, gazing up at the camera. In 2017, it was of a woman hiking in one of the U.S. national parks. The best-selling image had changed from focusing on what a woman looks like to what she's doing, from being passive to being active. Furthermore, working in concert with Sheryl Sandberg and her Lean In initiative, Getty Images has made a proactive effort to include more diverse and empowering photographs of women in their collection.[93]

Getty Images/Stephan Hoeck

The prevalence of culturally diverse photos in Getty's and other image collections influence attitudes and perceptions of what is possible. By presenting cultural and gender differences as a natural part of the communication landscape, image collections also increase our comfort with diversity. Could this shift, in part, be due to the fact that social media allow us to represent ourselves, and we expect marketers to depict us in much the same ways? The popularity of posts on apps like Facebook, Snapchat, Pinterest, and Instagram, together with videos we upload to sites such as YouTube, attest to our fascination with, and reliance on, visual, word-independent communication.

Getty Images/Jordan Siemens

We have become a visually oriented culture. When online, many of us use photos to establish our online identity. Based on others' photos and assessments of appearance, we then decide whether or not to engage. With this in mind, and because we try to manage our self-presentations, many of us are likely to select—or create with editing software—a complimentary picture in the effort to put the best version of ourselves forward.

In addition, by using avatars we try to make even a better impression than we think we could without them.[94] Imagining different selves is freeing. We can have a disembodied identity—more than one body that exists in actions and words online. Avatars let us be deceptive. We can exist in many worlds and play different selves simultaneously.

SKILL BUILDER

Assessing Your Virtual Presence

1. Describe your virtual physical presence. How is it different from your actual physical presence? Explain what it means to you to be virtually involved.

2. To what extent do others interact with you differently online than when face-to-face?

3. Do you find it easier to convey genuine feelings when online or face-to-face? Why?

4. If you were in an intimate relationship and one of you engaged in cybersex with someone else, would you consider it cheating?

5. Identify at least one nonverbal skill you use to be effective in communicating online.

DO SUBSTITUTES FOR FACIAL EXPRESSIONS AND GESTURES WORK?

Although we experience the most social presence when face-to-face, when online we have **emoticons** and **emoji** to replace physical gestures and facial expressions, substitute for nonverbal cues, and help us convey action, emotion, and emphasis in our online interactions. Emoticons and emoji are relational icons that add personalization and emotional expressiveness to online dialogue. We use them to indicate subtle mood changes. They are a way to approximate the warmth and intimacy of face-to-face interactions. They also help us establish our online personas.

Online we are most likely to seek out and affiliate with those whom we perceive to be like us, who seem to share our needs and interests. On the other hand, online it is easy to present multiple aspects of ourselves and multiple identities. Some of us adopt more than one screen name, pose as members of the opposite sex or another race. We use emoticons and emoji either to conceal who we really are as we perform the role of someone else or to reveal one or more aspects of ourselves that we have kept hidden. We manufacture or present an alternative identity to get the reaction we want from others and/or to test others' reactions to those parts of ourselves we have kept submerged.

Online communication advances continue. Years back, future-casters predicted that we soon would have wearable computers. Such computers are now built into our glasses and the watches we wear—always accessible. Chatbots—computer programs designed to mimic human interaction—are more commonplace. Humans and computers now converse.

COMMUNICATION SKILLS
Practice Using and Observing Nonverbal Cues

Developing the ability to make valid judgments and decisions on the basis of nonverbal cues takes work. When observing communication in action, practice the following behaviors.

Observe body language.
What does each communicator's facial expression reveal? Assess the extent to which you believe the displayed facial expressions are genuine.

- Analyze significant bodily cues.

- Assess the extent to which the individuals mirror each other's posture. Ask yourself how posture supports or contradicts their status relationship. Analyze when and why they alter their postures.

- Watch the eye behavior of the communicators. Determine if one looks away more than the other. Note if one stares at the other.

Listen for vocal cues.

Assess if the people you are observing are using appropriate vocal volume and rates of speaking, given their situation. Determine if and how the way each says something verbally supports or contradicts what is being said. Analyze the use of silence. Be responsive to signals of nervousness and changes in pitch.

Evaluate appearance, clothing, artifacts, and color.

Determine how the appearance, clothing, and artifacts of the communicators affect the impression they make. Decide if their dress, role, and behavior are congruent. Assess if the colors worn by each person and those adorning the space they are in have any influence on their behavior toward one another.

Assess the effects of time, touching, and smell.

Speculate on how each person treats time. Analyze the meanings of touch or touch-avoidance behavior. Watch to see if and when participants actually touch one another and with what effect. Identify if touching behavior was appropriate to the situation. Also identify the extent to which smell was a factor in attracting or repelling their interaction.

Explore the environment.

Assess the extent to which the setting did or did not affect the interaction. Determine if other people present had any impact on the people being observed. Speculate on whether color and décor had any effect on the nature and tone of communication. Analyze the amount of space available to them and the amount of space they used. Assess if architectural features or the positioning of furniture altered their interaction in any way.

Make predictions based on your observations of nonverbal behavior.

Develop a series of statements you feel are accurate descriptions of the people observed and could influence your decision about whether or not to approach them in the future.

> " The eyes of men converse at least as much as their tongues.
>
> —Ralph Waldo Emerson

COMPLETE THIS CHAPTER 5 CHECKLIST

5.1 I can define *nonverbal communication* and explain its characteristics. ☐

Nonverbal communication includes all the human responses that are not expressed in words. Over 65% of the meaning of a message is communicated nonverbally. Perceiving and analyzing nonverbal cues help us to understand what is really happening as people interact.

5.2 I can describe the functions of nonverbal communication. ☐

Nonverbal cues function to reinforce, negate, substitute for, intensify, and/or regulate verbal messages.

5.3 I can explain the following types of nonverbal messages: body language, voice, space and distance, appearance, colors, clothing and artifacts, time, touch, and smell. ☐

Nonverbal messages fall into the preceding main categories. All are significant sources of information.

Body language, or kinesics, includes facial expressions, posture, eye gaze and eye contact, and gestures.

Voice, or paralanguage, includes the analysis of pitch, volume, rate, and pauses—factors affecting the expressiveness of the human voice.

Space and distance, or proxemics, factors include considering both the distance that exists between people when they communicate and the way we organize the space in which we are located.

Appearance includes aspects of attractiveness, height, and weight.

Color includes a consideration of both psychological and physiological effects.

Clothing and artifacts include dress, hair, and body adornments. People are apt to make inferences about us based on our appearance or dress.

Time or chronemics finds us focusing on how time is organized, used, and responded to. Touch or haptics includes an analysis of messages sent through the presence or absence of touch.

Smell, or olfactics, includes the consideration of how smell influences perceptions of people and behavior.

5.4 I can describe how nonverbal cues can help distinguish truth telling from lying. ☐

Deception detection is important for societal, professional, and personal reasons. Accuracy in determining truthfulness depends on the ability to decipher leakage cues.

5.5 I can identify the ways in which differences in gender influence nonverbal behavior. ☐

The use of nonverbal cues reflects societal practices. To a large degree, people modify their use of nonverbal messages depending on the gender with which they identify.

. . . .

5.6 I can identify the ways in which differences in cultural background influence nonverbal behavior. ☐

Culture influences the expression of emotion and intimacy, judgments of beauty, attitudes toward distance and touch, and attitudes toward the environment.

. . . .

5.7 I can discuss technology's effect on nonverbal communication. ☐

Nonverbal messaging is affected by whether communication occurs online or in person. When interacting online, we often use expressive and relational icons called emoticons and emoji to substitute for actual facial expressions and gestures; emoticons and emoji add personalization and emotional expressiveness to online dialogue.

. . . .

5.8 I can apply skills to interpret nonverbal cues and make valid judgments and decisions. ☐

We improve our communication effectiveness by observing people and focusing on analyzing and interpreting all aspects of nonverbal behavior.

. . . .

BECOME A WORD MASTER

artifactual communication 120

chronemics 122

civil inattention 112

contact cultures 127

emoji 130

emoticons 130

facial management techniques 111

fixed-feature space 118

habitual pitch 114

haptics 123

informal space 117

intimate distance 116

kinesics 110

low-contact cultures 127

markers 118

mixed message 109

nonfluencies 115

nonverbal communication 107

olfactics 124

paralanguage 114

personal distance 117

pitch 114

proxemics 116

public distance 117

rate 115

semi-fixed-feature space 117

silence 115

social distance 117

territoriality 118

visual dominance 126

volume 115

iStock/MangoStar_Studio

6

Listening, Feedback, and Critical Thinking

6.1   Define *listening*, differentiate it from hearing, and explain its role in communication.

6.2   Distinguish among the four types of listening: appreciative, comprehensive, critical, and empathic.

6.3   Use the HURIER model to explain the six stages of listening.

6.4   Identify problematic listening behaviors.

6.5   Summarize the kinds of feedback listeners can provide.

6.6   Discuss critical thinking and its impact on listening.

6.7   Explain how gender influences listening.

6.8   Explain how culture influences listening.

6.9   Explain how media and technology influence listening.

6.10 Demonstrate effective listening skills.

> To get what you want in your career, stop talking and start listening.
>
> Anonymous

Does it frustrate you when someone tells you that she can multitask while listening to you? Is it possible for one person to really listen to another person while simultaneously involving themselves in a second activity, such as texting?

What about yourself? How often do you multitask while listening in class? Perhaps, you check Facebook or Instagram, or secretly text a friend. Can any of us listen effectively while distracted by competing interests? Studies reveal that if you multitask while listening, you are not absorbing as much as you think you are and often are unaware of what you missed.[1]

In contrast, do you know someone whose attention never wavers when engaged in conversation with you, whose eyes lock on yours, whose facial expressions announce interest in you, and whose questions and ability to paraphrase demonstrate an understanding of you? If you do, then you know a person who realizes what it means to be an effective listener.[2]

The Chinese character for "listening" (Figure 6.1) combines a number of symbols representing the ears, the eyes, and the heart, suggesting that when listening, we

FIGURE 6.1
Chinese Character for "Listening"

Ear

Eyes

Undivided
Attention

Heart

need to give our undivided attention and should not rely on our ears alone. Rather, we should use our ears, eyes, and hearts simultaneously. In your opinion, do most of the people you know accomplish this goal? Do you? ■

LISTENING AND COMMUNICATION

Famed American author Ernest Hemingway is believed to have said, "I like to listen. I have learned a great deal from listening carefully. Most people never listen." On the basis of your personal experiences, do you think Hemingway's conclusion is right? Do most people never listen?

TRUE "NOT LISTENING" STORIES

One college student, Brett Banfe, convinced that he had failed miserably in listening to others, vowed to correct his failing by remaining silent for a year. Banfe said, "I noticed I wasn't really listening to people. I was just waiting for people to stop talking so I could chime in."[3] He also noted, "I'd wait for them to stop talking, then I'd start talking. Because . . . my opinion was the right one anyway. It was like, 'Thanks a lot for your input, but here's how it really happened.'"[4]

Banfe was conscious of his problem. Many others are not. Recognizing this, the bestselling self-help book author Stephen Covey tells the following story:

A father once told me, "I can't understand my kid. He just won't listen to me at all."

"Let me restate what you just said," Covey replied to the father. "You don't understand your son because he won't listen to you?"

"That's what I said," the father impatiently replied.

Convey countered: "I thought that to understand another person, you needed to listen to him."

"Oh!" said the father. There was a long pause. "Oh!" he said again, as the light began to dawn. "Oh yeah! But I do understand him. I know what he's going through. I went through the same thing myself. I guess what I don't understand is why he won't listen to me."

Covey observes that the man didn't have a clue what was going on inside his boy's head. He had looked into his own head and imagined he saw his boy's world.[5]

While you may think that the action taken by Brett Banfe seems extreme, it is true that listening is something we often take for granted, as Covey's anecdote illustrates. However, listening is a difficult, intricate skill and, like other skills, it requires training and practice.

WE ALL DO IT!

Listening affects all kinds of communication. From the moment the alarm clock rings in the morning, until the late-night shows wind up, we are inundated with things to listen to. As we proceed through our day, and as we move from person to person, from class to lunch, from formal discussion to casual conversations, we are constantly called on to listen. We are expected to listen whenever we interact face-to-face with friends and acquaintances, use the phone, attend meetings, participate in interviews, take part in arguments, give or receive instructions, make decisions based on information received orally, and generate and receive feedback.

ARE YOU LISTENING?

Answer the following questions about how you listen.

1. When involved in a conversation with another person, how often do you find yourself thinking that what the other person is saying is unimportant?

   a. always   b. sometimes   c. never

2. How frequently do you find yourself silently criticizing the mannerisms or the appearance of an individual with whom you are conversing?

   a. always   b. sometimes   c. never

3. How often do you find yourself becoming emotional about something another person says?

   a. always   b. sometimes   c. never

4. How often do you find yourself jumping ahead of the person speaking—perhaps even completing her thoughts?

   a. always   b. sometimes   c. never

5. How frequently do you interrupt a person speaking with you?

   a. always   b. sometimes   c. never

6. How often do you fake paying attention to someone?

   a. always   b. sometimes   c. never

7. How frequently do you find yourself distracted by something while listening?

   a. always   b. sometimes   c. never

8. How often do you try to avoid listening to difficult content?

   a. always   b. sometimes   c. never

9. How often do you find yourself personally antagonized by another person using emotion-laden words?

   a. always   b. sometimes   c. never

10. How often do you refuse to give your complete attention to someone expressing a point of view that conflicts with yours?

    a. always   b. sometimes   c. never

Score your answers as follows: if your answer to a question is always, award yourself 1 point. If your answer is sometimes, award yourself 5 points. If your answer is never, award yourself 10 points. Total your score. If you score lower than 50, you're not listening when you should be. If you score between 50 and 70, you have listening potential. If you score between 70 and 90, you are a fair to good listener. If you score between 90 and 100, you are an accomplished listener. Based on your answers and resulting score, describe and, if necessary, critique your listening behavior.

LISTENING IS MORE THAN HEARING

Listening and hearing are not the same thing. Most people are born with the ability to hear.

Defining Hearing

Hearing is a process that occurs automatically and requires no conscious effort on our part. If the physiological elements within our ears are functioning properly, our brain will process the electrochemical impulses received, and we will hear.

Defining Listening

What is listening? **Listening** is a deliberate process through which we seek to understand and retain aural (heard) stimuli. Unlike hearing, listening depends on a complex set of skills that must be acquired. Whereas hearing simply happens to us and cannot be manipulated, listening requires us to make an active, conscious effort to comprehend and remember what we hear. Listening requires analysis and the desire for full understanding.

Who we are affects what we listen to. In any environment, from minute to minute, far too many sounds bombard us for us to be able to pay attention to each one. Thus, in listening, we process the external sounds of our environment to select those that are relevant to us, our activities, and our interests. But listening is also an internal process. We listen to the sounds we hear, and we listen to what others say, but we also listen to what we say aloud and what we say to ourselves in response. Observing our *self-talk*—what we say to ourselves—can help us make sense of the way we listen to and react to the people in our life. (Do you ever talk to yourself? Are you your own best listener? Most of us are.)

LISTENING TAKES EFFORT

While all of us continually engage in activities that require us to listen, some of us fail to pay enough attention to the role listening plays in these activities and in our relationships.

How Responsive a Listener Are You?

Although we expect others to listen to us, sometimes we ignore our ethical responsibility to listen to them. We fake listening or do not listen as carefully as we could. Consequently, problems due to ineffective listening occur.

At one time, a poll of American teenagers indicated that as many as half of them believed that communication between themselves and their parents was poor and that a primary cause was poor listening. Parents, too, often feel that communication is failing. One woman was convinced that her daughter must have a severe hearing problem and took her to an audiologist. The audiologist tested both ears and reported back to the distraught parent: "There's nothing wrong with her hearing. She's just tuning you out."

A leading cause of the high divorce rate (approximately half of all marriages in the United States end in divorce) is the failure of husbands and wives to interact effectively. They don't listen to each other or respond to each other's messages. Presidents of major companies similarly identify listening as one of their major communication problems.[6] Why is this? A nationwide survey revealed that 14% of each workweek is wasted as a result of poor listening. That amounts to about seven weeks of work per year.[7] A survey of personnel managers also identified listening as the skill most needed at work if work teams are to succeed.[8]

When we make the ethical commitment to listen to others, we focus and attend fully to them without allowing competing thoughts or stimuli to divert our attention. In effect, we practice **mindfulness**—by emptying our minds of personal concerns and interfering emotion and by choosing to focus on the person and what is happening in the present—a skill many of us would be wise to master.[9]

When we are mindful, we fully engage ourselves in the moment, paying careful attention to the here and now. We focus completely on what another person says and does. We do not judge the other but demonstrate our interest in understanding his ideas. If we fail at listening, does it mean that we are mindless?

Effective listeners—those of us who not only know how to listen but also want to listen—make better employers and employees, doctors and patients, friends, and significant others.[10] Many people even enroll in professional courses focused on how to improve listening skills.[11]

Do You Prepare to Listen?

Think back over the years you have spent as a student. Did you receive training in writing? Speaking? Reading? The answer to each of these questions is probably yes. In fact, many children now learn to read and write before they start school, and reading and writing skills are taught and emphasized throughout our educational careers. But what about listening? Of the four communication skills—reading, writing, speaking, and listening—it is listening that has received the least attention from educators. Yet listening is the fundamental process through which we initiate and maintain relationships, and it is the primary process through which we take in information.

Do You Use Listening Time Wisely?

A study revealed that college students spend as much time listening to media as engaged in interpersonal communication. Altogether, some 55.4% of a college student's day is now spent listening, while only 17.1% of it is spent reading, 16.1% speaking, and 11.4% writing.[12] These results hold true on the job, where listening is an integral element in creating relationships with others at work.[13] In fact, employees of Fortune 500 companies spend the majority of their day—approximately 60% of it—listening.[14]

Complications Caused by the Digital Domain

The use of digital media complicates this picture by distracting you. What happens when you are digitally distracted? Does being used to receiving quick bursts of information or tweets make it more difficult to listen to and make sense of more detailed and complex information?[15] Imagine a typical digital day for you (Table 6.1). According to a study by the Kaiser Family Foundation, young people use media 7 hours, 38 minutes a day. But that number is actually more like 10 hours and 45 minutes when the time spent multitasking is factored in—more time than is spent on a typical day at a full-time job or in school.[16]

Review Your Personal Situation

Take a moment to review your personal listening situation. Think of interactions you have had that were complicated because you or someone else failed to listen effectively. For

TABLE 6.1 A DIGITAL DAY

AVERAGE DAILY MEDIA USE, INCLUDING MULTITASKING, AMONG 8- TO 18-YEAR-OLDS	
Television content	4 hours, 29 minutes
Music/audio	2 hours, 31 minutes
Computer	1 hour, 29 minutes
Video games	1 hour, 38 minutes
Movies	25 minutes

Source: "Generation M²: Media in the Lives of 8- to 18-year-olds," Kaiser Family Foundation, January 2010.

example, when was the last time you jumped to a wrong conclusion? Missed an important word? Had earbuds in your ears and could hear nothing else? Failed to realize you were not being understood? Reacted emotionally or let yourself become distracted? Far too often, instead of listening, we daydream our way through our daily contacts. In other words, we adopt destructive behaviors, illustrative of poor listening.

Most people estimate that they listen with 70% to 80% accuracy. This means they believe that they can listen to others and accurately retain 70% to 80% of what is said. However, researchers such as Ralph Nichols tell us that most of us actually listen at only 25% efficiency; instead of retaining 75% of what we hear, we lose 75%.[17]

Do You Listen Accurately?

Although most of us, supposedly, have had years and years of listening practice, listening errors are extremely common. According to communication theorist William Haney, we frequently run into problems when we use **serial communication**, or chain-of-command transmissions, to relay messages (Figure 6.2). In serial communication, Person 1 sends a message to Person 2; Person 2 then communicates her perception of Person 1's message (not Person 1's message itself) to Person 3, who continues the process.

Whenever one person delivers a message to a second person, the message occurs in at least four different forms:[18]

1. The message as it exists in the mind of the speaker (his thoughts)

2. The message as it is spoken (actually encoded by the speaker)

3. The message as it is interpreted (decoded by the listener)

4. The message as it ultimately remembered by the listener (affected by the listener's personal selectivity and rejection)

In traveling down this unwieldy chain of command from person to person, ideas are distorted by as much as 80%.

Several factors are responsible. First, because passing along complex, confusing information poses many problems, we generally like to simplify messages. As a result, we unconsciously (and sometimes consciously) delete information from the messages we receive before transmitting these messages to others. Second, we like to think the messages we pass along to others make sense. (We feel foolish if we convey a message we ourselves do not

FIGURE 6.2

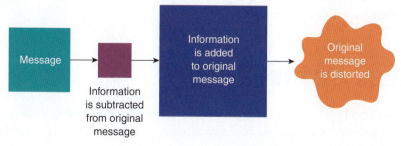

Message → Information is subtracted from original message → Information is added to original message → Original message is distorted

understand or deliver a message that appears illogical.) Thus, we try to make sense of a message before communicating it to someone else. We do this by adding to, subtracting from, or otherwise altering what we have heard. Unfortunately, as we see in Figure 6.2, once we make sense of the message, it may no longer correspond to the message that was originally sent. Such errors occur even though, as we noted, we have had years of practice in listening. Estimates are that a 20-year-old person has practiced listening for at least 10,000 hours and a typical 40-year-old, 20,000 or more hours.[19] Research, however, suggests that we have been practicing poor listening.

Do You Listen Ethically?

By listening ethically, we help avoid communication difficulties and breakdowns and increase our chances of being well liked and appreciated by others.[20] Who has the primary responsibility for clear and effective communication—the speaker or the listener? A proverb says, "Nature gave us two ears and one mouth so that we can listen twice as much as we speak." Actually, because everyone functions as both sender and receiver, everyone must assume 51% of the responsibility for communication. This practice might not be mathematically sound, but it certainly would increase the effectiveness of our interpersonal, small group, public, and mediated communication.[21]

ARE YOU A RECEPTIVE LISTENER?

There is a relationship between a speaker's acts and a listener's responses. Typically, speaker gaze coordinates this relationship. Although listeners usually look more at the speaker than the reverse, at key points, a speaker will look directly at the listener, signaling that the speaker is seeking a response. If the listener is attentive, this creates a period of mutual gaze known as the *gaze window*. When this occurs, the listener responds with a nod, a "hmm," or another verbal or nonverbal reaction that confirms that she is listening and collaborating in the dialogue or conversation.[22]

Phrases such as "I'm listening," I hear you," and "I get it" are affirmations listeners use to signify their respect, understanding, and acceptance.[23]

ARE YOU READY TO LISTEN BEYOND WORDS?

We need to listen to more than the words spoken. We also need to listen to the tone and cadence of a speaker's words. We need to interpret the speaker's gestures and facial expressions. We need to pay attention to what speakers don't tell us. Sometimes, what speakers omit is more important than what they say.

TYPES OF LISTENING

The type of listening in which we engage relates to our purpose for listening. Theorists identify four different types of listening: appreciative, comprehensive, critical, and empathic.

APPRECIATIVE LISTENING

Do you spend time listening to music on your smartphone or at concerts? Why? Is it because you enjoy it? When our primary motivation for listening is pleasure or relaxation—to unwind, to escape, or to be entertained—we are listening appreciatively. Listening to music, a movie, or a comedy routine are just a few examples of the kinds of **appreciative listening** we engage in.

Courses in music or film appreciation teach us how to listen appreciatively. Unlike the other three types of listening, appreciative listening usually does not require us to focus on organizing or remembering what we have listened to.

iStock/Rawpixel Ltd

COMPREHENSIVE LISTENING

When we listen to gain knowledge, we are listening comprehensively. Examples of **comprehensive listening** include listening to directions, a lecture, a job description, or a person's position on an issue of concern.

CRITICAL LISTENING

At times, we seek not only to gain knowledge but also to evaluate the worth of what we have listened to. When we listen critically, we listen to determine the usefulness, soundness, and accuracy of messages. During **critical listening**, our critical thinking skills also come into play as we decide whether to accept or reject a message. We talk more about comprehensive and critical listening later in this chapter.

EMPATHIC LISTENING

The goal in **empathic listening** is to understand the feelings and point of view of another person. Sometimes we serve as a relative's sounding board, listen to the troubles of a friend, or help a coworker talk through problems. In doing this, we also help to restore that person's sense of emotional balance, because we seek to understand him or her as he or she desires to be understood, interpreting the situation he is facing as if it were our own. Imagining ourselves in another's place is essential in empathic listening.[24]

Decenter

According to author Daniel Goleman, empathic listeners are effective at *decentering*—placing the focus on others rather than on themselves. They listen from the speaker's point of view, using three different skills to accomplish this: *empathic responsiveness* (the experience of an emotional response that corresponds to the emotions of another person),[25] *perspective listening* (placing oneself in another person's shoes),[26] and *sympathetic responsiveness* (feeling concern and compassion for the situation that the other person faces). If you use only sympathetic responsiveness, however, you fall short of empathic listening. If we only *feel for* a person, without using perspective taking and empathic responsiveness, our attempt to *feel with* that person cannot succeed.[27]

Skills to the Rescue

Empathic listeners rely heavily on two communication skills: the ability to read the nonverbal cues of others, including their eye contact, physical contact (touching), and facial expression, and the ability to paraphrase, which lets those they are listening to know that they care enough to listen, understand what is said, and respond to the expressed feelings.

When you paraphrase, you engage in listening actively, which means you put yourself in the speaker's place in an effort to understand her feelings and send back to her what you believe she communicated when delivering her total message; that is, you internalize and reflect back to the speaker the message's verbal content as well as the speaker's feelings.

How do you paraphrase? **Paraphrasing** is a three-step process in which you:

1. Make a tentative statement that invites correction—for example, "If I'm not mistaken . . . "
2. Repeat the basic idea or ideas in your own words.
3. Check your interpretation with the other person: "Is that correct?"

For example:

Person 1: I am so mad at my professor. He's making me rework my entire paper. I worked forever on it.

Person 2: If I'm not mistaken, your professor is asking you to rewrite the paper you turned in. You're feeling frustrated because you worked hard on it. Do I have it right?

Empathic Listening Fosters Healthy Relationships

Empathic communication and paraphrasing have roles to play in promoting healthy relationships.

Research reveals that listening to family stories and reminiscing about the past may be both physically and emotionally healing for both the storyteller and the listener, contributing to each's sense of overall well-being.[28]

iStock/Cecilie_Arcurs

Findings from medical research also underscore the importance of effective listening. Medical school curricula now include courses that teach medical students how to listen, ask open-ended questions, and establish productive, caring, and empathic relationships with patients.[29] Doctors who do not practice empathic listening frequently interrupt their patients, which can prevent them from eliciting relevant background on the patient's life circumstances and symptoms. The result? Costly mistakes.[30] Far too often doctors fail to paraphrase what a patient says, cutting off the patient's words after a scant 18 seconds—rarely sufficient time for the patient to reveal what is troubling him.[31]

THE STAGES OF LISTENING: MORE THAN MEETS THE EAR

A model of listening developed by listening researcher Judi Brownell, called the <mark>HURIER model,</mark> takes a behavioral approach to listening, suggesting that listening is composed of both mental processes and observable behaviors.[32] The model focuses on six listening stages: (1) hearing, (2) understanding, (3) remembering, (4) interpreting, (5) evaluating, and (6) responding (Figure 6.3).

HEARING

The first stage of listening is *hearing*. Sounds fill our world and compete to be noticed. Usually, however, we hear what we listen for, meaning that we choose to attend to some aspects of what we hear while ignoring the rest. Once we *attend* to a message—demonstrating our willingness to organize and focus on what we are hearing—if the message holds our attention, we will then seek to understand it.

FIGURE 6.3

The HURIER Model Stages of Listening

UNDERSTANDING

During Stage 2, *understanding* or listening comprehensively, we relate what we have listened to to what we already know. We refrain from judging the message until we are certain we have comprehended it. We might, for example, ask questions about or paraphrase what we believe another person has said to us during the hearing stage.

According to Ralph Nichols and Leonard Stevens, the authors of *Are You Listening?*, words that cause listeners to react emotionally interfere with understanding. Nichols calls these words red-flag words. <mark>Red-flag words</mark> produce emotional deafness, sending listening efficiency plummeting to zero.[33] Among the words known to function as red flags for some listeners are *AIDS* and *income tax*.

Other factors that interfere with understanding are the environment (e.g., it could be too hot, too cold, too messy) and people themselves (they

might speak too fast, too slow, too loudly, or too softly). We also can think faster than others speak. This is called the **speech–thought differential**. A person usually speaks at a rate of 125 to 150 words per minute. We think, however, at over 500 words per minute, meaning that we have excess time during which we can take mental excursions and daydream. To use the speech–thought differential to enhance understanding, we need to fill our excess thinking time by internally summarizing, questioning, and paraphrasing what is being said.

REMEMBERING

Once our brain assigns meaning to a message, the next stage is *remembering*, in which we try to retain what we have listened to for future use. We personally decide how much of what we have listened to is worth storing in memory and how much we can forget. Intense feelings or the reinforcement of a message increases our chances of remembering. However, we cannot possibly remember everything. Some forgetting is necessary for mental health.

We have two kinds of memory, short-term and long-term. Most of what we listen to, we store briefly in our short-term memory. Unless we use and apply what we have stored in short-term memory, we likely will forget it before being able to transfer it into long-term memory. This helps explain why we remember only 50% of a message immediately after listening to it and approximately 25% after a period of time has passed. Long-term memory, our more permanent memory bank, plays a key listening role by connecting new experiences to past ones.

We use three key tools to enhance recall. The first is *repetition*. The more we repeat an idea, the more likely we are to recall it later. The second tool is the now-familiar three-step *paraphrase*. By restating in your own words what a person just told you, you not only check on your understanding of what was said but also help yourself recall it. The third tool is *visualization*. By picturing what someone has said to you—connecting a visual image to a name, a place, or numbers—you can help improve your recall. For example, you might picture a person named John Sanderson as standing atop a large sand pile. Many memory problems are not due to faulty memory but rather to individuals losing their ability to pay attention. Attention and focus build memory.[34]

INTERPRETING

During the fourth stage, *interpreting*, we make sense of a message using *dual perspective taking*—considering the message from the sender's perspective as well as our perspective. If we are successful, we do not impose our personal meaning onto another person's message.

EVALUATING

During Stage 5, *evaluating*, we weigh the worth of a message and critically analyze it. (Evaluating is a type of listening referred to earlier in this chapter as critical listening.) During the evaluating stage, we distinguish facts from inferences, assess the evidence provided, and identify any prejudices or faulty arguments that could slant meaning. We stay mindful rather than mindless, listening between the lines and being careful not to jump to conclusions.

RESPONDING

During the last stage, *responding*, we react to what we have listened to and offer feedback to let the speaker know our thoughts and feelings about the message. We become the speaker's radar. (We cover feedback in more depth later in this chapter.)

MORE ON THE ETHICS OF LISTENING: IDENTIFYING PROBLEM BEHAVIORS

Of course, we do not—and probably cannot—listen at full capacity all the time. But we should be aware of our ineffective listening behaviors, especially if they prevent us from understanding what could be important. Many factors contribute to ineffective listening, and the following kinds of ineffective listeners are certainly not the only types we can identify. However, we have probably interacted with most of those identified here at some point in the past.

- **Fraudulent listeners.** Fraudulent listeners are pseudo-listeners. They look at the speaker, nod their heads appropriately in agreement or disagreement, and offer remarks such as "mm" or "uh-huh" that imply they are paying attention. In actuality, the speaker's words are falling on deaf ears. Just ask them to paraphrase what they have just heard and you'll see how far they are from understanding.

- **Monopolistic listeners.** Monopolistic listeners want you to listen to them, but they have neither the time nor desire to listen to you. Frequently egocentric, and as a result intrigued and obsessed with their own thoughts and ideas, monopolistic listeners deny your right to be listened to, while defending their right to express themselves, no matter the cost.[35]

Many years ago, researcher Alfie Kohn determined that men were more likely than women to be monopolistic listeners. Kohn found that men interrupted women's statements more frequently than women interrupted men's statements. In fact, in his research, 96% of the interruptions in male–female interactions were initiated by men.[36] Do you feel this finding is still valid today?

- **Completers.** Completers are gap fillers; they never quite get the whole story when they listen. To make up for what they miss or misinterpret, they manufacture information to fill in the gaps. Although their impression is that they got it all, they have missed important elements.

- **Selective listeners.** Selective listeners are like bees going after the pollen in a flower; they zero in on only those portions of a speaker's remarks that interest them or have particular importance to them. Everything else the speaker says is considered irrelevant or inconsequential and thus is rejected. Selective listeners, in their search for pollen, often miss the flower.

- **Avoiders.** Avoiders figuratively wear earmuffs; they close their eyes to information they would rather not have to deal with. Sometimes they pretend not to understand what you tell them, or they act as if they did not hear you at all. Sometimes they simply forget, in short order, what you have told them.

- **Defensive listeners.** Defensive listeners tend to perceive the remarks of other people as personal affronts or attacks. Usually insecure, they are apt to pounce when another person asks a simple question, or they are likely to perceive a threat in the comments of another, when none actually exists. When we listen defensively, we assume others are going to criticize or belittle us; we assume that they do not like, trust, or respect us. As a result, an innocent question such as "Did you do your report?" may be interpreted as criticism for our having spent too much time playing video games.

- **Attackers.** Attackers wait for you to make a mistake, so that they can undercut and challenge what you say. They lie in wait, hoping to gather ammunition that they can use to diminish your effectiveness. They also are not above distorting your words to advance their personal goals. Attackers are apt to precipitate defensiveness in the person they are listening to. Rather than working to understand meaning and conducting a discussion that is open and fair, they compete with you in an effort to outdo you.

ETHICS AND COMMUNICATION

Talk, Talk, Talk

Talk radio is a mediated version of interpersonal communication. Radio call-in programs allow a higher level of psychological comfort than do face-to-face interactions, because callers can remain relatively anonymous. Programs featuring argumentative hosts often demonstrate deficient listening skills as conversations become either yelling matches or love fests between the host and a caller who disagree with or support each other's views.

Why is this? In her book *The First Word: The Search for the Origins of Language*, Christine Kenneally offers insight into a cause of poor listening behavior. She describes an experiment in which two apes, skilled in sign language, were engaging in meaningful communication; however, when a disagreement arose, they had an arm-waving, sign-shouting match, with neither ape willing to listen to the other.[37]

Are we hardwired to prefer listening to ideas with which we agree? Do we enjoy listening more to ourselves than to others? What do you think? What's the solution?

RESPONDING WITH FEEDBACK

The feedback process is intimately connected with the listening process. Developing an understanding and appreciation of the way feedback works is essential to improving listening skills.

WHAT IS FEEDBACK?

The term *feedback* implies that we are feeding someone by giving something back to her. Feedback consists of all the verbal and nonverbal messages that a person consciously or unconsciously sends out in response to another person's message. As students, you continually provide your instructors with feedback. Many of you, however, are probably not completely honest when you send feedback. At times when you are confused or bored, you may nevertheless put on an "I'm interested" face and nod smilingly, indicating that you understand and agree with everything your instructor is saying. Unfortunately, such behavior tends to encourage the sending of unclear messages.

Sometimes we send feedback consciously in an attempt to evoke a particular response. For example, if you laugh at a speaker's story, you may be doing so because you want the speaker to feel that you enjoyed the story and hope he will tell another.

Some of the feedback we transmit is sent unconsciously and evokes unintended or unexpected responses. Often, when our words or behaviors prompt a reaction that we never intended, we respond with phrases such as "That's not what I meant!" or "I didn't mean it that way!" or "What I meant was . . . "[38]

TYPES OF FEEDBACK

What we intend to convey by feedback may not be what others perceive. Sometimes others intentionally choose not to perceive our messages. At other times, confusion results because feedback that we consider to be neutral (or nonevaluative) in tone is interpreted as judgmental (or evaluative). Distinguishing between these two types of feedback will help us use both effectively and appropriately.

Evaluative Feedback

When we provide another person with **evaluative feedback**, we state our opinion about a matter being discussed. For example, "How did you like my speech?" will almost always evoke a response that will be perceived as evaluative. When we give evaluative feedback, we make judgments—either positive or negative—based on our own system of values. By its very nature, the effect of evaluative feedback is either positive and rewarding or negative and punishing.

Positive Evaluative Feedback. Positive evaluative feedback tends to keep communication and its resulting behaviors moving in the direction they are already heading. If a company places an advertisement and achieves a tremendous growth in sales, the company will tend to place the same or a very similar ad in the same or similar media in the future. If a person wearing a new hairstyle is complimented, he or she will tend to keep that hairstyle.

Negative Evaluative Feedback. Negative evaluative feedback serves a corrective function in that it helps extinguish undesirable communicative behaviors. When we perceive feedback as negative, we tend to change our performance accordingly. For example, if you were to tell an off-color story that your listeners found in bad taste, they might send you negative responses. They might turn away, attempt to change the subject, or simply maintain a cold, lengthy silence. Each cue would indicate that your message had overstepped the bounds of propriety; as a result, you would probably discontinue your anecdote.

SKILL BUILDER

Looking at Faulty Listening and Future Me

1. Describe your experiences with the kinds of faulty listeners depicted in this section: fraudulent listeners, monopolistic listeners, completers, selective listeners, avoiders, defensive listeners, and attackers.

2. Explain what would have to happen for each situation discussed to be replayed more successfully.

3. Finally, identify which of the faulty listening behaviors you personally have been guilty of exhibiting, and describe the steps you will take to prevent these behaviors from interfering with your exhibiting effective listening behaviors in the future.

Formative Feedback. Timed negative evaluative feedback is **formative feedback**. Don Tosti, an industrial psychologist, and others discovered that in a learning situation, it is best to provide positive feedback immediately after someone displays a desired behavior.[39] Thus, comments such as "You did a good job" and "Keep up the good work" should be offered immediately, because these responses give people a sense of pride and pleasure in themselves and their work.

However, Tosti suggests that what he calls "formative negative" feedback be given only just before an undesired behavior (or similar behavior) is about to be repeated. Tosti believes that withholding negative feedback until the person can use it constructively makes the feedback seem more like coaching than criticism. Comments such as "OK, team, let's eliminate the errors we made last time" and "When you go out there today, try to . . . " reduce the extent to which others perceive negative feedback as harmful rather than helpful. Thus, giving formative feedback just before an activity is to be performed again can help eliminate the feelings of rejection that sometimes accompany negative feedback.

Nonevaluative Feedback

In contrast to evaluative feedback, **nonevaluative feedback** makes no overt attempt to direct the activity of a communicator. Thus, we use nonevaluative feedback when we want to learn more about a person's feelings or when we want to help another person formulate thoughts about a particular subject. When we offer nonevaluative feedback, we make no reference to our own opinions or judgments; instead, we simply describe, question, or indicate an interest in what the other person is communicating to us.

Despite its nonjudgmental nature, nonevaluative feedback is often construed as being positive. That is, other people's behaviors are reinforced when we probe, interpret their messages, and offer support as they attempt to work through a problem. Nonevaluative feedback reaches beyond positive feedback, however, by providing others with the opportunity to examine their own problems and arrive at their own solutions. For this reason, carefully phrased nonevaluative feedback can be enormously helpful and sustaining to people who are going through a difficult period.

We consider four kinds of nonevaluative feedback here. Three—probing, understanding, and supporting—were identified by David Johnson. The fourth—"I" messages—was identified by Thomas Gordon.[40]

CAREER BUILDER: CULTURAL IMPLICATIONS OF FEEDBACK

Are you culturally sensitive when giving feedback? For example, many Japanese, in contrast to Americans, prefer to use an indirect style of communication. Thus, when interacting with someone from Japan, if you give feedback directly (e.g., telling someone outright, "You are not working hard enough"), the feedback, instead of being viewed as helpful, might be viewed as threatening. And, if it is perceived as a threat, it could well be ineffective. An American giving feedback to another American, however, can give feedback more directly.

How might we change the way we provide feedback to conform to the preferences of another culture other than Japan? Explain with reference to a particular culture of your choosing.

Probing. When we ask people for additional information to draw them out and to demonstrate our willingness to listen to their problems, we are **probing**.[41] Suppose that a student is concerned about her grades in a particular course and says to you, "I'm really upset. All my friends are doing better in geology than I am." If you use probing, you might ask, "Why does this situation bother you?" or "What do you suppose caused this to happen?" Responding in this way gives the other person the chance to think through the overall nature of the problem while also providing her with an opportunity for emotional release. In contrast, comments like "So what? Who cares about that dumb class?" or "You really were dumb to stop studying" would tend to stop the student from thinking through and discussing the problem and, instead, would probably create defensiveness.

Understanding. When we offer understanding, we seek to comprehend what the other person is saying to us, and we check ourselves by paraphrasing what we believe we have heard. Doing this shows that we care about other people and the problems they face.

> Examine the following paraphrases to develop a feel for the nature of this kind of response.
>
> Person 1: I don't think I have the skill to be picked for the team.
>
> Person 2: You believe you're not good enough to make the team this year?
>
> Person 1: I envy those guys so much.
>
> Person 2: You mean you're jealous of the people on the team?

If we use understanding early in a relationship, in effect, we communicate that we care enough about the interaction to want to be certain that we comprehend what the other person is saying to us. Such a response strengthens the relationship, because it encourages the other person to describe and detail his feelings.

ANN PATCHANAN/Shutterstock.com

Supportive Feedback. When we give **supportive feedback**, we indicate that a problem that the other person deems important and significant is also important and significant to us.

Suppose a friend comes to you with a problem that he feels is extremely serious. Perhaps your friend has worked himself into a state of high anxiety and implies that you cannot possibly understand the situation. In offering supportive feedback, you would attempt to calm your friend down by assuring him that the world has not ended and that you do understand the problem.

Offering supportive feedback is difficult. We have to be able to reduce the intensity of other people's feelings while letting them know that we consider their problems real and serious. Such comments as "It's stupid to worry about that" and "Is that all that's worrying you?" are certainly not supportive. A better approach might be to say, "I can see you're upset. Let's talk about it. I am sure you can find a way to solve the problem." When we use supportive feedback, we judge the problems to be important, but we do not attempt to solve them ourselves; instead, we encourage people to discover their own solutions.

"I" Messages. When we deliver an "I" message, we do not pass judgment on the other person's actions but simply convey our own feelings about the nature of the situation.

According to Gordon, when people interact with us, they often are unaware of how they affect us. We have the option of providing these people with either evaluative or nonevaluative feedback. Neither type is inherently good or bad. However, far too often, the way we formulate our evaluative feedback adversely affects the nature of our interactions and relationships. For example, do any of these statements sound familiar? "You made me angry!" "You're no good!" "You're in my way!" "You're a slob!" What do these statements have in common? As you probably notice, each one contains the word *you*. Each also places the blame for something on another person. When relationships experience difficulties, people tend to resort to name-calling and blaming others. Such feedback messages create schisms that are difficult and sometimes impossible to bridge.

To avoid this situation, Gordon suggests that we replace ==**"you" messages**== with ==**"I" messages**==. If, for example, a parent tells a child, "You're pestering me," the child's interpretation will probably be "I am bad," and this interpretation will evoke a certain amount of defensiveness or hostility toward the parent ("I am not bad!"). But if the parent tells the child, "I'm really very tired, and I don't feel like playing now," the child's reaction is more likely to be "Mom is tired." Such an approach is more likely to elicit the type of behavior the parent desires

iStock/ALLVISIONN

than would name-calling and blaming. Using "I" messages as feedback will not always evoke the behavior you want from the other person, but it will help prevent the defensive, self-serving behaviors that "you" messages frequently elicit.

"I" messages have one other aspect you should be aware of. It is quite common to say, "I am angry" to another person. Anger, however, is a secondary emotion. We are angry because of a stimulus or stimuli. In actuality, we develop anger. For example, if your child ran into the street, your first response would probably be fear. Only after the child was safe would you develop anger, and then you probably would share your anger—rather than your fear—with the child. When formulating an angry "I" message, be certain to look beyond or beneath your anger and ask yourself *why* you are angry. Try to identify the forces that precipitated your anger—these are the feelings that should be expressed. Thus, if someone says something that hurts you, find ways to express the initial hurt rather than the resulting anger.

> Visit the interactive e-Book to access the Skill Builder feature "'I' Not 'You, Plus Future Me,'" in which you will practice using three-part "I" statements and consider their impact on conversations and relationships.

THE IMPORTANCE OF CRITICAL THINKING

While you listen to information, you interpret and assign meaning to the spoken words. Your primary focus is on gaining and retaining information. When you go the next step and engage in **critical thinking**, you think carefully about what another person has said to you and you evaluate the believability of the spoken message. Just as speakers can get carried away with their message's urgency and importance, so listeners can end up believing false or dangerous ideas that have been made to appear reasonable. Consequently, it is essential for you as a listener to stay alert, so that you are ready to challenge and raise questions about what you are listening to. When functioning as a critical thinker, you make a commitment to think for yourself. Thus, your primary goal is no longer simply to understand information; it also is to evaluate the person you are listening to and her ideas, deciding whether that individual is credible and ethical and whether she is drawing a reasonable conclusion.

WHAT CRITICAL THINKERS THINK ABOUT

What do critical thinkers think about? Critical thinkers seek to identify the unstated assumptions that underlie a speaker's message, the strengths and weaknesses of the speaker's viewpoint, if the message contains distortions or suggestions of bias, and the implications (positive and negative) of accepting that message. Critical thinkers also check themselves by asking if they are being fair-minded in their assessment of the speaker's message.[42] In other words, as a critical thinker, you determine if there is a logical connection between ideas and feelings. Rather than falling prey to strong emotional appeals, you examine the evidence on which conclusions are based and establish if they are valid or contain weaknesses and inconsistencies.

Critical thinkers listen carefully in an effort to determine if what they are listening to makes sense and is worth retaining or acting on.[43] Thus, when engaging in critical thinking, you raise questions that will help you draw well-reasoned conclusions. You consciously avoid thinking in egocentric or self-serving ways. You don't accept or reject what you hear simply because you feel you have to. Instead, you live up to the obligation to question the basis for your beliefs and your response.

THE CRITICAL VERSUS THE UNCRITICAL THINKER

The following characteristics differentiate a critical thinker from an uncritical one.

The Critical Thinker

1. Knows what he does not know
2. Is open-minded and takes time to reflect on ideas
3. Pays attention to those who agree and disagree with her
4. Looks for good reasons to accept or reject expert opinion
5. Is concerned with unstated assumptions and what is not said, in addition to what is stated outright

6. Insists on getting the best evidence

7. Reflects on how well conclusions fit premises and vice versa

The Uncritical Thinker

1. Thinks he knows everything

2. Is closed-minded and impulsive, jumping to unwarranted conclusions

3. Pays attention only to those who agree with her

4. Disregards evidence as to who is speaking with legitimate authority

5. Is concerned only with what is stated, not with what is implied

6. Ignores sources of evidence

7. Disregards the connection or lack of connection between evidence and conclusions[44]

Critical thinkers do not rush to judge another's words. Instead, they exhibit a willingness to reexamine ideas. Thus, they withhold their evaluation until they have had sufficient opportunity to assess the information being given to them.

QUESTIONS TO FACILITATE CRITICAL THINKING

You can ask yourself a number of questions to facilitate the critical thinking process.

1. Is the speaker's message plausible? Could it have reasonably occurred? Does it have a high probability of being true?

2. Does the support provided by the person speaking back up his claims? Are the claims he makes verifiable?

3. What do I know of the speaker's credibility or authority? Is the speaker reliable; that is, is she someone I should trust?

4. Is the speaker's message free of inconsistencies or contradictions?

When you think critically about what other people say to you, you do much more than merely hear their words.

KEEP IN MIND THE MINDFULNESS FACTOR

Effective listeners and critical thinkers are mindful, possessing self-awareness, thoughtfulness, and knowledge of how to connect meaningfully in the present moment with others. Mindful communicators make certain they are fully present and in touch with their feelings. They work to understand what others are sharing and how their cultures and ways of thinking differ from their own. Even more important, they are willing to pause to reflect before they respond. As a result, communicators who are mindful are more patient, more likely to understand what is happening, and more apt to react appropriately.

GENDER AND LISTENING STYLE

Women and men are likely to exhibit different listening styles. Women tend to search for relationships among message parts; they rely more on their feelings and intuition. They zoom in on emotional messages. They listen to enhance their understanding as well as to establish personal relationships.

Women also demonstrate a greater ability to switch between competing messages. Women appear able to split their focus and listen to two people at the same time. Men, in contrast, tend to concentrate their reactions on only one speaker at a time.

Women are more receptive, in general, than are men to what is happening around them. Thus, women are more likely than men to be engaged in conversation with one person and still pick up on the words of another person who is conversing with someone else nearby. Also, because women place great value on relationships, they listen to confirm the relationship as well as the person.[45]

Men are more at home with comprehensive listening—hearing a message's facts or informational dimension—than they are handling emotional content. Men tend to listen to solve problems, not to offer support.[46]

ETHICS AND COMMUNICATION

Would You Ask for and Listen to Directions?

When feeling lost or uncertain about how to get from place A to place B, what kind of directions are we likely to find most helpful? Women prefer directions containing landmarks to guide them in getting from one place to the next (start at Grove Street and then go until you see a bookstore), whereas men typically prefer receiving Euclidean information, instructions that tell them where to start and how far to go (start at Grove Street and go east for three blocks).[47] But which sex finds it easier to ease into the listening mode and ask for directions? Before answering, consider this:

According to linguist Deborah Tannen, men desire dominance so strongly that they would prefer to drive right past a police officer than to stop and ask for directions. For men, listening to directions implies inferiority. But according to Tannen, American women are so used to asking for help that they tend to ask strangers for directions even when they are well aware of where they are going.

What do you think? Do men and women listen differently? Explain your answer with examples.

Women also use head nodding and facial expressions to indicate their interest in a conversation. Because they view talk as a relationship developer, women also provide more vocal and verbal feedback when speaking with others. Women consider it important that others perceive them as receptive and open.[48] Thus, they use more listening cues than men and excel at empathizing and at identifying moods.

Men, in comparison, are more at home with comprehensive listening and less at home with the emotional content of messages. Men are more likely to focus on the message's structure or pattern. Their tendency is to direct their listening efforts toward a goal. Men listen to solve problems.[49] As a result, they listen primarily to get the facts in an effort to get to the bottom line. Men also will play up their expertise and use it to control or dominate conversations. Their goal is to have others respect them. As a result, they tend to interrupt women. Men penalize women for speaking, by interrupting them and talking over them instead of listening to them. Women have to work harder to make their voices heard.[50]

Additionally, in contrast to women, who exhibit more eye contact when listening than men do, men tend to survey the environment and direct their gaze away from the person they are conversing with.[51]

Of course, gender differences continue to be redefined. In your experience, have any of the trends described in this section changed? Which do you believe are still valid?

CULTURAL INFLUENCES ON LISTENING

As the psychological distance between people who live in different countries shrinks, our need to listen to others who neither live in the country we live in nor have the same native language increases. The globalization of business and our personal thirst for traveling to diverse geographical locations demand that we become more aware of cultural differences in listening styles and behavior.

When listening to another person, depending on our purpose and preferences, we tend to favor using one of four primary listening styles: people-oriented, content-oriented, action-oriented, or time-oriented.

PEOPLE-ORIENTED LISTENERS

Those of us who are **people-oriented listeners** display a strong interest in others and concern for their feelings. People-oriented listeners tend to be *we*, not *me* oriented, likely to focus on emotions, and eager to connect with others. As a result, people-oriented listeners are often considered empathetic.

CONTENT-ORIENTED LISTENERS

Those of us who are **content-oriented listeners** are more concerned with what is said than with the people involved or their feelings. Content-oriented listeners focus on facts, evidence, and credibility.

ACTION-ORIENTED LISTENERS

Action-oriented listeners are focused on task and concerned with outcomes—what will be done, by whom, and when. Sometimes their particular interest in action and outcomes is interpreted by others as impatience.

TIME-ORIENTED LISTENERS

Listeners who are **time-oriented** let the clock direct their listening. Concerned with time management, they limit the time they have available for listening, having brief or hurried interactions that tend to annoy others.

MIXING STYLES

Most of us use more than one style depending on the circumstances. What we need to keep in mind is that we can make the conscious effort to change listening styles. We can become more people-, content-, action-, or time-oriented depending on the situation and our interaction partner's needs. Interestingly, individuals from different cultures are likely to use different styles.

According to C. Y. Cheng, the Chinese place greater emphasis on the receiving process and less emphasis on the sending process, reflecting the East Asian concern for interpretations and anticipation.[52] In Japan, anticipatory communication is the norm. Speakers rarely tell or ask directly for something they want, leaving receivers to guess and accommodate speakers' needs. This communication style helps speakers and receivers save face in case what the speaker wants done cannot be accomplished.[53] In comparison, Germans practice action-oriented listening. They are inquisitive and exhibit a direct style. Israelis, who carefully analyze information, prefer the content style of listening. Collective in orientation, they tend to de-emphasize the personal aspects of interactions. The individually oriented Americans, on the other hand, exhibit a people-oriented style, focusing more on the feelings and concerns of the people involved in an interaction and emphasizing the interaction's social aspects. At the same time, however, they are focused on the time that interaction consumes.[54]

DIALOGIC LISTENING

Dialogic listening focuses on what happens between people as they respond to each other, work toward shared understanding, and build a relationship.[55] Too frequently, life's pressures keep us from adopting open-ended, tentative approaches to conversation. We seem to prefer certainty, closure, and control. Whereas people from Eastern cultures practice more speculative, metaphoric thinking, believing that people should listen more than they talk, members of Western cultures are less open and tentative in their listening behaviors, preferring specifically focused and concrete thinking.[56]

Within the United States, listening rules vary depending on the racial group with which you identify. African Americans, in general, display a more participative listening style than do European Americans. When listening to a speaker, African Americans are likely to shout out responses as means of demonstrating their interest and involvement. By acknowledging that people from different regions and countries differ both in how they listen and respond, we become less apt to misinterpret someone's words or actions.[57]

TECHNOLOGY'S INFLUENCE ON LISTENING AND CRITICAL THINKING

How are social media and technology changing the listening landscape? What roles are they playing in challenging our abilities to listen and learn?

OUR SHRINKING ATTENTION SPAN

Are the Internet and social media shortening our attention spans? Blame is placed on quickly changing visual images, especially in advertising and entertainment media, which researchers believe may overstimulate and permanently rewire a brain in the process of developing.[58]

Podcasts, radio, and music account for significant amounts of what we listen to. Increasingly, segments are being shortened and simplified for fear we will not pay attention if they are long, discuss complicated information, or contain descriptions of complex feelings. In the place of complex information, more and more graphics are being substituted. Visual culture does not place demands on us to listen.

IS THE COMPUTER REALLY OUR "FRIEND"?

Despite decades of work, scientists have yet to devise a computer, chatbot, or other device that functions as a virtual best friend, one that is able to listen sensitively and empathically to a user.[59] Although chatbots, for example, may "listen in" and potentially invade our privacy, they are not necessarily "listening and responding" with our best interests in mind. Others criticize our relationship with computers for another reason, believing that our connections to computers, e-mail, and Facebook—all visual stimuli—are impeding our ability to listen.

Visit the interactive e-Book to access the Skill Builder feature "Listening Gains and Losses," which will help you discern how technology influences listening-based communication.

LISTENING ETIQUETTE

Interpersonal etiquette appears to be at an all-time low. The world has become our phone booth. Even when we are face-to-face with another person, perhaps at lunch, on a walk, or out for a drive, one of us may be using a smartphone to talk or text a third person. Texting during classes, as noted earlier, appears to be a habit, causing instructors to wonder how many students are actively listening. Fifty-two percent of students say they text friends in the same classroom.[60] Perhaps we need smartphone-free zones so that we can listen more attentively to the person we are with.[61] Perhaps listening is too complex an activity for us to multitask at all if we want to do it well.

WE ARE BEING OVERSTIMULATED

In addition to being surrounded by smartphone users, according to David Shenk, author of *Data Smog*, we are being inundated with information that envelopes us within a toxic environment of continuous overstimulation,[62] supersaturating our minds, and making it difficult for us to separate fact from fiction.[63] When so much information is directed at us, deciding who and what to listen to becomes a challenge. It is probable that one outcome of this overload is a decrease in listening effectiveness.

MORE LISTENING WRINKLES

Advances in technology will continue to add listening wrinkles. For example, in the past when we listened, we were generally face-to-face with the speaker, and we engaged in real-time, synchronous listening. Then came the telephone, and we had the option of not having to share the same space when conversing. Then we entered the era of voice mail; we could have serial conversations (asynchronous listening) with a person who was in a different location and could not hear our words as we spoke them. More and more of our conversations are occurring asynchronously.[64]

Continuous advances add to the listening challenge. In fact, people are reporting having little time to concentrate and reflect on what they're receiving. With all the texting and tweeting going on, they're also finding it hard to be "present" and listen to family, significant others, friends, and coworkers in their immediate environment.[65] So everyone uses smartphones, but is anyone really talking and listening? Research reveals that talking on smartphones is now less than half of the traffic on mobile networks. Users see talking as intrusive and time consuming, with many reporting no patience for talking to only one person at a time. They would rather multitask conversations by texting or tweeting.[66] Do you consider the people who follow others on Twitter to be "listening" to them? Is following someone on Twitter and listening to her in person the same thing?

On the other hand, texting has made it easier for deaf people to communicate with others. Wives now text their deaf husbands as a hearing wife might call to a husband in the basement and deaf teens now blend in with others in the mall. Texting has made the deaf more independent.[67]

MORE OPTIONS

What we do know is that we can now be more selective about our willingness to listen at all. Caller ID allows us to see who is calling and to decide whom we want to listen to. Call waiting, of course, makes it possible for us not to miss a call from someone important to us. We can now line up our listeners! Or we can accept and add callers to a call we're already on.

We now have gadgets that listen to and obey our commands. For example, we can ask our smartphones and other devices to play songs, direct us to a local bakery, or convert voice mail into e-mail. We ask "Alexa" and "Siri" for information we don't possess and discover that often "she" does indeed have the answer.[68]

In the future, will even more of our machines be listening in on us and listening to us, and following up by obeying not only our stated demands but our implicit desires as well? Will we listen to and obey them? Do we now? Does it concern you that these virtual personal assistants are equipped with smart microphones that, unless disabled, are always on, waiting for us to wake them up by calling their names? Sometimes they even pipe up because they misheard us.[69]

CROSSING BARRIERS

With the exception of films in theaters, media or computer-generated messages are usually processed by people viewing or listening to them alone or in small groups. Because we now process messages from around the world, our ears are habitually crossing national boundaries and helping erase cultural and informational barriers.

The real-time transmission of voice is possible over the Internet. Skype, FaceTime, and other services enable you to use your computer as a telephone with pictures. Videoconferencing programs make it possible to chat across the Internet. Video conferencing is offered by many corporations. You probably have participated in an interview using videoconferencing technology.[70]

Visit the interactive e-Book to access the Exploring Diversity feature "Questions for Global Listeners," in which you will consider how interactions work in global and cyber contexts.

Because much of what we listen to is carried via newer media, are we listening less to each other? How actively can we listen to another human being in our immediate environment when technological advances are absorbing our attention and propelling us across national boundaries and into settings far removed from the ones with which we are most familiar?

COMMUNICATION SKILLS
Practice Listening Skills

Listening is a critical skill in every communication context from intrapersonal communication to interpersonal communication, from group communication to public communication, from face-to-face interaction to online interaction, from chatting to skyping. How effective you are as a friend, family member, significant other, and coworker depends on your listening skills.

Focus on mastering and maintaining these skills as you work to eliminate ineffective behaviors.

Use your listening time wisely.

Rather than assume you know what another person is going to say, fully tune in and listen attentively to understand what the other person says. Summarize and ask yourself questions about the substance and meaning of what you are hearing. Use thinking time to identify the other person's major points and reasons given to justify or support them.

Give real, not pseudo, attention.

Too many of us fake attention when listening. Although our external cues (e.g., making eye contact, smiling, nodding our heads) say that we are listening, we are only pretending. Instead, focus on interpreting the meaning contained in the other person's words.

Withhold judgment.

When we prejudge a person or his message, we uncritically accept or reject both the person and his ideas. Understanding needs to precede evaluation.

Maintain emotional control.

Sometimes we distort the ideas of others merely because we do not like or agree with them. Listening involves processing, not manufacturing, information. Rather than allow an emotional eruption to cause a listening disruption, we need to work harder when our emotions cause us to become aroused, defensive, alienated, elated, or outraged. Feelings of rapture and hero worship can limit understanding as much as can anger or hostility.

Be willing to see another person's viewpoint.

Willingness to look at a situation from another's perspective increases the likelihood that you will be able to see and feel what the other person is experiencing. You do not have to agree with another person, but it helps to understand where thoughts and feelings come from.

Listen with your whole body.

Listening is an active, not passive, process. By displaying an attentive posture and making meaningful eye contact, your body helps your mind increase its readiness to listen.

> Listening is not just hearing what someone tells you word for word. You have to listen with a heart.

Anna Deavere Smith

COMPLETE THIS CHAPTER 6 CHECKLIST

6.1 I can define *listening*, differentiate it from hearing, and explain its role in communication. ☐

Listening is a deliberate process dependent on a complex set of skills through which we seek to understand and retain aural (heard) stimuli. It requires training and practice. Listening is more than hearing. Hearing is an unconscious and automatic process, whereas listening is conscious and deliberative.

6.2 I can distinguish among four types of listening: appreciative, comprehensive, critical, and empathic. ☐

When we listen appreciatively, we are listening for pleasure. When we listen comprehensively, we listen to gain knowledge. When we listen critically, we seek to determine the usefulness, soundness, and accuracy of a message. When we listen empathically, we listen to understand the feelings and point of view of another person.

6.3 I can use the HURIER model to explain the six stages of listening. ☐

The HURIER model takes a behavioral approach to listening. Using it can help you develop listening skills. The model focuses on the six key states of listening: hearing, understanding, remembering, interpreting, evaluating, and responding.

6.4 I can identify problematic listening behaviors. ☐

The behaviors exhibited by fraudulent, monopolistic, completing, selective, avoidant, defensive, and attacking listeners impedes understanding.

6.5 I can summarize the kinds of feedback listeners can provide. ☐

Feedback is a prerequisite of effective listening. Feedback consists of all the verbal and nonverbal messages that one person consciously or unconsciously sends out in response to another person's communication. There are two main types of feedback: (1) Evaluative feedback gives an opinion, positive or negative, and attempts to influence the behavior of others. (2) Nonevaluative feedback gives emotional support. Probing, understanding (or paraphrasing), supportive feedback, and "I" messages are all forms of nonevaluative feedback that help sustain interpersonal relationships.

6.6 I can discuss critical thinking and its impact on listening. ☐

When you engage in critical thinking you think carefully about what another person is telling you, and you evaluate the believability of the message. You also seek to determine if there is a logical connection between ideas and feelings.

many of us use more than one style depending on the circumstances.

6.7 I can explain how gender influences listening. ☐

Recognizing how gender influences your listening preferences can enhance your ability to develop more effective listening practices. Women are likely to listen for emotional messages, whereas men are more apt to listen for facts.

6.8 I can explain how culture influences listening. ☐

Culture influences listening style and behavior. People tend to favor using one of four primary listening styles: people-oriented, content-oriented, action-oriented, or time-oriented. Although our culture may lead us to have a preference,

6.9 I can explain how media and technology influence listening. ☐

New technological advances, despite giving us the ability to listen globally, also compete for our listening time. Some fear that the Internet and social media are shortening our attention spans and therefore impeding our listening effectiveness.

6.10 I can demonstrate effective listening skills. ☐

By using your listening time wisely, offering real attention, being willing to withhold judgment, controlling your emotions, displaying a willingness to see from another's perspective, and listening with your whole body, you increase your listening effectiveness.

BECOME A WORD MASTER

action-oriented listener 158

appreciative listening 143

comprehensive listening 143

content-oriented listener 157

critical listening 143

critical thinking 154

dialogic listening 158

empathic listening 143

evaluative feedback 149

formative feedback 150

hearing 138

HURIER model 145

"I" messages 153

listening 138

mindfulness 139

nonevaluative feedback 150

paraphrasing 144

people-oriented listener 157

probing 151

red-flag words 145

serial communication 141

speech–thought differential 146

supportive feedback 152

time-oriented listener 158

"you" messages 153

iStock/MangoStar_Studio

Iryna Inshyna/Shutterstock.com

7

Understanding Relationships

AFTER COMPLETING THIS CHAPTER, YOU SHOULD BE ABLE TO:

7.1 Describe the functions relationships serve together with the needs they fulfill.

7.2 Discuss the role of conversation in relationships.

7.3 Explain the significance of depth and breadth in relationships.

7.4 Analyze relationships according to their stages, digital media influences, cost–benefit/social exchange implications, and relationship dialectics.

7.5 Explain how deception and trust affect relationships.

7.6 Describe laughter's role in relationships.

7.7 Explain how gender influences relationship formation, maintenance, and termination.

7.8 Explain how culture influences relationship formation, maintenance, and termination.

7.9 Discuss technology's impact on relationships.

7.10 Apply skills to improve the effectiveness of relationships.

> When you start out with someone, you're essentially driving a strange car for the first time, and none of the controls are labeled.
>
> Jerry Seinfeld

• •

The Bachelor, *The Bachelorette*, and *Bachelor in Paradise* feature men and women who, in exchange for celebrity, money, and/or the hope of finding that "special someone," permit us to observe them in action from their very first face-to-face meeting with a potential partner to the relationship's natural or unnatural outcome. Over succeeding weeks, we bear witness to "case studies" in relationship dynamics, as the participants decide to whom they're attracted and make decisions regarding which relationships they want to develop further and which they choose to end. By the last episode, the bachelor or bachelorette is left with but a single potential life partner.

Why do *Bachelor*-type reality shows receive such high ratings? Could it be because we enjoy the voyeur experience, watching and eavesdropping as people converse, reflect on, and express their feelings when beginning relationships, negotiating their ground rules, and deciding whether a relationship should continue? Or is it that relationships are the primary content of our social lives, and we hope that, by viewing and vicariously experiencing others' relationships, we will profit from their experiences and end up making wiser relationship choices for ourselves? Whatever your answer, for most of us, nothing is more consequential than our interpersonal relationships. ■

WHAT IS AN INTERPERSONAL RELATIONSHIP?

An **interpersonal relationship** is a meaningful dyadic connection in which two once independent people, to varying degrees, become interdependent, engaging in communication by exchanging information of a more or less personal nature, developing a shared history, and responding to each other's needs. By definition, a relationship dyad is indivisible. During our life span, we share a multitude of personal and professional relationships, some more complicated, meaningful, and/or important to us than others. A number of these relationships will succeed and last for years, perhaps even a lifetime. Others will be short-lived or fail totally. What makes the difference? If your answer is communication, you are right! Communication is the largest single factor affecting all of our relationships.[1]

In this chapter, we explore the nature of our relationships, how satisfied we are with them, and steps we can take to improve their outcomes.

WHY RELATIONSHIPS MATTER

How important are your existing relationships? Why are they important? Let's find out.

We Need Connections

We humans need personal connections. In fact, having effective relationships positively affects mortality.[2] People devoid of meaningful relationships are more likely to fall ill and die. Social isolation compromises the immune system and weakens physical and psychological resilience—whether or not people enjoy being alone.[3]

Relationships Fulfill Different Ends

Whether we connect digitally or face-to-face, the relationships we form fulfill different ends. For instance, a relationship makes different demands on us depending on its context, that is, whether we are in a doctor–patient, professor–student, work, friendship, or romantic relationship. Unique communication patterns also differentiate one relationship from another. Some, such as therapist–patient or employer–employee, depend on our being able to coordinate action with another person so that we are able to solve a problem or complete a task or project. Others are social and provide us friendship or intimacy, thereby helping us to avoid feeling socially isolated or lonely. Some relationships are impersonal and brief, as when we encounter a clerk in a store or chat with another person when in line for a movie. Such brief relationships have little, if any history, and demand little personal involvement. Other relationships are more personal and longer lasting, as are the relationships we have with some family members, friends, coworkers, and significant others.

So, whereas some relationships are purely professional, we invest the most effort in our longer-term, more personal relationships.

SKILL BUILDER

A Self-Assessment of My Relationships

Make two lists of relationships. On the first list, identify all the interpersonal relationships in which you have participated during the past month that you consider successful and likely to endure for at least another five years. On the second list, identify those interpersonal relationships you experienced during the same time period that either have already ended or that you expect not to last much longer.

1. Identify characteristics of the relationships on your two lists that contributed to their survival, demise, or uncertainty.

2. Explain what the identified characteristics tell you about the qualities necessary to sustain a relationship?

3. Which of the relationships on your first list do you consider most important? What makes you value these relationships more than the others?

RELATIONSHIPS MEET NEEDS

According to theorist William Schutz, we meet our needs for inclusion, control, and affection through friendships, work, and romantic relationships.[4] Schutz's theory, **Fundamental Interpersonal Relations Orientation**, highlights these three needs and offers insights into the reasons we decide to initiate, maintain, or end a relationship.

The Need for Inclusion

Inclusion has to do with the varying degrees to which we all need to establish and maintain feelings of mutual connection with other people—a sense that we take an interest in others, and they take an interest in us. We want others to pay attention to us, to take time to understand us. Wanting to be included is normal. Each of us can recall how it feels to be left out—to be the last person asked to join a team, to not be invited to an important party, to be ignored during an online conversation, or to be omitted from a Facebook photo. When such things happen, we suffer from FOMO—fear of having missed out. When our inclusion need is satisfied, we tend to feel worthwhile and fulfilled. When it goes unmet, however, we experience feelings of loneliness, and our health may even decline.

What exactly is loneliness? **Loneliness** is an all too common affliction of the 21st century.[5] We often don't know the names of our neighbors, and although we may have oodles of friends or followers on various social networking sites, we likely don't know many of them personally. Loneliness begins with a recognition that the interpersonal relationships we do have are not the kinds we want.[6] It causes us to think that our friends and loved ones don't care enough about us.[7] Interestingly, loneliness is not dependent on the number of relationships we have, but instead on our perception of their quality and meaningfulness. Thus, loneliness results from a perceived discrepancy between desired and achieved social relationships.[8] The truth is that we may be judging those with whom we share relationships too harshly. Avoiding feeling lonely might require that we readjust our perceptions and reach out more to others. Reconnecting is possible.[9]

iStock/FatCamera

The Need for Control

Control deals with the need to establish and maintain satisfactory levels of influence and power in our relationships. To varying degrees, we like to believe that we can take charge of situations when we choose to. When our control need goes unmet, we may conclude that others are failing to respect or value our abilities and that they are viewing us as incapable of making sound decisions, directing others, or taking charge of our own future.

The Need for Affection

Affection involves our need to give and receive love and to experience emotionally close relationships. If our need for affection goes unfulfilled, we are likely to conclude that we are unlovable and that others will remain emotionally detached from us—that is, they won't establish close ties with us. In contrast, if our experiences with affection have been more pleasant, we probably are comfortable handling both close and distant relationships and most likely recognize that not everyone with whom we connect will necessarily care for us in the same way.

These Needs Are Not All Met at the Same Time

These three basic needs are not met at once. Inclusion comes first, because the need for inclusion impels us to establish a relationship in the first place. By comparison, our control and affection needs are met largely through our already established relationships. As William Schutz notes, "Generally speaking, inclusion is concerned with the problem of in or out, control is concerned with top or bottom, and affection with close or far."[10] And this occurs whether we're talking about face-to-face or online relationships. In both contexts, we connect with others whom we hope will help us feel we belong, can exert influence, and are worthy of affection.[11]

CONVERSING: CONNECTING THROUGH INTERPERSONAL DIALOGUE

When writing about flirting, one person observed:

> "Woman spots man, Man spots woman. Woman smiles. Male looks away. Woman looks away. Man looks back. Will they speak to each other?"[12]

Flirting can create either an awkward moment or the start of a relationship. To be sure, technology complicates the act of flirting. When we're texting, we can't hear the tone of voice that a person is using or read their body language as we can do during face-to-face flirting. Not having such cues accessible can cause us to misinterpret everything. Is someone merely being friendly, or are they interested in more? The fact is flirting is more successful when we engage in face-to-face conversation. We need to talk to relate to others.[13]

TALK MATTERS

Talking is a fundamental consideration in every phase of a relationship—whether it is beginning, continuing, stabilizing, or ending. Conversation helps develop and reinforce a sense of connectedness as well as provide opportunities to discuss feelings and empathize. By speaking to others, we increase our understanding and appreciation for one another.[14] Typically, the more time we spend conversing in a relationship, the healthier that relationship is.[15] Although it may be easier to post photos of others or text others to demonstrate our connections with them, it is through face-to-face conversation and the attention paid to everyday talk that we are able to enact our social and work lives more fully.[16]

COMPETING CONCERNS

Certainly, devices may compete for our attention when we are face-to-face with another person. In fact, when was the last time you held an uninterrupted conversation, one in which you or your conversational partner did not have your heads down focusing on a smartphone for at least part of the time? When two of us are talking, the mere presence of a smartphone can change what we talk about and the degree of connection we feel with one another. When splitting our attention between smartphone and a physically present person, we become more disconnected from the physically present person, less observant of her or his nonverbal cues, and, therefore, less tuned into his or her feelings. As a result, we become less apt to empathize. Instead,

iStock/danchooalex

we become more likely to limit our talk to topics that are interruptible—which are those subjects not terribly important to us.[17]

BEING FULLY PRESENT

What happens when we are fully present in a conversation? How do we proceed? According to Steven Duck's **serial construction of meaning model**, before we engage in conversation with another person, we may share things in common with that person, expressed as *commonality*. As we converse about something that we share in common, we establish *mutuality*, and seek to determine if we evaluate the shared experience similarly. Once we establish the *equivalence of our evaluation*, we then process what Duck calls *shared meaning*. In other words, it is through conversation that we create a shared world.[18] The fact is that we seek to converse with people who resemble us and share our attitudes.[19]

THE FIVE-STEP PATTERN

Many of our conversations follow a five-step pattern (even though they may not divide neatly into five steps): (1) open, (2) provide feedforward, (3) elaborate on your goal by getting down to business, (4) reflect back on what you have said, and (5) close.

The Open

The opening typically involves a verbal greeting, for example, "Hi there," and/or a nonverbal greeting, perhaps a fist bump. You might introduce yourself, ask a question, or make an opening statement. (If conversing online, you might open with a greeting line containing an emoji.)

Feedforward. During the feedforward phase, you might widen the conversational opening by engaging in **phatic communication**, offering surface clichés designed to keep the channels of communication open. You could, for example, say, "What's up? How are you doing?" or perhaps discuss the weather, and then provide a preview of the conversation's purpose, perhaps saying something like, "You need to know about this."

Goal Elaboration

In the next step, goal elaboration, you explain your goal or purpose, making statements of fact such as "I really support PETA" or statements of feeling such as "I think Juana really is into Joe, and it's making me jealous."

Reflection

During the fourth step, you reflect back on what you have discussed and seek common ground, for example, by saying, "Isn't that ridiculous?" or "So, what do you think will happen?"

The Close

In the last phase of the conversation, you close and say your good-byes, called *leave taking*, again using verbal and/or nonverbal cues.

Take Turns

The expectation is that a conversation finds the parties to the relationship taking turns speaking and listening. By either taking turns or refusing to take turns, we influence the direction and nature of the conversation and relationship.

By offering *turn-yielding cues*, we let the other person know that we have finished commenting and are now prepared to listen. In contrast, if we ignore *turn-requesting cues*—messages that signal the other person's desire to speak—opting instead to continue dominating the conversation, it may turn off the other person, boding ill for our relationship's future.

The more skillful we are at keeping a conversation going, perhaps by using self-disclosure techniques to draw the other person into the conversation and not dividing our attention between a person and our device, the greater is the likelihood that such conversations will achieve mutual understanding and empathy. It is through them that we will develop our lasting personal and professional friendships.[20]

CAREER BUILDER: THE GRAPEVINE AND THE GOSSIP MILL

When we perceive a workplace threat and management has done a poor job at putting our minds at ease, in order to reduce our feelings of insecurity and uncertainty, we may turn to the **grapevine**—a type of informal, conversational network existing in organizations—to share key messages. Although research reveals the grapevine to be uncannily speedy and accurate, the messages it carries are not necessarily being delivered to others intact. In fact, they sometimes emerge quite distorted and incomplete.[21] By tapping into the grapevine, however, you can uncover clues regarding what's happening in organizational circles that could affect you.

Gossip mills differ from grapevines. The **gossip mill** is the network through which people in the organization spread unverified information. When we converse with someone about another individual who is not present, we are spreading gossip. Why do we gossip? Perhaps because we're addicted to it and use it to enhance our status. Gossip gets us into

inner circles and provides us with even more information to pass on. By sharing gossip, we signal that we trust the other person not to use the information we are sharing to harm us.[22]

The gossiper frequently hypothesizes about the behavior of an absent party, spreads malicious or false information about him or her, and muses about the person's future. Thus, although gossip may make you feel important, it also can lead to others perceiving you more negatively. Gossip is risky business.

1. Identify a time when you used the grapevine to learn information you could use.

2. Identify a time when you were the recipient of gossip. What did you do with the information divulged to you?

3. Identify a time when you gossiped but were betrayed by the person you trusted?

4. What advice would you pass on to others about office grapevines and gossip mills?

Who Don't You Want to Talk To?

Good conversations are not necessarily easy. Sometimes we say something like, "I just can't talk to ____." What makes us make such a pronouncement? Is it because we feel we have nothing in common and don't see things the same way? Is it because we find the other person's opinions clash with ours? Although this may be so, there are means we can use to have difficult conversations.

First, we need to be curious and keep an open mind. It is possible to learn from a person with whom we disagree. Second, we need to seek to understand rather than to agree or disagree. Third, always need to show respect. Fourth, we need to empathize. Fifth, we need to stay the course. And last, we should end the conversation by expressing our appreciation for the other person sharing her or his thoughts with us. Following these guidelines will provide a foundation for future conversations.[23]

RELATIONSHIPS DIFFER IN BREADTH AND DEPTH

We can describe every relationship—whether with a friend, coworker, family member, or significant other—in terms of two concepts: breadth and depth. **Breadth** has to do with how many topics we and our relational partner discuss. **Depth** has to do with how central the topics are to our self-concept and how much we reveal.

FIGURE 7.1
Breadth and Depth

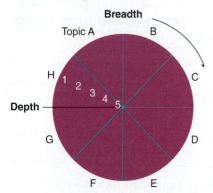

Sample Topics (breadth of topics)

A. Leisure
B. Career goals
C. Relationship with friends
D. Family relations
E. Health
F. Romance
G. Secrets
H. Self-concept

SOCIAL PENETRATION THEORY

A diagram of the relationship theory of social psychologists Irwin Altman and Dalmas Taylor, known as **social penetration theory**, is shown in Figure 7.1.[24] Central to social penetration theory is the idea that relationships develop incrementally beginning with relatively narrow breadth (we speak about only a few topics) and shallow depth (we do not penetrate the inner circles) and progress over time in intensity and intimacy as both breadth and depth increase. Thus, our relationships move from our discussing few to many topics and from superficial topics (the periphery of the circle) to intensely personal topics (the center of the circle). Figure 7.2 is an exercise using these concepts.

The social penetration model serves two key functions. First, it enables us to visualize the nature of our relationships by indicating the range of topics we communicate about and the extent to which we reveal ourselves through our discussions. Second, the model explains why some of our relationships are stronger than others.

SELF-DISCLOSURE AFFECTS RELATIONSHIP BREADTH AND DEPTH

Together, the nature and the amount of information we share with another person affect the strength and quality of our relationship. By deliberately revealing information about ourselves to another person, particularly information that we consider significant and that, without our personal intervention, would not be known to that individual, we increase both the breadth of information about us that the person has access to and the depth of understanding that she or he has for what makes us tick.

Self-disclosure is the voluntary revelation of confidential personal information about ourselves that we purposely reveal to others that they otherwise would not have access to or knowledge of. The amount of disclosing we do with another person is a gauge of how close we feel to the person or how close we want to become.

In contrast, when a relationship begins to wane, usually we decrease the breadth and the depth of our disclosures. We stop talking about some topics and discuss other topics in less depth. Changes like these signal that we are becoming less personal or intimate and instead have begun the de-penetration, or pulling away, process. In these ways, self-disclosure reflects a relationship's health. When disclosure between relationship partners is reciprocal and honest, partners feel more secure about the relationship and comfortable sharing their humanness.

FIGURE 7.2

Casual and Intimate Relationships. Use the following drawings to distinguish how breadth and depth differ in a casual and intimate relationship that you share.

Casual relationship

Intimate relationship

Layers (depth)
1. Most superficial layer
   (food, clothing, likes, dislikes)
2. Impersonal layer
   (job, education information)
3. Middle layer
   (political leanings, social views)
4. More personal layer
   (goals, values, beliefs, fears, secrets, dreams)
5. Most personal layer—the inner core—
   self-concept

PRIVACY NEEDS AFFECT RELATIONSHIP BREADTH AND DEPTH

Although social penetration theory reveals the breadth and depth of the information we are willing to share in our various relationships, it is **communication privacy management theory** that describes the establishment of boundaries and borders that we decide others may or may not cross. For each of our relationships, we compute a "mental calculus" to guide us in deciding whether to share information with another or keep it private. If we opt to keep it private, we avoid disclosure by engaging in the deliberate withholding of information.[25] At times, we may want to conceal what another person wants us to reveal. Such disagreements can lead to *boundary turbulence*, the tension created when the parties to a relationship are unable to agree on the boundaries of self-disclosure.

What might cause us to decide to secure a boundary? Should we discover a partner revealing a secret, spying on us, or otherwise violating our confidence, the likelihood that we will keep personal information private increases and so does the likelihood that the curtain will drop on the relationship.

ANALYZING RELATIONSHIPS

Among the ways we can make sense of relationships is with reference to their stages, digital influences, costs and benefits, and dialectical perspectives.

RELATIONSHIP STAGES: A DEVELOPMENTAL MODEL

Our relationships are complex and ever-changing. As we evaluate them, we decide that some of them are right for us, but others are wrong.[26] As they evolve, they proceed through a number of stages during which they either will strengthen, stabilize, or dissolve.[27] As a relationship fluctuates, the parties to it move up or down a figurative relationship staircase, either moving closer to or further from committing to one another. We can advance, stay put, or retreat should we decide that a more superficial relationship is what we really desire. We also might terminate a relationship only to decide that we want to begin it anew.

We move through relationship stages at our own pace. The relationship stage in which we're situated also determines the nature of our conversations, perhaps by limiting our talk to safe topics or by allowing probing questions in the effort to discover more about each other.

As we describe each relationship stage, consider how it applies to a close relationship of yours (Figure 7.3).

Stage 1: Initiating

Making contact and looking for signals that either lead us to begin a conversation or tell us that we have nothing to gain by conversing are instrumental in <mark>initiating</mark> a relationship. If we decide to converse, we search for an appropriate conversation opener, for example, "Nice to meet you" or "What are you up to?"

FIGURE 7.3

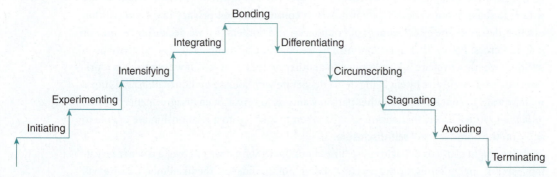

Bonding
Integrating — Differentiating
Intensifying — Circumscribing
Experimenting — Stagnating
Initiating — Avoiding
Terminating

Stage 2: Experimenting

If successful at initiating contact, we next try to find out more about the other person; we begin to probe the unknown. This stage is called **experimenting**. In an effort to get to know one another, we exchange small talk, such as telling the other person where we're from and whom we know. Small talk, which helps put people at ease, serves a number of purposes:

1. It creates opportunities for more penetrating conversations.
2. It serves as a friendship audition or a means of increasing the scope of a current friendship.
3. It offers a safe procedure for revealing who we are and how the other person can get to know us better.
4. It lets us maintain a sense of community with our fellow human beings.[28]

Small talk is like a game—its goal is to keep the conversational ball in the air.[29] Flirting is a form of small talk. At this stage, relationships lack depth; instead, they are casual and superficial. Many of our relationships never progress any further.

Stage 3: Intensifying

When a relationship progresses beyond experimenting, it enters the third stage, **intensifying**. During this stage, people become good friends. They start sharing things, disclose more, become better able to predict the behavior of the other, adopt nicknames for each other, and exhibit similar postural cues and clothing. The transformation from being an "I" to becoming a "we" begins.

Stage 4: Integrating

During Stage 4, **integrating**, two individuals have now become a team, a pair, a couple, or "a package." Interpersonal synchrony heightens as we dress, act, and speak more alike, perhaps even sharing a song ("our song") or a bank account.

Stage 5: Bonding

In Stage 5, **bonding**, the two people in the relationship announce that they're formalizing their commitment to one another. To accomplish this, they may institutionalize their relationship with a formal contract such as a wedding license or a written business agreement. The relationship takes on a new character. It is now guided by specified rules and regulations. Initially, this change can cause discomfort or rebellion as the two people in the relationship attempt to adapt.

Natalia Zasłona/Shutterstock.com

Stage 6: Differentiating

In Stage 6, **differentiating**, instead of continuing to emphasize their "we-ness," the two people try to reestablish their "I" orientations in an effort to regain their unique identities. They ask, "How are we different?" "How can I distinguish me from you?" It is at this point that previously designated joint possessions take on a more individualized character. "Our friends" become "my friends." "Our bedroom" becomes "my bedroom." Our child" becomes "your son" (especially when he misbehaves). The urge to differentiate the self from the other is common (we need to be individuals as well as in relationships), but if it persists, it can signal relationship troubles and the beginning of the process of uncoupling.

Stage 7: Circumscribing

In Stage 7, **circumscribing**, both the quality and the quantity of communication between relationship partners decreases. Sometimes a careful effort is made to limit discussions to what's considered safe. Other times there's no decrease in breadth of topics, but instead subjects no longer are discussed with any depth. Fewer and less intimate disclosures occur, signaling that one or both partners desire to withdraw mentally and/or physically from the relationship.[30] Dynamic communication ceases. Feelings of exhaustion and shrinking interest come to characterize the relationship.

Stage 8: Stagnating

As circumscribing continues, the relationship stagnates. In Stage 8, **stagnating**, we feel that we no longer need to relate to each other, because we know the end result. We conclude it is better to say nothing. Our communication is at a standstill. We mark time by going through the motions of being in a relationship, but we feel nothing. The only thing we now share is an environment.

Stage 9: Avoiding

During the **avoiding** stage, we go out of our way to be apart. To increase the psychological distance between the two of us, we avoid making eye contact. Although sometimes communicated more directly than at other times, the dominant message of this stage is "I don't want to see you anymore; I don't want to continue this relationship." The end of the relationship is in sight.

Stage 10: Termination

At Stage 10, **termination**, relationship bonds are severed and the relationship ends. Depending on if we agree on termination, this stage can be brief or drawn out. The relationship can end cordially or bitterly. All relationships eventually end (with the death of one party if not before), but this does not mean that saying good-bye is easy or pleasant. Breaking up, especially in the age of social media, can be very hard to do.

Some breakups are more difficult than others. According to communication researcher Steven Duck, as a relationship breaks up, we typically pass through four stages:[31]

1. *The self-talk stage*, in which we place our focus on relationship negatives, consider withdrawing totally from the relationship, and explore the potential positives of entering into an alternative relationship.

2. *The interpersonal communication stage*, in which we decide to confront, negotiate, and discuss possibilities for relationship repair and reconciliation, assess the

ramifications of withdrawing from the relationship, and ultimately decide to separate.

3. *The group and social communication stage*, during which we consider how to relate after breaking up. We may, for example, gossip about each other, tell stories, and place blame as a means of saving face.

4. *The grave dressing and public stage*, during which we offer a relationship postmortem—providing our respective publics with our own version of the breakup. Many former couples, for example, use social networks to tell their versions of the split, offering a stream of sometimes angry or sad posts. Although therapeutic for the person posting, they can be mortifying for the partner being attacked.[32]

Revisiting this approach to relationship dissolution, Duck and Julia Wood next conceptualized the breakup as composed of five processes:[33]

1. *Intrapsychic processes*, in which we brood about problems and our dissatisfaction with our relationship.

2. *Dyadic processes*, in which the rules and established patterns governing our relationship break down.

3. *Social support processes*, in which we air the relationship's dirty laundry for others outside the relationship, expecting others we know to take sides.

4. *Grave-dressing processes*, during which we determine the explanation we will give to friends, children, coworkers, and others for our breakup.

5. *Resurrection processes*, during which we enter and move forward into a future—minus a partner.

A SPECIAL CASE: RELATIONSHIP TERMINATION CAUSED BY A LOVED ONE'S PASSING

What happens when death takes a loved one away? When such a passage happens, we often experience feelings of grief that need to be worked through. Bereavement (i.e., how we adjust to the death of a loved one) is an individual matter; however, there is a process we can use to explain it.

The Grief Process

During the **grief process**, we pass through a series of stages (Figure 7.4). The first stage, denial, finds us rejecting what has happened. Denial eventually ebbs, however, as we acknowledge the impact of our loss and our accompanying feelings. During the second stage, anger, we feel helpless and powerless, striking out and railing against the loss. The third stage finds us experiencing guilt—we turn our anger against ourselves. We feel bad about

iStock/RichLegg

FIGURE 7.4
Grief Process

things we said or did to hurt the person who has died. We experience a sense of unfinished business. In the fourth stage, depression, we feel that nothing will ever be right again. Looking forward feels impossible. We feel lonely, empty, and isolated. The fifth and last stage is acceptance. At this point, we acknowledge that things will not be the same, but we believe that we will make it through, and we will be able to go on with life.[34]

How do we get to the fifth stage? By processing and expressing our feelings instead of trying to suppress and walk around our sadness. With the help and support of others, we become able to handle, rather than submerge, our grief, recover from grief's effects, and continue living by reengaging in consummate partnerships and new relationships.[35]

How Others Help

Others help us in bereavement by knowing how to address our feelings. They comfort us in a number of ways. First, they help by addressing our pain, not ignoring it. ("I'm so saddened by Adam's passing. I'm going to miss him a lot and so will everyone who knew him.") Second, they express their sympathy. ("I'm so sorry you are having to go through this. Please know my thoughts are with you and your family.") Third, they offer a statement reflective of something positive that the person's loved one represented. ("Adam was always there to listen to my problems. I'll always remember his helping me through a really tough time.") Fourth, they do not say that they know how the bereaved person feels. Attention remains on the person who suffered the loss. Finally, they offer help. Instead of asking the bereaved to call them if she or he needs anything, they take control, saying something like, "I'll call you tomorrow to let you know when to expect some food I'm ordering for you."

DIGITAL MEDIA AND RELATIONAL PROCESSES

Digital media are redefining not only the very nature of our relationships but also the processes our relationships go through, beginning with how we start one.[36] Many relationships have non-IRL (in real life) existences. Some users prefer it that way, because they feel vulnerable and are likely to shy away from physical encounters. Instead, they choose to flirt or even have "casual" phone sex in their fantasy worlds but with no intention of ever meeting the other person face-to-face. What is more, if others are discerning, they can use the messages we post to uncover our thoughts and aspects of our personality, including whether or not we're extroverted, how agreeable we are, our emotional stability, our openness to experience, and our conscientiousness.[37]

Tinder-Like Apps

When using an app such as Tinder, we expose ourselves to an expanded pool of partner possibilities. Then we simply can swipe right (if a photo of someone appeals to us) or left (if it doesn't) to indicate whether we would like to begin a relationship with a person. We can decide later if we want to turn it into a real-life relationship. Thus, digital media make it easier for us both to flirt and to follow up on our initial flirtations by messaging interest. We get an ego boost when discovering that an expressed interest is mutual.[38]

Alex Ruhl/Shutterstock.com

Dropping Relationship Breadcrumbs

To keep relationships going and a partner "hanging on" and connected even though a relationship has plateaued, digital adherents may offer their online relationship partners "breadcrumbs" through which they check in, seeking to maintain the relationship in name only, piquing the other person's interest, but making absolutely no commitment to get together or take the relationship further. These are not conversations but, rather, connectors meant to keep someone "on relationship hold."[39]

It's Over

Digital media also make it easier for us end a relationship. We may use digital assistance to help us end a relationship, such as the Breakup Shop, a firm that will send a breakup message for you.[40] We also can end a relationship ourselves merely by signaling a change of status, untagging photos, burying past posts, editing our Facebook walls, defriending a former partner without telling him or her ahead of time, or simply blocking his or her access to us. Before the digital age, we might not have been so mean or blunt in ending a relationship. Usually, we'd at least try to engage in face-to-face dialogue before calling it quits.[41] Now, we have a stream of endless apps we can use.[42] When we rely on digital media, however, our communication easily can become more impersonal. Somehow, texting that a relationship is over seems colder than breaking up in person.

It Ended . . . but Not Really

Prior to the digital age, we might pack up photos and other relationship reminders and either put them away or throw them out. Digital images on the Web, in contrast, persist. Online, it also seems as if the whole world is watching and privy to our breakup when it occurs.[43] As a result, online apps such as Mend exist to help the brokenhearted. On Mend, users meet an animated avatar, whose reassuring voice offers advice on how to recover from feeling like an emotional basket-case, encouraging the brokenhearted to move forward rather than give in to the shame some associate with breaking up.[44]

What happens online when either a relationship or a partner's life ends? Social media profiles persist. The former relationship or partner can be dead, yet present. Digital mementos of online relationships survive the demise of a relationship or person. Digital gravesites such as Facebook's "memorial profiles" are becoming places of mourning allowing grieving to occur online.

RELATIONSHIPS COME WITH COSTS AND BENEFITS

Feelings of acceptance are necessary for relationship satisfaction. The energy we are willing to commit to a relationship influences its outcome. Unless the people in a relationship continue to grow together and adapt to their continually changing environment, the relationship will deteriorate.

According to **cost–benefit/social exchange theory**, we work to maintain a relationship only as long as the benefits we perceive for ourselves outweigh the costs.[45] These benefits include feelings of self-worth, a sense of personal growth, a greater sense of security, additional resources for accomplishing tasks, and an increased ability to cope with problems. In comparison, costs include the time spent trying to make the relationship work, psychological and physical distress, and a damaged self-image. We enter our relationships with a **comparison level** in mind. We have a general idea, standard, or expectation of the kinds of rewards and profits that we believe we ought to get out of the relationship. When the rewards we receive equal or surpass our comparison level, we usually feel satisfied with the relationship. However, we also have a **comparison level for alternatives**. We compare the rewards we get from a current relationship with the ones we think we would be able to get from an alternative relationship. If we believe the present relationship rewards are below those we could receive from an alternative relationship, then we might decide to exit our present relationship and enter a new one.

Consider relationships in economic terms: Each partner acts out of a self-oriented goal of maximizing profits. When relationship rewards or profits are high and relationship costs are low, the more satisfying the relationship is and the more likely it is to continue.[46] Once costs outweigh benefits, however, we could begin to think seriously about terminating the relationship. Cost–benefit/social exchange theory predicts that the worth of a relationship influences its outcome. Positive relationships simply are more apt to endure.

RELATIONSHIPS EXPERIENCE TENSIONS

According to relational dialectics theorists, relationships are not linear but rather consist of the oscillation between contradictory personal goals. During relationship development, relational partners seek to meet goals, a number of which may be incompatible. As opposing goals meet, they create **dialectical tensions**. Three central relational dialectical tensions affecting relationships are connection and autonomy, predictability and novelty, and openness and privacy.[47] Let's explore each in turn.

Connection Versus Autonomy

We want to be independent of our significant others as well as to experience intimacy with them. We want to be close and separate. Perhaps you have found yourself saying something like this about a partner: "He barely spent any time with me," "She made me feel trapped," "He just wouldn't commit to being together," or "I need my freedom." If any of these statements sound familiar, then you and a partner had conflicting desires for connection and independence.

Because we want to establish more intimate connections with others we care about, we cherish the sharing of experiences. At the same time, however, we seek to preserve an independent identity. We don't want our relationships to erase our individuality.

Some relationships don't survive the connection–autonomy, self–other negotiations. Instead of working out an acceptable balance that preserves individuality while creating intimacy, partners may break up. In contrast, when they resolve connection–autonomy disagreements, they can redefine their relationship and even become closer.[48]

Predictability Versus Novelty

We desire both the excitement of change and the comfort of stability. We like routine as well as spontaneity. Too much routine, however, becomes boring. Perhaps these words sound familiar: "We always do the same things." "I want to do something different." "I know everything there is to know about her." Variety adds spice to normal routines. The challenge for relationship partners is to find the right mix between desire for predictability and the need to keep the relationship fresh and interesting.

Openness Versus Privacy

We wrestle with tensions between disclosure and silence or concealment. For many of us, complete openness is intolerable. Just as there are times we want to share our inner selves with those whom we care deeply about, there are times when we don't feel like sharing and desire privacy instead. Desiring privacy some of the time doesn't mean a relationship is broken. Our desire for openness or concealment waxes and wanes. We go through periods of disclosing and periods of withholding.[49] During every stage of our relationship, our desires for openness and privacy can fluctuate.

Dialectical Tension Resolutions

When a relationship is successful, partners are able to use a number of strategies to manage the dialectical tensions. First, they can negotiate a balance between connection and autonomy, predictability and novelty, and openness and closedness. Second, they can choose to favor one dialectic and ignore the other. Third, they can segment each of the dialectics by compartmentalizing different areas of their relationship and assigning each dialectic to different times or spheres. Fourth, they can reframe the dialectics by defining them as not contradictory at all.[50] It is not terribly effective to handle dialectical tensions by denying their existence. The fact is that ignoring relationship challenges rather than confronting them rarely succeeds long term.

LYING, TRUST, AND RELATIONSHIPS

Have lying, deception, and "post-truth" become characteristic of our 21st-century lives? After all, it is probable that during a typical week many of us do tell more than one lie.[51] And we are not just talking about politicians and actors. We lie to people with whom we share all kinds of relationships: We lie to our parents, professors, significant others, friends, family members, coworkers, and even ourselves. How can we explain this?

Telling the truth and lying are part of being human.[52] They are ways of relating, and we can use one or the other as a means of getting the outcome we desire.[53] In your opinion, is it always harmful, unethical, or immoral to lie consciously, whether deceiving another person or yourself? Would you ever want someone to lie to you? What would you never be willing to lie about either to another person or yourself?

THE EFFECTS OF LYING

Do you agree with the following statement? "Everyone is entitled to his (or her) own opinion, but not to his (or her) own facts."[54] When we lie, we make up facts or bend them to suit ourselves. Thus, a lie is the deliberate presentation of information that we know to be untrue.

We can lie either by commission or omission. When we lie by omission, we deliberately withhold relevant information, thereby contributing to others drawing an erroneous conclusion. When we lie by commission, we make a statement that we know to be false.

Sometimes, we lie so to continue to satisfy the basic needs that a particular relationship fulfills. Other times, we lie to increase desired or decrease undesired affiliations, to present a false image, to inflate our self-image and protect our self-esteem, or to achieve personal satisfaction.[55] We also lie to cover up something we did that was wrong. Most often, the lies we tell benefit ourselves, although some lies are designed to protect the person we are lying to, and a few benefit a third party. We lie to protect and acquire more resources. We lie to enhance our social attractiveness or present ourselves as more competent than we think we are. We lie to avoid conflict.[56]

Sometimes we **equivocate**, that is, we use purposefully vague language to finesse a response in an effort to avoid having to tell someone the unvarnished and unpleasant truth. Being deliberately vague helps us spare another's feelings and/or relieves us of having to address our anger. For example, if asked how we like a gift given to us, we might reply, "It's really special," when actually we think it's tasteless. Or, if asked how we like someone's hairstyle, we might say, "It's really you," when we believe it's unflattering. Equivocating takes the teller of the lie off the hot seat. It also helps the receiver save face. Would you rather have someone equivocate or tell you the truth?

Why Lying Takes a Toll

Studies of deception reveal that the act of lying strains the lie-teller both psychologically and physically. Just the act of information suppression causes thoughts to flood our consciousness, which contributes to our looking and sounding tenser.[57] On the other hand, sometimes we want to be lied to, because we don't know how to handle the truth. Does the blame for lying then fall on both the liar and the person lied to?

Once a lie is spoken, how does it affect the liar, the person who was lied to, and their relationship? Once a lie is uncovered, it changes how we feel about the relationship. Imagine sharing a relationship, no matter how ideal in other aspects, in which you were unable to rely on what the other person said or did? The information you exchanged would become virtually worthless. You might become resentful, disappointed, and suspicious. You might feel wronged and wary of what could come next. You might become angry with yourself for letting yourself be duped—for your inability to determine what was and what was not true. You might also feel shame for having been in denial or for having ignored warning signs. You likely would reevaluate everything based on the lie(s) that had come to light.[58]

While bending the truth to sustain a relationship may be a common practice, unless trust and truthfulness are present, it is only a matter of time before the relationship will die. Lying functions as a catalyst in precipitating a relationship crisis. Many breakups are attributed directly to the discovery of a major deception.

ETHICS AND COMMUNICATION

Self/Other Reflection

Interview three people from cultures other than your own regarding their experience of being lied to and of lying to someone else.

1. Ask each person to identify who lied to them, the nature of the lie and its context, and their reactions on discovering that they had been lied to.

2. Ask each person to describe the nature of the lie they told, their reason for lying, and the other person's reaction on discovering she or he had been deceived.

3. Whether they were the person lying or being lied to, ask them the specific effect(s) the lie had on their relationship with the other individual.

Switch focus. In your opinion, could telling someone the truth sabotage trust, the way lying does? Explain.

THE EFFECTS OF TRUST

There is a potential for trouble in any relationship. As we now recognize, one cause of trouble is lying, primarily because once discovered, it eats away at trust. **Trust** is an outgrowth of interpersonal communication. It is a reflection of how secure we are that another person will act in a predicted and desirable way. When we trust someone, we are confident that this person will behave as we expect and that he or she will not use whatever personal information we have confided in him or her to harm us.

Some of us are more trusting than others. How trusting a person are you?

The Trust Paradox

Whether or not we trust someone depends on whether prior relationships have reinforced trusting behavior or contributed to our being fearful about exhibiting trusting behavior. Trust creates a paradox. To be able to trust, we must be willing to risk trusting another person. When we take that risk, we risk being wrong. If we fail to take the risk, however, we never can be right.[59]

How Well Do You Tolerate Vulnerability?

The degree of trust we place in another person to accept information we disclose without hurting us or the relationship is a measure of our **tolerance of vulnerability**. This varies from person to person, topic to topic, and situation to situation. Researcher William Rawlins designed a matrix, shown in Figure 7.5, which we can use to analyze the amount of trust we place in different people at different times in our relationship's development. We also can use this matrix to determine which of our relationships have more stability or staying power. A relationship in which the partners have difficulty trusting one another is a troubled one.

Hurtful Messages

Troubled relationships typically involve the sending of **hurtful messages** that are designed to upset or cause emotional pain that further hamper trust. If the hurtful messages are intense, making it difficult for their target to ignore or forget them, they can poison the relationship by making it impossible to sustain closeness or derive satisfaction from it.

How do you respond when you're the target of a hurtful message? Some of us may end up simply accepting the hurtful message without challenging it, especially if the hurtful message makes us feel particularly vulnerable and causes us significant emotional pain. The less painful the message is, however, the more able we are to communicate our invulnerability. When a relationship is healthy and satisfying, the more likely it is that we will respond actively when we are the target of a hurtful message.[60]

FIGURE 7.5
Rawlins's Trust Matrix

	High need to be open	Low need to be open
High amount of trust in other's discretion	I Very tolerant of vulnerability (reveal)	III Judgment required
Low amount of trust in other's discretion	II Judgment required	IV Intolerant of vulnerability (conceal)

LAUGHTER AS INTERPERSONAL TOOL

iStock/monkeybusinessimages

Like trust, laughter also may serve us as an interpersonal tool. Every day we give and receive social laughter when interacting with friends, coworkers, and significant others. Laughter punctuates our conversations so often that we may not stop to appreciate its value. If, however, laughter disappeared from any of our important relationships, we would miss it sorely. By triggering the release of "feel good" chemicals in our brain, laughter impels us to connect with others. It also supports the creation of relationship depth.[61]

Humor can help us cope with anything, even the loss of someone we love. Once we are able to laugh again, we know that we are regaining control. Laughter also helps reduce stress by releasing excess energy. Like other interpersonal competencies, it enables us to develop fresh perspectives on events large and small by freeing us of anxious feelings and frustrations.

Laughter, called "rhythmic bursts of social glue" by one commentator, is contagious.[62] When we hear laughter, we typically begin laughing ourselves. The infectious nature of laughter can have dramatic effects on our relationships. Laughter helps synchronize both our mood and behavior, solidifying our relationship.

Like any relationship tool, laughter can have a downside. The opposite of joyful laughter is jeering, malicious laughter, laughter that is designed to punish, belittle, or exclude rather than include. In this case, rather than express our sociability, laughter signals our disdain for, and power over, someone else.

GENDER AND RELATIONSHIPS

When polled regarding their reasons for desiring intimacy in relationships, 20 of the top 25 reasons given by men and women were the same. Included among these were feeling attracted to the person, experiencing affection for the person, and a desire to express their love.[63] Gender also makes itself visible in non-hetero relationships. Lesbian relationships tend to be higher in disclosure and in partner equality, while gay male couples are more likely to limit both disclosiveness and emotional expressiveness.[64] Gay and lesbian men and women also engage in less stereotypical role-playing than do heterosexual partners.[65]

THE BENEFITS OF A FEMINIST PARTNER

In a study titled "The Interpersonal Power of Feminism: Is Feminism Good for Romantic Relationships?" the authors answered the question they posed in their article's title with a yes.

For both men and women, having a feminist partner was perceived as a benefit. In fact, feminist women were the most likely to be in romantic relationships characterized as healthier in terms of perceived relationship quality, equality, stability, and intimacy.[66]

FLIRTING MATTERS

Men and women may differ in behavior exhibited during the preliminary stages of a romantic relationship—particularly when flirting. For men, flirting is a form of foreplay —a verbal power struggle. For women, it often is more of "a way of making a connection."[67]

WHO'S SORRY?

When in a relationship, women are likely to apologize more than their male partners. They do so not because they *actually* have done something wrong—they just *think* they have. Women and men interpret "wrong" differently. It appears that a woman's threshold for offensive behavior is lower than a man's. Because men have a higher tolerance for offensive behavior, they sometimes fail to apologize for things that women think are worthy of an apology.[68]

WHO ENGAGES MORE WITH SOCIAL MEDIA?

Women are more engaged in using social media in their relationships than are men. They also are less apt than men to project their own feelings onto a partner.[69] Whereas men may post more videos online, women (particularly teenagers), in their effort to please someone who interests them, sext more—sending sexually explicit messages of themselves to the other person. When such images get into the wrong hands, they can end up being posted online for all to see. Frequently when this happens, cyberbullying attacks ensue. Women also post more, in general, on social media, perhaps because they have been taught to be social, communal, and to make stories about themselves. In contrast, men have not been taught to engage in confessional or emotional communication.[70]

WHO FOCUSES ON MAINTENANCE?

Women focus more on relationship maintenance than do men. They rely on maintenance strategies, including the use of personal and disclosive talk, to acquire personal information about a partner.[71] Because women desire a partner who demonstrates care and concern and who is empathetic, they model those same behaviors. Women engage in more relationship monitoring and assume primary responsibility for caring for the relationship. In lesbian couples, partners tend to assume mutual responsibility for nurturing the relationship and providing emotional support. This may be why lesbian couples, in general, report more satisfaction with romantic relationships than do either heterosexual or gay couples.[72]

WHAT WE SHARE

Women and men share many commonalities in their views about relationships. Both value same-sex friends and seek friends whom they can trust. They also value those who accept and will help them. People who have fulfilling same-sex friendships report higher levels of personal well-being. Those who share effective sibling relationships do as well.[73]

CULTURE AND RELATIONSHIPS

Do people from diverse cultures desire the same things in and from their relationships?

Attitudes toward the self and others influence the effectiveness of relationships shared by people from different cultures. Whereas some cultures emphasize social relationships and instruct individuals to give preference to the interests of others over their own private interests, other cultures, including U.S. culture, stress individualism. Americans find it natural to begin and end relationships; in contrast, Asian cultures believe that relationships should be long-lasting and characterized by loyalty and the fulfillment of obligations.

Not all cultures treat all relationships similarly. Some cultures, for instance, have different rules for heterosexual relationships and same-sex relationships, and others have men and women performing different relationship roles. Whereas same-sex marriage is legal across the United States and much of the developed world, in some countries same-sex couples face ostracism or severe consequences, including arrest or death.

In the United States, both men and women can begin and end their romantic relationships. We typically believe that any person has the right and ability to dissolve a relationship that makes him or her unhappy. This is not true in all cultures. In some cultures, parents select relationship partners for their children. Sometimes, their goal is to bring two families together. Other times, it is to reap a financial reward.

MORE ON TECHNOLOGY AND RELATIONSHIPS

Have you considered how technology is affecting your relationships? As we have seen, in increasing numbers, we are beginning and building our personal relationships online, with many of us having online romances. Dating sites continue to multiply, signaling the eroding role that family, friends, and coworkers are playing in fostering love connections.[74] Many of us now rely on swiping to make a connection that could lead to our meeting for a drink. We then text to sustain our connection, sending out streams of brief updates in the effort to build and develop feelings of closeness.[75]

DOES TECHNOLOGY HELP?

To be sure, technology is making it easier for us to find and connect with others. Technological advances have enabled us to overcome traditional barriers of space and time as we traverse both time zones and international borders. However, somewhat surprisingly, we also find ourselves relying on technology in order for us to relate with people living and working in close proximity to our actual physical location. As society puts more and more emphasis on using technology, some fear the result, believing it will show that we place too little emphasis on our personal relationships—whether they are work, friendship, or romantically based. In fact, some assert, for all practical purposes, we stopped talking to one another in about the year 2010—when the use of instant messaging and text messaging exploded.[76]

POPULARITY IS QUANTIFIABLE, BUT IS THIS APPROPRIATE?

Technology has also contributed to our being able to quantify popularity. The metrics are available for all to see. We count likes. We count views. We share our counts. Digital and physical lives merge, with digital popularity transforming people into "influencers" who are seen as desirable to hang out with, much like the prom queen and king used to be. We pose

pixabay/soyvanden

for selfies that will look good online but are quite ridiculous looking in person.[77]

How is technological connectivity impacting the nature of our social and professional relationships? Is it contributing to or accelerating the pace of face-to-face disconnections? Are we paying less attention to those people who share the space we're in, so that we may pay more attention to those who are more physically remote? Are we treating digital connectivity as if it were the same as, and more important than, face-to-face connectivity?[78]

FACTORS HAMPERING RELATIONSHIP DEVELOPMENT ONLINE

What are some differences between face-to-face and online communication that could hamper relationship development? First, in cyberspace a person remains invisible to us unless we FaceTime, Skype, or post photos. Second, because of fewer nonverbal cues, we may misinterpret the intended meaning of a message sent to us. Third, because it is more difficult to control the pace of online interaction, some of the spontaneity and immediate feedback that characterize and animate face-to-face interactions are lacking. Fourth, because we don't have access to as much information (verbal and nonverbal) as face-to-face communication offers, it may be harder for us to decide if we trust the other person. Fifth, simply due to the inelasticity of time, the more time we spend on online interaction the less time we have for face-to-face interpersonal interaction. As we become more active in the online social scene, we may scale back or cut off our more traditional interactions. Sixth, fakers can click their way into online relationships. Because it is easier to conceal true identities online, it is wise to proceed cautiously, being careful not to reveal personal information that could put your personal security at risk.

SOME FIND IT EASIER

Despite such drawbacks, as we've noted, some do find it easier to begin a relationship online. At least until photos are shared or a video uploaded, appearance remains on the back burner.

Whether a relationship that is begun online continues depends on the rapport-building skills of the users. Additionally, those who are homebound are able to use social networks to overcome feelings of isolation and loneliness. Many find it easier to disclose information online that we usually keep secret. However, it also becomes easier for our innermost secrets to be exposed. On one site aptly named PostSecret.com, there are a plethora of secrets that others have posted because they are seeking self-clarification and/or catharsis. Anyone can read them. Although privacy gives us the right

iStock/edgardr

to keep our personal feelings secret, many post their secrets anyway. In fact, many people troll their friends just to see what secrets they might be revealing to others.[79] What is not shared with us directly may still be discoverable online.

Ending a friendship or romance online is frequently a one-sided event that is accomplished with a simple click on Facebook, a practice called *defriending*—a term that first entered the *Oxford English Dictionary* in 2010. Contrast this with the more gradual, mutual fading away that tends to occur in the physical world. In contrast, individuals who find themselves defriended online often report having been blindsided.

COMMUNICATION SKILLS
Practice Improving Interpersonal Relationships

Whether to begin, develop, and perhaps terminate a relationship in the digital world or the physical world is up to you. The fact that this now is a choice attests to the power of virtual worlds in our lives. But which domain, the physical or the digital, fosters more accurate perceptions of a person, enabling us to perceive him or her based on more than our wants and needs alone?[80] Whatever you prefer, building a relationship that satisfies will take work. What should we do to enhance that possibility?

Actively seek information from others, and allow others to seek information from you.

People who fail to initiate contact or fail to reinforce the communication and conversation efforts of others are less likely to build stable foundations for effective relationships. Passive, restrained

(Continued)

(Continued)

communicators are instead more likely to remain chronically lonely. Although we all experience short-term loneliness from time to time, sustained loneliness can lead to social apathy.

Recognize that relationships evolve.

Ours is a mobile and increasingly technological society in which each change we experience has the potential to bring us different relationships. Be prepared for changes in relationships. Recognize that in your life you are likely to experience a certain amount of relational turnover and change. As you grow and develop, so will your relationships.

Know when to sever a relationship.

Although one party to a relationship may desire to sustain it, not all relationships or connections are meant to continue forever. When a relationship drains you of your energy and confidence, or when it becomes unhealthy, you need to extricate yourself from it before it destroys you.

Recognize that communication is the lifeblood of a relationship.

Without communication, relationships are sure to shrivel and die. Any relationship that is worth time and energy depends on effective communication to sustain and nourish it. The desire and motivation to communicate are key ingredients in a relationship's establishment and growth.

> People meet and separate. But funny things happen in between.
>
> Mark L. Knapp

COMPLETE THIS CHAPTER 7 CHECKLIST

7.1 I can describe the various functions of relationships and the needs they fulfill. ☐

Any interpersonal relationship is a meaningful, dyadic, person-to-person connection in which two interdependent people engage in communication of a personal nature, develop a shared history, and try to meet each other's social needs. Relationships play many roles in our lives, including fulfilling our inclusion, control, and affection needs.

7.2 I can discuss the role conversations play in relationships. ☐

Conversation plays a fundamental part in our relationships. In fact, we enact our relationships through our conversations. Most conversations can be divided into five steps: (1) open, (2) provide feedforward, (3) elaborate on your goal, (4) reflect back on what you have said, and (5) close. It is through conversation that we are able to create a shared world with another person.

7.3 I can explain the significance of depth and breadth in relationships. ☐

Every relationship we share is unique and varies in breadth (how many topics relational partners discuss) and depth (how much they are willing to reveal their feelings to one another). According to the social penetration model, most relationships develop by beginning with narrow breadth and shallow depth. Over time, some relationships increase in breadth and depth, becoming wider, more intimate, or both.

7.4 I can analyze relationships according to their stages, digital media influences, cost–benefit/social exchange implications, and relationship dialectics. ☐

Researchers have identified a number of stages through which our relationships may pass: initiating, experimenting, intensifying, integrating, bonding, differentiating, circumscribing, stagnating, avoiding, and termination. A relationship may stabilize at any stage. Digital media influence relational processes, providing non-IRL (in real life) existences and redefining the nature of our relationships and the stages they go through, including how we start, maintain, and end them. Cost–benefit/social exchange theory holds that we work to maintain those relationships that yield the greatest personal profits and fewest costs. Relational dialectics explore the oscillation that occurs between conflicting relationship goals.

7.5 I can explain how deception and trust affect relationships. ☐

Telling the truth and deception are each a way of relating. Telling the truth leads to others trusting us. Lying causes others to be wary of continuing a relationship.

7.6 I can describe laughter's role in relationships. ☐

By triggering the release of "feel good" chemicals in our brain, laughter impels us to connect with others. It also supports the creation of relationship depth and health.

7.7 I can explain how gender influences relationship formation, maintenance, and termination. ☐

Gender affects how we approach, form, sustain, and dissolve relationships. It affects the nature of the communication occurring between the parties in the relationship and influences how the parties view the relationship itself.

7.8 I can explain how culture influences relationship formation, maintenance, and termination. ☐

Not all cultures process and treat relationships similarly. Members of diverse cultures differ in their approach to social relationships with some giving preference to the interests of others over their own interests and others stressing individualism.

7.9 I can discuss the impact of technology on relationships. ☐

How we communicate plays a key part in determining whether our relationships are as effective and rewarding for us as they could be. Changes in the channels we rely on to communicate have both positive and negative relationship ramifications. Some fear that digital connectivity is becoming more consequential than face-to-face connectivity.

7.10 I can apply skills to improve the effectiveness of my relationships. ☐

Because communication is the lifeblood of every relationship, it is important we learn to use it to avoid loneliness, foster meaningful relationships that evolve as we grow, and end those relationships that are no longer meant to continue.

BECOME A WORD MASTER

affection 170

avoiding 178

bonding 177

breadth 174

circumscribing 178

communication privacy management theory 175

comparison level 182

comparison level for alternatives 182

control 170

cost–benefit/ social exchange theory 182

depth 174

dialectical tensions 182

differentiating 178

equivocate 184

experimenting 177

Fundamental Interpersonal Relations Orientation 169

gossip mill 173

grapevine 173

grief process 179

hurtful messages 186

inclusion 169

initiating 176

integrating 177

intensifying 177

interpersonal relationship 168

loneliness 170

phatic communication 172

self-disclosure 175

serial construction of meaning model 172

social penetration theory 174

stagnating 178

termination 178

tolerance of vulnerability 186

trust 185

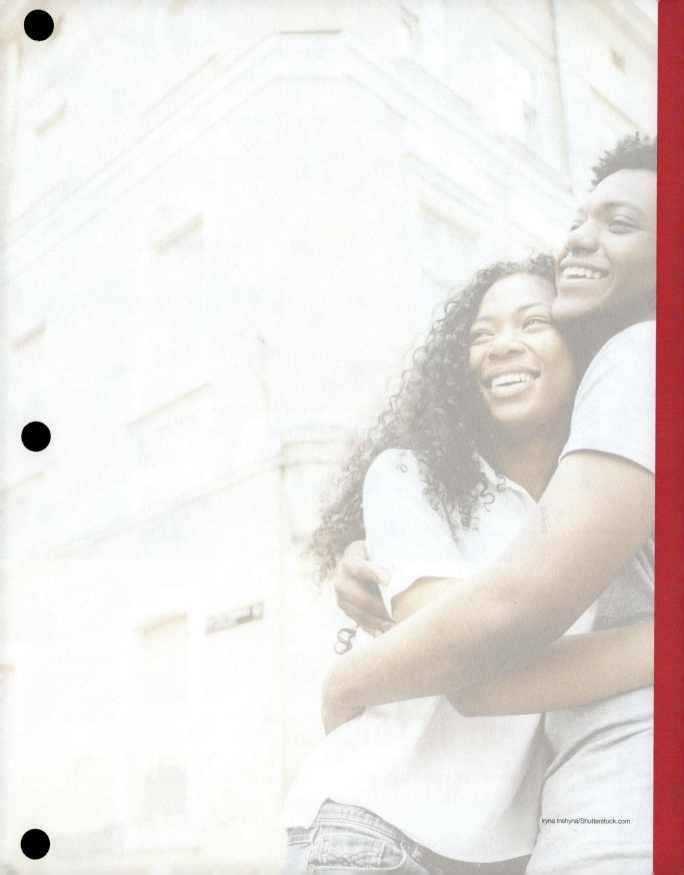

Iryna Inshyna/Shutterstock.com

Jacob Lund/Shutterstock.com

8

Person to Person: Handling Emotions and Conflict

8.1 Explain five factors contributing to relationship interest.

8.2 Discuss how uncertainty reduction and predictability impact a relationship's success.

8.3 Identify and distinguish among the following kinds of relationships: acquaintanceship, friendship, and romantic, family, and work relationships.

8.4 Define *emotional intelligence* and discuss its relationship effects.

8.5 Describe the importance of expressing our feelings in a relationship.

8.6 Define *relational conflict* and identify techniques to manage it.

8.7 Discuss technology's influence on the quantity and quality of our relationships.

8.8 Apply skills for handling conflict and standing up for emotional rights in relationships.

> People change and forget to tell each other.
>
> Lillian Hellman

. . . .

The Real Housewives franchise of shows introduced us to an array of friends, family members, lovers, and working professionals as they navigated their relationships. We observed as friends became frenemies or romantically involved and as family members experienced and resolved conflicts. Many of the interactions we were privy to were emotionally raw. We imagined what it would be like to be the people involved.

No matter their context, relationships require that we understand emotions, be able to express and process feelings, and be equipped to handle conflict. In our successful relationships, we communicate clearly and effectively about what we want. Along the way, we develop greater insight into ourselves and others. ■

FIVE FACTORS CONTRIBUTING TO RELATIONSHIP INTEREST

Why are we drawn to some people but not to others? Why are some people interested in getting to know us better while others display no such interest? Researchers have identified variables that we can use to answer these questions.[1] Among the factors consistently named are attractiveness, proximity, similarity, reinforcement, and complementarity.

ATTRACTIVENESS

There are three aspects to attractiveness: physical attractiveness, social attractiveness, and task attractiveness.

The first kind of information we process when interacting with another person is his or her outward attractiveness, or looks. However, there is no single standard of what an attractive person looks like because what we find appealing in a person's looks is subjective.

When it comes to social attractiveness, we tend to like those people whose personality is pleasant and who have a demeanor we admire. We simply feel comfortable with them. Of course, judgments of what constitutes a pleasant personality also are subjective.[2]

As for task attractiveness, we enjoy being with those people whom we enjoy working with. Thus, what starts off as a business relationship may in time develop into something more.

PROXIMITY

Proximity is the second factor influencing interest. Living physically close to another person or working nearby them, gives us ample opportunities for interaction. It becomes easier and more natural for us to talk, share activities, and form an attachment. As a result, the closer two people are geographically, the more likely it is that they will be drawn to each other, become a couple, or marry.

We should, however examine an opposite effect of proximity. Being proximate can also lead to feelings of dislike. Thus, whereas nearness may be a necessary condition for a relationship, it is likely that it also is a necessary condition for hatred.[3] What have your experiences taught you?

REINFORCEMENT

A third factor appearing in practically all theories of interpersonal interest is reinforcement. We feel positive about people who reward us or who we associate with our being rewarded. In contrast, we feel animosity or dislike for those people who punish us or are associated with our punishment. Thus, we tend to like people who praise us, like us, and cooperate with us more than with those who criticize us, dislike us, and oppose our efforts or compete with us.

Of course, reinforcement can backfire: If others become overzealous in their praise and fawn over us too much, we question their sincerity and motivation. But, in general, as social psychologist Eliot Aronson notes, "We like people whose behavior provides us with a maximum reward at minimum costs."[4]

SIMILARITY

The interest we have in others is also affected by similarity. We are drawn to people whose attitudes and interests and likes and dislikes match ours. Typically, we like people who agree with us more than those who disagree with us, especially when we are discussing issues we consider salient or important. Similarity provides social validation.

COMPLEMENTARITY

Not all evidence suggests that we are drawn to only attitudinal clones of ourselves. **Complementarity** can also be an appealing characteristic. We often find ourselves interested in people who differ from us in one or more ways, which explains why we fall in love with people who possess characteristics we admire but do not have ourselves. A dominant person might seek a submissive partner and a socially awkward person might appreciate someone who possessed social poise.

Take a moment to rank these five factors in order of their importance to you. What does it tell you about yourself?

UNDERSTANDING THE UNCERTAINTY FACTOR

Before a relationship develops, the parties to it are strangers. No matter how close we may become eventually, that was our beginning. A lot of what happens next depends on our goal. What is your goal when you meet someone for the first time?

STRATEGIES FOR REDUCING RELATIONSHIP UNCERTAINTY

According to relationship theorists, we want to reduce the amount of uncertainty we feel about another person.[5] We prefer the known to the unknown. Thus, to create understanding, we need to gain knowledge. By reducing uncertainty about another person, we not only find out what the other person is like, but we also figure out how to act with him or her.[6]

We rely on three key strategies to reduce uncertainty and increase relationship predictability: (1) passive strategies, through which we unobtrusively observe the other person while she or he is engaged in doing something, preferably interacting with others; (2) interactive strategies, through which we communicate directly with the other person, perhaps asking probing questions that encourage the person to talk about herself or himself; and (3) active strategies, through which either we get information about this person from a third party, manipulate a situation that enables us to observe the other person, or set up a situation in which we can have someone else observe as we talk with the other person. The more we interact with and converse with the person, the more our uncertainly decreases. The more we and the other person share things, the more our uncertainty wanes. The more we and the other person share a communication network—that is, interact with the same people—the more uncertainty is reduced.

Because interpersonal ignorance is uncomfortable, the urge to reduce uncertainty motivates our communication. Once we reduce uncertainty to the point that we are comfortable being in the situation, our interaction will increase and the relationship can continue. Just as reducing uncertainty acts as a bridge to relational development, so it also can be used to bridge some cultural gaps.[7]

PREDICTING RELATIONSHIP OUTCOMES

Another factor affecting relationship development is the predicted outcome value of the potential relationship. Researchers believe that we formulate a personal hypothesis regarding whether or not a given relationship will be rewarding.

As we've discussed, because we typically have limited information at the outset of a relationship, we may base our initial judgment on a person's physical appearance, the behaviors we observe, or information we get from others.[8] As we reduce our uncertainty, our ability to make more accurate predictions about the relationship's future improves. How accurate have you been at predicting the success or outcomes of your relationships?

TYPES OF RELATIONSHIPS

Relationships are colored by the life contexts in which they occur. By exploring the different kinds of relationships that we share with others, we can develop our abilities to strike a balance between closeness and distance, based at least in part on whether the relationship is with an acquaintance, a friend, a family member, a lover, or a partner at work.

ACQUAINTANCESHIPS

We have **acquaintanceships** with people whom we know by name, with whom we converse when the chance arises, but with whom our interaction is usually limited in scope and quality. Unless we want to turn an acquaintance into a friend, we rarely go out of our way to see that person, preferring instead to leave our meetings to chance.

FRIENDSHIPS

A number of our acquaintanceships develop into friendships. **Friendships** are voluntary. Those who share what they consider to be a good friendship report that the following qualities are present: *enjoyment* (they enjoy each other's company most of the time), *acceptance* (they accept each other as they are), *trust* (both parties assume that one will act in the other's best interest), *respect* (each assumes that the other will exercise good judgment in making choices), *mutual assistance* (they are willing to assist and support each other), *confidences* (they share experiences and feelings with each other), *understanding* (they have a sense of what the other thinks is important and why the other believes as she or he does), and *spontaneity* (they feel free to be themselves).[9]

iStock/molchanovdmitry

Keeping Friends

What actions do we take to keep our friends? First, we are proactive in making time to spend with them. We look for opportunities to be together. Second, we focus on and are responsive to them, refraining from selfishly placing the focus on ourselves. Third, we are willing to self-disclose. As friends, we share our feelings with one another. Of course, we might be closer to some friends than others. It is to our very closest friends that we confide our most private thoughts and feelings. Fourth, we offer each other emotional support, especially when either of us feels emotionally or psychologically vulnerable. Friends help each other. And last, we manage any conflicts in ways that meet each person's needs.[10]

A Model of Friendship

As friendships develop and become closer, our knowledge and trust in each other—and the breadth and depth of our relationship—increases. Bill Rawlins's six-stage model depicts how friendships develop (Figure 8.1).[11]

According to Rawlins, friendship begins with **role-limited interaction**, during which two people make initial contact in some context. At this point, there is uncertainty around whether the relationship will develop, and we act tentatively in relating to each other. The next interaction stage, **friendly relations**, finds us exploring whether we have enough in common to continue building the relationship. During the **moving toward friendship** stage, we step beyond conventional social rules and make small personal disclosures to indicate that we'd like to expand the friendship. We invite the other person to interact with us in a context outside those that happen serendipitously.

As the other person echoes our moves toward friendship, we enter the **nascent friendship** stage and begin to consider ourselves friends. We substitute our own rules in place of the social stereotypes and standards that regulated communication between us to this point. We plan activities to share together. Our interactions become more regular. We enter the **stabilized friendship** stage once we decide that our friendship is secure and will continue. We trust in each other and respond in ways that display our trustworthiness.

If friends begin to drift apart, they enter the **waning friendship** stage. Sometimes this happens when friends take their friendship for granted. Other times, one or both make less of a personal effort to keep the friendship going. Perhaps career or family obligations get in the way. Maybe a trust is violated or one person develops new interests that the other doesn't share. Friendships don't maintain themselves, so when one or more of the preceding situations occur, the friendship may dissolve.

FIGURE 8.1

Rawlin's Six-Stage Model of Friendship

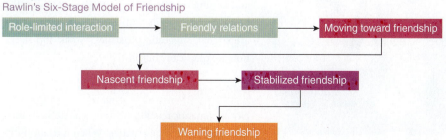

Variant Forms of Friendship

A variant form of friendship, called *friends with benefits* (FWB), involves friends who share a sexual relationship with no strings attached in addition to friendship. Traditional dating on college campuses is being upstaged by *hookups*, relationships in which bonds between young men and women are short-lived and sexual. Some attribute the prevalence of hookups to the fact that there are more women than men on many college campuses, creating increased competition for access to men and contributing to relationships becoming sexual more quickly. Dating, in such instances, may follow rather than precede sex.[12]

A term we use to describe a person whom we're not quite certain is a friend, but who pretends to be one, is frenemy. A *frenemy* is someone about whom we have ambivalent feelings; their intensions confuse us. Do they have our best interests at heart, or are they rivals out to best us? They may smile to our face, but we suspect they are jealous, have ulterior motives, or are likely to gossip about us, belittle us, or tell lies to make us look bad. Do you have any frenemies?

ROMANTIC RELATIONSHIPS

Romantic love is different from the kind of love we feel for our friends or our family members. Although statistics reveal that over half of all marriages in the United States end in divorce, when we enter into marriage, we expect it will last. In fact, it is the expectation of permanence that helps distinguish a romantic relationship from other kinds of relationships.

Unique Characteristics

Three additional characteristics unique to romantic relationships are commitment (the intention to remain in the relationship even if trouble arises), passion (intensely positive feelings of attraction), and intimacy (sustained feelings of closeness and connection). Although any one of these can exist without the others, all three are essential to a successful romantic relationship.[13]

Stages and Changes

Like friendships, romantic relationships pass through stages reflective of each person's perception of the amount of self-disclosing that is occurring and the kind of intimacy shared. Here the presence of trust is essential, because trust frees partners to share their feelings and innermost thoughts.

iStock/AntonioGuillem

When a romantic relationship sours and one partner rejects the other, it can really hurt. In fact, as far as our brains are concerned, getting burned and getting dumped feel about the same. For the brain, physical pain and intense emotional pain are similar, suggesting that heartbreak and rejection are physically harmful.[14]

Dysfunctions

Not all romantic relationships are healthy. Some turn dark and become destructive. When a relationship becomes dysfunctional, **toxic communication**, including verbal abuse, and/or physical or sexual aggression or violence, is present. Although spousal abuse is all too common, the highest incidence of violence in romantic relationships occurs between unmarried cohabiting couples.[15] Relationship well-being is more secure in relationships that develop along traditional pathways.[16]

Dysfunctional romantic relationships also move through a series of stages, but these stages are cyclical, not linear. During the first stage, relational tensions build in the abusing partner, who blames the other partner for problems and seeks an excuse to vent anger. In the second stage, the tensions erupt into violence. In the third stage, the abusing partner apologizes and promises to make it up to the victim, assuring her or him that it will never again happen. In the fourth stage, there is a lull in violent activity, during which the victim again feels loved. Ultimately, however, the relational tensions again build, and the cycle of abuse continues (Figure 8.2).[17]

FAMILY RELATIONSHIPS

Most of our earliest relationships occur within the family. Family members mutually influence one another as they work out the nature of their relationships. Family members are expected to play certain roles in relation to each other and to the family as a whole. Among the roles family members enact are wage earner, homemaker, financial manager, and child-care provider. These roles may be shared or may be the primary responsibility of one person. In healthy families, role relationships evolve as family members grow, develop, and enter different life stages.

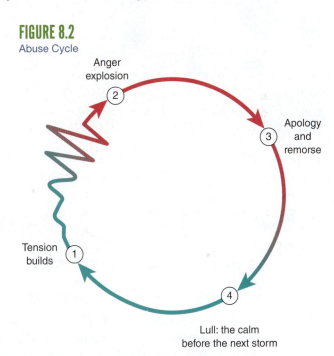

FIGURE 8.2
Abuse Cycle

Anger explosion

2

Apology and remorse

3

Tension builds

1

4

Lull: the calm before the next storm

Expectations

Family members have expectations for each other. They expect to receive emotional support from others in the family. They expect family members to pull together to preserve the family unit. The rules that guide family interaction help regulate the behavior of family members. They reveal how family members divide tasks—who is in charge of what and the like. To thrive in a family, we need either to follow or to renegotiate successfully the rules that prescribe family member behavior.

Healthy Versus Unhealthy Communication

When a family practices healthy communication, members offer emotional and physical support to each other, reveal their feelings and thoughts to each other, meet each other's needs, and display flexibility and a willingness to adapt to change. In contrast, when a family's communication practices become dysfunctional—when they prohibit members of the family from expressing their feelings or needs adequately or contain messages that are physically, sexually, or emotionally abusive—then family relationships are in danger and deteriorate.[18]

Evolving Composition

Family composition continues to evolve in the United States. No longer is the once-dominant nuclear family comprised of a wife, a husband, and biological children the norm. The United States is now a composite of an array of family types, including single-parent, step, unmarried, multigenerational, and same-sex. Young people today are marrying later if at all and, in many cases, choosing to cohabitate instead. Unmarried adults now represent more than half of all households.[19]

Making Sense

The behavior of a family does not occur in a vacuum. When one family member acts out, all have to adjust. Because families are composed of people and people change as they age, families continually find themselves adapting and transitioning. As members work out their relationships, they work out an array of issues such as power, intimacy, and trust.

SKILL BUILDER

My Family Network

To better understand your family, draw a family network map.[20]

1. Get a large sheet of paper and, using a felt-tipped pen, draw a circle to represent each family member. If grandparents are part of the household, include circles for them. If someone was a part of the family but now is gone, represent that person with a filled-in circle.

2. Show how family members are connected by drawing lines between the different pairs or roles. For example, a family may have marital pairs, parent–child pairs, and sibling pairs.

3. Add network lines to the map by linking every family member with every other family member. As the lines for each person are drawn, think about the particular relationship that person has with every family member, identify the roles the family member performs, and describe what you feel about each connection.

WORK RELATIONSHIPS

At work, we develop social networks that have benefits both in the office (they enhance our job satisfaction) and out of the office (the office serves as a top marital hunting ground).[21]

Friendship affects our sense of well-being in the workplace. Having friends at work helps make the workplace fun; we know we can count on our coworkers for support, especially those coworkers whose levels of power and responsibility are similar to our own. Because of power and status differences, we are less likely to be close friends with our superiors or our subordinates (a word that actually is out of favor).[22]

There also is a downside to some office friendships. In too many organizations, what has come to be known as "bro culture"—the exclusionary, male-centric atmosphere akin to that found in some college frat houses—affects relationships among men and women at work, causing festering issues of inequality and harassment.[23]

When we work in an organization, we share interdependent relationships with others in that organization. When we are knowledgeable about how to build person-to-person, on-the-job relationships, we put ourselves in a better position to nurture both our personal

CAREER BUILDER: WHAT ATTITUDE DO YOU BRING TO WORK?

Do you consider yourself an optimist or a pessimist? Which is most helpful to you in doing your job?[24] Although both outlooks can be beneficial to your performance at work, being very cheerful has its risks in that you might not seek input from others and could underestimate barriers to completing an assignment. In addition, if the workplace's culture is "fun," people could fail to speak up when they see a threat or problem.

Feeling moderately pessimistic, in contrast, can create just enough worry in you to cause you to prepare yourself better. It can also contribute to your being more sensitive to the moods of others, improving chances for career success.

Explore the moods described in the following table. Indicate where you fall and how you think the description that you identify with could benefit or hinder you as an employee.

Positive Mood

DOWNSIDE	UPSIDE
Apt to ignore threats	More creative
Excessive risk taking	Better relationships
More trusting	Mentally and physically healthier
Lacking appropriate levels of guilt	Willing to explore

Negative Mood

DOWNSIDE	UPSIDE
Overly cautious	More detail oriented
Less creative	More motivated
At risk of stressing out	More polite and attentive to others
More close-minded	On the lookout for threats

growth and the organization's development. The notion of the rugged individual in the organization is no longer current. Replacing it is the *team player*—a person effectively working with others within and between groups. Team players realize the potential to work together to develop meaningful partnerships with many others in the organization.

The relationship level is where most of an organization's work gets done. When we perceive interaction with others to be supportive, open, and honest, we tend to find our jobs more satisfying. A culture of openness makes the genuine expression of ideas and feelings possible. The relationship level also is where many of the organization's difficulties surface. If, for example, we fear punishment for revealing our thoughts and feelings, we will suppress them. Bullying or sexual harassment can make a workplace dysfunctional.

EMOTIONS AND RELATIONSHIPS

The main characters of the film *Inside Out* were emotions. Joy, Sadness, Fear, Disgust, and Anger were portrayed working both in harmony and, when contentious, in disharmony, as they do in our inner lives when they grapple for control of our minds.

WE ALL HAVE THEM

Emotions are present and play a role in all relationships. When a relationship is healthy, relational partners are aware of how their emotions affect their relationship and how their relationships affect their emotions.

WE BENEFIT FROM EMOTIONAL INTELLIGENCE

Emotional intelligence includes the ability to motivate oneself, to control impulses, to recognize and regulate one's moods, to empathize, and to hope.[25] By learning to regulate powerful feelings, we also enhance our well-being.[26] The success of the relationships we share depends to a great degree on how emotionally intelligent and in control of our feelings we are. If, for example, we can understand and manage our emotions and also be sensitive to others' feelings, then we are better equipped to get along with a broad array of people in diverse contexts.

How well do you read and express feelings in the relationships you share? For example, are you able to tell and react appropriately when a friend, family member, or coworker is feeling happy, grows sad, becomes angry, or experiences jealousy? Can they do the same for you?

THE RANGE OF EMOTIONS

Most of us experience a normal range of emotions. Typically, we reach our highest levels of happiness when we are in a stable, long-lasting, and contented relationship. For example, in a romantic relationship, our contentment usually lasts until something happens, such as when a partner passes away or falls out of love with us, breaking our heart. When this occurs, then happiness's emotional counterpart, sadness, disturbs our happy state.

Because we need both negative and positive emotions, sadness (unless it persists for an extended period of time) is neither a disease nor an emotion to stigmatize or silence. Rather, it is a normal reaction when a hope, dream, or relationship fails.[27] It is, in part, because of sadness that we recognize happiness and vice versa.[28] Suffering through emotional pain can help us appreciate happiness and also can make us more resilient and better able to make choices that are right for us down the line.[29]

We don't all experience or express our emotions in the same way. As Carroll Izard observes, "The joyful person is more apt to see the world through 'rose colored glasses,' the distressed or sad individual is more apt to construe the remarks of others as critical, and the fearful person is inclined only to see the frightening object (tunnel vision)."[30] Our ability to accept another's unique reactions indicates an awareness that their experience and response to an event or situation is separate and distinct from our own.

SKILL BUILDER

The Expression of Angry Feelings

Why are so many people today experiencing intense and frequent angry feelings? Is it because they are modeling the extreme examples of anger regularly displayed and reported in the media? On political talk shows, in blogs, in political columns, we find people engaging in extremely angry, hate-filled tirades. We see them ranting, calling other people names, using derogatory language, and exhibiting very dark behaviors, indicative of an inability to express their anger civilly. What about you? Are you effective at sharing anger civilly even when our technologically oriented culture makes it easy to post an angry and/or hateful message?

1. Identify three instances when you became very angry because of what another person said or did to you. Explain how you addressed the anger in each situation, evaluating your response on a scale from 1 to 5, with 1 being extremely ineffective and 5 being extremely effective. Do you think that you handled your anger as effectively as possible in each situation?

2. When we practice anger management—that is, when we express anger constructively by sharing our angry feelings in an assertive rather than aggressive way—we help to redirect our anger and we also calm ourselves down. Research and identify anger management techniques.

Visit the interactive e-Book to access the Skill Builder feature "More Expression of Angry Feelings," which discusses how anger affects our health and how men and women express anger differently.

PRIMARY AND MIXED EMOTIONS

Psychiatrist Robert Plutchik identifies eight primary emotions: surprise, anger, fear, sadness, disgust, acceptance, anticipation, and joy. He notes, however, that these eight emotions can combine like paint on a canvas to form mixed emotions: remorse (a mixture of disgust and sadness), love (joy and acceptance), awe (fear and surprise), submission (acceptance and fear), disappointment (sadness and surprise), contempt (anger and disgust), optimism (anticipation and joy), and aggressiveness (anger and anticipation).[31]

By developing a greater understanding of the amalgams of emotions we experience—amalgams that sometimes conflict with one another—we can describe our feelings more accurately, develop a keener awareness of their effect on us, and process and respond to them more appropriately.

ARE FEELINGS CATCHING?

Have you ever put on a happy face? What happened? Did you discover that smiling actually made you feel happy? How did your smile affect those around you? Facial expressions by themselves elicit feelings. They are not merely the visible signs of our emotions.[32] Putting on a sad, happy, or frightened face can produce in ourselves and others the feelings that the expression represents.

Moods also are contagious. If you've ever started your day in a great mood, gone to class or work, and then ended up in a bad mood, you may want to consider the possibility that someone gave you that nasty mood. The more empathetic we are, the more susceptible we are to **emotional contagion**—catching another's mood. Empathetic people unconsciously mirror and/or imitate the moods and emotions of others.[33]

ETHICS AND COMMUNICATION

Rx for Emotional Contagion

Emotional Intelligence author Daniel Goleman contends that moods are contagious. In fact, the more emotionally expressive we are, the more likely we are to transmit our mood when communicating with someone else. The transmission of emotion appears to occur both instantaneously and unconsciously.

If we accept this as true, should a person who is experiencing a bout of sadness or a similar depressive emotion be kept isolated from others so as not to "infect" anyone else with the same feelings? Would we be better off if we were exposed only to people who were in good moods? What do you think?

EXPRESSING AND SHARING FEELINGS

From our feelings, we learn about our needs and the state of our relationships.[34] Those of us who share healthy relationships are able to pay direct attention to the emotional reactions that occur. We take time to become aware of the emotions at work by periodically asking ourselves, "What am I feeling?" Once we identify the feeling, our next step is to estimate its strength: "How strong is this feeling?" Next, we ask, "How did I get to feel this way? Where did the feeling come from? How did I contribute?" In our healthy relationships, we report an emotion as we experience it: "I'm getting angry and I'm beginning to say things I really don't mean." Healthy relationships are not comprised totally of positive feelings.

Unfortunately, many of us lack the commitment, courage, and skill we need to express our feelings—particular when they aren't positive—or to allow others to express their feelings to us. Some of us are reluctant to think our feelings through. Instead, we ignore or deny them, keeping them too much in check, until they become unmanageable and we express them ineptly.

EXPRESSION PROBLEMS

Did you know that the majority of people who are fired from their jobs are asked to leave not because of incompetence but because of personality conflicts? Many of our problems with friends, parents, or employers are due to the inability to express or accept messages about feelings. When we sacrifice or disregard feelings, we inevitably create relationship problems.

What can we do to control our feelings so as not to do irreparable harm to a relationship? We have the choice to intervene by doing the following instead of reacting automatically: (a) We can choose to seek out or avoid responding to an emotional scenario. (b) We can take action to ease or modify the difficult circumstance we find ourselves in. (c) We can look elsewhere—to divert our attention and distract ourselves. (d) We can sideline unhealthy feelings by reappraising our response. (e) We can let it out—because regularly suppressing pent-up emotions can take a toll on us.[35]

SUPPRESSING AND DISCLOSING FEELINGS

The way we handle feelings influences a relationship's course and trajectory. In any relational context, we face choices: Do we bury our feelings, express them, or unleash them uncontrollably?

Censoring Feelings

At times, we act as if feelings were the enemy of healthy relationships. They are not. Some of us simply grew up afraid of revealing how we felt, perhaps because important people in our lives expressed sentiments similar to the following:

> "You shouldn't feel depressed by what happened."

> "If you can't tell me you like the way it looks, then don't say anything."

"Don't scream at me! You have no right to be angry with me."

"Why are you such a baby? There's no reason to be scared."

As these examples imply, we often treat feelings and emotions as if they were dangerous, harmful, or shameful. As a result, we censor them and become overly hesitant to express them, fearing that others would perceive us as emotionally volatile or irrational. Instead, we exhibit freely only socially approved feelings.

We present ourselves as the "nice guy." We want others to like us and are willing to pretend to feel what we do not. As we try to protect ourselves from an exchange of feelings, we seek to avoid emotional entanglements, becoming **emotional isolationists** as a result.[36] Emotional isolationists also over-intellectualize every experience in an attempt to render their emotions impotent. These are counter-productive techniques and lead to relationship and health issues.

Display Rules

Unwritten laws, or display rules, guide us in deciding if and when to show our emotions. For instance, when we are young, we may be told not to cry in school, not to yell in front of strangers, or not to kiss on public transportation. As adults, we may be advised not to flirt at office parties, not to show any anger when criticized, or not to be too outspoken in a meeting.

iStock/Geber86

Gender's Effect

When in a relationship, men and women communicate differently. Women expect their friends to be emotionally supportive. They expect them to be understanding, to display empathy, and to engage in self-disclosure.[37] Men, in contrast, base their friendships on engaging in activities together, engaging in friendly competition, and making fewer intimate disclosures.[38]

Although feelings don't discriminate based on gender and although we all are equally capable of expressing emotions of all kinds, society deems it appropriate for men and women to behave differently when it comes to expressing their emotions. For example, only 9% of women report dealing with anger by directly confronting the person they're angry with. Instead they bottle their anger up and play out a "no anger" script.[39]

Gender identity also influences our reactions when someone tears up or cries. Although in many situations, including a loved one's illness or death, crying is accepted as perfectly normal, if you tear up or cry at work, some view it as manipulative or a sign of instability. Again, crying on the job does more damage to a woman's career than a man's.

Culture's Effect

Culture also modifies rules for displaying emotions. For example, in some African societies, people will assume that you are friendly until you prove them wrong. When they smile, it means that they like you. If they don't smile, it means that they distrust you. In contrast, the Japanese often laugh and smile to mask anger, sorrow, or disgust. People belonging to Mediterranean cultures often intensify emotional expression, whereas the British de-intensify or understate theirs.

Personal Values Play Their Part

We also can decide for ourselves under what conditions and with whom we will share freely. You might, for instance, feel it inappropriate to express anger to a parent, but you might readily reveal it to a romantic partner. You might choose not to express your innermost thoughts to a professor or employer, but you might readily do so to a close friend.

Our personal experiences could also lead us to develop a characteristic style of emotional expressiveness. We might become *withholders* and try never to show how we feel, or we might become *revealers* and try always to show how we feel, or we might balance our actions.[40] If we hesitate to put out what we really are, how can others come to know us? Dissembling and concealing feelings can lead to significant stress, adversely affecting our health. When we don't reveal our feelings, we encourage others to continue to behave in ways of which we may disapprove.

Effects of Disclosing Feelings

By honestly revealing feelings, we make it less risky for others to reveal their feelings to us. We demonstrate that we care enough to disclose our feelings so risk taking can be shared. By revealing our feelings, we show others how we want to be treated. It also demonstrates that emotions are acceptable, enabling people to experience the whole person that is their relationship partner. The expression of feelings also gives us opportunities to resolve relationship conflicts more productively, a topic we address next.

EXPERIENCING RELATIONAL CONFLICT

Conflict, or perceived disagreement about views, interests, and goals, is a part of every relationship. Relationship disagreements are normal. Their presence does not signal relationship trouble, but how we manage a conflict is an indicator of our relationship's health. How we disagree—the tone of voice and the words we use, whether we hear each other out fairly—can make all the difference.[41]

SOURCES OF RELATIONAL CONFLICT

How and why does conflict arise? Conflict is a clash of opposing beliefs, opinions, values, needs, assumptions, and goals. It is likely to occur whenever human differences meet. Misunderstandings and anger contribute to conflict arising. We can experience conflict within ourselves and with others.

Self-conflict, also known as **intrapersonal conflict**, occurs when we find ourselves having to choose between two or more mutually exclusive options—two cars, two classes, two potential dates, two activities. **Interpersonal conflict** involves the same type of struggle but between two or more people. It arises because of differences in our perception and interests, perhaps due to a scarcity of resources or rewards, or interpersonal rivalry. When experiencing either intra- or interpersonal conflict, we feel ourselves pulled in different directions.

CATEGORIES OF RELATIONAL CONFLICT

We can categorize conflict in different ways.

Classifying Conflict by Goal

First, we can classify a conflict by the goal or objective around which the conflict revolves. This can be shareable (we both can attain the goal) or one of us can fully possess it (only one of us attains the goal).

Classifying Conflict by Intensity

Second, we can categorize a conflict according to its level of intensity. In a **low-intensity conflict**, we work together to devise an acceptable way to control our communications to permit us to discover a solution that's beneficial to us both. In a **medium-intensity conflict**, we each commit to winning, but winning is seen as sufficient. We feel no need to destroy one another. In a **high-intensity conflict**, one of us intends to destroy or at least seriously hurt the other. Total victory is perceived to be the only option.

Classifying Conflict by Type

Conflicts also can be categorized by their underlying causes. A **pseudo-conflict** is not really a conflict but gives the appearance of one. It occurs when we believe mistakenly that two or more of our goals can't be achieved simultaneously. Pseudo-conflicts frequently revolve around false either–or judgments ("Either I get my way or you get your way") or around simple misunderstandings (failing to realize that you both really agree). A pseudo-conflict is resolved once relational partners realize that no conflict actually exists.

A **content conflict** occurs when relational partners disagree over matters of fact: the accuracy or implications of information, the definition of a term, or the solution to a problem. Once we accept that facts can be verified, inferences tested, definitions checked, and solutions evaluated against criteria, we can settle a content conflict rationally.

A **value conflict** arises when we hold different views on a particular issue, for example, the American welfare system. A person who values individual independence and self-assertiveness will have opinions about public welfare that differ markedly from those of someone who believes that we are responsible for the well-being of others. The realistic outcome of such a conflict would be that we would disagree without becoming disagreeable—that is, we would discuss the issue and learn something from one another, even though we might continue to disagree. We would agree that it's okay to disagree.

An **ego conflict** occurs when we believe that whether we win or lose is a reflection of our self-worth, prestige, or competence. When this happens, the issue itself is no longer important because we each perceive ourselves to be on the line. It becomes nearly impossible for us to deal with the disagreement rationally. Ego conflicts have the greatest potential to destroy a relationship.

Particular conflict-generating behaviors affect each of us differently. It's good to take some time to discover the sources of conflict to which you're most sensitive and how you respond to them. Making such observations helps you understand the types of issues that draw you into disharmony with others and how you are likely to behave in such situations.

Classifying Conflict by Functionality

Of course, we can also categorize conflicts based on whether they are functional (and strengthen a relationship) or dysfunctional (and weaken it). A lot depends on how we manage the conflict. In a functional conflict, we listen to our partner and come to better understand them and their feelings. If, however, we verbally attack our partner, make accusations, behave passive aggressively, communicate contempt, get defensive, or stonewall them, we are harming our relationship.[42]

iStock/PeopleImages

MANAGING RELATIONAL CONFLICT

There are definite benefits to handling a conflict effectively. When we handle a conflict appropriately, we can reduce or even eliminate the probability of a more serious conflict between us in the future. Working to manage the conflict can foster innovation by helping us acquire new ways of looking at things, new ways of thinking, and new behaviors. It also can develop our sense of cohesiveness and togetherness by increasing our closeness and trust. How we approach conflict also provides us with an invaluable opportunity to measure a relationship's strength and viability.[43]

Conflict tests every relationship we share, producing outcomes that range from highly constructive to highly destructive. In healthy relationships, conflict occurs regularly. If we handle a conflict well, it helps us to develop a clearer picture of the other, cementing and strengthening our relationship. If we handle it poorly, however, it will widen schisms, inflict psychological scars, inflame hostilities, and cause lasting resentments.[44]

Crazy-Making Behavior

If we resort to using **crazy-making behaviors**, we use conflict-producing techniques that can figuratively drive a partner crazy. For example, imagine the outcome of the following conversation between a husband and wife after the husband has been waiting for his wife, who arrives very late:

HE: Why are you late?

SHE: I tried to make it on time.

HE:	Yeah. Your mother is never on time either.
SHE:	That's got nothing to do with it.
HE:	The heck it doesn't. You're just as sloppy as she is.
SHE:	You don't say! Who picks your dirty underwear off the floor every morning?
HE:	I happen to go to work. What do you do all day?
SHE:	I'm trying to get along on the money you don't make. That's what I do all day.
HE:	Why should I put myself out for a lazy ingrate like you?

This exchange between the two illustrates a technique called "gunnysacking," in which the user saves all of his or her complaints, as though stuffing them into a gunnysack, and then makes a mess of things by emptying the sack during a heated moment, allowing an abundance of complaints to cascade out. Such a technique precipitates the exchange of insults.

Other crazy-making options include "guiltmaking" (one party makes the other responsible for causing pain) and "beltlining" (making comments that "hit below the belt," such as bringing up a person's unattractiveness or perceived lack of intelligence).

Effective Conflict Management

Instead of resorting to crazy-making behavior, when a conflict arises, follow these guidelines:

1. Be specific when you introduce a complaint.

2. Ask for change that will make things better.

3. Be tolerant of your partner.

4. Attack the issue, not the person.

5. Think about what you have to say before you say it.[45]

Managing relational conflict is a skill. We manage a conflict skillfully when we don't deny its existence but engage each other in a dialogue. We manage it skillfully when, instead of criticizing or attacking the other's behavior, we speak respectfully in language absent of threats. We manage it skillfully when we converse to be understood, not to win. You may have your perspective and another person may have his or her perspective, but there likely are other perspectives as well. For a description of how to resolve conflict, see Figure 8.3.

> Visit the interactive e-Book to access the Skill Builder feature "Assessing My Conflict-Handling Abilities," which will help you determine the best strategies for de-escalating a conflict.

FIGURE 8.3
You Say You Want a Resolution

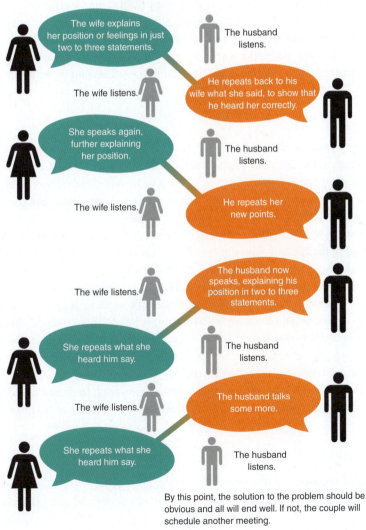

You Say You Want a Resolution
HOW TO TALK YOUR WAY TO A HEALTHIER AND HAPPIER CONCLUSION TO CONFLICT

Call a 'couple's meeting'. Agree to talk without looking for a solution.
Set a time limit of 15 minutes.

Flip a coin to see who speaks first—only one person at a time. (In our scenario, the wife wins the toss.)

The wife explains her position or feelings in just two to three statements.

The husband listens.

The wife listens.

He repeats back to his wife what she said, to show that he heard her correctly.

She speaks again, further explaining her position.

The husband listens.

The wife listens.

He repeats her new points.

The wife listens.

The husband now speaks, explaining his position in two to three statements.

She repeats what she heard him say.

The husband listens.

The wife listens.

The husband talks some more.

She repeats what she heard him say.

The husband listens.

By this point, the solution to the problem should be obvious and all will end well. If not, the couple will schedule another meeting.

CONFLICT RESOLUTION STYLES

Our emotions and how we handle them, together with our preferred style of approaching conflict, can make or break a relationship. The three primary styles of handling emotionally charged or conflict-producing situations are nonassertively, aggressively, or assertively. Which do you tend to use most frequently, and how is it working for you?

Nonassertiveness

Have you ever felt afraid to let others know how you felt when facing a potential conflict, especially one in which you perceived yourself to be treated unfairly? Perhaps you felt intimidated by the other person and hesitated to express your feelings honestly. If you have done this, then you know what it is to behave nonassertively. When exhibiting **nonassertiveness**, we keep our real feelings bottled up. We function much like a weathervane, changing direction to preserve the peace. We become an echo of the feelings expressed by those around us rather than giving voice to ours. Unfortunately, either because they are lazy, apathetic, shy, or fearful, nonassertive people rarely take the steps needed to improve their relationships. As a result, they often end up with something they don't want.

Aggressiveness

In contrast to nonassertive people, who let others victimize them, people who display **aggressiveness** insist on standing up for their points of view and what they want by ignoring and violating the rights of others. Although some of us deliberately defy a bully, in general, aggressive people manage to have more of their needs and wants met than do nonassertive people. Unfortunately, this is often at another's expense.

In a relationship, an aggressor aims to dominate and win; breaking even is not enough. The message of the aggressive person is selfish: "This is how I see it. If you see it differently, you're stupid. This is what I want. What you want doesn't count or matter to me." Because the aggressive person begins by attacking, he or she often escalates conflict.

Why do people act aggressively? Sometimes it's because they feel vulnerable and attempt to protect themselves from feeling powerless. Other times it's because being aggressive is the only way they think they get their ideas and feelings across to another person. They may never have learned to handle their aggressive impulses, or a pattern of past nonassertion may have led to their feeling hurt, disappointed, or bewildered. They may be experiencing a sense of personal violation from their past nonassertion that now has risen to the boiling point. Damaged or destroyed relationships often result from aggression.[46]

Assertiveness

The intent of nonassertive behavior is to avoid conflict of any kind. The intent of aggressive behavior is to dominate. By contrast, the intent of assertive behavior is to communicate honestly, clearly, and directly and to support your beliefs and ideas without harming others or allowing yourself to be harmed.

When we display ==assertiveness==, we protect ourselves from being victimized during conflict. We meet more of our interpersonal needs, make more decisions about our own life, and say what we believe. As a result, we are able to work through conflict and establish closer relationships without infringing on the rights of other people.

Assertive people know how to stop themselves from sending inappropriate nonassertive or aggressively charged messages. This involves saying "no," "yes," "I like," and "I think." The focus of assertiveness is negotiation. The aim is to find mutually satisfying solutions to relationship issues. This involves attending to feelings and using very specific verbal and nonverbal skills to alleviate interpersonal problems.

Use a DESC Script[47]

By using a ==DESC script== (DESC stands for describe, express, specify, and consequences), we facilitate self-assertion when in conflict. A script assumes characters (you and another

> Visit the interactive e-Book to access the Skill Builder features "Assessing My Verbal Aggressiveness and Future Me," which will help you assess the ways in which verbal aggressiveness manifests itself in you and others, and "Assessing Past Conflict-Producing Situations and Future Me," which will help you determine your areas of internal conflict.

person), a plot (an event or situation that has left you at a disadvantage), a setting (the time and place of your interaction), and a message (verbal and nonverbal).[48]

Begin the script by *describing* as specifically and objectively as possible, the behavior of the other person that troubles you or makes you feel uncomfortable. The act of identification helps you handle it better. Use simple, concrete, specific, and unbiased language to describe the other's actions. For example, instead of saying, "You're always overcharging me, you dirty cheat!" try "I was told the repairs would cost $100 and now I'm being charged $150." Instead of guessing at motives by saying, "You resent me and wish you were with Lisa," say, "The last two times we've gone out to eat with Jack and Lisa, you've criticized me in front of them."

Once you write a direct description of the behavior bothering you, add a few sentences *expressing* how you feel and what you think about the behavior. This requires you to get in touch with your emotions and to use personal statements, making it clear that you're referring to what you are feeling and thinking. The distinguishing feature of a personal statement is a pronoun such as *I, me,* or *my;* for example, "I feel," "My feelings," and "It appears to me."

There are a number of ways you can express your feelings. You can name a feeling: "I feel disappointed." You can use comparisons: "I feel like used gum." Or you can indicate the type of behavior prompted by your feelings: "I feel like leaving the room."

Once you have described the troubling behavior and expressed your feelings or thoughts, *specify* different behavior you would like substituted. For example, "Please stop playing the drums after midnight." Finally, note possible *consequences*—positive and negative—in terms of your own and the other person's behavior.

GENDER, CULTURE, AND CONFLICT

When people of different gender identities and cultures communicate, they carry their assumptions, beliefs, and perceptions with them into their relationships. This often leads to their approaching conflict in diverse ways.

Gender and Conflict

From childhood on, men generally are taught to be more competitive and aggressive, whereas women are encouraged to exhibit more cooperative behaviors. Men, more concerned with power, tend to make demands—frequently without providing rationales. Women, being more concerned with relationship maintenance, tend to make proposals, often supplying reasons for their suggestions.

Sexual orientation similarly plays a role in conflict management. Gay men and lesbians tend to be nicer than straight people during intimate relationship conflicts. Less fearful, belligerent, and domineering, they also are more apt to use humor to diffuse conflict.[49] Gay men, however, have more difficulty than lesbians and heterosexuals making up or repairing their relationships after a conflict ends.[50]

No matter your sexual orientation, conflict will affect your relationships. For example, if one of the parties to a conflict engages while the other withdraws, both are likely to be left feeling unhappy. Negative marital interactions, including name calling and disdain-signaling nonverbal cues such as eye rolling, have an adverse effect on participants' health, especially the health of women. In fact, how often women are the target of eye rolls can predict how often they need to go to the doctor.[51]

Culture and Conflict

Different cultures socialize their members to behave differently when facing conflict. Members of individualistic cultures, such as the United States, tend to display a direct approach, emanating from their belief that individuals have a right to defend themselves. Members of collectivistic cultures, in contrast, often find such behavior rude, believing instead that harmony, restraint, and nonconfrontation are paramount.[52] Thus, hesitant to refuse a request directly, members of a collectivistic culture might say, "Let me think about that" instead of "No." When evaluating a conflict, Americans tend to see one side as right and the other as wrong; Chinese are more apt to see the validity of both sides. Members of collectivist cultures are less likely to express their disagreement overtly and tend not to engage in or condone personal attacks on one another. Rather, they display their respect by not saying what they think if it might hurt others.[53]

Similarly, maintaining calmness during conflict is characteristic of some cultures but not others. For example, in African and Arab cultures, conflict is characterized by the expression of intense emotions. Because they value emotional expressiveness, they do not restrain their passion. If they did, others might judge them insincere or unconcerned. In contrast, among Caucasian Americans, rationality and calmness are preferred.[54]

By becoming sensitive to such differences and recognizing the assumptions on which they're based, we can approach conflict more sensitively.

TECHNOLOGY, RELATIONSHIPS, AND THE COMMUNICATION OF EMOTION

Two points of view: (1) Social media is life. (2) Social media destroys life.[55] Do you ascribe to either? If not, what statement summarizes your relationship with social media?

EFFECTS ON SELF-EXPRESSION

The Internet is making seismic changes in how we express ourselves and share our feelings. It has extended our relationships' reach far beyond what it was before the social media age. It is the ultimate *noncontact* person-to-person network. Online social networking sites let us "get out" and socialize or "make friends" with those we hardly know by encouraging us to declare our friendships on the basis of the flimsiest of connections. Despite this, we talk with one another very casually and with a familiarity incongruous with the weakness of the ties between us.[56] When online, it is easy to spend more time with people who think like us and less time with those who think differently. It lets us create echo chambers of affirmations.[57]

EGO EFFECTS

Online, we are able to sustain our egos by acting like micro-celebrities collecting fans of choice.[58] Longing to be liked and constantly aware that others are watching us, we style our selfies hoping to create a meme, share thoughts about sex, and obsess over popularity and looks, always working on touching up the self we present to others. We become the masters of our social circles. We get to decide again and again whether to accept or reject someone as a friend.

Friendship decisions in the physical world rarely are so direct. Often, because we don't want to come off as rude, we end up accepting friend requests online.[59] In terms of "online presence," quantity of contacts can count more than the quality of our contacts. Social media gamify the idea of friendship as we compete for likes.[60] Professional athletes tend to be judged based on their stats. Has it become the same for us?

Research shows that liking other people's status updates and photos can contribute to our liking ourselves less.[61] On average, we keep in touch with about 120 to 150 people via social networking. Despite having an inflated sense of connection, people who seek excessive connectivity actually tend to be lonelier than those who don't go overboard.[62]

ETHICS AND COMMUNICATION

Computing Relationship Stats[63]

Baseball players earn a batting average, which reflects how often they get a hit versus strike out. What if those with whom you shared important social and professional relationships were able to award you and publish your relationship batting average? Your boss, for example, might report that you began strong with a .500 average but have become complacent and have now trailed off to a middling .245. What if your family reported that you scored .125 in your ability to rebound from relationship letdowns? And what if you could do the same for them?

What are the ethical implications of treating people in this way? In what ways does reducing relationships to statistical averages trivialize them? And if someone's average got too low, for example, would we be right to jettison her or him from our relationship line-up? In what ways is this akin to counting Facebook likes?

TUNED INTO FEELINGS

Might the machines we're creating contribute to our de-emphasizing the importance of genuine friendship?[64] In part to combat feelings of loneliness and engender connection, online and smartphone apps are tuning into our feelings. We exchange messages with virtual assistants like Siri and Alexa. Introduced in the last decade, these assistants have a hold on us. They can recall details from our earlier exchanges with them and have been engineered to demonstrate their interest in us by asking us how we're feeling. They are programmed with a database of responses to follow up on ours. When we talk with them we reveal information about our daily routines and preferences.[65] The idea of friending a computer and sharing your feelings with it strikes some as problematic.

GET REAL

Many people are fans of Snapchat because on it they are able to reveal how they really look and feel. They can be transparent, share unbecoming photos, and be negative—primarily because the messages are being shared with smaller, more intimate groups of people and are short-lived. Snapchat's messages disappear after being viewed.

In contrast, using psychology and data mining, start-up companies like Emotient, Eyeris, and Affectiva are building algorithms to analyze people's faces and discover their deepest feelings. Using such technology, a person might be able to determine if her or his partner was lying.[66] How would you feel if your emotions were revealed without your consent?

DRAWBACKS AND CONSEQUENCES

Not all online or digital relationships are pleasant. There are drawbacks too. When online or texting, it's easy to respond without considering the consequences of our words and actions.

Most of the personal threats targeted at us today come to us via social media or texts, rather than being delivered in person.[67] Sexting is prevalent. People circulate images of genitalia—often without permission. An increasing number of online interactions produce conflict, with people hurling insults at one another, engaging in cyberbullying, or demonstrating their verbal aggression by daring others to say things they'd never say face-to-face. A 2017 study conducted by the Cyberbullying Research Center found that 70% of the 5,600 students surveyed said that rumors had been spread about them online.[68] When critiques and feedback are delivered online, they are not sugarcoated.

As we can do in the physical world, when attacked or criticized online, we can choose to withdraw or reply. What do you usually do?

COMMUNICTION SKILLS
Practice Handling Feelings Effectively

Many of us have trouble expressing our feelings. Either we behave nonassertively and keep our emotions too much in check, or we behave aggressively and become excessively demanding or belligerent.

It is unfortunate that few of us are taught to reveal our emotions in ways that will help our relationships. The key to using our feelings to promote effective relationships is to express them effectively, including when involved in conflict. The following advice can help you communicate feelings in positive ways that enrich the quality of your relationships.

Face the difficulties you have expressing or handling feelings.

By now you should have a good idea of what feelings you have trouble expressing or responding to. Now is the time to concentrate on expressing and responding to them when they arise. A first step is to reveal to others the feelings that cause problems for you.

When involved in a disagreement, stand up for your emotional rights.

When we sacrifice our rights, we teach others to take advantage of us. When we demand rights that are not ours, we take advantage of others. Not revealing your feelings and thoughts to others can be just as damaging as disregarding the feelings and thoughts of others.

Check your perceptions.

What about the other person's feelings? Sometimes our interpretations of the feelings of another are determined by our own. Checking your perceptions requires that you express your assessment of the other's feelings in a tentative manner. Sample perception checks include "Were you surprised at what Beckham said to you?" "I get the feeling that what I said annoyed you. Am I right?" and "I'm not certain if your behavior means you're confused or embarrassed."

(Continued)

(Continued)

Show respect for feelings.

Don't try to persuade yourself or others to deny honest feelings. Comments like "Don't feel that way," "Calm down," and "Don't cry over spilled milk" communicate that you believe the other person has no right to a particular feeling. Feelings are potentially informative and constructive, and should not be denied or treated as if they were destructive.

If you respond inappropriately, be willing to apologize.

Apologies, when genuine, work wonders, diffusing tension and hostility and restoring good will. When apologizing, begin by taking responsibility for your behavior and identifying what you said or did wrong. Acknowledge how what you said or did must have affected the other person's feelings. Explain how you have responded differently by acknowledging one or more alternative ways of behaving. Express your sorrow and regret. Correct your behavior. End by asking for forgiveness.

Practice basic assertive behaviors.

Practice the following assertive responses:

1. Substitute declarative statements in place of requests for permission. Instead of saying "Do you mind if I . . ." say, "I'd like to . . . ."

2. Show others that you have the confidence to look them in the eye.

3. Instead of looking down or to the side (cues that signal uncertainty or insecurity), look into the eyes of the other person.

4. Talk slowly and deliberately; doing otherwise can give the impression that you lack self-assurance or are unprepared.

5. State whether or not you concur with another person clearly.

6. Say "no" calmly, firmly, and quietly. Say "yes" sincerely and directly. Say "I want" without fear or guilt.

> **If you want to change the way people respond to you, change the way you respond to people.**
>
> Timothy Leary

COMPLETE THIS CHAPTER 8 CHECKLIST

8.1 I can explain five factors contributing to relationship interest. ☐

Among the factors contributing to our establishing relationships with some people but not others are attractiveness (we favor people who are physically attractive and who have pleasing personalities), proximity (we are more apt to interact with those whom we live near or work with), reinforcement (we like being around people who reward us), similarity (we enjoy being with people whose attitudes and interests are similar to ours), and complementarity (we sometimes find ourselves attracted to people dissimilar to us).

8.2 I can discuss how uncertainty reduction and relational predictability impact a relationship's success. ☐

Because we prefer the known to the unknown, we take pains to reduce our uncertainty or lack of knowledge about others. Based on what we discover, we make predictions over whether a relationship will succeed.

8.3 I can identify and distinguish among the following kinds of relationships: acquaintanceships, friendship, and romantic, family, and work relationships. ☐

Although interaction with acquaintances is usually limited in scope and quality,

some do develop into friendships. As friendships become closer, relationship breadth and depth are enhanced. The expectation of permanence distinguishes romantic relationships from other kinds of relationships. We play roles in both family and work relationships. In families that practice healthy communication, family members pull together to preserve the family unit. Members of an organization who are "team players" recognize their interdependence with others.

8.4 I can define emotional intelligence and discuss its relationship effects. ☐

Emotional intelligence, the ability we have to motivate ourselves, control our impulses, recognize and regulate our moods, empathize, and hope, determines how effective we are at handling feelings in our relationships.

8.5 I can describe the importance of expressing our feelings in a relationship. ☐

When we censor or fail to disclose our feelings, our interactions can become shallow and unfulfilling. By expressing feelings honestly and clearly rather than concealing them or uncontrollably unleashing them, together with perceiving the impact of personal preferences, gender, and culture on how we approach conflict and handle feelings, we take steps toward developing relationships that are healthier.

8.6 I can define *relational conflict* and identify techniques to manage it. ☐

We can classify conflict as intrapersonal or interpersonal, and as pseudo, content, value, or ego based. There are three ways of expressing feelings in emotionally charged or conflict-laden situations: assertively (we express our feelings and thoughts honestly without infringing on others' rights), nonassertively (we fail to express our actual feelings), and aggressively (we stand up for our rights while ignoring or violating others' rights). Managing conflict constructively takes skill.

8.7 I understand technology's influence on the quantity and quality of our relationships. ☐

Cyberspace has expanded the number of relationships we are capable of developing while at the same time diverting our attention from individuals in the physical world. It also offers a platform for the expression of incivility and bullying.

8.8 I can apply my skills to better handle feelings and conflict in my relationships. ☐

A relationship devoid of conflict is not a genuine relationship. Working on how to handle feelings and standing up for our emotional rights as we work to manage relational conflict are key.

BECOME A WORD MASTER

acquaintanceships 200

aggressiveness 216

assertiveness 217

complementarity 199

conflict 211

content conflict 212

crazy-making behaviors 213

DESC script 217

ego conflict 213

emotional contagion 208

emotional intelligence 206

emotional isolationists 210

friendly relations 201

friendships 200

high-intensity conflict 212

interpersonal conflict 212

intrapersonal conflict 212

low-intensity conflict 212

medium-intensity conflict 212

moving toward friendship 201

nascent friendship 201

nonassertiveness 216

pseudo-conflict 212

role-limited interaction 201

stabilized friendship 201

toxic communication 203

value conflict 212

waning friendship 201

Jacob Lund/Shutterstock.com

iStock/Jacob Ammentorp Lund

9

Teamwork: Strategies for Decision Making and Problem Solving

9.1 Define a *group*, distinguishing a *team*
as a special kind of group.

9.2 Identify the characteristics and
components of groups.

9.3 Describe the advantages and
disadvantages of using a group to make
decisions and solve problems.

9.4 Distinguish among task, maintenance,
and self-serving group roles.

9.5 Compare and contrast cooperative
and competitive goal structures and
defensive and supportive behaviors.

9.6 Describe the means groups use to
achieve their goals, including decision-
making methods, reflective thinking, and brainstorming.

9.7 Explain how gender, culture, and technology affect group interaction.

9.8 Apply skills for improving group effectiveness.

Most of the decisions that affect our lives are not made by individuals, but by small groups of people in executive boardrooms, faculty meetings, town councils, dormitory rooms, kitchens, locker rooms and a host of other meeting places.

Arthur Jensen

Have you ever been part of a group composed of members whom you perceived to be difficult to work with? Might some of the group's members have behaved in ways that undermined your group's ability to function?

A number of television programs—such as *The Celebrity Apprentice*, *Big Brother*, *VEEP*, and *Silicon Valley*—are built on the premise that group members have difficulty working together. In these shows, we regularly find cast members undermining the people with whom they work. We laugh at and make fun of them, but when we find ourselves part of real-world groups, this sort of behavior is no laughing matter.

How a group's members interact with one another affects not only the group's success but also whether we want to stay in or leave the group. The goal is to learn how to make working in groups work for us. When it comes to your future, the ability to work in groups and teams is one of the most important communication skills

to master.[1] Global organizations need people skilled in teamwork and able to work together to innovate, solve problems, and make decisions. In fact, many contemporary organizations are emphasizing team building as the key to improving the functioning, satisfaction, and productivity of work-group members.[2] Teamwork and the ability to collaborate with others are valued abilities on the open market.[3] ◼

GROUPS, TEAMS, AND YOU

How important are groups and teams in your life? Try to visualize what your personal and professional life would be like if you belonged neither to groups nor teams. What would you miss?

We have spent, and will continue to spend, a great deal of time in groups. A large part of our socialization (i.e., our adaptation to society), for example, occurs in groups,

especially our family group. Much of our leisure time is spent in the company of groups, particularly our group of friends and/or team members if we're on a sports team. If we attend religious services regularly, we become part of that group. If we belong to Weight Watchers, Alcoholics Anonymous, or a study group, we are in a support group. If we serve on a jury, we are part of a decision-making group. If we participate in student government, we are part of a policy-making group. As a class member, we also belong to a group. Thus, from our earliest days, we have been members of a multitude of groups.

Many of the groups we belong to, such as the group of friends we meet for dinner once a week or the sports team members we scrimmage with, are social. Others are more formally organized, such as the Parent-Teacher Association. Some, such as the Rotary Club, serve both public and private purposes. Others exist primarily to meet the needs of the organization for which we work. Thus, groups provide much of the social fabric of our lives but are also the basic building blocks of organizations. In fact, when it comes to the world of work, team management is fast becoming the norm.

FIGURE 9.1
Key Dimensions of Teams

Nominal Team		Real Team
Functional Group	**Identification**	Team
Independence	**Interdependence**	Interdependence
High	**Power Differentiation**	Low
Distant	**Social Distance**	Close
Forcing, Accommodating, Avoiding	**Conflict Management Tactics**	Confronting, Collaborating
Win-Lose	**Negotiation Process**	Win-Win

DIFFERENTIATING GROUPS AND TEAMS

A **group** is a collection of people who interact verbally and nonverbally, occupy certain roles with respect to one another, and cooperate to accomplish defined goals.

A **team** is a type of group composed of people with a strong sense of their collective identity acting collaboratively. The members of a team agree on their need for each other to accomplish their goals. Unlike other groups, teams by definition are composed of people who have *diverse skills* and bring *different resources* to a problem or task. Teams depend on members' pooling their abilities, knowledge, and insights to solve problems and make better decisions than any single individual on the team acting alone.

All teams are groups. However, because not every group has members contributing specialized knowledge or different resources, not every group is a team.[4] See Figure 9.1 for a look at the differences in behavior the members of nominal (in name only) and real (functioning) teams exhibit.

THE BENEFITS OF GROUPS AND TEAMWORK

We profit from working together in groups, including teams. Research suggests that teamwork often is its own reward. Investigators note that just as eating dessert and making good money cause many of us to experience delight, so does cooperating with each other to achieve a goal. Using magnetic resonance

wavebreakmedia/Shutterstock.com

imaging (MRI) to examine brain activity, researchers have shown that humans experience pleasure when they choose to forgo immediate personal gain and opt instead to cooperate with others for the long-term common good.[5]

THE PREVALENCE OF GROUPS AND TEAMWORK

Over two thirds of U.S. companies use formal work teams to accomplish their objectives.[6] Employees now participate in more groups and teams and attend more meetings than ever before. It is commonplace for committees of employees to make the kinds of decisions that "dictatorial" executives once handled. **Self-directed teams**, for instance, are autonomous groups in which employees possessing an array of skills and talents work together, empowered to make decisions and even supervise themselves. Among the major companies championing such approaches are Xerox, Proctor and Gamble, and General Electric.[7] Do you feel prepared to become a part of such groups?

CHARARACTERISTICS AND COMPONENTS OF GROUPS

Identifying the characteristics that groups have in common will help you understand how to function more effectively when part of one. Although social groups are important, in these chapters we focus on the work-related decision-making/problem-solving group, also called the *task group*.

GROUP MEMBERSHIP

The members of a group recognize the other individuals who are part of the group, have certain kinds of attitudes toward these people, and obtain some degree of satisfaction from belonging to or participating in the group with them. They acknowledge the do's and don'ts of group life—the norms that specify and regulate the behavior expected of the group's members. Furthermore, communication within a group involves more than the casual banter that occurs between strangers at bus stops or in department stores.

GROUP SIZE

What is the optimal size for a group? In task-oriented groups, it is the smallest number of people capable of handling the assigned task.[8] The larger the group is, the more difficult it becomes to schedule meetings, share information, and equalize opportunities for participation.

Most group theorists and practitioners set the lower limit of group size at three members. For most tasks, groups of five to seven people work best. Such a group enables members to communicate directly with each other as they work on a common task or goal, such as solving problems, exchanging information, or improving personal relationships.

GROUP GOALS, STRUCTURE, AND CLIMATE

Every group establishes its own **group goals** (the end state desired), **group structure** (member positions and roles), **group patterns of communication** (patterns of message flow), **group norms** (informal rules for interaction), and **group climate** (emotional atmosphere).

Every participant in the group typically has a stake in the outcome of the group, develops relationships with the other members of the group, and assumes roles and relationships relating to the group's task(s) that either foster or impede the group's effectiveness. Thus, the members' styles of interaction have an impact on the kind of atmosphere, or climate, that develops in the group. Conversely, the climate affects what members say to each other and how they say it. Have you ever belonged to a group with a "hot" climate—one in which members were intolerant of each other and tempers flared? Have you ever belonged to a group that had too "cold" a climate—in which members were aloof, sarcastic, unconcerned about hurting one another's feelings, or too self-centered to notice that the needs of others were not being adequately met?

A group's climate tends to persist. If the group's climate is cold, closed, mistrustful, or uncooperative, individual members frequently react in ways that perpetuate those characteristics. In contrast, if the group's climate is warm, open, trusting, and cooperative, members usually react in ways that reinforce those characteristics. In the book *Communication Within the Organization*, Charles Redding suggests that an effective climate is composed of the following five characteristics: (1) supportiveness, (2) participative decision making, (3) trust among group members, (4) openness and candor, and (5) high performance goals.[9] The healthier the group climate is, the more cohesive the group will be.

Group climate affects group norms—the explicit and implicit rules that members internalize concerning behavior in the group. In some groups, members exhibit certain behaviors that they would dare not exhibit in others. For example, do you belong to any groups in which you feel free to ask a question that might be considered "dumb," interrupt someone who is talking, express disagreement with another member, openly express support for an unpopular position, point out that someone is not making sense, offer a comment unrelated to the topic, or simply not attend a meeting? In some groups, interaction is formal and stuffy; in others, it is informal and relaxed. Groups invariably create standards that they expect members to live up to. In this way, a group is able to foster a certain degree of uniformity.

Characteristics of Effective Groups

In Chapter 10 we take a closer look at leadership behaviors and the development and resolution of problems that develop in groups. For now, let us recognize that certain attributes facilitate the group process, whereas others work against it. Douglas McGregor, a recognized expert in organizational communication, summarized the characteristics of an effective and well-functioning group as follows:

1. The group's atmosphere tends to be informal, comfortable, and relaxed.

2. Members engage in a lot of discussion with virtually everyone participating; the group's discussion is relevant to the group's task.

3. Members accept and understand the group's task or objective. After a period of free discussion, members are able to commit themselves to it.

4. The members listen to each other. Every idea is given a hearing. Unafraid of appearing foolish, members offer a creative idea even if it seems somewhat odd.

5. Disagreement is allowed rather than being suppressed or overridden by premature action. The reasons for disagreeing are diligently explored, with the group seeking to resolve disagreements rather than overpowering or diminishing the value of dissenters.

6. Most decisions are made by consensus in which it is apparent that everyone generally agrees and is willing to support the decision. Formal voting is discouraged; the group does not accept a simple majority as a proper basis for action.

7. Criticism is encouraged and accepted. Members do not personally attack one another.

8. Feelings are expressed freely with members sharing ideas about the problem and how the group is functioning.

9. When action is taken, clear assignments are made and accepted.

10. The chairperson of the group functions as a group member so that the group's leadership is able to shift from person to person, without any one person dominating the group. There is little evidence of a struggle for power as the group operates. The issue is not who is in control but how to get the job done.

11. The group is self-conscious of its own operation.[10]

THE DYNAMICS OF GROUP DEVELOPMENT

Once a group is in place, its development occurs in stages. According to researchers, the five key stages that a group moves through during its life are forming, storming, norming, performing, and adjourning (Figure 9.2).[11]

Forming

iStock/mapodile

On joining a new group, we may experience some initial confusion or uncertainty. We are unsure about how to behave or interact with others and unclear about the roles that we will have in the group. We need to figure out who is in charge and why we were brought together. Thus, in the *forming stage* of a group, our primary objective is to fit in and be perceived as likable. We also make an effort to find out about other group members and the group's task. Once we feel valued and accepted, we begin to identify with the group.

Storming

Invariably, members experience some conflict as they determine how to work together. Typically, groups experience both task and relational conflicts. During the *storming stage*, the group's members experience tension that results from members' disagreeing and/or struggling to exert leadership as they work to clarify both the goals and the roles members will have in the life of the group. During this stage, rather than being concerned with fitting in, members now focus on expressing their ideas and opinions and securing their place in the group power structure.

FIGURE 9.2
Stages of Group Development

Adjourning

Performing

Norming

Storming

Forming

Norming

Over time, a clear group structure emerges. Members firm up roles, and a leader or leaders emerge. During the *norming stage*, the group solidifies its behavioral norms, especially those relating to conflict management. In addition, the group forms a sense of identity as member awareness of interdependence and the need to cooperate with each other increases.

Performing

The emphasis of the group next switches to task accomplishment. During the *performing stage*, often considered the most important phase, members combine their skills, knowledge, and abilities to overcome obstacles and realize the group's goals.

Adjourning

Finally, during the *adjourning stage*, members review and reflect on their accomplishments or failures and determine how or whether to end the group and the relationships that have developed during the group's existence. Ending a group can involve having a celebration or simply saying good-bye to each other or it can be more complicated and prolonged, with some groups opting to continue working together on a new or different task, and some members choosing to continue relationships that developed during the group's life.[12]

iStock/skynesher

How a group develops through each of these stages determines how effectively it is able to function.

USING GROUPS TO MAKE DECISIONS AND SOLVE PROBLEMS

We form small groups to share information, to solve common problems, and to make decisions about achieving identified common goals. But why do almost half of us think that meeting as a group is waste of time (Figure 9.3)? For those who think this way, the disadvantages of meeting in groups outweigh the advantages. To be sure, group meetings can be frustrating to the person who enjoys working alone and making decisions independently. However, when we work together effectively, groups can facilitate problem solving and be rewarding.

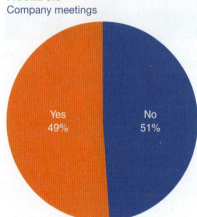

FIGURE 9.3
Company meetings

Yes 49%

No 51%

ADVANTAGES OF THE SMALL GROUP

In many ways, using a group to solve a complex problem is more logical than relying on one individual. Group problem solving offers a number of important advantages.

Pooling Resources

Groups permit a variety of people with different information and points of view to contribute to the problem-solving/decision-making process. That is, a small group facilitates the pooling of resources. The broader the array of knowledge that is brought to bear on any problem, the more likely it is that an effective solution will be found.

Motivation Enhancement

Participating in a group also apparently increases individual motivation. Group efforts lead to greater commitment to finding a solution and to greater commitment to that solution's implementation.

Error Elimination

Group functioning makes it easier to identify other people's mistakes and to filter out errors before they become costly or damaging. Groups are better equipped than individuals to foresee difficulties, detect weaknesses, visualize consequences, and explore possibilities. As a result, they tend to produce superior decisions and solutions.

Better Received Decisions

The decisions or solutions of a group tend to be better received than those of an individual. As the saying goes, "There is strength in numbers!" The person or people to whom a group solution is reported will tend to respect the fact that a number of people working together came to one conclusion.

More Pleasant Experience

Working as part of a group is generally more pleasant and fulfilling than working alone. The group provides companionship, a chance to affirm ideas and feelings, and an opportunity for self-confirmation. It is rewarding to have our thoughts and concerns accepted by others (Table 9.1).

DISADVANTAGES OF THE SMALL GROUP

Despite these advantages, group work may have drawbacks.

Shirking of Responsibility

When we are working with a number of other people, it sometimes becomes very tempting to let someone else handle the duties and responsibilities. A lazy group member can maintain a low profile and simply coast along on the efforts of others.

Goal Conflicts

Personal goals sometimes conflict with group goals. As a result, people may try to use the group to achieve self-oriented objectives that could interfere with or even sabotage the achievement of group objectives.

Decision Domination

The decision-making/problem-solving process may be dominated by a few forceful, persistent group members who do not take the time to ensure that all members in the group have a chance to speak and be heard. Actual or perceived status plays a part here. Group members may be hesitant to criticize the comments of high-status people, and low-status people may be reluctant to participate at all. Consequently, position and power can affect whether ideas are offered, listened to, or incorporated into group decisions.

TABLE 9.1   WHY USE TEAMWORK?

ADVANTAGES	DISADVANTAGES
Various resources can be pooled.	Laziness is encouraged.
Motivation and commitment are increased.	Personal goals may conflict with group goals.
Errors are easier to identify.	A few high-status members may dominate.
Decisions are better received.	Stubbornness leads to deadlock.
Rewards of working with others are provided.	Riskier decisions are made.
	Reaching a decision takes longer.

Refusal to Compromise

Certain people who are set on having their ideas, and only their ideas, accepted may be unwilling to compromise. When this happens, the group decision-making machinery breaks down, and frequently no solution can be agreed on. In other words, the group becomes deadlocked.

The Risky Shift

The decisions reached and the actions taken after group discussion are often riskier than the decisions any one individual would have made or the actions that any one individual would have taken. The knowledge that blame will be shared, in the case of a bad outcome, makes people more willing to take a chance on a longshot. This phenomenon is known as a *risky shift*.

It Takes Longer

It often takes longer to reach a group solution than an individual decision. In business and industry, where time is frequently equated with money, the group can be a costly tool. (See Table 9.1 for a summary of these drawbacks.)

ETHICS AND COMMUNICATION

Golden Rules of Decision Making

We often talk about the need to act ethically when making a decision, but our behavior does not always reflect our words. For example, investigate the behavior and events that contributed to the nation's financial crisis in 2008, the rise of White nationalist movements, or another movement or event of your own choosing that you believe involved a series of ethical challenges. Based on what you discover, why do you imagine that some question whether people in organizations or government know how to make ethical decisions?

What about yourself—do you know how to make an ethical decision? First, describe the ethical guidelines or golden rules that you believe should guide group decision making. Then, think of a recent decision you made in collaboration with others and evaluate it in light of your guidelines and these questions.

1. Would I be happy if this decision were made public?
2. What if everyone did this?
3. How would I feel if someone did this to me?
4. Will a good result come from my actions?
5. Will the action reflect positively on my character or my organization's character?
6. Is the action consistent with my values and principles?

WHEN TO USE A GROUP FOR DECISION MAKING AND PROBLEM SOLVING

In view of these pros and cons, we ask: When does it make sense to use a group? At what point do the advantages outweigh the possible disadvantages?

Experience suggests that we use a group rather than an individual to make decisions and solve problems if the answer to most of the following questions is *yes*:

1. Is the problem to be solved complex rather than simple?
2. Does the problem have many parts or facets?
3. Would any one person be unlikely to possess all the information needed to solve the problem?
4. Would it be advisable to divide the responsibility for problem solving?
5. Are many potential solutions desired, rather than just one?
6. Would an examination of diverse attitudes be helpful?
7. Are group members more likely to engage in task-related than non-task related behavior?

In these complex times, it often makes sense for individuals of varied expertise to pool their knowledge and insights to solve problems. Group efforts become futile if all the members pool is ignorance and obstinacy. The more information the members can gather and share, the more likely they are to rid themselves of bias and, in turn, the more objective their work becomes.[13]

UNDERSTANDING THE ROLES GROUP MEMBERS PLAY

The authors of the book *Tribal Leadership: Leveraging Natural Groups to Build a Thriving Organization* contend that although the members of every group are different, they are performing the same set of roles.[14]

Roles are patterns of behavior. There are roles that we expect group members to play because they contribute to the group's effectiveness (functional roles) and roles that we expect group members to refrain from playing because of their harmful effects on the group (dysfunctional roles).

GROUP ROLE-CLASSIFICATION MODEL

Even though Kenneth Benne and Paul Sheats formulated their group role-classification model almost a half century ago, the system is still commonly used. It describes the kinds of roles that group participants should seek to perform—together with those that they should seek to avoid—during the life of a group.[15] Benne and Sheats considered goal achievement (completing the task) and group maintenance (building relationships) the two basic objectives of any group. They further reasoned that eliminating self-serving roles (nonfunctional behaviors) is a requirement that must be met if the group's goals are to be realized. Guided by these assumptions, Benne and Sheats identified three categories of roles: task-oriented roles, maintenance roles, and self-serving roles.

Task-Oriented Roles

The following are among the **task-oriented roles** that help a group realize its goals:

Initiating. The member defines a problem; suggests methods, goals, and procedures; and starts the group moving along new paths or in different directions by offering a plan.

Information seeking. The member asks for facts and opinions and seeks relevant information about the problem.

Opinion seeking. The member solicits expressions of feeling and value to discover the values underlying the group effort.

Information giving. The member provides ideas and suggestions and supplies personal experiences as well as factual data.

Opinion giving. The member supplies opinions, values, and beliefs and reveals his or her feelings about what is being discussed.

Clarifying. The member elaborates on the ideas of others, supplies paraphrases, offers examples or illustrations, and tries to eliminate confusion and increase clarity.

Coordinating. The member summarizes ideas and tries to draw various contributions together constructively.

Evaluating. The member evaluates the group's decisions or proposed solutions and helps establish standards for judgment.

Consensus testing. The member checks on the state of group agreement to see if the group is nearing a decision.

Maintenance Roles

The following **maintenance roles** help the group run smoothly:

Encouraging. The member is warm, receptive, and responsive to others and praises others and their ideas.

Gatekeeping. The member attempts to keep communication channels open; he or she helps reticent members contribute to the group and works to keep the discussion from being dominated by one or two members.

Harmonizing. The member mediates differences between participants and attempts to reconcile misunderstandings or disagreements; he or she also tries to reduce tension by using humor or other forms of relief at appropriate junctures.

Compromising. The member is willing to compromise his or her position to maintain group cohesion; he or she is willing to admit error and modify beliefs to achieve group growth.

Standard setting. The member assesses whether group members are satisfied with the procedures being used and indicates that criteria have been set for evaluating group functioning.

Self-Serving Roles

The following **self-serving roles** prevent the group from working effectively:

Blocking. The member is disagreeable in an effort to ensure that nothing is accomplished.

Aggression. The member criticizes or blames others and works to deflate the egos of other group members in an effort to enhance his or her own status.

Recognition seeking. The member attempts to become the focus of attention by boasting about his or her own accomplishments rather than dealing with the group task; he or she may speak loudly and exhibit behavior that is unusual.

Dominating. The member insists on getting his or her own way, interrupts others, and gives directions in an effort to run or control the group.

Joking. The member appears cynical or engages in horseplay or other inappropriate or irrelevant behaviors.

Self-confessing. The member uses other group members as an audience and reveals personal feelings or insights that are not oriented toward group concerns.

Help seeking. The member tries to elicit sympathy or pity from other members.

UNDERSTANDING GROUP MEMBER RELATIONSHIPS

In addition to the various roles played by group members, the nature of the relationships that members share is also highly significant in determining whether the group will operate effectively. Although it appears natural for human beings to cooperate, never is this more evident than when we face a crisis.

In 2010, 33 Chilean miners were trapped 2,300 feet underground. Leaders emerged among the group to establish rules and to organize the miners into teams to look after one another. We do the same thing in the workplace under much less extreme conditions. To what extent do members of a group cooperate or compete with one another? To what extent do the members foster a defensive or a supportive environment?[16]

COOPERATION VERSUS COMPETITION

Obviously, the personal goals of each member have an impact on a group's operation. If individual members view their goals as congruent or coinciding, an atmosphere of cooperation can be fostered. However, if individual members see their goals as contradictory, a competitive atmosphere will develop. Too frequently, group members attempt to compete with one another when cooperating would be more beneficial to the group.

The term *goal structure* describes the way members relate to each other. Under a **cooperative goal structure**, the members of a group work together to achieve their objectives, and the goals of each person are perceived as compatible with those of the others. Group members readily pool resources and coordinate their efforts to obtain what they consider common aims. In contrast, when a group develops a **competitive goal structure**, members do not share resources or coordinate efforts. Consciously or unconsciously, individuals work to hinder one another's efforts to obtain the goal. According to psychologist Morton Deutsch, group members who have a competitive orientation believe that they can achieve their goals only if other members fail to do so.[17]

SUPPORTIVENESS VERSUS DEFENSIVENESS

Defensive behavior occurs when a group member perceives a threat. When you feel yourself becoming defensive, you may experience one or more of the following symptoms: a change in your voice tone (as you become nervous, your throat and vocal mechanism grow tense and your vocal pitch tends to rise), a tightening of your muscles and some degree of rigidity throughout your body, and a rush of adrenaline accompanied by an urge to fight or flee.

Why We Become Defensive

In general, we become defensive when we perceive others as attacking our self-concept. In fact, when we behave defensively, we devote a great amount of energy to defending the self. We become preoccupied with thinking about how the self appears to others, and we become obsessed with discovering ways to make others see us more favorably. When a member of a group becomes overly concerned with self-protection, he or she may compensate either by withdrawing or by attacking other members. When this happens, the conditions necessary for the maintenance of the group begin to deteriorate.

Defensive behavior on the part of one group member gives rise to defensive listening in others. The postural, facial, and vocal cues that accompany words also can raise the defensiveness level. Once the defensiveness of a group member is aroused, that person no longer feels free to concentrate on the actual meaning of messages that others are trying to send. Instead, the defensive member distorts the messages sent.

The upshot: As group members become more and more defensive, they become less and less able to process each other's emotions, values, and intentions accurately. For this reason, the consequences of defensiveness include destroyed or badly damaged individual relationships, continuing conflicts, increased personal anxiety within the group, wounded egos, and hurt feelings.

Behaviors That Raise and Reduce Perceived Threat Levels

Before we can eliminate or reduce defensiveness in our group relationships, we must understand the stimuli that contribute to our becoming defensive in the first place. In a classic study, sociological researcher Jack Gibb identified six behaviors that cause defensiveness and six contrasting behaviors that allay the perceived level of threat (Table 9.2).[18]

TABLE 9.2 BEHAVIORS CHARACTERISTIC OF DEFENSIVE AND SUPPORTIVE CLIMATES

DEFENSIVE CLIMATE	SUPPORTIVE CLIMATE
Evaluation	Description
Control	Problem orientation
Strategy	Spontaneity
Neutrality	Empathy
Superiority	Equality
Certainty	Provisionalism

Source: Jack R. Gibb, "Defensive Communication," *Journal of Communication, 2* (1961), pp. 141–148.

Evaluation Versus Description. Group relationships may run into trouble if a member makes judgmental or evaluative statements. As Gibbs notes in the article "Defensive Communication," "If by expression, manner of speech, tone of voice, or verbal content the sender seems to be evaluating or judging the listener, then the receiver goes on guard."[19] Although most people do not mind having their actions praised, most of us object to having our actions condemned. Moreover, whether judgment is positive or negative, the anticipation of judgment can hinder the creation of an open communication climate. In contrast to evaluative statements, descriptive statements recount particular or observable actions without labeling those behaviors as good or bad, right or wrong. Instead of making an evaluative statement, simply report or question what you saw, heard, or felt.

Control Versus Problem Orientation. Communication that group members see as seeking to control them also may arouse defensiveness. In other words, if your intent is to control other group members, to get them to do something or change their beliefs, you are likely to evoke resistance. How much resistance you meet depends on how openly you approach others and on whether your behavior causes them to question or doubt your motives. When we conclude that someone is trying to control us, we also tend to conclude that he or she considers us ignorant or incapable of making our own decisions.

In contrast, a problem orientation promotes the opposite response. When senders communicate that they have not already formulated solutions and will not force their opinions on us, we feel freer to cooperate in solving the problems at hand.

Strategy Versus Spontaneity. Our defensiveness increases if we feel that another group member is trying to put something over on us. No one likes to be conned or to be the victim of a hidden plan. We are suspicious of strategies that are concealed or tricky. We do not want others to make decisions for us and then try to persuade us that we made the decisions ourselves. Thus, when we perceive we are being manipulated, we become defensive and self-protective. In contrast, spontaneous behavior that is honest and free of deception reduces defensiveness. Under such conditions, the receiver feels no need to question the motivations of the sender, and trust is engendered.

Neutrality Versus Empathy. Neutrality is another behavior that increases defensiveness in group members. We want others to empathize with us, like us, and value us. We want to feel that others care about us and will take the time to establish a meaningful relationship with us. If a group member communicates neutrality or indifference, we may well perceive this as worse than rejection.

Superiority Versus Equality. Our defensiveness is aroused if another group member communicates feelings of superiority about social position, power, wealth, intelligence, appearance, or other characteristics. We tend to react to such a message by competing with the sender, by feeling frustrated or jealous, or by disregarding or forgetting the sender's message altogether. On the other hand, a sender who communicates equality decreases our defensiveness. We perceive him or her as willing to develop a shared problem-solving relationship with us, as willing to trust us, and as feeling that any differences between us are unimportant.

Certainty Versus Provisionalism. The expression of absolute certainty or dogmatism on the part of a group member will probably succeed in making us defensive. We are suspicious of those who believe they have all the answers, view themselves as our guides rather than our fellow travelers, and reject all information that we attempt to offer. In contrast, an attitude of provisionalism or open-mindedness encourages the development of trust. We perceive those who communicate in a spirit of provisionalism—instead of attempting to win arguments, to be right, and to defend their ideas to the bitter end—as flexible and open.

DECISION MAKING IN GROUPS: REACHING GOALS

In our society, we usually relegate critical decisions to groups. Depending on the group and its task(s), a wide variety of decision-making strategies or approaches may be used. In this section, we investigate the diverse methods members can adopt to arrive at a decision, as well as the advantages and disadvantages of each approach.

STRATEGIES OF DECISION MAKING

Before we examine the different methods that groups use in making decisions, consider the following list to decide which decision-making strategy or strategies a group you belong to would employ most often if you had your way. Do this by ranking the possibilities from 1 (your first choice) to 8 (your last choice).

_____ Ask an expert to decide.

_____ Flip a coin.

_____ Let the majority rule.

_____ Let the group leader decide.

_____ Stall until a decision no longer needs to be made.

_____ Let the minority rule, because that is sometimes fair.

_____ Determine the average position because this is least likely to be offensive to anyone.

_____ Reach a decision by consensus; that is, be certain all have had input into the discussion, understand the decision, can rephrase it, and will publically support it.

Then consider the implications of your rankings.

An effective group bases its decision-making strategy on a number of variables, including the nature of the problem, the time available to solve the problem, and the kind of climate in which the group is operating or would prefer to operate.

Thinking About the Effectiveness of Decision-Making Methods

Experience reveals that methods of group decision making vary considerably in their effectiveness.

Majority Vote. Majority vote is the method used most frequently. Most elections are decided and many laws are passed on the basis of the vote of at least 51% of a group's members.

Averaging. Another popular decision-making strategy is averaging, by which the most popular decision becomes the group's decision.

Let the Expert Decide. Letting the expert member decide what the group should do is also fairly common. In this case, the group simply defers its decision-making power to its most knowledgeable member.

Let the Leader Decide. In many groups, the leader retains all the decision-making power. Sometimes this is done after consultation with group members; at other times, it is done without consultation.

The Nominal Group. The _nominal group technique_ uses limited discussion and secret voting to reach a decision. It is especially valuable when group members are reluctant to voice their opinions, perhaps because the issue under discussion is controversial or because members do not want their ideas attacked. The method enables each group member to contribute equally. The system combines individual work and group discussion and follows a series of steps: (1) The problem is defined for group members. (2) Without having any discussion, every group member writes down ideas for possible solutions to the problem. (3) Going in round-robin sequence, each member, in turn, offers one idea on his or her list. The offered ideas are recorded in order and presented so that everyone can see them, until ideas are exhausted. Duplicate and overlapping ideas on the list are combined. (4) Members clarify ideas. (5) Privately and in writing, every member ranks the listed suggestions. (6) Member rankings are combined to produce a group ranking. (7) Discussion, clarification, and reordering, if necessary, ensue. (8) The ideas with the highest rankings are put into practice.

The Delphi Method. The Delphi method depends on a selected group of experts, who do not communicate directly with each other but instead respond to a series of questionnaires. It is especially useful when you want to involve all members in finding a solution but it would be inconvenient or impossible to get participants physically together in the same location and you don't desire to meet virtually. It also prevents a dominant member from unduly influencing other members. Like the nominal group technique, the Delphi method contains a series of steps: (1) The problem is defined and the contribution needed from each member is specified. (2) Each member contributes ideas in writing. (3) The ideas provided by all members are combined and redistributed to the members. (4) Members choose the three or four best ideas. (5) Another list is created using these contributions and is distributed to members. (6) Members select and submit one or two ideas from the new list. (7) Using these responses, another list is created and distributed to members. (8) The solutions are identified and shared with all members.

Quality Circles. **Quality circles** are groups of employees, often with different areas of expertise and from different levels in an organization's hierarchy, whose task it is to explore and make recommendations for improving the quality and usually the profitability of an organizational function. They use any problem-solving technique available to achieve their goal. This technique empowers employees by involving them in the decision-making process, helping to increase their morale and bond them to the organization.

iStock/PeopleImages

Decision by Consensus. Although each of the previously mentioned methods can bring success, the most effective decision-making strategy is decision by consensus. When a group achieves consensus, all members agree on the decision. Even more important, all of them help formulate the decision by voicing their feelings and airing their differences of opinion. Thus, they all understand the decision and will support it.

EXPLORING DIVERSITY
Group Polarization

Group polarization is a phenomenon in decision making in which discussion is found to strengthen the average inclination of group members. For example, when business students were asked to decide hypothetically whether to invest more money in failing projects in the hope of preventing losses, individually, 72% chose to reinvest money, whereas among those working in groups, 94% came to that decision.[20] Discussion with like-minded people strengthens existing views.

How might such a trend influence the beliefs of prejudiced and unprejudiced people when it comes to issues involving racial profiling, affirmative action, and those responsible for increases in crime? How might it influence the thinking of like-minded online fringe groups?

The Communication Playbook

Factors to Consider in Weighing Decision Method Effectiveness

The greater the involvement of members in the decision-making process, the more effective the decision will be.

Of course, decisions by a leader, by an expert, or by a majority or minority vote all take less time than consensus. However, it is the group that will usually be responsible for implementing the decision. If members disagree with a decision or do not understand it, they may not work very hard to make it succeed. A leader may make routine decisions or may be called on to make decisions when little time is available for a real discussion of the issues. Under most circumstances, however, one person cannot be the best resource for all decisions.

A drawback of the decision-by-expert method is that it is sometimes difficult to determine who the expert is. Also, decision by an expert—like decision by a leader—fails to involve other group members.

Decision by averaging, on the whole, is superior to either decision by a leader or decision by an expert. With averaging, all members can be consulted, individual errors will cancel each other out, and an average position usually will not dissatisfy anyone too much. On the other hand, an average position usually does not satisfy anyone very much. Thus, commitment to the decision tends to be rather low.

Under most circumstances, the quality of decision making and the satisfaction of the participants are higher when a group seeks consensus. Consensus puts the resources of the entire group to effective use, permits discussion of all issues and alternatives, and ensures the commitment of all members. It is not the decision alone that is important in group interaction. The reactions and feelings of group members also matter.

QUESTIONS FOR DECISION MAKERS: FACTS, VALUES, AND POLICIES

The actual content of decision making is based on three key kinds of questions: questions of fact, questions of value, and questions of policy.

Questions of Fact

Questions of fact focus on the truth of a statement. Existing information may be inconsistent or contradictory, and group members try to ferret out the truth. For example, a group might seek to determine whether evidence proved beyond a doubt that Lee Harvey Oswald acted alone in assassinating President John F. Kennedy, or that O. J. Simpson killed his former wife, or that President Trump and his aides facilitated Russian involvement in the 2016 U.S. presidential election.

Questions of Value

In contrast, **questions of value** involve subjective judgments. "Who was the best president to serve in the past 100 years?" and "How desirable are extreme physical fitness programs?" are questions of value.

Questions of Policy

Questions of policy help us determine what future actions, if any, we should take. In fact, the key word in a question of policy is the word *should*: "What should colleges do to prevent student suicides?" or "What should the United States do to discourage populism?"

A FRAMEWORK FOR DECISION MAKING: REFLECTIVE THINKING

The quality of a group's decisions depends, at least partly, on the nature of its decision-making system. There is a generally agreed-on structure, consisting of several stages, which, if used properly, can increase the problem-solving effectiveness of most groups. This is called the **reflective-thinking framework**. It was first proposed by John Dewey in 1910. It probably is still the most commonly used sequence.[21]

The reflective-thinking framework has six basic components:

1. What is the problem? Is it clearly defined? Do we understand the general situation in which it is occurring? Is it stated so as not to arouse defensiveness? Is it phrased so as not to permit a simple yes or no answer? (E.g., "What should the college's policy be toward final exams for seniors?" instead of "Should the college stop wasting the time of its seniors and eliminate final exams?")

2. What are the facts of the situation? What are its causes? What is its history? Why is it important? Whom does it affect and how?

3. What criteria must an acceptable solution meet? By which and whose standards must a solution be evaluated? What are the principal requirements of the solution? How important is each criterion?

4. What are the possible solutions? How would each remedy the problem? How well does each satisfy the criteria? What are the advantages and disadvantages of each?

5. Which is the best solution? How would you rank the solutions? Which offers the greatest number of advantages and the smallest number of disadvantages?

6. How can the solution be implemented? What steps need to be taken to put the solution into effect?

To make this framework function effectively, every member of the group must suspend judgment. Group members must be open to all available ideas, facts, and opinions. They must guard against early concurrence, which could force them to conclude discussion prematurely. All data and alternative courses of action must be appraised thoroughly. Instead of insisting on your own position and closing yourself to new information, you need to explore all the major variables that contributed to the problem and investigate all the major issues that may be involved in producing a workable solution.

As you make your way through the framework, ask yourself if (a) the resources of all group members are being well used, (b) the group is using its time to advantage, (c) the group is emphasizing fact-finding and inquiry, (d) members are listening to and respecting one another's opinions and feelings, (e) pressure to conform is being kept to a minimum while an honest search for diverse ideas is made, and (f) the atmosphere is supportive (noncritical), trusting (nonthreatening), and cooperative (noncompetitive). Remember, if group members are afraid to speak up, closed-minded, reluctant to search for information, or unmotivated, they will not perform effectively.

THE SEARCH FOR BETTER IDEAS: BRAINSTORMING

According to Jay Cocks, a business theorist and writer, "In an era of global competition, fresh ideas have become the most precious raw materials."[22] Where do fresh ideas come from?

Where Ideas Come From

Betty Edwards, author of *Drawing on the Right Side of the Brain*, believes that fresh ideas come from developing creative problem-solving skills, as well as from encouraging creativity in the workplace.[23] To prepare students to meet the demands of the 21st century, colleges and universities across the country are offering entire courses on creativity and creative problem solving.

In his now-classic 1939 book on idea generation, *A Technique for Producing Ideas*, advertising copywriter James Webb Young suggested that any new idea owes its birth to the ability of others to see new relationships between known facts. In other words, we create new ideas by combining old elements in new ways. Young's book offers a guide to jump-starting idea generation, a skill much needed in an age of increased global competition.[24] If you can come up with new creative solutions, you may find yourself of greater value to the companies and corporations of today and tomorrow.

James Webb Young was not alone in searching for creative ways to develop new ideas. Following on Young's contributions, management consultants introduced **brainstorming**, a key technique we rely on to thaw frozen patterns of thinking and encourage creativity.

What Is Brainstorming?

A number of researchers suggest that the best way to have a good idea is to have lots of ideas. Frequently, however, instead of suspending judgment and permitting ideas to develop freely, problem solvers tend to grasp at the first solution that comes to mind.

Recognizing that this practice inhibits the search for new avenues of thought, Alex Osborn devised a technique called brainstorming.[25] This method promotes a free flow of ideas and is easily incorporated into the problem-solving process. For instance, although groups use brainstorming most frequently when members are attempting to identify a solution, it can also be used to help identify the factors causing a problem, the criteria that a solution should meet, and ways to implement the solution.

Guidelines for Brainstorming

Although most people know what brainstorming means, few have been taught to do it correctly.[26] To ensure your group brainstorming sessions are conducted appropriately, group members need to follow these guidelines:

1. Temporarily suspend judgment. That is, do not evaluate or criticize ideas. Instead, adopt a "try anything" attitude. This will encourage rather than stifle the flow of ideas.

2. Encourage freewheeling. The wider the ideas that are offered, the better. It is easier to tame a wild idea later than it is to replace or invigorate an inert idea. At this point, the practicality of an idea is not of primary importance.

3. Think of as many ideas as you can. At this stage, it is the quantity, not the quality, of ideas that is important. The greater the number of ideas the group generates, the better the chance the group will find a good one. Thus, in a brainstorming session, no self-censorship or group censorship is permitted. All ideas should be expressed.

4. Build on and improve or modify the ideas of others. Work to mix ideas until they form interesting combinations. Remember, brainstorming is a group effort.

5. Record all ideas. This ensures that the group will have available all the ideas that have been generated during the session.

6. Only after the brainstorming session is finished should group members evaluate the ideas for usefulness and applicability.

Brainstorming is effective because it lessens the inhibitions of members and makes it easier for them to get their ideas heard. It promotes a warmer, more playful, enthusiastic, and cooperative atmosphere, and it encourages each individual's potential for creativity. But the unique aspect of brainstorming—and perhaps its most important benefit—is suspended judgment.

What Can Go Wrong?

Too often, one or two group members stifle the creative-thinking effort of a brainstorming group. Despite the lip service they may pay to suspending judgment, they may have come to the problem-solving experience with an evaluative mind-set. According to Sidney Parnes, who studied creative thinking, this attitude pops up in **killer phrases** like "That won't work," "We tried that before," and "You've got to be joking!" Such comments stop the flow of ideas.[27]

This behavior strikes at the heart of brainstorming. It replaces the green light of brainstorming not so much with a yellow light of criticism or thoughtful evaluation as with a red light of frozen judgment. Killer phrases are often accompanied (or replaced) by **killer looks**—facial expressions that discourage or inhibit the generation of ideas. By gaining insight into these types of killers and their effects, you can increase your ability to analyze your own behavior and change it if necessary.

Ways to Foster Creativity

Pamela Well Moore is an executive at Synectics, a creativity consulting firm. One technique she recommends to limber up the minds of tightly focused corporate managers is "sleight of head." While working on a particular problem, she'll ask clients to pretend to work on something else. In one real-life example, a Synectics-trained facilitator took a group of product development and marketing managers from the Etonic shoe corporation on an "excursion," a conscious walk away from the problem, in this case, to come up with a new kind of tennis shoe.

The facilitator asked the Etonic people to imagine they were at their favorite vacation spot. "One guy," Moore says, "was on a tropical island, walking on the beach in his bare feet. He described how wonderful the water and the sand felt on his feet, and he said, 'I wish I could play tennis barefoot.' The whole thing would have stopped right there if somebody had complained that while his colleague was wandering around barefoot, they were supposed to come up with a shoe. Instead, one of the marketing people there was intrigued, and the whole group decided to go off to play tennis barefoot on a rented court at 10 at night."

While the Etonic people played tennis, the facilitator listed everything they said about how it felt. The next morning, the group looked at her assembled list of comments, and they realized that what they liked about playing barefoot was the lightness of being without shoes and the ability to pivot easily on both the ball of the foot and the heel. Nine months later, the company produced an extremely light shoe called the Catalyst, which featured an innovative two-piece sole that made it easier for players to pivot.[28]

Brainstorming is also related to what researcher Rosabeth Moss Kanter calls **kaleidoscope thinking**. According to Kanter:

A kaleidoscope takes a set of fragments and forms them into a pattern. But when the kaleidoscope is twisted or approached from a new angle, the same fragments form a different pattern. Kaleidoscope thinking then involves taking existing data and twisting it or looking at it from another angle in order to see and analyze the new patterns that appear.[29]

Fishboning is a structured brainstorming technique groups use to search for solutions to problems, such as poor gas mileage. When using this technique, group members first create a diagram that resembles a fishbone. As shown in Figure 9.4, the problem or effect is placed at the fishbone's head, on the right side of the diagram, and the problem's possible cause or effects in their order of probable occurrence or significance are positioned as if growing out of the fishbone's spine. Subcauses are also shown as contributors to the primary causes.

FIGURE 9.4
Fishbone Technique

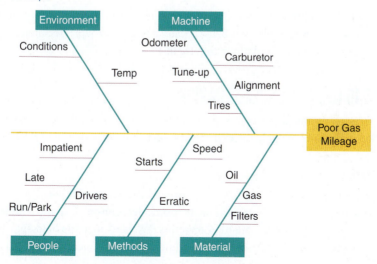

FOCUS ON FOCUS GROUPS

Organizations often rely on a special kind of information-sharing group when conducting market or policy research. Focus groups (typically composed of approximately 10 to 12 people) are assembled when individuals are solicited to participate in an in-depth group interview. The purpose is to discover what individuals, in general, think about a subject, issue, candidate, or product. For example, a series of focus groups might be formed to determine what people with different political party preferences think about National Football League (NFL) players taking a knee during the singing of the national anthem to protest racial discrimination.

The focus group leader is more like an interviewer or professional facilitator. She or he explains how a focus group functions, the general goals of the session, and the time constraints. The facilitator then asks a series of questions to the group in the effort to uncover the thoughts, attitudes, and beliefs of the group's members, making certain that all members of the group offer input and that no one member dominates the discussion.

The purpose of a focus group is not for the group to solve a problem on its own or to reach consensus, but rather to identify how members react to questions, to gauge the strength of their feelings, and to see if the responses of one member influence the responses of others. Sometimes the people who funded the focus group are seated behind a one-way mirror to observe the group in action, paying careful attention to member nonverbal cues and reactions to one another.

Once focus groups are complete, the organization can then apply what they've learned to hone their product, packaging, policy, and/or persuasive strategies.

GENDER, CULTURE, TECHNOLOGY, AND GROUP INTEGRATION

The gender and the cultural backgrounds of a group's members provide a set of unstated assumptions and rules that guide their behavior and affect the group.[30] Technology makes it possible for members to meet and problem solve in cyberspace.

GENDER AND GROUP MEMBER BEHAVIOR

Gender affects group membership and member behavior in a number of ways including participation in decision making, the exercise of power, and the nature of problem solving.

Decision Making

Although 52% of all middle managers in corporations are now women, there has been a leveling off in the number of women serving on the prime decision-making and control groups in corporations, including on the board of directors. Women currently hold approximately 14.8% of seats on boards of Fortune 500 companies.[31] However, according to Catalyst, an organization focused on women in the workplace, companies with more female directors not only outperform their rivals financially but also end up having more female managers. Female directors help diffuse stereotypes about women in the workplace and serve as powerful role models for more junior colleagues.[32]

Exercising Power

Whether serving on boards or working in other kinds of work groups, on average, men and women are likely to focus on different aspects of a group's life and exercise their power differently. Whereas men tend to be more goal oriented, concentrating on the group's task-related matters, women tend to pay more attention to the relationships among group members, displaying more signs of liking or immediacy toward each other.

In addition, in contrast to men, who display more signs of power or potency, women tend to be more patient, offering positive responses to one another. Men also are more likely to offer comments that are more objective, compared with women, who tend to be more comfortable sharing subjective opinions.[33]

When it comes to the perception of their power in groups, most men perceive power as finite, something to be guarded for oneself and used to enhance personal status. Most women, on the other hand, perceive power as unlimited, as something to share, and as a resource for empowering others.[34]

Problem Analysis

Women tend to analyze problems holistically, whereas men are more apt to analyze problems in a more linear fashion, looking for cause-and-effect relationships. Studies of mixed-sex groups indicate that because men and women contribute in unique ways to a group, having them work together enhances group productivity.[35]

CULTURE AND GROUP MEMBER BEHAVIOR

Culture has a profound impact on decision-making approaches and the ways people behave in groups.

Openness to Ambivalence

When we see a situation as black and white, with one clear-cut solution that just needs to be found, we are less likely to display decisional ambivalence. Although more difficult, thinking in shades of gray and evaluating all sides of a problem lets us perceive a problem's complexity. It also symbolizes our ability to live with uncertainty and empathize with others' points of view, and it is usually interpreted as a sign of maturity.

Culture probably plays a role in determining your ambivalence quotient. Although black-and-white thinkers make decisions more quickly, if they are unable to see others' points of view, their certainty may lead to conflict.

People in Western cultures are more apt to label something as wholly good or bad. Being adept at seeing good and bad simultaneously is less common. In Eastern cultures, however, dualism is the norm and something can be one thing *and* another.[36]

Problem Solving and Member Satisfaction

The cultural backgrounds of group members similarly affect the nature of communication in the group. Increasing group member diversity can create challenges, but it also leads to more effective problem solving and enhances the satisfaction of members.[37]

When working in a diverse group, members need to understand how cultural factors influence behavior. For example, because African American culture in the United States is an oral culture, both verbal inventiveness and playfulness are highly valued. As a result, African Americans are apt to rely on back-channel responses (saying things such as "That's right" or "Go on") to indicate their interest and involvement in the discussion. Because European Americans do not use back-channel responses as frequently, African Americans may perceive them as underreactive in the group's communication. In contrast, European Americans may perceive African Americans as overreactive.

Member Orientations

Whereas members of collectivist cultures have a strong need for group consensus, people in the United States are more analytical, basing their decision making on objective facts rather than on feelings or faith. People from collectivistic cultures, such as those of Japan, China, and Pakistan, generally are more conforming in groups than are people from individualistic cultures, such as the United States, Great Britain, Australia, and Canada, countries in which individuals place greater emphasis on competition and dissent. In Japan, for instance, an organization's members have been taught to feel a sense of obligation to those who provide them with security, care, and support. When this obligation is paired with a developing sense of dependency, a force called *on* results. *On* links people in a group forever, because the Japanese believe obligation continues throughout life. Hence, because nothing can be decided without a consideration of how the outcomes will influence everyone involved, consensus seeking becomes a priority.[38]

Because collectivists use group norms rather than individual goals to guide their participation, they also are likely to be group players and stress harmony and cooperation.[39] Individualists, on the other hand, are more apt to dominate group discussions and more prone to want to win in decision making. Individualistic culture members are more likely to voice their disagreements, whereas collectivists prefer to slowly assess the feelings and moods of group members without verbalizing their objections or doubts. Consensus seeking does not come as easy to individualists as it does to collectivists.[40]

Globalization Effects

Globalization has led to a plethora of culturally mixed work groups with managers having to interact with peers from diverse cultures. Group members from Western cultures soon discover that people from collectivist cultures find it more difficult than they do to be free and open in their expressions of opinion. More commonly, members of collectivist cultures refrain from bringing issues they question into the open because of the difficulty they have expressing their personal views directly.

Faced with this practice, in order to ensure effective discussion and decision making, some Western corporations are encouraging the use of a number of foreign-inspired decision-making practices among their collectivist partners, including the coaxing of group members to speak up and challenge each other and advocating for consensus decision making in place of the sometimes required unanimous consent, where members accept a decision without questioning it. With practice, group members are also finding that common goals help overcome cultural differences.[41]

Group Composition and Goals

The makeup of a group also influences the nature of the group's goals and whether they will be short or long term in nature. Members of Western cultures tend to focus on short-term goals that deliver more immediate payoffs, whereas members of East Asian cultures are more patient and willing to defer gratification and thus more likely to seek long-range goals. Group members need to work out their differences in goal orientation for them to be able to work together harmoniously.

Generational Diversity

Another variant of culture, the age or generational diversity of group members, is leading companies to grapple with how generational differences affect teamwork.

In contemporary workplaces, it is not uncommon to have members from three postwar generations working together on a single project. Age-diverse, multigenerational groups, present different kinds of challenges, as is discussed in a book called *4genR8tns*.[42] For example, a group's more mature members may become irritated by the impatience exhibited by their group's younger members who think that group meetings take too long to plan and, once planned, consume too much of their time. Members from earlier generations soon realize that their group's younger members want the time they spend working in groups to be not only meaningful but also enjoyable. In addition, while members from the boomer generation may prefer to display their group's work via a PowerPoint presentation, younger members might favor report methods that are more interactive. Because younger members also seek regular feedback on the contributions they make toward their group's goal, the group's more mature members can improve group effectiveness by remembering to offer such input regularly.[43]

iStock/Rawpixel

It is not advisable to follow blanket stereotypes, but it is important to recognize that on average, each generation has different preferences regarding group work. Boomers, for example, tend to be competitive and driven to succeed and like being singled out for praise. Gen X-ers tend to be skeptical and independent minded, dislike bureaucracy and formality, and prefer casual meetings. Gen Ys tend to favor teamwork, feedback, and the use of technology. As a result, participating in multigenerational work teams requires each generation to adjust and shift attitudes as they work out their differences. The development of an inclusive workplace culture facilitates this process.

TECHNOLOGY AND GROUPS

Groups commonly meet virtually. When meeting online, the best way to solve a problem is to rely on an extensive network. In the online world, the person who provides needed information, advice, or an answer to a problem may be on the periphery of a group, as compared to in the face-to-face world, when group members share extremely strong links and typically know each other better.

The Social Network Paradigm

Individuals and groups in disparate locations link with others using social networks that have woven themselves into the fabric of group life by putting people in touch with one another and giving users access to larger, more interrelated pools of information.[44] In effect, online social networks have migrated group communication into alternative meeting environments. When online, highly creative teams interact via a "pulsing star" pattern, in which they fan out to gather information and then regroup to share what they discover.[45]

LinkedIn is a social network for professionals, who join primarily to connect with other professionals whom they use to help them solve daily business problems. One LinkedIn product, Company Groups, automatically gathers all the employees from a company who use LinkedIn into a single, private Web forum. Once in the forum, employees can ask and answer questions, share and discuss information about themselves and their responsibilities, and collaborate on projects.

Similar to LinkedIn are TownSquare and SharePoint, each of which enable a company's employees to follow one another's activities.[46] Connectbeam is a consultancy that sets up secure social networks for the corporate Internets of Fortune 500 companies that do not want workers putting information on social networking sites such as Facebook, which use servers beyond the company's control. Some companies use Yammer, a system similar to Twitter, but open only to employees. Yammer lets people brag, share information, and learn about what others are doing in the company, facilitating their collaboration.[47] Thousands of workplace teams also use Slack, an internal messaging and archiving program, to encourage communication between members.

Other companies bring workers together by having them meet in sites such as Second Life. Their avatars—alter egos of the employees—meet in the company's own virtual workspace. Many organizations use Second Life, a virtual reality operation with 900,000 active users to hold meetings.[48]

Benefits of Online Groups

Group members who use virtual sites report feeling more comfortable talking and expressing ideas or calling others' views into question. They may not display such behavior in real-world meetings because of feelings of intimidation. Social networking gets employees talking, brainstorming, and cooperating across the organization, fostering the sharing of information and the collection of ideas. To make the most of virtual collaboration, companies also tap the wisdom of a crowd—a practice known as crowdsourcing—in which they invite, either publicly or semipublicly, a community to provide input, effectively enlarging their brainstorming efforts.[49]

Drawbacks of Online Groups

On the flip side, using technology and social media in the workplace also can have negative effects for both employees and employers. It may blur the lines between personal and professional identities. Because of heavy social media use, employees worry that everyone has access to the information they place online. At the same time, employers worry that employees are misusing social media, spending valuable meeting time tweeting or game-playing when they should be working.[50]

Social media can encourage other bad habits besides distraction. Participants in virtual meetings sometimes behave as if they have less accountability than people meeting face-to-face. People need to show up physically and mentally for a face-to-face meeting. When a meeting is held online, attendees are not always as prepared and willing to participate actively, preferring to have side conversations or check sports scores.[51]

Virtual meetings also disrupt some of the communication channels we rely on in person. It becomes more difficult to read nonverbal cues, making it more likely for misunderstandings to occur. When you can't tell if someone is confused or uneasy, agreeing or disagreeing, it becomes more difficult to be certain you're interpreting the words being exchanged correctly. The increasing sophistication of videoconferencing technology removes some of these obstacles. Telepresence systems enable members who are not actually present to appear virtually, often via life-sized video screens. The high-definition system simulates face-to-face meetings by allowing group members to make eye contact and observe body language.[52]

Generally, it is important to keep in mind that what works face-to-face may not translate to the virtual world. The members of virtual teams may not share the same culture or make the same effort to see things from colleagues' points of view. Thus, although social media offers a relatively inexpensive way for colleagues around the world to connect, it also presents new and considerable challenges.

CAREER BUILDER: WHAT CAN WE LEARN FROM ONLINE SPEAK?

Do you think interaction in either online or face-to-face groups would improve if groups capitalized the words *You* and *We* but visualized or used a lowercase *i* when referring to themselves?

Because English is the only language that capitalizes the word *I*, we can only guess if and how such changes might affect our individualistic tendencies. Some people who regularly e-mail or text tend to use lowercase *i* instead of capitalized *I*, preferring to eradicate all capitalization from the messages they send. But why not do as Caroline Winter suggested in an article titled "Is the Vertical Pronoun Really Such a Capital Idea?"[53] "i suggest," she wrote, "that you try as an experiment, to capitalize those whom You address while leaving yourselves in the lowercase. It may be a humbling experience." It may also remind us of the importance of teamwork!

COMMUNICATION SKILLS
Practice Tips for Improving Group Communication

If a problem-solving group is to be effective in either a physical or online setting, certain characteristics need to be present and concerned members must work to develop these qualities. By becoming aware of the difference between optimal problem-solving behaviors and the actual behaviors you and your fellow group members exhibit, you can begin to improve your group's method and style of operation.

Ensure your group has the following characteristics.

Group goals are clearly understood and cooperatively formulated by the members.

As theorists Bobby R. Patton and Kim Griffin stressed, "If we aim at nothing, we are pretty apt to hit it."[54]

All members of the group are encouraged to communicate their ideas and feelings freely.

Key phrases are "I think," "I see," and "I feel." These phrases reveal a personal point of view and indicate that you recognize that someone else may feel, think, or see differently than you do.

Group members seek to reach a consensus when the decision is important.

Input from all members is sought. Each member's involvement is considered critical. Thus, the decision is not left to an authority to make on the basis of little or no discussion.

Consideration is given to both the task and the maintenance dimensions of the problem-solving effort.

Both the quality of the decision and the well-being of the group members are considered important.

Group members do not set about problem solving haphazardly.

A problem-solving framework is used and an outline is followed that aids the group in its search for relevant information.

Motivation is high.

Group members are eager to search for information, speak up, listen to others, and engage in an active and honest search for a better solution.

An effort is made to assess the group's problem-solving style.

Group members identify and alleviate factors that impede the group's effectiveness as well as identify and foster factors that enhance its effectiveness.

The environment is open and supportive.

Group members feel free to contribute ideas and feelings. They also believe that others will listen to their ideas.

The climate is cooperative.

To guard against destructive competition and foster a cooperative orientation, members need to work to demonstrate mutual trust and respect. Participative planning is essential. Coordination, not manipulation, is key.

The group encourages continual improvement.

Group members pay careful attention to how their behavior affects one another. They continually make the effort to improve and facilitate effective group interaction.

> "Groups can bring out the worst as well as the best in man."
>
> Irving L. Janis

COMPLETE THIS CHAPTER 9 CHECKLIST

9.1 I can define *group*, distinguishing a *team* as a special kind of group. ☐

A group is a collection of people who interact verbally and nonverbally, occupy certain roles with respect to one another, and cooperate with each other to accomplish a definite goal. A team, a special kind of group, contains people who have diverse skills and bring different resources to bear on a problem or task.

9.2 I can identify the characteristics and components of groups. ☐

To operate effectively, group members develop effective patterns of communication; establish group norms; act supportively; exercise participative decision making; show trust, openness, and candor; and set high performance goals. The healthier the group climate is, the more cohesive the group becomes. There are five stages in a group's development: forming, storming, norming, performing, and adjourning.

9.3 I can describe the advantages and disadvantages of using a group to make decisions and solve problems. ☐

The advantages in group problem solving are that resources can be pooled, motivation is increased, errors are more likely to be detected, decisions are more readily accepted by those outside the group, and group members can enjoy the companionship and rewards of working with others. Among the potential disadvantages are that it may encourage laziness among some members, conflict may arise between personal and group goals, a few people may dominate the group, one or two stubborn members may create a deadlock, the group may make an excessively risky decision, and it usually takes longer to reach a decision.

9.4 I can distinguish among task, maintenance, and self-serving group roles. ☐

Group members have specific group roles to perform. Members contribute to the group's objective when they assume task-oriented roles (behave in ways that promote the accomplishment of the task) or maintenance roles (helping to maintain relationships among the group members). However, members undercut effectiveness by playing self-serving roles (seeking to satisfy only their own needs and goals).

9.5 I can compare and contrast cooperative and competitive goal structures, and defensive and supporting behaviors. ☐

A group benefits from cooperation and a lack of defensiveness among members. Sharing resources and working together to achieve objectives help the group maintain itself, whereas competition and power plays hinder group functioning and promote defensiveness in members.

∙∙∙∙∙∙∙∙∙∙∙∙∙∙∙∙∙∙∙∙∙∙∙∙∙∙∙∙∙∙∙∙∙

9.6 I can describe the means groups use to achieve their goals, including decision-making methods, reflective thinking, and brainstorming. ☐

Groups use a variety of methods to make decisions—decision by an expert, by chance, by majority, by the leader, by the minority, by the average of individual decisions, and by consensus—or the group can defer a decision entirely. Making decisions by consensus is considered the most effective strategy. Using the reflective-thinking framework, a systematic six-step approach to decision making improves decision making. Brainstorming is also a useful technique because it encourages the discovery of new solutions.

∙∙∙∙∙∙∙∙∙∙∙∙∙∙∙∙∙∙∙∙∙∙∙∙∙∙∙∙∙∙∙∙∙

9.7 I can explain how gender, culture, and technology affect group interaction. ☐

The gender and cultural backgrounds of group members provide a set of unstated assumptions and rules that guide behavior, affecting the group. Increasing group diversity enhances both problem solving and member satisfaction. Additionally, online social networks have moved groups into alternative meeting environments and methods.

∙∙∙∙∙∙∙∙∙∙∙∙∙∙∙∙∙∙∙∙∙∙∙∙∙∙∙∙∙∙∙∙∙

9.8 I can apply skills for improving group effectiveness. ☐

By understanding and stating the goals of the group clearly, encouraging members to communicate ideas and feelings freely, paying attention to task and maintenance needs, keeping motivation high, honestly assessing the group's problem-solving style, fostering an open and supportive climate, and building a cooperative member orientation, members contribute to the group's effectiveness.

∙∙∙∙∙∙∙∙∙∙∙∙∙∙∙∙∙∙∙∙∙∙∙∙∙∙∙∙∙∙∙∙∙

BECOME A WORD MASTER

iStock/Jacob Ammentorp Lund

iStock/Tinpixels

10

Leading Others and Resolving Conflict

10.1 Define *leadership* and distinguish among the following leadership styles: type X, type Y, autocratic, laissez-faire, and democratic.

10.2 Compare and contrast trait, situational, functional, and transformational theories of leadership.

10.3 Analyze conflict styles and explain the dangers of conflict avoidance.

10.4 Discuss how personal characteristics, gender, cultural factors, and technology influence approaches to leadership and conflict.

10.5 Use skills to handle conflict more constructively.

> Man is the only animal that can remain on friendly terms with the victims he intends to eat until he eats them.
>
> Samuel Butler

In the reality program *Undercover Boss*, each episode finds a leader of a different organization disguising himself or herself as a worker and going undercover to discover how the firm's employees are functioning and what they think of him or her. Every chief executive officer (CEO) hears firsthand how various employees actually feel about working for the organization and, more specifically, how they feel about working under the CEO. Frequently, this turns out to be a revelatory experience for the CEO. Leaders may know exactly what their goals are. And they may think that those working for them understand their vision. Often, however, they find out otherwise.

What if you could eavesdrop on what others had to say about you as a leader or potential leader of a group? How do you imagine they would describe your leadership style, your ability to work with others, your openness to ideas, especially if your ideas differ significantly from theirs? What would they say about your approach to and ability to handle conflict? According to organizational psychologist Robert Sutton, "The best groups will be better than their best individual members, and the worst groups will be worse than the worst individual."[1] The difference is likely due to the nature of the leader–follower relationship.

We have a dual focus in this chapter as we explore both leadership and the management of group conflict. By gaining insight into how each of these forces affects us, we can prepare ourselves to analyze and improve our own leadership and conflict resolution behaviors in groups. ■

APPROACHES TO LEADERSHIP: THE LEADER IN YOU

What is leadership? What qualities does a good leader possess? Are effective leaders born or made? What sets a leader apart from the pack? Why should anyone be led by you?[2] These are some of the questions we address in this section.

WHAT IS LEADERSHIP?

Leadership is the ability to influence others. Thus, every person who influences others can be said to exert leadership.[3] Leadership may be either a positive or a negative force. When its influence is positive, leadership facilitates task accomplishment by a group. But if its influence is negative, it inhibits task accomplishment. Every group member is a potential leader.[4] Whether this potential is used wisely or is abused, used effectively or ineffectively, depends on individual skills, personal objectives, and commitment to the group.

Groups, especially problem-solving groups, need effective leadership to achieve their goals. One or more members of a group can demonstrate such leadership. Note that there is a difference between being appointed a leader and exhibiting leadership behaviors. Whenever you function as a **designated leader,** an outside force has selected you to be the leader and given you the authority to exert your influence within the group. When you engage in effective leadership behavior without being appointed or directed to do so, you function as an **achieved leader**.

In lieu of a designated team leader, more and more companies are requiring team members to share leadership, so that the person in charge at any moment in the group's life is the person who has the key knowledge, skills, and abilities called for at that moment. For example, in one *Survivor*-style competition designed to build team building skills, 15 United Airlines employees had to work together using clues and solving puzzles in order to escape from a locked room within 60 minutes. Ultimately, the person who led the group to freedom was the intern.[5] Teams that have a shared leadership structure tend to be higher performing than teams dominated by any one appointed leader.[6]

Effective leaders perform combinations of the task-oriented and maintenance roles introduced in Chapter 9. They demonstrate role versatility. Such leaders help establish a group climate that encourages and stimulates interaction. They make certain that an agenda is planned for a meeting. They take responsibility for ensuring that group communication proceeds smoothly. When group members go off track, this type of leader asks relevant questions, offers internal summaries, and keeps the discussion going. When discord occurs, they resolve clashes and conflicts so that the team may continue its work.[7] This is also the kind of leader who encourages continual evaluation and improvement by group members.

LEADERSHIP STYLES

Theorists have identified a number of leadership styles. Among them are type X, type Y, autocratic, laissez-faire, and democratic leadership.

Type X and Type Y Leaders

Our assumptions about how people work together influence the type of leadership style we adopt. The following are eight assumptions that a leader might make about how and why people work. Choose the four with which you are most comfortable.

1. The average group member will avoid working if he or she can.

2. The average group member views work as a natural activity.

3. The typical group member must be forced to work and must be closely supervised.

4. The typical group member is self-directed when it comes to meeting performance standards and realizing group objectives.

5. A group member should be threatened with punishment to get him or her to put forth an adequate effort.

6. A group member's commitment to objectives is related not to punishment but to rewards.

7. The average person prefers to avoid responsibility and would rather be led.

8. The average person not only can learn to accept responsibility but actually seeks responsibility.

If you picked mostly odd-numbered items in the preceding list, you represent what management theorist Douglas McGregor calls a **type X leader.** If you selected mostly even-numbered items, you represent what McGregor calls a **type Y leader.**[8]

The type Y leader is more of a risk taker than the type X leader. Type Y leaders are willing to let each group member grow and develop in order to realize his or her individual potential. In contrast, type X leaders do not readily delegate responsibility. Type X leaders are not concerned with group members' personal sense of achievement.

Are you satisfied with the set of assumptions you have chosen? What consequences, down the line, could they have for you and those who work with you?

CAREER BUILDER: SHAKESPEARE, POP CULTURE, AND LEADERSHIP LESSONS

A number of the historic plays of William Shakespeare offer explorations of leadership. The lessons contained in *Henry V*, for example, reveal leadership's burdens as we observe Henry motivate his troops and see him walk disguised among his followers as he seeks to understand them. From this and other of Shakespeare's works, we realize the importance of timing in achieving goals, the value of courage in facing challenges, and the value of identifying a firm, clear vision.[9]

Despite not being up to the standard set by Shakespeare's plays, media offerings of the recent past, including *VEEP*, *Designated Survivor*, *House of Cards*, *Mad Men*, *The Celebrity Apprentice*, *The Office*, *Parks and Recreation*, and *Survivor*, also offer us case studies of leaders and teams in action. As we recognize the types of leaders, we come to understand them and their methods and even imagine how to handle the challenges they face.

Select a recent film or television show. Identify and discuss one or more leadership lessons you learned from viewing it. Also, explain how the leader and one or more of the follower characters deepened your awareness of the behavior exhibited by those you work with or interact with daily. Describe the depicted leader's strong and weak qualities, problem-solving abilities, conflict resolution techniques, and preferred decision-making methods. How might you use the lessons learned from this analysis in the future?

Autocratic, Laissez-Faire, and Democratic Leaders

In most discussions of leadership styles, three categories in addition to type X and type Y usually come up: the autocratic leader (the "boss"), the democratic leader (the "participator"), and the laissez-faire leader (the "do your own thing" leader).[10] Let's examine each briefly.

iStock/SteveLuker

Autocratic, or authoritarian, leaders are dominators who view their task as directive. In a group with an **autocratic leader**, the leader determines all policies and gives orders to the other group members. In other words, this person becomes the sole decision maker. Although such an approach may be effective and efficient during a crisis, the usual outcome of this behavior is low group satisfaction.

The opposite of the autocratic leader is the **laissez-faire leader**. This type of leader adopts a "leave them alone" attitude. In other words, this person diminishes the leadership function to the point where it is almost nonexistent. The result is that group members are free to develop and progress on their own. This style is most effective when a minimal amount of interference fosters teamwork. Unfortunately, the members of a laissez-faire group often are distracted from the task at hand and lose their sense of direction, with the result that the quality of their work suffers.

In between these two positions we find **democratic leaders**, who use a style that has proved most effective. In groups with democratic leadership, members are directly involved in the problem-solving process; the power to make decisions is neither usurped by an autocrat nor abandoned by a laissez-faire leader. Instead, the leader's behavior represents a reasonable compromise between those two extremes. Democratic leaders do not dominate the group with one point of view, but they do attempt to provide direction to ensure that both task-oriented and maintenance functions are carried out. The group is free to identify its own goals, follow its own processes, and reach its own conclusions. Most people prefer working in groups with democratic leadership. Morale, motivation, group-mindedness, and the desire to communicate all increase under the guidance of a democratic leader.

THEORIES OF LEADERSHIP

Where does leadership ability come from? Why are some people more effective leaders than others? Are some individuals born to be leaders? Or does every situation create its own leader? Or is leadership a matter of learned abilities and skills? Over the years, theorists have given various answers to these questions.

TRAIT THEORY

The earliest view of leadership was trait theory. According to **trait theory**, leaders are born to lead.[11] Trait theorists also believe there are special built-in, identifiable leadership traits. Accordingly, attempts have been made to design a test that could predict whether a person would become a leader.

iStock/sampsyseeds

After many years of research, proof of trait theory is still lacking. Personality traits are not surefire predictors of leadership. For one thing, no one set of characteristics is common to all leaders, and leaders and followers share many of the same characteristics. Also, the situation, at least in part, appears to determine who will come forward to exert leadership. This is not to suggest, however, that trait research has not yielded valuable findings. In fact, although it is not valid to state "Leaders must possess the following personality traits," the research enables us to note that certain traits are indeed more likely to be found in leaders than in nonleaders.

According to researcher Marvin Shaw, the characteristics identified in Table 10.1 are indicative of leadership potential. Shaw notes that a person who does not exhibit these traits is unlikely to become a leader.[12] Of course, having leadership potential does not guarantee that you will actually emerge as the leader. A number of group members may have the qualities of leadership, but the final assertion of leadership will depend on more than potential.

TABLE 10.1 EVALUATING YOUR LEADERSHIP TRAITS: RATE YOURSELF

TRAIT	LOW				HIGH
Dependability	1	2	3	4	5
Cooperativeness	1	2	3	4	5
Desire to win	1	2	3	4	5
Enthusiasm	1	2	3	4	5
Drive	1	2	3	4	5
Persistence	1	2	3	4	5
Responsibility	1	2	3	4	5
Intelligence	1	2	3	4	5
Foresight	1	2	3	4	5
Communication ability	1	2	3	4	5
Popularity	1	2	3	4	5

Source: Marvin Shaw, *Group Dynamics: The Psychology of Small Group Behavior*, 3rd ed. New York: McGraw-Hill, 1981.

SITUATIONAL THEORY

A second theory of leadership is **situational theory**, which posits that whether an individual displays leadership skills and exercises actual leadership depends on the situation.[13] The development and emergence of leadership can be affected by such factors as the nature of the problem, the social climate, the personalities of the group members, the size of the group, and the time available to the group to accomplish the task. As organization behavior theorist Keith Davis notes in *Human Relations at Work*, leaders and their followers interact not in a vacuum but at a particular time and within a specific set of circumstances.[14] A leader is not necessarily a leader for all seasons.

Fred Fiedler's contingency theory and Paul Hersey and Ken Blanchard's readiness theory are both situational theories. Fiedler's theory contends that predicting a group's leader is contingent on three situational factors: leader–member relations, task structure, and position power.[15] Hersey and Blanchard's theory contends that the readiness level of a group (the degree to which members are willing and skilled enough to perform a task) determines the degree of task or relationship behavior a leader needs to emphasize.[16] This means that the relationship behavior, task behavior, and maturity of group members all come into play as a leader determines the style called for. For example, when groups are new, a *telling* style of leadership may be effective. The leader needs to provide direction, training, and instruction. When a group has some confidence in its skills, a *selling* style of leadership, in which the leader uses both task and relational behavior to persuade members to accomplish tasks, is called for. When group members take on more responsibility and become more independent, the leader becomes more equal to other group members. In this case, the leadership style of *participating* is used and decision making is shared. Finally, when the group is ready to provide its own leadership, a *delegating* style is appropriate.

FUNCTIONAL THEORY

In contrast to trait theory and situational theory, which emphasize the emergence of one person as a leader, **functional theory** suggests that several group members should be ready to lead because various actions are needed to achieve group goals.

Functional theorists believe that any of the group's task or maintenance activities can be considered leadership functions. In other words, when you perform any needed task or maintenance function, you are exercising leadership. Thus, according to functional theory, leadership shifts from person to person and is shared. Of course, sometimes one or two group members perform more leadership functions than others do. Consequently, one member might become the main task leader, whereas another might become the main emotional leader. However, the point is that we can enhance our leadership potential by learning to perform needed group functions more effectively.[17]

From the functional viewpoint, then, leadership is not a birthright, nor is it simply a matter of being in the right situation at a critical juncture. Instead, we are all capable of leadership and what is required is enough self-assertion and sensitivity to perform the functions that are needed as they are needed. In effect, this theory is asserting that good membership is good leadership. And the converse is also true: Good leadership is good membership.

TRANSFORMATIONAL THEORY

A **transformational leader** transforms a group by giving it new vision, strengthening its culture or structure. The transformational leader does not merely direct members, elicit contributions from members, or wait for members to catch up with his or her thinking. Instead, the transformational leader helps group members imagine and visualize the future they can build together.

According to neuroscientists, a transformational leader may actually think differently than others. Research reveals that transformational or visionary leaders tend to show much higher levels of brain activity than nonvisionaries in the areas associated with visual processing and organization of information. They also appear to have more efficient left brains, possibly indicating more charisma.[18] Transformational leaders inspire, motivate, and intellectually stimulate group members to become involved in achieving the group's goals. They function as the group's guiding force.[19]

Phil Stafford/Shutterstock.com

LEADING THE WAY THROUGH CONFLICT MANAGEMENT

How a group handles **conflict**, which can occur at any point in the group's existence and be started by any member of the group, makes a difference in member satisfaction as well as in the decision-making and problem-solving effectiveness of the group. How we feel about conflict and whether we view it positively or negatively reveals how we might act when facing it. The self-assessment in the accompanying Skill Builder will help you understand your personal attitudes toward conflict. Also see Table 10.2 to evaluate your feelings about conflict.

> Visit the interactive e-Book to access the Skill Builder feature "Conflict Self-Assessment," which will help you clarify your perspective on conflict.

Somehow, many of us grow up thinking that nice people do not fight, do not make waves. Some believe that if they do not smile and act cheerful, other people will not like them and they will not be accepted or valued as group members.[20] This should not be the case. Conflict is an inevitable part of group work, organizational life, and our lives in general. However, the way it is managed and responded to makes a difference. The route to resolving a conflict is to understand it. This requires that neither party assert that the other is wrong but tries to empathize with the other's position instead. It also requires that we choose appropriate styles of conflict management so that our disagreement does not become dysfunctional.[21]

TABLE 10.2

EVALUATING YOUR FEELINGS ABOUT CONFLICT: SCORE YOURSELF						
Good	1	2	3	4	5	Bad
Rewarding	1	2	3	4	5	Threatening
Normal	1	2	3	4	5	Abnormal
Constructive	1	2	3	4	5	Destructive
Necessary	1	2	3	4	5	Unnecessary
Challenging	1	2	3	4	5	Overwhelming
Desirable	1	2	3	4	5	Undesirable
Inevitable	1	2	3	4	5	Avoidable
Healthy	1	2	3	4	5	Unhealthy
Clean	1	2	3	4	5	Dirty

GOALS AND STYLES: A CONFLICT GRID

A number of paradigms, or models, have been proposed to represent the ways we try to manage and resolve conflicts. Among them is Robert Blake and Jane Mouton's **managerial grid** (Figure 10.1) which subsequently was adapted to describe five different conflict resolution styles.[22] The grid has two scales, both ranging from 1 (low) to 9 (high). The horizontal scale represents the extent to which a person wants to attain personal goals ("concern for production of results"). The vertical scale represents the extent to which the person is concerned for others ("concern for people"). On the basis of these measures, five main conflict styles emerge. As you consider the grid and the following description of the five styles, try to identify your own conflict style.

A person with a 1.1 conflict style can be described as an **avoider**; the avoider's attitude can be summed up as "lose and walk away." If you have a 1.1 style, your goal is to maintain neutrality at all costs. You probably view conflict as a useless and punishing experience, one that you would prefer to do without. Rather than tolerate the frustrations that can accompany conflict, you physically or mentally remove yourself from the conflict situation.

A person with a 1.9 style is an **accommodator**, whose attitude is "give in and lose." If you are a 1.9, your behavior demonstrates that you overvalue the maintenance of relationships and

FIGURE 10.1
Conflict Grid

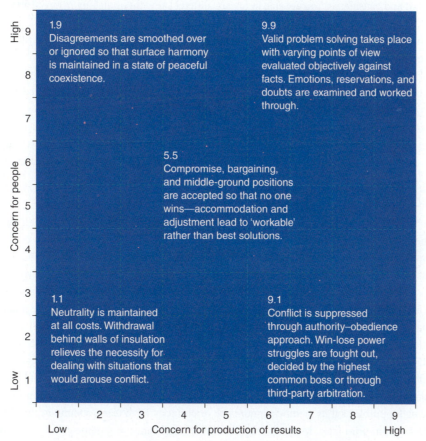

undervalue the achievement of your own goals. Your main concern is to ensure that others accept you, like you, and coexist in peace with you. Although conflicts may exist in your world, you refuse to deal with them. You feel a need to maintain an appearance of harmony at all costs, leading to an uneasy, tense state characterized by a great deal of smiling and nervous laughter.

A person with a 5.5 style is a **compromiser**, someone who wants to find a middle ground. You work to find a way to permit each participant in a conflict to gain something. Compromise is, of course, a valid strategy in some cases, but it can be a problem if you always settle for a workable solution because you are afraid the conflict may escalate if you try to find the best solution. It is undeniable that "half a loaf is better than none" and this conflict style will leave participants half-satisfied, but it can also leave them half-dissatisfied. Thus, compromise is sometimes as bad as the lose-lose approach.

A person with a 9.1 style is a **competitive forcer** who takes a win-lose attitude. If you are a 9.1, attaining your personal goals is far more important to you than is concern for other people. You have an overwhelming need to win and dominate others; you will defend your position and battle with others, whatever the cost or harm to them.

A person with a 9.9 style is a **problem-solving collaborator** who takes a win-win attitude. If you are a 9.9, you actively seek to satisfy your own goals (you are results-oriented) as well as those of others (you are person-oriented). This, of course, is the optimum style when you are seeking to reduce conflict. As a problem solver, you realize that conflicts are normal and can be helpful; you also realize that each person in a conflict holds legitimate opinions that deserve to be aired and considered. You are able to discuss differences without making personal attacks.

According to Alan Filley, effective conflict resolvers rely, to a large extent, on problem solving (9.9) and accommodating (1.9), whereas ineffective conflict resolvers rely extensively on forcing (9.1) and avoiding (1.1).[23]

If we are to develop and sustain meaningful group relationships, we need to learn to handle conflicts constructively. A conflict has been productive if all the participants are satisfied with the outcomes and believe they have gained something.[24] In other words, no one loses, everyone wins. In contrast, a conflict has been destructive if all participants are dissatisfied with the outcomes and believe that they have lost something. Perhaps one of the most important questions facing each of us is whether we can turn our conflicts into productive rather than destructive interactions.

STEER CLEAR OF GROUPTHINK

A body of research suggests that "smart people working collectively can be dumber than the sum of their brains."[25] This premise seems to have been at work in the tragedy involving the loss of the space shuttle *Columbia* and its crew in February 2003. Investigators looking into this disaster questioned the analysis by mission engineers after falling foam struck the shuttle during launch. NASA quickly concluded that the incident did not pose a danger to the crew and shuttle's safety and allowed the mission to proceed as planned. *Columbia* broke up on reentry; the foam had damaged the shuttle's wing and left it unable to withstand the atmospheric forces. Further investigation revealed that the decision-making culture at NASA was indicative of groupthink.

Groupthink has also been identified as a cause of numerous other fiascos, including the sinking of the *Titanic*, the surprise attack on Pearl Harbor, the failed Bay of Pigs invasion of Cuba, the escalation of the Vietnam War, and the wars in Iraq and Afghanistan. We can tell when a team is heading for problems if its members ignore risk or obstacles. Such teams attempt to shield those in power from grim facts. Meetings may contain an abundance of statements but not enough questions. Members acquiesce, seek as much credit as possible for themselves, argue to look smart, and eagerly place blame on others.[26]

So, what is **groupthink**, what does it have to do with conflict, and how does it come about? According to Irving Janis, author of *Groupthink*, it occurs when groups let the desire for consensus override careful analysis and reasoned decision making.[27] In the case of the *Columbia* disaster, some NASA engineers suspected that the damage caused by the falling foam was severe, but they were unwilling to voice a differing opinion for fear of creating conflict and dissension. In

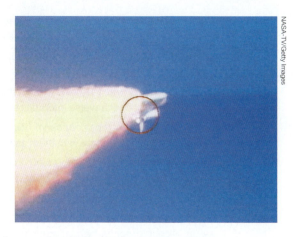

NASA-TV/Getty Images

effect, then, groupthink is an extreme way of avoiding conflict. Cohesiveness is normally a desirable group characteristic, but when carried to an extreme, it can become dysfunctional or even destructive.

Why is dissenting and risking finding ourselves in conflict with others a hard thing for many of us to do? Researchers have demonstrated that when asked to rate the attractiveness of facial photographs, young men changed their ratings significantly up or down based on how they believed their peers had rated the same photographs, revealing a bias fostered by a perceived social pressure to conform. Standing apart from a group not only leads us to think that we are different but also can cause us to think we are wrong.[28] On the other hand, dissenters—those who distinguish themselves by refusing to conform—become more willing to go the distance in defying the herd when they believe they have allies. If a dissenter thinks others support him or her, will be on his or her side in a potential conflict situation, then he or she is more likely to stand firm and make the effort to influence others in the group.[29]

When group members engage in sloppy thinking, they can fall prey to irrationality—behavior that causes them not only to make poor decisions but also to become involved in unnecessary conflicts. For example, one professor typically begins a class he teaches on negotiation skills by auctioning off a $20 bill. Because it is difficult to see a decision-making bias at work, not once in all the years that this professor has taught the class has the bidding halted below $20. In fact, it was not uncommon for the bids for the $20 to go as high as several hundred dollars. Getting caught in the raw power of herd behavior can cause group members to swear that black is white, merely because everyone else says so.[30] They may be decisive in their actions, but they are "decisively wrong."[31] Conformity by suppressing conflict impedes rational decision making.

Groupthink damages a group's ability to work through potential conflicts functionally to reach a good decision. To help combat groupthink, look out for the following symptoms:

iStock/HAYKIRDI

- *Illusion of invulnerability*: Group members believe they are virtually beyond harm, making them even more vulnerable to excessive risk taking.

- *Rationalization*: Members find reasons to disregard any warning of potential problems or negative information.

- *Mind guarding:* Members protect the leader and one another from hearing or being notified about adverse information or potential problems that could shatter the status quo.

- *Stereotyping those opposed:* Members have an "us versus them" mind-set; they view those who disagree with them as weak, foolish, and not worthy of serious consideration.

- *Self-censorship:* Members do not voice their doubts or concerns.

- *Assumption of morality:* Members believe in the inherent goodness of their actions or cause. Therefore, any opposition is perceived as immoral.

- *Illusion of unanimity:* Differences of opinion are not discussed, causing members to assume, sometimes incorrectly, that everyone agrees.

- *Pressure to conform:* Members put real pressure on one another to agree, to go along with the group, to be a team player.

SKILL BUILDER

What Kind of Thinker Are You?

Do you engage in groupthink? To find out, answer yes or no to each of the following questions, and explain your answers with examples.

1. Have you ever felt so secure about a group decision that you ignored all warning signs that the decision was wrong? Why?

2. Have you ever been party to a rationalization justifying a group decision? Why?

3. Have you ever defended a group decision by pointing to your group's inherent sense of morality?

4. Have you ever participated in feeding an "us versus them" feeling? Have you depicted those opposed to you in simplistic, stereotyped ways?

5. Have you ever censored your own comments because you feared destroying the sense of unanimity in your group?

6. Have you ever applied direct pressure to dissenting members in an effort to get them to agree with the will of the group?

7. Have you ever served as a "mind guard"? That is, have you ever attempted to preserve your group's cohesiveness by preventing disturbing outside ideas or opinions from becoming known to other group members?

8. Have you ever assumed that the silence of other group members implied agreement?

Each time you answered yes to one of these questions, you indicated that you have contributed to an illusion of group unanimity; in effect, you let a tendency to agree interfere with your ability to think critically. In so doing, you became a groupthinker. Groupthink impedes effective group functioning; the fact is, when all group members think alike, no one thinks very much.

COOPERATIVE VERSUS COMPETITIVE CONFLICT: WIN-WIN OR WIN-LOSE

A lion used to prowl about a field in which four oxen dwelled. Many a time he tried to attack them, but whenever he came near, they turned their tails to one another, so that whichever way he approached them, he was met by the horns of one of them. At last, however, they fell a-quarreling among themselves, and each went off to the pasture alone in a separate corner of the field. Then the lion attacked them one by one and soon made an end to all four.[32]

How does this story from *Aesop's Fables* apply to our study of conflict? Unlike the oxen, you can learn to handle your conflicts constructively; you can learn to disagree without becoming disagreeable. In general, people enter into a conflict situation with one of two orientations or perspectives: competition or cooperation. People who have a **competitive set** perceive a conflict situation in all-or-nothing terms and believe that to attain victory, they must defeat the other participants. They do not believe that their own interests and those of others are compatible. By contrast, people with a **cooperative set** believe that a way to share the rewards of the situation can be discovered.

If people bring a competitive orientation to a conflict, they will tend to be ego-involved and will see winning as a test of personal worth and competence. If a conflict is defined as competitive, then participants become combatants: They believe that, to attain victory, they must defeat the other side. In contrast, if people bring a cooperative orientation to a conflict, they are likely to look for a mutually beneficial way to resolve the disagreement. For a conflict to be defined as cooperative, each participant must demonstrate a willingness to resolve it in a mutually satisfactory way. If the people involved in a conflict are treated with respect by all the others involved, if they are neither demeaned nor provoked, and if communication is free and open instead of underhanded and closed, the disagreement may be settled amicably.

We can define a conflict as a win-lose situation, or we can define it as a win-win situation. If we define it as win-lose, we will tend to pursue our own goals, misrepresent our needs, avoid empathizing with or understanding the feelings of others, and use threats or promises to get others to go along with us. If we define a conflict as win-win, we will tend to view it as a common problem, try to pursue common goals, honestly reveal our needs to others, work to understand the other side's position and frame of reference, and make every effort to reduce rather than increase defensiveness.[33]

To transform a conflict from competitive to cooperative, you must use effective communication techniques.[34] There are a number of workable strategies that you can practice using until you come to rely on them unconsciously. One strategy is **role reversal**—that is, acting as if you were the person(s) with whom you are in conflict. This strategy can help those involved in a conflict understand each other, find creative ways to integrate their interests and concerns, and work toward a common goal. Reversing roles helps you avoid judging others by enabling you to see things from their perspective. Once you can replace a statement like "You're wrong" or "You're stupid" with one like "What you believe is not what I believe," you will be on your way to developing a cooperative orientation.

EXPLORING DIVERSITY

Win-Win

The following apocryphal story offers a lesson on how culture, in general, influences attitudes toward competition and a more specific lesson on how it influences attitudes toward competition among the Navajo:

> A new teacher arrived at a Navajo reservation. Each day, something like the following occurred: The teacher would ask five of her young Navajo students to go to the chalkboard and complete a simple mathematics problem. All five students would go to the chalkboard, but not one of them would tackle the problem. Instead, they would all stand silent and motionless.
>
> The instructor, of course, wondered what was going on. She repeatedly asked herself if she might be calling on students who were unable do the problems. Discounting that possibility, finally, she asked her students what the problem was. Their answer displayed a depth of understanding not many have.
>
> The students knew that not everyone in the class would be able to complete the problems correctly. But they respected each other and they understood the dangers of a win-lose approach. In their opinion, no one would win if anyone was embarrassed or humiliated, and so they refused to compete publicly with each other.

Where do you stand? Would typical American schoolchildren behave similarly? Why or why not? Should they behave more like the Navajos? Explain your answer.

THE INFLUENCE OF GENDER, CULTURE, AND TECHNOLOGY ON LEADERSHIP AND CONFLICT MANAGEMENT

How do our gender expectations, cultural mores, and prevailing online norms influence the performance of leadership and the handling of conflict? How does socialization impact approaches to both leadership and conflict management?

GENDER, LEADERSHIP, AND CONFLICT: COMPARING APPROACHES

Are we shifting away from traditional leadership approaches emphasizing stereotypical masculine attributes, such as competitiveness, aggression, and control, to a paradigm reflective of more stereotypically feminine attributes, such as collaborative problem solving, connectedness, and supportiveness? Some say that is the case.[35]

Gendered Leaders and Relationships

Men continue to be perceived as better at strategic planning, more in control of emotional expression, and more willing to take the kind of risks that facilitate innovation.[36] Women are perceived as dependable while men are seen as visionary.[37] Despite these views, studies show that women in leadership roles enhance profitability.[38] Indeed, women generally score higher than men in people-oriented leadership skills such as empathizing, keeping people informed, providing feedback, sharing responsibilities, demonstrating sensitivity to the needs of others, and creating environments in which people can learn, grow, think, and achieve together.[39]

A prevailing expectation is for women to excel at relationship building and participative leadership and for men to excel at being work-directed and assertive. On the other hand, a man can exhibit a feminine leadership style, just as a woman can display leadership behaviors that are masculine. Indeed, the most effective leadership style may be blended, drawing on both masculine and feminine strengths.

Unfortunately, sex-role stereotypes persist in influencing perceptions of and expectations for male and female leadership styles, with people evaluating the same message differently, depending on whether a man or a woman delivered it. Thus, women are labeled as bossy or overly emotional, whereas men delivering the same messages are seen as responsible and as exercising leadership.[40] Too often, when a woman is perceived to be acting like a man, others misinterpret or devalue her leadership efforts. Women leaders such as Hillary Clinton, Meg Whitman, Elizabeth Warren, and Nancy Pelosi have found themselves enacting their "alpha-ness," whereas it has become somewhat more acceptable for men to shed the "strongman" stereotype.[41]

Gendered Leaders and Conflict

Women and men have been socialized to approach conflict differently.[42] Whereas most men have been socialized to be demanding and competitive, women have been taught to practice cooperativeness, compromise, and accommodation instead. Men tend to become verbally aggressive and adopt a fight mentality, whereas women are more likely to engage in protracted negotiation in the attempt to avoid a fight.[43] When asked to describe how their style of handling conflict differed from that of men, women noted that men are overly concerned with power and content issues and less concerned with relational issues. Women place more emphasis on preserving their relationships during conflict than men do; instead of focusing on the content, they focus on feelings.[44]

Men, however, are more likely than women to withdraw from a conflict. Researchers believe this may occur because men become substantially psychologically and physiologically aroused during conflict and may opt to withdraw from the conflict rather than risk further escalation or a confrontation that turns physical.[45] Women prefer to talk about conflict in an effort to resolve it.[46] Women are more likely to reveal their negative feelings and become emotional during conflict. Men, on the other hand, are more apt to keep their negative feelings to themselves.[47]

CULTURE, LEADERSHIP, AND CONFLICT: COMPARING VIEWS

Culture influences group interaction. Although cultural variations often enhance a group's operation, at times cultural clashes impede it, resulting in conflict.[48] For example, when Corning and the Mexican company Vitro made a cross-border alliance, cultural misunderstandings hurt their communication efforts. According to business leaders, problems developed in the relationship because of stereotypes as well as the different decision-making and work-style approaches employed by the two companies. Whereas the Americans were accustomed to working lunches in the office, the Mexicans were used to going out for leisurely meals. The Mexicans typically put in much longer workdays because of their longer lunches and conducted evening meetings, whereas the Americans wanted to keep business matters to daytime hours. The Mexicans saw the Americans as too direct, and the Americans viewed the Mexicans as too polite. But the decision-making methods of the two companies created the most potential for conflict between the two groups: Because Mexican businesses tend to be much more hierarchical, the decisions were made by the top executives, which slowed down the decision-making process. The Mexicans, unlike the Americans, displayed an unwillingness to criticize. As a result, the conversations of the Americans were more direct.[49]

As is true of the Mexican style of decision making, the Japanese decision-making style also differs from the American approach. Whereas Americans tend to value openness in groups, the Japanese value harmony. Americans emphasize individual responsibility, in contrast to the Japanese, who stress collective responsibility.[50] Thus, there is a tendency among the Japanese to lose individual identity within the group.[51] We see that people in one country who need to work on a team with people in another would be wise to learn about each other in order to alleviate any discomfort they feel with the cultural differences that could provoke conflict. For example, Middle Easterners expect members to engage in small talk to build rapport rather than get straight to the group's agenda.

> Visit the interactive e-Book to access the Exploring Diversity feature "Which Cultural Differences Affect a Group's Functioning?," which will ask you to consider how diversity within a group can help or hinder the group's cohesion.

Overcoming Cultural Challenges to Reach Common Understandings

Reaching common understandings in culturally diverse groups poses challenges. Indian workers, for example, may not be used to the fairly forward or aggressive Western styles, so Western executives who are used to discussing business after the workday is over may need to stick to small talk at such occasions. Attitudes toward time also can affect meetings. Asians, for example, are usually unconcerned when it comes to the time a meeting will end. If the meeting is going well, time is not a factor; they will keep the meeting going.

Even though group membership and group identity are highly valued in collectivistic cultures, participating in decision-making groups does not appear to give group members actual decision-making power. In one study of 48 Japanese organizations, members were encouraged to contribute ideas, but the decision-making power remained with the CEO and managers high in the organizational hierarchy.[52]

As we see, culture influences both membership and leadership style, with the group's cultural makeup affecting the group's potential to develop shared leadership. Even though the generalizations we are about to make are not true of every person in every country, in general, they are thought to be valid. According to researchers, people in a large number of countries, including Arab countries, Brazil, Chile, Greece, Mexico, Pakistan, and Peru, tend to accept unequal distribution of power in their institutions and organizations and consequently prefer participating in groups with a centralized decision-making structure. Part of the leader's reluctance to share leadership in these cultures is because leadership is perceived as the sole prerogative of the appointed leader, who believes others will perceive him or her as weak if he or she attempts to share control. In contrast, countries in which power is distributed more equitably, such as Australia, Canada, Denmark, Israel, and the United States, tend to be more comfortable practicing decentralized or shared decision making.[53]

Cultures differ along a continuum that ranges from nurturing to aggressive. Societies tending toward the aggressive end of the scale include Arab countries, Hong Kong, Mexico, and the United States. Group members from these countries focus on goal achievement and are likely to be more assertive and competitive even if it comes at others' expense. In general, members from aggressive societies tend to vie for control rather than work toward shared leadership, unless sharing leadership is paired with outsmarting or beating the competition. By contrast, group members from more nurturing cultures, such as Finland, Italy, Brazil, and France, tend to emphasize concern for developing the potential of all, preferring to share rather than compete. In the United States, recognition of one's work is a great reward. In Russia, compromise is viewed as a weakness. The Chinese expect to build strong relationships with their negotiating partners before reaching an agreement.

Whether members come from individualistic cultures, such as those in Argentina, Austria, Canada, and the United States, or collectivist cultures, such as those in Greece, Indonesia, Spain, and Turkey, also influences how easy or hard members find it to share leadership. People from individualistic cultures tend to be more independent and self-reliant. Enjoyers of personal freedom, they often are less inclined to meet the demands of teamwork. In contrast, people from collectivistic cultures are more predisposed to helping the team even if it comes at a personal cost.[54]

We should note that companies also are mixing age groups in teams—looking for a mix of skills and experiences, trying to create environments where senior people understand what younger workers bring to the table, and vice versa, so that all member regardless of age feel appreciated and valued. Human resources consultant Betty Price coined the term *gen-blending* to describe the practice of having workers from different generations come together in groups to solve problems.[55]

Rawpixel.com/Shutterstock.com

My Way or the Highway

On the basis of your understanding of leadership, the nature of conflict, and the value of effective conflict management, agree or disagree with this excerpt from Deborah Tannen's book *Talking From 9 to 5*. Supply reasons and examples from both research and your own life that support the stance you take, and indicate whether or not you think intransigence is ethical.

> When decisions are made by groups, not everyone has equal access to the decision-making process. Those who will take a position and refuse to budge, regardless of the persuasive power or intensity of feeling among others, are far more likely to get their way. Those who feel strongly about a position but are inclined to back off in the face of intransigence or very strong feeling from others are much less likely to get their way.[56]

LEADING GROUPS AND HANDLING CONFLICT IN CYBERSPACE

It is quite common for groups to hold virtual meetings—teleconferences, video conferences, or Web conferences—that link participants in remote locations. Besides facilitating discussion

among people in diverse places, online groups have several other advantages as well. When working to resolve conflict, they tend to be less influenced by member status and less subject to dominance by a single member. Separated from the physical workplace, they are able to focus more on work and less on interpersonal frictions or the dynamics of office politics.[57] However, the online groups that members most enjoy are those in which members take active responsibility for their group's progress by adequately preparing for meetings, and ones in which the responsiveness of group members to each other is high, enhancing conflict resolution and promoting collaboration.[58]

Foursquare, a social media platform, turns real-world spaces into a game and pits friends and coworkers against one another in potentially conflict-producing competitions. Users of Foursquare vie to be the leader or "mayor" of a particular location, which might be a bar, a store, a restaurant, an office or conference room, or even a bridge, a parking spot, or trash-filled alley. The player who checks into the particular location the most within a 60-day period is named its mayor. Foursquare precipitates conflict as it generates turf battles, often petty and vicious, because users become emotionally invested. The application taps into the desire to win, especially in competition with peers, even if users need to break the rules to secure a place to call their own. Some users who believe others are cheating—perhaps checking in from a car or from the comfort of their own couch—will shame them on other sites, even posting photos on Twitter, accusing them of deception.[59]

Unfortunately, a dysfunctional online behavior, cyberbullying, is occurring more and more frequently and producing conflict in school, the workplace, and our social lives. For example, one supervisor checked out an employee on Facebook and downloaded some pictures, which he sent to colleagues in his group with this note, "Look at these two gay boys," creating a hostile work environment.[60] By exhibiting characteristics of the competitive forcer mentioned earlier in the chapter, workplace bullies make themselves feel better by putting their coworkers down. About one in three workers reports having witnessed someone being bullied on the job. The Workplace Bullying Institute notes that 37% of U.S. workers have reported being bullied—subjected to repeated, health-harming verbal abuse; threatening, humiliating, or offensive behavior, or other forms of interpersonal sabotage.[61] How would you handle these occurrences?

COMMUNICATION SKILLS

Practice Tips for Ethical Conflict Management

Conflict can be managed productively by applying the principles of effective communication. The following suggestions are a basic guide to handling conflict effectively.

Recognize that conflicts can be settled rationally.

Act like a capable, competent problem solver by expressing your feelings openly, directly, and constructively. Recognize unproductive or irrational behaviors such as insulting, attacking, or withdrawing from others. Focus on issues, not personalities. Be willing to listen and react appropriately to the other person.

Define the conflict.

Ask questions such as "Why are we in conflict? What is the nature of the conflict? Which of us feels more strongly about the issue? What can we do about it?" It is important to send "I" messages ("I think it's unfair for me to do all of the work around here"; "I don't like going to the library for everyone else") and to avoid sending blame messages ("You do everything wrong"; "You are a spoiled brat").

Check your perceptions.

In conflict-ripe situations, we often distort the behavior, position, or motivation of the other person involved. We may deny the legitimacy of any position other than our own. To combat this, let each person take the time to explain his or her assumptions and frame of reference to others, and be sure to listen to one another. Along with active listening, role reversal can help people in conflict to understand the other side.

(Continued)

(Continued)

Suggest possible solutions.

Working as a group, come up with a variety of solutions without evaluating, condemning, or mocking any of them. Suspend judgment and allow for any number of resolutions to the conflict.

Assess alternative solutions and choose the one that seems best.

Try to determine which solutions make everyone lose, which let one side win, and which let everyone win. Once all of the solutions have been assessed, you are in a position to determine if one of the mutually acceptable choices is clearly superior.

Try your solution and evaluate it.

During the "try out" stage, you try to ascertain who is doing what, when, where, and under what conditions, and you ask how all this is affecting each person in the group. Then you see how well the chosen solution has solved the problem and whether the outcome has been rewarding to everyone. If not, begin the process again.

> You can't eat your friends and have them too.

Budd Schulberg

COMPLETE THIS CHAPTER 10 CHECKLIST

10.1 I can define leadership and distinguish among the following leadership styles: type X, type Y, autocratic, laissez-faire, and democratic. ☐

Leadership is the ability to influence others. There are different leadership styles. A type X leader believes group members need to be closely controlled and coerced to work. A type Y leader believes members are self-directed and seek responsibility as well as opportunities for personal achievement. The autocratic leader dominates and directs all the other members of the group, whereas the laissez-faire leader lets them do their own thing. In most situations, the democratic leader, a leader who encourages all members to be involved constructively in decision making and problem solving, is preferred.

10.2 I can compare and contrast trait, situational, functional, and transformational theories of leadership. ☐

There are four principal explanations of how people become leaders. Trait theory holds that some men and women are simply born to lead. Situational theory holds that the situation itself—the nature of the problem and the characteristics of the group—determines who assumes leadership. Functional theory holds that a number of group members can and should share the various leadership functions that need to be performed if the group is to achieve its goals. A transformational leader helps group members imagine and visualize the future so group members can hold together, strengthening the group's culture.

10.3 I can analyze conflict styles and explain the dangers of conflict avoidance. ☐

Blake and Mouton's managerial grid has been adapted to map different styles of handling conflict. The avoider walks away from the conflict. The accommodator gives in. The compromiser finds middle ground. The competitive forcer seeks to win at any cost. The most productive style is that of the problem-solving collaborator who takes a win-win approach and has high concern both for results and the feelings of other people.

Groupthink develops where a group allows the desire for consensus to override careful analysis of a problem, the effective handling of functional conflicts, and reasoned decision making.

10.4 I can discuss how personal characteristics, gender, cultural factors, and technology influence approaches to leadership and conflict. ☐

Personal factors, like the tendency to cooperate or compete, and attitudes toward leadership and conflict related to gender and cultural preferences play roles in influencing group member behavior. So does technology. Virtual meetings, the ability to have a telepresence, and online sites that foster conflict are providing both benefits and challenges when it comes to the leading of groups and the handling of conflicts.

10.5 I can use my skills to handle conflict more constructively. □

First, recognize that by focusing on issues, instead of personalities, conflicts can be settled rationally. Next, define the conflict and check the accuracy of perceptions by using "I" messages, empathic listening, and role reversal, as appropriate. Then, suggest and assess a variety of solutions to the conflict. Finally, choose the one that is mutually acceptable, and try it out.

BECOME A WORD MASTER

accommodator 269

achieved leader 262

autocratic
    leader 264

avoider 269

competitive
    forcer 270

competitive set 273

compromiser 270

conflict 268

cooperative set 273

democratic
    leaders 265

designated
    leader 262

functional theory 267

groupthink 271

laissez-faire
    leader 264

leadership 262

managerial grid 269

problem-solving
    collaborator 270

role reversal 273

situational
    theory 266

trait theory 265

transformational
    leader 267

type X leader 263

type Y leader 263

iStock/Tinpixels

iStock/recep-bg

11

Public Speaking and You

11.1 Describe the sources of, and potential remedies for, public speaking anxiety.

11.2 Explain how to approach public speaking systematically.

11.3 Explain why conducting a comprehensive self-analysis facilitates the speechmaking process.

11.4 Analyze your audience so that you can tailor your speech to them.

11.5 Explain how the nature of the occasion influences a speech.

11.6 Identify topic selection criteria.

11.7 Narrow your topic, formulate a thesis statement, and develop main points for your speech.

11.8 Apply skills for improving speech preparation.

> In the United States, there are more than twenty thousand different ways of earning a living, and effective speech is essential to every one.
>
> Andrew Weaver

Our technologically rich environment is dependent on both written and visual user-generated content. Every day, we provide some of that content. We send and receive e-mail, texts, and tweets. We blog, create podcasts, and post on social media. In this section of the text, it's time to apply our content-generation skills to a different communication venue: the public speech, an important means of sharing information, opening minds, and advocating for ideas.

Even in our age of abundant digital connections, public speakers are in demand with the number of platforms open to them increasing. From corporate meetings to trade shows, from educational conferences to political rallies, from town halls to your classroom, from YouTube to Facebook, from Ted.com to Twitter, public speakers have key roles to play. Public speaking is like a form of currency, only instead of providing access to the marketplace of goods and services, it provides access to the marketplace of ideas. From Mark Zuckerberg or Sheryl Sandberg to a local school superintendent or a concerned parent, from Oprah and Bono to you and your peers, we share the responsibility to make our voices heard.

There is no shortage of advice on how to improve your ability to speak so that others listen. From blogs to self-help books, from DVDs to this text, resources exist to help you become more effective and at ease speaking in public.

No matter your age, sex, or ethnic or racial background, becoming effective at speaking in public is an important skill to develop. Because speaking before others is likely to play an important role in your future, let's prepare to meet that challenge. ■

BUILDING PUBLIC SPEAKING CONFIDENCE

Public speaking is the act of preparing, staging, and delivering a presentation to an audience. We speak every day. Under ordinary circumstances, we rarely give our speaking skills a second thought—that is, until we are asked to speak before an audience and deliver a speech. Once we know this is what we're going to have to do, if we're like most Americans, we fear it more than we fear bee stings, accidents, or heights (Figure 11.1).[1] In fact, when asked how they feel about speaking in public, many people answer that they'd rather be in the casket than be delivering the eulogy.

Is the day when you will have to step in front of the class and give your first presentation drawing closer? Experiencing stress at the thought of speaking in front of other people isn't restricted to students. Kings, presidents, actors, and professors find this stressful it as well. Some people fear stuttering (as did King George VI of the United Kingdom, whose experiences speaking in public were dramatized in the film *The King's Speech*). Others fear saying the wrong thing or putting the audience to sleep. You may feel so anxious that you wonder if you'll really be able to gather your courage and do it. The answer is, of course, you will!

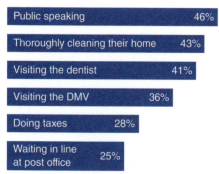

FIGURE 11.1
Activities Adults Say They Dread

Activity	Percentage
Public speaking	46%
Thoroughly cleaning their home	43%
Visiting the dentist	41%
Visiting the DMV	36%
Doing taxes	28%
Waiting in line at post office	25%

Source: USA Today, May 14–16, 2010, p. 1A

We can overcome whatever anxiety we feel about speaking in public by understanding the sources of our anxieties, learning to cope with our fears, using strategies to handle the physical and mental symptoms produced by our anxiety, and preparing and rehearsing our presentations thoroughly. When a speaker is energetic and passionate about a speech, the audience reciprocates, as illustrated by one prominent motivational speaker who begins his presentations like this:

I couldn't sleep last night. I finally got up at 4 this morning. I got dressed and went through this presentation 37 times. And guess what? You loved it. (Gentle laughter.) And let me tell you one thing I'll never forget about this group. That is, when I got introduced, everyone was standing. (More laughter.) Tell you what I'm going to do. I'm going to reintroduce myself, and what I want you to do is just give me the welcome you gave me this morning. Just pump it up. OK? Are you ready? (Music pulses.) Ladies and gentlemen, all the way from Atlanta, GA. If you forget everything I say, don't forget this . . . You are the best at what you do because of one main thing: Attitude. (The audience stands and cheers.)[2]

What is your attitude toward speaking in public? If you experience a certain amount of apprehension before, during, or even after presenting a speech, rest assured that you are not alone.[3] The key is not to allow your fears to get the better of you. Instead, by following the suggestions in this chapter, you can learn to use your anxiety as a positive force.

CAREER BUILDER: TED'S GOT TALENT

1. Watch five TED Talks presentations at www.ted.com.

2. Rank the five presentations from least effective to most effective.

3. Describe in detail what makes the most effective TED presentation a winner from your perspective. Include attributes of both the speaker and the speech in your analysis.

4. Contrast the most effective presentation with the one you perceived to be least effective. Describe the particular characteristics of the speaker and the speech that contributed to this speech being least effective.

5. What did you learn from each of the TED speakers that you can apply when planning and presenting your own speeches in educational, business, and public arenas?

UNDERSTAND YOUR FEARS

Let's look at how to make **public speaking anxiety** (fear of speaking to an audience) work in your favor. Public speaking anxiety affects some 40% to 80% of us.[4] It has two dimensions: process anxiety and performance anxiety. *Process anxiety* is fear of preparing a speech. *Performance anxiety* is fear of presenting a speech.

Public speaking anxiety also is a form of **communication apprehension**, which is fear of communicating no matter the context. Communication apprehension affects about 20% of the U.S. popula-

iStock/mokee81

tion. Those affected exhibit "trait" apprehension, meaning they have a predisposition to being apprehensive. In contrast, more of us experience occasional or "state" apprehension when facing a specific situation like public speaking.[5] To determine your communication anxiety and communication apprehension scores, you can complete the "Self-Assessment of Speaking Anxiousness" Skill Builder and access the Perceived Report of Communication Apprehension (PRCA) developed by James McCroskey at http://www.jamescmccroskey.com/measures/.

SKILL BUILDER

Self-Assessment of Speaking Anxiousness

How anxious are you about delivering a speech? Use the following assessment to find out. Although this evaluation is not a scientific instrument, it should give you some indication of your level of fear. Note that it is normal to display some level of anxiety. If you had no apprehension about speaking in public, you would not be typical; what's more, you probably would not make a very effective speaker either.

On the line before each of the following statements, enter the number in the rating scale that best represents your feelings about each statement:

Not at all concerned 1 2 3 4 5 Extremely concerned

1. _____ I will forget what I plan to say.

2. _____ My thoughts will confuse listeners.

3. _____ My words will offend listeners.

4. _____ Audience members will laugh at me when I don't mean to be funny.

5. _____ I'm going to embarrass myself.

6. _____ My ideas will have no impact.

7. _____ I will look foolish in front of my audience, because I won't be able to look them in the eyes and/or I won't know what to do with my hands.

8. _____ My voice and body will shake uncontrollably.

9. _____ I will bore my audience.

10. _____ Audience members will stare at me unresponsively.

To determine your score, add together the numbers you selected:

TOTAL SCORE _____

To determine your fear level, refer to the scale below:

41–50 You have speech anxiety.

31–40 You are very apprehensive.

21–30 You are concerned to a normal extent.

10–20 You are very confident.

UNDERSTAND SOURCES OF PUBLIC SPEAKING ANXIETY

What makes some of us fear speaking in front of others?

Fear of Failure

We all fear failure.[6] If we choose not to take risks because we visualize ourselves failing rather than succeeding, if we disagree with what we hear or read but choose to keep our thoughts to ourselves, then we are probably letting our feelings of inferiority limit us.

Fear of the Unknown

Some of us fear what we do not know or have not had successful experience with. The unknown leaves much to the imagination, and far too frequently, we irrationally choose to imagine the worst thing that could happen when making a speech.

Fear of Evaluation

Some of us also fear that others will judge our ideas, how we sound or look, or what we represent. When given a choice, we prefer not to be judged.

Fear of Being the Center of Attention

We also may fear being conspicuous or singled out. Audience members usually focus directly on the speaker. Some of us interpret receivers' gazes as scrutinizing and hostile rather than as revealing a genuine interest in us.

Fear of Difference

Ethnocentricity—the belief that one's own group or culture is better than others—makes some of think that we share nothing in common with the members of our audience. Feelings of difference make it more difficult to find common ground, which in turn, increases anxiety about making a speech.

Fear Due to Cultural Background

Culture may influence our attitudes toward speaking in public. For example, research suggests that Filipinos, Israelis, and other Middle Eastern peoples are typically less apprehensive about public speaking than are Americans.[7] In these cultures, children are rewarded for effort, making judgment and communication anxiety a less intrusive force.[8]

CONTROLLING SPEECHMAKING ANXIETY

One of the best ways to cope with fear of giving a speech is to design and rehearse your speech carefully. Being prepared is a confidence builder. While we still might feel anxious, there are steps we can take to control both the physical and mental effects we experience.

The first thing to do is to recognize the bodily sensations and thoughts that accompany and support feelings of nervousness. Make a list of the physical symptoms you experience and the fear-related thoughts that occur to you. Then compare your list with the symptoms and thoughts that others in the class identified. Do the lists include any of these physical symptoms?

Rapid or irregular heartbeat

Stiff neck

Stomach knots

Lump in the throat

Shaking hands, arms, or legs

Nausea

Dry mouth

Dizziness

Were statements like these included on the lists?

"I just can't cope."

"I'm under too much pressure."

"This is my worst nightmare."

"I know something terrible is going to happen."

Once you identify the physical and mental sensations that accompany fear, the next step is to learn how to control your reactions.

Use Deep-Muscle Relaxation to Overcome Physical Symptoms

Muscle tension commonly accompanies fear and anxiety. Whereas it can be difficult to intentionally relax a muscle, you can tense it further. Once you stop, the muscle will relax more fully. Deep-muscle relaxation is a technique that takes advantage of this fact.

Try this. Tense one arm. Count to 10. Now relax your arm. What feelings did you experience? Did your arm seem to become heavier? Did it seem to become warmer? Next, try tensing and relaxing one or both of your legs. When you examine what happens, you'll see that you can calm yourself by systematically tensing and relaxing various parts of your body.

Use such techniques several times before you actually present a speech. Some students report that butterflies or tension tends to settle in particular body sections. It can be helpful to check the bodily sensations you feel when anxious and personalize the "tense and relax" approach to focus on your individual symptoms.

> Visit the interactive e-Book to access the Skill Builder feature "Tense and Relax" in which you will practice transitioning from a tense state to a "de-tensed" one.

Use Thought Stopping to Overcome Mental Symptoms

Anxiety is not simply a physical phenomenon. It also manifests in our thoughts. Thus, it's important to work to eliminate the thoughts associated with anxiety, as well as the bodily symptoms.

Many people use the word *relax* to calm themselves. Unfortunately, the sound of the word *relax* itself is not very relaxing because of the harshness of the voiced "x." It is better to substitute the word *calm* with its soft vowel and soothing "m."

A variation on the "calm technique" is to precede the word *calm* with the word *stop*. When you begin to think upsetting thoughts, say to yourself, "Stop!" Then follow that command with "Calm." For example:

"I just can't get up in front of all these people. Look at their cold stares and mean smirks."

"Stop!"

"Calm."

You may find that you can adapt this thought-stopping technique to help you handle symptoms of anxiety in interpersonal situations as well.

Use Visualization to Picture Yourself Succeeding

Sports psychologists use a technique called *visualization* to help athletes compete more effectively. The athletes are guided in visualizing the successful completion of a play or a game. They are asked to imagine how they will feel when they win. Eventually, when they go out on the field to compete, it is almost as if they have been there before—and have already won.

You may want to try the technique of visualization to boost your speaking confidence. Sit in a quiet place. Picture yourself approaching the front of the classroom. See yourself delivering your presentation. Then hear your audience applaud. After you have delivered the speech, answer these questions: Did the experience help you to control your anxiety? Did it help you succeed?

iStock/RyanKing999

Other Techniques

Speakers report that other techniques also can help reduce speech apprehension. Some try to include a bit of humor early in the speech in order to elicit a favorable response from the audience right away. They say that such a reaction helps them calm their nerves for the remainder of the presentation. Others look for a friendly face and talk to that person for a moment or two early in the speech. Others use visuals aids, like slides, to help them organize the material. The visual shows the next major point to be covered, eliminating the necessity for the speaker to remember it or refer to notes. Still others report that they rehearse a speech aloud, standing in front of an imaginary audience and "talking through" the material again and again. Some even deliver their speech to their pets. What other techniques have you found helpful?

Remember, no matter how you choose to deal with it, fear is a natural response. Although you probably can never eliminate it completely, you do need to learn to cope with your fears if you're to deliver a successful presentation.

If we take the time to analyze and practice successful behaviors, we can learn to handle ourselves more effectively as speakers. With practice, we can develop the understanding and master the skills that will turn us into articulate presenters who are organized, confident, and competent and able to communicate in such a way that others will be interested in us and persuaded by us.

We begin our exploration of public speaking by putting the entire speechmaking process into a logical sequence that you can follow. The process serves as a road map that you can use to prepare every public presentation you'll ever make.

APPROACHING SPEECH MAKING SYSTEMATICALLY: A PRIMER FOR GIVING YOUR FIRST SPEECH

How do you respond to the challenge of public speaking? Some of us may believe that speech making is an inborn skill: "I talk a lot, so this public speaking business is not a problem for me." Others of us may view it as torture: "I'm shaking like a leaf at the thought of speaking in public. This is going to be traumatic!" These attitudes represent two extremes, and either can cause problems. Why? Because those of us who are overconfident run the risk of being inadequate speakers. If we feel we know it all, we are apt to conduct too little research and expend too little effort. As a result, we likely show up ill-prepared. Similarly, those of us who are overly anxious find it terribly trying and nerve-racking to stand before an audience and deliver a presentation. Our nerves control us instead of vice versa. We lose focus and distract ourselves from the task at hand.

The most effective among us are those who display a healthy respect for the challenges involved in delivering a speech and who work systematically to create, prepare, and present an admirable presentation. Let's all make the effort to belong to this group.

PROCEED STEP-BY-STEP

The staircase-like chart in Figure 11.2 illustrates a systematic, step-by-step approach to public speaking. As you make your way up the staircase, you move from one speechmaking phase into another. There is a logical order to speech making that can be reduced to four main phases, represented in the figure by staircase landings. They are:

1. Topic selection and self-analysis and audience analysis
2. Speech development, support, and organization

FIGURE 11.2
Systematic Speaking Process

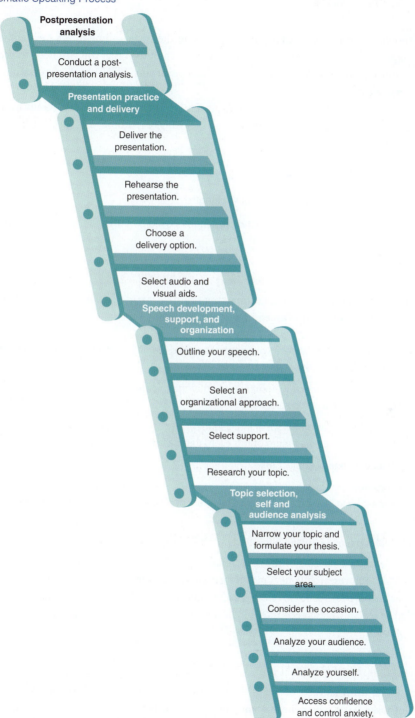

Postpresentation analysis

Conduct a post-presentation analysis.

Presentation practice and delivery

Deliver the presentation.

Rehearse the presentation.

Choose a delivery option.

Select audio and visual aids.

Speech development, support, and organization

Outline your speech.

Select an organizational approach.

Select support.

Research your topic.

Topic selection, self and audience analysis

Narrow your topic and formulate your thesis.

Select your subject area.

Consider the occasion.

Analyze your audience.

Analyze yourself.

Access confidence and control anxiety.

3. Presentation practice and delivery

4. Postpresentation analysis

Although the primary focus of this chapter is on the steps leading to the first landing of the speechmaking staircase, we will briefly review each of the tasks you will need to accomplish as you ascend to the staircase's top—at which point you will be able to successfully give and then evaluate your speech.

Before we preview each of these tasks, let us remind you that the staircase is only as strong as its foundation. To ensure your foundation is strong, each time you speak, ask yourself these questions:

- Am I handling my topic as ethically as possible?

- Am I applying principles of critical thinking?

- Am I as sensitive as I can be to the challenges posed by the diversity inherent in my audience?

First Landing: Topic Selection and Self-Analysis and Audience Analysis

To reach the first landing of the speechmaking staircase, *topic selection and self-analysis and audience analysis*, you need to ascend five steps, completing the following tasks:

1. Analyze yourself to assess your confidence and identify your interests, concerns, and areas of special knowledge.

2. Analyze your audience to identify ways that their interests, needs, and knowledge could affect your topic selection.

3. Identify the occasion for speaking, including any special requirements assigned by your instructor or the nature of the event that calls for the speech.

4. Choose a general subject area.

5. Concentrate on making that subject increasingly specific. By narrowing your scope, you will be able to select a clear thesis statement and cover the topic in the time allotted you.

Second Landing: Speech Development, Support, and Organization

To reach the second landing of the speechmaking staircase, *speech development, support, and organization*, you research your topic and gather supporting materials you can use to clarify your speech's purpose. You also select presentation aids. Finally, you organize all the materials you plan to use in your speech into a logical sequence that facilitates the communication of your message.

Third Landing: Presentation Practice and Delivery

To reach the third landing of the speechmaking staircase, you need to complete another series of tasks. First, you rehearse your presentation, taking pains to revise it during the rehearsal phase as needed. Your ultimate goal is to deliver a presentation that flows, has maximum impact, and is readily comprehensible. You also need to prepare for the audience's reaction and anticipate the questions the members of your audience may ask. Once all this is done, you can focus on harnessing the energy produced by nerves and excitement and put it to work for you as you deliver your speech.

Fourth Landing: Postpresentation Analysis

After presenting your speech, compare and contrast your expectations with what you actually experienced during the delivery process.

Effective speakers criticize their speechmaking performances. They know that they and their receivers will be changed in some way by the speechmaking experience. They know that their words, once spoken, leave an impression and they want to be certain that they learn as much as possible from the speech so that they can apply the lessons learned to the next speech.

The speechmaking staircase is one you will climb over and over, working your way from one speech experience to the next. In time, you will master the ins and outs of giving presentations. For the remainder of this chapter, we look more specifically at the steps involved in ascending to the first landing: topic selection and self-analysis and audience analysis. We begin with self-analysis.

ANALYZE YOURSELF

Thorough self-analysis is a prerequisite for effective speech making. Although at times topics may be assigned, under many circumstances the choice of what to speak about will be left to you. Even when a topic is specified, we recommend that you undertake a self-analysis to help you uncover aspects that you may find particularly interesting or appealing. Such an analysis also can become the basis for personal narratives or anecdotes that you then can integrate into your speech.

There are more topics for speeches than you can possibly exhaust during this course. Elie Wiesel, Holocaust survivor and Nobel Peace Prize winner, acknowledged that "I don't know where to start" is an all too familiar lament. Wiesel wrote, "But where was I to start? The world is so vast, I shall start with the country I know best, my own. But my country is so very large. I had better start with my town. But my town, too, is large. I had best start with my street. No, my home. No, my family. Never mind, I shall start with myself."[9]

At the outset of your preparation, take some time for what corporate trainers call a front-end analysis—a preliminary examination of possibilities. The following sections describe four useful formats that you can follow to produce a front-end analysis of yourself.

REVIEW YOUR LIFE: YOUR NARRATIVE

Begin by reviewing your life in terms of potential topics.

1. Divide your life (thus far) into thirds: early, middle, recent. Compose one sentence to sum up what your life consisted of during each segment (e.g., "I lived with my two brothers and mother in Gary, Indiana, where I went to elementary school.")

2. Under each summary statement, identify your main interests and concerns at that time of your life.

3. Examine the interests and concerns you listed. Which of them recur in more than one life segment? Which have you left behind? Which have you developed only recently?

CONSIDER THE MOMENT: THIS MOMENT

A second approach is to consider this very moment as a source of potential topics:

1. On the left side of a sheet of paper, list sensory experiences: everything you are able to see, hear, taste, smell, or touch from your present vantage point.

2. When you have listed 10 to 15 items, go back over the list and note topics that might be suggested by each observation or experience. Arrange these in a corresponding list on the right side of the paper. For example, if you list "passing train" in the left column, you might enter "mass transportation" in the right column. Note: If you're not satisfied with the topics you generated, move to another location and begin the process anew.

SEARCH THE NEWS

A third approach is to focus on the news as a source of potential topics.

1. Peruse a series of news articles and compile a list of topics suggested by them. For example, the September 17, 2017, issue of the *New York Times Book Review* featured a review of a book on the controversy surrounding the building of the Vietnam Veterans Memorial in Washington, D.C.[10] Imagine the possible speech topics that this review could suggest: the purpose of war memorials, the nature of memorials in general, disputes over Confederate and other memorials, or how art commemorates war, just to name a few.

2. Do not prejudge your ideas. Simply work your way through the articles looking for possibilities.

3. Alternately, view a nightly local or national newscast or newsmagazine program, taking notes as you watch. Divide your notes into two columns: "Stories Presented" and "Ideas Generated by the Story." Work your way through the program, looking for possibilities.

USE TECHNOLOGY

Explore websites such as About.com, Quamut.com, eHow.com, ExpertVillage.com, Squidoo. com, Ted.com, and YouTube.com to find examples of presentations on a vast array of subjects from the basics of football, to how to make sushi, to how to do your hair like a rock star, and on and on. Such sites are likely to include advice from both experts and amateurs. Be sure to use the speech examples you find to fuel your topic search; do not copy the presentation itself.

A number of other websites also can help with topic generation. Try using the follow topic generators:

www.speechmastery.com/speech-topics.html

www.tallmania.com/topicgenerator/topicgenerator.htm

ANALYZE YOUR AUDIENCE

Having conducted research on yourself, it's now time to figure out how your audience fits in. A pitfall for many speakers is speaking to please themselves—approaching speech making with only their own interests and points of view in mind and neglecting the needs and interests of their audience. Such speakers often choose an inappropriate topic, dress improperly, or deliver a presentation that either is too simple or too technical for the audience. We have all heard medical experts address general audiences using such complex language that their listeners become baffled and bored. We have also heard speakers address highly educated groups in such simple language and about such mundane topics that not only was everyone bored, they felt insulted.

iStock/ferrantraite

Your focus during the initial stages of speech preparation, therefore, should not be solely on yourself. Be prepared also to consider potential topics from the audience's perspective. Just as you bring your own background and experiences to a presentation, the audience members will bring theirs. As a result, it's important to consider what your listeners are thinking about and what their needs and hopes are.

Answering the following questions can guide you in designing a speech that your audience will tune in to:

- To whom am I speaking?

- How do they feel about my topic?

- What would they like me to share with them?

- What kind of presentation do they expect me to deliver?

- What do I hope to accomplish?

- How important is my presentation to them?

- What do they know, want to know, and need to know about my subject?

- How do they feel about me?

- What problems or goals do the members of the audience have?

- What should I do to gain and maintain their interest and attention?

If you don't find out the answers to questions like these, you risk your words falling on deaf ears. Of all the steps in the process of public speaking, audience analysis is most often overlooked.

ETHICS AND COMMUNICATION

The Magic Bullet of Speech Making

What is the magic bullet of speech making? Practitioners and consultants offer varied answers to this question. One analyst says that to deduce the answer, listen to and view masters of speech making, such as Winston Churchill, Martin Luther King Jr., Sheryl Sandberg, Elizabeth Warren, and Barack Obama on YouTube.[11] Another believes the answer lies in embodying both style and substance, in other words, that leadership and communication go hand-in-hand.[12] A third writes that the key to communication is being likable.[13]

What do you think the magic bullet is? Is it being emotionally involving, likable, or something else? If you choose being likable, is that more or less important than giving receivers information that they need to have but may not enjoy being told? If you choose being emotionally involving, what happens when what you share is not in the best interests of receivers, but you succeed in connecting with them and motivating them to listen to accept your message?

GATHERING AUDIENCE INFORMATION

Information about your audience comes from two key sources: your personal experience with the group and original research.

Personal Experience

The best source of information about your audience is your personal experience with the group, either as speaker or as an audience member. If you've attended several functions or are a member of the class or organization that you will be addressing, you have personal knowledge of the audience. Thus, you will be able to formulate reasonably accurate predictions about the appropriateness of your material for that group.

Research

What if you've had no prior contact with the group you're going to speak to? If that's the case, you might ask the program planner to provide you with relevant information. For instance, if you've been asked to speak at a professional meeting, you would be concerned with the makeup of the audience: How many are expected in attendance? Will interns be present? These and other factors would have to be taken into account in preparing and customizing the presentation.

Another way to gather information about a group is to obtain copies of the group's public relations material. Recent news releases about the organization may help put you on the same footing as your audience. Reading corporate newsletters and visiting the corporate website also will be valuable, as can a trip to the local library for information describing the organization.

The library and the Internet also hold clues to the backgrounds and interests of potential audience members. Use both to discover what local, regional, and national opinion polls reveal about the views potential audience members might have on a variety of social and political issues.

To further enhance your knowledge, you also might survey potential receivers. You can use the results of a well-thought-out questionnaire to help estimate how much your listeners already know about your subject and gauge their attitudes toward it. Questionnaires usually contain the following question types: closed ended, scaled, and open ended. Closed-ended questions are highly structured, requiring respondents only to indicate which of the provided responses most accurately reflects their own. The following are examples of closed-ended questions:

What is your marital status?

☐ Married   ☐ Single   ☐ Divorced   ☐ Widowed   ☐ Separated

Do you think prayer should be permitted in public schools?

☐ Yes   ☐ No   ☐ Undecided

Scaled questions allow respondents to indicate their views along a continuum ranging between extremes such as strongly agree to strongly disagree. The following is a scaled question:

To what extent do you agree or disagree with the following statement? Condoms should be dispensed in public high schools.

Strongly agree   Agree   Neutral   Disagree   Strongly disagree

Open-ended questions allow respondents even more answering freedom. For example:

Respond to this statement: A politician's private life is not the public's business.

Original research also takes the form of direct discussion with members of the audience. Talking at length to potential audience members can provide information that you can use to help establish rapport with the audience so that even if they are not inclined to agree with your views, you may be able to render them friendly enough to listen. Understanding receivers helps you to connect with them. For example, drawing on her awareness of what new college graduates expected to hear from her, in her commencement speech to the graduates of Tulane

University, comedian Ellen DeGeneres told them: "Follow your passion. Stay true to yourself. Never follow someone else's path unless you're in the woods and you're lost and you see a path. Then by all means, you follow that."[14] Her remarks drew a big laugh, establishing a connection.

DRAW A DEMOGRAPHIC PROFILE

A **demographic profile** is a composite of characteristics, including age; gender; educational level; racial, ethnic, or cultural ties; group affiliations; and socioeconomic background. For example, let's suppose you were going to speak to two different audiences on the value of using socioeconomic diversity as a consideration in college admissions. You learn that the first audience you are going to speak before is composed primarily of middle-aged, well-educated, wealthy people employed in professional or executive jobs. Your second audience is composed primarily of middle-aged, high school–educated people who live in the city and work in service or trade jobs. Which group would you expect to be more sympathetic to your position? Without compromising your own stance on the issue, how might you adapt your message to the less sympathetic group?

Irina Kozorog/Shutterstock.com

We speak before homogeneous and heterogeneous audiences. A **homogeneous audience** is one whose members are of approximately the same age and who have similar characteristics, attitudes, values, and knowledge. Speaking to such a group is rarer than speaking before audiences that are **heterogeneous**, composed of people of diverse ages with different characteristics, attitudes, values, and knowledge. When the audience is diverse, be sure to include all groups, paying attention to the demographic data you can use to help enhance communication. How would you describe your class audience?

Age Considerations

We would not give the same presentation to a group of elementary school children as we would give to our class. Make it your goal to diminish the age difference between you and your audience if one exists. Use events and trends that serve as generational markers to guide you in appealing to different age segments of your audience. Be sensitive to references you employ and the words you use. Ask yourself questions like these:

- Will audience members give the same meanings to my words?
- Will they be able to identify with my examples and illustrations?
- Are they old or young enough to be familiar with the people and events I refer to?

Of course, age is more relevant to some topics than others. For example, the age of listeners is crucial if you're speaking about retirement planning but likely less important if your topic were the history of the environmental movement.

Gender Considerations

Study your potential audience before drawing any conclusions. Although the same topics may appeal to both men and women, gender may influence how audience members respond. For example, a discussion of rape may elicit a stronger emotional reaction from the women, whereas a discussion of the rights of the accused in a rape trial may elicit a stronger response from men. Be aware, though, that the so-called traditional roles of men and women are changing and that stereotypes once attributed to both groups are crumbling.

Sexual Orientation Considerations

Sexual orientation is often an invisible variable, so it is important to acknowledge that not everyone in your audience will share the same orientation as you. Just as using racially insensitive remarks is inappropriate, so is speaking disparagingly of, or displaying a bias against, any sexual orientation. By making the effort to include supporting materials that feature the LGBTQ community and heterosexuals, you ensure that you include all receivers. For example, if you were to speak about adoption, you might include information about local and state resources for married and unmarried heterosexual, same-sex, and transgender couples who seek to adopt.

Family Orientation

Are receivers single? Married? Divorced? Widowed? From one-parent or two-parent homes? These factors might influence audience reactions to your speech. The concerns of one group are not necessarily the concerns of another.

Religion

If you are speaking to members of a religious groups with which you have little familiarity, make a point of discussing your topic in advance with some of the group's members. Some groups have very clear guidelines regarding issues such as divorce, birth control, and abortion. It's important for you to understand the audience and its feelings if you hope to be able to relate to them effectively.

Cultural Background

Use your knowledge of an audience's culture and mind-set to bond with listeners. Ensure your speech reflects a diversity of thinking rather than one knowledge system.[15] By identifying racial, ethnic, religious, or cultural differences, you can prevent potential misunderstandings. For example, receivers from low-context cultures expect a speaker to explicitly explain his or her message, whereas those from high-context cultures prefer more indirection.

Occupation

People are interested in ideas and issues that relate to their work and the work of those important to them. If you are speaking before an audience whose members belong to a particular occupational group, attempt to find or create examples and illustrations that reflect their interests and concerns.

Socioeconomic Status

There are psychological and economic differences among different socioeconomic classes. Having or lacking discretionary income, power, or prestige influences our attitudes and beliefs. Because our society is socially mobile, in theory, and has a "move-up" philosophy, as a speaker, you usually can assume that your audience members want to get ahead and improve their positions in life, and you can adjust your presentation to appeal to those desires.

Educational Level

Although it's important to determine the educational level of receivers, don't let your findings trap you into making unwarranted assumptions regarding their intellectual abilities. Still, on the whole, the higher people's level of education is, the more general their knowledge and the more insightful their questions will be. In addition, the more knowledgeable members of your audience may possess specific data to dispute your stand on controversial issues. An educated and sophisticated audience may also be more aware of the impact of various political and social programs than might a group of high school dropouts. A less educated audience may need background information that a more educated audience may already have.

Whatever the educational level of receivers, keep these three recommendations in mind:

1. Don't underestimate the intelligence of the audience. Don't speak down to receivers.

2. Don't overestimate their need for information. Don't try to do too much in the time available to you.

3. Don't use jargon if there's a chance that audience members are unfamiliar with it. They will tune out what they don't understand.

Additional Considerations

You may want to consider several additional variables as you prepare your speech. For example, if your audience is your class, do class members belong to particular campus organizations or groups? Do they involve themselves in any particular types of projects? Do class members have any identifiable goals, fears, frustrations, loves, or hates that you could tie in to your presentation?

DRAW A PSYCHOGRAPHIC PROFILE

After considering audience demographics, the next step is to try to predict the attitudes of your receivers. Learning about audience members' **psychographics**—how they see themselves, their attitudes toward various issues, their motives for being there, and how they feel about your topic, you, and the occasion or event—provides additional clues to their likely reactions.

Understand Receivers' Values, Beliefs, and Attitudes

Values are the principles important to us; they guide what we judge to be good or bad, ethical or unethical, worthwhile or worthless. Knowing that respect for elders is among the core values shared by Chinese people, machismo and saving face are important to Mexicans, devoutness and hospitality are valued by Iraqis, and family, responsibility to future generations, and a healthy environment are valued by many in the United States can help you adapt your speech.

Beliefs are what we hold to be true and false. They are the building blocks that help to explain our attitudes. For example, those who believe that citizens make better decisions with their money than does the government often favor lower taxes. The more important the beliefs we hold are to us, the harder we work to keep them alive and the less willing we are to alter them.

Our values and beliefs feed into our **attitudes**, the favorable or unfavorable predispositions that we carry with us everywhere. Our attitudes direct our responses to everything—including a speech. Some of us, for example, hold favorable attitudes toward school voucher programs; others do not. Whatever your topic, try and predict your audience members' reaction to the stance you take. When speaking to an audience, your objective is to move them closer to agreeing with you. This becomes easier to do if you first establish common ground by stressing the values and beliefs that you share.

To help in this effort, answer the following questions:

1. What do the audience members know about my topic?
2. To what extent do they care about my topic?
3. What are their current attitudes toward my topic?

Before class, make small talk with your peers in an effort to discover the answers to these questions. Even just listening to what's on their minds as they chat with others can provide you with clues to their mind-set.

Should you be unsuccessful at gathering information about how your audience feels about your topic, you may find it useful to take the pulse of public opinion, in general, by familiarizing yourself with the results of several public opinion polls on the subject. Log on to a website that features public opinion polls, such as www.gallup.com or www.washingtonpost.com, or www.norc.uchicago.edu (the National Opinion Research Center) in an effort to acquire the information you seek. These are well-known and respected polling organizations that conduct polls on a broad array of topics, from attitudes toward the presidency and government to attitudes toward trustworthiness of the press.

Understand How the Audience Perceives You

No matter how audience members feel about your topic, if they believe you to be a credible source, they will be more likely to pay careful attention to your speech. Identify what you can do to help the audience view you favorably. For example, if you think audience members might not believe you to be an authority on your topic, you can work into your presentation experiences you've had that qualify you to speak on your topic. One student who asked his audience to accept that the U.S. government should increase social services to the homeless made his message stronger by relating his own experiences as a homeless person some years earlier.

In addition to focusing on your receivers and their reactions to you, whenever you give a speech, you also should have a clear idea of the nature of the speechmaking occasion and how your topic relates to it. Both the occasion and your subject will affect how you develop, stage, and deliver your presentation.

ANALYZE THE OCCASION

Even if you are to speak in class, it's wise to think about "the occasion" and your role. Fortunately, much, if not all, of what we need to find out about the occasion is relatively easy to determine. Essentially, it helps to specify the following:

- The nature of the occasion
- The date and time of the presentation
- The time constraints of the presentation
- The expected size of the audience

DATE AND TIME: WHEN AND HOW LONG?

Date and time are the most obvious, and among the most important, bits of information we need to acquire. On some occasions, students make assumptions about when they'll speak and end up being unprepared when told "It's your turn." Timing also influences how receivers evaluate a professional speaker's effectiveness. For example, one well-known speaker arrived late at an event and found a hostile audience that had been waiting nearly an hour. Some professional speakers schedule their engagements so close together—giving two or three a day—that they must rush out the door rudely as soon as a talk is completed. In such situations, the audience may react angrily.

The length of the presentation also may influence judgments of its effectiveness. For example, one student was supposed to deliver a 5- to 7-minute informative speech. His chosen topic was "The History of the Corvette." Although the instructor suggested that he limit his consideration of the topic to two or three major model changes, the student attempted to discuss every body and grill alteration in the Chevrolet Corvette from 1954 to the present. The instructor made several attempts to stop him, but the speech exceeded its time limit and was still going strong when the instructor announced a class break. The student responded, "That's fine. I'll just continue." And he did even though the majority of his audience had departed. Whereas the student's passion for his subject was admirable, his speech was not.

Are you able to plan a presentation to ensure that you will not run over or under your time limit?

LOCATION: WHERE?

Familiarizing yourself with the location for your presentation and the people directly connected with it is also necessary. Although this may seem obvious, it sometimes is neglected, with absurd and embarrassing results. For example, at a speech given by a world-famous psychologist whose audience consisted of members of the host college and the surrounding community, early in his speech, the eminent Dr. M. mumbled what seemed to be the name of another college, although most of the audience failed to notice. The second time, however, he clearly announced how happy he was to be at X College, mentioning the wrong institution again. (Doubly unfortunate was the fact that X College was a rival of the host college.) By then, some audience members appeared embarrassed for the speaker and others appeared hostile. The third time, the psychologist mentioned not only the wrong school but the wrong town, too. At this point, there was sufficient commotion in the audience for him to realize his error and in evident confusion he turned to the college president to ask where he was.

How can we avoid such a problem? The minister who officiated your authors' marriage had a possible solution. During the wedding rehearsal, a page in his Bible was marked with a paper clip that held a slip of paper, and later we asked him about it. The minister showed us that it had our names clearly written on it. He explained that, because he was somewhat nervous when conducting a wedding, he tended to forget the names of the two people he was marrying, even if they had belonged to his congregation for years. The slip of paper provided an unobtrusive reminder. Taking our cue from this experience, we now attach a slip of paper to the first page of our notes whenever we speak before a new group. The slip bears the name of the organization, its location, the name of the person introducing us, the names of the officers, and other important information. Thus, the data we need are at our disposal, to be integrated into our remarks as appropriate. You can use the same technique to avoid unnecessary embarrassment or loss of credibility.

OCCASION SPECIFICS: WHY? HOW MANY?

Although every occasion is unique, it's wise to ask some general questions to clarify your reason for speaking. Right now, it's probably a class assignment, but in the future, it could be a sales meeting, a management planning session, a convention, a celebration, or a funeral. Is your presentation part of the observance of a special event? For instance, is the occasion in honor of a retirement? A promotion? Some other type of recognition? Who else, if anyone, will be sharing the program with you? Factors like these can affect the nature of your talk. A suitable topic for a retirement party might be considered inappropriate for a more formal occasion. Similarly, a speech delivered at a celebratory luncheon will have a different tone than one delivered on Memorial Day to honor fallen soldiers. The occasion for your speech influences audience expectations.

We also need to take into account audience size. Is a large or small number of people expected to be present? This is not always easy to determine. In a classroom situation, for example, on one day the room may be filled, but on another day a speaker may arrive and find that a number of students are out sick or off on a special project for another course. The same problem confronts the professional speaker. It's a good idea to both multiply and divide the sponsor's estimate by 2 to give yourself a reasonable range. Thus, you can be prepared, if 40 are expected, to speak to a group of between 20 and 80 people.

You're not likely to have an advance person to assist you when preparing to speak before others (at least not yet), so you need to do all the advance thinking for yourself. Make it a habit to complete an analysis of both your audience and the occasion before completing work on any presentation. The predictions you make will serve you well as you continue preparing your speech.

SELECT YOUR TOPIC

Review the list of possible topics that you have generated thus far. To continue preparing your speech without deciding on a subject—on the basis of self-analysis, audience analysis, and occasion analysis—would be like trying to buy an airline ticket without knowing your destination. During this examination, you evaluate your ideas according to four specific criteria: (1) apparent worth, (2) appropriateness, (3) interest, and (4) availability of material.[16]

IS THE TOPIC WORTHWHILE?

It is best to determine if a potential topic is important both to you and those who will compose your audience. Many speakers, including college students and businesspeople, often fall into the trap of choosing topics that are of little value to the audience. One of the authors recalls a time in a military training institute when he heard one colonel tell another, "After 25 years as an officer, I'm expected to waste my time hearing how to inspect a fork!" To that audience of high-ranking officers, the topic "Fork Inspection Techniques"

was clearly trivial. You may also find that some topics others choose are trivial from your perspective. They may be so commonplace—how to set a table, for example—that they don't merit the time and energy you will expend in listening to them. Many subjects that are acceptable for interpersonal discourse are inconsequential when presented in a public setting where the speaker's purpose is to inform or persuade. Which topics do you judge to be worth your time? Which, in your opinion, are unworthy of consideration?

IS THE TOPIC APPROPRIATE?

We've already discussed how important it is to determine if a topic is appropriate to you and your personal interests. But we also need to weigh whether the topic is appropriate to the audience and to the occasion. Let's consider each in turn.

By this time, you should have developed an audience profile. You either have researched or made educated guesses about the age, gender, and education level of the majority of the people in your audience. That done, you next need to ask which of your possible topics is most appropriate for the mix of people who will listen to your speech. Sometimes, this decision is easy. For instance, we would not ordinarily give a talk about the evils of the Internet to Silicon Valley employees. Nor, ordinarily, would we opt to speak on the advantages of a women's college to an audience already attending a women's college. Every subject area must be seen through the eyes of its intended audience. Just as an automobile is customized for a particular owner, so a subject area must be customized to reflect the needs of a particular group of listeners. Just as the car is painted, detailed, and upholstered with an owner or a type of owner in mind, so you as a speaker must "outfit" your topic to appeal to the audience members you hope to engage.

You also need to consider the topic's appropriateness to the occasion. For example, you can probably think of any number of occasions on which a humorous topic might be ill-conceived. Can you think of occasions when a humorous topic might be an asset?

IS THE TOPIC INTERESTING?

Some speakers err by selecting topics that they *think* they should speak about rather than topics that they *want* to speak about. Student speakers, for instance, sometimes select a topic because it sounds important. One student insisted on talking about labor–management relations simply because it sounded like an impressive subject. Unfortunately, she had spent little time in the labor force and no time in management. And because she did not care enough to do much—if any—research, the entire subject remained foreign to her. Not surprisingly, the delivered speech was dull and disjointed.

John Silverstein, a spokesperson for General Dynamics, put it this way: "You need to believe in your idea. This is very important. What a listener often gauges is how convinced the speaker is. If he (or she) has lived it, breathed it, and is himself (or herself) really sold on it, it generally is enough to sell the argument."[17] Of course, selecting a topic that's appealing to you is a personal matter and can be relatively simple, but determining what will interest your audience can be somewhat more challenging.

Here, students have an advantage. As a student, you know your fellow students, and you should be able to come up with topics that will interest them. When speaking before less familiar audiences, however, feel free to return to your audience analysis and make some educated guesses. Determining an audience's interests is a never-ending challenge—one that unadventurous speech makers prefer not to tackle. One corporate executive, for instance, once delivered a speech that was gratifyingly well received. Unfortunately, he then delivered essentially the same speech for the next 5 years, although times and needs kept changing. Topics need to be updated to match the moods, needs, and concerns of listeners.

When considering audience member interests, ask yourself how your subject relates to them. Ask yourself what they stand to gain from listening to you. Create an inventory for each of your possible subjects. If you can't identify significant ways your audience will benefit from hearing about a topic, there is good reason for you not to speak about it.

IS SUFFICIENT RESEARCH MATERIAL AVAILABLE ON THE TOPIC?

Before settling on a topic, be certain that material on the subject exists and that you can find it readily. We don't want any last-minute panicking because information you requested doesn't arrive on time or you do not find sufficient resources to develop a first-rate presentation.

Avoid this pitfall by checking your library databases during the selection phase of your preparation.

For practice, select a possible topic and determine the extent to which it meets all the preceding criteria.

NARROW THE TOPIC AND CLARIFY YOUR PURPOSE

Time is of the essence. Your topic has to be narrowed to fit your time limit. More than once, an army chaplain demonstrated his skill at handling time constraints. The chaplain's job was to speak to groups of recruits during basic training and on each occasion he was given only 3 minutes to get his message across. One day his objective was to persuade soldiers not to use foul language. (It was his belief that such a practice degraded both individuals and the service.) Realizing that he could accomplish only so much in the time allotted, he chose to focus on a single word—the particular word that he found most offensive. During his 3-minute talk, he suggested that the troops avoid using just that one term. By doing this, the chaplain demonstrated that he understood how important it is to narrow a topic to manageable proportions and, incidentally, succeeded in his objective. (After his speech, the abused word was heard much less frequently around the base.)

There is a strategy you can use to avoid biting off more than you can chew—or talk about. Select a topic and place it at the top of a topic cone. Then subdivide it into constituent parts; that is, break it down into smaller and smaller units, as shown in Figure 11.3. The smallest unit should appear on the lowest level of the cone. This process is like whittling or carving a

FIGURE 11.3
Topic Cone

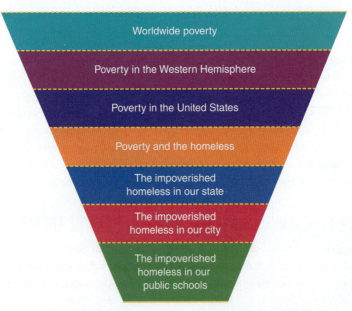

- Worldwide poverty
- Poverty in the Western Hemisphere
- Poverty in the United States
- Poverty and the homeless
- The impoverished homeless in our state
- The impoverished homeless in our city
- The impoverished homeless in our public schools

stick of wood. The more you shave off, the narrower the topic becomes. Like the carver, you decide what shape to give your topic and when to stop shaving.

Let's say that you want to speak on the need to save the rain forest. One way to narrow your topic would be to focus on how indigenous people can save the rain forest. Your topic could be focused even further. You might explore how their harvesting of native plants can stop deforestation or, more specifically, how their harvesting of fruit can help preserve the ecological balance.

> Visit the interactive e-Book to access the Skill Builder feature "Topic Cone," in which you will practice developing topic cones and determine a topic's effectiveness in a speech.

FORMULATE A PURPOSE STATEMENT

Once you have chosen a topic and narrowed its scope, reexamine exactly why you are speaking. What is your purpose? What do you hope to accomplish? What kind of response do you seek from your audience? What would you like your listeners to think or do as a result of your presentation? What is your ultimate objective?

Most speeches fulfill one of two general purposes: to inform or to persuade; that is, speakers aim either to share new information or insights with the audience or to convince audience members to believe in or do something. Thus, when speaking informatively, your aim is to provide a learning experience for receivers, to share with them information they did not possess before your talk. When speaking persuasively, your aim is to reinforce or change an audience's beliefs or to cause audience members to behave differently.

Whatever your general purpose, you'll want to express your specific purpose statement in an infinitive phrase that specifies and summarizes your goal. For example, in a speech about self-driving cars, your specific purpose might be "to inform my audience about three ways self-driving cars will impact society." If speaking about Zika, your specific purpose might be "to persuade my audience to fear the Zika virus."

You then rely on the specific purpose to help you develop your thesis or central idea.

COMPOSE A THESIS

A thesis expresses the central or main idea of your speech in just one sentence. It focuses the attention of audience members on what they should know, feel, and/or do after experiencing your speech. It also reinforces your specific purpose. Here is an example of a thesis statement directly derived from the specific purpose statements provided in the previous subsection:

> Self-driving cars will change the way we live and get around in three ways: (1) by reducing accidents, (2) by permitting overnight travel, and (3) by fundamentally changing the taxicab, Uber, Lyft, and ride-sharing industries.

> We should fear the Zika virus because it causes birth defects and serious illnesses, and responses to it have been far from effective.

The thesis is the core idea or bottom line of your speech. It is your speech in a nutshell. Along with the specific purpose, the thesis statement acts as a road map for building your speech. You next move is to develop the main points that flesh out the thesis.

IDENTIFY YOUR SPEECH'S MAIN POINTS

Once your specific purpose and thesis are clearly stated, it is easier to identify your speech's main points—the major ideas you will communicate to the audience. Most of your speeches will contain two or three main points, with each main point supporting your expressed thesis.

For example, let's look at the last thesis statement identified in the previous section. Its three main points might read:

I. There is fear of a surge in birth defects due to the Zika virus.

II. Members of the general population can contract serious illnesses attributed to the Zika virus.

III. Responses to protect the general population from Zika have been ineffective.

Once you formulate the main points, your next move is to locate and select supporting materials, and outline your speech, which we cover in Chapter 12.

SKILL BUILDER

Score Your Subject

Answer each of the following questions about your subject by assigning a score from 1 to 10, where 1 represents "No, not at all" and 10 represents "Yes, very." The highest score is 100.

1. Is your subject worthwhile?

    _____ from your perspective

    _____ from your audience's perspective

2. Is your subject appropriate?

    _____ from your perspective

    _____ from your audience's perspective

3. Is your subject interesting?

    _____ from your perspective

    _____ from your audience's perspective

4. Is sufficient information available?

    _____ from your perspective

    _____ from your audience's perspective

5. Have you narrowed your topic to fit the situation? _____

6. Have you prepared fully and to the best of your ability? _____

    Total Score: _____

COMMUNICATION SKILLS
Practice Tips for Improving Speech Preparation

Effective speech makers approach speech making systematically. Careful preparation precedes the actual speechmaking experience. Every speaker, from novice to professional, will benefit from following the suggestions listed here.

Conduct a systematic self-analysis as a preparation for speech making.

Take the time you need to survey your own likes, dislikes, and concerns. Effective speakers know themselves well. They know what they care about, and they know what ideas they'd like to share.

Analyze your audience.

Effective speakers adapt their ideas to reflect the needs and interests of their receivers. Speeches are delivered with the specific purpose of informing or persuading others—of affecting others in certain specific ways. The degree to which you will succeed is directly related to how well you know your audience and how accurately you're able to predict their reactions.

Analyze the occasion.

It's essential that you learn why, when, where, and for how long you are expected to speak. Without this information, your preparation will be incomplete and insufficient.

Determine if your topic is supported by your interests, your audience's interests, and the demands of the occasion.

Be certain to evaluate your subject according to the following criteria: Is the topic worthwhile? Is the topic appropriate? Is the topic interesting? Is sufficient research material available?

Narrow and clarify your topic.

Ask yourself: Have I sufficiently narrowed my focus? Are my specific purpose, thesis, and main points clear?

> We like to hear what makes us feel comfortable and self-assured. Yet this is exactly what we have no need of hearing; only those who disturb us can improve us.
>
> Sidney Harris

COMPLETE THIS CHAPTER 11 CHECKLIST

11.1 I can describe the sources of, and potential remedies for, public speaking anxiety. ☐

Public speaking is the act of preparing, staging, and delivering a presentation to an audience. Some degree of anxiety or fear affects most speech makers. One of the best ways to cope with speech fright is to plan and rehearse your presentation. Once you recognize fear's causes, as well as the physical and mental sensations that accompany feeling fearful, you can learn to use a variety of techniques such as deep muscle relaxation, thought stopping, and visualization to control your reactions. These techniques help eliminate the tension, thoughts, and symptoms associated with fear—the first by eliminating stress, the second by stopping the fear-inducing process, and the third by boosting confidence.

11.2 I can explain how to approach public speaking systematically. ☐

There is a logical order to speech making: (1) topic selection, self-analysis, and audience analysis; (2) speech development, support, and organization; (3) presentation practice and delivery; and (4) postpresentation analysis.

11.3 I can explain why conducting a comprehensive self-analysis facilitates the speechmaking process. ☐

Self-analysis is a prerequisite for preparing an effective speech. A self-analysis lets you take your interests, thoughts, and limitations into account when selecting a topic.

11.4 I can analyze the audience so that I can tailor my speech to them. ☐

By conducting demographic and psychographic analyses of your receivers, you keep their background, needs, and interest in mind. By considering potential topics from the audience's point of view, you focus attention and adapt the speech to those people you hope to reach.

11.5 I can explain how the nature of the occasion influences a speech. ☐

Identifying the occasion and your role in it is another essential step toward delivering an effective speech. Once you determine the date, time limit, and location of the speech, as well as the nature of the occasion, you can tailor your presentation accordingly.

11.6 I can identify topic selection criteria. ☐

Carefully examine the list of possible topics generated during self, audience, and occasion analyses in an effort to identify which best reflect the following criteria: apparent worth, appropriateness, interest, and material availability.

11.7 I can narrow my topic, formulate a thesis statement, and develop main points for my speech. □

Once you choose your topic, you need to reexamine your purpose for speaking. Most speakers have one of two general objectives: to inform listeners or to persuade listeners. To ensure that your purpose is clear, you should develop a specific purpose, an infinitive phrase summarizing what you want to accomplish. Using the specific purpose, you next formulate a thesis statement, a declarative sentence that directs the course of your speech, helping you to identify the main points that your speech will develop.

. . . .

11.8 I can apply skills for improving speech preparation. □

Careful preparation, including adhering to a series of necessary steps, paves the way for a more successful speechmaking experience.

. . . .

BECOME A WORD MASTER

attitudes 303

beliefs 303

communication
apprehension 287

demographic
profile 300

heterogeneous
audience 300

homogeneous
audience 300

psychographics 302

public speaking 286

public speaking
anxiety 287

values 302

iStock/Jacob Ammentorp Lund

Researching, Supporting, and Outlining Your Speech

**AFTER COMPLETING THIS CHAPTER,
YOU SHOULD BE ABLE TO:**

12.1 Conduct primary and secondary research for your speech both online and offline.

12.2 Explain how to use support to enhance a presentation.

12.3 Summarize the types and features of linear and configural speech formats.

12.4 Discuss the speech framework and its relationship to outlining stages and principles, including the identification of main and subordinate ideas.

12.5 Identify characteristics of effective introductions and conclusions.

12.6 Apply skills to evaluate a speech's supporting material, organizational format, and outline.

> **Research is the process of going up alleys to see if they're blind.**
>
> Barstow Bates

Now that you have looked at your subject from both your perspective and the point of view of the audience and taken the occasion into account, it is time to focus on researching, selecting support, choosing an organizational approach, and outlining your speech—the next steps on the way up the speechmaking staircase (Figure 12.1).

As you turn your attention to research, the goal is to discover an array of supporting materials, including illustrations, statistical evidence, expert opinions, and quotations, to use in your speech. These materials will enable you to answer the questions that audience members will be asking themselves when listening to you speak. As you deliver your speech, the members of your audience will weigh your words, using "self-talk" to ask themselves questions such as the following: What do you mean? Why should I accept what you say? Why should I care? If you develop your speech

FIGURE 12.1

On your way to the halfway point

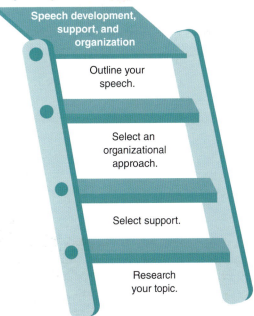

Speech development, support, and organization

Outline your speech.

Select an organizational approach.

Select support.

Research your topic.

with care, being certain to support and organize your ideas, you will have no difficulty providing the audience with sound answers to their questions. ■

RESEARCH YOUR TOPIC

When trying to pick a movie you want to see, you likely start by accessing Fandango or some other online service. Similarly, when it comes to choosing a new restaurant at which to dine, you probably ask your friends for advice or consult review services and restaurant home pages on the Internet. What do these research methods have to do with public speaking? The research we do when preparing to speak in public is much like the personal research we conduct daily. However, because a speech is likely to be shared with others in a somewhat more formal setting, we use a more formal approach.

Research sources available to speakers include primary and secondary sources. Primary sources are other people you consult directly (and can include yourself). Secondary sources are comprised of already published works, including statistics, texts and articles by experts, and media and personal documents. If, for instance, you are speaking on some aspect of sports medicine, and have yourself suffered an injury when playing a sport, you may choose to share that personal experience in your speech. If your topic has to do with business or technology, you may likewise choose to use examples from your work in an industry that relates directly to your topic. Far too often, speakers fail to realize that they can use their personal experiences to establish credibility and add interesting and pertinent examples in addition to citing the secondary research provided in journal articles, books, statistics, and other sources.

RESEARCH BOTH ONLINE AND OFFLINE

Suppose you are going to speak on the role that that the practice of *framing* plays in society, and you want to explore how both government supporters and dissenters are using framing to make their cases regarding the United States' progress in the war on terror. Where would you go to get your information? What sources would you turn to in order to learn what framing is, how it functions, why it is used, what its effects are, and whether it is ethical? For instance, both supporters and those opposed to continuing the wars in Iraq and Afghanistan frame their respective positions by telling stories about the successes and failures of the war on terror. Might a comparison of such framed stories serve as good examples for your speech? As you conduct your research, you become better able to answer such questions.

Get to Know the Library

A library is a storehouse and retrieval system for information. It contains resources invaluable for every type of research. The library is one of the few real bargains left in society. A huge array of material is available there for free; other materials and services (those available through a variety of photographic and electronic systems) may be yours for only a minimal cost. In addition, every academic and public library has on its staff knowledgeable people who have been trained to aid you with your investigative work. In addition to your college library, you can consult the following Internet libraries: the Internet Public Library (www.ipl .org), the Library Spot (www.libraryspot.com), and the Reference Desk (www.Refdesk.com).

When you begin library research, consult an array of reference sources to compile a preliminary bibliography. Your first step may well be the library's electronic catalog. Next, you may move on to a variety of newspaper, magazine, and journal indexes. Depending on your subject, you may also consult bibliographical sources, encyclopedias, and almanacs. And you almost certainly will conduct online searches.

Use Reference Works

The *World Almanac*, *Statistical Abstract of the United States*, and *Information Please Almanac* are only three of many such reference works that can provide the speech maker with interesting factual and statistical evidence.

Biographical materials can be located in the *Dictionary of National Biography*, the *Dictionary of American Biography*, and even the *New York Times Obituary Index*. Similarly, *Current Biography* can help you research the lives of contemporary public figures.

Use Online References and Databases

Libraries are user friendly. You can visit yours in person or access it from a distance. In fact, you can conduct much of the research for your speech online by using your library's computerized system when in the library or by using passwords and following log-on procedures that give you access when at home or in another remote location. In preparation for conducting online research, your first step should be to attend a live orientation in your library or to take an online tutorial. Meet the reference librarian and find out what research databases your college library subscribes to. At the same time, familiarize yourself with the library's electronic catalogs and reference room.

During your research, you will want to consult a variety of online reference works and databases, including the Reader's Guide to Periodical Literature (www.hwwilson.com), and LexisNexis (www.lexisnexis.com). Of course, you also can use Google and Google Scholar, popular online databases, or newspapers such as the *New York Times* and the *Wall Street Journal* online. Among other databases, you may want to consult the *American Statistics Index* (ASI).

You also may want to consult the online encyclopedia Wikipedia, but be wary of using it as a speech source. Wikipedia may offer a quick overview of a subject, but because it can be inaccurate, many people in higher education simply do not view it as a definitive source.

Use E-Mail

You can use e-mail to write to knowledgeable potential sources, a group, or a listserv—an e-mail list of potentially hundreds of people who have interest in and knowledge of a particular topic. Search CataList (http://www.lsoft.com/catalist.html), a directory of listservs, for any that are relevant to your topic. Ask whether new members are welcomed and then follow the instructions to join, in order to explore potentially useful listservs. Before sending any messages or contacting users, try to identify the types of messages members send and their usefulness to you. Also read the frequently asked questions (FAQ) file so that you do not ask questions that have already been answered.

Using e-mail, you may also have access to (or be able to create) a listserv for your class. Once one is in place, you can use it to ask your peers to fill out questionnaires that reveal their attitudes toward your chosen topic. You can also use the class listserv to seek and receive feedback after your speech.

Check Newsgroups and Subreddits

Newsgroups facilitate the exchange of ideas on a broad array of topics through discussion forums. The Internet contains a multitude of newsgroups, also known as Usenet. In a newsgroup, you can post messages, read the posts of others, and respond to them. Like listservs, newsgroups bring together people interested in sharing ideas about a topic. As with a listserv, before joining a newsgroup, be sure you read through the FAQ file; doing so will ensure you receive maximum benefits from the newsgroup. You can use binsearch.info or giganews.com to search newsgroups for information on requested topics.

Subreddits are networks of niche communities within the website reddit.com whose members are devoted to the sharing of information on specific topics. Users both post information and ask and answer questions. Content on the site is voted up or down by the site's members.

Access the World Wide Web

Almost any kind of content you can find in print is also available on the Web. You can subscribe to various special interest groups or use a search engine to browse for information on your selected topic. While browsing, you might, for example, visit the Associated Press online, peruse copies of historical documents or the Congressional Record. With the Internet, you have easy access to information that exists on numerous campuses and every continent.[1]

Search engines can help you find relevant articles and websites. You can also search for relevant video. Google, for example, uses speech recognition technology to create searchable transcripts of videos.[2]

Corporate websites will provide you with access to annual reports and other information. Remember to bookmark your favorite sites to facilitate future access.

Be Certain to Evaluate What You Find

Whereas the information contained in traditional research sources, including books, magazines, and journal articles, is typically reviewed and checked by editors and experts before being published, virtually anyone can post information on a website or to a newsgroup. Thus, verifying and thinking critically about the information you find online is a serious responsibility. As you decide what and what not to include in your speech from your Web search, ask yourself who a site's sponsor is. For example, CNN, MSNBC, and Fox are established news organizations, as are major newspapers that also operate websites. As you evaluate Web-based information from other sources, it is important to determine if the source has an apparent or hidden bias. Ask yourself if postings are specific or general. Do the claims they make seem justifiable? Do not trust a source simply because it is published on the Internet. Seek out sources that can confirm what you discover.

Your college library most likely also has criteria for you to refer to when checking the accuracy and validity of online sources. Compare your library's suggestions with the criteria we offer here.

1. Evaluate the author. Who is the author? How credible is she or he to write about the topic?

2. Evaluate the publisher. Who sponsors the site? What does the extension at the end of the site's URL reveal about its sponsor? Don't blindly trust the top-level domain.

3. Evaluate the timeliness of information on the site. When was the website created and last updated?

4. Pursue the links identified on the site. Do they connect you to sources that are credible or questionable? What connections exist between the site and its links?

5. Evaluate the site's purpose. Why does the site exist? Is its primary function to inform, persuade, sell, or entertain?

6. Determine if the information contained in the site can be confirmed. Compare the site's contents with the contents of other available sources to see if there are any major disagreements or discrepancies.

CONDUCT PRIMARY RESEARCH

Primary research involves the collection of original research, information that has not already been published. It enables you to give your audience members a firsthand report based on your personal observations and experience, informal surveys you conduct, and/or interviews you hold.

Personal Observations and Experience

One of the best ways to research a topic is to examine what you know about it. Search your own background and experiences for materials you might want to integrate into your presentation.

If your topic is one for which direct observation of an event, a person, or a phenomenon would be appropriate, then by all means go out and observe. An observational excursion might take you to a biology interactive workshop, an airport, a supermarket, or a construction site, for example. When conducting direct observation, be sure to take careful notes. If possible, take a video of the observation on your phone. Sit down immediately after the experience and record your thoughts and feelings. File your firsthand notes with the materials gathered during your library research.

Informal Surveys

Developing a reliable scientific survey instrument is complicated. However, informal surveys can provide a speaker with useful and often entertaining information. Let's say you are investigating adding an online degree at your college; a survey of students currently at your school may produce data you can use. (For instance, you might be able to discover the percentage of students who would be more interested in obtaining an online degree.)

Informal surveys normally consist of no more than 10 questions. To conduct an informal survey, you need to identify yourself to your prospective interviewee and state the purpose of your survey:

"Hello, I'm _____. I'm investigating the feasibility of incorporating an online degree into the regular curriculum of the college." The survey can be conducted either orally, in writing, or online. A sample of 25 to 50 people and some simple mathematical calculations should provide adequate statistical information to integrate into your presentation. When you conduct an informal survey, you may gain more than expected. Respondents may offer interesting remarks that you can incorporate into your speech.

Interviews

An interview is similar to a survey except that it is usually more detailed and assumes that the person being interviewed is in some way an expert on the topic under investigation. On your campus, in your community, or in an online discussion group, you will probably find knowledgeable people to interview about current issues and many other topics. Political, business, and religious leaders, for instance, can often be persuaded to talk to student speakers. And, of course, the faculty members of a college are often eager to cooperate.

CAREER BUILDER
WHAT DO THEY KNOW?

According to essayist Ralph Waldo Emerson, "Every fact depends for its value on how much we already know." Consider the following subjects related to today's workplaces: sexual harassment, work–life balance, unconscious hiring bias, the gender–wage gap, and diversity practices. What do you already know about these subjects? Do you think you know more or less than the average citizen? Identify an organization you would like to work for, and conduct research to determine its policies related to any one of the subjects just identified or another workplace-related topic of your choosing. Investigate what employees in the organization know about those policies. What new information were you able to add to your own knowledge base?

RECORD INFORMATION DERIVED FROM RESEARCH

When conducting research, the information you gather from books, articles, and other sources should be easy for you to retrieve. Either buy a pack of 4 × 6 inch notecards to record your information or use a computer to compile your notes. When the time comes, either approach will let you move information around to wherever you need or want to use it in the speech. Try this approach:

- Use a bibliography card or page for each basic article or source you reference.

- Record the title, author, and subject on the top of each card or page.

- Record one bit of information per card.

FIGURE 12.2
Notecard Derived From an Interview

Raymond Robinson, Mayor of Ourtown, NJ

"During the storm, many people had to be evacuated.

Otherwise they would have been caught in grave danger.

This was a storm that caught us completely by surprise."

Interview 1/16/11, 4 p.m.

For an example of what your notecards and pages might look like, see Figures 12.2 and 12.3. Notice how each one contains either a direct quotation or paraphrased information taken from a source.

Whenever you research, be sure to give each source correct attribution to avoid plagiarizing. The word **plagiarism** derives from the Latin word *plagiarius*, meaning "kidnapper." When you plagiarize, you kidnap or steal the ideas and words of another and

FIGURE 12.3
Sample Notecards

Bibliography Card

Mark Hosenball, "Airplanes: Dangerous Descents,"

Newsweek. January 10, 2005, p.6.

Direct Quotation Card

From Hosenball, "Airplanes: Dangerous Descents," p.6.

"A series of mysterious incidents in which powerful laser beams were flashed into the cockpits of low-flying passenger planes has jolted the air-travel system."

Paraphrase Card

From Hosenball, "Airplanes: Dangerous Descents," p.6.

Commercial airlines landing at airports reported laserbeams flashed into the cockpit. A pilot could suffer eye injury from laser beams. Homeland Security has been concerned but feels the incidents are probably either accidental or mischievous in nature.

claim them as your own. An increasing percentage of students are guilty of "cut and paste plagiarism," in which the student takes sections from the works of a number of other people and weaves them together into a "new" work that the student then claims as his or her own.

Here are three simple steps to follow to avoid passing off some else's ideas or words as your own.

1. Attribute the source of every piece of evidence you cite in your speech. Never borrow the words or thoughts of a source without acknowledging them.

2. Tell your audience when you are quoting a statement; otherwise, paraphrase it.

3. Use and credit a variety of sources.

Following these guidelines will demonstrate your respect for the audience and also will help you earn their respect. The unique expression of ideas matters. Giving sources the credit due them not only protects you but also increases your credibility.

Audience members expect and deserve oral citations (also known as oral footnotes) when you refer to the ideas of others. Such citations are easy to include in your presentation as long as you have done your research and recorded your information carefully. What do you say in an oral citation? If you are citing a speech or article, you might say,

In a speech honoring those killed and wounded in the largest mass shooting that ever occurred in the United States, the mayor of Las Vegas, the city where the shooting occurred, told those assembled . . .

If you are using a direct quotation, state the name of the author and the source:

In her book *Confidence*, researcher and Harvard Business School professor Rosabeth Moss Kanter tells readers . . .

If you are paraphrasing a book or article, you might say to your audience,

Howard Gardner, author of the book *Changing Minds*, feels that most of us change our minds gradually. According to Gardner, the notion that mind change happens suddenly is wrong.

As you build your speech, the experts you bring onto your team give your speech more impact. Be sure to include each source you use in a Works Cited page (for sources actually mentioned during your speech) or in a Works Consulted page (for all the sources you referred to when conducting your research). The MLA (Modern Language Association) and APA (American Psychological Association) formats are the most popular. For examples, see the Words Consulted of the sample speech outline at the end of this chapter and the speeches included in Chapters 14 and 15. Also see the Quick Guide to Citation provided here.

FIGURE 12.4
Quick Guide to Citations

QUICK GUIDE	APA	MLA
Book	Last name, A. A., & Last name, B. B. (date). *Title of book*. City: Publisher.	Last name, First name and First name Last name. *Title of Book*. City: Publisher, date.
Journal	Last name, A. A. (date). "Title of article." *Journal Name, volume,* page numbers.	Last name, First name. "Title of Article." *Journal Name*, volume (date): page numbers.
Magazine	Last name, A. A. (date). "Title of Article." *Magazine name, volume,* page numbers.	Last name, First name. "Title of Article." *Magazine name*, date: page numbers.
Newspaper	Last name, A. A. (date). "Title of Article." *Newspaper name*, page numbers.	Last name, First name. "Title of Article." *Newspaper name*, date: page numbers.
Internet	Organization. (date). Title. Retrieved from <address>. Date.	Document Title Site. Date. Organization Publishing site. Retrieval date. <address>
Email	Email is not included in APA.	Last name, First name. Personal email. Date.
Interview	Interviews are not included in APA.	Last name, First name. Personal telephone interview. Date.

FIGURE 12.5
Guide for APA Style Citations

Book—One Author

Family name, Initial. Initial. (date). *Title of book*. City: Publisher.

King, S. E. (2013). *Doctor sleep*. New York: Scribner.

Book—Two Authors

Family name, Initial. Initial., & Family name, Initial Initial. (date). Title. City: Publisher.

Jason, F., & Hanson, D. H. (2013). *Remote: Office not required*. New York: Crown Publishers.

Journal Article

Family name, Initial. Initial. (date). Title. *Journal Title, volume number*, page numbers.

Alibali, M. W., Phillips, K. O., & Fischer, A. D. (2009). Learning new problem-solving strategies leads to changes in problem representation. *Cognitive Development, 24,* 89–101.

Magazine

Family name, Initial. Initial. (year, month, week or day). Title of article. *Magazine Name*, page numbers.

Seabrook, J. (2013, October 14). The doctor is in: A technique for producing number one songs. *The New Yorker*, 44–56.

Newspaper

Family name, Initial. Initial. (year, month, day). Title of article. *Newspaper Name,* page numbers.

Berkman, S. (2013, October 19). Bronx renaissance. *The New York Times*, p. D1.

Internet

Organization publishing website. (date). Document title. Retrieved date, from address.

National Football League. (2013). *Football 101: Offense*. Retrieved October 1, 2013, from http://www.nfl.com/news/story/0ap.

Email

Email messages are categorized as personal information in the APA and are not included in a reference list. You can refer to them in your speech.

Interview

The interview is categorized as personal information in the APA system and is not included in a reference list. You can refer to interviews during your speech.

FIGURE 12.6
Guide for MLA Style Citations

Book—One Author

Family name, First name. *Title of the Book*. City: Publisher, date.

Hosseini, Khaled. *The Kite Runner.* New York: Penguin Books, 2004.

Book—Two Authors

Family name, First name and First name, Last name. *Title of the Book*. City: Publisher, date.

Mahzarin, R. Banaji and Anthony G. Greenwald. *Blindspot: Hidden Biases of Good People*. New York: Random House, 2013.

Journal

Last name, First name. "Title of Article." *Journal Name*, date: page numbers.

Olson, Kathryn. "An Epidectic Dimension of Symbolic Violence in Disney's *Beauty and the Beast*." *Quarterly Journal of Speech*, November, 2013: 448–480.

Magazine

Last name, First name. "Title of Article." *Magazine Name.* Date: page numbers.

Wallace-Wells, Benjamin. "The Truly Paranoid Style in American Politics." *New York Magazine.* 25 November 2013: 31–43. Print.

Newspaper

Family name, First name. "Title of Article." *Newspaper Name*, date: page number. Print.

Eisenberg, Ann. "When Algorithms Grow Accustomed to your Face." *The New York Times*. 1 December 2013: B3. Print.

Internet

Organization website. (date). *Article Title*. Retrieved date, from Web address.

International Association of Skateboard Companies. (2013). *Just One Board*. Retrieved December 1, 2013 from http://thelasc.org.

Email

Family name, First name. "Subject Line." Email to Family name. Date.

Robinson, James. "My Attempts at Rope Climbing." Email to Johnson, Judy. 3 August 2013.

Interview

Family name, First name. Personal telephone interview. Date.

Guiliano, Edward. Telephone interview. 10 April 2012.

SELECT THE BEST SUPPORT POSSIBLE

Taken together, the research you conduct along with your experiences should yield a wealth of information that you then can consider integrating into your presentation.

Making your research and experiences come to life for an audience is not an easy task. In fact, it is a key challenge. Following are some tried and true ways to use different kinds of support to make research speak to the audience.[3]

DEFINITIONS

It is especially important to use **definitions** when members of the audience are unfamiliar with terms you are using or when their association for words or concepts might differ from yours. Only if you can explain what you mean by a term can you hope to share your meaning with the audience.

In a speech on how post-traumatic stress disorder affects soldiers returning from serving in Iraq and Afghanistan, speaker Megan Solan defined *psychological injury* as "that which soldiers suffer when they lose their peace of mind, their ability to function in society, and their belief in the existence of human virtues."[4] She went on to flesh out this definition with specifics: "Soldiers learn skills such as the art of deception; the capacity to respond instantly with violent, lethal force; and the suppression of such emotions as compassion, horror, guilt, tenderness, grief, and disgust, all necessary skills for combat, but all skills with dangerous potential within civilian society and severe consequences for the human psyche."[5]

STATISTICS

Statistics are simply facts expressed in numerical form. Speakers cite them to explain relationships or to indicate trends. To be used effectively as support, statistics must be honest and credible. If used appropriately, they can make the ideas you are presenting memorable and significant.

In a speech on why criticisms of what it costs the United States to support the United Nations are unjustified, the former U.S. Permanent Representative to the U.N. Susan E. Rice said, "Let me provide a bit of perspective. Out of every tax dollar you pay, 34 cents go to Social Security and Medicare, 22 cents to national security and our amazing military, and a nickel to paying interest on the national debt. Just one-tenth of a single penny goes to pay our U.N. dues."[6]

EXAMPLES AND ILLUSTRATIONS

Examples are representative cases; as such, they specify particular instances.[7] **Illustrations**, on the other hand, tell stories and thus create more detailed narrative pictures. Both examples and illustrations may be factual or hypothetical. When used effectively, they turn the general into the specific, the unfocused into the focused, and the dull into the interesting, breathing life into a speech.

Solomon D. Trujillo, chairman, president, and CEO of US West, Inc., used a series of examples to demonstrate for audience members that one idea can make a difference:

We've seen how the idea that all people are created equal can find expression in an African-American woman on a bus in Alabama, or in a student on a soda-fountain stool in North Carolina, or even in a young Hispanic businessman in Cheyenne, Wyoming.

A few weeks back I was at the University of Colorado talking to a group of business students, and I told them that I would not be in the job I have were it not for Affirmative Action.

When I joined the old Bell system, AT&T had just entered into a consent decree with the government. Before I joined the company, people like me . . . for some reason . . . weren't likely to get hired. Those who were hired . . . for some reason . . . weren't in management jobs.

But people with courage and foresight knew that our nation's promise of freedom and justice for all was an empty one if you had the wrong color of skin, if you were female, if you spoke with an accent, or if your last name ended in a "z" or a vowel.[8]

Illustrations are more detailed than examples. Built like a story, they open, reveal a complication, contain a climax, and describe a resolution. Emotionally compelling, illustrations add a sense of drama to a speech as they focus attention on the issue at hand.

In a speech on the power of "positive deviance," Risa Lavizzo-Mourey, MD, the Alvin M. Poussaint Visiting Lecturer at Harvard Medical School, used the following illustration to demonstrate the importance of Alvin M. Poussaint to her career:

When I showed up here for medical school in the 1970s, only 12 Black physicians had graduated from Harvard Medical School in the preceding two decades. Nationally in that era annually there were only 300 African Americans out of about 10,000 first-year med students in the entire country—and half of them were at Howard or Emory. The other half made up only 1.4% of all first-year students in the more mainstream medical schools like Harvard. Not long afterward, I added to that statistic. I was young, naïve, and consumed with a passion to become a physician. Not just any physician—but one educated and trained at the best of the best, by the best of the best. There was only one hand-up. Some of the school's old guard was still unhappy about admitting either minorities or women. They questioned the capability of our brains. Complained we were not good enough. "Not Harvard material." In my second year, a senior faculty member—biochemist renowned in his field—attacked us in an article in the *New England Journal of Medicine*. "Faculty lowered standards," he said, so we could pass. Our medical degrees were awarded on a "charitable basis." The professor scolded that we were like airline pilots who'd flunked landing. Patients, like passengers, might die in our care and on our watch. He even suggested it could be considered "criminal." We were furious. Frustrated. Maybe even a little bit frightened. That's when Doctor Poussaint became our hero. Right from day one, he was there for us.[9]

TESTIMONY

Whenever you cite some else's opinion or conclusions, you are using testimony. Testimony gives you an opportunity to connect the ideas in your speech with the thoughts and attitudes of respected and competent people, both modern and historical. When using testimonials, be sure to consider whether the people you cite as authorities are credible sources, whether their ideas are understandable, and whether their comments are relevant to your purpose.

In a speech on life after graduation from college, best-selling author and motivational speaker Harvey Mackay used testimony to emphasize the importance of listening, telling his audience:

Bill Marriott, chairman and CEO of Marriott International, the world's largest hotel chain, described the biggest lesson he has learned through the years: "It is to listen to your people. I find that if you have senior managers who really gather their people around them, get their ideas and listen to their input, they make a lot better decisions."[10]

As we can see, testimony reinforces a speaker's claims. It may be quoted directly, as in the preceding example, or it may be paraphrased. Use direct quotations when you believe that the language and the length of an expert's remarks are appropriate for your audience. Paraphrase when you need to summarize an expert's opinion in fewer words or when you need to simplify its language.

COMPARISONS AND CONTRASTS

Comparisons stress similarities between two entities; contrasts stress differences. Speakers use both to help audiences understand something that is unknown, unfamiliar, or unclear.

William L. Laurence combined comparison and contrast when he described the atomic bombing of Nagasaki:

> As the first mushroom floated off into the blue, it changed its shape into a flowerlike form, its grand petals curving downward, creamy white outside, rose-colored inside . . . Much living substance had gone into those rainbows. The quivering top of the pillar was protruding to a great height through the white clouds, giving the appearance of a monstrous prehistoric creature with a ruff around its neck, a fleecy ruff extending in all directions, as far as the eye could see.[11]

REPETITION AND RESTATEMENT

When a speaker uses repetition, the same words are repeated verbatim. When a speaker uses restatement, an idea is presented again but in different words. If used sparingly, these devices help add impact to a speech maker's remarks and thereby increase memorability.

One of the most famous examples of successful use of repetition is the speech delivered by Martin Luther King, Jr. in 1963 at the Lincoln Memorial:

> I say to you today, my friends, so even though we face the difficulties of today and tomorrow, I still have a dream. It is a dream deeply rooted in the American dream. I have a dream that one day this nation will rise up . . . live out the true meaning of its creed—we hold these truths to be self-evident, that all men are created equal. . . .

> I have a dream that my four little children will one day live in a nation where they will not be judged by the color of their skin but by the content of their character. I have a dream today.

Francis Miller/The LIFE Picture Collection/Getty Images

> I have a dream that one day every valley shall be exalted, and every hill and mountain shall be made low, the rough places shall be made plain, and the crooked places shall be made straight and the glory of the Lord will be revealed and all flesh shall see it together.[12]

SKILL BUILDER

Reliable Sources and Support

Identify a reliable source whose testimony you could use in a speech on any one of the following topics (or another of your choosing) to enhance the credibility of your ideas:

Recycling

Introversion

Hatred

Medical errors

Fake news

Statues to the Confederacy

The benefits and risks of vaccinations

Next, identify an interesting fact, statistic, or illustration you also could use in the speech.

LINEAR AND CONFIGURAL FORMATS

An audience has to be able to follow your speech for it to be effective and fulfill its purpose. Without good organization, your speech's message will remain fuzzy and hard to follow. Because receivers rarely interrupt speakers during a speech to seek clarification and because they usually don't have access to transcripts or tapes of presentations, speakers need to organize the ideas contained in their speeches so that receivers are able to comprehend them the first time they hear them.[13]

Generally, speeches exhibit either a linear or a configural (nonlinear) format. Western cultures typically favor a linear organization, whereas non-Western cultures commonly prefer otherwise. In the book *The Geography of Thought: How Asians and Westerners Think Differently . . . and Why*, Richard Nisbett observes that human cognition and reasoning preferences differ, depending on whether one grows up in a Western or an Eastern culture.[14] According to Nisbett, East Asians are more holistic and contextual in their perceptions, whereas Westerners have more of a tunnel-vision perceptual style that depends on identifying with what is prominent in a situation and remembering it. People from Eastern cultures tend to tolerate subtleties and deal in relationships, stressing intuitive thinking and informal logic, not the use of categories.

Nisbett asserts that people from Western cultures tend to be analytic, preferring absolutes and information that is grouped. They stress categorization and rational, logical thinking. East Asian people start out by focusing on the context and zero in on the object of interest, whereas Westerners start by focusing on a central object.

These diverse preferences affect how people from Eastern and Western cultures organize their ideas. According to Nisbett, in the West, we begin with a general statement and give suggested solutions, present evidence and refute objections, then summarize and offer a conclusion. In the East, people cycle back to the same topic from different directions.[15] Nisbett offers the following example—from an English professor and thus focused on writing, but it could equally apply to public speaking—to demonstrate this difference in methodology:

> I was surprised when one of my students who had been a teacher in China before coming here told me that she didn't understand the requirements of essay structure. I told her to write a thesis statement and then prove its three points in the following paragraphs. She told me if she wrote this way in China she would be considered stupid. "In China," she said, "essays are written in a more circular fashion moving associated ideas closer and closer to the center."[16]

Although we need to be cautious about overgeneralizing, especially since people from one culture who spend time in another culture tend to align their thinking style with the culture with which they are interacting, we will see these differences surface as we explore both linear and nonlinear organizational formats.

LINEAR ORGANIZATIONAL FORMATS

Linear formats are typically used by North American speakers to make sense of information. A speech has a linear organization if its main points develop and relate directly to the thesis or topic sentence that comes early in the presentation. We will look at five traditional approaches to ordering materials: (1) chronological (or time) order, (2) spatial order, (3) cause-and-effect order, (4) problem-and-solution order, and (5) topical order.

Chronological Order

Developing an idea or a problem in the order it occurs or occurred in time is called **chronological order**.

One student, for example, used chronological order to inform receivers about the evolution of the right to privacy in the United States.

Purpose: To inform the audience about the evolution of the right to privacy.

Thesis: Americans believe they have a fundamental right to privacy.

   I. More than a century ago, Justice Louis D. Brandeis called privacy "the right to be let alone."

  II. Within a decade, the courts began to recognize the right to privacy.

 III. The Supreme Court relied on a privacy rationale in reaching its famous and controversial decisions on birth control and abortion.

 IV. Threats to privacy abound today.

As you can see, this student has considered the steps leading to the present situation in the order they occurred. In addition, each main point the speaker used covers a particular time period. Because the main points describe a sequence of happenings, they help the audience keep track of where the speaker is in time.

Any event that has occurred in time can be examined chronologically. When using a time-ordered presentation, you decide where to begin and end your chronology, whether to move forward or backward through the chronology, and what events to include. As you might expect, time order is used most often in informative speeches.

Spatial Order

Spatial order describes an object, a person, or a phenomenon as it exists in space. An object, for example, might be described from one of the following perspectives:

Top to bottom

Bottom to top

Left to right

Right to left

Inside to outside

Outside to inside

With spatial order, you must select one orientation and carry it through. Like chronological order, spatial order is used more frequently in informative speeches. Here is an example of how a speaker used a spatial pattern in talking about Stonehenge.

Purpose: To inform the audience of the appearance of the mysterious monuments of Stonehenge.

Thesis: The mystery of Stonehenge is revealed in its five circles of stones.

   I. The outermost circle of Stonehenge is called the Outer Sarsen Circle.

  II. The first circle is called the Outer Bluestone Circle.

 III. The second circle is the Inner Sarsen Trilithons.

 IV. The third circle is the Inner Bluestone Horseshoe.

  V. The innermost circle is the Altar Stone.

> Visit the interactive e-Book to access the Skill Builder feature "Speaker's Choice," in which you will practice using spatial order as a method of description.

Cause-and-Effect Order

When you use **cause-and-effect order**, you categorize your material into factors related to the causes of a problem and factors related to its effects. In a speech on drunk driving, you might begin by discussing the percentage of drivers during a certain period who were drunk when involved in a car accident (cause). You might then discuss the number of deaths each year that are attributed directly to drunk driving (effect).

You can vary this approach by discussing the effect before the cause. In the following example, a student used effect-and-cause order to discuss the causes of excessive stress among college students:

I. The number of students suffering from stress-related ailments is increasing at an alarming rate.

II. Experts on such ailments have identified four major explanations for this increase.

Both approaches are used in informative and persuasive speeches.

Problem-and-Solution Order

Problem-and-solution order requires you to determine the problems inherent in a situation and the solutions to remedy them. Thus, you might discuss the problems that develop when many students entering college are deficient in writing skills. In the second portion of your speech, you can then suggest a number of ways the identified problem might be alleviated (perhaps, for example, by expanding tutoring programs or offering noncredit remedial courses).

The next example also illustrates a problem–solution pattern. Notice how the emphasis is on how the problem can best be resolved.

Purpose: To convince my audience that national health insurance can help solve our health care problems.

Thesis: National health insurance will solve many of the problems caused by rising health care costs.

I. Rising health care costs have resulted in an uninsured class of people.

II. Implementing national health insurance will solve this problem.

When using a problem-and-solution format, you may discuss the advantages of the solution as well. In that case, the body of the speech would include three main points:

I. The problem

II. The solution

III. The advantages of adopting the solution

Problem-and-solution order is most frequently employed in persuasive speeches.

Topical Order

At times, a speech may not fit neatly into any of the patterns described previously. When this happens, you may choose to develop or cluster your material by arranging it into a series of appropriate topics. This is **topical order**. Speeches that discuss the advantages and disadvantages of a proposal; the social, political, and economic factors that contribute to a problem; or perceptions of upper-class, middle-class, and lower-class people on an issue are organized topically. When you use a topical order, you may find that you can intermingle cause-and-effect, time, problem-and-solution, or spatial order within the topical order.

One student used topical order to speak about the pros and cons of using animals for medical and product research.

Purpose: To inform audience members of the advantages and disadvantages of using animals for medical and product research.

Thesis: Using animals for medical and product research presents both advantages and disadvantages.

I. There are two advantages to using animals as research subjects.

   A. Using animals is more effective than simply using results of test tube experiments.

   B. During the early stages of research, using animals is more effective than using human subjects.

II. There are two disadvantages to using animals in research.

   A. Animals are often mutilated and experience pain.

   B. Animals do not respond in precisely the same manner that human subjects do.

ETHICS AND COMMUNICATION

Sound Bites With Bite

A sound bite is a brief, catchy, and memorable statement that a speaker uses to communicate the essence of his or her message. Sound bites are designed to be picked up and spread by the media. Sometimes, however, they oversimplify or misrepresent complex subjects, causing some to question if they are ethical.

How capable must a speaker be to be able to deliver a sound bite to attract supporters and urge action? Which, if any, organizational formats do you believe best lends itself to this type of abbreviated presentation? Is 90 seconds or less enough time to deliver a message designed not just to inform but also to influence?

Try your hand at it. Create a sound bite on any of the following topics or another of your choosing: the advantages of public education, the benefits or drawbacks of sororities or fraternities, nuclear proliferation, how to create a successful personal brand. Describe the organizational approach you used to express your thoughts concisely.

Internal Previews, Summaries, Transitions, and Signposts

Audience members who think linearly will count on you to use transitional tools as you move from one idea to the next. The devices that speakers using linear logic use to create a sense of presentation coherence and unity are internal previews, internal summaries, transitions, and signposts.

An **internal preview** precedes information the speaker will discuss. Internal previews help to prepare the audience for important information to follow as well as what to look for as the speech progresses. For example, in a presentation on genetic engineering, a speaker told her audience: "We will next consider a technique that allows biologists to transfer a gene from one species to another. It is called recombinant DNA technology."

Internal summaries follow information the speaker has presented. They are designed to help receivers remember the content, for example, "The four characteristics we have considered thus far are . . . ." **Transitions**—connective words and phrases— help the audience recall material and facilitate the speaker's movement from one idea to another. In effect, transitions bridge gaps between ideas so that there are no abrupt switches.[17]

Speakers use **signposts**, signaling cues such as "equally important" or "furthermore," to indicate that additional information is forthcoming. They also use them to make receivers aware that they are about to explain something, share an important idea, or let the audience know where they are in the progression of a speech. Commonly used signposts include the words *first*, *second*, and *third*; phrases that focus attention, such as "above all else, remember this"; phrases that indicate an explanation is forthcoming, such as "for example"; or rhetorical questions (queries that you ask and also answer), such as "What steps can we take to make things better?" To signal that you will be discussing a cause-and-effect relationship, you can use the expressions "as a result" or "consequently." To introduce a contrasting view, you could use "after all," and "yet," "in spite of," or "on the other hand." Signposts also signal the end of a speech. When a speaker says something like "finally" or "to sum up," he or she is signaling that the speech is about to conclude. So, in addition to moving a speech forward, signposts draw it to a close.

CONFIGURAL ORGANIZATIONAL FORMATS

As we have seen, linear formats develop ideas step-by-step, relying on facts and data to support each main point. In contrast, **configural formats** are more indirect and less explicit in offering hard evidence and proof in defense of a point. Whereas a number of us prefer to use linear logic to develop our ideas, others of us—including some people from Native American, Asian American, or Latino cultures—do not.

Instead of previewing, spelling out, and discussing each key point, one at a time, people who prefer configural thinking approach their subject from a variety of perspectives and rely on examples and stories to carry the crux of their message. They also rely on receivers to understand the messages implied by the examples and stories they use. Because they believe that explicitly stating a message is unnecessary, speakers who use a configural style do not bluntly tell receivers their conclusion or call on them to make a specific response; instead, the speakers lead them to their conclusion indirectly and by implication. Thus, configural frameworks require receivers to do more work.

Although people in cultures who favor the use of configural patterns might not categorize them in this way, Westerners identify three kinds of configural systems of organization. First is the *deferred-thesis pattern*, in which the main points of a speech gradually build to the speaker's thesis, which he or she does not indicate until the speech is nearly over. Second is the *web pattern*, in which threads of thought refer back to the speaker's central purpose; whereas to Western receivers the speaker may seem to be "off topic" at points, to receivers in other cultures the tangents the speaker explores are connected to the speaker's topic and make it more meaningful. Third is the *narrative pattern*, in which the speaker tells a story without stating a thesis or developing it with main points. When using a narrative pattern, the speaker uses a series of illustrations and parables to help receivers discover the speech's main points. The speaker uses indirection and implication rather than bridges or transitions to circle and connect ideas, establish their point, and ultimately help the audience members arrive at their conclusion.[18]

The following speech outline is organized configurally, using a narrative pattern.

Purpose: To persuade my audience that *E. coli* presents problems for our food supply.

    I.   A hypothetical food worker, Jake, who is employed in a meatpacking plant, inadvertently infects the plant's meat supply with *E. coli*.

    II.   Jake's carelessness contributes to the infection of a number of people in an array of cities across the United States.

    III.   The plant is closed because of *E. coli* contamination.

    IV.   Today, member of the families of those who were sickened by *E. coli* ask the federal government, "How can our food supply be made safe?"

Looking at the preceding example, you can see that it has four main points. First, the speaker sets the scene for receivers, introducing the subject and the situation. The speaker next describes the sequence of events as they occurred. Then, she or he discusses the situation's effects. Finally, the narrator points to a solution. If you choose narration, tell a solid story, use descriptive language, intersperse dialogue when possible, build interest or suspense, and help your audience identify with the people involved. When serving as a narrator, you can place yourself there and tell the story in the first person, use the second person and help audience members imagine themselves in such a situation, or use the third person (as the speaker in the provided example did) and describe what happened.

As the speaker embellishes each of the ideas identified in the outline during his or her presentation, it is up to the receivers to interpret the meaning of the speaker's narrative from the stories, examples, and testimony offered. The speaker will not state directly what receivers should think or do but will rely on them to draw their own conclusions and come up with their own solutions.

EXPLORING DIVERSITY
Is Attention Cultural?

Edward T. Hall suggested that "culture . . . designates what we pay attention to and what we ignore." If this is so, what can you do to ensure that audience members who belong to other cultural groups or who prefer an organizational pattern other than the one that you have chosen to use will pay attention to the right things in your speech? In other words, what can you do to target crucial ideas and emphasize key points?

For example, let's say a speaker from a low-context culture such as the United States were asked to give a speech on how climate change affects the economy to an audience composed of economists from Saudi Arabia or Mexico. How might the speaker adapt his or her speech's organizational pattern to appeal to members of a high-context culture? [19]

In your opinion, does changing the organizational structure of a speech also change the speech's content? Is a speaker who makes such adaptations no longer being true to himself or herself? Explain your position.

Recall from Chapter 2 that members of low-context cultures such as the United States usually are more direct in how they convey information to others than are members of high-context cultures, such as Latin America, Japan, and Saudi Arabia. To low-context receivers, the speaker from a high-context culture may come off as vague or deceptive because of his or her reluctance to be direct, explicit, or obvious. In contrast, high-context receivers prefer to receive information through examples, illustrations, and other indirect means of expression.[20]

According to most intercultural communication theorists, English is primarily a speaker-responsible language, but other languages, including Japanese, Chinese, and Arabic, are more listener responsible. Native users of speaker-responsible languages typically believe it is up to the speakers to tell receivers exactly what they want them to know. In contrast, native speakers of listener-responsible languages typically believe that speakers need indicate only indirectly what they are speaking about and what they want receivers to know. They believe it is up to audience members, not the speaker, to construct the message's meaning.[21] To which thought group do you belong?

OUTLINING YOUR SPEECH: BUILDING A SPEAKING FRAMEWORK

Once you have decided what format to use for your speech, you are ready to prepare an outline. Just as an architect develops a plan for a building, so you must develop a plan for your speech. Organizing your ideas helps to facilitate communication with your audience. How can you accomplish this? Communication theorists have developed guidelines to help you with this phase.

As we saw in Chapter 6, not everyone is a skillful listener. For this reason, you should base your organization on the *principle of redundancy*. In other words, to ensure comprehension, you will need to build a certain amount of repetition into your speech. Only if this is done will listeners be able to follow your ideas easily. The basic developmental principle is often expressed as follows:

Tell them what you are going to tell them.

Tell them.

Tell them what you have told them.

One of the best ways to organize a speech is the introduction-body-conclusion format (Figure 12.7), which we call the **speech framework**, because it provides a frame, or skeleton, on which any speech or other formal presentation can be built.

Use this framework to organize your speech. Your introductory remarks and your concluding statements should each take up approximately 10% to 15% of the total presentation. That leaves 70% to 80% of your time for developing the ideas contained in the body of your speech. Because the body will be the main portion of your presentation, it is often advisable to begin by preparing this part of the speech. Once the body is set, you can move on to develop the introduction and the conclusion.

CREATING YOUR OUTLINE

As you begin to organize the body of your speech, you will want to build a suitable structure onto which you can place your ideas. Your audience is unlikely to recall a long, wandering, unstructured collection of data, so you need a clear organization to be understood. When you take the time to prepare an easy-to-follow structure for your speech, in addition to enhancing receiver perception of your competence and adding to the personal credibility you have in their eyes, your efforts also help fulfill receiver expectations. That is, the main points of a speech alert receivers to listen for supporting information. Because they are not struggling to make sense of a disordered array of information, the audience is able to focus instead on the thesis of your speech and the support you offer.

Taking time to develop an outline has another benefit. Because you identify the information you are using to support each main point, your delivery will be improved. With your ideas already carefully laid out, you can focus on establishing a good relationship with the audience instead of what to say next.

Outlining Principles

After completing your research, you will need to develop an outline that distinguishes between your **main ideas**—the two to five subtopics that directly support your thesis—and your **subordinate ideas**—those ideas that function as support or amplification for your main ideas.

In many ways, subordinate ideas are the foundation on which larger ideas are constructed (Figure 12.7). Consequently, you should begin the organizational process by arranging your materials into clusters of main and subordinate ideas. As you do this, you will be able to determine which evidence supports the main ideas and which supports the subordinate ideas.

If you are developing a speech on affirmative action programs, you should begin by laying out your purpose and thesis:

Purpose: To inform the audience about affirmative action.

Thesis: The definition, uses, and results of affirmative action have contributed to its being a policy under fire (Figure 12.8).

You are off to a good start. The first stage of outline development is to create a *preliminary working outline.* This sparse outline has points containing one or two words that eventually will achieve fuller form in the second stage, the full sentence outline. Your preliminary working outline on affirmative action might look something like this:

I. Definition

II. Purposes

III. Outcomes

IV. Why under attack

FIGURE 12.7
Construction of an idea

Main Idea

Subordinate

Subordinate

FIGURE 12.8
Dividing a Thesis Into Major Parts

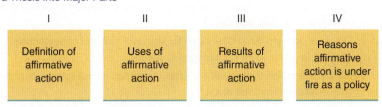

I	II	III	IV
Definition of affirmative action	Uses of affirmative action	Results of affirmative action	Reasons affirmative action is under fire as a policy

Next, and only after you have researched and fully developed the ideas of your speech, develop these major points into complete sentences using parallel structure—that is, using sentences with similar or matching styles—to create your *full sentence outline.*

I. Affirmative action can be defined as any action taken to ensure or affirm equal opportunity for oppressed or previously disadvantaged groups.

II. Affirmative action is used in hiring and college admissions decisions.

III. Affirmative action has benefits and drawbacks.

IV. Affirmative action is under fire for being reverse discrimination.

Now flesh out each main idea with subordinate points and evidence (or support). The basic structure should look something like this:

I. Main idea

   A. Subordinate idea

      1. Support for subordinate idea

      2. Support for subordinate idea

   B. Subordinate idea

      1. Support for subordinate idea

      2. Support for subordinate idea

Notice that the outline you develop indicates the relative importance of each item included in it. The main points—Roman numerals I, II, III, and so on—are the most important points you want your audience to remember. Your subpoints—capital letters A, B, C, and so on—are supportive of, but less important than, the main points.

Be sure to line up the entries in your outline correctly. Locate the main ideas closer to the left margin. The subpoints should be tabbed in. The sub-subpoints are indented below that.

An outline for a speech with the purpose "To inform audience members about the fears and questions concerning the H5N1 avian flu (bird flu)" might look like this:

I. Several fears concerning the H5N1 avian flu are prevalent in society today.

   A. Many people fear that H5N1 avian flu is the next pandemic.

      1. Cases of human infection of H5N1 avian flu among people who handled infected birds have been reported in a number of countries, including China, Cambodia, Turkey, and Iraq.

      2. There is concern that H5N1 avian flu virus will mutate spontaneously, giving it greater ability to jump from person to person.

      3. There is concern that travel, especially by air, will accelerate transmission of the disease around the world.

   B. Currently, chances of contracting H5N1 avian flu are small for people who are not in constant contact with birds.

      1. Not a single bird in the United States has been found to suffer from avian influenza.

      2. Casual contact with birds will not spread flu because of the species barrier.

II. Many questions remain regarding future efforts to protect against a pandemic strain of avian flu.

    A. Developing a vaccine to attack a pandemic avian flu virus was problematic.

        1. Whether Tamiflu and Relenza would be effective against the pandemic version of the avian flu virus was unclear.

        2. Because scientists do not know what a pandemic flu virus will look like, it is difficult to make an effective vaccine.

        3. Scientists hope that the H5N1 vaccine in use since April 17, 2017, will provide at least some protection in a pandemic.

    B. Improving international cooperation is critical.

        1. We need to increase awareness of the threat.

        2. We need to improve surveillance and diagnosis of the disease in birds.

    C. Biosecurity is key.

        1. The president signed an executive order adding pandemic influenza to the list of quarantine worthy diseases.

        2. The N95 mask provides some protection from the droplets that spread the virus.

        3. Discouraging personal stockpiling, the government is calling for the maintenance of national and regional supplies.

BEGINNINGS AND ENDINGS

Once you have outlined the body of your speech and considered the need for transitional devices, you are ready to "tell them what you are going to tell them" and "tell them what you told them." In other words, it is time to develop the introduction and conclusion.[22]

THE INTRODUCTION

All too frequently, the introduction is overlooked or neglected because speakers are in too much of a hurry to get to the heart of the matter. However, in public speaking, just as in interpersonal communication, first impressions count. Thus, it is essential for you to make the first few minutes of your speech particularly interesting.

Functions of the Introduction

The functions of your introduction are to gain the attention of the audience members, to make them want to listen to your speech, and to provide them with an overview of the subject you will be discussing. The art of designing introductions is much like any other art: It requires creative thinking. As you design yours, consider your purpose for speaking, the body of the speech, your analysis of the audience, and your own abilities.

The opening moments of contact, whether with one person or with a multitude, can affect a developing relationship either positively or negatively. Unquestionably, the first few moments of your speech will affect your audience's willingness to give your speech a fair hearing. It is at this point that audience members will decide whether what you have to say is interesting and important or dull and inconsequential. If your introduction is designed poorly, your audience may tune out the remainder of the speech. On the other hand, a well-designed introduction can help you develop a solid rapport with the audience and thus make it easier for you to share your ideas.

Select the material you will include in your introduction with care. In all likelihood your listeners have not been waiting eagerly to hear you speak, so you will need to work to spark their interest. You will need to motivate them to listen to you. Student speakers sometimes go overboard in trying to accomplish this objective. Some have been known to yell or throw books across the room. Besides being inappropriate and potentially dangerous, such over-the-top attention-getting attempts can turn the audience against you. Other speakers look for a joke—any joke—to use as an attention getter. Unfortunately, a poorly chosen joke can confuse or even alienate listeners rather than interest and involve them. (A well-chosen anecdote, however, can be very effective.) Some speakers insist on beginning with statements like, "My purpose here today is" or "Today I hope to convince you." Such openings suggest mainly that the speech maker has forgotten to consider motivation and attention.

Years ago, television shows began simply by flashing the title of the program onto the screen. Today, however, it is common to use a teaser to open a program. The teaser usually reveals segments of the show designed to arouse the interest of potential viewers, to encourage them to stay tuned. Without this device, many viewers would probably switch channels. Your listeners, of course, cannot switch speakers, but they can decide not to listen actively to what you have to say. Therefore, you, too, must design a teaser to interest and appeal to your audience.

Types of Introductions

Effective speech makers begin in a number of different ways. They might cite something unusual, ask a question, offer a compliment, refer to the occasion, or use a humorous or suspenseful story. Audiences respond to stories about people. If you have selected a topic because you have personal interest in it, you also can use a personal anecdote to begin your presentation. Let us examine a few examples of these approaches.

Some of the most effective introductions use relevant humor, as in the following example from a speech about changes the U.S. Army has made delivered by David H. Petraeus, then commander of U.S. Central Command and later head of the CIA.

> Earlier today, as I was talking with my wife about tonight's speech, she reminded me of a story about a young schoolboy's report on Julius Caesar. "Julius Caesar was born a long time ago," the little boy explained. "He was a great general. He won some important battles. He made a speech. They killed him."
>
> I'll try to avoid Caesar's fate.[23]

When used in introductions, illustrations can add drama, as is seen in the remarks singer-songwriter Pink delivered at the 2017 MTV Video Music Awards:

> Recently, I was driving my daughter to school and she said to me, out of the blue, "Mama?" I said, "Yes, baby?" She said, "I'm the ugliest girl I know." And I said, "Huh?" And she was like, "Yeah, I look like a boy with long hair." And my brain went to, "Oh my god, you're six. Why? Where is this coming from? Who said this? Can I kick a 6-year-old's ass, like what?"

But I didn't say anything. Instead I went home and I made a PowerPoint presentation for her. And in that presentation were androgynous rock-stars and artists that live their truth, are probably made fun of every day of their life, and carry on, wave their flag, and inspire the rest of us.[24]

Student Adrienne Hallett uses suspense to make her point. Adrienne's speech began this way:

He showed all of the classic symptoms. His response time was slowed, his judgment was impaired, but he thought he could handle it. As he drove home along the interstate, his car swerved onto the shoulder of the road, running over and killing a man who was trying to change a flat time. When the police questioned him later, he didn't remember a thing. What caused this Ohio man's actions is something we have all been guilty of, yet we won't readily admit it. Although the U.S. Department of Transportation estimates that it kills 13,000 people annually, no one will be taking the keys, calling a cab or taking a stand on this issue. Whenever we get into the driver's seat, we must be prepared for the risks presented by an impaired driver—surprisingly, not from alcohol but from lack of sleep.[25]

Another student began a speech by asking a rhetorical question:

Do you know who you voted for in the last presidential election? I bet you don't. I bet you think you voted for the Democratic, Republican, or Independent candidate. But you didn't. You voted to elect members of the Electoral College.

Another student used frightening facts to jolt her audience:

In the time that it takes me to complete this sentence, a child in America will drop out of school. In the time that it takes me to complete the sentence, a child in this country will run away from home. Before I finish this presentation another teenage girl will have a baby.

Finally, speakers also use startling statistics to capture the audience's attention. The following example from Romaine Seguin's speech, "Becoming Visible: Insights for Working Women From the Women of Hidden Figures," demonstrates the speaker's use of statistics to spark interest:

Here's a number: 1,176,000,000. What does this number mean to me? Let me explain: 20 years of this event taking place, 4,200 attendees on average per event and 14,000 women-owned businesses. The number seems impressive when we talk about women that are making an impact in today's world, but there are an estimated 3.2 billion women in the world. So, the number suddenly doesn't seem so big, right? But there is a lot hidden behind that figure.[26]

THE PREVIEW

If your speech is organized in a linear fashion, after you have used your introduction to spark interest and motivate your audience to continue listening, it is necessary for you to preview the speech. That is, you need to let your audience members know what you will be discussing. Consider the following example of a preview.

There are three "weight classes" of people in our society: the overweight, the underweight, and those who are the right weight. Unfortunately, many people fail to understand the role weight plays in their lives. Your weight affects how your body functions. Let's explore how.

Your preview should correspond to your purpose statement. It should let your audience know what to listen for. Additionally, by presenting it after you have gotten your listeners' attention and motivated them to continue paying attention, you ensure that your purpose statement will get a fair hearing.

THE CONCLUSION

The conclusion summarizes the presentation and leaves your listeners thinking about what they have just heard. It provides a sense of completion.

Functions of the Conclusion

The conclusion's summary function may be considered a preview in reverse. During your preview, you look ahead, revealing to your listeners the subject of your efforts. During the summary, you review for them the material you have covered. For example, a summary might begin, "We have examined three benefits you will derive from a new town library." During the remainder of this summation, the three benefits might be restated to cement them in the minds of the listeners.

Inexperienced speech makers sometimes say that the summary appears to be superfluous. ("After all, I've just said all of that not more than two minutes ago.") However, it is important to remember that you are speaking for the audience, not for yourself. The summary provides some of the redundancy mentioned earlier; it enables audience member to leave with your ideas freshly impressed on their minds. In addition to refreshing your listener's memory, the conclusion can help clarify the issues or ideas you have just discussed.

Besides serving as a summary, your conclusion should be used to heighten the impact of the presentation. You can do this in a number of ways. One popular technique is to refer to your introductory remarks; this gives your speech a sense of closure. If, for example, you are speaking about child abuse and you begin your presentation by showing pictures of abused children, you might paraphrase your opening remarks and show the pictures again to arouse sympathy and support. Quotations and illustrations also make effective conclusions. For example, if you are speaking about the problems that veterans of the war on terror face, you could provide a moving conclusion by quoting some veterans or relating some of the challenges they face. You also are free to draw on your own experiences when designing a conclusion. Keep in mind that, as with introductions, audiences respond to conclusions that include personal references, surprising statements, startling statistics, and relevant humor.

Types of Conclusions

Let's examine how some conclusion techniques work in practice. The director of the New Jersey School Boards Association used this illustration in her conclusion to a speech on why public schools must thrive.

One of the students being honored as an unsung hero in Ocean County had suffered through a childhood filled with taunts and ridicule because he had a birth defect that affected his balance and made him fall. As a teen, he had major surgery and is now described as a handsome young man who you'd never know suffered from such problems. In his freshman year, he accompanied to the prom a girl with such crippling health issues she could barely stand to three feet tall. Yet this empathetic young man treated her with respect; he spent the evening dancing with her on his knees so that he was her height.[27]

In a speech on skin cancer, university student Jessy Ohl concluded with a startling statistic.

Regularly examine your body for skin cancer. Skin cancer usually begins in oddly shaped moles that often bleed or don't heal. If you see something like this, do yourself and your family a favor and ask your physician. Be the first line of defense and do not assume that your doctor will check for skin cancer. The *Journal of Dermatology* reports that, unless asked, physicians provide skin cancer examinations to only 1.5 percent of patients.[28]

Quotations can increase a conclusion's impact. Former attorney general Robert Kennedy often ended his speeches with the following words by the playwright George Bernard Shaw:

Some men see things as they are, and ask, "Why?"

I dare to dream of things that never were, and ask, "Why not?"[29]

Humor, when used appropriately, can help keep people on your side. One student ended a speech directed at first-year college students with the following "letter."

Dear Mom and Dad:

Just thought I'd drop you a note to clue you in on my plans.

I've fallen in love with a guy named Buck. He quit high school between his sophomore and junior years to travel with his motorcycle gang. He was married at 18 and has two sons. About a year ago he got a divorce.

We plan to get married in the fall. He thinks he will be able to get a job by then. I've decided to move into his apartment. At any rate, I dropped out of school last week. Maybe I will finish college sometime in the future.

Mom and Dad, I just want you to know that everything in this letter so far is false. NONE OF IT IS TRUE.

But it is true that I got a C in French and a D in math.

And I am in need of money for tuition and miscellaneous.

Love, Your daughter.

A Sample Outline

The following is a student's full sentence outline, containing an introduction, body, transitions, and a conclusion. What do you think are the outline's strengths and weaknesses?

Granny Dumping

Specific Purpose: To explain the growing abandonment problem that thousands of our elderly experience.

Thesis: Increased family stresses and a lack of government assistance are causing families in the United States and abroad to abandon their older relatives.

Introduction

   I. Just about a half-century ago, the late playwright Edward Albee wrote *The Sandbox*, a drama telling the story of a family who bring their grandmother to a playground and dump her in a sandbox.

   II. Back then, Albee's play was labeled as absurd.

   III. Now that this is happening in many countries, it is all too real.

   IV. Today, I would like to talk to you about the growing problem of granny dumping that the elderly face.

(*Transition:* Let's begin by examining the story of one elderly person.)
   Body

   I. Thousands of families in the United States are abandoning aging parents.

   A. John Kingery, 82, was abandoned outside a men's room in Post Falls, Idaho.
      1. His clothes were stripped of their labels.
      2. An Alzheimer's sufferer, Kingery was not able to remember his name.

   B. Thousands of older Americans face similar situations, often being left in hospitals.
      1. The American College of Emergency Physicians estimates that 70,000 elderly relatives are abandoned each year in hospital emergency rooms.
      2. Most of the families who abandon relatives do so because they cannot pay for the necessary care.
      3. Many have suffered financially in the recession, making them vulnerable to predators who too often are also family members.

(*Transition:* This is not only an American problem. In South Korea, China, and India, the elderly face similarly uncertain futures.)

   II. In South Korea, the breaching of the Confucian social contract has left many elderly people to fend for themselves.

   A. Denied welfare, thousands of South Koreans age 65 and older commit suicide.
      1. One 78-year-old widow staged her death as a final act of public protest against a society she said had abandoned her by drinking pesticide in front of her city hall.
      2. South Koreans are denied welfare because their children are capable of supporting them.

   B. Thousands of older Chinese face equally horrific fates.
      1. Chinese parents invest heavily in their children's education, thinking the children will repay the debt to them later in life.
      2. The children do not live up to their responsibilities.
      3. Elderly parents find themselves with no financial reserves.

    C. The elderly in India also are being abandoned.
       1. Every year, thousands of grown Indian children abandon their parents.
       2. With society no longer parent-oriented, the elderly in India are left to fend for themselves.

(*Transition:* Why are family members and governments not living up to their responsibilities?)

  III. Responsibilities are overwhelming those here and abroad who in the past would have cared for elderly relatives.
    A. The social fabric of societies is fraying.
    B. Governments have not responded to the erosion of the family structure.
    C. Caregivers suffer physical and mental stress.
       1. Exhausted caregivers become susceptible to high blood pressure and strokes.
       2. Caregivers suffer from depression.
       3. Caregivers experience guilt.

(*Transition:* So much for the reality of granny dumping; what about the future?)

  IV. There are a number of ways to ensure granny dumping ends.
    A. Families can do more.
       1. They can avoid placing all the responsibilities on one person.
       2. Relatives can help out with the never-ending stack of paperwork required by government agencies.
   B. Governments can do more.
       1. Programs need to be added so that patients can be cared for outside the home at least part of the time.
          a. This would provide variety for the elderly parents.
          b. Such programs would also give a much-needed rest to the family so they could avoid burnout.
       2. Suicide prevention centers need to be established.
          a. The government needs to protect its people.
          b. The elderly need to feel there is hope.
       3. A holistic approach to elder care needs to be adopted.

Conclusion

  I. Though Albee's *The Sandbox* was labeled as an example of absurdism some 50 years ago, granny dumping has become an all too real and all too tragic way of life for tens of thousands of people around the world.
  II. It is time to treat our aging and elderly relatives with the respect and dignity they deserve.

Works Consulted
"Abuse Underreported in Many States," *USA Today*, April 2004, p. 3.
Edward Albee, *The Sandbox*. New York: New American Library, 1961.
Alzheimer's Association, www.alz.org.

"Avoiding Granny Dumping," *Daily Utah Chronicle*, January 10, 2008, www.dailyutahchronicle.com/news/2008/10/News/Avoiding.Granny.Dumping3148735.shtml.

Rachel Boaz and Charlotte F. Muller, "Why Do Some Caregivers of Frail Elderly Quit?" *Health Care Financing Review*, 13(2), Winter 1991, pp. 41-47.

Keith Bradsher, "In China, Families Bet It All on College for Their Children," *New York Times*, February 16, 2013, https://www.nytimes.com/2013/02/17/business/in-china-families-bet-it-all-on-a-child-in-college.html.

Robert Butler, "Health Care for All: A Crisis of Cost and Access," *Geriatrics*, 47, September 1992, pp. 34-48.

"Elder Abuse: A Hidden Tragedy," *Biotech Week*, October 20, 2004, p. 195.

"Granny-Dumping by the Thousands," *New York Times*, March 29, 1992, https://www.nytimes.com/1992/03/29/opinion/granny-dumping-by-the-thousands.html.

Homewatch CareGivers, https://www.homewatchcaregivers.com. A support group of caregivers for people who suffer from Alzheimer's disease.

Paul Krugman, "Does Getting Old Cost Society Too Much? *New York Times Magazine*, March 9, 1997, pp. 58-60.

Rebecca Ley, "Why Do So Many Children Abandon Parents in Their Darkest Hour?" *Daily Mail*, May 28, 2014, http://www.dailymail.co.uk/femail/article-2642006/Why-DO-children-abandon-parents-darkest-hour-Im-stunned-Ian-Botham-didnt-visit-dementia-stricken-father.html.

Judy Lin, "Honor or Abandon: Societies' Treatment of Elderly Intrigues Scholar," *UCLA Today*, January 7, 2010, http://newsroom.ucla.edu/stories/jared-diamond-on-aging-150571.

Choe Sang-Hun, "As Families Change, Korea's Elderly Are Turning to Suicide," *New York Times*, February 17, 2013, https://www.nytimes.com/2013/02/17/world/asia/in-korea-changes-in-society-and-family-dynamics-drive-rise-in-elderly-suicides.html.

Stacy Singer, "Lawyers Warn of Granny Dumping," *Palm Beach Post*, June 14, 2011.

COMMUNICATION SKILLS

Practice Tips for Speech Design and Organization

In order to document your progress in designing and organizing your speech, ask yourself the following questions. Until you can answer each question with a yes, you have more work to do.

Have I made the specific purpose of my speech clear?

If you can't answer this question with a yes, revise your speech until you can.

Have I expressed the main idea or thesis of my speech as effectively as I can?

Everything in your speech should support your thesis. If this is not the case, alterations are now in order.

Does my speech contain an introduction that includes both an attention-getter and a preview?

All components of the introduction should be expressed as effectively as possible. If they are not, you have work to do.

Have I developed a clear outline of my presentation?

The outline should clearly delineate each main point. If it does not, it is not yet ready.

In developing each main point in the speech, did I present sufficient verbal or visual support?

Identify which of the main points is currently the most fully developed and then work to bring the others up to its level.

Have I taken the cultural backgrounds of receivers sufficiently into account?

If not, take steps now to broaden the speech's interest and appeal.

Do I offer sufficient internal previews and summaries, as well as transitions and signposts, to facilitate comprehension and recall in my audience members?

If not, work on integrating these now.

Does my speech contain a conclusion that summarizes it? Does it use psychological appeals to promote receiver interest and heighten my speech's impact?

Each of the conclusion's components needs to be as effective. If they are not, this is the time to make those changes.

> A speech is like a love affair. Any fool can start it, but to end it requires considerable skill.
>
> Lord Mancroft

COMPLETE THIS CHAPTER 12 CHECKLIST

12.1 I can conduct primary and secondary research for my speech both online and offline. ☐

Researching the content of your speech using online and offline resources is among your first tasks in preparing a speech. For example, when working offline, you may consult published works, including books, journals, magazines, and newspapers. When working online, you have the Internet and its many resources at your disposal.

In addition to using secondary research, or work already published, speakers also use primary research, making personal observations and conducting informal surveys or personal interviews to gather information for their speeches. Informal surveys consist of approximately 5 to 10 questions that you ask people affected by or familiar with your topic. Interviews are similar to surveys except that they are more detailed and assume that the person whom you interview is an expert on your topic.

12.2 I can explain how to use support to enhance a presentation. ☐

Among the kinds of verbal support that speakers use to make their research interesting and understandable to audience members are definitions (explanations of what words or concepts mean), statistics (facts expressed in numerical form), examples (representative cases), illustrations (stories and narrative pictures), and testimonials (someone else's opinions, conclusions, or quotations). They also use comparisons that express similarities and contrasts that express differences, repetition (the same words repeated verbatim), and restatement (the same idea in different words) to increase the impact and memorability of their speech.

12.3 I can summarize the types and features of linear and configural speech formats. ☐

There are five common linear approaches to order the ideas in a speech: (1) chronological order, (2) spatial order, (3) cause-and-effect order, (4) problem-and-solution order, and (5) topical order. When you use linear logic, the body of your presentation contains internal previews and summaries. Internal previews prepare receivers for important information to follow. Internal summaries help receivers recall content. Transitions facilitate movement from one idea to another. Signposts indicate that additional information is forthcoming. Together, these devices help listeners follow and recall the speech's content.

Configural, or nonlinear, speech formats often use implication, examples, stories, and different perspectives to convey a message to the audience. Speakers from a number of cultural groups prefer using configural logic to structure their ideas. They may use a deferred-thesis pattern, a web pattern, or a narrative pattern to organize a speech.

12.4 I can discuss the speech framework and its relationship to outlining stages and principles, including the identification of main and subordinate ideas. □

A speech framework or outline is composed of an introduction, body, and conclusion. An outline is developed in stages. First, the speaker creates a preliminary outline, then a full sentence outline, and ultimately an extemporaneous outline or speaker's notes. Main ideas are the primary points of the speech. Subordinate ideas amplify the main ideas.

12.5 I can discuss the characteristics of effective introductions and conclusions. □

The introduction should gain the attention of audience members, make them want to listen to your speech, and provide them with an overview of the speech. Devices used to enhance introductions and conclusions include humor, illustrations, questions, surprising statements, and statistics.

12.6 I can apply my skills to evaluate supporting materials, organizational format, and the speech outline. □

Speakers select supporting materials by evaluating them for currency, accuracy, reliability, sufficiency, appropriateness, and effectiveness. They build a framework for their speech and prepare a detailed outline to ensure the parts of the speech have coherence and will be easy for receivers to follow and digest.

BECOME A WORD MASTER

cause-and-effect order 331

chronological order 329

configural formats 333

definitions 324

examples 325

illustrations 325

internal preview 333

internal summaries 333

linear formats 329

main ideas 337

plagiarism 321

primary research 319

problem-and-solution order 331

signposts 333

spatial order 330

speech framework 336

statistics 325

subordinate ideas 337

testimony 326

topical order 332

transitions 333

iStock/gilaxia

Using Presentation Aids and Delivering Your Speech

13

13.1 Explain how to use presentation aids, including PowerPoint, to enhance the content and delivery of a speech.

13.2 Distinguish extemporaneous speaking from other styles of delivery, including manuscript, memorized, impromptu, extemporaneous, and sound bite speaking.

13.3 Identify speech rehearsal and delivery strategies, including the effective use of nonverbal cues.

13.4 Analyze a speech maker's performance (including your own) in terms of content, organization, wording, and delivery.

13.5 Apply skills to improve speech delivery.

> If all my talents and powers were suddenly taken from me by some inscrutable Providence, and I were allowed to keep only one, I would unhesitatingly ask to be allowed to keep my Power of Speaking, for with that one, I would quickly regain all the others.
>
> Daniel Webster

Let's continue ascending the speech maker's ladder. You are just about prepared to present—only a few steps stand between you and success. By now, you have chosen a topic and adapted it to your audience and the occasion. You have conducted research, selected support, chosen an organizational approach, and outlined your speech. It's time to shift your focus and begin thinking about how you might illustrate the content of your speech; that is, you need to decide if adding audio and visual aids to your speech will make it stronger (Figure 13.1). ■

FIGURE 13.1

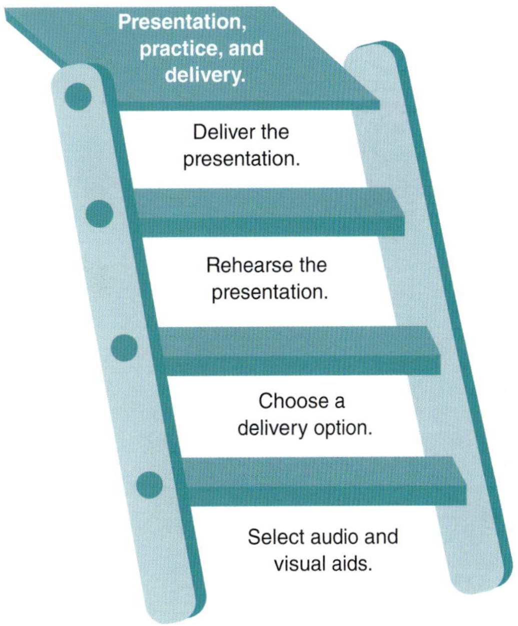

Presentation, practice, and delivery.

Deliver the presentation.

Rehearse the presentation.

Choose a delivery option.

Select audio and visual aids.

SELECTING AND PREPARING PRESENTATION AIDS

Consider this observation by former presidential adviser and communication and media relations specialist Merrie Spaeth:

When Moses came down from the mountain with clay tablets bearing the Ten Commandments, it was perhaps history's first example of a speaker using props to reinforce his message. It wouldn't have had the same impact if Moses had simply announced: "God just told me 10 things, and I'm going to relay them to you."[1]

We are more attracted to messages with visual appeal than to those that appeal solely to our ears. Visual aids have become a tool of choice for speakers in the public arena. In fact, at congressional hearings, it is common for senators and representatives to use aids with text large enough to be seen by the cameras.

WHY USE PRESENTATION AIDS?

Presentation aids make it easier for the audience to follow, understand, respond to, and remember your speech. When deciding whether to use an audio or visual aid, begin by asking yourself if it will fulfill at least one of the purposes identified here:

- **Facilitating comprehension.** We process more than 80% of all information we receive through our sense of sight.[2]

- **Directing attention and controlling interest.** A dramatic photograph, object, or graph holds a listener's attention more compellingly than do words alone.

- **Increasing persuasiveness.** Speakers who use presentation aids in their presentations are perceived as stronger communicators and are 43% more likely to persuade their audiences than are speakers who rely exclusively on spoken words.[3]

- **Promoting content organization.** By displaying main ideas visually, you help receivers follow your speech's structure and better understand it.

- Enhancing recall. We remember only about 10% of what we read, 20% of what we hear, and 30% of what we see. But we remember more than 50% of what we see and hear simultaneously.[4]

- **Communicating concisely.** Presentation aids facilitate the sharing of information that might otherwise appear too complex or take up too much time.

iStock/GlobalStock

For example, displaying a three-dimensional model of the molecular structure of a virus might create more interest than your words alone could provide. Visuals depicting the damage that cigarette smoke does to human lungs or sound effects that re-create the breathing of patients with lung cancer similarly can add impact. A chart dramatizing the number of babies who succumb to sudden infant death syndrome each year can reinforce the spoken message. Audio and visual aids impel audience members to pay attention and care about a speech in ways that they otherwise might not.[5]

Once you commit to using presentation aids, you will need to make a number of other decisions. Initially, you will have to identify precise points in your speech where such aids will be effective. One way to prepare yourself to make such judgments is to examine how producers of newscasts select audio and visual aids to complement the work of on-camera reporters. After all, in many ways you are the "producer" of your speech.

You also might want to spend some time brainstorming. Examine your outline, consider the information you have, and repeatedly ask yourself the following question: Which specific pieces of information will be improved with either audio or visual aids? Keep a record of each idea that comes to mind, being sure to indicate how you would actually integrate the audio or visual support into your speech.

TYPES OF VISUAL AIDS

Let's now examine a sampling of visual aid choices. Remember to check with your instructor regarding his or her specific rules and guidelines for embedding visual aids into your speech.

Objects and Models

In your brainstorming session, you may have decided that it would be good to use an object to illustrate a particular concept. If legal, easily transportable, and not dangerous to others, the object you choose can be the real thing—for example, a set of earphones, a piece of amber, or a fragment of coal.

However, keep in mind that using an actual object sometimes can prove impractical: automobiles are obviously too large to transport, and microelectronic chips may be too small to see. In such cases, it may be better to use a model instead. A model can be made of clay, papier-mâché, wood scraps, or other materials. If used creatively, inexpensive materials can work very well. Your aim simply is to make a reasonable facsimile of the object—something that will let you share your information more meaningfully.

The following photograph shows one celebrity, spokesperson Sean "Diddy" Combs, using himself as a model and wearing the message that he sought to share with receivers. Do you think a speaker's attire should be made a part of the speaker's message?

Objects and models make it easier for you to pull the audience into your speech. Because objects and models are tangible, they also can make your points more realistic while adding drama to your presentation.

Frank Micelotta/Getty Images

Graphs

The use of graphs may make an effective presentation even more successful.

A **pie graph** (or circle graph) is a circle with the various percentages of the whole indicated by wedges. Because the entire circle represents 100%, the pie graph is an effective way to demonstrate percentage relationships or proportions. In a speech on how to meet the challenges posed by diversity in the workplace, one student used a pie graph to provide a snapshot of the extent to which employees perceive diversity in the workplace to have changed over the course of a single decade (Figure 13.2).[6]

If your goal is to show the performance of one variable over time, a **bar graph** might be appropriate. A bar graph is used to compare quantities or magnitude. In a speech on how tornadoes form, a student used the bar graph in Figure 13.3 to compare and contrast the average number of tornadoes in years past with the huge number that occurred in April 2011.

Like a bar graph, a **line graph** is used to illustrate trends, relationships, or comparisons over time. In a speech on incarceration in the United States, one student used a line graph to make the point that although violent crime has abated, harsher sentencing for less serious crimes has caused a dramatic increase in the national prison population.[7] The line graph, in addition to showing the number of people in prison, also illustrates an upward trend. If a line graph contains more than one line, the presenter should color-code each line for clarity,

FIGURE 13.2

Workplace Diversity

Has the level of diversity in your workplace changed from 10 years ago?

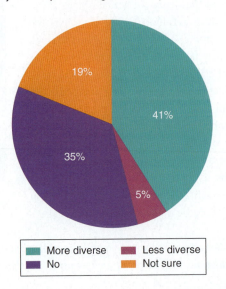

Source: "Census Projects More Diversity in Workforce: Changes Could Affect Training, Education," *USA Today*, August 14, 2008, p. A4.

FIGURE 13.3

Average Number of Tornadoes in the United States

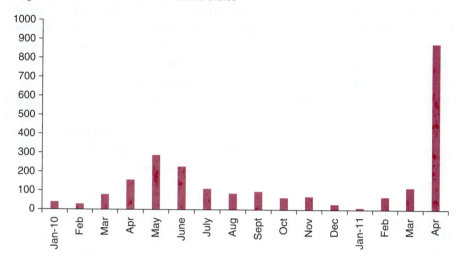

Source: "New Study Shows Rival for 'Tornado Alley': Ground Zero for Twisters Now May Be in the Southeast USA," *USA Today*, April 26, 2011, p. A3.

as did the speaker in a speech on the growing influence of minorities in the United States (Figure 13.4). When well designed, the line graph is one of the easiest types for audiences to read and follow.

FIGURE 13.4

Growing Minority Population

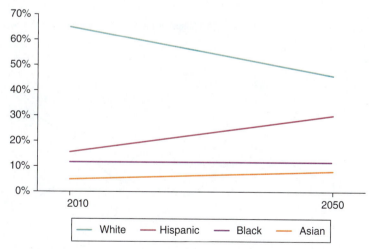

Source: "Census Projects More Diversity in Workforce: Changes Could Affect Training, Education," *USA Today*, August 14, 2008, p. A4.

Infographics, composites of information, illustration, and design, help speakers relay information in more interesting ways. They are particularly useful in helping audience members visualize data.[8] A simplified version of an infographic, the **pictograph**, uses sketches of figures to represent concepts. In the speech on incarceration, the speaker incorporated a pictograph (Figure 13.5) to compare and contrast the percentages of men and women, Whites, Hispanics, and Blacks who were currently serving prison terms. As you work on your speech, keep a lookout for materials you can turn into pictographs to help audience members visualize your message.

The general rule to follow in making and using graphs of all varieties is that a single graph should be used to communicate one concept or idea. Consider the line graph in Figure 13.6. This graph is far too cluttered for an audience to read easily and quickly. Your goal in devising a graph is to eliminate extraneous information and to focus the audience's attention. Emphasize the essentials.

FIGURE 13.5

U.S. Prison Population, 2016

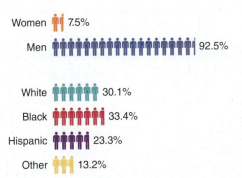

Source: Bureau of Justice Statistics, "Prisoners in 2016," https://www.bjs.gov/content/pub/pdf/p16.pdf.

FIGURE 13.6

Poorly Designed Line Graph

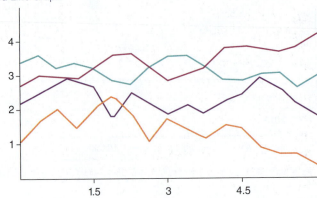

Drawings, Photographs, and Maps

Drawings and photographs are used to help generate a mood, clarify a concept, or identify something. You may find that using drawings and photographs add interest to your presentation as well as make your topic more concrete. For example, one student used a graphic created by the National Oceanic and Atmospheric Administration of rip currents (Figure 13.7).

Maps, similarly, are useful in illustrating geographic information. One speaker used a map showing where Hispanics live in the United States to illustrate a speech on immigration (Figure 13.8).

GUIDELINES FOR EVALUATING WHICH VISUALS TO USE

When evaluating visuals, remember that they must be appropriate to the audience, the occasion, the location, and the content of your speech. You also need to be comfortable using them.

In developing and selecting visual materials, keep these four criteria in mind: simplicity, clarity, visibility, and authenticity. *Simplicity* means that the visuals, if not integrated into slides, should be as transportable and as easy to use as possible. Give careful consideration to the size and weight of large items. Ask yourself if you will be able to display the visual without disrupting the environment. Ask yourself if you can set it up and take it down in a minimal amount of time. With regard to *clarity*, remember that the visual aid's purpose is to enhance understanding, not to cause confusion. Ideally, each visual should depict only one idea or concept, or at least should be displayed so that only the relevant portions are visible at the appropriate point in your speech. *Visibility* is the third criterion. Visual aids serve no purpose if they cannot be seen and read; thus, you must determine if your audience will be able to see and read them. Make sure that the lettering is tall enough and that photographs or pictures are large enough.

Authenticity means that the visual is a true depiction of what you're illustrating and that it has not been doctored or Photoshopped in an effort to misrepresent evidence and deceive receivers. For example, in May 2012, after Navy SEALS killed Osama bin Laden, fake death photos of the terrorist-leader spread on the Web. In one, a frame from the film *Black Hawk Down* had been used to create a photo of Navy SEALS carrying bin Laden's body. Fabrications like this one succeeded in fooling some newspapers,

FIGURE 13.7

Rip Currents

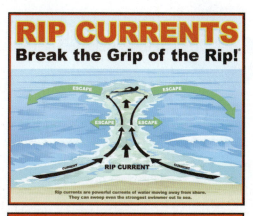

Source: National Oceanic and Atmospheric Administration

FIGURE 13.8

Hispanic Origin Persons

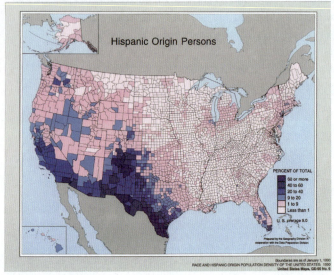

Source: Census.gov

which then unfortunately published them.[9] Too often, insatiable hunger for images fuels the use of unauthenticated photographs, forcing newspapers to issue retractions and harming the credibility of their reporting in the process. When you use a visual, your goal is to boost your credibility, not detract from it. Unless giving a presentation on the nature or effects of fake photos or fake footage, avoid using such visuals.

When relying on DVDs instead of embedded video in a slide, you'll need to cue up the DVD before you begin your speech. Far too many speakers press the Play button only to find that they have no picture or

ETHICS AND COMMUNICATION

Visually Speaking

The old maxim was that "a picture is worth a thousand words." Why was this believed? Because it was thought to be proof of reality. A photograph was considered incontrovertible evidence. Do you think that this still is true today?

Computer programs make it easy to distort actual images, even to the point of fabricating events that never occurred. Like a magician creating an illusion, unethical presenters are able to manipulate their audiences by altering visuals. For example, after the tsunami that devastated Japan's coast on March 11, 2011, images appeared on Twitter and Facebook purporting to be photographic evidence of the event. Unfortunately, many were fakes. Bogus charity organizations posted the fake footage on social media in order to solicit money from unsuspecting people.

Receivers should expect speakers to substantiate the authenticity of any visuals. For example, a university admitted to doctoring a photo on its brochure cover by inserting Black students into a crowd of White football fans because it wanted an image of diversity in its recruitment literature.[10]

At what point do you think that retouching or alteration of a visual puts the speaker on ethically thin ice?

sound on the screen. Audiences today are not willing to sit and wait while you and others tinker with electronic gadgetry. Prepare video carefully in advance, and rehearse using it.

AUDIO AIDS

Like video, audio is readily available and easy to use as an accompaniment to a speech via either a computer or CD player. Because speech makers often find it advantageous to integrate a brief excerpt from a song, an interview segment, or a newscast into their presentations, sound has become a popular support medium. One student, for example, reinforced an informative presentation titled "The Speech Capabilities of Dolphins" with a few moments of dolphin sounds that she had recorded during a visit to an aquarium.

If using a CD player, be sure to cue it to the precise point at which you want to begin. Do this prior to arriving at the front of the room to deliver your speech.

COMPUTER-ASSISTED PRESENTATIONS

Of all the visual aids explored, computerized presentations are the most popular. You can use your outline to build an effective PowerPoint presentation integrating video clips, text, animation, photographs, drawings, and charts in it. PowerPoint contains a clip art library enabling you to select images to enhance the meaning of your words. It also allows you to generate backgrounds, formats, layouts, and colors that you believe best reflect your presentation's purpose. The computer-generated visuals you create can be shown directly on a computer, printed out in handout form, or blown up for display.

You can create your own graphics or use professionally created ones as one student did when explaining how the Ebola virus works (Figure 13.9).[11] To create your own graphic, begin by organizing your data. Select the type of graphic you want—for example, pie chart, bar chart, or some other graphic—and the software will produce the visual and, in many cases, even generate a legend. Microsoft Excel, Word, or PowerPoint offer this functionality. Figure 13.10 shows a sample of a computer-generated graph. If possible, use a variety of dark, rich colors to add contrast to a graphic. But remember, unless it is large enough to be seen, it will not increase your audience's attention or strengthen your presentation.

Embedding brief video clips in a speech can establish your credibility at the same time it increases audience member interest, memory, and understanding. Imagine speaking about football and the risk of injury and then showing a brief video segment of a player being tackled during a game and suffering a concussion. Having the video embedded and playing it during your speech will provide an immediate dramatic impact. You can find videos at YouTube, Vimeo, MetaCafe.com, and DailyMotion.com, among other sources. To be effective, your video clip must be short, usually consuming no more than 30 seconds of a 5-minute speech.

FIGURE 13.9
Red Squiggles

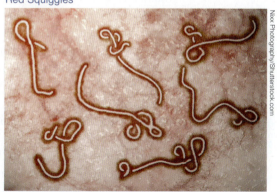

Nixx Photography/Shutterstock.com

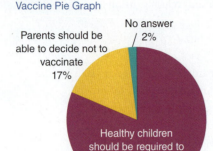

FIGURE 13.10
Vaccine Pie Graph

No answer / 2%

Parents should be able to decide not to vaccinate 17%

Healthy children should be required to be vaccinated 81%

Source: Pew Research Center, "Vast Majority of Americans Say Benefits of Childhood Vaccines Outweigh Risks," February 2, 2017, http://www.pewinternet.org/2017/02/02/vast-majority-of-americans-say-benefits-of-childhood-vaccines-outweigh-risks.

When evaluating visuals, try using the *glance test*: Your receivers should be able to process the message contained in each of your slides in 2 to 3 seconds. Receivers should not be distracted from what you are saying to read a slide that is designed more like a technical manual. (See the sample computer-assisted slide presentation in the Skill Builder on p. 361.)

To deliver an effective PowerPoint presentation, you need to think visually. By connecting the right words with the right visuals, you will succeed in unifying thought and emotion in audience members. For this to happen, the pictures or images you use need to be the right ones, and the message needs to be succinct. When planning a PowerPoint presentation, think in bullets. Supporting, not replacing your spoken speech, PowerPoint slides help you illustrate your talk.

According to MIT psychology professor Steven Pinker, when used effectively, PowerPoint gives visual shape to an argument. Says Pinker, "Language is a linear medium: one damn word after another. But ideas are multidimensional . . . When properly employed, PowerPoint makes the logical structure of an argument more transparent. Two channels sending the same information are better than one."[12]

Pitfalls of PowerPoint

Although computerized presentations are the standard in business and education, if not prepared with care or if allowed to upstage the speaker, they can overpower the message and drain a speech of its vitality.[13] Some years back, reflecting the growth in PowerPoint presentations, the chairman of the Joint Chiefs of Staff was reported to have told U.S. military bases around the globe, in essence, "Enough with the bells and whistles—just get to the point."[14]

When effective, PowerPoint helps tell a story. When it runs smoothly, PowerPoint improves audience member recall by showing receivers why your message should matter. This does not mean it is not without drawbacks.

Critics of PowerPoint warn that dazzling PowerPoint presentations can be used to cover up weak content.[15] Technology's role is not to elevate format over content but to promote communication. Although fiddling with fonts and slide shows is fun, it's more important to do adequate research. Another criticism is that by enabling speakers to rely on bullet points that are deliberately vague or lacking specificity, PowerPoint stifles critical thinking and thoughtful decision making.[16] One blogger, for instance, pointed out that there is nothing inherently visual about bullet points. Imagine, the blogger wrote, if the renowned orator and prime minister of Great Britain, Sir Winston Churchill, had used PowerPoint when rallying his country to meet the challenges of World War II:

Where We Will Fight Them:

- beaches
- hills
- trenches[17]

Another fear is that you will use too many slides and fill them with too many words. In fact, one U.S. computer company distributed guidelines to its employees about PowerPoint presentations that require presenters to adhere to the "Rule of Seven": seven bullets or lines per slide, seven words per line.[18] PowerPoint gets a bad rap when a speaker forgets that its role is to enhance a speech, not to *be* the speech. By limiting the number of slides and taking

SKILL BUILDER

Evaluating a PowerPoint Presentation

Technology is helping to transform ordinary presentations into extraordinary ones. Examine the following sample PowerPoint presentation, and answer each of the questions posed.

1

Whirlwinds

Tornadoes in Your Life

2

What Is a Tornado?

The National Weather Service defines a tornado as a violently rotating column of air in contact with the ground. It is a pendent from a thunderstorm.

3

How Tornadoes Work

- Vortex of air rises into a cloud.
- Vortex becomes a funnel.
- Vortex wind speed can reach 300 mph.

4

A spinning tube of air formed by low-level wind shear is lifted into the supercell thunderstorm, causing it to rotate.

5

A downdraft splits the tail end of the tube into two columns—one spinning clockwise, the other spinning counterclockwise.

6

The updraft stretches the counterclockwise spinning column into the rotating storm; when the storm and column connect, a tornado often is formed.

7

Tornado Warnings

- A major storm approaches.
- The atmosphere feels unsettled.
- Wind becomes more and more violent.

8

The Fujita Scale Wind Speed

- F0-Up to 72 mph. Broken tree limbs and signs.
- F1-Up to 112 mph. Trailer homes flipped.
- F2-Up to 157 mph. Roofs torn off; trailer homes demolished.

9

The Fujita Scale Wind Speed

- F3-Up to 206 mph. Roofs and walls torn down; trains thrown from tracks.
- F4-Up to 260 mph. Frame homes leveled.
- F5-Over 260 mph. Homes and buildings completely destroyed.

10

How Large are Tornadoes?

- Average 500 feet in width
- Travel 5 miles on ground
- Last only a few minutes

11

Where do Tornadoes Occur Most Often?

- South in early spring
- Midwest in May
- The Texas and Oklahoma Panhandles are sometimes known as Tornado Alley in the spring and early summer.
- Later in the summer, tornadoes are found in the eastern part of the country.

12

Who Chases Tornadoes?

- People who work for the National Weather Service
- Tourists
- A travel agency in Amarillo, Texas, plans two-week tours every summer for amateur tornado chasers.

13

Protection from Tornadoes

- Listen to weather reports.
- Get inside a building away from glass.
- Basements are the safest places.

14

AVOID!

- TRAILER HOMES
- OVERPASSES ON THE HIGHWAY
- TRYING TO CHASE A TORNADO

15

WHIRLWINDS

DON'T LET THEM CAUSE TURBULENCE IN YOUR LIFE!

1. The first slide introduces the topic to the audience. The slide's background should reflect the presentation's tone. *What do you think of the background provided here?*

2. The second slide introduces the speech's first main point. How did the speaker add credibility to the definition provided? In your opinion, could the speaker have done more to orient receivers visually to the topic before defining this key term?

3. The third, fourth, fifth, and sixth slides introduce the second main point of the speech by summarizing how tornadoes work. *In your opinion, will these slides sustain receiver interest? Why or why not?*

4. The seventh slide introduces the third point of the speech by revealing the warning signs of an approaching tornado. *To what extent, if any, might the speaker have made the slide more interesting?*

5. In the eighth, ninth, and tenth slides, the speaker develops the fourth main point of the speech, telling how tornadoes are rated and offering examples. *What feedback can you offer the speaker?*

6. In the eleventh and twelfth slides, the speaker develops the fifth main point of the speech, summarizing where and when tornadoes are likely to occur and the people who track them. *In your opinion, are any of these slides too wordy? What could the speaker do to enhance receiver engagement in this phase of the speech? For example, should the speaker have included a slide showing the devastation caused by a tornado?*

7. The thirteenth and fourteenth slides focus on the speaker's last main point—what receivers can do to protect themselves in case of a tornado. *Do you find the advice credible?*

8. The final slide wraps up the speech by supporting the speaker's concluding words and providing closure. Would the speaker have benefitted from using a slide prior to this one, summarizing what the speech had accomplished? If so, what might that slide have contained?

9. Are there any other slides that you think the speaker should have added to this presentation or that you feel the speaker could have done without?

10. How many slides did the speaker use that you believe contain too many words or bullets? Shorten these slides to make them more effective.

pains to ensure that nothing that comes out of your mouth is replicated word for word on the slides that you display, your slides will enhance rather than overshadow you and your presentation.[19]

PREPARING TO SPEAK

After selecting audio and visual aids, and indicating where in your speech you will integrate or embed them, it's time for you to take another look at your speech's wording. What are you looking for? You want to be sure that you are using an oral rather than a written style when delivering your speech; that is, you want to be certain that you have prepared your speech to be heard, and not read, by audience members. To do this, you need to keep in mind the specific ways that oral and written styles differ.

First, an oral style is more *personal*. When presenting using an oral style, you speak directly to the audience, invite their participation, and adapt to their reactions (feedback) in ways that a writer cannot. Second, an oral style is more *repetitive*. Because your receivers cannot replay your words, you will need to use repetition and reinforcement, repeating and restating key ideas. Third, an oral style is more *informal*. Whereas written discourse commonly contains abstract ideas, complex phrasing, and a sophisticated vocabulary, the use of simpler sentences and shorter words and phrases characterize the oral style.

The public speaker's language is less like the language of an essayist and more like that of a skilled conversationalist. Filling your speech with everyday colloquial expressions, clear transitions, personal pronouns, and questions that invite participation is more effective than using abstract language, complex sentences, and impersonal references.

For these reasons, keep the following in mind:

- Speak in short units.

- Avoid using jargon or technical language if the audience is unfamiliar with the subject.

- Use words that are simple, concrete, appropriate, and vivid.

By following this advice, you won't sound as if you're reading an essay or a manuscript.

Speakers generally select one of five general styles of delivery depending on the nature of the specific speechmaking purpose and occasion: manuscript, memorized, impromptu, extemporaneous, and sound bites or Twitter speak.

Jose Gil/Shutterstock.com

MANUSCRIPT SPEECHES

A **manuscript speech** is written out word for word and then read aloud by the speaker. It is a scripted presentation. Manuscript speeches are most commonly presented when it is imperative that the speaker use very precise language. For example, because presidential addresses are likely to be under close scrutiny throughout the world, they traditionally are read by the president from a typed page or a teleprompter.

Unfortunately, the use of a manuscript tends to reduce eye contact between speaker and audience. Furthermore, speakers reading aloud often sound as if they are reading to, rather than talking to, the audience. As a result of the diminishment of a conversational tone, the connection between speaker and receivers can suffer unless the presenter is particularly skilled. At this point in your development as a speaker, there is no reason for you to speak from a manuscript.

MEMORIZED SPEECHES

A **memorized speech** is a manuscript or scripted speech that the speaker commits to memory. Unskilled speakers can take on a canned tone and be less responsive to feedback from the audience. Additionally, there is the problem of retention. Speech makers who insist on memorizing their presentations word for word often find themselves suffering memory lapses, leading to long, awkward silences, during which they valiantly try to recall forgotten material. You may want to memorize certain key words, phrases, or speech segments, but at this point in your speaking career you should not try and commit your speech to memory.

IMPROMPTU SPEECHES

An **impromptu speech** is one you deliver spontaneously, or on the spur of the moment, without formal preparation. When asked to speak impromptu, you need to think on your feet. Often, you will have no more than a few seconds or minutes to gather your thoughts. An impromptu speaking situation may arise, for example, when a boss unexpectedly asks an employee to discuss the status of a project. If you are faced with such a request, you will need to rely on what you have learned about patterning your ideas. Using the introduction-body-conclusion format will help you organize and format your remarks.

EXTEMPORANEOUS SPEECHES

An **extemporaneous speech** is researched, outlined, and then delivered after careful rehearsal. Extemporaneous speaking is more audience-centered than any of the preceding options. Because extemporaneous speakers both prepare and rehearse in advance, they are freer to establish eye contact with audience members and to respond to their feedback. In addition, extemporaneous speakers may use notes; they are neither constrained by the need to commit entire presentations to memory nor handicapped by a manuscript that must be read word for word, inhibiting their adaptability to and connection with the audience.

Before delivering an extemporaneous speech, you will want to generate speaker's notes, also known as an *extemporaneous outline*. The extemporaneous outline contains brief reminders of the key parts of your speech as well as references to support you will use to develop each of your main points. More specifically, the extemporaneous outline you prepare should include reminder phrases for your speech's introduction; a statement of your central idea or thesis; brief notes on your main point and subpoints, including the complete names of sources or citations for oral references; transition reminders; and reminder phrases for the speech's conclusion. Also feel free to incorporate delivery cues in the outline's margin, such as "emphasize" or "hold up the model," much as an actor marks up a script.

Keep your extemporaneous outline purposefully brief. This will prevent you from being tempted to read your notes instead of maintaining eye contact with receivers. A key to using the extemporaneous outline effectively is to begin practicing your speech using the more detailed full sentence outline you developed earlier in the process. Once you rehearse a few times using that outline and are comfortable and familiar with your speech's content, make the switch and rely only on your speaker's notes during remaining practice sessions. (For a sample of a card containing brief speaker's notes, see Figure 12.3.)

Preparing and delivering an extemporaneous speech builds speaker confidence. It is the method most preferred by public speaking instructors and experienced speakers alike.

SOUND BITE SPEAKING (TWITTER SPEAK)

We live in a "headline society."[20] According to some observers, contemporary audiences lack the patience to listen to long-winded speakers who, as a result, are going the way of the dinosaurs.[21] Although some instructors caution students to steer clear of using sound bites or Twitter speak in class, you may be involved in some speaking situations that require it.

During political conventions or events, after the delivery of speeches by public figures, or in the course of introducing new policies or programs, spokespeople, pundits, and politicians "spin their messages," frequently spouting sound bites—short, memorable statements that can be tweeted and repeated after being delivered orally. Consider this answer that Timothy Geithner offered when asked by a reporter to describe his role as Secretary of the Treasury during the last major financial crisis: "It's like you're in the cockpit of the plane—your engine's burning, smoke's filling the cabin, it's filled with a bunch of people that are fighting with each other about who's responsible, you have terrorists on the plane and people

CAREER BUILDER: CAN YOU MAKE IT BITE SIZE?

The ability to make spoken comments memorable and succinct is a skill valued in the workplace.

Read the following pairs of statements. In each case the first statement is dull, whereas the second version, prepared by a professional, is more engaging.[23]

Pair 1

A. To construct an amalgam, you have to be willing to split open its component parts.

B. To make an omelet, you have to be willing to break a few eggs. (Robert Penn Warren)

Pair 2

A. Capital will not produce great pleasure, but it will remunerate a large research staff to examine the questions proposed for a solution.

B. Money won't buy happiness, but it will pay the salaries of a large research staff to study the problem. (Bill Vaughan)

Now it's your turn. Select any speech from *Vital Speeches* or another source and distill its message down to memorable sound bite size. Also create a 6-second video to accompany it.

want you to come out of the cockpit and put them in jail. And you have to land the plane. That terrifying core objective in a crisis is to make sure you first put out the fire."[22] In your opinion, do Geithner's remarks make for an effective sound bite? Because audiences today are impatient, speakers need to be able to distill their messages effectively in order to hold their attention.

REHEARSING

In the entertainment industry, producers, directors, and performers never open a show without first holding a series of dress rehearsals, also known as tryouts or preview performances, in front of an audience. Such practice sessions make it possible for them to experience audience reactions and alter the performance prior to the actual opening. As a speaker, you can benefit by giving yourself a similar opportunity. At your fingertips are visual, vocal, and verbal tools that, if mastered during your rehearsals, will reinforce your speechmaking performance and enable audience members to accept you as a credible source—meaning that they will judge you to be more competent, trustworthy, and dynamic.

How do you communicate your credibility? Obviously, at least in part, it can be conveyed verbally, through the content and structure of language. However, speakers also can convey it through the visual and vocal cues they use. Thus, during rehearsals, both the visual and vocal dimensions of your speech, together with your verbal message, merit careful attention. The sound of your voice, your appearance, and your demeanor need to work in concert to support your message. The only way to get it right is to rehearse.

CONDUCT TRYOUTS: REHEARSE, REFINE, REHEARSE

Your extemporaneous outline is complete. It's now time for you to become your own audience and explore the sound and feel of your speech prior to delivering it to others. For this, you will need three essential tryout tools: your speaker's notes, a stopwatch, and a recording device (audio or video) so that you can review the exact words you use to express your ideas.

Before starting, check the time and turn on the recorder. Then stand, face an imaginary audience, and begin presenting your speech. In effect, you now are delivering a "rough oral draft" of your presentation. Deliver the entire speech a number of times, conducting your tryouts over several days, sometimes alone, at other times before a small group of friends or relatives. Be certain to integrate any audio and visual aids you plan to use. Also practice giving the speech from a couple of different spaces. Your goal is to develop a flexible and adaptable delivery—one that will enable you to meet the unique demands of presenting before a live audience.

What will you do and discover during rehearsals? First, you'll determine if your speech is too short or too long. If you are supposed to give a 5-minute speech but run overtime, you need to trim it. If, on the other hand, your speech is running significantly under the allotted time limit, you will need to gather more material to incorporate. Second, be alert for ideas that you may not have expressed as clearly as possible. Third, you may discover that you are sharing the same ideas again and again and again—more than is necessary for redundancy. Fourth, you may realize that the structure of your speech is confusing as a result of missing or inappropriate transitions, or that you need to remind yourself to stress certain important points.

Just as a playwright reworks a scene, the tryout period is your chance to rework sections of your speech. If you discover that your main attention getter isn't as effective as desired, improve it. If the supporting material under, say, the second main point in the body of your speech is unclear, rewrite it. If an illustration is too long and drawn out, shorten it. Your goal during tryouts is to refine your speech until it's as close as possible to the one you will present to your audience.

CONDUCT A VISUAL TUNE-UP

Let's consider visual cues. How do you think a speech maker should look when standing before an audience? Close your eyes and picture his or her attire, posture, gestures, movements and facial expressions, and use of eye contact.

Attire

In deciding what to wear when you deliver your speech, you should consider the topic, the audience, and the occasion. Sometimes, speakers make thoughtless errors in dress. For example, one student delivered a serious tribute to Nelson Mandela while wearing a shirt emblazoned with a huge Mickey Mouse emblem. (When asked why he wore that shirt, he responded, "I didn't think anyone would notice.") The clothes you wear should not distract receivers from focusing on the ideas in your speech. What speech topic, audience, and occasion, if any, might wearing a Mickey Mouse shirt be appropriate for?

Posture

Most public speakers stand when presenting their speeches. Unless you are physically challenged, you likely will be on your feet. The problem is that standing (or sitting for that matter) is something that many of us don't do very well.

Consider the anchors of broadcast and cable news shows. They stand (or sit) erectly. Their backs are straight. Posture communicates. It sends a potent message to the audience. Speakers often seem to forget this, assuming a stance that works against rather than for them. For instance, some speakers lean on the lectern or actually drape themselves over it—giving the impression that they would fall if it were not there to support them. Some prop themselves against a wall, giving the impression that they want to disappear into it. Others simply slouch.

To prepare yourself to exhibit proper posture when delivering a speech, assume your natural posture, and ask others to evaluate it. Are you too

iStock/monkeybusinessimages

stiff? Do you slouch? Do you appear too relaxed? Feedback can help you put your best posture forward when presenting before others.

Gestures

As we noted in Chapter 5, gestures are movements of a person's hands and arms. The gestures that you use when speaking in public should be purposeful and help to reinforce the content of your speech. Purposeless gestures detract from your message.

Gestures also may be cultural. For example, people in the United States point with one finger, whereas the Chinese point with an open hand. A problem most of us encounter is that we have certain favorite gestures of which we are unaware—gestures like neck scratching, putting our hands into and out of our pockets, jingling keys or jewelry, or smoothing our hair. Such mannerisms often intensify when we find ourselves facing a situation that is stressful such as speaking in public. In fact, when we are nervous, we typically add new gestures to our repertoire of annoying mannerisms. Some nervous speakers will tap a pencil or finger ring on the lectern, or even crack their knuckles—things they would never do in normal circumstances.

Using meaningful gestures, however, serves a number of useful speaking purposes. They help to emphasize important points, enumerate ideas, or suggest shapes or sizes.

Movements and Facial Expressions

Your presentation is under way as soon as you are introduced or called on to speak—that is, it begins well before you speak your first syllable. What is more, your presentation does not end until you return to your seat in the audience and the next speaker rises to speak, or the class is over.

The way you leave your seat in class and approach the speaker's stand communicates a first impression of you to the audience. In like fashion, your facial expressions as you walk back to your seat on completing delivering it also send the audience important signals. Far too many speakers approach the front of the room in inappropriate ways. For example, they may grimace and walk in ways that broadcast a lack of preparation, rather than approach the front of the room confidently and smile at the audience. Some even verbalize their lack of confidence by mumbling something like "I'm really not ready. This will be awful." Others apologize for a poor showing all the way back to their seats.

Consider carefully what your face reveals to others and how you move to and from the speaker's stand. Each act communicates whether you are in control. You may have noticed that confident people move with head erect, follow a straight rather a circuitous path, proceed at an assured rather than a hesitant or frenetic pace, use open rather than closed arm movements, and exhibit facial expressions that engage others.

Eye Contact

Eye contact also communicates. Sadly, some speakers "talk" to walls, smartboards, windows, trees, or the floor rather than to the members of their audience. Some speakers seem embarrassed to look at any audience members; others seek the attention of one person and avoid looking at anyone else. Some student speakers avoid meeting the eyes of the instructor during a speech. Others focus on the instructor exclusively.

Be sure that your gaze includes all the members of the audience. Look at each individual as you deliver your speech. Such eye contact will draw even the most reluctant listeners into your presentation. Remember that in the United States, direct eye contact conveys sincerity.

CONDUCT A VOCAL TUNE-UP

Obviously, the voice is one of our main tools in speech making. In Chapter 5, we considered four basic vocal dimensions: volume, rate, pitch, and quality. Review this material during your rehearsals, keeping in mind that your goal when delivering a speech is to use your voice to reinforce your speech's content.

To respond to the ideas contained in your speech, you audience must be able to hear you. Maintaining your voice at an appropriate volume is your responsibility. If you are to address a group in a large auditorium, a microphone will probably be provided. However, if you're speaking before a group in a smaller room, you will need to make yourself heard without amplification. By observing the reactions of people in the rear of the room, you should be able to judge if you're speaking loudly enough for them to hear you easily. If you notice that any audience members look confused or upset, speak up. On the other hand, if your voice is normally loud, and you notice that those seated nearest to you are cringing, turn down your volume a bit.

With regard to pitch, try not to fall into the monotone trap. Maintaining one predominant tone only bores the audience. Instead, vary pitch to reflect the emotional content of your materials and to create interest.

Like volume and pitch, speaking rate also communicates. Speaking too quickly or too slowly can impede understanding. Thus, respond to audience feedback and speed up or slow down your pace as appropriate.

Nonfluencies are a problem every public speaker needs to consider. "Uhs" and "ums" are normal in interpersonal conversations, but they are not expected when making a speech. During person-to-person interactions, we understand that people are thinking about or planning what they're going to say next. In contrast, we expect public speakers to have prepared their remarks carefully, and as a result we are less tolerant of their nonfluencies. Consequently, make it your business to eliminate them from your delivery as much as possible.

CONDUCT A VERBAL TUNE-UP

Although we have already spoken about developing the verbal aspects of your speech (see Chapter 12), when rehearsing, take the time you need to double-check that your word choices are clear and vivid.

Visit the interactive e-Book to access the Exploring Diversity feature "Culture and Delivery," which will help you consider how cultural backgrounds affect a person's nonverbal cues.

When trying out your speech, ask yourself if it contains any unnecessary or confusing words or expressions. If so, eliminate them. For example, instead of saying "a sufficient supply of," say, "enough." In general, choose simpler and more familiar words over those that could cause audience members difficulty in deciphering their meaning. Thus, say "plan" rather than "strategize." This especially holds true for idioms when speaking before audiences composed of people from diverse cultures. Also remember to use transitions to guide your audience from one point to the next.

How do you make your words live in the minds of audience members? As you rehearse, ask yourself if your speech contains vivid words, including strong and active verbs, and figures of speech and images to enliven your presentation by helping receivers form mental pictures. Avoid using tired words such as "very interesting" or clichés such as "cool as a cucumber." Phrases like these are used so often that audiences find them meaningless. Language that helps others not only understand but also see, hear, and feel your message is the goal.

PREPARING FOR THE Q&A

The question-and-answer (Q&A) session plays an integral role in most presentations. The Q&A session gives audience members a voice by providing an opportunity to ask you questions about your speech. The Q&A also gives you one more chance to demonstrate your preparedness and expertise to the audience.

The rehearsal or tryout period is the time when you anticipate the questions—especially difficult ones—that members of the audience might ask you at the end of your speech. Anticipating questions lets you think through your answers in advance. As a result, when the time comes for you to respond to the actual questions that the members of your audience ask, you will be better positioned to build understanding by answering every question politely and to the best of your ability.

THE REHEARSAL–CONFIDENCE CONNECTION

Rehearsal—careful practice of your presentation—gives you the confidence needed to deliver an effective speech. Now that you have prepared and tried out your extemporaneous outline, integrating appropriate presentation aids, you should feel more confident. Rehearsal is your key to synthesizing all that you have done into a polished performance.

PRESENTING: KEYS TO REMEMBER

If you follow the developmental plan outlined in this book, you should find yourself ready and eager to deliver your speech. Not only will you have carefully prepared and rehearsed it, you also will have at your disposal tested techniques to help you control any nerves. At this juncture, we offer only a few additional pointers:

1. Arrive at your speaking location with ample time to spare. If required or available, be sure that you have prepared equipment to hold your notes and presentation aids.

2. If you are going to use a microphone and/or other technology, test it so that you will not have to adjust anything during your presentation.

3. Consider your attire. Confidence and believability increase when you look the part.

4. Let your audience know you are prepared by the way you rise when introduced and by walking confidently to the front of the room.

5. When delivering the speech and during the Q&A, work to transmit a sense of enthusiasm and commitment to the audience.

6. Complete your presentation before returning to your seat. You have worked hard to communicate your credibility to audience members. Don't ruin it in the last few seconds. Last impressions, like first impressions, count.

BEYOND THE PRESENTATION: ASSESSING YOUR EFFECTIVENESS

As soon as you complete your presentation, the first question you will ask yourself is "How did I do?" No doubt you also will want to know what your peers and your instructor thought of your performance. You and your listeners can evaluate your speech making by analyzing how effectively you were able to handle the content, organization, wording, and delivery.

When it's time for the members of the audience to comment on your speech, they, like you, should review the positive dimensions of your presentation before making improvement recommendations. Speaker and audience alike need to remember that critique is designed to be constructive. It should help build confidence and growth. It should never destroy a speaker's desire to try again.

Your instructor probably will provide you with a specific means of analyzing your work, perhaps by using an evaluation form similar to the one shown in Figure 13.12. For now, you may find it helpful as a personal guide.

FIGURE 13.12

Name: _____ Speech: _____

Specific purpose: _____

1. Content

_____Based on accurate analysis of speaking situation.

_____Specific goal of speech was apparent.

_____Subject appropriate, relevant, and interesting to intended audience.

_____All material clearly contributed to purpose.

_____Had specific facts and opinions to support and explain statements.

_____Support was logical.

_____Handled material ethically.

_____Used audio and/or visual aids when appropriate.

_____Included a variety of data—statistics, quotations, etc.

2. Organization

_____Began with effective attention-getter.

_____Main points were clear statements that proved or explained specific goals.

_____Points were arranged in logical order.

_____Each point was adequately supported.

_____Concluded with memorable statement that tied speech together.

3. Language

_____Ideas were clear.

_____Ideas were presented vividly.

_____Ideas were presented emphatically.

_____Language was appropriate for intended audience.

4. Delivery

_____Was prepared to speak.

_____Stepped up to speak with confidence.

_____Maintained contact with audience.

_____Sounded extemporaneous, not read or memorized.

_____Referred to notes only occasionally.

_____Sounded enthusiastic.

_____Maintained good posture.

_____Used vocal variety, pitch, emphasis, and rate effectively.

_____Gestured effectively.

_____Used face to add interest.

_____Articulation was satisfactory.

_____On finishing, moved out with confidence.

_____Fit time allotted.

Additional comments:

Whether or not your instructor uses the form in Figure 13.12, you will find it helpful as a personal guide.

Another means of evaluating your own effectiveness as well as the effectiveness of other speakers is to assess the credibility of the evidence included in the presentation. For this, see the evaluation checklist at the end of Chapter 15.

CONTENT

Was the subject of your speech appropriate? Was it worthwhile? Was your purpose communicated clearly? Did you research the topic carefully? Were your presentation aids helpful? Did you use a variety of support? Were your main points adequately developed? Were the main divisions of your speech effectively bridged by transitional words and phrases?

ORGANIZATION

How effective was the organizational approach you used? Did you begin with material that engaged the audience, capturing their attention? Did you preview each main point? Were your main points arranged in a logical sequence? Was the number of main points appropriate for the time allotted? Was your organizational design easily discernible? Did your conclusion provide a logical wrap-up of your main parts? Did the speech motivate receivers to continue thinking about your presentation or take action?

WORDING

Did you use the right words to explain your ideas? Were your word choices vivid? Did your speech sound as if it should be listened to rather than read? Could any of the words or phrases in your speech have been considered offensive by any audience members?

DELIVERY

Did you approach the speaking situation confidently? Did you maintain effective eye contact with the members of the audience? Were you able to use an extemporaneous style of delivery? Could you be heard easily? Was your speaking rate appropriate? Did you articulate clearly? Were you able to convey a sense of enthusiasm as you spoke? Did your gestures help reinforce your content?

COMMUNICATION SKILLS
Practice Tips For Evaluating Your Speech

By reviewing and critiquing your presentation and comparing your expectations with your actual experience, you will learn what changes you need to make to become more effective at presenting to others. Be sure to compare your evaluation with those offered to you by your instructor and peers.

Assess the introduction.

The introduction should capture attention, convey the thesis, preview main points, and engage receivers by connecting the topic to them.

Critique the body.

The body should communicate each main point, contain transitions between main points, and integrate materials that support each main point.

Determine the effectiveness of the conclusion.

The conclusions should restate the thesis, summarize the main points, and motivate receivers to think and/or act.

Weigh the effectiveness of presentation aids.

Presentation aids should be designed and integrated into a speech to enhance the speaker's message. Designed to strengthen key points in the speech, they also should help to enhance the speaker's credibility and ability to connect with receivers.

Evaluate delivery.

The speaker should use vocal cues to create interest and convey meaning, use eye contact to connect with receivers, and use gestures and movements that are natural and effective.

> The human brain is a wonderful thing. It operates from the moment you're born until the first time you get up to make a speech.

Howard Goshorn

COMPLETE THIS CHAPTER 13 CHECKLIST

13.1 I can explain how to use presentation aids, including programs such as PowerPoint, to enhance the content and delivery of a speech. ☐

Integrating visual images and audio clips in a speech helps to reinforce, clarify, and dramatize its content. Among the presentation aids speakers can use in a speech are objects, models, graphs, photographs, drawings, maps, PowerPoint slides, DVDs, and sound from CDs. If used to enhance rather than overpower a presentation, presentation aids are effective tools.

13.2 I can distinguish among five styles of delivery: manuscript, memorized, impromptu, extemporaneous, and sound bite speaking or Twitter speak. ☐

A manuscript speech is written out word for word and then read aloud by the speaker. A memorized speech is one that the speaker commits to memory. An impromptu speech is a speech a speaker delivers on the spur of the moment without formal preparation. An extemporaneous speech is one the speaker researches, outlines, and then delivers using speaker's notes after rehearsing conscientiously. A sound bite or Twitter speak is a short, memorable statement that can be tweeted and repeated subsequent to being shared.

13.3 Identify speech rehearsal and delivery strategies, including the effective use of nonverbal cues. ☐

During rehearsals or speech tryouts, speakers time their presentation, refine the clarity and vividness of their words, edit out unnecessary redundancy, and add needed transition and delivery reminders. They also consider how to dress for the presentation and work on supporting their speech with appropriate posture, gestures and body movement, facial expressions, and vocal cues. On the day of their presentation, they arrive prepared and make sure any equipment they will use is working.

13.4 I can assess the speechmaking effectiveness of myself and others in terms of content (including the integration of presentation aids), organization, wording, and delivery. ☐

The speaker and the audience evaluate the speech's effectiveness seeking to determine the extent to which the speaker succeeded in fulfilling speechmaking goals.

13.5 I can apply skills to improve my speech delivery. ☐

By using my skills to prepare and integrate presentation aids, and employing effective visual and vocal cues when practicing my speech, I take steps to improve my speech's delivery.

BECOME A WORD MASTER

bar graph 354

extemporaneous
speech 364

impromptu
speech 364

infographic 356

line graph 354

manuscript
speech 363

memorized
speech 364

pictograph 356

pie graph 354

iStock/Tomwang112

Informative Speaking

14.1 Define *informative speaking.*

14.2 Distinguish among three informative speaking categories.

14.3 Follow guidelines to increase audience engagement and comprehension.

14.4 Apply skills to enhance informative speaking presentations.

Life is very different than it was just a decade ago. We have access to the world's information wherever we can get a cell phone signal. Establishing connections to information has been simplified for us. The question is this: Are we able to thoughtfully process all the information that is now accessible to us? ■

> There are things that are known and things that are unknown; in between are doors.
>
> Anonymous

SHARING AND CONCEPTUALIZING INFORMATION

Information, when it is turned into knowledge, confers power. Once in possession of, and able to make sense of, the *right* information, we are able to comprehend what we otherwise might not have understood and accomplish things we otherwise might not have done. But is it possible that we now have the ability to possess too much information? Whereas the amount of information available to us continues to explode, our individual capacities for absorbing information have not increased. Every day, we face a deluge of new, and often conflicting, data. As a result, we are expected to be able to filter, process, and edit all the information we receive.[1]

What is more, we have another increasingly important responsibility, which is to conceptualize. In fact, while information remains essential, we are transitioning—moving beyond the information age and into the conceptual age—to a time when people with the ability to understand and interpret meaning, think differently, detect patterns, recognize opportunities, and edit and put the pieces together in new ways will be in demand, especially in professional sectors.[2] Do you have these skills? Would you like to develop and improve them?

AVOID INFORMATION OVERLOAD OR UNDERLOAD

Becoming a conceptualizer requires that you get a handle on information glut and **information anxiety**—the psychological stress we experience when **information overload** confuses

iStock/Siphotography

us or makes it difficult for us to make sense of the never-ending accumulation of information.[3]

Just as serious a problem as information overload is information underload—the failure to provide the members of the audience with sufficient information. Whether because of a lack of research on your part, the erroneous belief that receivers will be unable to understand the information being presented, or an unwillingness to communicate complex information in a way that makes it understandable and relatable, information underload will make your goals as a speaker difficult to achieve.

CAREER BUILDER: ASSESSING THE EFFECTS OF INFORMATION OVERLOAD

How overloaded with information do you feel? How many of the following statements can you answer with a firm "yes"?

1. My thoughts frequently drift off, making it difficult for me to concentrate on what's before my eyes.

2. I find myself forgetting what I think I should retain.

3. I feel tired when I think of all the information I have to acquire.

4. I often put off making a decision because I want to get more information.

5. After I make a decision, I wonder if I chose the right option because of all the possible choices I had before me.

6. When I go online, I think about all the other things I have to do.

7. I check my online networks repeatedly, because I'm concerned that if I don't, I'll miss something important.

8. I feel like my texts, e-mails, and voice messages pile up, causing me to use up too much of my time trying to keep up with them.

9. I'm distracted by new information, which makes it hard for me to process the information that I already have.

10. It's hard for me to separate what I need to know from what's interesting and nice to know.

While many of us experience a normal amount of information overload, for some of us, information obsessiveness becomes debilitating. When it's never enough, that's usually too much to process—and could impede rather than enhance understanding, making it less likely that we will transmit knowledge.

MAKE IT RELEVANT

What's also important is to be able to process and understand information that is not extraneous to our purpose but will add to knowledge. Here, the informative speech has an important role to play in our lives. Our world is filled with informative messages that we depend on. Some of these messages are informal, but others are carefully planned, structured, and rehearsed to achieve maximum impact. Some three quarters of the U.S. labor force hold jobs that require the production, storage, delivery, or interpretation of information. Educators in schools and businesses, sales professionals, medical practitioners, and consultants and managers in a wide array of fields depend on their skill in giving and receiving information for their livelihoods. They all share the need to make their messages clear, relevant, and useful to receivers.

Monkey Business Images/Shutterstock.com

Informative speakers face three primary challenges: (1) to identify information that has importance for others; (2) to put themselves in the position of their receivers and make the information they deliver understandable to them, and (3) to communicate and conceptualize information in ways that create interest, enhance learning, and help audience members remember the messages delivered to them.

Being able to convey information and to conceptualize meaning to others are among the most useful skills you can acquire. That is what this chapter prepares you to do—to share information you have with people who lack it but need it, or who possess it but do not understand it fully. Let's get started.

TYPES OF INFORMATIVE PRESENTATIONS

What's going on? What is it? What does it mean? How does it work? These are the kinds of questions that informative speeches answer. Whenever you present an **informative speech**, your goal is to offer your audience members more information than they currently possess on a topic. Your objective is to update and add to their knowledge, refine their understanding, or provide background.[4]

The main purpose of an informative speech is to educate, not advocate. There is an unlimited number of topics about which we can share information and develop understanding. Whether you are a student, parent, employer, or employee, speaking informatively is a part of your daily life. You likely describe, demonstrate, or explain something to other people regularly. For organizational purposes, we divide informative speaking into the following categories: speeches about objects and ideas, about events and people, and about processes and procedures. Although these categories are far from exhaustive, they represent the most common ways public speakers package information (Table 14.1).

What Can You Do to Handle the Glut of Information?

What ethical guidelines should speakers use to determine how much data to share with receivers? We live in the age of "big data." Vast numbers of American workers are paid to gather and interpret the morass of information collected. We possess not only an overabundance of information but also so many competing expert opinions that it becomes virtually impossible for us to apply logical approaches to deliberation and problem solving. For example, well over 100,000 studies now exist on the topic of depression. How is any doctor or patient to even begin to make sense of all that information and craft a treatment plan? Because of a sheer quantity of information, our attempts to draw conclusions often lead to "paralysis by analysis." How much information is too much information? Could endless information result in perpetual argumentation but no conclusion?

What advice can you offer regarding how to avoid overwhelming audience members with data? What steps might speakers take to minimize the effects of "data smog"?

TABLE 14.1 INFORMATIVE SPEECH TYPES AND TOPICS

SPEECH TYPE	SAMPLE TOPICS
Objects/Ideas	Self-Driving Cars Gene Therapy Instagram September 11 Memorial The Tomb of Tutankhamun Privacy Flight Sustainable Energy Yoga
Events/People	The Repair of the Hubble Space Telescope The Publication of *Go Set a Watchman* Comic-Con The Cannes Film Festival Harvey Milk J. K. Rowling Kanye West
Processes/Procedures	How to Change a Flat Tire How to Speed Read How to Prepare for a Job Interview How to Perform the Heimlich Maneuver

SPEECHES ABOUT OBJECTS AND IDEAS

When speaking of an object, we usually describe it and tell about its uses. When we speak of an idea or concept, we typically define and explain it.

Speaking About an Object

An object speech can cover anything tangible—a machine, building, structure, place, or phenomenon (see Table 14.1 for examples). The chosen object (or thing) may be animate or inanimate, moving or still, visible or invisible to the naked eye. Whatever object you choose, the goal remains the same: to paint an accurate and information-rich picture of it.

Once you select an object for your topic, the next step is to create a specific purpose that identifies the particular aspect of the object on which you will focus. The following are sample purpose statements for informative speeches about objects:

> To inform my audience about types of volcanoes

> To inform my audience about the nature of the Egyptian pyramids

> To inform my audience about the anatomy of the human brain

Organizing Speeches About Objects. Speeches about objects lend themselves to topical, spatial, and chronological organizational formats. A topical format allows you to divide your subject into groups or major categories; when speaking about volcanoes, for example, you might focus first on extinct volcanoes, second on dormant volcanoes, and third on active ones. A spatial or physical framework enables you to discuss one major component of the object at a time as you might do when discussing the entrance, antechamber, and burial chamber of an Egyptian pyramid. And finally, a chronological format is most appropriate if you are going to stress how a design or phenomenon evolved over time (e.g., the formation of the Hawaiian Islands).

Whichever organizational framework you select, be sure to review and follow the guidelines discussed in Chapter 12.

Speaking About an Idea

What does the word *existentialism* mean? What is *bullying*? What is *a hostile work environment*? How do we clarify the nature of *double jeopardy*? In a speech about an idea, also known as a concept speech, your goal is to explain your topic in such a way that audience members agree on two things:

1. The idea has relevance and importance for them.

2. They want you to clarify or elaborate on it.

General or abstract ideas usually work best for concept speeches, as they allow for the most creative analyses and interpretations. For example, you might discuss free speech, Buddhism, or inequality (see Table 14.1 for more suggestions).

When we conceptualize ideas, audience members may have different interpretations of the words we use—primarily because personal experiences influence meaning. This is particularly likely for nontangible topics such as injustice and religion. By using language that is concrete to make your interpretation clear, as well as analogies to increase common understanding, you can help audience members conceptualize your subject similarly.

As with a speech about an object, your next step after selecting a topic is to create a purpose statement. The following are sample purpose statements for informative speeches about ideas:

To inform my audience about the meaning of injustice

To inform my audience about basic tenets of Buddhism

To inform my audience about different philosophies of religion

Organizing Speeches About Ideas. You can easily develop a speech about an idea using a topical order, enumerating and discussing, in turn, key aspects of the idea. For instance, you might explain the ways racial prejudice affects its victims economically, politically, and socially.

Speeches about ideas also lend themselves to chronological development. When speaking about sexual harassment, you might explain how our understanding of the term has changed over time.

Topics such as the meaning of emotional intelligence, shyness, or implicit bias are really speeches of definition. How would you define *shyness*? You might offer examples of what it feels like to be shy, describe how a shy person behaves, and then go on to discuss shyness's consequences. On the other hand, you could discuss the causes of shyness and then focus on different types or categories of shyness.

> Visit the interactive e-Book to access the Exploring Diversity feature "Conveying Information to Diverse Audiences," which will ask you about how informative speaking and cultural perspective intersect.

SPEECHES ABOUT EVENTS AND PEOPLE

Many of us are interested in the remarkable people and events of both our time and history. Both make solid informative speech topics. Can you describe an event or person for receivers so that the event or person comes alive and audience members form a mental close-up in their minds?

Speaking About an Event

A speech about an event focuses on something that happens regularly (a holiday, a birthday) or something that happened once (D-Day, the first moon landing), something that marks our lives (graduations, funerals) or something that left us with a lasting impression (the Las Vegas shooting, Hurricane Maria). The event you discuss might be one you personally witnessed (a political rally) or one you choose to research (the Constitutional Convention, the passage of the Nineteenth Amendment giving women the vote, or the removal of monuments to the Confederacy). Whatever your topic, your goal is to bring the event to life so that your audience can visualize and experience it.

Speaking About a Person

If instead of an event, you opt to tell about the life of a person—someone famous or someone you know personally, someone living or dead, someone admired by or abhorrent to all—your goal is to make that person come alive for audience members, to enable them to appreciate the person's unique qualities, and to help them understand the impact the individual has had on others. In other words, you seek to answer the question: Why is the person worthy of our attention?

A speech on Jeffrey Dahmer would become interesting if the speaker used it to explore the mind of a mass murderer. A speech on Amy Schumer could develop an understanding of comedic originality, and a speech on Salman Rushdie (the author of *The Satanic Verses* and *The Golden House*) could help audiences comprehend the free-speech challenges of writers.

Organizing Speeches About Events and People

Speeches on events and people lend themselves to a variety of organizational approaches; chronological, topical, and causal patterns are especially useful. Look to the purpose of your speech to help you choose your organizational approach. For example, if your speech aims to explain the history of an event or person—say Hurricane Maria—you probably would choose a chronological sequence. In contrast, if you wanted to approach the subject from a different angle and discuss, for instance, the social, economic, and political effects of Hurricane Maria, a topical organization would better suit your needs. And if you wanted to inform audience members why Hurricane Maria proved so destructive to Puerto Rico, you likely would choose a causal order.

SPEECHES ABOUT PROCESSES AND PROCEDURES

How do you do that? Why does this work? Can I make one, too? When we answer questions like these, we share our understanding about processes and procedures, the third category of informative speeches.

Here are examples of purpose statements about processes and procedures:

To inform my audience about how photosynthesis works

To inform my audience about the workings of the Electoral College

To inform my audience how to change the oil in a car

If you are delivering a "how" speech, then your primary goal is to increase audience understanding of your subject:

How a Slot Machine Works

How Colleges Select Students

How Tsunamis Develop

How the Jet Stream Works

If, however, you are delivering a "how-to" speech, then your primary goal is to communicate not only information but also specific skills so audience members can learn how to do something:

How to Cut Your Own Hair

How to Housebreak a Dog

How to Avoid Identity Theft

How to Lobby Your Legislators

There is virtually no end to the list of processes and procedures about which you can speak.

iStock/stevecoleimages

Organizing Speeches About Processes and Procedures

When delivering a speech that focuses on a process or procedure, you probably will find it most useful to arrange your ideas in either chronological or topical order.

Chronological order works well because it naturally reflects the sequence, approach, or series of steps used from start to finish in making or doing something. For example, in a speech on how scientists could save planet Earth from collision with a meteor, you might detail four key steps in the process from detecting the meteor, determining when contact will occur, sending a spacecraft to intercept it, and blowing it up.

Other times, you might find it more useful to discuss the major principles, techniques, or methods receivers need to understand to master the process or procedure. Then topical order is your best choice. For example, you could focus your speech on how scientists prepare for a potential meteor on a collision course with Earth, beginning with their researching the effects of past meteor collisions and then describing what researchers are doing to improve meteor detection technology.

Keep your speech clear and comprehensible. One that contains too many main points, or step after step after step with no logical categorization, usually is too difficult for audience members to interpret and remember. This makes it unlikely they will engage and be able to follow what you're sharing. By keeping your main points manageable, you facilitate better understanding of the process or procedure.

SKILL BUILDER

Assessing an Informative Speech

Because informative speaking is a prime means of sharing what you know with others, it is essential for speakers to recognize diversity and adapt to difference.

In the following speech, titled "What It Means to Be Deaf," student Andi Lane addresses a diversity issue when she shares her understanding of what it means to be hearing impaired. Notice how she uses her own experiences as a starting point.

After reading the transcript of the speech, answer these questions:

1. To what extent did the speech's introduction succeed in getting your attention? To what extent was the speaker successful in achieving closure by tying her introduction and conclusion together?

2. What means did the speaker use to establish and maintain her credibility? Which kinds of information were most useful? Most memorable?

3. Are you now able to understand what it means to be deaf? If so, what did the speaker do to help you internalize such an understanding? If not, what could the speaker have done to promote better understanding?

4. Were the supporting materials that the speaker used effective? How many different kinds of supporting materials did the speaker use? In what ways did these supporting materials facilitate your understanding? Your emotional involvement?

5. Focus on the speaker's use of transitions. How effectively did the speaker move from one point to the next? To what extent was it easy to identify the speaker's main points?

6. What did the speaker do to widen receiver appreciation of diversity issues?

7. What might the speaker change to enhance her speech?

8. Based on this transcript, pretend you are the speaker, and develop first an outline and then speaker's notes to use when delivering the speech.

(Continued)

(Continued)

What It Means to Be Deaf

At the beginning of this year I moved into an apartment.

SN 1
Introduction, with personal anecdote

When I arrived at my new place, my roommate was there to greet me, and she saw my stereo. She got really excited, and she said, "Great you have a stereo for us to listen to." I laughed and told her that was a pretty funny joke, as I turned and ran up the stairs. But Sarah never knew I said that. You see, Sarah is profoundly deaf and relies upon lip reading as her primary source of communication. Living with Sarah has taught me many things.

SN 2 Thesis and preview of speech's contents

Prime among them is this: The deaf and hearing impaired face many problems on a daily basis. My interest in this subject led me to take a basic sign language and communication with the hearing impaired course. In the course I discovered that understanding the deaf culture, learning to communicate with them, and accepting them can alleviate many of the problems that deaf and hearing-impaired people face. Let's explore these points together.

SN 3 First main point

"What exactly is deaf culture?" you might ask. This is a legitimate question, since even those who are deaf and involved in the deaf culture have a difficult time explaining it. In his book, *Sign Language and the Deaf Community*, William Stokes says that there are several characteristics that can help us define the deaf culture. The deaf culture is closed and limited only to those who are deaf. Members have a common language that they share and common beliefs about others who are deaf and also those who are hearing. They also have shared goals; one of their primary goals is a goal of acceptance—acceptance in employment, politics, and every aspect of life.

SN 4 Second main point; use of comparison and contrast and specific examples

It's also interesting to compare the hearing world to the deaf culture. In deaf culture there's less emphasis on personal space; people have to be close together in order to read each other's signs. There's also less importance placed on time. People are not always punctual; there's a more relaxed feeling in the deaf culture.

Eye contact is lengthy, necessary, and polite in the deaf culture. Also, when you do introductions—we usually greet each other; we meet each other; we exchange names. In the deaf culture, you exchange first names, last names, and where you attended school.

And my final point, the difference between the hearing world and the deaf culture, is that the hearing world is more reserved whereas the deaf culture is more tactile. An illustration of this is that in the hearing world we shake hands. In the deaf culture—usually they exchange hugs. These are just some of the important differences that Dr. Kenya Taylor, an audiologist, points out.

Daily life is, of course, very different for those who have a hearing problem. Communication is the main distinguishing factor. Sign language is usually taught to children at a very early age to provide them with a sense of vocabulary—a way to communicate their thoughts and ideas.

There are many different types of sign language, and these vary from area to area much as spoken language does, much like a dialect. The two most common types are signed English and the American Sign Language. Sign language, basic sign, is usually taught to beginners and follows the main sentence structure as spoken English does. ASL is used by those who are hearing impaired. It's a shortened, more abbreviated form. While the same signs are used, it's the format that differs, according to Greenburg in his book *Endless Sign*.

As mentioned before, children are usually taught sign language at a very early age. It is later that they acquire lip reading or speech skills, if they acquire them at all. Most deaf people can lip read to some extent. Now, of course, this presents special problems for the person. They must always be alert and aware of what's going on. And imagine being in a dimly lit room or trying to talk to a person who has a habit of looking away. Also, when you are talking to a deaf person they can't hear the sarcasm in your voice; you need to say what you mean.

Nonverbals are important; they pick up information any way they can get it. It's funny, because now I have a habit of flipping on the interior light when I get in my car at night. This is because I'm accustomed to riding with Sarah. Even when she's not in the car, the light's on, because it's impossible for us to communicate without the interior light on.

SN 5 Personal experiences add credibility

Right now, I'm going to paint a hypothetical situation for you, and I would like for you to put yourself in it. And it's a situation where you will be trying to communicate with a deaf person. Let's say you're at a restaurant; you're working there. It's a real busy place, the most popular place in town. One night a man comes in, alone, and is seated in the back corner, which is dimly lit. You're in a rush, and you go over to him, and you pour his water. And as you're pouring his water, you say: "May I take your order?" And you look up, and he doesn't say anything. First of all, he doesn't know you are addressing him, and second of all, he has no idea what you said. So you repeat yourself, "May I take your order?" And the man says, "I am deaf." But you don't know what he said because you don't know sign language. He speaks, and you can't understand him, and you're about to panic. In this situation, what you don't need to do is panic. You need to remember that the only difference between you and him is that you can hear and he can't. Communication is always possible, even if you have to point at the menu or write notes.

SN 6 Hypothetical illustration involves receivers

This leads me into my final point, the importance of accepting those with hearing problems. The more aware we are of the problems faced by the deaf and the greater our understanding, the less prejudiced we are going to be. The main difference, the only difference, in fact, between us—those who can hear and people who can't hear—is that we hear sounds with our ears, while they hear words and expressions with their eyes. And they feel with

SN 7 Transition into final main point

(Continued)

(Continued)

their hearts just like we do. We can't measure a person's intelligence by the degree of a hearing loss or the way that they speak. They are our equals.

SN 8 Citation of authoritative source 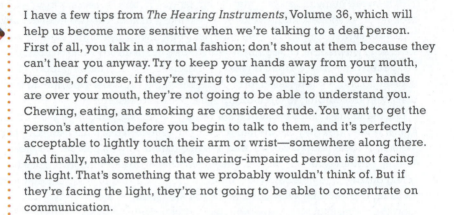 I have a few tips from *The Hearing Instruments*, Volume 36, which will help us become more sensitive when we're talking to a deaf person. First of all, you talk in a normal fashion; don't shout at them because they can't hear you anyway. Try to keep your hands away from your mouth, because, of course, if they're trying to read your lips and your hands are over your mouth, they're not going to be able to understand you. Chewing, eating, and smoking are considered rude. You want to get the person's attention before you begin to talk to them, and it's perfectly acceptable to lightly touch their arm or wrist—somewhere along there. And finally, make sure that the hearing-impaired person is not facing the light. That's something that we probably wouldn't think of. But if they're facing the light, they're not going to be able to concentrate on communication.

SN 9 Summary Today I've shared with you some background information about the deaf culture, ways in which deaf people are able to communicate, and the importance of accepting deaf people for who they are. In the short time I've lived with Sarah, I've learned so much. I learned that you don't talk to her when your back is turned or when you're in another room. I've learned that I can scream as loud as I want to in the apartment, and it wouldn't make any difference at all. I can achieve the same end result by just telling her I'm upset. And I've learned that one of my most dear friends has a profound hearing loss, but I still love her.

GUIDELINES FOR INFORMATIVE SPEAKERS

An effective informative speaker motivates audience members to want to learn more about the topic, communicates the information clearly by providing information balance, emphasizes key points, involves audience members in the presentation, provides information in ways that make it memorable, draws on the strengths of novelty and creativity, and integrates presentation aids.

CREATE INFORMATION HUNGER

One of the informative speaker's tasks is to ensure that audience members find the presentation interesting, intellectually stimulating, and relevant (i.e., significant or personally valuable). This means you want to increase each receiver's need to know and make them hungry to receive your message.

You will be more adept at creating information hunger if you have analyzed your audience conscientiously (see Chapter 11). Then, by using appropriate vehicles, you will be able to generate the interest that motivates audience members to listen to you. Remember to use the attention-getting devices shared in Chapter 13. For example, you can tell stories about your own experiences or the experiences of others, you can ask rhetorical questions, or you can draw analogies for your receivers to consider. You also can arouse the audience's curiosity and you can incorporate humor or use eye-catching visual aids.

OFFER INFORMATION BALANCE

Your speech will inform receivers only if they are capable of processing the information you are sharing. A common danger in informative speaking is information overload. Information overload occurs when two conditions are met: (1) The speaker delivers far more data about the topic than the audience needs or wants, confusing receivers and causing them to tune out; and (2) the speaker presents ideas in words that receivers don't understand. Instead of using clear and simple language, the speaker creates frustration among audience members by using unfamiliar jargon or words that soar beyond the listeners' vocabulary.

On the other hand, speakers who go out of their way to avoid information overload sometimes overcompensate and create a situation known as *information underload*. Information underload occurs when the speaker underestimates the audience's sophistication or intelligence and ends up sharing with them what they already know.

The goal is to strike a balance, providing neither too little nor too much information. Don't underestimate or overestimate the audience's capability. Instead, motivate receivers to want to fill in information gaps.

As you share information, pace, don't race. When delivering your informative speech, don't race to see how much new information you can cram into the brains of receivers in a mere 5 to 7 minutes. The real challenge is to know not only what to include but also what to exclude.

EMPHASIZE KEY POINTS

As we discussed in Chapter 12, emphasis can be created through repetition (saying the same thing over again) and restatement (saying the same thing in another way). As long as you do not become overly repetitious and redundant, these devices will help the audience process and retain the main points of your speech.

The organization of your speech also can reinforce your main ideas. Remember that you can use your introduction to preview ideas in your conclusion and to help make those ideas memorable. Transitions and internal summaries also help create a sense of cohesiveness.

INVOLVE THE AUDIENCE

With so many communication options at their fingertips, contemporary audiences tend to be restless. Public speakers need to work to channel the nervous energy of the members of the audience who will learn more as they become involved with the material being presented to them.[5] Effective speakers don't view the audience as a passive receptacle. Rather, they work to find ways to let the audience take an active part in their presentation. Say that you're giving a speech on how to reduce stress. To involve the audience, you might have your receivers try one or two stress-reducing exercises.

MAKE INFORMATION MEMORABLE

Audience members work to understand and remember information that they perceive as relevant to their own lives. You might not have much interest in a speech on the development of bees. If, however, you heard about a new species of killer bee that is resistant to common insecticides and that droves of these bees are on the way to your community, you probably would develop an intense interest quickly.

Similarly, audiences want to learn new information. In this case, the term *new* means "new to them." A historical blunder may be new in this sense, and it may be relevant to a college or business audience today.

DRAW ON NOVELTY AND CREATIVITY

An effective speaker looks for ways to approach information from an unusual direction. If you are the fifth speaker that your audience will be listening to speak on the homeless, you must find a different slant or approach to the topic or you may bore the audience from the outset. You might try taking a different point of view—what homelessness looks like through the eyes of a child, for example. Also work to create analogies to help bring a topic home to the audience: "The number of people entering teaching today is diminishing. The teaching profession is like a stream drying up." Try other ways to complete this analogy. As you prepare your presentation, remember that you're looking for creative ways of bringing your topic to life for your receivers.

INTEGRATE PRESENTATION AIDS

Presentation aids have important roles in informative presentations. Remember first, though, that you are your primary visual aid. The way you stand, walk, talk, and gesture is extremely important to the effectiveness of your presentation.

Bring objects, or make simple models if you cannot bring the objects themselves. Use PowerPoint charts, graphs, and drawings when appropriate.

In addition, consider using brief video and audio clips to create or sustain audience interest. One student, for example, showed a brief YouTube segment of a chemical reaction that could not have been demonstrated safely in the classroom. Keep in mind that you can find abundant images, charts, and graphs on the Internet and incorporate them into your presentation to help communicate your message.

COMMUNICATION SKILLS

Practice Tips for Achieving Informative Speaking Goals

Being effective at informative speaking will serve you personally and professionally throughout your life. To achieve mastery, continually apply the following strategies.

Select a topic of importance to you and others.

Speakers should bore neither themselves nor their receivers. By acquiring and sharing information that increases knowledge, understanding, and/or skills, you open yourself and others to the excitement of learning.

Use informing approaches appropriate to your subject.

Selecting the right approach will support your efforts to make your message clear and useful to the audience. Integrating definitions, explanations, descriptions, and narratives makes it easier for receivers to learn by helping in transferring information and creating teaching moments that are fun and exciting.

Frame your message strategically to enhance its relevance.

Inform about issues, places, policies, processes, objects, or events that receivers will profit from learning more about. Draw receivers into your speech by making your topic compelling and memorable. Once receivers understand their vested interest, and become involved, their motivation to listen to and learn from you increases.

> Take your mind out every now and then and dance on it. It is getting all caked up.
>
> Mark Twain

COMPLETE THIS CHAPTER 14 CHECKLIST

14.1 I can define *informative speaking.* ☐

The goal of the informative speaker is to offer audience members more information than they presently have about a topic. Informative speaking aims to update and add knowledge, refine understanding, or provide background.

14.2 I can distinguish among three informative speaking categories. ☐

Three categories of informative speaking are speeches on objects and ideas, speeches on events and people, and speeches on processes and procedures. In order to develop their speeches, informative speakers enhance them with messages of explanation, messages of description, messages of definition, and messages that tell a story.

14.3 I can follow guidelines to increase audience engagement and comprehension. ☐

A primary goal of the informative speech is to increase each receiver's need to know and hunger to receive the information in the speech. To do this, speakers analyze the audience and use appropriate attention-getting devices to generate receiver interest. At the same time that speakers work to create interest in the audience, they also need to avoid overloading or underloading receivers with information.

14.4 I can apply skills to enhance informative speaking presentations. ☐

Honing the ability to share information effectively also promotes continued personal and professional success. In every informative speech, the right topic, the right approach, and the right frame should work in sync to enhance the sharing and understanding of information.

BECOME A WORD MASTER

information anxiety 379

information overload 379

informative speech 381

iStock/Tomwang112

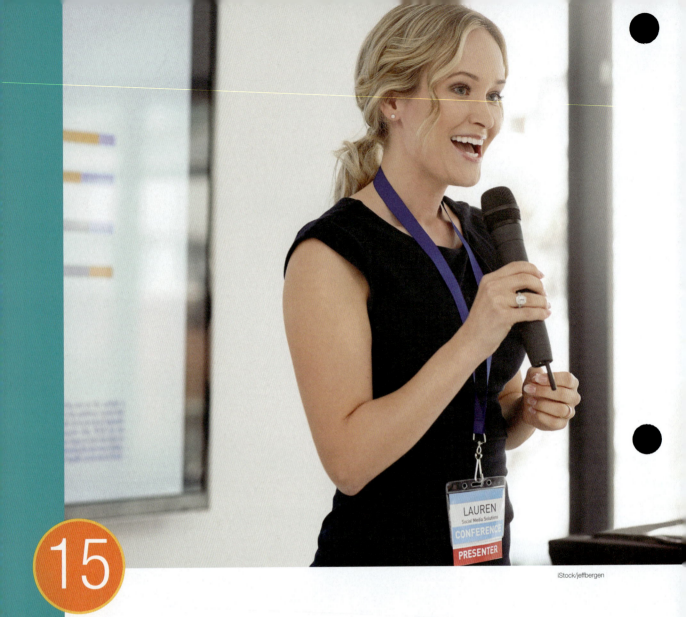

iStock/jeffbergen

15

Persuasive Speaking

AFTER COMPLETING THIS CHAPTER, YOU SHOULD BE ABLE TO:

15.1 Define the purpose of persuasion.

15.2 Distinguish between types of persuasive propositions and speeches.

15.3 Describe and use Monroe's motivated sequence.

15.4 Discuss what it means to persuade responsibly, strategically, and credibly.

15.5 Follow guidelines for persuading effectively.

15.6 Apply skills to enhance persuasive presentation effectiveness.

> Man is the only animal that laughs and weeps; for he is the only animal that is struck with the difference between what things are and what they ought to be.
>
> William Hazlitt

We are all persuasive targets. "Vote for me," demands the candidate. "Buy me," reads the ad. "Support my cause," cajoles the lobbyist. "Attend my rally," the community organizer cries out. "Give money to the cause," pleads the fund raiser. How do you respond?

We are all persuasive advocates. Can you imagine yourself speaking in favor of opening U.S. borders to increased numbers of immigrants, or do you see yourself advocating for closing them? Would you speak in support of a woman's right to choose, or are you a proponent of the right-to-life movement? Would you speak against or for the death penalty?

Persuasion, the process of using communication to change or strengthen others' attitudes, beliefs, values, and/or behavior, permeates society.[1] Advertisers, public relations professionals, politicians, religious leaders, and numerous others have the same primary goal: persuading us. When choosing sides, are you among those likely to take shortcuts or those who seek to make reasoned decisions? Do you look for easy answers, or do you have the skill needed

to see nuances and possibilities that escape others? And most important, do you see yourself as able to make a positive difference in your college, community, and world?

No matter if you are a persuasive target or advocate, choice and change are constants of life in the 21st century.[2] The positions we take on the issues of our day, and our efforts to convince others to hold those positions that we believe correct, have real and meaningful effects. The fact is, persuaders can change the world!

Our aim in this chapter is to increase your ability to prepare, present, and process persuasive speeches by showing you how to apply your general knowledge and skills to this special type of discourse. ∎

THE PURPOSE OF PERSUASION

A **persuasive speech** aims to modify the thoughts, feelings, or actions of the members of an audience. The speaker's hope is that as a result of listening to a speech or series of speeches, audience members will modify those attitudes, beliefs, or behaviors of which the speaker does not approve and instead adopt attitudes and behaviors more compatible with the speaker's goals and worldview.

Because persuasion is omnipresent, our communication environment demands effective persuasive skills. In fact, with the exception of class lectures, a majority of the presentations that others direct at us probably are persuasive. So are the majority of presentations that we make to others. As a result, being able to exert influence is a necessary and vital talent.

When was the last time you tried to change another person's mind? Maybe you wanted to be given the opportunity to improve a grade on a paper and had to develop reasons why your instructor should allow you "a do over." Or you may have sought to persuade your employer to give you a raise or more responsibility. Whatever your persuasive goal, it is the attitudes, beliefs, and values of the person(s) on the receiving end of your persuasive appeals that you rely on to frame and support your case. So, whether you are negotiating to buy property, arguing that the jury should acquit your client, working in support of Amnesty International, or making an appeal for any one of thousands of other causes, understanding your receivers enables you to decide how best to approach persuasive discourse.

GOALS OF PERSUASION

A speaker may believe that flying saucers exist even though most of the audience may not; oppose bilingual education while others support it; or want audience members to become organ donors when audience members feel reluctant to make that commitment. The speaker's goal, referred to as the **proposition** of the speech, indicates the type of change that she or he seeks in audience members.

Typically, speakers desire one or both of two general outcomes: They want to convince receivers that something is so (i.e., they want you to change the way you think), and/or they want to cause audience members to take an action (i.e., they want you to change the way you behave). Whatever the general nature of the speech proposition, it likely will reflect at least one of the following persuasive goals: adoption, discontinuance, deterrence, or continuance.[3]

When the goal is *adoption*, the speaker's hope is to persuade the audience to accept a new idea, attitude, belief, or behavior (e.g., that genetically modified food is hazardous to our health or that audience members should march to protest racial injustice).

When the goal is *discontinuance*, the speaker's hope is to persuade audience members to stop doing something they currently do (e.g., stop drinking alcohol while pregnant or limit fast food consumption).

When the goal is *deterrence*, as opposed to discontinuance, the speaker's hope is to persuade the audience to avoid an activity or a way of thinking that they do not already engage in and that the speaker does not want them to start engaging in (e.g., "If you believe that every woman has the right to exercise control over her own body, don't vote for candidates who would make abortions illegal.")

Finally, if the speaker's goal is the *continuance*, then she or he encourages receivers to continue to think or behave as they now currently do (e.g., keep limiting sun exposure or reaffirm belief in freedom of the press).

Can you develop a list of things that you'd like to persuade others to think, feel, or do? Adoption and discontinuance goals involve asking receivers to alter their ways of thinking or behaving, whereas deterrence and continuance goals involve asking them not to alter their thinking or behavior but to reinforce or sustain it. In general, it is easier to accomplish deterrence and continuance objectives than adoption or discontinuance goals. However, if you use a variety of appeals, a sound organizational format, and build your credibility, then these goals also are within your reach.

TYPES OF PERSUASIVE SPEECHES

Persuasive speeches focus on questions of fact, value, or policy. Selecting which kind of speech to present is among your first tasks. By choosing one question type over the others, you are deciding to speak on what is or what is not (a **proposition of fact**), how good or bad something is (a **proposition of value**), or what ought to be (a **proposition of policy**).

PROPOSITIONS OF FACT

The following are sample propositions of fact that seek to influence receiver's beliefs:

Civility is teachable.

Self-driving cars make driving safer.

Education prevents poverty.

Social media use decreases interpersonal skills.

The federal deficit is a threat to our economic security.

Good propositions of fact are not resolvable with simple yes or no answers. Rather, they are open to debate. When delivering a speech on any proposition of fact, your goal is to persuade the audience of its truth by using an array of evidence and arguments to convince them that your interpretation is valid, your assertion is true and accurate, and your conclusion is undeniable.

Organizing the Question of Fact Speech

Your challenge in speaking on a proposition of fact is to convince receivers that you based your conclusion on objective evidence. To do this, you need to present the facts as persuasively as possible.

It is common to use a *topical organization* to organize speeches on questions of fact, with each main point offering the audience a reason to agree with you.

However, if you believe that you can best achieve the goals of your presentation by describing an issue as worsening over time or by describing a subject spatially—for example, how a specific issue under consideration has global implications—then instead of using a topical organizational format, you might choose to use a chronological or spatial organizational format. In addition, the cause–effect pattern is also effective in organizing the question of fact speech.

PROPOSITIONS OF VALUE

The following are propositions of value that seek to influence receivers' opinions:

Discrimination against transgender people is wrong.

Grade inflation decreases the value of a college education.

Solitary confinement is cruel and unusual punishment.

The use of chemical weapons is immoral.

Fetal tissue research is morally justifiable.

Propositions of value explore the worth of an idea, a person, or an object. Like propositions of fact, they require more than a simple answer, in this case, a true or false response. When speaking on a proposition of value, you need to convince the audience that the evaluation contained in your proposition is valid. This likely requires that you also explore one or more propositions of fact. For example, you probably will not be effective advocating the premise that fetal tissue research is morally justifiable until you establish that such research is necessary.

In analyzing a proposition of value, you need to do the following:

- Define the object of evaluation and support that definition.
- Provide value criteria for determining what the evaluative term means; that is, how do you define what is "proper," what is "wrong," or what is "immoral"?

In the next example, the speaker explains why she believes it is immoral to fund research to clone human beings. By referring to the work of Richard A. McCormick, who was a professor of Christian ethics at the University of Notre Dame, she hopes to build support for her stance.

Cloning would tempt people to try to create humans with specific physical or intellectual characteristics. It would elevate mere aspects of human beings above what University of Notre Dame theologian Richard A. McCormick says is the "beautiful whole that is the human person." But who among us should decide what the desirable traits are, what the acceptable traits are?

Organizing the Question of Value Speech

Speeches on propositions of value often use a <mark>reasons approach</mark>, a type of topical organization in which each reason in support of the position is presented as a main point. One student used this kind of format to explain why she believes that keeping the detention center at Guantanamo Bay open is contrary to the country's values. After hearing her speech, another student was motivated to deliver a speech supporting an opposing set of values, which calls for a <mark>refutation format</mark>. When arguing against a previously stated position, you first note the stance being refuted, state your position, support it, and demonstrate why your position undermines the one previously stated. In this case, the student defended the proposition, "It is morally right to keep the detention facility at Guantanamo Bay open."

PROPOSITIONS OF POLICY

The following are sample propositions of policy that seek to influence receivers to take action:

National health insurance should be provided to all U.S. citizens.

To be culturally literate, all college students should study a foreign language.

College athletes should be paid.

Artificial sweeteners should be banned.

Childhood immunizations should be mandatory.

When speaking on a proposition of policy, you go beyond questions of fact or value. Instead, you work to demonstrate a need for the policy; you seek to earn audience approval or support for the policy in question. By asking audience members to support a proposition of policy, you are asking them to support a course of action. Audience members may agree on the facts surrounding an issue and even share a similar value orientation, but they may disagree regarding what to do. Whatever the nature of the policy disagreement, there are four aspects of any controversy that as a speaker you'll want to address:

Christopher Halloran/Shutterstock.com

- Is there a problem with the status quo?
- Is it fixable?
- Will the proposed solution work?
- Will the costs of fixing the problem outweigh the benefits of fixing the problem—that is, will the proposed solution help, or will it create new and more serious problems?

Organizing the Question of Policy Speech

The following are among the most popular formats for speeches on questions of policy: problem-causes-solution, comparative advantages, and Monroe's motivated sequence (discussed separately following this section), all of which are variants of topical organization.

Sometimes, a proposition of policy speech divides naturally into a *problem-causes-solution* organizational framework. The speech's first main point describes the nature and seriousness of the problem, the second main point explains the problem's causes, and the third main point proposes the solution and describes its practicality and benefits.

If the audience is well informed about the problem and convinced of a need for action, you can spend the bulk of your time explaining your plan and its viability. In this case, a *comparative advantages* format works well. In this format, you use each main point to explain how your plan is better than the alternative. For example, in a speech supportive of running more in-person classes on campus as opposed to increasing the number of online courses the college offers, your main points might be that in-person classes are more effective learning environments, that they better foster social skills, and that they are more effective at preventing cheating than are online classes.

Many topics can be approached as propositions of fact, value, or policy. For example, let's say we selected as our topic the effects of corporate influence on U.S. foreign policy. Our three possible proposition options might read as follows:

Proposition of fact: Corporations influence U.S. foreign policy positively and negatively.

Proposition of value: It is wrong for corporations to influence U.S. foreign policy.

Proposition of policy: Write your representatives and express your displeasure regarding corporate influence over U.S. foreign policy.

Given the preceding example, identify how you might approach a topic of interest to you by formulating a proposition of fact, a proposition of value, and a proposition of policy for it.

> Visit the interactive e-Book to access the Exploring Diversity feature "Persuasion and Assumed Similarity," in which you will reflect on the effects cultural upbringing has on persuasive speaking.

UNDERSTANDING MONROE'S MOTIVATED SEQUENCE

Monroe's motivated sequence is another organizational framework useful in motivating receivers to act in response to a speaker delivering a speech on a proposition of policy. Alan Monroe, a speech professor at Purdue University, developed the framework more than half a century ago.

Based on the psychology of persuasion, Monroe's motivated sequence has five phases that move the audience toward accepting and acting on a proposition of policy.

Phase 1: *Attention*. At the speech's outset, you must arouse the audience's interest.

Phase 2: *Need.* Show audience members that there's a serious problem with a present situation by stating explicitly the need, illustrating it with an array of supporting materials, and relating it to their interests and desires.

Phase 3: *Satisfaction*. After you demonstrate for your audience that there is a need, you must then satisfy their desire for a solution. Present your plan and explain it fully. Help the audience understand that alleviating the problem will also satisfy their interests and desires.

Phase 4: *Visualization*. Show the audience how your proposal will both benefit them and improve the situation. Asking receivers to visualize what the world will be like if they fail to act as you request also can be effective.

Phase 5: *Action*. Tell audience members specifically what you would like them to do, and conclude with an appeal that reinforces their commitment.

The following outline illustrates how the motivation sequence can be used to design a presentation advocating that a drowsy driver should not drive.[4]

Introduction

(Attention) I. It was after midnight when six students walking to a fraternity party were killed when Brandon Kallmeyer fell asleep at the wheel of the pickup truck he was driving, veered off the road, and hit them.

II. Over 100,000 accidents occur every year because drivers fall asleep at the wheel.

III. The problem of people driving while drowsy is increasing.

IV. Today I would like to explore why it is important to us to examine this problem, why it continues to escalate, and what steps we can take to help alleviate it.

Body I. We have put sleep on the back burner.

(Need) A. Everyone needs approximately eight hours of sleep a day to function effectively the next day, but we average only about six hours of sleep a day.

  B. The most important sleep stage is the REM stage, which occurs in cycles throughout sleep.

II. Sleep-deprived people pose serious dangers on the road.

  A. Highway patrol officers report stopping motorists who appear drunk only to discover they are fatigued.

  B. Drowsy driving is approaching a national epidemic.

(Satisfaction) III. The drowsy driving problem can be alleviated once we fully understand its causes.

  A. We are poor judges of our own sleeplessness.

  B. Alcohol consumption contributes to becoming sleepy behind the wheel.

  C. Boredom is a contributing factor to becoming tired.

(Visualization) IV. Tragedy can be prevented if we take the proper steps.

      A. Imagine what would happen if the Federal Highway Administration added more rumble strips designed to wake us up when we began to veer off the road.

      B. Imagine what would happen if every car were equipped with cameras that emit rumble strip-like sounds when a driver drifts out of a lane.

(Action) V. There are some steps we can take personally to protect ourselves.

      A. We can take naps to fight fatigue.

      B. We can sleep the recommended seven to eight hours a night.

(Conclusion) I. Six innocent students were killed because someone didn't take action to avoid a tragedy.

II. It is time to get the sleep that could save our lives and the lives of others.

By using Monroe's motivated sequence, the speaker was able to anticipate the questions and concerns of audience members. Observe how the outline established the topic's relevance, isolated the issue, identified a solution, helped receivers visualize the positive outcomes resulting from the solution, and appealed to them to take action.

PERSUADING RESPONSIBLY, STRATEGICALLY, AND CREDIBLY

Whenever we desire others to change their beliefs, attitudes, or behavior, or whenever others seek to influence us, we are engaged in the persuasive process. Responsible persuaders understand that persuasion is not coercion or manipulation. When someone is successful

ETHICS AND COMMUNICATION

Big and Little Lies

To be considered ethical, should you always reveal your real motive for speaking? For years, the pharmaceutical industry has paid tens of thousands of dollars to medical professionals to speak to their colleagues at sponsored events. In many cases the speeches were written for them by the drug companies sponsoring the events. The goal of the speeches was to convince those attending to use the drug company's featured products. The speakers, however, failed to disclose that they were being paid and failed to reveal that their presentations were canned. In your opinion, do such speakers violate the principle that the words you speak should be your own? Should it be required that the audience be informed of the speakers' relationship to event sponsors?

at persuading you to do or believe what she or he asks, you *choose* to think or act differently because you want to, not because you believe that you have to. Ethical persuasion is honest and in the best interest of receivers. Its success is not dependent on the spread of false or misleading information.

What makes one person more persuasive than another? Over 2,000 years ago, the Greek philosopher Aristotle identified three tools that contemporary theorists still believe persuaders should use to achieve their persuasive goals: logos, pathos, and ethos.

Logos is logical proof. The more effective your proof—the more reasonable your arguments and the more convincing your reasons—the greater the chance your message will make rational sense to receivers and the more likely they will be to accept it.

Pathos is emotional proof. Pathos develops empathy and passion in the members of your audience, touching them by arousing their feelings, often through the use of expressive and emotional language and the telling of stories high in human interest. Such stories may contain testimony; recount suffering; arouse fear, anger, or compassion; or use humor. When moved by pathos, audiences are more likely to agree with your message, because they believe what you are sharing could also affect them or a loved one personally.

a katz/Shutterstock.com

Ethos is the audience's judgment of your character or credibility. The more credible your audience believes you to be, the more likely they are to accept you as a source and your message as true.

BUILDING PERSUASIVE CREDIBILITY

Credibility is based on the audience's judgment of a source's expertise on a particular topic. Thus, in large measure, your success as a speaker is based on what the members of your audience think of you—in other words, it is based on their assessment of your credibility or ethos. When we use the term *credibility*, we are *not* talking about what you actually are like but about what members of the audience *perceive* you to be like. As a result, it's important for you to see yourself through their eyes.

For audience members to accept you as credible, they need to believe that you are a person of good character (trustworthy and fair), knowledgeable (trained, competent to discuss your topic, and a reliable source of information), and personable (dynamic, charismatic, active, and energetic). If these criteria are met, then your ideas are likely to receive a fair hearing. However, if audience members believe that you are untrustworthy, incompetent (not sufficiently knowledgeable about your topic), and/or passive (lacking in dynamism), then they are unlikely to respond favorably to your presentation.

It is entirely possible—even probable—that receivers may consider you to be more credible on some topics than others. For example, which statement in the following pairs of

Krista Kennell/Shutterstock.com

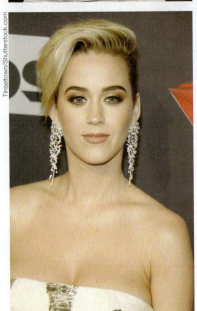

Tinseltown/Shutterstock.com

hypothetical statements would you be more willing to accept given the stated source?

The United States must never negotiate with terrorists. Strength is the only language they will understand.

—former Secretary of State Hillary Clinton

The United States must never negotiate with terrorists. Strength is the only language they will understand.

—Katy Perry

The world of contemporary music has room in it for everyone. The message music sends is tolerance.

—Bono

The world of contemporary music has room in it for everyone. The message music sends is tolerance.

—President of the United States, Donald J. Trump

If you are like most people, you find the first statement in each pair to be more credible. The source cited for the first statement is more closely connected to the subject and therefore likely to be more knowledgeable about the subject.

Regardless of the circumstances, however, it's up to you to build your credibility by giving audience members reasons to consider you competent, trustworthy, and dynamic.[5] To help the audience see you as competent, you can describe your experiences with the subject and suggest why you feel that you've earned the right to share your ideas. You can help receivers see you as trustworthy by demonstrating respect for different points of view and communicating a sense of sincerity. To help them see you as dynamic, speak with energy, use assured and forceful gestures, and create vocal variety.

The audience's assessment of your credibility can change at any time during your presentation or as a result of it. In fact, we identify three stages of credibility:

Initial credibility: the audience's assessment of your credibility before you start to deliver your presentation

Derived credibility: the audience's assessment of your credibility during your presentation

Terminal credibility: the audience's assessment of your credibility at the presentation's end

Of course, if your initial credibility is high, your task becomes easier. But keep in mind that the speech you deliver can help lower or raise your initial credibility. What you say and how you say it are important determiners of credibility.

Evan El-Amin/Shutterstock.com

Frederic Legrand - COMEO/Shutterstock.com

> Visit the interactive e-Book to access the Career Builder feature "Building My Persuasive Credibility in My Community," which will ask you to imagine your role in a scenario where persuasive speaking is key.

GUIDELINES FOR PERSUADING EFFECTIVELY

Persuasion usually occurs in steps. Audience members don't usually surrender their current ways of thinking and behaving easily or, for that matter all, at once. However, if you offer convincing arguments, solid evidence, and a clear message in a number of persuasive speeches that you plan incrementally and deliver over time, receivers gradually may alter their positions.

Your persuasive goal needs to be based on an accurate analysis of the beliefs and attitudes of the audience. For instance, if your goal is to convince members of the National Rifle Association (NRA) that the nation's gun-control laws need overhauling, rather than advocating against the sale of all guns to the public, you might start by working to convince receivers that there are some problems with existing gun laws. Simply reducing the strength of the audience's current stance on gun control would be a step forward that repeated persuasive efforts could then build on. Let's examine what you can do to increase your personal persuasiveness as a speaker.

BE CLEAR ABOUT YOUR GOAL

Clearly define your purpose. Unless you are clear about what you would like your listeners to think, feel, or do, your objective remains fuzzy. To clarify your goal, answer these questions:

- What response do I want from audience members?
- Would I like audience members to think differently, act differently, or both think and act differently?
- Which of their attitudes or beliefs am I trying to change? Why?

CONSIDER RECEIVERS' ATTITUDES AND BELIEFS

How do audience members feel about your goal? Are they in favor of a change? How important is your proposition to them? What's at stake? By understanding the attitudes, beliefs, and values of audience members, you position yourself to overcome the objections they will present when theirs are challenged.

First, you need to try to understand the favorable and unfavorable mental sets or predispositions that audience members bring with them to your speech. That is, you need to understand their attitudes. The more ego-involved the members of your audience are, the more committed they will be to their current attitudes and positions, and the harder it will be for you to reach them.

Second, you need to understand audience member beliefs. Receiver attitudes and beliefs are related to each other as buildings are related to bricks, beams, boards, and so on. Beliefs are the building blocks of attitudes. The belief system is made up of everything that a person agrees is true. The disbelief system is comprised of everything that a person does not think is true. Together, these affect the processing of information.[6] The more central or important a belief is, the harder audience members will work to defend it, the less willing they will be to change it, and the more resistant they will be to your persuasive efforts.

USE THE INFLUENCE PRINCIPLES OF CONSISTENCY AND SOCIAL PROOF

Persuaders need to be aware of two significant principles: We all have a desire to be consistent with what we have already done, and we all respond to social proof.

With regard to the first principle, consistency theory tells us that once we take a stand we tend to behave consistently with that commitment.[7] Therefore, it's important to consider how your speech can engage this tendency toward **consistency**. If you can find a way to get audience members to make a commitment (to take a stand or go on record), you will have set the stage for them to behave in ways consistent with that stand.

With regard to the second principle, one way we determine what is right is to find out what other people think is right.[8] You can use the actions of others to convince your audience that what you are advocating is right. This is **social proof**. In fact, because 95% of us are imitators and only 5% initiators, most audience members will be persuaded more by the action of others than by anything else.[9]

GAIN YOUR AUDIENCE'S ATTENTION

Before you can persuade or convince audience members, you must first capture their attention. Find ways to encourage them to listen. Work to put them in a receptive frame of mind.

Compliment them. Question them. Say something to surprise them. Relate your message directly to their interests. Once you have their attention, it is up to you to hold it.

EVOKE RELEVANT NEEDS AND ISSUES

Balance is a state of psychological health or comfort in which our actions, feelings, and beliefs are in sync. When in a balanced state, we are content and satisfied. Thus, we engage in a continual struggle to keep ourselves in balance. What does this mean for you as a persuasive speaker? If you want to convince audience members to change their attitudes or beliefs, you need first to demonstrate to them that a current situation or state of affairs has created an imbalance in their lives and that what you are advocating for them to believe or do can help to restore their balance. The simple introduction of imbalance, or dissonance, motivates change in thinking or behaving. Thus, speakers may deliberately create dissonance in receivers and then suggest what their receivers need to think or do for them to alleviate their dissonance and restore themselves to a state of balance. It is our inner drive for balance that helps to explain our positive responses to an array of persuasive appeals.

Remember that human behavior depends on motivation. In order to persuade others to believe and do what you would like them to, align your message with their needs and goals. One popular device used to analyze human motivation is a schematic framework devised by the renowned psychologist Abraham Maslow.[10]

In **Maslow's hierarchy of needs**, motivation is depicted as a pyramid, with our most basic needs at its base and our most sophisticated needs at its apex (Figure 15.1). Maslow defined survival (physiological) needs as the basic necessities of life: shelter, food, water, and procreation. The second level of the hierarchy, safety needs, includes the need for security and the need to know that our survival requirements will be satisfied. At the third level are

FIGURE 15.1
Maslow's Hierarchy of Needs

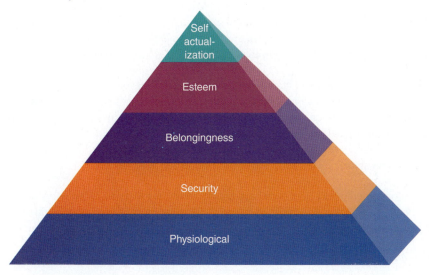

love and belonging needs. Once these are met, our esteem needs can be addressed. Esteem needs include self-respect and the respect of others. Our efforts to succeed often are attempts to satisfy our esteem needs, because success tends to attract respect and attention. At the peak of Maslow's hierarchy is the need for self-actualization. When we satisfy this need, we have realized our potential; that is, we have become everything we are capable of becoming.

Of what value is Maslow's hierarchy to persuasive speakers? The point is that salient needs make salient motives. Your goal is to help audience members connect a proposal you make with their needs.

> Visit the interactive e-Book to access the Skill Builder feature "Climbing the Motivational Pyramid," which will ask you to practice persuasive argumentation with various topics and audiences.

MAKE THE AUDIENCE FEEL AND THINK

Appeals to emotion (pathos) also can add to a speech's power. Why do you think that a student included the following passage in her speech on the issue of Palestinians jailed without trial in Israel? In the passage, a Palestinian prisoner writes to an Israeli officer who himself was imprisoned for refusing to serve as a jailer for the political detainees because of his belief that administrative detention was wrong:

Who are you, officer?

I want to write to you, but first I have to know who you are. I have to know the reasons that moved you to act as you did. I have to know how you arrived at this principled decision of conscience; how you chose such a unique rebellion, so unexpected.

What's your name? Where do you live? What do you do? How old are you? Do you have children? Do you like the sea? What books do you read? And what are you doing now in the cell where you are held? Do you have enough cigarettes? Is there someone who identifies with you over there? Do you ask yourself, "Was it worth paying the price?"

Can you see the moon and stars from the cell window? Have your ears grown accustomed to the jangle of the heavy keys, to the creak of the locks, to the clang of the metal doors? . . . Do you see in your sleep fields of wheat and kernels moving in the wind? Do you see expanses of sunflowers, and are your eyes filled with yellow, green and black hues, and the sun tans you, and you smile in your sleep, and the walls of the cell tumble and fall, and an unknown person waves his hand to you from afar? . . .

Don't you have regrets? Didn't you have doubts when they told you: "They're dangerous; they belong to Hamas, to Islamic Jihad and the Popular Front? Don't you trust our security services? Do you really believe that we are ready to throw innocent people in jail?"

Why do I feel as if I know you? . . .

Anonymous lieutenant, whatever your name is, sleep well; sleep the peaceful slumber of someone whose conscience is clear.

Many changes in human behavior result from messages that combine emotional appeals, designed to make listeners feel, with rational reasons. Remember, it is necessary to appeal to both the hearts and the heads of the audience.

REASON LOGICALLY

Rational or logical proof (logos) includes arguments, reasoning, and evidence that add substance to a speaker's claim. Included in evidence are quotations or testimony from authoritative sources, conclusions from relevant studies and reports (sometimes presented in the form of statistics), and examples and illustrations provided in support of a proposition. By offering logical reasons why the audience should support what you advocate, you increase your chances of persuading them.

Talk show hosts are known for taking a social or political issue and turning it into an argument with a guest. Although such transformations often entertain us, when we analyze them critically, the arguments they make often turn out to be illogical and lacking in sound reasoning principles.

Effective persuaders reason with their audiences by including evidence and arguments to move the audience closer to the speaker's view. In the book *The Uses of Argument*, author Stephen Toulmin shows that reasoning should contain the following components to be effective:

A claim. The proposition or thesis you hope to prove, for example, *College football should be banned.*[11]

Data. Reasons, facts, and evidence for making the claim, for example, College football should be banned *because it has no academic purpose.*

A warrant. A logical and persuasive relationship that explains how you get to your claim from the data you offer, for example, *The primary focus of a college is academics.*

The backing. Supporting information that answers other questions of concern and strengthens the warrant when it is controversial, for example, *Football is a distraction benefiting alumni and coaches but not students or players. Coaches make obscene millions while players receive no compensation. The majority of the student body receives no benefit because tuition costs continue to rise while colleges continue to slash budgets.*

The qualifier. Limitations placed on the connection between the data and warrant, usually symbolized by words such as *often, rarely,* or *always,* for example, *Colleges often lose money on their football programs.*

The rebuttal. Potential counterarguments, at times proffered during the initial argument, for example, *The student athlete is a false concept. Any Division I college player will tell you the demands of the game make the student aspect superfluous.*

In diagram form, the **Toulmin reasonable argument model,** shown in Figure 15.2, suggests that if you state your claim clearly and qualify it so as not to overgeneralize an issue, support it with reasons, and connect it to the evidence you offer via the warrant, you increase the chances of persuading others to accept it.

FIGURE 15.2
Toulmin Reasonable Argument Model

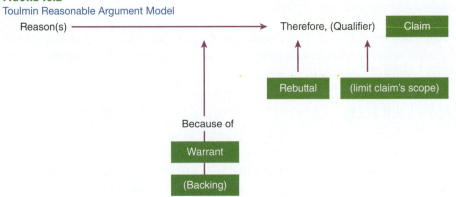

Stephen Toulmin, *The Uses of Argument*. Cambridge University Press. 1958/2003

There are four methods of reasoning you can use to move receivers to affirm or act on your goal: deductive reasoning, inductive reasoning, causal reasoning, and analogical reasoning.[12]

Deductive Reasoning

Deductive reasoning offers general evidence that leads to a specific conclusion. It takes the form of a **syllogism**, which is a pattern used to structure an argument. A syllogism has three parts:

1. A major premise, that is, a general statement or truth; for example, *We must condemn speech that precipitates violence.*

2. A minor premise, which is a more specific statement that describes a claim made about a related object; for example, *A speech by the grand wizard of the Ku Klux Klan will precipitate violence.*

3. A conclusion derived from both the major premise and the minor premise; for example, *Therefore, we must condemn the grand wizard's speech.*

You can evaluate examples of deductive reasoning using these criteria:

- Both the major and minor premises must be true.
- The conclusion must follow logically from the premise.

When using deductive reasoning, you first introduce audience members to your general claim. One of the potential disadvantages of the deductive approach is that those who oppose your claim may tune out and not pay attention to the specifics you offer in the minor premise. They may be preoccupied rebutting your initial contention.

Additionally, keep in mind that wrong premises can lead to faulty conclusions. For example:

All protestors are liberal.

James is a protestor.

James is a liberal.

Inductive Reasoning

Inductive reasoning progresses from a series of specific observations to a more general claim or conclusion. You offer the audience specific reasons why members should support your generalization. The following is an example of inductive reasoning as it moves from the specific to the general—from a series of facts to a conclusion:

Fact: One of every three children violates the "no drinking before the age of 21" law by the age of 12.

Fact: Businesses benefit from violations of the "no drinking before the age of 21" law.

Fact: Parents commonly permit their children to violate the "no drinking before the age of 21" law.

Conclusion: The "no drinking before the age of 21" law is disregarded widely in our society.

You can determine if a speaker's use of inductive reasoning is effective by answering these two questions:

- Are enough reasons given to justify the conclusion drawn?
- Are the instances cited typical and representative?

Causal Reasoning

When using **causal reasoning**—that is, reasoning that unites two or more events to prove that one or more of them caused the other—a speaker either cites observed causes and infers effects, or cites observed effects and infers causes. We frequently use causal reasoning. Something happens and we ask, "Why?" We hypothesize about the effects of actions. The next series of statements illustrates causal reasoning:

Effect: Women are discriminated against in the workplace.

Cause 1: Women earn less than men in most occupations.

Cause 2: Women are not offered the same training opportunities as men.

Cause 3: Society expects women but not men to put family before their jobs.

Of course, causal reasoning can be fallacious. Just because one thing happens and another follows, does not necessarily mean that the first event was the cause of the second event. Evaluate the soundness of causal reasoning by asking:

- Is the cause cited real or false?
- Is the cause cited justified or an oversimplification?

Remember, causal reasoning associates events that precede an occurrence with events that follow. It shows us that antecedents lead to consequences.

Reasoning From Analogy

When **reasoning from analogy**, we compare like things and conclude that because they are comparable in a number of ways, they are comparable in another new respect as well. For example, if you propose that the strategies used to decrease welfare fraud in San Francisco would also work in your city, you would first have to show that your city was like San Francisco in a number of important ways—perhaps the number of people on welfare, the number of social service workers, and the financial resources. If you can convince audience members that the two cities are alike, except for the fact that your city doesn't yet have such a system in place, then you would be reasoning by analogy.

Use these two questions to check the validity of an analogy:

- Are the objects of comparison in the speech alike in essential respects? That is, are they more alike than different?

- Are the differences that do exist between them significant?

The best speakers combine several kinds of reasoning to justify their position. Thus, your reasoning options are open. If you are going to speak ethically, however, you do not have the option of becoming unreasonable—that is, of using an argument that has only the appearance of valid reasoning without the substance.

REASON ETHICALLY

Ethical speakers do not rely on logical fallacies to persuade others. A fallacy is an error in logic. It is flawed reasoning. The following are among the most common fallacies you will want to avoid using or accepting from other speakers:

Hasty Generalizations

You make a hasty generalization when you jump to a conclusion on the basis of too little evidence. To avoid this reasoning error, review enough typical causes to validate a claim.

Post Hoc Ergo Propter Hoc

The phrase *post hoc ergo propter hoc* is Latin for "after this; therefore, because of this." Reasoning suffers from this fallacy when you assume that merely because one event preceded another, the first caused the second. The sunrise is not caused by a rooster crowing. Neither did it rain yesterday because you washed your car.

Slippery Slope

You find yourself on a **slippery slope** when asserting that one action will set in motion a chain of events. Though all choices have consequences, they rarely are as serious as users of slippery slope reasoning would have you conclude. The following is an example of a slippery slope: "First, they ban pornography, next, they'll ban comic books, and finally they'll ban all books."

RED HERRING

When you put a **red herring** in your speech, you lead your audience to consider an irrelevant issue instead of the subject actually under discussion. In an effort to defend the right of individuals to smoke in public places, for example, one speaker tried to deflect his listeners' concerns by focusing instead on the dangers of automobile emissions.

FALSE DICHOTOMY

When you use a **false dichotomy**, you require the audience to choose one of two options, usually polar extremes, when in reality there are many options in between. This polarizes receivers and reduces a complicated issue to a simple choice that all too often obscures other legitimate possibilities. "If you are not part of the solution, you are part of the problem" is an example of the false dichotomy at work.

False Division

A **false division** infers that if something is true of the whole, it is also true of one or more of its parts. For instance, just because a boat can float on water doesn't mean its motor can. What is true of the whole may not be true of its constituent parts.

Personal Attacks

When you engage in name-calling, you give an idea, a group, or a person a bad name ("Little Marco," "Crooked Hillary") so that others will condemn your target without thinking critically or examining the evidence.

Glittering Generalities

A **glittering generality** is the opposite of a personal attack. Here the speaker associates an idea with things that the audience values highly (such as democracy and fairness). Again, however, the aim is to cause audience members to ignore or gloss over the evidence.

Bandwagon Appeals

If everyone jumps off a cliff, would you jump off it, too? Also known as the appeal to popular opinion, the **bandwagon appeal** tells receivers that because "everyone is doing it," they should as well. Just because many people believe something, however, doesn't make it so.

Appeal to Fear

A speaker who instills fear in the audience in order to accomplish his or her goal often ends up pandering to prejudices or escalating their legitimate fears. Once audience members are "running scared" because the dangers alluded to by the speaker have been exaggerated beyond what is reasonably likely to occur, they rarely are able to think critically and rationally about the issue.

Appeal to Tradition

When appealing to tradition, you ask the audience to accept your idea or plan because that's the way it's always been done or to reject a new idea because the old way of doing things is better. Because it was or is that way now doesn't necessary make it better or best.

Appeal to Misplaced Authority

When a speaker asks us to endorse an idea because a well-liked personality who is not an expert on the subject has endorsed it, we should question the request. Name recognition doesn't equal expertise.

Straw Man

When you respond to another's position by distorting, exaggerating, or misrepresenting it, you are depending on a **straw man** in an attempt to create the illusion that you refuted the other's stance successfully. Effectively, you misrepresent another's position to make it easier to attack.

The preceding fallacies are dishonest and undermine reason. Because they distort truth, they are inherently invalid.

CAREER BUILDER: FACT CHECKING PINOCCHIO AT WORK AND IN PUBLIC LIFE

Being able to identify fallacies and other ethical faults that people use in different life spheres, including the workplace or mediated panels, can function as your personal alert system.

Over a period of a week, keep a fact check log: Write down every time you hear a fact that you think has been shaded—either exaggerated or deemphasized—or is contradicted by other information and therefore potentially false or in error. Also pay attention to anyone who takes remarks out of context, plays with the truth, or tells an outright lie in the effort to motivate you and others to change the way you think or behave. Note how many of these occur in the workplace and how many occur in more public spheres.

Examine the "Pinocchio" scale that the *Washington Post* uses to rate and fact check truthfulness in public figures. Is there any public figure you observed the same week to whom you would award either one (uses some fact shading), two (significantly omits or exaggerates information), three (tried to pass off as fact a statement contradicted by other information), or four Pinocchios (tells a whopper of a lie)? What does your research reveal about attitudes toward honesty in workplaces and public spaces?

PROMISE A REWARD

When speaking persuasively, demonstrate how your proposal can satisfy the personal needs of audience members. Stress how your ideas can benefit those whom you are trying to persuade. Reveal to them how it will supply a reward. This reward may not be something tangible; think about the benefits of clean air or an impartial judiciary.

It is important to keep in mind that usually we are preoccupied with how something will benefit us personally. Your audience members, whoever they are, will want something in return for thinking or behaving as you would like them to do.

SKILL BUILDER

Assessing a Persuasive Speech

In the speech that follows, the goal was to persuade the audience that people need to be careful to not spread misinformation and to engage in informed sharing instead. As you review the speech, consider whether it succeeds by responding to these questions:

1. To what extent do you think the speech's introduction and conclusion fulfilled their functions?

2. Was the proposition of the speech clearly stated? What action was the speaker encouraging receivers to take?

3. What evidence is there that the speaker considered the attitudes, beliefs, and values of receivers?

4. Did the speaker demonstrate that there was a problem with the status quo?

5. Was the solution proposed by the speaker to fix the existing problem viable?

6. Was the organizational framework of the speech effective?

7. What might the speaker add or change to improve the speech?

8. Based on this transcript, pretend you are the speaker and develop first an outline and then speaker's notes to use when delivering the speech.

Informed Sharing

Some years back, a story broke reporting that the Los Angeles Police Department had ordered 10,000 jet packs for their officers. Pretty cool, right? Until you realize that they cost 1 million dollars each. Not cool. Especially for a police force that couldn't even buy new squad cars. The story becomes a little less cool when you learn that it isn't even true.

SN 1
Introduction, with surprising piece of information

(Continued)

The story caught on like wildfire and, according to Cracked.com, was even picked up by national news outlets. While this anecdote is amusing, it isn't that important, is it? I mean, who cares about a story now and then that isn't true? However, given the false news stories circulating during the 2016 presidential election and continuing now, there are now more lies on the internet than we ever imagined possible. And I'm not just talking about articles from *The Onion*, or the *Babylon Bee*. Even trusted news sources sometimes get it wrong today.

SN 2
Preview of speech contents

Let's first look at why it's important to know the truth behind the articles that we read and share, then at how we can vet the information we take in, and finally examine the benefits of what I call informed sharing.

According to the World Economic Forum, one of the 10 most important issues facing the world is the "rapid spread of misinformation." In 2014 and 2015, the BBC published an article of 7 news events that were not read. Eighteen more were reported by PolitiFact, and the *Washington Post* highlighted 15 stories that were lies, including one that nude photos of Emma Watson were leaked. Not that it couldn't happen, but it didn't. Saul Eslake writes in a 2006 paper that "Accurate, reliable and timely information is vital to effective decision-making in almost every aspect of human endeavor." This should be the goal of every article we crack open: to educate ourselves in order to improve our decision-making process, and ultimately our lives.

The concern here is that every time we get on Facebook or Twitter, we are bombarded with news stories from all kinds of sources written by all kinds of people, and many of them are not true. And then we click "share" spreading the lies to all our friends, who likely do the same.

This makes it imperative for us, as consumers of media, active or passive, to know the truth behind the article before we share it with others. Plus, there is also the possibility you will embarrass yourself later when you reference a story you thought was true, but that everyone else knows was fake.

SN 3
Rhetorical question involves receiver

In a social web that is woven with posts, stories, articles, and memes, how is any sane person supposed to cipher through all the material they encounter? Well, you can't. But that just means that the things you do choose to read or share need to be taken seriously. The first thing I do when I see a headline that catches my attention is look at the source. If it's not one I know or trust, I am likely to skim over it.

Secondly, Melanie McManus suggests in her article titled, appropriately, *10 Ways to Spot a Fake News Story*, that you check other news sources. This will not only legitimize the article, but cross check the details. If multiple sources are coming to similar conclusions on an issue, then it is probably safe to say that it's legitimate. The headline itself can also be very telling. McManus lists several types of headlines that are almost always a hoax, or at the least, unverifiable. End of the world announcements, or claims to have found cures to major illnesses often fall into this category. Other types of headlines that can be "internet garbage" are those that invoke a deep emotion. When the author uses loaded language that automatically makes you angry, it's possible that they are playing with your emotions just to get you to read the article.

SN 4 Citation of reliable source

Other ways we can avoid sharing bad information is simply reading the article in its entirety. Most people who have any common sense can tell that a story lacks validity just by reading it. It is when we read a headline, and immediately share the story without reading the article itself that we can be contributing to the spread of misinformation.

Informed sharing can stop the spread of internet garbage. By checking our facts, reading entire articles, and reading other articles on the topic, we can reduce the amount of misinformation that is shared. Fact checking may not be important to everyone, but according to Larry Margasak of the News Literacy Project, it is for those "who want to base their decisions on accurate information." And that should be important to everyone. By checking your facts, both those that you read, and those that you share, you add another layer of validity to the information on the web. Finally, by calling out authors or advocates of false stories you find, you not only make yourself look smart, but you educate others.

The spread of misinformation goes beyond the LAPD spending $10 million on jet packs. It reaches into the fabric of our lives in the political, social, religious, and even personal arenas. Lies and false stories permeate the media, and it's up to you to evaluate the sources and determine the validity of the things you believe and share with others. By understanding the dangers of misinformation, doing your part to be informed, and recognizing the benefits of informed sharing, hopefully together we can make the world a smarter place.

SN 5 Reiteration of theme achieves closure

COMMUNICATION SKILLS
Practice Tips for Achieving Persuasive Speaking Goals

Effective persuasive speakers use both reason and emotion to convince others. They provide their receivers solid evidence, effective appeals, and reasons to trust them. Focus on mastering and maintaining these skills as you prepare to present your persuasive speech.

Develop an effective attention getter to pique the audience's interest.

Receivers need to be drawn into your speech. This can be done by connecting your topic to their concerns and demonstrates the serious problem or issue you are addressing.

Research and use the most effective forms of evidence and reasoning.

Offer relevant facts, statistics, examples/illustrations, and testimony in support of your speech's proposition. Reason logically, not fallaciously, to ensure your analysis is airtight.

Appeal to the salient need levels of receivers.

Remember Maslow's hierarchy. Audience members need to have their lower order needs met before you can motivate them using higher level needs. An appeal to esteem needs will likely fail unless the audience's physiological, security, and belongingness needs have been satisfied.

Use both positive and negative appeals to motivate receivers.

In a positive motivational appeal, you note how your proposal benefits audience members and improves their quality of life. However, a negative motivational appeal, such as a fear appeal, attempts to reach receivers by using the possibility that something bad will happen if they don't support what you are advocating. In order for the fear appeal to work, audience members need to believe you are a credible source, the threat is real and not exaggerated, and taking action to remove the threat will restore them to a balanced state.

Never put the best in the middle.

Use both primacy and recency theories as guides when positioning the persuasive points in your speech. Either put your strongest points up front to win receivers to your side early in your presentation, or put your strongest argument last to build momentum as you approach the speech's conclusion. The middle position is weakest. Position arguments strategically to be more persuasive.

> Don't raise your voice; improve your argument.

Desmond Tutu

COMPLETE THIS CHAPTER 15 CHECKLIST

15.1 I can define the purpose of persuasion. ☐

Persuasion is the attempt to change or reinforce the attitudes, beliefs, values, or behaviors of others. Persuasive speaking is the means a speaker uses to modify the thoughts, feelings, or actions of audience members; it is the effort to convince receivers to adopt attitudes and behaviors compatible with the speaker's interests and worldview.

15.2 I can distinguish between types of persuasive propositions and speeches. ☐

The speaker's objective, often referred to as the proposition of the speech, indicates the type of change the speaker seeks in receivers. Most propositions reflect at least one of the following persuasive goals: adoption, discontinuance, deterrence, or continuance of a way of believing or behaving. When speaking on a proposition of fact, you seek to convince others of what is or is not; you argue that something is or is not so. A proposition of value focuses on how good or bad something is; it focuses on the worth of a given statement. When speaking on a proposition of policy, you seek to convince receivers to take action; you argue for what should happen to solve an existing problem.

15.3 I can describe and use Monroe's Motivated Sequence. ☐

Monroe's motivated sequence contains five key phases designed to move receivers toward accepting and acting on a proposition of policy: attention, need, satisfaction, visualization, and action.

15.4 I can discuss what it means to persuade responsibly, strategically, and credibly. ☐

Responsible speakers neither coerce nor manipulate the members of the audience. Strategic persuaders use logos (logical proof), pathos (emotional proof), and ethos (judgments of the speaker's character) to advance their goals. Another word for ethos is credibility. In order for audiences to judge a speaker to be credible, they need to believe that the speaker is a person of good character, knowledgeable, and personable. Assessments of speaker credibility can change during the course of a speech.

15.5 I can follow guidelines for persuading effectively. ☐

Effective persuaders are clear about their goal, consider their receivers' attitudes and beliefs and make sure to gain their attention by highlighting the needs and issues of receivers. Persuaders use both logic and emotion to convince others. They provide their receivers with solid evidence, effective appeals, and reasons to trust them.

15.6 I can apply skills to enhance persuasive presentation effectiveness. □

Persuasive speakers who develop effective attention getters use effective reasoning and evidence, address the salient needs of receivers, motivate by using appropriate positive and negative appeals, and remember not to put the best in the middle are more strategically persuasive.

. . . .

BECOME A WORD MASTER

backing 411

balance 409

bandwagon
  appeal 415

causal
  reasoning 413

claim 411

consistency 408

credibility 405

deductive
  reasoning 412

derived
  credibility 406

ethos 405

false dichotomy 415

false division 415

glittering
  generality 415

inductive
  reasoning 413

initial
  credibility 406

logos 405

Maslow's hierarchy
  of needs 409

Monroe's motivated
  sequence 402

pathos 405

persuasion 397

persuasive
  speech 398

*post hoc ergo
  propter hoc* 414

proposition 398

proposition of
  fact 399

proposition of
  policy 399

proposition of
  value 399

qualifier 411

reasoning from
  analogy 414

reasons
  approach 401

rebuttal 411

red herring 415

refutation
  format 401

slippery slope 414

social proof 408

straw man 416

syllogism 412

terminal
  credibility 406

Toulmin reasonable
  argument
  model 411

warrant 411

iStock/jeffbergen

iStock/monkeybusinessimages

APPENDIX

Interviewing and Developing Professional Relationships

AFTER COMPLETING THIS APPENDIX, YOU SHOULD BE ABLE TO:

16.1 Define and explain the nature of the *employment interview*, including the identification of common interviewee fears.

16.2 Describe tools to use and tasks to complete to secure an interview.

16.3 Explore employment interview specifics, including interview stages, the kinds of questions asked, and the roles and responsibilities of the interviewee.

16.4 Explain the practice of impression management.

16.5 Explain your rights as an interviewee under the law.

16.6 Identify how diversity and technology influence the job search and the interview.

16.7 Apply skills to improve interviewing effectiveness.

> Twenty years from now, the typical American worker will have changed jobs four times and careers twice and will be employed in an occupation that does not exist today.
>
> Jeffrey Hallet

What does a job interview have to do with communication? A lot! In fact, when it comes to the kinds of skills that job recruiters look for, interpersonal skills top the list.[1] An employment interview is much like the interactions users experience on Match.com or other dating sites. However, instead of two people seeking to discover if they have what it takes to make a love connection, during the job interview, the candidate and the employer meet, virtually and/or face-to-face, to decide if the corporate culture and needs of the potential employer's organization are a good match with the applicant's values and abilities.

During the course of our lives, many of us will take part in job interviews. From our vantage point, the job interview incorporates many of the topics and principles of communication that we already have discussed. Culture, self-concept, perception, listening, feedback, language and meaning, nonverbal cues, and assertiveness, together with team building, leadership, and presentation skills, have parts to play in determining your job interviewing success. Let us explore the interview process and what you can do to succeed as an interviewee. ■

THE EMPLOYMENT INTERVIEW: BEYOND CASUAL COMMUNICATION

In comparison to ordinary conversation, the conversations we have during employment interviews are planned and designed to achieve specific objectives. An **employment interview** is the most common type of purposeful, planned, decision-making, person-to-person communication. The individual(s) doing the hiring and the candidate seeking to be hired engage in a process of personal contact and behavior exchange, giving and receiving information, in order for each to make an educated career-related decision.

The employment interview offers a unique opportunity for the potential employer and employee to share meaningful information that should permit each to assess whether their future professional association would be beneficial and productive. It gives all parties to the interview a chance to test each other by asking and answering relevant questions.

EMPLOYER AND EMPLOYEE PERSPECTIVES

During the interview, the employer hopes to gather information about you that your résumé, references, and any personality tests you may have been asked to take do not provide. In general, employers also believe that the person-to-person approach is an effective way to sell their organization to you. As an applicant, you use the interview as an opportunity to seek information about the employer and the job for which you are applying. In the process, based on your interactions with the interviewer, you assess your long-term relationship with the firm and imagine what life in the organization would be like were you to accept a job offer.

Some interviews are over almost before they begin. Why? Because the interviewer asks a question that he or she thinks is easy but that the interviewee cannot answer. For example, on being asked what she had to offer the company, all one interviewee could respond was, "Hmm, that's a toughie." Then she added, "I was more wanting to hear what you could do for me." That candidate did not get the job. How would you have replied if asked, "What do you have to offer the company?"

It is as a result of a hiring or selection interview that we find ourselves accepted or rejected by prospective employers. The better prepared we are to interview, the better our chances will be of performing effectively and realizing our job objectives. Remember, an interview is not "just a talk."[2]

COMMON INTERVIEWEE FEARS

How do you feel about interviewing for a job? Listed here are some fears that interviewees express frequently. Do you share them? To find out, circle the numbers that most accurately reflect your level of interview apprehension: 0 = completely unconcerned; 1 = very mild concern; 2 = mild concern; 3 = more apprehensive than not; 4 = very frightened; 5 = a nervous wreck.

1. I will be asked questions I cannot answer.

    0   1   2   3   4   5

2. I will not dress appropriately for the interview.

    0   1   2   3   4   5

3. I will appear to be nervous.

    0   1   2   3   4   5

4. I will appear incompetent.

    0   1   2   3   4   5

5. The interviewer will cross-examine me.

    0   1   2   3   4   5

6. I will be caught in a lie.

    0   1   2   3   4   5

7. I will talk too much or too little.

    0   1   2   3   4   5

8. I will have poor rapport with the interviewer.

    0   1   2   3   4   5

9. I will undersell or oversell myself.

    0   1   2   3   4   5

10. I won't be hired.

    0   1   2   3   4   5

Total the numbers you circled to arrive at your "interviewee anxiety" score.

Your scores indicate how frightened you are of assuming the role of interviewee. If you accumulated 45 to 50 points, you are extremely nervous; if you scored 35 to 44 points, you are very frightened; if you scored 20 to 34 points, you are somewhat apprehensive; if you scored 11 to 20 points, you are too casual; if you scored 10 points or less, you are not at all concerned—that is, you simply do not care.

Contrary to what you might assume, not being concerned at all about participating in an interview is just as much of a problem as being a nervous wreck, and being too casual can do as much damage as being too frightened. An interviewee should be apprehensive to a degree. If you are not concerned about what will happen during the interview, then you will not care about making a good impression and, as a result, you will not perform as effectively as you could.

SECURING THE INTERVIEW: TOOLS AND TASKS

There are a number of actions you can take to facilitate your job search, including networking, preparing an effective cover letter and résumé, and engaging in preliminary prepping.

NETWORKING AND THE JOB SEARCH

Networking may be responsible for 50% of the people who are looking for a job finding one, which means it makes sense for you to follow the ABCs of networking: **A**lways **B**e **C**onnecting. Although being on social networking sites such as LinkedIn and Facebook can be helpful, they are not the only answers. How else should you be making connections?

Networking is not something you do just when you're looking for a new position. Networking should happen even when things are going well.[3] The following are among the networking options you should consider using:

- Join a professional networking group. This would require you to attend regular meetings, reach out to others, and follow up on leads.

- Seek membership in industry and professional associations in or related to your field. Joining such groups will enable you to make industry connections and stay up with developments in your area of interest.

- Become a member and stay active in your college alumni association. This group can further your career and business life as well as your social life.

- Keep databases containing names of family, friends, and friends of family members. Using friend and family ties—even if weak—can aid your job search.

- Join civic organizations and clubs. You can be active in and make contacts through organizations such as Rotary, the Chamber of Commerce, and parent–teacher associations, or sports teams and clubs.

- Supplement your education by obtaining an internship—even if unpaid. Interning or even volunteering gives you on-the-job experience that can set you apart from your competition. In fact, a survey by the National Association of Colleges and Employers (NACE) reveals that 42.3% of graduates with internship experience receive at least one job offer compared to only 30.7% of graduates without internship experience.[4]

- Use social networks. If not misused or relied on exclusively, social networks can enhance your job search. Social networks such as Facebook, Twitter, and LinkedIn are effective ways to build your contact network by making it easy for you to reach out to former associates and classmates, as well as industry professionals and alumni. A Jobvite survey revealed that 80% of companies either now use, or are planning to use, social networking sites to fill job openings.[5]

Keep in mind, however, that you are more likely to be eliminated from consideration than to be hired because of what you reveal on your social networking sites. According to Careerbuilder.com, companies regularly remove applicants from consideration because of their social networking mistakes such as posting provocative or inappropriate photographs and information or revealing a lack of interpersonal or communication skills.[6] Here is a rule to follow: If you wouldn't want your grandparent to see it, keep it offline!

PREPARING THE COVER LETTER AND RÉSUMÉ

The job of the applicant is to prepare fully for the interview. By completing two documents—a cover letter and a résumé—that are well written and register a positive impression, you provide the interviewer with a preview of who you are and why you are qualified for the open position.

The Cover Letter

The cover letter introduces you to the interviewer. One career coach advises that it even be as short as 120 words because your average reader reads approximately 6 words per second and will give your letter about 20 seconds, providing it looks good to begin with.[7] The well-written cover letter reveals your purpose and whether you are replying to a posting, following up on a referral, or writing an unsolicited introduction. Whatever type of cover letter you write, it should fulfill the following six criteria: (1) It expresses your interest in a position, (2) it tells how you learned of the position, (3) it reviews your primary skills and accomplishments, (4) it explains why these qualify you for the job, (5) it highlights any items of special interest about you that are relevant to your ability to perform on the job, and (6) it contains a request for an interview. Although a résumé is always included with a cover letter, your cover letter needs to make a compelling statement about the value you will bring to the firm. This means putting in two or three important, high-impact accomplishments from your résumé that you think will interest the reader.

The Résumé

The résumé summarizes your abilities and accomplishments. It details what you have to contribute that will meet the company's needs and help solve the employer's problems. Although formats differ, the résumé typically includes the following, in order:

1. Contact information—your name, address, telephone number, and e-mail address
2. Job objective—a phrase or a sentence or two that focuses on your area of expertise
3. Employment history—your job experience, both paid and unpaid, beginning with the most recent
4. Education—schools attended, degree(s) completed or expected, dates of completion, and a review of courses that relate directly to your ability to perform the job
5. Relevant professional certifications and affiliations
6. Community service
7. Special skills and interests you possess that are relevant to the job
8. References—people who agree to elaborate on your work history, abilities, and character; state only that references are available on request unless you are asked to provide specific references at the time you submit your résumé

Because the average résumé gets about 5 seconds of the reader's time, crafting an effective one is essential.[8] Although sending a video résumé may intrigue you, some companies may not accept them. You definitely will want to optimize your résumé for digital eyes, however. It is common for employers to scan résumés, sometimes by hand but increasingly by computer, for particular terms as a means of narrowing the applicant pool. This means taking the time to enumerate your skills clearly up top in your résumé and using key terms from the job ad/listing itself. Be specific. Generalized language won't appeal to the "machine parsers"; keywords will.[9]

Preliminary Prepping

More and more companies are saving time and money by using video-chat software such as Skype or GoToMeeting as their tool of choice when conducting preliminary screenings of job candidates in the effort to narrow the field. While such long-distance interviews may not be as good as meeting face-to-face, they tend to be better than phone calls.

When preparing for such a screening, be sure to:

- Set the stage. Clean up the area so the interviewer isn't looking at a messy room. Consider setting up in front of a curtain or hanging a clean, solid color sheet behind you. Be sure the space where you will be speaking is quiet—no barking dogs or loud music allowed. Make sure there's no bright light behind you, as this will darken your face. Be sure to adjust the microphone settings.

- Dress appropriately. Even though you are not meeting the interviewer in person, you are meeting visually so dress as if you were in the same room as the person interviewing you. Don't wear bold patterns, as these can be distracting, or white, which is noticed on a screen first.

- Be videogenic. The interviewer will also be able to see your facial expressions and read your body language. Remember to sit tall, but don't lean too close to the webcam as this offers the interviewer a close up of your nose. Decide on a flattering angle. Try swiveling your chair toward the corner of your screen. Look at the interviewer's image when she or he talks but when you answer, look at the camera so you make virtual eye contact with the interviewer. To look good on video, you need to look at the video lens. To sound good, you need to use your voice to communicate your enthusiasm for the opportunity being given you.[10] Just like when speaking in public, you need to rehearse aloud and via video prior to "showing up" for the actual virtual interview.

CONDUCTING AN INTERVIEW

Interviews develop in stages. The success of any interview depends on the questions that are asked and answered by both the interviewer and interviewee during each stage.

STRUCTURE: STAGES OF THE INTERVIEW

Most effective interviews have a clear structure. The beginning, or opening, is the segment of the process that provides an orientation to what will come. The middle, or body, is the longest segment and the one during which both parties really get down to business. The end, or close, is the segment during which the participants prepare to take leave of one another.

The Opening

Just as the right kind of greeting at the start of a conversation can help create a feeling of friendliness, so the opening of an interview can help establish rapport between interviewer and interviewee.[12] The primary purpose of the opening is to make it possible for both parties to participate freely and honestly by creating an atmosphere of trust and goodwill and by explaining the purpose and scope of the meeting. Conversational icebreakers and orientation statements perform important functions at this stage. Typical icebreakers include comments about the weather, the surroundings, and current events—or a compliment. The idea is to use small talk to help make the interview a human encounter rather than a mechanical one. Typical orientation remarks include an identification of the interview's purpose, a preview of the topics to be discussed, and statements that motivate the respondent and act as a conduit, or transition, to the body of the interview.

The Body

In the body of the interview, the parties really get down to business. At this point, the interviewer and interviewee might discuss work experiences, including the applicant's strengths, weaknesses, major accomplishments, difficult problems tackled in the past, and career goals. Educational background and activities or interests are relevant areas to probe during this phase of the interview. Breadth of knowledge and the ability to manage time also are common areas of concern.

The Close

During the close of the interview, the main points covered are reviewed and summarized. Because the interview can affect any future meetings between the parties, care must be taken to make the leave-taking comfortable.[13] Expressing appreciation for the time and effort given is important.[14] Neither interviewee nor interviewer should feel discarded. In other words, the door should be left open for future contacts.

QUESTIONS: THE HEART OF THE INTERVIEW

Questions are the primary means of collecting interview data. Not only do questions set the tone for an interview, but they also determine whether the interview will uncover valuable information. Using the interrogatives what, where, when, who, how, and why throughout the interview lays a foundation of knowledge on which to base decisions or conclusions.

During the course of an interview, closed, open, primary, and secondary questions may be used in any combination.[15] **Closed questions** are highly structured and answerable with a simple yes or no, or in a few words. Following are examples of closed questions:

- Where do you live?

- Did you graduate in the top quarter of your class?

- What starting salary do you expect?

Open questions are broader than closed questions and are less restricting or structured. As such, they offer more freedom with regard to the choice and scope of answers. Following are examples of open questions:

- Tell me about yourself.

- How do you judge success?

- Why did you choose to interview for this job?

- Describe a time you failed.

- Describe a time when you failed to solve a conflict.

Open questions give you a chance to express your feelings, attitudes, and values. For example, let's consider the first question above. The question "Tell me about yourself" is not a request for your life story. The interviewer is really asking, "Why should I hire you?" Thus, your task when answering a question like this is to showcase your communication skills by crafting a statement shorter than 2 minutes—about the length of an elevator ride—that lets the interviewer know more about you and what you can do for the company, that is, the benefits you will bring to your employer.[16]

Open and closed questions may be either primary or secondary. **Primary questions** introduce topics or begin the exploration of a new area. "What is your favorite hobby?" and "Tell me about your last job" are examples of primary questions—the first is closed, the second is open.

Interviewers also use **secondary questions**—sometimes called probing questions—to follow up primary questions. They ask for an explanation of the ideas and feelings behind answers to other questions, and frequently they are used when answers to primary questions have been vague or incomplete. Following are examples of secondary questions:

- Go on. What do you mean?

- Can you give me an example?

INTERVIEWEE ROLES AND RESPONSIBILITIES

An employer will use the interview in three ways: to assess your probable performance if hired, to determine if you and the organization's team can work well together, and (assuming the first two goals result in a yes answer) to persuade you that the organization is a good one to work for.

What are your roles and responsibilities during this process? You need to speak and listen and to provide information to help convince the interviewer that you are the right person for the job. At the same time, you need to collect information that will help you decide whether to accept the job if it is offered to you. To accomplish these goals, you need to research the organization to which you are applying and try to anticipate the questions the interviewer will ask. In addition, to help control the interview's direction and content, you also need to plan to ask questions. As your questions are answered, you will learn about work conditions and prospects for advancement.

Assess Yourself

Effective interviewees work hard at self-assessment. In effect, they take stock of themselves to determine who they are, what their career needs and their goals are, and how they can best sell themselves to an employer.

As a prospective interviewee, you will find it useful to prepare by answering the following questions:

- For what types of positions has my training prepared me?

- What has been my most rewarding experience?

- What type of job do I want?

- Would I be happier working alone or with others?

- What qualifications do I have that make me feel I would be successful in the job of my choice?

- What type or types of people do I want to work for?

- What type or types of people do I not want to work for?

- How do I feel about receiving criticism?

- What salary will enable me to meet my financial needs?

- What salary will enable me to live comfortably?

- What will interviewers want to know about me, my interests, my background, and my experiences?

Prepare to Withstand Pressure

In addition to conducting a self-survey, interviewees need to prepare themselves to withstand the pressure of interview situations. Are you prepared to maintain your composure while being stared at, interrupted, spoken to abruptly, or asked difficult questions? Have you practiced enough to keep cool when on the interview hot seat? How do you think you would react if asked tough questions? The following questions are favorites among interviewers. How would you respond to them?

- Tell me about yourself.

- What do you think you're worth?

- What are you good at?

- If we hired you, what about this organization would concern you most?

- What attributes do you think an effective manager should possess?

- What are your short-term goals? How are they different from your long-term goals?

- How has your background prepared you for this position?

- What are your major strengths and weaknesses?

- How would a former employer or instructor describe you?

- Why did you leave your last job?

- What do you consider your greatest accomplishment?

- What is wrong with you?

- What would you do if I told you I thought you were giving a very poor interview today?

- How long do you plan to remain with us if you get this job?

- What would you like to know about us?

Some interviewers prefer to ask even more searching questions, such as the following:

- Tell me how you handled the last mistake you made.

- Are there things at which you aren't very good?

- At your weekly team meetings, your boss unexpectedly begins aggressively critiquing your performance on a current project. What would you do?

Practice in answering questions like these—under both favorable and unfavorable conditions—is essential.[17] It is important that you know what you want to say during the interview and that you use the questions you are asked as an opportunity to say it. Along the way, you can compliment the interviewer by offering comments such as "I think you've touched on something really important."

Identify Personal Qualifications

The interviewer can, of course, consult a résumé to ascertain information about the applicant—educational background and previous positions held, for example. However, gathering enough information to evaluate the personal qualities of an applicant is more difficult. Following is a list of personal qualifications and the questions interviewers typically ask to evaluate them.

1. *Quality*: Skill in managing one's own career

   Question: What specific things have you done deliberately to get where you are today?

2. *Quality*: Skill in managing others

   Question: What are some examples of things you do and do not like to delegate?

3. *Quality*: Sense of responsibility

   Question: What steps do you take to see that things do not fall through the cracks when you are supervising a project?

4. *Quality*: Skill in working with people

   Question: If we assembled in one room a group of people you have worked with and asked them to describe what it was like to work with you, what would they be likely to say? What would your greatest supporter say? What would your severest critic say?

S.T.A.R.

When it comes to answering questions about items listed on your résumé, one career coach suggests using the acronym S.T.A.R (situation, task, action, result) as a guide. For example, let's say your résumé notes that you turned around a sales territory in decline, ultimately increasing sales by 10% in your first year. The interviewer asks: "How did you do that?" Your job is to walk the interviewer through the process by revealing the **s**ituation you faced, how you assessed your **t**ask, the **a**ction you took, and the **r**esult you achieved.[18]

Interview Categories

Most employment interviews can be grouped into one of three categories: the behavioral, the case, and the stress interview.

In the **behavioral interview**, an employer is looking for specific examples from the prospective employee of times when he or she has exhibited specific skills. When asked a question such as "Tell me about a time you acted in a leadership role," the interviewee might respond, "I was the director of a fund-raising group," or "I was an officer in Women in Communications."

In the **case interview**, a company presents the interviewee with a business case and asks him or her to work through it. To help prepare yourself for such an interview, check out the company website beforehand. Some companies post sample cases on their sites.

The third type of interview, the **stress interview**, typically includes more than one interviewer firing questions at the interviewee to see how that person handles himself or herself during a stressful situation.

Remember to Ask Questions

Because the interview is a conversation and not an interrogation, you should ask questions of the interviewer as a means of demonstrating interest in the job and the company.[19] When you ask questions, the interview becomes more balanced. What kinds of questions should you ask when in the interviewee role? You should not ask questions that you can answer easily by visiting the company's website. You should, however, ask questions that seek clarification; for example, "I read on your site that you will be introducing new products. Could you tell me more about how you plan to roll them out?"

> Visit the interactive e-Book to access the Skill Builder feature "Let's Get Tough," which presents an example of a tough job interview question and discusses how different answers may come across to the interviewer.

In general, interviewees ask questions about the company and corporate culture (rather than about salary or benefits), the industry, the position, and the people in the company. Following are some examples.

- Why is this position open?

- What would you say are the main challenges of this job?

- What will be the priorities in the first 90 days?

- With whom will I be working?

- How is the department organized, and what will my role be?

- How will performance be measured and evaluated?

- How are conflicts resolved?

- How are decisions made?

- Why do you like working here?[20]

To be effective, both interviewer and interviewee need to work hard. Questioner and respondent constantly exchange information. While one speaks, the other conveys nonverbal information through posture, facial expression, gestures, and so on. You may stop talking during an interview, but that does not mean that you stop communicating. Know what you want to accomplish with your verbal and nonverbal messages.

IMPRESSION MANAGEMENT AND INTERVIEWEE PRESENCE

How well do we need to know someone before we believe we understand him or her? Experience says not very long. According to psychologists Nalini Ambady and Frank Bernieri, the power of first impressions arms us with a kind of prerational ability or intuition for making judgments about others that colors the other impressions we gather over time.[21] It becomes a self-fulfilling prophecy. We assume that the way someone behaves in an interview is indicative of the way that a person always behaves. Thus, in an effort to manage the impression the interviewer forms of the interviewee, the interviewee makes a concerted effort to influence the interviewer's perceptions of his or her image and interview presence by engaging in behavior that causes the interviewer to view the interviewee favorably.

The adage that first impressions count apparently holds true for job interviews.[22] In fact, the word *interview* is derived from the French word *entrevoir* meaning "to see another" or "to meet." What happens when an interviewer and an interviewee meet for the first time? What variables influence the impressions the interviewer forms of the interviewee? Most interviewers make their decisions about an applicant during the course of the interview. In fact, although most decide in the last quarter of the interview whether or not to invite the applicant back, a bias for or against the candidate is established earlier in the interview, often during the first four to six minutes.

What can you do to help the interviewer judge you positively from the outset? Look like the professional the interviewer wants to hire. Keep in mind that you are going on an interview and not a date. Be smart going in. Know about the company, the competition, and industry trends. Be enthusiastic and show that you are happy to be there. Smile, sit up, lean slightly forward, and maintain eye contact. Communicating a high level of energy works in your favor. Vary your pitch and volume. The interviewer will view you more positively if you do not speak in a monotone, whisper, or shout and if you speak without exhibiting vocal hesitations or signs of physical tension.[23]

According to researcher Lois Einhorn, the amount of time allotted for an interview also sends an important message.[24] She found that interviewees who were not hired had participated in shorter interviews than those of successful applicants. She also found that successful interviewees spoke a greater percentage of the time than their unsuccessful counterparts. In fact, the successful applicants spoke for some 55% of the total interview time, whereas the unsuccessful applicants spoke only 37% of the time. Seeming to control the interview also leaves an impression. In Einhorn's research, successful applicants initiated 56% of the comments made during the interviews, whereas unsuccessful applicants were viewed as less assertive or involved—they initiated only 37% of the comments. When interviewing, it is important for you to send messages that you are active, not passive.

Companies are toughening their interviews, using more challenging techniques to sort through job candidates. Thus, you need to be prepared so that you make as good an impression as possible. Here's where your team-building and presentation skills come in handy. You need to equip yourself to propose solutions to hypothetical or real problems. Employers want to know if you can think on your feet and stay composed. You need to prepare yourself to deliver an on-the-spot presentation about yourself—sometimes in front of your competition—so pay attention to their presentations as well, because employers also want to see how you treat others. Some employers conduct group interviews; in this case, try to pay attention to each person, addressing each by name, if possible.

The interviewer's assessment of you will determine whether or not you get the job. The following are some of the negative factors that turn off the interviewer and lead to applicant rejection:

- Arrogance

- Lack of motivation

- Immaturity

- Poor communication skills

- Unclear goals

- Unwillingness to relocate or travel

- Deficient preparation for the interview

- Lack of experience

- Excessive sloppiness or slickness in appearance[25]

In contrast, factors associated with receiving job offers include the following:

- A pleasant personality (likableness)

- Enthusiasm

- Interpersonal skills

- Ability to function as part of a team

- Knowledge of the field

- Computer literacy

- Creativity

- Clear purpose and goals

- Flexibility and the ability to handle change

- Confidence in what you are doing and who you are

- Integrity and moral standards

- Global perspective

- Sense of humor [26]

You can cement a positive image in three ways.

1. Never ask about vacation, company benefits, and personal days during the first interview. Work, instead, to display your knowledge of the company, understand its goals, and identify how you fit in by asking questions that touch on strategic and tactical issues.

2. End an interview by reaffirming your interest in the position and restating why you believe you will be an asset to the company.[27] View this as your sales opportunity; that is, ask for the order. Saying something like "I'm very interested in the position. I would welcome the opportunity to work with you and your team" helps communicate that you really want the job.

3. Remember to send a thank-you note or e-mail to the person or people who interviewed you. An essential step in the job-seeking process, sending a thank-you note is a task job seekers most often forget.[28] One successful job candidate sent her thank-you note via overnight carrier. Another who had interviewed for a job with Google delivered a handwritten thank-you along with cupcakes for the recruiter and five other officials who interviewed him. One letter of the Google name appeared atop each cupcake.[29] Do you think he was hired?

LOOKING AT THE LAW: ILLEGAL INTERVIEW QUESTIONS

We have seen that some interview questions are tough and probing. Others that concern age, race, marital status, and other personal characteristics protected under antidiscrimination statutes are illegal to ask. Despite this, surveys reveal that half of all Americans report being asked questions that could be used to discriminate against a protected class.[30] The Equal Employment Opportunity Commission (EEOC) is the arm of the federal government responsible for monitoring discriminatory practices in hiring decisions. The guidelines are updated periodically, and the laws of the EEOC apply in all 50 states.

According to the EEOC, criteria that are legally irrelevant to job qualifications are discriminatory. Interviewees are protected from answering questions about race, ethnicity, marital status, age, sex, and disability. Some states have additional protected categories. It is important for both interviewers and interviewees to realize which questions are legally impermissible in employment interviews. Both parties to the interview have to be well versed in their rights to be able to protect them. The determining factor in whether a question is lawful is simple: Is the information sought relevant to your ability to perform the job? The following are among the most commonly asked illegal questions.

- Are you physically disabled?

- How old are you?

- Are you married?

- Do you have or are you planning to have a family?

- What political party do you belong to?

- Is English your native language?

- What is your religion?

- Will you need to live near a mosque?

- Is it hard for you to find child care?

- Are you a United States citizen?

- Where were your parents born?

- Who lives with you?

- When did you graduate from college?

- What was the date of your last physical exam?

- To what clubs or social organizations do you belong?

- Have you had any recent or past illnesses or operations?

- How is your family's health?

- If you have been in the military, were you honorably discharged?

- What's your current or most recent salary?

The last question on the list is our most recent addition. Taking past salary into account when setting starting pay at a new job often handicaps women and those whose pay disparity otherwise would follow them from one job to another.[31]

On the other hand, it is legal to ask the following questions:

- Are you authorized to work in the United States?

- What languages do you read or speak fluently (if relevant to the job)?

- Are you over 18?

- Would you relocate?

- Would you be willing to travel as needed?

- Would you be able and willing to work overtime as necessary?

- Do you belong to any groups that are relevant to your ability to perform this job?

- What education do you have?

- Have you ever been convicted of a crime?

- In what branch of the armed forces did you serve?[32]

What if an interviewer asks you an illegal question? You can object diplomatically and remind the interviewer that the question is inappropriate. Doing so, however, can make the interviewer defensive and less willing to select you for the job. Another option is to respond to the illegal question with only information that the interviewer legally could have sought from you. That is, you handle the question by answering the part you do not object to without providing any information you do not wish to offer. For example, if the interviewer asks whether English is your native language, you can respond, "I am fluent in English." If he or she asks whether you belong to a political group, you can respond, "The only groups with which I affiliate that are relevant to this job are the Public Relations Society of America and the American Society for Training and Development."

DIVERSITY, TECHNOLOGY, AND THE INTERVIEW

Both diversity and technology influence the nature of present-day interviews, affecting the practices and performance of the participants.

CULTURE AND THE INTERVIEW

Culture influences the conduct of interviewees and interviewers during interviews. For example, in collectivistic cultures such as those in China, Japan, and Korea, interviewees habitually display modesty. If Americans, who are used to stressing their positive qualities, were interviewing in any of those countries, they could be perceived as arrogant and self-centered. On the other hand, if people from a collectivistic culture were to interview in the United States, they could come across as unassertive, lacking in confidence, and unprepared to assume leadership. Whereas Western culture encourages people to be assertive and showcase strengths, Eastern culture traditionally teaches members to be more modest and humble about their personal achievements, qualifications, and experience. Similarly, Native American culture teaches that cooperation is a benefit and that one leads through deeds, not words. Thus, not wanting to appear boastful, Native Americans could also be hesitant to discuss their personal strengths.[33]

There also are gender differences in what employees seek in a job. Survey results reveal that most men value compensation above all else, whereas most women put employee benefits first. Compensation is ranked third on most women's lists, after opportunities for skill development.[34] Job postings also can lead to gender differences in response rates by applicants. For example, "pink-collar" jobs often are sought by women, which can be a turn-off for men, even though they are often in growth areas like health care. Researchers attribute this to the feminine language used in the job ads, which attracts women to respond disproportionately. The same is true of job postings for careers traditionally dominated by men with words in the ads catering to male stereotypes. Employers are being cautioned to use gender-neutral words in ads to try and attract an equal number of responses from male and female candidates.[35]

Age also influences what employees desire most in a job. In contrast with all other groups, job candidates in their 30s do not even rank benefits among their top five concerns. What is important to most persons in this age bracket are opportunities to develop skills, chances for promotion, compensation, vacations, and an appealing culture and colleagues.[36]

Interviewers need to be sensitive to and demonstrate their respect for all cultures. Not hiring someone on the basis of age, sexual preference, national origin, or religion is illegal. Despite this, many Muslim workers report having thought about changing their last names to avoid alienating potential employers.[37] Similarly, despite corporate diversity efforts, African Americans still face discrimination. Candidates with White-sounding names are about one-third more likely to be invited to interview than candidates with Black-sounding names who have similar work experience and credentials.[38] Would you ever change you name if you thought doing so would help you get the job you want? Why or why not?

The good news, however, is that an increasing number of companies are seeking to increase employee diversity in the effort to create more effective teams and evolve ways of reaching consumers of varied ethnicity, age, gender, and sexuality.[39]

TECHNOLOGY AND THE JOB SEARCH

The Web has changed how we search for and find jobs. Job searchers now regularly search online classified ads for job opportunities. In addition to Monster.com, aggregator sites such as Indeed.com and SimplyHired.com link you to job ads all over the Internet, including companies' career pages. Additionally, networking websites such as LinkedIn can help you connect with business professionals in your field without your knowing them well or at all.[40]

Applicants should use a company's home page to get background information on the organization and its culture and to find instructions on how to apply for a job. Following are some websites you can consult to gather information on companies and jobs.

Company Information

www.wsj.com the website of *The Wall Street Journal*

www.nytimes.com the website of *The New York Times*

www.glassdoor.com a site that lets you access company reviews and salary information

Job Information

http://stats.bls.gov the Bureau of Labor Statistics website, which offers information on positions by state, listing the average salary

www.careerbuilder.com a job search site

www.snagajob.com a source of hourly employee information

www.monster.com a job search and career advice site

Usenet newsgroups, listserv mailing lists, and blogs are three other Internet resources you can use to learn about employment possibilities and company cultures. Of the three, blogs are becoming increasingly popular in electronic recruiting, functioning as a prime means that applicants use to find out about companies. Often, they contain information such as what it's like to work at a company as well as what's going on in an industry.[41]

Personal Job-Seeking Websites

Job seekers can also create their own home pages, featuring both their résumés and business cards.[42] By posting your résumé on a home page, you increase the likelihood that an employer looking for someone with your background and qualifications will access your résumé and contact you directly. It also is possible to create a multipage, online portfolio that contains samples of your work, a page of references, and testimonials. It is advisable to provide your résumé in different formats such as Microsoft Word, ASCII text, and PDF. This gives the employer a choice regarding how to download it. When posting your résumé online, you may want to be more private. You might, for example, not include your home address but feature an e-mail address. Some people use a Google Voice phone number that keeps your actual phone number private.

A variety of online resources and computer programs exist to help you prepare your résumé. Many provide you with templates that you can complete or customize. You can also post your résumé online at a number of job listing sites.

Electronic Résumés

More and more companies require potential employees to submit electronic résumés, which can be machine read.[43] Electronic résumés require standard formats. Line breaks and block letters may be used, but no boldface type, underlining, or bullets. The text is all that matters. Once the résumé is added to the company's tracking system, when a job becomes available, the employer can efficiently search the résumés contained in the database by the keywords that describe a candidate qualified for the position. In cases such as these, you may also be asked to submit a résumé in the PDF file format, which can be formatted more attractively.

To facilitate the initial résumé screening, which will be done by a bias-free computer, an electronic résumé should typically contain blocks of keywords for each job you have held. Unlike your traditional résumé, which probably contains actions such as "communicates well," your electronic résumé should contain nouns such as "organizational skills." A number of Internet sites can help you prepare an electronic résumé.

Online Interviews and Assessment

As we've also noted, employers use webcams to add flexibility to currently available interviewing channels. By conducting a webcam-based interview, employers are able to conduct preliminary conversations with candidates geographically dispersed from them. In increasing numbers, in addition to telephones and video conferences, employers also are conducting interviews via e-mail and chat groups. Although these channels do not enable interviewer and interviewee to shake hands with each other, and despite the fact that such interviews will probably not replace face-to-face interviews, they do expand the information resources used by organizations and can be used to supplement face-to-face interviews.[44]

Some applicants may endure multiple rounds of interviews and assessments before they even encounter a human. More and more frequently, candidates for a job are being asked to play a set of online games and submit videos of themselves responding to questions about how they would tackle challenges of the job. These games have been designed to assess skills such as ability to concentrate under pressure and short-term memory. Algorithms then are used to sort the candidates. The last step is the person-to-person interview.[45]

Online Blunders to Avoid

You will want to avoid the following five blunders commonly made by those who use the Internet to search for a job.[46]

1. *Mismatched cover letters.* The interviewee sends a letter that expresses the desire to put skills to work for a company when applying for a job with another company.

2. *Goofy personal e-mail addresses.* Using a name like Snickerdoodle@pastrylover.com or egotisticalking@sold.com can make you look like a less than serious candidate. Use a professional-sounding e-mail address instead.

3. *Fun with fonts.* It is a mistake to use bright colors and exotic fonts in résumés or e-mails. Unless you are applying to be a graphic designer, use a common typeface like Times New Roman and black text.

4. *Playing out of your league.* Because the Internet makes applying for a job so easy, many applicants apply for jobs for which they are not qualified.

5. *Thinking "send" is the end.* Your work is not done when you click "send." Networking and follow-up remain essential components of any job search. Indeed, 61% of people surveyed report that networking and referrals remain the best sources for new jobs.[47]

Finally, here are some other warnings.

1. Do not post anything online, including on blogs and discussion boards, that you would not want an employer to see.

2. Do not request an interview or follow-up using the too casual tone of text-speak. Managers who were interviewed believe that text-speak, including the use of emoticons, has no place in interview communications.[48]

Getting a job today has much in common with reality-show contests. Hundreds of job candidates compete, but there will be just one winner. You want to be awarded the rose!

> Each party has questions in the interview—both you and the employer. The essence of the interview is to find out the answer to those questions.
>
> Richard N. Bolles

COMPLETE THIS CHAPTER 16 CHECKLIST

16.1 I can define and explain the nature of the *employment interview*, including a description of common interviewee fears. ☐

The employment interview is the most common type of purposeful, planned, decision-making, person-to-person communication. Among the fears interviewees have when it comes to interviewing for a job are not being able to answer questions, not dressing properly, appearing nervous, and not being hired.

16.2 I can describe tools to use and tasks to complete in order to secure an interview. ☐

To secure an interview, interviewees need to prepare an effective cover letter and résumé and prepare themselves for a webcam-based screening interview.

16.3 I can explain the stages of an interview, the kinds of questions asked, and interviewee roles and responsibilities during employment interviews. ☐

Effective interviews are well-structured interactions. They have a beginning, which provides an orientation to what is to come; a middle, when the participants get down

to business; and an end, when the main points are reviewed and the participants take leave of one another. Good interviewees work hard during an interview, functioning simultaneously as information seekers, information givers, and decision makers.

16.4 I can explain the practice of impression management. ☐

Impression management, in the context of interviewing, has the interviewee making a concerted effort to influence the interview's perceptions of his or her image by engaging in behavior that causes the interviewer to view the interviewee favorably. To accomplish this, the interviewee dresses professionally, is knowledgeable about the company, uses verbal and nonverbal cues to convey his or her enthusiasm for the job, never asks about benefits during the first interview, ends the interview by affirming interest in the position, and remembers to send a thank-you note following the interview.

16.5 I can identify my rights as an interviewee under the law. ☐

According to the Equal Employment Opportunity Commission, criteria that are legally irrelevant to job qualifications are discriminatory. Interviewees in all states are protected from answering questions about race, ethnicity, marital status, age, sex, disability, and arrest records.

· ·

16.6 I can identify how diversity and technology affect the job search and the interview. ☐

To avoid misunderstandings, interviewees need to be aware of how cultural differences can affect the interview. They also need to be adept at using the Web to research job openings and promote themselves.

· ·

16.7 I can apply skills to improve interviewing effectiveness. ☐

When interviewees prepare thoroughly, demonstrate the ability to send and receive clear messages, listen expertly, communicate with conviction, use powers of observation, critically consider the interview's outcome, and commit to continually assessing personal progress, they improve their chances of succeeding.

· ·

BECOME A WORD MASTER

behavioral
   interview   435

case interview   435

closed
   questions   431

employment
   interview   426

open
   questions   432

primary
   questions   432

secondary
   questions   432

stress
   interview   435

Answer Key

Blindering Problem (page 68)

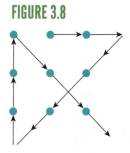

FIGURE 3.8

Glossary

A

accommodation   the means by which co-culture members maintain their cultural identity while striving to establish relationships with members of the dominant culture

accommodator   a person who, when faced with a conflict, overvalues the maintenance of relationships and undervalues the achievement of his or her own goals

achieved leader   a person who exhibits leadership without being appointed

acquaintanceships   relationships with persons we know by name and with whom we converse when the chance arises

action-oriented listener   a person focused on task and concerned with outcomes—what will be done, by whom, and when

affection   the need to experience emotionally close relationships

aggressiveness   the expressing of one's own thoughts and feelings at another's expense

appreciative listening   listening for enjoyment or relaxation

artifactual communication   the use of personal adornments

assertiveness   the expressing of one's thoughts and feelings while displaying respect for the thoughts and feelings of others

assimilation   the means by which co-culture members attempt to fit in with members of the dominant culture

attitudes   predispositions to respond favorably or unfavorably toward a person or subject

attribution theory   a theory describing how we explain our own behavior and that of others by coming up with motives and causes

autocratic leader   authoritarian leader, directive leader

avoider   a person who, when faced with a conflict, uses the unproductive strategy of mentally or physically fleeing the situation

avoiding   the relationship stage during which the participants intentionally avoid contact

B

backing   support that answers concerns of others

balance   a state of psychological comfort in which one's actions, feelings, and beliefs are related to one another as one would like them to be

bandwagon appeal   an appeal to popular opinion

bar graph   graph used to show the performance of one variable over time or to contrast various measures at a point in time

behavioral interview   an employment interview in which an employer looks for the employee to provide specific examples of specific skills

beliefs   confidence in the truth of something

bonding   the relationship stage in which two people make a formal commitment to each other

brainstorming   a technique designed to generate ideas

breadth   the number of topics one discusses with another person

bypassing   miscommunication that occurs when individuals think they understand each other but actually miss each other's meaning

C

case interview an employment interview in which the interviewee is presented with a business case by the employer and asked to work through it

causal reasoning speculation about the reasons for and effects of occurrences

cause-and-effect order an organizational format that categorizes a topic according to its causes and effects

channels media through which messages are sent

chronemics the study of the use of time

chronological order an organizational format that develops an idea using a time order

circumscribing the relationship stage in which both the quality and the quantity of communication between two people decrease

civil inattention the polite ignoring of others so as not to infringe on their privacy

claim debatable conclusion or assertion

closed questions highly structured questions answerable with a simple yes or no or in a few words

closure the tendency to fill in missing perceptual pieces in order to perceive a complete world

co-cultures groups of persons who differ in some ethnic or sociological way from the parent culture

collectivistic cultures cultures in which group goals are stressed

communication the deliberate or accidental transfer of meaning

communication apprehension fear of communication, no matter what the context

communication presence the composite of characteristics we present both in the physical and online world

communication privacy management theory theory that describes the establishment of the boundaries and borders that we decide others may or may not cross

comparison level an expectation of the kinds of rewards and profits we believe we ought to derive from a relationship

comparison level for alternatives the comparing of rewards derived from a current relationship with ones we expect to get from an alternative relationship

competitive forcer a person who, when faced with a conflict, adopts a win-lose orientation in which the attaining of personal goals is paramount

competitive goal structure a goal structure in which members hinder one another's efforts to obtain a goal

competitive set a readiness to perceive a conflict in all-or-nothing terms

complementarity the attraction principle that states that opposites attract

comprehensive listening listening to gain knowledge

compromiser a person who, when faced with a conflict, tries to find a middle ground

configural formats organizational patterns that are indirect and inexplicit

conflict perceived disagreement

connotative meaning subjective meaning; one's personal meaning for a word

consistency the desire to maintain balance in our lives by behaving according to commitments already formed

contact cultures cultures that promote interaction and encourage displays of warmth, closeness, and availability

content conflict a disagreement over matters of fact

content-oriented listener a person more concerned with what is said than with the people involved or their feelings

context the setting

control the need to feel we are capable and responsible and are able to exert power and influence in our relationships

cooperative goal structure a goal structure in which the members of a group work together to achieve their objectives

cooperative set a readiness to share rewards to resolve conflicts

cost–benefit/social exchange theory the theory that we work to maintain a relationship as long as the benefits we receive outweigh the costs

crazy-making behaviors conflict-producing techniques that can figuratively drive a partner crazy

credibility the receiver's assessment of the competence, trustworthiness, and dynamism of a speaker

critical listening listening to evaluate the worth of a message

critical thinking the careful and deliberate process of message evaluation

cultivation theory a theory propounded by George Gerbner and colleagues focusing on the mass media's ability to influence users' attitudes and perceptions of reality

cultural imperialism the expansion of dominion of one culture over another culture

cultural pluralism adherence to the principle of cultural relativism

cultural relativism the acceptance of other cultural groups as equal in value to one's own

culturally confused lacking an understanding of cultural difference

culture a system of knowledge, beliefs, values, customs, behaviors, and artifacts that are acquired, shared, and used by members during daily living

D

deductive reasoning reasoning that moves from the general to the specific

defensive behavior behavior that occurs when one perceives a threat

definitions explanations of what a stimulus is or what a word or concept means

democratic leaders leaders who represent a reasonable compromise between authoritarian and laissez-faire leaders

demographic profile a composite of characteristics, including age; gender; educational level; racial, ethnic, or cultural ties; group affiliations; and socioeconomic background

denotative meaning dictionary meaning; the objective or descriptive meaning of a word

depth a measure of how central the topics you discuss with another person are to your self-concept

derived credibility a measure of a speaker's credibility during a speechmaking event

DESC script a four-step (describe, express, specify, and consequences) response that facilitates self-asssertion when in conflict

designated leader a person given the authority to exert influence within a group

dialectical tensions tensions that occur when opposing goals meet

dialogic listening listening that focuses on what happens to people as they respond to each other, work toward shared understanding, and build a relationship

differentiating the relationship stage in which two people identified as a couple seek to regain unique identities

digital and social media forms of electronic media through which users create online communities and share ideas, personal information, and other content

digital divide information gap

disclaimers remarks that diminish a statement's importance

distinctiveness theory the theory that states that a person's own distinctive traits are more salient to him or her than are the more prevalent traits possessed by others in the immediate environment

diversity the recognition and valuing of difference

dominant culture the culture in power; the mainstream culture

E

effect the communication outcome

ego conflict a disagreement in which persons believe that winning or losing is tied to their self-worth, prestige, or competence

emoji a small digital image or relational icon used to express an idea or emotion

emoticons symbols that replace nonverbal cues during machine-assisted communication

emotional contagion the catching of another person's mood

emotional intelligence the ability to motivate oneself, to control impulses, to recognize and regulate one's moods, to empathize, and to hope

emotional isolationists persons who seek to avoid situations that may require the exchange of feelings

empathic listening listening to help others

empathy experiencing the world from a perspective other than our own

employment interview   the most common type of purposeful, planned, decision-making, person-to-person communication

equivocate   use purposefully vague language to finesse a response

essentials of communication   those components present during every communication event

ethics   the moral principles, values, and beliefs that members of society use to guide behavior

ethnocentrism   the tendency to see one's own culture as superior to all others

ethos   audience's judgment of speaker's character or credibility

euphemism   a pleasant word that is substituted for a less pleasant one

evaluative feedback   a positive or negative judgment

examples   representative cases

experimenting   the relationship stage during which we begin to probe the unknown, often through the exchange of small talk

extemporaneous speech   a speech that is researched, outlined, and delivered after careful rehearsal

external feedback   a response from another

F

facework   the means used to present a public image

facial management techniques   the means we use to control the expressions we reveal to others

fact   that which is known to be true based on observation

false dichotomy   reasoning requiring the audience to choose one of two options when, in reality, there are many options in between

false division   the polarization of options when, in fact, many options exist

feedback   information returned to a message source

feminine cultures   cultures that value tenderness and relationships

figure–ground principle   a strategy that facilitates the organization of stimuli by enabling us to focus on different stimuli alternately

fixed-feature space   space that contains relatively permanent objects

formative feedback   timed negative feedback

friendly relations   the friendship stage in which we explore whether we have enough in common to continue building a relationship

friendships   relationships characterized by enjoyment, acceptance, trust, respect, mutual assistance, confidences, understanding, and spontaneity

functional theory   the leadership suggesting that several members of a group should be ready to lead because various actions are needed to achieve group goals

Fundamental Interpersonal Relations Orientation   a theory of interpersonal relations highlighting the needs for inclusion, control, and affection and their influence on interpersonal dynamics

G

gender-lects   Deborah Tannen's term for language differences attributed to gender

glittering generality   reasoning that associates an idea with things that the audience values highly

globalization   the increasing economic, political, and cultural integration and interdependence of diverse cultures

gossip mill   the network through which unverified information is spread

grapevine   a type of informal, conversational network existing in organizations

grief process   a mourning process composed of five stages: denial, anger, guilt, depression, and acceptance

grit   a combination of passion and perseverance for a singularly important goal, together with resilience and a tolerance for feeling frustrated

group   a collection of individuals who interact verbally and nonverbally, occupy certain roles with respect to one another, and cooperate to accomplish a goal

group climate   the emotional atmosphere of a group

group communication   interaction with a limited number of persons

group goals   a group's motivation for existing

group norms   informal rules for interaction in a group

group patterns of communication patterns of message flow in a group

group role-classification model a model that describes functions participants should seek to assume and to avoid in groups

group structure group member positions and roles performed

groupthink an extreme means of avoiding conflict that occurs when groups let the desire for consensus override careful analysis and reasoned decision making

H

habitual pitch the characteristic pitch one uses

haptics the study of the use of touch

hearing the involuntary, physiological process by which we perceive sound

heterogeneous audience an audience characterized by diversity

high self-monitors people highly attuned to impression management efforts

high-context communication a tradition-bound communication system that depends on indirectness

high-intensity conflict a conflict in which one person intends to destroy or seriously hurt the other

high power distance cultures cultures based on power differences in which subordinates defer to superiors

homogeneous audience an audience whose members are of approximately the same age and who have similar characteristics, attitudes, values, and knowledge

human capital what we know, our skills, knowledge, and experience

HURIER model a model of listening focusing on six skill areas or stages

hurtful messages messages designed to upset or to cause emotional pain that further hampers trust

I

"I" messages nonevaluative responses that convey our feelings about the nature of a situation

illustrations stories; narrative pictures

impression management the creation of a positive image designed to influence others

impromptu speech a speech delivered spontaneously or on the spur of the moment

inclusion the need for social contact

individualistic cultures cultures in which individual goals are stressed

inductive reasoning reasoning that moves from specific evidence to a general conclusion

inference an assumption with varying degrees of accuracy

infographics visuals that are composites of information, illustration, and design

informal space space that is highly mobile and can be quickly changed

information anxiety psychological stress attributed to information overload

information overload the situation that occurs when the amount of information provided by a speech maker is too great to be handled effectively by receivers

informative speech a speech that updates and adds to the knowledge of receivers

initial credibility a measure of how an audience perceives a speaker prior to the speechmaking event

initiating the relationship stage during which contact is first made

integrating the relationship stage in which two people are identified as a couple

intensifying the relationship stage during which two people become good friends

intercultural communication interaction with individuals from different cultures

interethnic communication interaction with individuals of different ethnic origins

internal feedback a response one gives oneself

internal preview content that prepares the audience for what follows in a speech

internal summaries rhetorical devices designed to help listeners remember content

international communication communication between persons representing different nations

interpersonal communication the relationship level of communication

interpersonal conflict conflict between two or more people

interpersonal relationship a meaningful connection, such as friendship, between two persons

interracial communication the interpreting and sharing of meanings with individuals from different races

intimate distance a distance ranging from the point of touch to 18 inches from a person

intracultural communication interaction with members of the same racial or ethnic group or co-culture as one's own

intrapersonal communication communication with the self

intrapersonal conflict conflict between two mutually exclusive options

J

jargon a specialized vocabulary of technical terms that is shared by a community of users

Johari window a model containing four panes that is used to explain the roles that self-awareness and self-disclosure play in relationships

K

kaleidoscope thinking the taking of existing data and twisting it or looking at it from another angle

killer looks looks that discourage or inhabit the generation of ideas

killer phrases comments that stop the flow of ideas

kinesics the study of the relationship between human body motion, or body language, and communication

L

laissez-faire leader a nondirective leader

language a unified system of symbols that permits the sharing of meaning

leadership the ability to influence others

line graph graph used to illustrate trends, relationships, or comparisons over time

linear formats an organizational system in which main points develop and relate directly to the thesis

linguistic determinism the belief that language influences how we interpret the world

linguistic prejudice the use of prejudiced language

linguistic relativity the belief that persons who speak different languages perceive the world differently

listening the deliberate, psychological process by which we receive, understand, and retain aural stimuli

logos logical proof

loneliness the perceived discrepancy between desired and achieved social relationships

low-contact cultures cultures that maintain more distance when interacting

low-context communication a system that encourages directness in communication

low-intensity conflict a conflict in which the persons involved work to discover a solution beneficial to all parties

low power distance cultures cultures that believe that power should be used only when legitimate

low self-monitors individuals who pay little attention to how others respond to their messages

M

main ideas the main points of a speech; the subtopics of a speech

maintenance roles group roles designed to ensure the smooth running of a group

managerial grid a style leadership model developed by Robert R. Blake and Jane Mouton

manuscript speech a speech read from a script

markers items that reserve one's space

masculine cultures cultures that value aggressiveness, strength, and material symbols of success

Maslow's hierarchy of needs a model that depicts motivation as a pyramid with the most basic needs at the base and the most sophisticated at the apex

mass communication the transmission of messages that may be processed by gatekeepers prior to being sent to large audiences via a channel of broad diffusion

medium-intensity conflict a conflict in which each person feels committed to winning, but winning is seen as sufficient

melting pot philosophy the view that different cultures should be assimilated into the dominant culture

memorized speech a manuscript speech committed to memory

message the content of a communicative act

mindfulness emptying one's mind of personal concerns and interfering emotions, and choosing to focus on the person and the here and now

mixed message message that occurs when words and actions contradict each other

monochronic an approach to time in which people schedule time carefully, one event at a time, preferring to complete an activity before beginning another

Monroe's motivated sequence a speech framework composed of five phases—attention, need, satisfaction, visualization, and action

moving toward friendship the friendship stage in which we make small personal disclosures demonstrating the desire to expand our relationship

multiculturalism engagement with and respect toward people from distinctly different cultures

N

nascent friendship the friendship stage that finds us considering each other friends

need for affection the need to express and receive love

need for control the need to feel we are capable and responsible

need for inclusion the need for social contact

negative feedback a response that extinguishes behavior in progress

noise anything that interferes with or distorts the ability to send and receive messages

nonassertiveness the hesitation to display one's feelings and thoughts

nonevaluative feedback nondirective feedback

nonfluencies meaningless sounds or phrases that disrupt the flow of speech

nonverbal communication the kinds of human messages and responses not expressed in words

O

olfactics the study of the sense of smell

online speak the informal communication style that marks electronic communication

open questions questions that offer the interviewee freedom with regard to the choice and scope of an answer

organizational communication messaging conducted with larger, more stable collections of people who work together to achieve the organization's goals

P

paralanguage vocal cues that accompany spoken language

paraphrasing restating in one's own words what another person has said

pathos emotional proof

people-oriented listener a person who displays a strong interest in others and concern for their feelings; an empathic listener

perception the process by which we make sense out of experience

perceptual sets expectations that produce a readiness to process experience in a predetermined way

personal distance a distance ranging from 18 inches to 4 feet from a person

persuasion the attempt to change or reinforce attitudes, beliefs, values, or behaviors

persuasive speech a speech whose primary purpose is to change or reinforce the attitudes, beliefs, values, and/or behaviors of receivers

phatic communication communication designed to open the channels of communication

pictograph graph that uses sketches to represent concepts

pie graph (or circle graph) a circle with the various percentages of the whole indicated by wedges; a means of showing percentage relationships

pitch the highness or lowness of the voice

plagiarism the practice of taking someone else's work or ideas and passing them off as one's own

polarization the use of either/or language that causes us to perceive and speak about the world in extremes

polychronic an approach to time in which people give in to distractions and interruptions, even choosing to tackle several different problems or hold several different conversations at the same time

pop language words and phrases used to sell oneself as hip or cool

positive feedback a behavior enhancing response

post hoc ergo propter hoc the identification of a false cause

predicted outcome value theory a theory positing that when we first meet another person, based on our first impression of the person, we are able to predict the probability outcome of our relationship

prejudice a biased, negative attitude toward a particular group of people; a negative prejudgment based on membership in a social category

primary questions questions used to introduce topics or explore a new area

primary research the collection of information that does not already exist

probing a nonevaluative technique in which we ask for additional information

problem-and-solution order an organizational format that identifies the problems inherent in a situation and presents a solution to remedy them

problem-solving collaborator a person who, when faced with a conflict, adopts a win-win orientation, seeking to satisfy his or her own goals as well as those of others

proposition a statement that summarizes the purpose of a persuasive speech

proposition of fact a persuasive speech with the goal of settling what is or is not so

proposition of policy a persuasive speech on what ought to be

proposition of value a persuasive speech that espouses the worth of an idea, a person, or an object

proxemics the study of the use of space

pseudo-conflict the situation that results when persons mistakenly believe that two or more goals cannot be achieved simultaneously

psychographics the study and classification of people according to their attitudes, aspirations, and other psychological criteria

public communication communication designed to inform, persuade, or entertain audience members

public distance a distance of 12 feet or farther from a person

public speaking the act of preparing, staging, and delivering a presentation to an audience

public speaking anxiety fear of speaking to an audience

Pygmalion effect the principle that states that we fulfill the expectations of others

Q

qualifier indication of the strength of the connection

qualifiers tentative phrases

quality circles small groups of employees who meet regularly to discuss organizational life and the quality of their work environment

questions of fact questions involving the truth or falsity of a statement

questions of policy questions designed to help determine future actions

questions of value questions involving subjective judgments

R

racial code words words that are discriminatory but not literally racist

rate speaking speed

reasoning from analogy reasoning by comparison

reasons approach a type of topical organization in which each reason in support of a position is presented as a main point

rebuttal   potential counterargument

receivers   persons who receive, decode, and interpret a message

red herring   a distraction used to lead the receiver to focus on an irrelevant issue

red-flag words   words that trigger emotional deafness, dropping listening efficiency to zero

reflective-thinking framework   a system for decision making and problem solving that is designed to encourage critical inquiry

refutation format   a presentation in which a speaker argues against a previously stated position

role reversal   a strategy in which persons in conflict each act as the other in order to understand the other's position

role-limited interaction   the beginning stage of friendship

S

Sapir–Whorf hypothesis   the belief that the labels we use help shape our thinking, our worldview, and our behavior

secondary questions   questions that follow up primary questions

selective attention   the tendency to focus on certain cues and ignore others

selective exposure   the tendency to expose oneself to information that reaffirms existing attitudes, beliefs, and values

selective perception   the means of interpreting experience in a way that conforms to one's beliefs, expectations, and convictions

selective retention   the tendency to remember those things that reinforce one's way of thinking and forget those that oppose one's way of thinking

self-awareness   the ability to reflect on and monitor one's own behavior

self-concept   everything one thinks and feels about oneself

self-directed teams   autonomous groups of employees empowered to make decisions and supervise themselves

self-disclosure   the process of revealing to another person information about the self that he or she would not otherwise know

self-esteem   how well one likes and values oneself

self-fulfilling prophecy   a prediction or an expectation that comes true simply because one acts as if it were true

self-image   the sort of person one perceives oneself to be

self-serving roles   group roles that impede the functioning of a group by preventing members from working together effectively

semi-fixed-feature space   space in which objects are used to create distance

senders   persons who formulate, encode, and transmit a message

separation   the means co-culture members use to resist interacting with members of the dominant culture

serial communication   a chain-of-command transmission

serial construction of meaning model   a theory explaining how relationships develop through talk, creating a shared world

signposts   verbal statements in a speech that are used to orient the audience

silence   the absence of both paralinguistic and verbal cues

situational theory   the theory of leadership that asserts that leadership depends on the situation

slang   informal vocabulary that bonds its users together while excluding others

slippery slope   reasoning falsely asserting that one action will set in motion a chain of events

social capital   social connections or networks

social distance   a distance ranging from 4 feet to 12 feet from a person

social penetration theory   the theory that states that our relationships begin with relatively narrow breadth and shallow depth and develop over time

social proof   the determination of what is right by finding out what other people think is right

spatial order an organizational format that describes an object, a person, or a phenomenon as it exists in space

speech framework a skeleton for speech development

speech–thought differential the difference between speaking and thinking rates

stabilized friendship the friendship stage in which we decide that our friendship is secure and will continue

stagnating the relationship stage during which communication is at a standstill

statistics facts expressed in numerical form

stereotype a generalization about people, places, or events held by many members of a society; a mental image or picture that guides our reactions to others

stigma extreme disapproval resulting from prejudice and stereotypes that leads to discrimination and the promotion of shame in those targeted

straw man misrepresenting another's position to make it easier to attack

stress interview an employment interview in which more than one person fires questions at an interviewee

subordinate ideas ideas that amplify the main ideas or subtopics of a speech

supportive feedback a nonevaluative response indicating that the receiver perceives a problem as important

syllogism a three-part pattern used to structure an argument

symbol that which represents something else

T

tag questions questions that are midway between outright statements and yes–no questions

task-oriented roles roles that help a group realize its goals

team a type of group composed of people with a strong sense of their collective identity acting collaboratively

terminal credibility a measure of a speaker's credibility at the end of a speechmaking event

termination the relationship stage during which the relationship ends

territoriality the need to demonstrate a possessive or ownership relationship to space

testimony someone else's opinions or conclusions

time-oriented listener a person concerned with time management and thus limits the time available for listening

tolerance of vulnerability the degree of trust we place in another person to accept information we disclose without hurting us or the relationship

topical order an organizational format that clusters material by dividing it in to a series of appropriate topics

Toulmin reasonable argument model a model that breaks a reasonable argument into six parts

toxic communication the consistent use of verbal abuse and/or physical or sexual aggression or violence

trait theory the theory of leadership that asserts that certain people are born to lead

transactional communication model a model depicting communication as a continuous circle with sending and receiving as simultaneous rather than separate acts

transformational leader a leader who gives a group a new vision, strengthening its culture or structure

transitions connective words and phrases

triangle of meaning a model that explains the relationship that exists among words, things, and thoughts

trust confidence in a person to act in a predictable and desirable way

type X leader a leader who does not trust group members to work and is unconcerned with the personal achievements of group members

type Y leader a leader who displays trust in group members and is concerned with their sense of personal achievement

U

unconscious bias attitudes or stereotypes formed outside our conscious awareness that affect the positions we hold

V

value conflict a disagreement that arises when persons hold different views on an issue

values the principles important to us; that which we judge to be good or bad, ethical or unethical, worthwhile or worthless

visual dominance a measure calculated by comparing the percentage of looking while speaking with the percentage of looking while listening

volume the degree of loudness of the voice

W

waning friendship the friendship stage during which friends begin to drift apart

warrant explanation of the relationship between the claim and the data

Y

"you" messages responses that place blame on another person

Notes

Chapter 1

1. Hilary Sheinbaum, "The Wi-Fi Version of Vanity Plates," *New York Times*, September 14, 2017, p. D6.

2. "Teens, Smart Phones & Texting," Pew Charitable Trusts, March 19, 2012, http://www.pewtrusts.org/our_work_report_detailaspx?id=858899377053&category=56.

3. Amanda Lenhart, "Teens, Social Media, and Technology Overview 2015," Pew Research Center, April 9, 2015, http://www.pewinternet.org/2015/04/09/teens-social-media-technology-2015.

4. Teddy Wayne, "The End of Reflection," *New York Times*, June 12, 2015, pp. ST1, ST8-9.

5. Robert D. Putnam, Bowling Alone: The Collapse and Revival of American Community. New York: Simon & Schuster, 2000.

6. National Association of Colleges and Employers (NACE), *Job Outlook 2015*, November 2014.

7. Elizabeth Fox-Genovese, *Feminism Without Illusions*. Chapel Hill: University of North Carolina Press, 1991, p. 20.

8. See Julia T. Wood, *Gendered Lives: Communication, Gender, and Culture*, 9th ed. Boston: Wadsworth, 2011.

9. O. Wiio, *Wiio's Law and Some Others*. Espoo, Finland: Welin Goos, 1978.

10. C. Wade and C. Tarvis, *Learning to Think Critically: The Case of Close Relationships*. New York: HarperCollins, 1990.

11. Marshall McLuhan, *Understanding Media*. Cambridge: MIT Press, 1994.

12. Lindsey Bahr, "'Ingrid Goes West' Satirizes Social Media Envy," *The Record*, August 18, 2017.

13. Melinda Gates, "I Spent My Career in Technology. I Wasn't Prepared for Its Effect on My Kids," *Washington Post*, August 24, 2017.

14. See, e.g., James A. Roberts, Luc Honore Petnji Yaya, and Chris Manolis, "The Invisible Addiction: Cell-Phone Activities and Addiction Among Male and Female College Students," *Journal of Behavioral Addiction*, 3(4), 2014, pp. 254-265.

15. William Schutz, *The Interpersonal Underworld*. Palo Alto, CA: Science and Behavior Books, 1966.

16. Lisa Katz, "Communication Is Next 'Top' Technical Skill," April 5, 2016, Report by the Workforce Intelligence Network for Southeast Michigan, http://www.crainsdetroit.com/article20160405/BLOG107/160409927/communications-is-next-top-technical-skill.

17. Diana Middleton, "Students Struggle for Words," *Wall Street Journal*, March 2, 2011, p. B8.

18. See, e.g., "Why Communication Education Is Important: The Centrality of the Discipline in the 21st Century," *Communication Education*, 57(2), April 2008, pp. 224-240.

Chapter 2

1. See Walter Lippmann, *Public Opinion*. New York: Macmillan, 1957, pp. 79-103; and C. S. Abbate, S. Boca, and P. Bocchiaro, "Stereotyping in Persuasive Communication: Influence Exerted by Disapproved Source," *Journal of Applied Social Psychology*, 34, 2004, p. 1192.

2. See Herb Jackson, "Muslim Leaders Angry Over Inquiry," *The Record*, March 10, 2011, p. A1. Also see Neil MacFarquhar, "Abandon Stereotypes, Muslims in America Say," *New York Times*, November 4, 2007, p. A12.

3. Devlin Barrett, "Emotions Run High at Hearing," *Wall Street Journal*, March 11, 2011, p. A5.

4. Pamela Constable, "Racial Survey Unearths Tensions," *The Record*, December 11, 2007, p. A6.

5. Marshall McLuhan, *The Medium Is the Message*. New York: Bantam Books, 1967; and Marshall McLuhan, *Understanding Media*. New York: Mentor, 1964.

6. Pew Research Center, "American Mobility," December 29, 2008, http://pewsocialtrends.org.

7. Robert D. Putnam, *Bowling Alone: The Collapse and Revival of American Community*. New York: Simon & Schuster, 2001.

8. See, e.g., Christopher Caldwell, "Diversity Is Not Black and White," *Financial Times*, August 12, 2007, p. 7; and Michael Skapinker, "Why the Workplace Is Diversity's Best Bet," *Financial Times*, September 18, 2007, p. 11.

9. See William B. Gudykunst and Young Youn Kim, eds., *Readings on Communicating With Strangers*. New York: McGraw-Hill, 1991.

10. U.S. Census Bureau, "2010 Census Shows America's Diversity," March 24, 2011, https://www.census.gov/newsroom/releases/archives/2010_census/cb11-cn125.html.

11. Sam Fleming, "Asians Projected to Overtake Hispanics as Largest Immigrant Group in the U.S. by 2065," *The Financial Times*, September 28, 2015, p. 1.

12. Hava El Nasser, "Multiracial No Longer Boxed in by the Census," *USA Today*, March 3, 2010, pp. 1A, 2A.

13. Edward T. Hall, *The Silent Language*. New York: Fawcett, 1959.

14. Wendy Griswold, *Cultures and Society in a Changing World*. Thousand Oaks, CA: Pine Forge, 2012, pp. 22-24.

15. Carley H. Dodd, *Dynamics of Intercultural Communication*. Dubuque, IA: Brown, 1997, p. 3.

16. See Geert Hofstede, *Masculinity and Femininity: The Taboo Dimension of National Cultures*. Thousand Oaks, CA: Sage, 2013.

17. William B. Gudykunst, *Bridging Differences*, 4th ed. Thousand Oaks, CA: Sage, 2003, pp. 12-13.

18. "Unhappy Meal for Muslims," *The Record*, June 8, 1993, p. C-3.

19. Griswold, p. 1.

20. Margaret H. DeFleur and Melvin I. DeFleur, "The Next Generation's Image of Americans: Attitudes and Beliefs Held by Teen-Agers in Twelve Countries," October 3, 2002, https://www.infoamerica.org/documentos_pdf/defleur.pdf.

21. Gudykunst, *Bridging Differences*, 4th ed.

22. Peter Holley, "A Black Man Went Undercover as a White Supremacist. This Is What He Learned," *Washington Post*, August 24, 2017.

23. Walter Lippmann, *Public Opinion*. New York: Macmillan, 1922.

24. Nicholas Kristof, "Our Biased Brains," *New York Times*, May 7, 2015, p. A29.

25. For more on prejudice, see M. L. Hecht, ed., *Communicating Prejudice*. Thousand Oaks, CA; Sage, 1998.

26. Deborah Tannen, You Just Don't Understand: Women and Men in Conversation. New York: Morrow, 1990.

27. Amelia Thompson-Deveaux, "America's Shifting Religious Identity Could Spell Problems for Both Parties," September 6, 2017, https://fivethirtyeight.com/features/americas-shifting-religious-makeup-could-spell-trouble-for-both-parties.

28. Daniel Cox, "America's Changing Religious Identity," Findings from the 2016 American Values Atlas, September 6, 2017, https://www.prri.org/research/american-religious-landscape-christian-religiously-unaffiliated.

29. Katy Steinmetz, "Move Over, Millennials," *Time*, December 28, 2015–January 4, 2016, p. 34.

30. Alex Williams, "Move Over, Millennials: Here Comes Generation Z," *New York Times*, September 20, 2015, p. ST1, ST18.

31. Judith Cornelia Pearson and Edward Nelson. *Understanding and Sharing: An Introduction to Speech Communication*, 6th ed. Dubuque IA: Brown & Benchmark, 1994, p. 193. See also Judy C. Pearson, Paul E. Nelson, Scott Titsworth, and Angela M. Hosek, *Human Communication*, 6th ed. New York: McGraw-Hill, 2017.

32. Wendy Griswold. *Cultures and Societies in a Changing World*. Thousand Oaks, CA: Pine Forge, 1994, p. 57.

33. M. P. Orbe, "Laying the Foundation for Co-Cultural Communication Theory: An Inductive Approach to Studying 'Nondominant' Communication Strategies and the Factors That Influence Them," *Communication Studies*, 47, 1996, pp. 157-176.

34. See Judith N. Martin and Thomas K. Nakayama, *Intercultural Communication in Contexts*, 2nd ed. Mountain View, CA: Mayfield, 2000, pp. 265-266. Also see 3rd ed., 2003.

35. G. Hofstede, *Cultures and Organizations*. London: McGraw-Hill, 1991.

36. Hall, *The Silent Language*.

37. Edward T. Hall, *The Dance of Life: The Other Dimension of Time*. New York: Anchor/Doubleday, 1983, p. 42.

38. See G. Hofstede, *Masculinity and Femininity: The Taboo Dimension of National Cultures*. Thousand Oaks, CA: Sage, 1998; and S. K. Ciccarelli and J. N. White, *Psychology: An Exploration*. Boston, MA: Pearson, 2016.

39. See Felicia Wu Song, *Virtual Communities: Bowling Alone, Online Together*. New York: Peter Lang, 2009; and Josh Meyrowitz, "Media Theory," in Erik P. Bucy, ed., *Living in the Information Age*. Belmont, CA: Wadsworth, 2002, p. 32.

40. See, e.g., Bill Bishop with Robert G. Cushing, *The Big Sort: Why the Clustering of Like-Minded America Is Tearing Us Apart*. New York: Houghton Mifflin.

41. Christopher Chabris and Daniel Simons, "The Internet: Is IT Reshaping Our Brains?" *The Record*, July 30, 2010, p. A21.

42. Clifford Stoll, "Further Explorations Into the Culture of Computing," in Erick P. Bucy, ed., *Living in the Information Age*. Belmont, CA: Wadsworth, 2002, p. 32.

43. Anjali Mullany, "Egyptian Uprising Plays Out on Social Media Sites Despite Government's Internet Restrictions," *Daily News*, January 29, 2011.

44. Larry A. Samovar and Richard E. Porter, *Intercultural Communication: A Reader*, 11th ed. Belmont, CA: Wadsworth, 2006, p. 5.

Chapter 3

1. Adam Liptak, "Often Wrong but Rarely in Doubt: Eyewitness IDs Will Get a Fresh Look," *New York Times*, August 23, 2011; and Erica Goode and John Schwartz, "Police Lineups Start to Face Fact: Eyes Can Lie," *New York Times*, August 29, 2011, p. A1, A3.

2. Ron Alsop, "The 'Trophy Kids' Go to Work," *Wall Street Journal*, October 21, 2008, pp. D1, D4.

3. Natalie Angier, "Blind to Change, Even as It Stares Us in the Face," *New York Times*, May 20, 2008, p. 5.

4. See Christopher Chabris and Daniel Simons, *The Invisible Gorilla and Other Ways Our Intuitions Deceive Us*. New York: Crown, 2010.

5. William V. Haney, *Communication and Organizational Behavior*. Homewood, IL: Irwin, 1973, p. 55.

6. Sara Reistad-Long, "Older Brain Really May Be a Wise Brain," *New York Times*, May 20, 2008, p. F5.

7. See Jonathan Foer, *The Art and Science of Remembering Everything*. New York: Penguin, 2011.

8. Chabris and Simons.

9. David A. Shaywitz, "The Future of Our Illusions," *Wall Street Journal*, June 11, 2010, p. W4.

10. See, e.g., Steve Freiss, "Memory Does Not Always Serve, and That's No Lie," *USA Today*, September 14, 2004, p. 9D; and Daniel L. Schacter, "The Fog of War," *New York Times*, April 4, 2004, p. A21.

11. E. Rubin, "Figure and Ground," in D. Beardslee and M. Werthimer, eds., *Readings in Perception*. Princeton, NJ: Van Nostrand, pp. 194-203.

12. See, e.g., C. N. Macrae and G. V. Bodenhausen, "Social Cognition: Categorical Person Perception," *British Journal of Psychology*, 92, 2001, pp. 853-864.

13. K. G. Wilson and S. C. Hayes, "Why It Is Crucial to Understand Thinking and Feeling: An Analysis and Application to Drug Abuse," *Behavior Analyst*, 23, Spring 2000, pp 25-43.

14. D. Cvencek, A. G. Greenwald, and A. N. Meltzoff, "Implicit Measures for Preschool Children Confirm Self-Esteem's Role in Maintaining a Balanced Identity," *Journal of Experimental Social Psychology*, 62, 2015, pp. 50-57.

15. C. Mruk, *Self-Esteem: Research, Theory, and Practice*. New York: Springer, 2005.

16. See D. Hamacheck, *Encounters With the Self*, 3rd ed. Fort Worth Texas: Holt, Rinehart & Winston, 1992, pp. 5-8.

17. See, e.g., Jessica Li Yexin, Katherine A. Johnson, Adam B. Cohen, Melissa J. Williams, Eric D. Knowles, and Chen Zhansheng, "Fundamental(ist) Attribution Error: Protestants Are Dispositionally Focused,"

Journal of Personality and Social Psychology, 102, 2012, pp. 281-290.

18. See Maureen Stout, *The Feel-Good Curriculum: The Dumbing Down of America's Kids in the Name of Self-Esteem.* New York: Perseus Books, 2000; and Mary Amorose, "Is Self-Esteem Overrated?" *The Record*, April 27, 2000, pp. HF-1, HF-3.

19. Roy E. Baumeister, Jennifer D. Campbell, Joachim I. Krueger, and Kathleen D. Vohs, "Exploding the Self-Esteem Myth," *Scientific American*, January 2005, pp. 84-91.

20. See Michele Orecklin, "Beware of the Crowd," *Time*, August 21, 2000, p. 69; and Valerie Strauss, "Most, Least Popular Kids Less Likely to Bully, Study Says," *Washington Post*, February 8, 2011, http://voices. washingtonpost.com/answer-sheet/bullying/most-least-popular-kids-less-1.html.

21. R. Baumeister, L. Smart, and J. Boden, "Relation of the Threatened Egotism to Violence and Aggression: The Dark Side of High Self-Esteem," *Psychological Review*, 103, 1996, pp. 5-33.

22. B. Bushman and R. T. Baumeister, "Threatened Egotism, Narcissism, Self-Esteem, and Direct and Displaced Aggression: Does Self-Love or Self-Hate Lead to Violence?" *Journal of Personality and Social Psychology*, 75, 1998, pp. 210-229.

23. Sharon Jayson, "Yep, Life'll Burst That Self-Esteem Bubble," *USA Today*, February 16, 2005, p. L7.

24. Roy F. Baumeister, Jennifer D. Campbell, Joachim I. Krueger, and Kathleen D. Vohs, "Does High Self-Esteem Cause Better Performance, Interpersonal Success, Happiness, or Healthier Lifestyles?" *Psychological Science in the Public Interest*, 4(1), May 2003, pp. 1-44.

25. J. Saunders, "The Role of Self-Esteem in the Misinformation Effect," *Memory*, 20(2), 2012, pp. 90-99.

26. Marlene Zuk, "A Case of Unwarranted Self-Regard," *The Record*, May 30, 2005, p. L7.

27. Angela Duckworth, "The Grit Factor," *New York Times*, April 10, 2016, p. EL7.

28. See Rosabeth Moss Kanter, *Confidence: How Winning Streaks and Losing Streaks Begin and End*. New York: Crown, 2004.

29. Sharon Begley, "Real Self-Esteem Builds on Achievement, Not Praise for Slackers," *Wall Street Journal*, April 16, 2003, p. B1.

30. Ashley Parker, "My Bitmoji, My (Better) Self," *New York Times*, October 4, 2015, ST12.

31. See A. Bandura, *Self-Efficacy: The Exercise of Control*. New York: Freeman, 1997.

32. Martin E. P. Seligman, interview in *Success*, July–August 1994, p. 41.

33. Judith Martin and Thomas Nakayama, *Experiencing Intercultural Communication: An Introduction*, 3rd ed. New York: McGraw-Hill, 2008, p. 95.

34. Justine Coupland, John F. Nussbaum, and Nikolas Coupland, "The Reproduction of Aging and Ageism in Intergenerational Talk," in Nikolas Coupland, Howard Giles, and John Wiemann, eds., *Miscommunication and Problematic Talk*. Newbury Park, CA: Sage, 1991, p. 85.

35. Kellie Ell, "Job Barriers Fading for Those With Disabilities," *USA Today*, August 24, 2017, p. 1B, 2B.

36. For example, check out what Google is doing. Chloe Cornish, "Google to Offer Depression Check," *Financial Times*, August 24, 2017, p. 11.

37. See, e.g., P. Watzlawick, "Self-Fulfilling Prophecies" in J. O'Brien and P. Kollock, eds., *The Production of Reality*, 3rd ed. Thousand Oaks, CA: Pine Forge, 2001, pp. 411-423.

38. David L. Kirp, "Don't Suspend Students, Empathize," *New York Times*, September 2, 2017, https://www.nytimes .com/2017/09/02/opinion/ sunday/dont-suspend-students-empathize. html?smid=nytcore-iphone-share&smprod=nytcore-iphone.

39. See Eric Berne, *Games People Play*. New York: Grove, 1964.

40. Joseph Luft, *Group Processes: An Introduction to Group Dynamics*, 2nd ed. Palo Alto, CA: Mayfield, 1970.

41. V. Benet-Martinez, J. Leu, F. Lee, and M. Morris, "Negotiating Biculturalism: Cultural Frame Switching in Biculturals With Oppositional Versus Compatible Cultural Identities," *Journal of Cross-Cultural Psychology*, 33, 2002, pp. 492-516.

42. See E. Goffman, *The Presentation of Self in*

Everyday Life. Garden City, NY: Doubleday, 1959; and *Relations in Public.* New York: Basic Books, 1971.

43. Peggy Orenstein, "I Tweet, Therefore I Am," *New York Times Magazine*, August 1, 2010, pp. 11–12.

44. Paul Chance, "Seeing Is Believing," *Psychology Today*, January-February 1989, p. 26.

45. M. Sunnafrank, A. Ramirez, and S. Metts, "At First Sight: Persistent Relational Effects of Get Acquainted Conversations," *Journal of Social and Personal Relationships*, 21(3), February 2005, pp. 361-379.

46. Marina Krakovsky, "Mixed Impressions." *Scientific American Mind*, January/February, 2010, p. 12.

47. Jessica Guynn, "Facebook Develops Unconscious Bias Training," *USA Today*, July 30, 2015, p. 3B.

48. Ibid. See also David Francis, "Employers Replies to Racial Names," National Bureau of Economic Research, November 22, 2017, http://www.nber.org/digest/sep03/w9873.html; and Marianne Bertrand and Sendhil Mullainathan, "Are Emily and Greg More Employable than Lakisha and Jamal? A Field Experiment on Labor Market Discrimination," *American Economic Review* 94(4), 2004, pp. 991-1013.

49. Sharon Begley, "Racism Studies Find Rational Part of the Brain Can Override Prejudice," *Wall Street Journal*, November 19, 2004, p. B1.

50. Irving J. Lee, *How to Talk With People.* San Francisco: International Society for General Semantics, 1980.

51. Alfred Korzybski, *Science and Sanity*, 4th ed. San Francisco: International Society for General Semantics, 1980.

52. Peggy Orenstein, "I Tweet, Therefore I Am," *New York Times Magazine*, August 1, 2010, pp. 11-12.

53. Julia T. Wood, *Gendered Lives: Communication, Gender, and Culture*, 9th ed. Belmont, CA: Wadsworth, 2011.

54. Diane Hales, *Just Like a Woman.* New York: Bantam, 1999, p. 136.

55. See, e.g., Susan Faludi, *Fear and Fantasy in Post 9/11 America.* New York: Metropolitan Books, 2008; and Wood.

56. J. S. Bagby, "A Cross-Cultural Study of Perceptual Predominance in Binocular Rivalry," *Journal of Abnormal and Social Psychology*, 54, 1957, pp. 331-334.

57. H. A. Elfenbein and N. Ambady, "Is There an In-Group Advantage in Emotion Recognition?" *Psychological Bulletin*, 128, 2002, pp. 243-249.

58. "Textbooks Show Students' Conflicting Views of Past," *Wall Street Journal*, August 6, 2007.

59. Richard Breslin, *Understanding Culture's Influence on Behavior.* Orlando, FL: Harcourt Brace Jovanovich, 1993, p. 47.

60. "Hey, I'm Terrific," *Newsweek*, February 17, 1992, p. 48.

61. Osei Appiah, "Americans Online: Differences in Surfing and Evaluating Race-Targeted Web Sites by Black and White Users," paper presented at the annual meeting of the Association for Education in Journalism and Mass Communication, Miami, FL, August 2002.

62. Sue Shellenbarger, "Why Students Might Not Know If This Story Is Fake," *Wall Street Journal*, November 22, 2016, p. A11, A12.

63. Richard Waters, Matthew Garrahan, and Tim Bradshaw, "The Harsh Truth About Fake News," *Financial Times*, November 22, 2016, p. 9.

64. V. Rohan, "Defining the Face of Evil," *The Record*, January 23, 2005, p. E1.

65. G. Gerbner, L. P. Gross, M. Morgan, and N. Signorielli, "The Mainstreaming of America; Violence Profile No. 11," *Journal of Communication*, 30, pp. 10-29; J. Shanahan and M. Morgan, *Television and Its Viewers: Cultivation Theory and Research.* New York: Cambridge University Press, 1999.

66. Jacqueline Howard, "Americans Devote More Than 10 Hours a Day to Screen Time and Growing," CNN, July 29, 2016, http://www.cnn.com/2016/06/30/health/americans-screen-time-nielsen/index.html.

67. Amanda Lenhart, "Teens, Social Media, and Technology Overview 2015," Pew Research Center, April 9, 2015, http://www.pewinternet.org/2015/04/09/teens-social-media-technology-2015.

68. Nancy Jo Sales, "How Social Media Is Disrupting the Lives of American Girls,"

Time, February 22-29, 2016, pp. 26-27.

69. See Nicholas Carr, *The Shallows: What the Internet Is Doing to Our Brains*. New York: Norton, 2010; and Sherry Turkle, *Alone Together: Why We Expect More From Technology and Less From Each Other*. New York: Basic Books, 2011.

70. Susan B. Barnes, *Online Connections: Internet Interpersonal Relationships*. Cresskill, NJ: Hampton, 2001, p. 102.

71. See, e.g., D. P. McAdams and E. Manczak, "Personality and the Life Story," in M. Mikulincer, P. R. Shaver, M. I Cooper, and R. J. Larsen, eds., *APA Handbook of Personality and Social Psychology*. Vol 4: *Personality Processes and Individual Differences*. Washington, DC: American Psychological Association, 2015, pp. 425-446.

72. Svetlana Shkolnikova, "Smartphones Dominate Kids' Lives," *The Record*, August 21, 2017, pp. 1A, 6A.

73. Brooks Barnes, "Hollywood Still Likes Its Women Skinny," *New York Times*, August 20, 2017, pp. AR1, AR10.

74. See, e.g., K. Wilcox and A. T. Stephen, "Are Close Friends the Enemy? Online Social Networks, Self-Esteem, and Self-Control," *Journal of Consumer Research*, 40, 2013, pp. 90-103; and J. W. Kim and T. M. Chock, "Body Image 2.0: Associations Between Social Grooming on Facebook and Body Image Concerns," *Computers in Human Behavior*, 48, 2015, pp. 331-339.

Chapter 4

1. "In 'Arrival,' the World Is Saved by Words," *Wall Street Journal*, December 4, 2016, p. SR8.

2. Clarence Page, "A Few Words—and an Image—About 2015," *The Record*, December 31, 2015, p. A11.

3. Connor Gaffey, "Lies, Damn Lies and Post-Truth," *Newsweek*, December 9, 2016, p. 57.

4. Barry Gottlieb, "My Word," *The Record*, February 18, 2009, p. A11.

5. C. K. Ogden and I. A. Richards, *The Meaning of Meaning*. Orlando, FL: Harcourt Brace Jovanovich, 1993.

6. Charles F. Vich and Ray V. Wood, "Similarity of Past Experience and the Communication of Meaning," *Speech Monographs*, 36, pp. 159-162.

7. For a discussion of how the mindless use of language affects behavior, see Ellen Langer, "Interpersonal Mindlessness and Language," *Communication Monographs*, 59(3), September 1992, pp. 324-327.

8. Jonah Berger, "Why 'Cool' Is Still Cool," *New York Times*, November 22, 2015, p. SR 10.

9. Anemona Hartocollis, "At Harvard, 'House Master' Is Discontinued as Job Title," *New York Times*, December 3, 2015, p. A22.

10. Jill Lawless, "Texting Terms Make Oxford," *The Record*, March 26, 2011, p. A8.

11. Michiko Kakutani, "When the Greeks Get Snide," *New York Times*, June 27, 2000, p. E1.

12. Laura Landro, "Taking Medical Jargon Out of Doctor Visits," *Wall Street Journal*, July 6, 2010, pp. D1, D2.

13. See, e.g., S. I. Hayakawa and Alan R. Hayakawa, *Language in Thought and Action*, 5th ed. Orlando, FL: Harcourt Brace Jovanovich, 1990.

14. "'Hi, Jack' Greeting to a Co-Pilot Causes Stir," *The Record*, June 8, 2000, p. A13. Used by permission of the Associated Press. Copyright 2000. All rights reserved.

15. See William V. Haney, *Communication and Organizational Behavior*, 3rd ed. Homewood, IL: Irwin, 1973, pp. 247-248.

16. For a discussion of names and how they affect us, see Mary Marcus, "The Power of a Name," *Psychology Today*, October 1976, pp. 75-76, 108.

17. Thomas N. Robinson, Dina L G. Borzekowski, Donna M. Matheson, and Helena C. Kraemer, "Effects of Fast Food Branding on Young Children's Taste Preferences," *Archives of Pediatric and Adolescent Medicine*, 161, 2007, pp. 292-297.

18. J. L. Cotton, B. S. O'Neill, and A. Griffin, "The 'Name Game': Affect and Hiring Reactions to First Names," *Journal of Managerial Psychology*, 23, 2008, pp. 18-39.

19. See M. Bertrand and S. Mullainathan, "Are Emily and Greg More Employable than Lakisha and Jamal? A Field Experiment on Labor Market Discrimination," *American Economic Review*, 94, 2004, pp. 991-1013.

20. B. Coffey and P. A. McLaughlin, "Do Masculine Names Help Female

Lawyers Become Judges? Evidence from South Carolina," *American Law and Economics Review*, 11, 2009, pp. 112-133.

21. Jori Finkel, "What's in a Name? Some Say Inclusion," *New York Times*, September 12, 2017, p. C7.

22. "Washington Wire," *Wall Street Journal*, October 14, 1994.

23. William Lutz, *The New Doublespeak: Why No One Knows What Anyone's Saying Anymore*. New York: HarperCollins, 1976.

24. Jennifer Lee, "A Call for Softer, Greener Language," *New York Times*, March 2, 2003, p. 24.

25. Liz Spayd, "When the Language of Politics Becomes a Minefield," *New York Times*, December 4, 2016, p. SR10.

26. See William Lutz, *Doublespeak Defined*. New York: Harper Resource, 1999; and National Council of Teachers of English, "The 1999 Doublespeak Awards," *ETC*, 56(4), Winter 1999-2000, p. 484.

27. Henry Beard and Christopher Cerf, *The Official Politically Correct Dictionary and Handbook*. New York: Villard Books, 1992.

28. Diane Ravitch, "You Can't Say That," *Wall Street Journal*, February 13, 2004, p. W15.

29. Donald. G. McNeil Jr., "The World: Taboos, Globally Speaking; Like Politics, All Political Correctness Is Local," *New York Times*, October 11, 1998, p. WK-5.

30. See Jean M. Twenge, "The Smartphone Generation vs. Free Speech," *Wall Street Journal*, September 2-3, 2017, p. C3.

31. John Zeaman, "There's Way Too Much Katakarktanq," *The Record*, February 15, 2004, pp. F1, F4.

32. Nicholas D. Kristof, "Chinese Relations," *New York Times Magazine*, August 18, 1991, pp. 8-10.

33. Guy Deutscher, "You Are What You Speak," *New York Times Magazine*, August 29, 2010, pp. 42-47; and Guy Deutscher, *Through the Language Glass: Why the World Looks Different in Other Languages*. New York: Metropolitan Books/Henry Holt, 2010.

34. Liz Sly, "In China, the Right Name Is Crucial," *The Record*, October 6, 1996, p. A31.

35. Elizabeth Llorente and Ovetta Wiggins, "Human Services Agency to Correct Letter," *The Record*, February 7, 1997. p. A3.

36. See, e.g., Deborah Tannen, Talking From 9 to 5: How Women's and Men's Styles Affect Who Gets Heard, Who Gets Credit, and What Gets Done at Work. New York: Morrow, 1994.

37. Tannen.

38. Michael Slackman, "The Fine Art of Hiding What You Mean to Say," *New York Times*, August 6, 2006, p. WK-5.

39. See, e.g., Carolyn Calloway-Thomas, Pamela J. Cooper, and Cecil Blake, *Intercultural Communication: Roots and Routes*. Boston: Allyn & Bacon, 1999, pp. 154-155; and William B. Gudykunst, *Bridging Differences: Effective Intergroup Communication*, 2nd ed. Thousand Oaks, CA: Sage, 1994, p. 83.

40. "Work Week," *Wall Street Journal*, p. A1.

41. J. J. Hemmer Jr., "Exploitation of Native American Symbols: A First Amendment Analysis," paper presented at the National Communication Association annual convention. New Orleans, LA, November 22, 2002.

42. Suzanne Daily, "In Europe, Some Fear National Languages Are Endangered," *New York Times*, April 16, 2001, pp. A1, A10.

43. Steven Komarow, "Some Germans Fear Language Is Being Infected by English," *USA Today*, May 16, 2001, p. 6A.

44. Andrew Jacobs, "Shanghai Is Trying to Untangle the Mangled English of Chinglish," *New York Times*, May 3, 2010 p. A12.

45. A. Nilsen, "Sexism as Shown Through the English Vocabulary," in A Nilsen, H. Bosmajian, H. Gershuny, and J. Stanley, eds., *Sexism and Language*. Urbana, IL: National Council of Teachers of English, 1977.

46. Sam Kean, "What's in a Name?" *New York Times Magazine*, October 28, 2007, p. 25.

47. Simon Romero, "A Culture of Naming That Even a Law May Not Tame," *New York Times*, September 5, 2007, p. A4.

48. Thomas Fuller, "In the Cultural Battle, Name-Calling Is Encouraged," *New York Times*, August 29, 2007, p. A4.

49. Michael Wines, "In a Land of Homemade Names, Tiffany Doesn't Cut It," *New York Times*, October 1, 2007, p. A4.

50. Albert Mehrabian, "Baby Name Report Card," http://www.kaaj.com/psych/namebk.html.

51. A. Mulac, J. Bradac, and S. Mann. "Male/Female Language Differences and Attributional Consequences in Children's Television," *Human Communication Research*, 11, 1985, pp. 481-506.

52. C. Kramer, "Stereotypes of Women's Speech: The Word From Cartoons," *Journal of Popular Culture*, 8, 1974, pp. 624-630.

53. C. Kramer, "Male and Female Perceptions of Male and Female Speech," *Language and Speech*, 20, 1978, pp. 151-161.

54. Patricia Hayes Bradley, "The Folk-Linguistics of Women's Speech: An Empirical Examination," *Speech Monographs*, 48, pp. 73-90.

55. Nancy M. Henley and Cheris Kramarae, "Gender Power and Miscommunication," in Nickolas Coupland, Howard Giles, and John Weimann, *Miscommunication and Problematic Talk*, Newbury Park, CA: Sage, 1991, p. 42.

56. Deborah Tannen, *You Just Don't Understand.* New York: Ballantine, 1991, p. 42.

57. M. Hiller and F. L. Johnson, "Gender and Generation on Conversational Topics: A Case Study of Two Coffee Shops," paper presented at the annual meeting of the Speech Communication Association, San Diego, CA, November 1996.

58. Cited in Craig Johnson and Larry Vinson, "Placement and Frequency of Powerless Talk and Impression Formation," *Communication Quarterly*, 38(4), Fall 1990, p. 325.

59. Cheris Kramarae, *Women and Men Speaking*, Rowley, MA; Newbury House, 1981, p. 1.

60. Deborah Tannen, *You Just Don't Understand.*

61. Sandy Ong, "From Bad to Curse," *Newsweek*, December 9, 2016, pp. 48-49.

62. "When Cheers Turn to Abuse, Colleges Need to Take Action," *USA Today*, March 7, 2008, p. A6.

63. Madeline Glover, "Experts See Epidemic of Foul-Mouthed Kids," *The Record.* February 28, 2008, p. A6.

64. Rachael Emma Silverman, "On the Job Cursing: Obscene Talk Is the Latest Target of Workplace Ban," *Wall Street Journal*, May 8, 2001, p. B12.

65. For example, James O'Connor, *Cuss Control: The Complete Book of How to Curb Your Cursing.* New York: Three Rivers, 2000.

66. Erez Levon, "Words Transition, Too," *Financial Times*, October 26, 2016, p. 11.

67. Randall Kennedy, *Nigger: The Strange Career of a Troublesome Word.* New York: Pantheon, 2002.

68. Anahad O'Connor, "In Bid to Ban Racial Slur, Blacks Occupy Both Sides," *New York Times*, February 25, 2007, pp. 23, 26.

69. Joseph Plambeck, "Dr. Laura Retreats After Use of Epithet," *New York Times*, August 19, 2010, p. C3.

70. DeWayne Wickman, "N-Word Has Become an Indelible Part of the American Lexicon," *USA Today*, January 11, 2011, p. 9A.

71. Stephanie Raposo, "Quick! Tell Us What KUTGW Means," *Wall Street Journal*, August 5, 2009, pp. D1, D3.

72. Kevin Maney, "There Are No Words. . ." *Newsweek*, April 8, 2016, pp. 46-47.

73. Amy Harmon, "Internet Changes Language for & ," *New York Times*, February 20, 1999, p. B-7.

74. See Katie Roiphe, "The Language of *Fakebook*," *New York Times*, August 13, 2010, https://www.nytimes.com/2010/08/15/fashion/15Culture.html.

75. Boyce Watkins, "Teacher Calls First-Graders 'Future Criminals,'" *The Root*, August 31, 2011, http://www.theroot.com/buzz/teacher-calls-first-graders-future-criminals.

76. For more information, see Richard Lacavo, "Mixed Signals on Sanctions," *Time*, December 17, 1990, p. 114.

Chapter 5

1. See, e.g., H. A. Elfenbein and N. Ambady, "Predicting Workplace Outcomes From the Ability to Eavesdrop on Feelings," *Journal of Applied Psychology*, October 2002, pp. 963-972.

2. Ray Birdwhistell, *Kinesics and Context.* Philadelphia: University of Pennsylvania Press, 1970; Albert Mehrabian, *Silent Messages*, 2nd ed. Belmont, CA: Wadsworth, 1981.

3. Mark L. Knapp, Judith A. Hall and T. G. Horgan, *Nonverbal Communication in Human Interaction*, 8th ed. Belmont, CA: Wadsworth, 2013.

4. A. Cuddy, "Your Body Language Shapes Who You Are," TED.com, https://www

.ted.com/talks/amy_cuddy_ your_body_language_ shapes_who_you_are/ transcript?language=en.

5. Kathleen Fackelman, "Look Who's Talking With Gestures," *USA Today*, July 5, 2000, p. 7D.

6. Daniel Goleman, "Sensing Silent Cues Emerges as Key Skills," *New York Times*, October 10, 1989.

7. S. Faeber, J. Kaufman, and S. Schweinberger, "Face Recognition: Early Temporal Negativity Is Sensitive to Perceived (Rather Than Physical) Facial Identity," *Journal of Vision*, 15, 2015, p. 677.

8. M. D. Licke, R. H. Smith, and M. L Klotz, "Judgments of Physical Attractiveness: The Role of Faces and Bodies," *Personality and Social Psychology Bulletin*, 12, 1986, pp. 381-389.

9. T. R. Levine et al., "The Lying Chicken and the Avoidant Egg: Eye Contact, Deception, and Causal Order," *Southern Communication Journal*, 71(4), December 2006, pp. 401-411; and D. S. Berry, "What Can a Moving Face Tell Us?" *Journal of Personality and Social Psychology*, 58, 1990, pp. 1004-1014.

10. See, e.g., S. Ho, T. Foulsham, and A. Kingstone, "Speaking and Listening With the Eyes: Gaze Signaling During Dyadic Interaction," *PLoS One*, 10(8), 2015, eo136906.

11. Helmut Morsbach, "Aspects of Nonverbal Communication in Japan," in Larry Samovar and Richard Porter, eds., *Intercultural Communication: A Reader*, 3rd ed. Belmont, CA: Wadsworth, 1982, p. 308.

12. See also, Arryn Robbins and Michael C. Hout, "Look Into My Eyes," *Scientific American Mind*, January/February 2015, pp. 54-69.

13. Rachel Uda, "Sealed With a Grin," *Psychology Today*, April 2016.

14. Stephanie M. Bucklin, "The Big Picture," *Psychology Today*, September/October 2017, p. 43-44.

15. V. Richmond, "Teach Nonverbal Immediacy: Use and Outcomes," in J. L. Chesebro and M. C. McCroskey, eds., *Communication for Teachers.* Boston: Allyn & Bacon, 2002, pp. 65-82; also see Frank Bruni, "Read These Lips," *New York Times*, May 25, 2014, p. SR3.

16. See Julie Woodzicka "Sex Differences in Self-Awareness of Smiling During a Mock Job Interview," *Journal of Nonverbal Behavior*, 32(2), June 2008, pp. 109-121.

17. Jane E. Brody, "Good Posture May Better Your Position," *New York Times*, December 29, 2015, p. D5.

18. Johannes Michalak, Judith Mischnat, and Tobias Teisman, "Sitting Posture Makes a Difference: Embodiment Effects on Depressive Memory Bias," *Clinical Psychology and Psychotherapy*, 21(6), November/December, 2014, pp. 519-524.

19. Jeanne Whalen, "Slouch at Your Own Peril," *Wall Street Journal*, June 25, 2014, p. D1, D2.

20. Stephanie M. Bucklin, "The Big Picture," *Psychology Today*, September/October 2017, p. 43-44.

21. See Nancy Henley, *Body Politics: Power, Sex, and Nonverbal Communication.* New York: Simon & Schuster, 1986.

22. Albert Mehrabian, "Significance of Posture and Position in the Communication of Attitude and Status Relationship," *Psychological Bulletin*, 71 (1969), pp. 359-372; also see Johannes Michalak, Judith Mischnat, and Tobias Teisman, "Sitting Posture Makes a Difference: Embodiment Effects on Depressive Memory Bias," *Clinical Psychology and Psychotherapy*, 21(6), November/December 2014, pp. 519-524.

23. Christina Binkley, "Heelpolitik: The Power of a Pair of Stilettos," *Wall Street Journal*, August 2, 2007, p. D8.

24. Del Jones, "The Bald Truth About CEOs," *USA Today*, March 13, 2008, pp. 1B, 2B.

25. Malcolm Gladwell, *Blink.* New York: Little, Brown, 2005.

26. Del Jones, "Does Height Equal Power," *USA Today*, July 18, 2007, pp. 1B, 2B.

27. Paul Ekman, W. V. Friesen, and J. Baer, "The International Language of Gestures," *Psychology Today*, May 1984, pp. 64-69.

28. See, e.g., Scott Shane, "Language Help From Um, Almost-Words," *Sunday Record*, September 12, 1999, pp. L3, L7.

29. Peter Jaret, "My Voice Has Got to Go," *New York Times*, July 21, 2003, p, G1.

30. Mehrabian.

31. See Hyun O. Lee and Franklin J. Boster,

"Collectivism-Individualism in Perceptions of Speech Rate: A Cross-Cultural Comparison," *Journal of Cross Cultural Psychology*, 23(3), September 1992, pp. 377-388.

32. F. Goldman-Eisler, "Continuity of Speech Utterance, Its Determinance and Its Significance," *Language and Speech*, 4, 1961, pp. 220-231.

33. See Adam Jaworski, *The Power of Silence: Social and Pragmatic Perspective*. Thousand Oaks, CA: Sage, 1993.

34. Pamela Paul, "A Failure to Communicate," *New York Times*, August 29, 2010, p. 6; also see Shiri Lev-Ari and Boaz Keysar, "Why Don't We Believe Non-Native Speakers? The Influence of Accent on Credibility," *Journal of Experimental Social Psychology*, 46, 2010, pp. 1093-1096.

35. Sarah E. Needleman, "Office Personal Space Is Crowded Out," *Wall Street Journal*, December 7, 2009, p. B7.

36. Edward Hall, *The Hidden Dimension*. New York: Doubleday, 1969.

37. Lizette Alvarez, "Where the Healing Touch Starts With the Hospital Design," *New York Times*, pp. F5, F10; and T. Field, *Touch*, 2nd ed. Cambridge, MA: MIT Press, 2014.

38. See J. K. Burgoon, "Privacy and Communication," in M. Burgoon, ed., *Communication Yearbook 6*. Beverly Hills, CA: Sage, 1982, pp. 206-249; J. K. Burgoon and L. Aho, "Three Field Experiments on the Effects of Violations of Conversational Distance," *Communication Monographs*, 49, 1982, pp. 71-88; and J. K. Burgoon and J. B. Walther, "Nonverbal Expectations and the Evaluative Consequence of Violations," *Human Communication Research*, 17(2), 1990, pp. 232-265.

39. See, e.g., A. G. White, "The Patient Sits Down: A Clinical Note," *Psychosomatic Medicine*, 15, 1953, pp. 256-257.

40. Jill Filipovic, "Donald Trump Was a Creep. Too Bad Hillary Clinton Couldn't Say That," *New York Times*, August 27, 2017, SR4, SR5.

41. See, e.g., Sarah Goodyear, "The Threat of Gated Communities," *CityLab*, July 5, 2013, https://www.citylab.com/equity/2013/07/threat-gated-communities/6198.

42. James McAuley, "French President Macron Has Spent $30,000 on Makeup Services in Just 3 Months," *Washington Post*, August 25, 2017.

43. Dahlia Lithwick, "Our Beauty Bias Is Unfair," *Newsweek*, June 14, 2010, p. 20; and Jessica Bennett, "The Beauty Advantage," *Newsweek*, July 26, 2010, pp. 46-48; and T. K. Frevert and L. S. Walker, "Physical Attractiveness and Social Status," *Sociology Compass*, 8, 2014, pp. 313-323.

44. See L. K. Guerrero, J. A. DeVito, and M. L. Hecht, eds., *The Nonverbal Communication Reader: Classic and Contemporary Readings*, 2nd ed. Prospect Heights, IL: Waveland, 1999; and Joseph Kahn, "Chinese People's Republic Is Unfair to Its Short People," *New York Times*, May 21, 2004, p. A13.

45. Choe Sang-Hung, "South Korea Stretches Standards for Success," *New York Times*, December 24, 2009, pp. A6, A10; Patricia Marx, "About Face: Why Is South Korea the World's Plastic-Surgery Capital?" *New Yorker*, March 23, 2015, pp. 50-55.

46. "Cold Shoulder for Fat Customers," *New York Times*, April 5, 2005, F6.

47. Lindsay Averill, "New Voices Are Striking a Blow Against Fat Shaming," *CNN*, July 7, 2017, http://www.cnn.com/2017/07/07/opinions/fat-shaming-hage-clarkson-opinion-averill/index.html.

48. Maureen Dowd, "Dressed to Distract," *New York Times*, June 6, 2010, p. D6.

49. Harriet Brown, "For Obese People, Prejudice in Plain Sight," *New York Times*, March 16, 2010, p. D6.

50. V. Ritts, M. L. Patterson, and M. E. Tubbs, "Expectations, Impressions, and Judgments of Physically Attractive Students: A Review," *Review of Educational Research*, 62, 1992, p. 413-426.

51. J. Kilbourne, "The More You Subtract, the More You Add: Cutting Girls Down to Size," in J. Spade and C Valentine, ed., *The Kaleidoscope of Gender*. Belmont, CA: Wadsworth, 2004, pp. 234-244.

52. Ruth La Ferla, "Generation E. A.: Ethically Ambiguous," *New York Times*, December 28, 2003, pp. ST1, ST9.

53. Ray Smith, "Dress for Success—and Perhaps Be a Success," *Wall Street Journal*, February 22, 2016, p. R2.

54. Catherine Porter, "Canada Judge Faces Heat for Wearing Trump Cap," *New York*

Times, August 24, 2017, p. A4.

55. Jackie Bischof, "This Dress Makes People Stand Back, Really," *Wall Street Journal,* May 28, 2014, p. D2.

56. John T. Molloy, *New Dress for Success.* New York: Warner, 1990.

57. See, e.g., M. S. Singer and A. E. Singer, "The Effect of Police Uniforms on Interpersonal Perception," *Journal of Psychology,* 119, 1985, pp. 157-161.

58. Pantone Color Institute, "Color of the Year 2017," https://www.pantone.com/color-of-the-year-2017.

59. See Kendra Cherry, "Color Psychology: How Colors Impact Moods, Feelings, and Behaviors, 2016, https://www.verywell.com/color-psychology-2795824.

60. Roy A. Smith, "The Color of Confidence," *Wall Street Journal,* September 25-26, 2010, p. D3.

61. Pam Belluck, "Reinvent Wheel? Blue Room. Defusing a Bomb? Red Room," *New York Times,* February 6, 2009, pp. A1, A15.

62. See, e.g., Vance Packard and Mark Crispin Miller, *The Hidden Persuaders.* New York: Ig Publishing, 2007.

63. Vanessa Friedman, "For the Royals Abroad, Pantone Politics," *The New York Times,* July 23, 2017, p. ST3.

64. Robert Levine, *A Geography of Time, or How Every Culture Keeps Time Just a Little Differently.* New York: Basic Books, 1997; see also T. J. Bruneau, "Chronemics: Time-Binding and the Construction of Personal Time," *ETC: A Review of General Semantics,* 69(1), p. 72.

65. See Alex MacKenzie, *The Time Trap.* New York: McGraw-Hill, 1975; see also R. L. Hotz, "Time and Status, or, Why the Boss Is Late for Everything," *Wall Street Journal,* July 22, 2014, p. D1, D2.

66. See Robert J. Samuelson, "The Sad Fate of the Comma," *Newsweek,* July 23, 2007, p. 41.

67. Marilyn Elias, "Study: Hugging Warms the Heart, and Also May Protect It," *USA Today,* March 10, 2003, p. 7D; see also Ashley Montagu, *Touching: The Human Significance of the Skin.* New York: Harper & Row, 1971.

68. Marilyn Elias, "Hugs Can Do a Heart Good," *USA Today,* March 8, 2004, p. 7D; Nicholas Bakalar, "Five-Second Touch Can Convey Specific Emotion, Study Finds," *New York Times,* August 11, 2008, p. D3; and Benedict Carey, "Evidence That Little Touches Do Mean So Much," *New York Times,* February 23, 2010, p. D5.

69. Barbara Bales, *Communication and the Sexes.* New York: Harper & Row, 1988, p. 60.

70. See D. F. Fromme, W. E. Jaynes, D. K. Taylor, E. G. Harold, J. Daniell, J. R. Roundtree, and M. Fromme, "Nonverbal Behaviors and Attitudes Toward Touch," *Journal of Nonverbal Behavior,* 13, 1989, pp. 3-14.

71. R. Hoder, "The End of Hugs," *The Record,* September 3, 2014, p. A11.

72. See, e.g., J. T. Wood, *Interpersonal Communication in Everyday Encounters,* 5th ed. Belmont, CA, Wadsworth, 2009.

73. Henley.

74. Sarah Nassauer, "Stores Lead Shoppers by the Nose," *Wall Street Journal,* May 21, 2014, pp. D1, D4.

75. N. Wade, "Scent of a Man Is Linked to a Woman's Selection," *New York Times,* January 22, 2002, p. F2.

76. N. Wade, "For Gay Men, Different Scent of Attraction," *New York Times,* May 10, 2005, pp. A1, A14.

77. Jim Beckerman, "A Whiff of Vanilla Seems to Please Us All," *The Record,* September 16, 2003, pp. F1, F2.

78. Lauren Neergaard, "Researchers Find Bad Times Really Do Stink," *The Record,* March 28, 2008, p. A6.

79. Alissa J. Rubin, Patrick Kingsley and Palko Karasz, "How Imam's Charm and Guile Built the Barcelona Terrorist Cell," *New York Times,* August 24, 2017, p. A1, A10.

80. M. G. Millar and K. U. Millar, "The Effects of Suspicion on the Recall of Cues to Make Veracity Judgments," *Communication Reports,* 11, 1998, pp. 57-64.

81. R. G. Riggio and H. S. Freeman, "Individual Differences and Cues to Deception," *Journal of Personality and Social Psychology,* 45, 1983, pp. 899-915.

82. D. B. Buller and J. K Burgoon, "Deception Strategic and Nonstrategic Communication," in J. Daly and J. M. Wiemann, eds., *Interpersonal Communication.* Hillsdale, NJ: Erlbaum, 1994.

83. Paul Ekman and Mark G. Frank, "Lies That Fail," in Michael Lewis and Carolyn

Saarni, eds., *Lying and Deception in Everyday Life.* New York: Guilford, 1993, pp. 184-200.

84. J. E. Dovidio, S.L. Ellyson, C. F. Keating, K. Heltman, and C. E. Brown, "The Relationship of Social Power to Visual Displays of Dominance between Men and Women," *Journal of Personality and Social Psychology*, 54, 1988, pp. 233-242.

85. Emma G. Fitzsimmons, "Dude, Close Your Legs: MTA Fights a Spread Scourge," *New York Times*, December 21, 2014, p. 1, 34.

86. Julia T. Wood, *Gendered Lives.* Belmont, CA: Wadsworth, 1994, p. 154.

87. N. G. Rotter and G. S. Rotter, "Sex Differences in the Encoding and Decoding of Negative Facial Emotions," *Journal of Nonverbal Behavior*, 12(2), 1998, pp. 139-148.

88. Jack Healy, "Montana Legislature Dress Code Angers Women," *New York Times*, December 14, 2014, p. 24; see also Claire Zillman, "Congress's "No Sleeveless Dress Code Is Another Arbitrary Barrier for Women," *Fortune*, http://fortune.com/2017/07/07/congress-dress-code.

89. Joanna Stern, "Alexa, Siri, Cortana: The Problem With All-Female Digital Assistants," *Wall Street Journal*, February 22, 2017.

90. P. Anderson, "Exploring Intercultural Differences in Nonverbal Communication," in L. Samovar and R. Porter, eds. *Intercultural Communication: A Reader*, 3rd ed. Belmont, CA: Wadsworth, 1982, pp. 272-282.

91. E. R. McDaniel, "Japanese Nonverbal Communication: A Review and Critique of Literature," paper presented at the annual meeting of the Speech Communication Association, Miami Beach, FL, November 81-21, 1993.

92. J. H. Langlois, L. E. Kalakanis, A. J. Rubenstein, A. D. Larson, M. J. Hallam, and M. T. Smoot, "Maxims or Myths of Beauty: A Meta-Analytic and Theoretical Review," *Psychological Bulletin*, 126, 2000, pp. 380-423.

93. Claire Cain Miller, "From Sex Object to Gritty Woman: The Evolution of Women in Stock Photos," *New York Times*, September 7, 2017, p. B2, https://www.nytimes.com/2017/09/07/upshot/from-sex-object-to-gritty-woman-the-evolution-of-women-in-stock-photos.html.

94. Jim Blascovich and Jeremy Bailenson, *Avatars, Eternal Life, New Worlds, and the Dawn of the Virtual Revolution.* New York: William Morrow, 2011.

Chapter 6

1. See, e.g., David Glenn, "Divided Attention," *Chronicle of Higher Education*, February 28, 2010, http://chronicle.com/article/Scholars-Turn-Their-Attention/63746.

2. Karen Arenson, "The Fine Art of Listening," *New York Times Education Life*, January 13, 2002, pp. 34-35; Faith Byrnie, "The Madness of Multitasking," *Psychology Today*, "Brain Sense" blog, August 24, 2009, https://www.psychologytoday.com/us/blog/brain-sense/200908/the-madness-multitasking.

3. Cesar G. Soriano, "News Flash: Teen Stops Speaking!" *USA Today*, August 9, 2000, p. 1D.

4. Brendon Schurr, "Teenager Vows Not to Speak for a Year," *The Record*, August 16, 2000, p. A-5.

5. Stephen R. Covey, *The 7 Habits of Highly Effective People.* New York: Simon and Schuster, 1989, pp. 239-240.

6. See Jane Allan, "Talking Your Way to Success (Listening Skills), *Accountancy*, February 1993, pp. 612-663; and John W. Haas and Christina L. Arnold, "An Examination of the Role of Listening in Co-Workers," *Journal of Business Communication*, April 1995, pp. 123-139.

7. The Office Team Survey, 2000, was cited in "Sssh! Listen Up!" *High Gain, Inc. Newsletter*, June 2000, p. 4.

8. K. W. Hawkins and B. P. Fullion, "Perceived Communication Skill Needs for Work Groups," *Communication Research Reports*, 16, 1999, pp. 167-174.

9. J. T. Wood, "Buddhist Influences on Scholarship and Teaching," *Journal of Communication and Religion*, 2004, pp. 323-339.

10. See, e.g., M. Levine, "Tell the Doctor All Your Problems but Keep It to Less Than a Minute," *New York Times*, June 1, 2004, p. F6; and M. Nichols, "Listen Up for Better Sales," *Business Week Online*, September 15, 2006, p. 12.

11. Jared Sandberg, "Bad at Complying? You Might Just Be a Very Bad Listener," *Wall Street Journal*, September 25, 2007, p. B1.

12. Richard Emanuel, Jim Adams, Kim Baker, et al. "How College Students Spend Their Time Communicating," *International Journal of Listening*, 22(1), 2008, pp. 13-28; D. Beard and G. Bodie, "Listening Research in the Communication Discipline," in P. J. Gehrke and W. M. Keith, eds., *A Century of Communication Studies: The Unfinished Conversation.* New York: Routledge, pp. 207-233.

13. Brigitta R. Brunner, "Listening Communication and Trust: Practitioners' Perspectives of Business/Organizational Relationships," *International Journal of Listening*, 22(1), 2008, pp. 73-82.

14. See A. D. Wolvin and C. G. Coakley, "A Survey of the Status of Listening Training in Some Fortune 500 Corporations," *Communication Education*, 40, 1991, pp. 152-164.

15. Denise R. Superville, "Hours Spent Wired Changing How Kids Think and Interact," *The Record*, May 15, 2010, pp. A1, A8.

16. See "Generation M²: Media in the Lives of 8- to 18-Year-Olds," Kaiser Family Foundation, January 2010.

17. For a detailed discussion, see Ralph G. Nichols and Leonard A. Stevens, *Are You Listening?* New York: McGraw-Hill, 1956. See also K. Watson and L. Barker, "Listening Behavior: Definition and Measurement," in R. Bostrom, ed., *Communication Yearbook 8*, Beverly Hills CA: Sage, 1984, pp. 178-197; Andrew Wolvin and Carolyn Gwynn Coakley, *Listening*, 4th ed., Dubuque, IA: Brown, 1988; Andrew Wolvin, ed., *Listening and Human Communication in the 21st Century.* New York: Wiley Blackwell, 2011; and P. C. Fontana, S. D. Cohen, and A. D. Wolvin, "Understanding Listening Competency: A Systematic Review of Research Scales, *International Journal of Listening*, 29(3), 2015, pp. 148-176.

18. John R. Freund and Arnold Nelson, "Distortion in Communication," in B. Peterson, G. Goldhaber, and R. Pace, eds. *Communication Probes.* Chicago: Science Research Associates, 1974, pp. 122-124.

19. Gerald Goldhaber, *Organizational Communication*, Dubuque IA: Brown, 1993.

20. See L. Wheeless, A. Frymier, and C. Thompson, "A Comparison of Verbal Output and Receptivity in Relation to Attraction and Communication Satisfaction in Interpersonal Relationships," *Communication Quarterly*, Spring 1992, pp. 102-115.

21. See, e.g., Judi Brownell, *Listening: Attitudes, Principles and Skills.* New York: Routledge, 2012.

22. James Beavin, Linda Coates, and Trudy Johnson, "Listening Responses as a Collaborative Process: The Role of Gaze," *Journal of Communication*, 52(3), September 2002, pp. 566-579.

23. Frank Luntz, *Win.* New York: Hyperion, 2011.

24. For insight into empathic listening, also see Judi Brownell, *Listening: Attitudes and Skills*, 5th ed. New York: Routledge, 2012.

25. B. L. Omdahl, *Cognitive Appraisal, Emotion and Empathy.* London: Psychology Press, 2014.

26. T. Holtgraves, *Language as Social Action: Social Psychology and Language Use.* London: Psychology Press, 2014.

27. See, e.g., J. B. Weaver III and M. B. Kirtley, "Listening Styles and Empathy," *Southern Communication Journal*, 60, 1993, pp. 131-140.

28. Karen S. Peterson, "Sharing Memorable Moments Can Calm the Soul, Heal the Body," *USA Today*, February 15, 1999, p. 4D.

29. Angela Delli Santi, "N.J. Doctors to Learn Cultural Sensitivity," *The Record*, April 11, 2005, p. 6D.

30. Nissa Simmon, "Can You Hear Me Now?" *Time*, August 18, 2003; and Kim Painter, "Getting Bad Reception," *USA Today*, October 3, 2005, p. 6D.

31. C. Crosen, "Blah, Blah, Blah," *Wall Street Journal*, July 10, 1997, pp. 1A, 6A; and Betsy Lehman, "Getting an Earful Is Just What the Doctor Needs," *The Record*, March 21, 1994, p. B4.

32. See also Judi Brownell, *Listening, Attitudes, Principles and Skills.* New York: Routledge, 2012.

33. Ralph G. Nichols and Leonard Stevens, *Are You Listening?* New York: McGraw-Hill, 1956.

34. Harry Jackson Jr., "Fear of Forgetting," *The Record*, April 5, 2005, pp. F1, F2.

35. See A. Vangelisti, M. Knapp, and J. Daly, "Conversational Narcissism," *Communication Monographs*, December 1990, pp. 251-171.

36. Alfie Kohn, "Girl Talk, Guy Talk," *Psychology Today*, February 1988, pp. 65-66.

37. Christine Kenneally, *The First Word: The Search for the Origins of Language.* New York: Viking, 2007.

38. Deborah Tannen, *The Argument Culture: Moving From Debate to Dialogue.* New York: Ballentine, 1998.

39. Don Tosti, "Operant Conditioning," speech presented at Operant Conditioning Seminar, New York, Fall 1983.

40. David W. Johnson, *Reaching Out: Interpersonal Effectiveness and Self-Actualization.* Englewood Cliffs, NJ: Prentice Hall, 1972; and Thomas Gordon, *Leader Effectiveness Training.* New York: Wyden, 1977.

41. For a discussion of the benefit of questioning, see John F. Monoky, "Listen by Asking," *Industrial Distribution*, April 1995, p. 123.

42. See Richard Paul and Linda Elder, *The Miniature Guide to Critical Thinking*, 6th ed. Tomales, CA: Foundation for Critical Thinking Press, 2014.

43. See R. Boostrom, *Developing Creative and Critical Thinking.* New York: McGraw-Hill, 2001.

44. Teri Gamble and Michael Gamble, *The Public Speaking Playbook.* Thousand Oaks, CA: Sage, 2017.

45. Deborah Tannen, *You Just Don't Understand: Women and Men in Conversation.* New York: Morrow, 1990.

46. See Julia T. Wood, *Gendered Lives: Communication, Gender, and Culture*, 10th ed. Boston: Wadsworth, 2013, p. 127.

47. See, e.g., Deborah M. Saucier, et al. "Are Sex Differences in Navigation Caused by Sexually Dimorphic Strategies or by Differences in the Ability to Use the Strategies?" *Behavioral Neuroscience*, 116(3), 2002, pp. 403-410, and Bia Kim, Sewon Lee, and Jaesik Lee, "Gender Differences in Spatial Navigation," *Proceedings of the World Academy of Science, Engineering and Technology*, 25, November 2007, pp. 297-300.

48. S. Petronio, J. Martin, and R. Littlefield, "Prerequisite Conditions for Self Disclosing: A Gender Issue," *Communication Monographs*, 51, 1984, pp. 282-292.

49. See also Michael Purdy and Deborah Borisoff, *Listening in Everyday Life: A Personal and Professional Approach.* Lanham, MD: University Press of America, 1997.

50. Susan Chira, "Women Interrupted," *New York Times*, June 15, 2017, p. B1, B2.

51. Judi Brownell, *Listening*, 2nd ed.

52. C. Y. Cheng, "Chinese Philosophy and Contemporary Communication Theory," in D. I. Kincaid, ed., *Communication Theory: Eastern and Western Perspectives.* New York: Academic Press, 1987.

53. Documented by T. S. Lebra in *Japanese Patterns of Behavior.* Honolulu: University Press of Hawaii, 1976.

54. C. Kiewitz, J. B. Weaver III, H. B. Borsius, and G. Wiemann, "Cultural Differences in Listening Style Preferences: A Comparison of Young Adults in Germany, Israel and the United States," *International Journal of Public Opinion Research*, 9(3), Fall 1997, p. 233.

55. John Stewart and M. Thomas, "Dialogic Listening: Sculpting Mutual Meanings," in J. Stewart, ed., *Bridges Not Walls: A Book About Interpersonal Communication*, 10th ed. New York: McGraw-Hill, 2011.

56. Larry Samover and Richard Porter, *Communication Between Cultures.* Belmont, CA: Wadsworth, 2016.

57. For more information on this topic, also see Julia T. Wood, *Gendered Lives: Communication, Gender and Culture.* Belmont, CA: Wadsworth, 2016.

58. D. A. Christakis, E. J. Zimmerman, D. L. DiGuiseppe, and C. A. McCarty, "Early Television Exposure and Subsequent Attentional Problems in Children, *Pediatrics*, 113, 2004, pp. 707-713.

59. See, e.g., "Personality Typing," *Wired*, July 1999, p. 17. See also Wu Youyou, "Computer-Based Personality Judgments

Are More Accurate Than Those Made by Humans," *Proceedings of the National Academy of Sciences*, September 2014.

60. Patricia Alex, "Texting in Class Getting out of Hand," *The Record*, October 11, 2010; see also Employee Handbook Store, https://www.the-guru-group.com/employee-handbook.html, for company policies on texting and cell phone usage.

61. Sharon White Taylor, "Wireless and Witless," *New York Times*, July 5, 2000, p A17; and "Cell Phone Rage: Helpful Hints," *New York Times*, July 8, 2000, p. A-14; also see Dawn Rosenberg McKay, "Rules for Using Cell Phones at Work," *The Balance*, October 25, 2016.

62. David Shenk, *Data Smog*. New York: Harper & Row, 1997; see also David Levitin, *The Organized Mind: Thinking Straight in the Age of Information Overload*. New York: Dutton, 2015.

63. Todd Gitlin, "Supersaturation, or the Media Torrent and Disposable Feeling," in E. Bucy, ed., *Living in the Information Age: A New Media Reader*, 2nd ed. Belmont CA: Thomson Wadsworth, 2005.

64. Sheila C. Bentley, "Listening in the 21st Century," paper presented at the annual convention of the National Communication Association, Chicago, November 1999.

65. Mickey Meece, "Who's the Boss, You or Your Gadget?" *New York Times*, February 6, 2011, pp. BU1, BU8.

66. Jenna Wortham, "Everyone's Using Cellphones, but Not So Many Are Talking," *New York Times*, May 14, 2010, p. BU4; see also Jenna Wortham, "Is Social Media Disconnecting Us From the Big Picture?" *New York Times*, November 22, 2016.

67. Jay Reeves, "Texting as Life-Changer," *The Record*, September 20, 2010, p. A4.

68. See, Carolyn Mohr, "6 Gadgets From the Consumer Electronic Show," *The World of Technology*, January 2017.

69. Haley Sweetland Edwards, "Alexa Takes the Stand: Listening Devices Raise Privacy Issues," *Time*, May 15, 2017, pp. 28-29.

70. Ronald Schlager, *Selecting Video Conferencing Solutions*. CreateSpace Publishers, 2017.

Chapter 7

1. Virginia Satir, *The New Peoplemaking*. Palo Alto, CA: Science and Behavior Books, 1998, p. 51.

2. J. O'Neill, "Help Others for a Longer Life," *New York Times*, November 2, 2002, p. F6.

3. Susan Pinker, "People Who Need People Have the Longest Lives," *Wall Street Journal*, June 27/28, 2015, p. C2; Maggie Fox, "Sick? Lonely? Genes Tell the Tale," September 13, 2007, Reuters, https://www.reuters.com/article/us-genes-loneliness/sick-lonely-genes-tell-the-tale-idUSN1338802820070913; and Kathleen Fackelmann, "For Lonely Hearts, 1 Can Be an Unhealthy Number," *USA Today*, August 27, 2007, p. 8D; C. M. Perissinotto, I. S. Genzer, and K. E. Covinsky, "Loneliness in Older Persons: A Predictor of Functional Decline and Health," *JAMA Internal Medicine*, 172, 1078-1084.

4. William C. Schutz, *The Interpersonal Underworld*. Palo Alto, CA: Science and Behavior Books, 1966, pp. 18-20.

5. Steve Duck, *Human Relationships*, 3rd ed. Thousand Oaks, CA: Sage, 1999, p. 57.

6. See, e.g., Robert A. Bell, "Conversational Involvement and Loneliness," *Communication Monographs*, 52, 1985, pp. 218-235; see also M. Z. Yao and Z. Zhong, "Loneliness, Social Contacts and Internet Addiction: A Cross-Legged Panel Study," *Computers in Human Behavior*, 30, 2014, pp. 164-170.

7. Guy Winch, "Solutions for the Solitary," *Psychology Today*, July/August 2017, pp. 32-34.

8. Robert A. Bell and Michael Roloff, "Making a Love Connection: Loneliness and Communication Competence in the Dating Marketplace," *Communication Quarterly*, 39(1), Winter 1991, pp. 58-74.

9. Winch.

10. Schutz, p. 24.

11. J. A. Bryant, A. Sanders-Jackson, and A. M. K. Smallwood, "IMing, Text Messaging, and Adolescent Social Networks," *Journal of Computer Mediated Communication*, 11, 2006, pp. 577-592.

12. Andrea Heiman, "Flirting Still Has Its Attractions," *Sunday Record*, March 20, 1994.

13. Robert E. Nofsinger, *Everyday Conversation.* Newbury Park, CA: Sage, 1991, p. 1.

14. Deborah Cameron, *Good Talk? Living and Working in a Communication Culture.* Thousand Oaks, CA: Sage, 2000; and Deborah Tannen, "Why Sisterly Chats Make People Happier," *New York Times*, October 26, 2010, p. D6.

15. Anita L. Vangelisti and Mary A. Banski, "Couples' Debriefing Conversations: The Impact of Gender, Occupation, and Demographic Characteristics," *Family Relations*, 42(2), April 1993, pp. 149-157.

16. Sherry Turkle, *Reclaiming Conversation: The Power of Talk in a Digital Age.* New York: Penguin Press, 2015.

17. Sherry Turkle, "Stop Googling. Let's Talk," *New York Times*, September 27, 2015, p. SR1, SR6.

18. See Steven W. Duck, *Human Relationships*, 4th ed. London: Sage, 2007; and Steven W. Duck, *Meaningful Relationships: Talking, Sense, and Relating.* Thousand Oaks, CA: Sage, 1994.

19. Matt Huston, "Finding Your Crowd," *Psychology Today*, July/August 2017, p. 9.

20. Karen Shafer, "Talk in the Middle: Two Conversational Skills in Friendship," *English Journal*, 82(1), January 1993, pp. 53-55.

21. Bob Smith, "Care and Feeding of the Office Grapevine," *Management Review*, 85, 1996, p. 6; and Lisette Hilton, "They Heard It Through the Grapevine," *South Florida Business Journal*, 21, August 2000, p. 53.

22. See Joann Klimkiewicz, "Society Has Become Addicted to Gossip," *The Record*, April 29, 2007, p. F4; and F. T. McAndrew, E. K. Bell, and C. M. Garcia, "Who Do We Tell and Whom We Tell On: Gossip as a Strategy for Status Enhancement," *Journal of Applied Social Psychology*, 37(7), July 2007, pp. 1562-1577.

23. Celeste Headlee, *We Need to Talk: How to Have Conversations That Matter.* New York: HarperCollins, 2018.

24. I. Altman and D. A. Taylor, *Social Penetration: The Development of Interpersonal Relationships.* New York: Holt, Rinehart & Winston, 1973.

25. Sandra Petronio, *Boundaries of Privacy: Dialectics of Disclosure.* Albany: State University of New York Press, 2003. See also Sandra Petronio, "Translational Research Endeavors and the Practices of Communication Privacy Management," *Journal of Applied Communication Research*, 35(3), August 2007, pp. 219-222.

26. John Kim, "Are You in the Wrong Relationship?" *Psychology Today*, May/June, 2017, pp. 38-39.

27. Mark L. Knapp and Anita L. Vangelisti, *Interpersonal Communication and Human Relationships*, 2nd ed. Boston: Allyn & Bacon, 1992, p. 33.

28. Knapp and Vangelisti.

29. Michael Korda, "Small Talk," *Signature*, 1986, p. 78.

30. See Lawrence B. Rosenfield and Daniella Bordaray-Sciolino, "Self-Disclosure as a Communication Strategy During Relationship Termination," paper presented at the national meeting of the Speech Communication Association, Denver, CO, November 1985.

31. Steve Duck, "A Topography of Relationship Disagreement and Dissolution," in *Personal Relationships 4: Dissolving Personal Relationships.* New York: Academic Press, 1982.

32. Leslie Kaufman, "When the Ex Writes a Blog, the Dirtiest Laundry Is Aired," *New York Times*, April 18, 2008, pp. A1, A23; and Emily Gould, "Exposed," *New York Times Magazine*, May 25, 2008, pp. 32-40.

33. See S. W. Duck and J. T. Wood, "What Goes Up May Come Down: Sex and Gendered Patterns in Relational Dissolution," in M. A. Fine and J. H. Harvey, eds., *The Handbook of Divorce and Relationship Dissolution*, Mahwah, NJ: Erlbaum, 2005, pp. 169-187; and J. T. Wood, *Gendered Lives: Communication, Gender and Culture*, 9th ed. Belmont, CA: Wadsworth, 2011.

34. See, e.g., Harold S. Kushner, *When Bad Things Happen to Good People.* New York: Schocken Books, 1981.

35. N. Stevens, "Re-engaging: New Partnerships in Late-Life Widowhood," *Aging International*, 27(4), Spring 2003, pp. 27-43.

36. Mary Murphy Marcus, "Online Love Is Easy Come, Easy Go," *USA Today*, February 4, 2011, p. 1A.

37. Matt Huston, "Insights," *Psychology Today*, July/August 2015, p. 9.

38. Teddy Wayne, "Swiping Them Off Their Feet," *New York Times*, November 9, 2014, p. ST14; Eli J. Finkel, "In Defense of Tinder," *New York Times*, February 8, 2015, p. SR9.

39. Jessica Bennett, "The Agony of the Digital Tease," *New York Times*, July 10, 2016, p. ST2.

40. Aimee Lee Ball, "Breaking Up? Let an App Do It," *New York Times*, December 27, 2015, ST1, ST2.

41. Lee Siegel, *Against the Machine: Being Human in the Age of the Electronic Mob*. New York: Random House, 2008.

42. Sam Slaughter, "A Medium for Every Message," *New York Times*, December 13, 2015, p. ST8.

43. Laura H. Holson, "Breaking Up in a Digital Fishbowl," *New York Times*, January 7, 2010, pp. E1, E6.

44. Sophia Kercher, "Modern Help for the Brokenhearted? It's Online," *New York Times*, February 2, 2017, p. D3.

45. J. W. Thibaut and H. H. Kelly, *The Social Psychology of Groups*. New York: Wiley, 1959.

46. See Richard West and Lynn H. Turner, *Introducing Communication Theory: Analysis and Application*. Mountain View, CA: Mayfield, 2000, pp. 189-190.

47. L. A. Baxter and B. M. Montgomery, *Relating Dialogues and Dialectics*. New York: Guilford Press, 1966; and L. A. Baxter, "Dialectical Contradictions in Relationship Development," *Journal of Social and Personal Relationships*, 7, 1990, pp. 69-88.

48. See Sandra Petronio, ed., *Balancing the Secrets of Private Disclosures*. Mahwah, NJ: Erlbaum, 1999.

49. C. A. VanLear, "Testing a Cyclical Model of Communication Openness in Relationship Development," *Communication Monographs*, 58, 1991, pp. 337-361.

50. J. G. Wood, L. Dendy, E. Dordek, M. Germany, and S, Varallo, "Dialectic of Difference: A Thematic Analysis of Intimates' Meanings for Differences," in K. Carter and M. Presnell, eds., *Interpretive Approaches to Interpersonal Communication*. New York: State University of New York Press, 1994, pp. 115-136.

51. K. B. Serota, T. R. Levine, and F. J. Boster, "The Prevalence of Lying in America: Three Studies of Self-Reported Lies," *Human Communication Research*, 36(1), 2010, pp. 2-25.

52. Yudhijit Bhattacharjee, "Why We Lie," *National Geographic*, June 2017, http://www.nationalgeographic.com/magazine/2017/06/lying-hoax-false-fibs-science.

53. See Mark L. Knapp, *Lying and Deception in Human Interaction*. Boston: Penguin Academics, 2008.

54. Cal Thomas and Bob Beckel, "Lies, Lies, Lies," *USA Today*, June 3, 2010, p. 11A.

55. C. Camden, M. T. Motley, and A. Wilson, "White Lies in Interpersonal Communication: A Taxonomy and Preliminary Investigation of Social Motivations," *Western Journal of Speech Communication*, 48, 1984, pp. 309-325.

56. See E. Bryant, "Real Lies, White Lies and Gray Lies: Towards a Typology of Deception: *Kaleidoscope: A Graduate Journal of Qualitative Communication Research*, 7, 2008, pp. 723-748.

57. J. J. Bavelas, A. Black, N. Chovil, and J. Mullett, *Equivocal Communication*. Newbury Park, CA: Sage, 1990, p. 171; and Benedict Carey, "I'm Not Lying, I'm Telling a Future Truth, Really," *New York Times*, May 6, 2008, p. F5.

58. Sissela Bok, *Lying*. New York: Pantheon, 1978; and Sissela Bok, *Secrets*. New York: Random House, 1989.

59. J. K. Rempel and J. G. Holmes, "How Do I Trust Thee?" *Psychology Today*, February 1986.

60. A. L. Vangelisti and L. P. Crumley, "Reactions to Messages That Hurt: The Influence of Relational Contexts," *Communication Monographs*, 65, 1998, pp. 173-196.

61. Abigail Fagan, "Bound by Laughter," *Psychology Today*, September-October 2017.

62. Natalie Angier, "Laughs: Rhythmic Bursts of Social Glue," *New York Times*, February 27, 1996, pp. C1, C5.

63. Seth Borenstein, "Why Have Sex?" *The Record*, August 1, 2007, p. A8.

64. N. S. Eldridge and L. A. Gilbert, "Correlates of Relationship Satisfaction in Lesbian Couples," *Psychology of Women Quarterly*, 14, 1990, pp. 43-62.

65. See, e.g., Charlotte J. Patterson, "Family Relationships of Lesbians

and Gay Men," *Journal of Marriage and the Family*, 62(4), November 2000, pp. 1052-1069.

66. L. A. Rudman and J. E. Phelan, "The Interpersonal Power of Feminism: Is Feminism Good for Romantic Relationships?" *Sex Roles*, 2007.

67. Heiman.

68. Sharon Jayson, "Women Say Sorry More Because of a Sense of 'I'm Wrong,'" *USA Today*, September 29, 2010, p. 5D.

69. Science Daily.com, "Women More Perceptive Than Men in Describing Relationships," www.sciencedaily.com/releases/2008/02/080213111055.htm.

70. Stephanie Rosenbloom, "Sorry Boys, This Is Our Domain," *New York Times*, February 21, 2008, pp. G1, G8.

71. J. D. Ragsdale, "Gender Satisfaction Level, and the Use of Relational Maintenance Strategies in Marriage," *Communication Monographs*, 63, 1996, pp. 354-369.

72. Eldridge and Gilbert, "Correlates of Relationship Satisfaction," pp. 43-62.

73. A. M. Sherman, H. E. Lansford, and B. L. Volling, "Sibling Relationships and Best Friendships in Young Adulthood: Warmth, Conflict, and Well-Being," *Personal Relationships*, 13, 2006, pp. 151-165.

74. Sharon Jayson, "Internet Changing the Game of Love," *USA Today*, February 11, 2010, pp. 8A, 8B.

75. Joanne Kaufman, "Romancing the Phone," *Wall Street Journal*, June

11, 2010, p. W8; and Judith Shulevitz, "Dating, Disrupted," *Atlantic*, November 2016, p. 52-53.

76. Sharon Jayson, "The Year We Stopped Talking," *USA Today*, December 30, 2010–January 2, 2011, pp. 1A, 2A.

77. Maureen O'Connor, "Social Media Ruined Social Climbing," *New York Magazine*, May 1-14, 2017, pp. 20-24.

78. Sherry Turkle, *Alone Together: Why We Expect More From Technology and Less From Each Other*. New York: Basic Books, 2011.

79. Sharon Jayson, "Thanks for Oversharing," *USA Today*, September 14, 2010, pp. 1D, 2D.

80. See, e.g., "Living a Second Life Online," *Newsweek*, July 28, 2008, p. 10.

Chapter 8

1. See S. W. Duck, "Interpersonal Attraction and Personal Relationships," in V. S. Ramachandran, ed., *Encyclopedia of Human Behavior*, 2nd ed. New York: Academic Press, 2012; and Ellen Bercheid and Elaine Hatfield Walster, *Interpersonal Attraction*, 2nd ed. Reading, MA: Addison-Wesley, 1978.

2. Wendy Paris, "Laws of Attraction," *Psychology Today*, July/August 2017, pp. 55-61; and Emily Prager, "The Science of Beauty," *New York Times*, April 17, 1994.

3. Bercheid and Walster.

4. Eliot Aronson, *The Social Animal*, 3rd ed. San Francisco: Freeman, 1980, p. 239.

5. See Katherine C. Maguire, "Will It Ever End? A (Re) Examination of Uncertainty in College Student Long-Distance Relationships," *Communication Quarterly*, November 2007, pp. 415-432; and Charles Berger, "Uncertainty and Information Exchange in Developing Relationships," in Steve Duck, ed., *Handbook of Personal Relationships*. New York: Wiley, 1988, p. 244.

6. C. R. Berger and R. J. Calabrese, "Some Explorations in Initial Interaction and Beyond: Toward a Developmental Theory of Interpersonal Communication," *Human Communication Research*, 1, 1975, pp. 98-112.

7. See, e.g., W. Gudykunst, "Uncertainty and Anxiety," in Y. Y. Kim and W. Gudykunst, eds., *Theories in Intercultural Communication*. Newbury Park, CA: Sage, 1988, pp. 123-156.

8. See A. Ramirez, M. Sunnafrank, and R. Goei, "Predicted Outcome Value Theory in Ongoing Relationships," *Communication Monographs*, 77, 2010, pp. 27-50; and M. Sunnafrank, "A Communication-Based Perspective on Attitude Similarity and Interpersonal Attraction in Early Acquaintance," *Communication Monographs*, 51, 1984, pp. 372-380.

9. Keith E. Davis, "Near and Dear: Friendship and Love Compared," *Psychology Today*, February 1985, pp. 22-30.

10. See C. I. Yee, G. C. Gonzaga, and S. I. Gable,

"Positive Emotions in Close Relationships," in M. M. Tugade, M. N. Shiota, and I. D. Kirby, eds., *Handbook of Positive Emotions.* New York: Guilford Press, 2014, pp. 215-228; W. Samter, "Friendship Interaction Skills Across the Lifespan," in J. O. Greene and B. R. Burleson, eds., *Handbook of Communication and Social Interaction Skills.* Mahwah, NJ: Erlbaum, 2003; Daniel Goleman, "'Friends for Life': An Emerging Biology of Emotional Healing," *New York Times*, October 10, 2006; and Alan K. Goodby and Scott A. Myers, "Relational Maintenance Behaviors of Friends With Benefits: Investigating Equity and Relational Characteristics," *Human Communication*, 11(1), Spring 2008, pp. 71-85.

11. W. K. Rawlins, "Friendship as a Communicative Achievement: A Theory and an Interpretive Analysis of Verbal Reports," doctoral dissertation, Temple University, Philadelphia, 1981.

12. Sharon Jayson, "Is Dating Dead?" *USA Today*, March 31, 2011, pp. 1A, 2A.

13. Robert J. Sternberg, "A Triangular Theory of Love," *Psychological Review*, 93, 1986, pp. 119-135; and Robert L. Sternberg, *The Triangle of Love: Intimacy, Passion, Commitment.* New York: Basic Books, 1988.

14. Alice Park, "Love Hurts," *Time*, April 11, 2011; Nanci Hellmich, "Heartbreak Hurts Physically, Too," *USA Today*, p. 1A; and Matt McMillen, "To the Brain, Getting Burned, Getting Dumped Feel the Same," March 29, 2011, http://www.cnn.com/2011/HEALTH/03/28/burn.heartbreak.same.to.brain/index.html.

15. See Sally A. Lloyd and Beth C. Emery, *The Dark Side of Courtship: Physical and Sexual Aggression.* Thousand Oaks, CA: Sage, 2000; and J. D. Cunningham and J. K. Antill, "Current Trends in Nonmarital Cohabitation: The Great POSSLQ Hunt Continues," in Julia Wood and Steve W. Duck, eds., *Understanding Relationship Processes, 6: Off the Beaten Track: Understudied Relationships.* Thousand Oaks, CA: Sage, 1995, pp. 148-172.

16. D. Holmberg, "So Far So Good: Scripts for Romantic Relationship Development as Predictors of Relational Well-Being," *Journal of Social and Personal Relationships*, 19(6), December 2002, pp. 777-796.

17. Julia T. Wood, *Gendered Lives*, 3rd ed. Belmont: CA: Wadsworth, 1999, p. 340.

18. Virginia Satir, *The New Peoplemaking.* Mountain View, CA: Science and Behavior Books, 1988, p. 79; and A. Vangelisti, K. C. Maguire, A. Alexander, and G. Clark, "Hurtful Family Environments: Links With Individual and Relationship and Perceptual Variables," *Communication Monographs*, 74(3), September 2007, pp. 357-385.

19. Sharon Jayson and Anthony DeBarros, "Young Adults Delaying Marriage," *USA Today*, September 12, 2007, p. 6D.

20. Satir, *New Peoplemaking*, pp. 182-193.

21. Deborah Gibbons and Paul M. Olk, "The Individual and Structural Origins of Friendship and Social Position Among Professionals," *Journal of Personality and Social Psychology*, 84(2), February 2003, pp. 340-352; and Tom Terez, "The Power of Nice," *Workforce*, 82(1), January 2003, pp. 22-24.

22. See P. M. Sias, "Workplace Relationships," in L. I. Putman and D. K. Mumby, eds., *The SAGE Handbook of Organizational Communication: Advances in Theory, Research, and Methods*, Thousand Oaks, CA: Sage, 2014, pp. 375-400; and Y. Venkataramini, G. Labianca, and T. Grosser, "Positive and Negative Workplace Relationships, Social Satisfaction and Organizational Attachment," *Journal of Applied Psychology*, 98, 2013, pp. 1028-1039.

23. Marco della Cava and Kevin McCoy, "'Bro Culture' Far From Tamed in the Office, Women Say," *USA Today*, August 22, 2017, p. 1B.

24. Sue Schellenbarger, "The Unexpected Benefits of Being a Worrywart at Work," *Wall Street Journal*, April 1, 2015, pp. D1, D2.

25. Daniel Goleman, *Emotional Intelligence.* New York: Bantam, 1995, p. 34; see also Goleman, *Social Intelligence: The New Science of Human Relationships.* New York: Bantam, 2006.

26. Steve Ayan, "How to Control Your Feelings—and Live Happily Ever After," *Scientific American Mind*, January 2015, pp. 48-53.

27. Alan V. Horwitz, Jerome C. Wakefield, and Robert L. Spitzer, *The Loss of Sadness: How Psychiatry Transformed Normal Sorrow Into Depressive Disorder.* Boston: Oxford University Press, 2007.

28. Eric G. Wilson, *Against Happiness.* New York: Farrar, Straus & Giroux, 2008.

29. John Cloud, "When Sadness Is a Good Thing," *Time,* August 27, 2007, p. 56.

30. Carroll E. Izard, *Human Emotions.* New York: Plenum, 1977, p. 10.

31. Robert Plutchik, "Emotions: A General Psychoevolutionary Theory," in Klaus R. Scherer and Paul Ekman, eds., *Approaches to Emotion.* Hillsdale, NJ: Erlbaum, 1984, pp. 197-218.

32. See Daniel Goleman, "A Feel-Good Theory: A Smile Affects Mood," *New York Times,* July 18, 1989, pp. C1, C9.

33. Ellen O'Brien, "Moods Are as Contagious as the Office Cold," *The Record,* November 15, 1993, p. B3.

34. Katherine J. Miller and Joy Koesten, "Financial Feeling: An Investigation of Emotion and Communication in the Workplace," *Journal of Applied Communication Research,* 36(1), February 2008, pp. 8-32.

35. Ayan.

36. Theodore Isaac Rubin, *The Angry Book.* New York: Macmillan, 1970; and Rolland S. Parker, *Emotional Common Sense.* New York: Harper & Row, 1986.

37. J. A. Hall, "Sex Differences in Friendship Expectations: A Meta-Analysis," *Journal of Social and Personal Relationships,* 28, 2011, p. 723-747.

38. Ibid.

39. Marilyn Elias, "The Traits of Wrath in Men and Women," *USA Today,* August 11, 1994, p. 1D.

40. Michael Ryan, "Go Ahead—Cry," *Parade,* January 5, 1997, p. 22.

41. Elizabeth Bernstein, "Fighting Happily Ever After," *Wall Street Journal,* July 27, 2010, pp. D1, D4.

42. J. Gottman, *Why Marriages Succeed or Fail: And How You Can Make Yours Last.* New York: Simon & Schuster, 1994.

43. Alan C. Filley, *Interpersonal Conflict Resolution.* Glenview, IL: Scott, Foresman, 1975.

44. See Denise H. Cloven and Michael E. Roloff, "The Chilling Effect of Aggressive Potential on the Expression of Complaints in Intimate Relationships," *Communication Monographs,* 60(3), September 1993, pp. 199-219.

45. See, e.g., Stella Ting-Toomey, "Managing Conflict in Intimate Intercultural Relationships," in Dudley D. Cahn, ed., *Conflict in Personal Relationships.* Hillsdale, NJ: Erlbaum, 1994.

46. See, e.g., Arthur J. Lange and Patricia Jakubowski, *Responsible Assertive Behavior.* Champaign, IL: Research Press, 1976.

47. See, e.g., Sharon Anthony Bower and Gordon H. Bower, *Asserting Yourself: A Practical Guide for Positive Change,* updated edition. Reading, MA: Perseus Books, 1991, pp. 11-113; also see https://www2.fgcu.edu/studentservices/StudentConduct/files/D.E.S.C._Script.pdf.

48. For exercises related to the topic, see Danny Saunders, "Exercises in Communicating," *Simulation/Games for Learning,* 21(2), June 1991, pp. 186-200.

49. J. M Gottman and R. W. Levinson, "Observing Gay and Lesbian and Heterosexual Couples' Relationships: Mathematical Modeling of Conflict Interaction," *Journal of Homosexuality,* 45(1), 2003, pp. 711-720.

50. Ibid.

51. Lori Oliwenstein, "Marry Me," *Time,* January 28, 2008, pp. 73-76.

52. See J. W. Pennebaker, B. Rime, and V. E. Blankenship, "Stereotypes of Emotional Expressiveness of Northerners and Southerners: A Cross-Cultural Test of Montesquieu's Hypotheses," *Journal of Personality and Social Psychology,* 70, 1996, pp. 372-380.

53. F. E. Jandt, *Intercultural Communication: An Introduction,* 3rd ed. Thousand Oaks, CA: Sage, 2001; and L. A. Samovar, R. E. Porter, and E. R. McDaniel, *Communication Between Cultures,* 4th ed. Belmont, CA: Thomson Wadsworth, 2007.

54. S. Ting-Toomey, K. K. Yee-Jung, R. B. Shapiro, W. Garcia, and T. Wright, "Ethnic Identity Salience and Conflict Styles in Four Ethnic Groups: African Americans, Asian Americans, European Americans, and Latino Americans," paper presented at the annual conference of the Speech Communication

Association," New Orleans, November 1994.

55. See, e.g., Mary Jo Sales, *American Girls: Social Media and the Secret Lives of Teenagers*. New York: Knopf, 2016.

56. Alan Wright, "Friending, Ancient or Otherwise," *New York Times*, December 2, 2007, p. WK4.

57. Frank Bruni, "How Facebook Warps Our Worlds," *New York Times*, May 22, 2016, p. 3SR.

58. Laurence Scott, *The Four-Dimensional Human: Ways of Being in the Digital World*. New York: Norton, 2016.

59. Craig Wilson, "Suddenly, You've Got a Friend—Tons of Them," *USA Today*, February 6, 2008, p. 1D; Steven Levy, "How Many Friends Is Too Many?" *Newsweek*, May 26, 2008, p. 15; Robin Dunbar, *How Many Friends Does One Person Need? Dunbar's Number and Other Evolutionary Quirks*. Cambridge, MA: Harvard University Press, 2010.

60. John Gapper, "Always Connected," *Financial Times*, March 11-12, 2017, p. 9.

61. Mai-Ly Steers, Robert E. Wickham, and Linda K. Acitelli, "Seeing Everyone Else's Highlight Reels: How Facebook Usage Is Linked to Depressive Symptoms," *Journal of Social and Clinical Psychology*, 33(8), 2014, pp. 701-731.

62. M. Z. Yao, Z. Zhong, "Loneliness, Social Contacts, and Internet Addiction: A Cross-Lagged Panel Study," *Computers in Human Behavior*, 30, 2014, pp. 164-170.

63. Joe Queenan, "Polls and Stats for Friends and Family," *Wall Street Journal*, September 9-10, 2017, p. C11.

64. John Markoff and Paul Mozur, "Program Knows Just How You Feel," *New York Times*, August 4, 2015, pp. D1, D2.

65. Nicholas Carr, "These Are Not the Robots We Were Promised," *New York Times*, September 10, 2017, p. SR12.

66. Elizabeth Dwoskin and Evelyn M. Rusli, "The Technology That Unmasks Your Hidden Emotions," *Wall Street Journal*, January 28, 2015, http://www.wsj.com/articles/startups-see-your-face-unmask-your-emotions-1422472398.

67. Jean M. Twenge, "The Smartphone Generation vs. Free Speech," *Wall Street Journal*, September 2-3, 2017, p. C3.

68. Svetlana Shkolnikova, "Smartphones Dominate Kids' Lives," *The Record*, August 21, 2017, pp. 1A, 6A.

Chapter 9

1. D. Johnson and F. Johnson, *Joining Together: Group Theory and Group Skills*, 12th ed. Boston: Pearson, 2016.

2. See www.bestcorporateevents.com for a sampling of current companies providing training in team building.

3. Henry Jenkins, "From YouTube to YouUniversity," *Chronicle of Higher Education*, February 16, 2007, p. B10. Also see "How to Build a Teamwork Culture," *The Balance*, 2017, www.thebalance.com/how-to-build-a-teamwork-culture-1918509.

4. See, for e.g., S. A. Beebe and J. T. Masterson, *Communicating in Small Groups: Principles and Practices*, 11th ed. Boston: Pearson, 2014.

5. Natalie Angier, "Why We're So Nice: We're Wired to Cooperate," *New York Times*, July 23, 2002, pp. F1, F8.

6. See, e.g., H. Lancaster, "The Team Spirit Can Lead Your Career to New Victories," *Wall Street Journal*, January 14, 1996, p. B1; and M. Ridley, "Which Makes Us Nicer, Teams or Trade?" *Wall Street Journal*, August 27, 2011.

7. See David Chaudron, "Nailing Jelly to a Tree: Approaches to Self-Directed Work Teams," 2008, www.organizedchange.com/selfdir.htm; Daniel S. Iacofano, *Meeting of the Minds*. New York: MIG Communication, 2001; M. A. Verpeij, "When You Put the Team in Charge," *Industry Week*, December 1990; and R. S. Wellins, C. W. Byham, and J. M. Wilson, *Empowered Teams: Creating Self-Directed Workgroups That Improve Quality, Productivity and Participation*. San Francisco: Jossey-Bass, 1991.

8. J. Hackman, "The Design of Work Teams," in J. Lorsch ed., *Handbook of Organizational Behavior*. Englewood Cliffs, NJ: Prentice Hall, 1987. See also *Handbook of Organization Behavior*, 2nd ed. New York: Wiley, 2009; and T. Clark, *Business Models for Teams*. New York: Penguin, 2017.

9. W. Charles Redding, *Communication Within the Organization*. New York:

Industrial Communication Council, 1972.

10. Douglas McGregor, *The Human Side of Enterprise.* New York: McGraw-Hill, 1960.

11. B. Tuchman, "Developmental Sequence in Small Groups," *Psychological Bulletin*, 63, 1965, pp. 384-399; and S. A. Wheelen and J. M. Hockberger, "Validation Studies of the Group Development Questionnaire," *Small Group Research*, 27(1), 1996, pp. 143-170.

12. See, for example, J. Keyton, "Group Termination: Completing the Study of Group Development," *Small Group Research*, 24, 1999, pp. 84-100.

13. See, e.g., Marshall Scott Poole, "Do We Have Any Theories of Group Communication?" *Communication Studies*, 41(3), 1990, p. 237.

14. Dave Logan, J. King, and H. Fisher-Wright, *Tribal Leadership.* New York: HarperCollins, 2008.

15. Kenneth Benne and Paul Sheats, "Functional Roles of Group Members," *Journal of Social Issues*, 4, 1948, pp. 41-49.

16. For a discussion of supportive leadership, see Peter G. Northouse, *Leadership: Theory and Practice*, 7th ed. Thousand Oaks, CA: Sage, 2015; and Teri Kwal Gamble and Michael Gamble, *Leading With Communication: A Practical Approach to Leadership Communication.* Thousand Oaks, CA: Sage, 2013.

17. Morton Deutsch, "A Theory of Cooperation

and Competition," *Human Relations*, 2, 1949, pp. 129-152.

18. Jack R. Gibb, "Defensive Communication," *Journal of Communication*, 2, 1961, pp. 141-148.

19. Ibid.

20. See Y. Oztubo, A. Masuchi, and D. Nakanishi, "Majority Influence Process in Group Judgment: Test of the Social Judgment Scheme Model in a Group Polarization Context," *Group Process and Intergroup Relations*, 5(3), July 2002, pp. 249-262; and D. G. Meyers, *Social Psychology*, 12th ed. New York: McGraw-Hill, 2012.

21. John Dewey, *How We Think.* Boston: Heath, 1910.

22. Jay Cocks, "Let's Get Crazy!" *Time*, June 11, 1990, p. 40.

23. Betty Edwards, *Drawing on the Right Side of the Brain*. New York: TarcherPerigee, 2012.

24. See James Webb Young, *A Technique for Producing Ideas.* New York: McGraw-Hill, 2015; and Luke Johnson, "How to Find Ideas for Challenging Times," *Financial Times*, June 18, 2008, p. 10.

25. Alex Osborn, *Applied Imagination.* New York: Scribner's, 2011; N. Michinov, E. Jamet, N. Metayer, and B. Le Henaff, "The Eyes of Creativity: Impact of Social Comparison and Individual Creativity on Performance and Attention to Others' Ideas During Electronic Brainstorming," *Computers in Human Behavior*, 42, 2015, pp. 57-67.

26. Kelly K. Spors, "Productive Brainstorms Take the Right Mix of Elements," *Wall Street Journal*, July 24, 2008, p. B5.

27. Sidney Parnes, *A Source Book for Creative Thinking*. New York: Scribner's, 1962. See also Robert Root Bernstein, *Sparks of Genius*. New York, Mariner Books, 2001.

28. Leslie Dorman and Peter Edidin, "Original Spin," *Psychology Today*, July 8, 1989, p. 46.

29. Rosabeth Moss Kanter, "How to Be an Entrepreneur Without Leaving Your Company," *Working Woman*, November 1986, p. 44. See also Rosabeth Kanter, *When Giants Learn to Dance*. New York: Touchstone, 1990.

30. G. Hofstede, *Culture and Organizations: Software of the Mind.* New York: McGraw-Hill, 1997.

31. Paul B. Brown, "A Defense of the Boss's Pay," *New York Times*, April 12, 2008, p. C5.

32. Francesco Guerrera, "Women Crack Glass Ceiling From Above," *Financial Times*, July 23, 2008, p. 3.

33. See, e.g., L. P. Stewart, P. J. Cooper, A. D. Stewart, and S. H. Friendley, *Communication and Gender*. Boston: Allyn & Bacon, 2003, p. 44-50.

34. S. Helgesen, *The Female Advantage: Women's Use of Leadership*. New York: Doubleday, 1990.

35. Julia T. Wood, *Gendered Lives*, 10th ed. Belmont, CA: Cengage Learning, 2006; and Iris Aaltio and Pila Lapiston, "Discursive Practice in Ways Male and Female Managers Talk About Careers," www.mngtworkato/ac/nz.ejrotconference2003/proceedings/gender/Aaltio.pdf.

36. Shirley S. Wang, "Why So Many People Can't Make Decisions," *Wall Street*

Journal, September 28, 2010, pp. D1, D2.

37. See, e.g., S. B. Paletz, K. Peng, M. Erez, and C. Maslach, "Ethnic Composition and the Differential Impact on Group Processes in Diverse Teams," *Small Group Research*, 35, 2004, pp. 128-157.

38. Delores Cathcart and Robert Cathcart, "The Group: A Japanese Context," in Larry Samovar and Richard Porter, eds. *Intercultural Communication: A Reader*, 14th ed. Belmont CA: Wadsworth, 2014.

39. Harry C. Triandis, Richard Brislin, and C. Harry Hul, "Cross Cultural Training Across the Individualism-Collectivism Divide." *International Journal of Intercultural Relations*, 12, 1988.

40. Cathcart and Cathcart.

41. Ichiyo Makamoto, "Modernizers Span a Cultural Divide," *Financial Times*, May 22, 2008, p. 14.

42. Erin White, "Making the Generation Gap Work for You," *The Record*, July 278, 2008, pp. J1-J2.

43. Stefan Stern, "Y's and Wherefores of a Multi-Generation Workplace," *Financial Times*, April 15, 2008, p. 12.

44. Laurie J. Flynn, "MySpace Mind-Set Finally Shows Up at the Office," *New York Times*, April 9, 2008, p. 7.

45. Clive Thompson, "Close Encounters," *Wired*, August 2008.

46. Brad Stone, "At Social Site, Only the Businesslike Need Apply," *New York Times*, June 18, pp. C1, C2.

47. Adam Bryant, "Views From the Top," *Wall Street Journal*, April 21, 2011, p. A11.

48. Mark Tuton, "Going to the Virtual Office in Second Life," CNN.com. See also Matt Weinberger, "This Company Was 13 Years Early to Virtual Reality and It's Getting Ready to Try Again," http://www.businessinsider.com/second-life-is-still-around-and-getting-ready-to-conquer-virtual-reality-2015-3.

49. Laura Rich, "Tapping the Wisdom of the Crowd," *New York Times*, August 5, 2012, p. B8.

50. David Gelles, "The Personal at Work Can Be a Disruptive Mix," *Financial Times*, April 20, 2011, p. 2.

51. Eileen Zimmerman, "Staying Professional in Virtual Meetings," *New York Times*, September 26, 2010, p. BU9; and J. Stepper, *Working Out Loud: For a Better Career and Life*. Farnborough, NH: Ikigai Press, 2015.

52. Joanne Lublin, "Video Comes to Board Meetings," *Wall Street Journal*, April 25, 2011, p. B6.

53. Caroline Winter, "Is the Vertical Pronoun Really Such a Capital Idea?" *New York Times Magazine*, August 3, 2008.

54. Bobby R. Patton and Kim Griffin, *Decision Making: Group Interaction*. New York: Harper & Row, 1978.

Chapter 10

1. Sutton, quoted in Jason Zweig, "How Group Decisions End Up Wrong-Footed," *Wall Street Journal*, April 25, 2009, p. B1.

2. Paul B. Brown, "What Sets Leaders Apart From the Pack," *New York Times*, February 5, 2006, p. BU8.

3. For a historical perspective and summary and critique of 114 studies of small groups, focusing on leadership, discussion, and pedagogy, see John F. Cragan and David W. Wright, "Small Group Communication Research of the 1970s: A Synthesis and Critique," *Central States Speech Journal*, 31, 1980, pp. 197-213; and Michael S. Frank, "The Essence of Leadership," *Public Personnel Management*, 22(3), Fall 1993, pp. 281-289.

4. For a discussion of how to develop leadership skills, see Teri Kwal Gamble and Michael W. Gamble, *Leading With Communication*. Thousand Oaks, CA: Sage, 2013; Stephen S. Kaagan, *Leadership Games*, Thousand Oaks, CA: Sage, 1999; Louis B. Harle and Charlotte S. Waisman, The *Leadership Training Activity Book*, New York: Amacom, 2004; and Rob Roy and Chris Larson, *The Navy Seal Art of War: Leadership Lessons From the World's Most Elite Fighting Force*. New York: Crown, 2015.

5. Robert Channick, "Corporate Team Building Starts Elevating Its Game," *The Record*, July 23, 2017, p. 28.

6. Craig Pearce, "Follow the Leaders," *Wall Street Journal*, July 7, 2008, pp. R8, R12.

7. Naomi Shragai, "Solving Clashes and Conflicts at Work," *Financial Times*, April 22, 2016, p. 10.

8. Douglas McGregor, *The Human Side of Enterprise*. New York: McGraw-Hill, 2006.

9. Norman Augustine and Kenneth Adelman, *Shakespeare in Charge*. New York: Miramax Books, 2001.

10. For a classic study on leadership style, see K. Lewin, R. Lippit, and R. K. White, "Patterns of Aggressive Behavior in Experimentally Created Social Climates," *Journal of Social Psychology*, 10, 1939, pp. 271-299; see also N. Bhatti, G. M. Maitlop, M. S. Hashmi, and F. M. Shaikh, "The Impact of Autocratic and Democratic Leadership Style on Job Satisfaction," *International Business Research*, 5(2), pp. 292-201; and K. Adams and G. J. Galanes, *Communicating in Groups Applications and Skills*, 9th ed. New York: McGraw-Hill, 2015, p. 260.

11. For an early study on trait theory, see Frederick Thrasher, *The Gang: A Study of 1313 Gangs in Chicago*. Chicago: University of Chicago Press, 1927.

12. Marvin Shaw, *Group Dynamics: The Psychology of Small Group Behavior*, 3rd ed. New York: McGraw-Hill, 1981.

13. See Fred Fiedler, *A Theory of Leadership Effectiveness*. New York: McGraw-Hill, 1967.

14. Keith Davis, *Human Relations at Work*. New York: McGraw-Hill, 1967.

15. See, e.g., F. E. Fiedler, "Personality and Situational Determinants of Leadership Effectiveness," in D. Cartwright and A. Zander, eds., *Group Dynamics Research and Theory*, 3rd ed. New York: Harper & Row, 1968.

16. P. Hersey and K. Blanchard, *Management of Organizational Behavior*, 10th ed. Boston: Pearson, 2012.

17. See Stephen Covey, *The 7 Habits of Highly Effective People*. New York: Simon & Schuster, 2013.

18. Phred Dvorak and Jaclyne Badal, "Neuroscientists Are Finding That Business Leaders Really May Think Differently," *Wall Street Journal*, September 20, 2007, pp. B1, B6; and Andrew Hill, "Beware the Inspirational Boss," *Financial Times*, April 28, 2016, p. 10.

19. See, e.g., M. Z. Hackman and C. E. Johnson, *Leadership: A Communication Perspective*, 6th ed. Long Grove, IL: Waveland Press, 2013; and M. Van Wart, "Lessons From Leadership Theory and Contemporary Challenges of Leaders," *Public Administration Review*, 73(4), pp. 553-565.

20. For an interesting discussion of how conformity pressures can hamper decision making, see Russel Proctor, "Do the Ends Justify the Means? Thinking Critically About 'Twelve Angry Men,'" paper presented at the annual meeting of the Central States Communication Association, Chicago, April 11-14, 1991. See also Russel Proctor, *Now Playing*. Oxford: Oxford University Press, 2009.

21. M. Afzalur Rahim, "Toward a Theory of Managing Organizational Conflict," *International Journal of Conflict Management*, 13(3), 2002, pp. 206-235.

22. Robert Blake and Jane Mouton, "The Fifth Achievement," *Journal of Applied Behavioral Science*, 6, 1970, pp. 413-426.

23. Alan Filley, *Interpersonal Conflict Resolution*. Glenview, IL: Scott Foreman, 1979; and W. W. Wilmot and J. L. Hocker, *Interpersonal Conflict*, 8th ed. New York: McGraw-Hill, 2013.

24. John Schwartz and Matthew L. Wald, "NASA's Curse!" *New York Times*, March 9, 2003, p. WK5.

25. Morton Deutsch, "Conflicts: Productive and Destructive," *Journal of Social Issues*, 25, 1969, pp. 7-43; H. Whitteman, "Group Member Satisfaction: A Conflict Related Account," *Small Group Research*, 22, 1992, pp. 24-58; and R. C. Pace, "Personalized and Depersonalized Conflict and Small Group Discussion: An Examination of Differences," *Small Group Research*, 21, 1991, pp. 79-96.

26. Jim Collins, *How the Mighty Fall*. New York: Random House, 2010.

27. Irving Janis, *Groupthink: Psychological Studies of Policy Decisions and Fiascos*. Boston: Houghton Mifflin, 1982.

28. Robert M. Sapolsky, "The Brain Science of Conformity," *Wall Street Journal*, April 22-23, 2017, p. C2.

29. Benedict Carey, "How to Turn a Herd on Wall St." *New York Times*, April 6, 2008, pp. WK1, WK4.

30. See Ori Brafman and Rom Brafman, *Sway: The Irresistible Pull of Irrational Behavior*. New York: Doubleday, 2008; and Robert Thaler and Cass Sunstein, *Nudge: Improving Decisions About Health, Wealth, and Happiness*. New Haven, CT: Yale University Press, 2008.

31. Joseph Nye, "Good Leadership Is Deciding How to Decide," *Financial Times*, April 1, 2008, p. 13.

32. Adapted from *Aesop's Fables*.

33. See, e.g., Larry Leslie, *Mass Communication Ethics: Decision Making in Post Modern Culture*, 2nd ed. Boston: Houghton Mifflin, 2003; Barbara Ehrenreich, "In Defense of Talk Shows," *Time*, December 4, 1995, p. 92; and Howard Kurtz, *Hot Air*. New York Basic Books, 1997.

34. For a description of how to promote a win-win approach to conflict, see Deborah Weider Hatfield, "A Unit in Conflict Management Communication Skills," *Communication Education*, 30, 1981, pp. 265-273; Joyce L Hocker and William Wilmot, *Interpersonal Conflict*, 3rd ed. Dubuque, IA: Brown, 1991; and Herb Cohen, *Negotiate This!* New York: Warner Books, 2007.

35. M. T. Claes, "Women, Men, and Management Styles," in Paula J. Dubeck and Dana Cunn, eds., *Workplace/Women's Place: An Anthology*, 2nd ed. Los Angeles: Roxbury, 2005; and A. H. Eagly and S. J. Karau, "Role Congruity Theory of Prejudice Toward Female Leaders," *Psychological Review*, 109(3), 2002, pp. 573-598.

36. R. I. Kabacoff, "Gender Differences in Organizational Leadership: A Large Sample Study," paper presented at the meeting of the American Psychological Association, San Francisco, CA, 1998.

37. Susan Chira, "Why Women Aren't CEOs," *New York Times*, July 27, 2017, pp. SR1, SR6-7.

38. Sarah Gordon, "Female Leaders Boost the Bottom Line," *Financial Times*, September 27, 2017, p. 9.

39. J. K. Fletcher, "The Paradox of Post Heroic Leadership: Gender Matters" (Working Paper No. 17). Boston Center for Gender in Organization, Simmons Graduate School of Management, 2003.

40. See, e.g., T. D. Daniels, B. K. Spiker, and M. J. Papa, *Perspectives on Organizational Communication*, 4th ed. New York: McGraw-Hill, 1997.

41. Jennie Yabroff, "Betas Rule", *Newsweek*, June 4, 2007, pp. 64-65.

42. Chira, pp. SR6-7.

43. Deborah Tannen, *The Argument Culture: Moving From Debate to Dialogue*. New York: Random House, 1998.

44. Joyce F. Benenson, Sheri. Aikins-Ford, and Nicholas H. Apostoleris, "Girls' Assertiveness in the Presence of Boys," *Small Group Research*, 29, 1998, pp. 198-211.

45. See, e.g., Daniel Canary, William Cupach, and Susan Messman, *Relational Conflict*. Thousand Oaks, CA: Sage, 1995.

46. Majaana Linderman, Tuja Harakko, and Lisa Keltilangas-Jarvinen, "Age and Gender Differences in Adolsecents' Reactions to Conflict Situations: Aggression, Prosociality, and Withdrawal," *Journal of Youth and Adolescence*, 26, 1997 pp. 339-351.

47. Canary, Cupach, and Messman.

48. J. Stier and M. Kjellin, "Communication Challenges in Multinational Project Work: Obstacles and Tools for Reaching Common Understandings," *Journal of Intercultural Communication*, 24, 2010, pp. 1-12.

49. Anthony DePalma, "It Takes More Than a Visa to Do Business in Mexico," *New York Times*, June 26, 1994.

50. Lea P. Steward, "Japanese and American Management: Participative Decision Making," in L. A. Samovar, R. E. Porter, and E. R. McDaniel, eds., *Intercultural Communication: A Reader*, 12th ed. Belmont, CA: Wadsworth, 2008.

51. Dolores Cathcart and Robert Cathcart, "Japanese Social Experiences and Concept of Groups," in L. A. Samovar, R. E. Porter, and E. R. McDaniel, eds., *Intercultural Communication: A Reader*, 4th ed. Belmont, CA: Wadsworth, 1985.

52. Marie Brennan, "Mismanagement and Quality Circles: How Middle Managers Influence Direct Participation." *Employee Relations*, 13, 1991, pp. 22-32.

53. Pearce, 2008.

54. Ibid.

55. Rebecca Knight, "When Three Generations Can Work Better Than One," *Financial Times*, September 15, 2009, p. 10.

56. Deborah Tannen, *Talking From 9 to 5*. New York, Morrow, 1994.

57. Keith Ferrazzi, "How to Manage Conflict in Virtual Teams," *Harvard Business Review*, November 19, 2012, https://hbr.org/2012/11/how-to-manage-conflict-in-virt.

58. Eric Timmerman and Craig Scott, "Virtually Working: Communicative and Structural Predictors of Media Use and Key Outcomes in Virtual Work Teams," *Communication Monographs*, 73, 2008 pp. 108-136.

59. Simone S. Oliver, "Who Elected Me Mayor? I Did." *New York Times*, August 19, 2010, pp. E1, E2.

60. David Gelles, "The Person at Work Can Be a Disruptive Mix, *Financial Times*, April 20, 2011, p. 2.

61. Teresa McAleavy, "Don't Let Bullies Do a Job on You," *The Record*, October 23, 2007, p. B3.

Chapter 11

1. David Wallechinsky, Irving Wallace, and Amy Wallace, *The Book of Lists.* New York: Morrow, 1977, p. 469. See also K. K. Dwyer and M. M. Davidson, "Is Public Speaking Really More Feared Than Death?" *Communication Research Reports*, 29, April-June 2012, pp. 99-107.

2. Ellen Joan Pollock, "The Selling of a Golden Speech," *Wall Street Journal*, March 12, 1999, p. B1.

3. Halina Ablamowicz, "Using a Speech Apprehension Questionnaire as a Tool to Reduce Students' Fear of Public Speaking," *Communication Teacher*, 19, July 2005, pp. 98-102.

4. See, e.g., R. R. Behnke, A. N. Finn, and C. R. Sawyer, "Audience Perceived Anxiety Patterns of Public Speakers," *Communication Quarterly*, 51(4), 2003, pp. 470-481; R.

R. Behnke and C. R. Sawyer, "Milestones of Anticipatory Public Speaking Anxiety," *Communication Education*, 48, 1999, pp. 165-172; See also A. N. Finn, "Public Speaking: What Causes Some to Panic?" *Communication Currents*, 4(4), 2009, pp. 1-2.

5. J. D. Mladenka, C. R. Sawyer, and R. R. Behnke, "Anxiety Sensitivity and Speech Trait Anxiety as Predictors of State Anxiety During Public Speaking," *Communication Quarterly*, 46, 1998, pp. 417-429; and Penny Addison, Ele Clay, Shuang Xie, Chris R. Sawyer, and Ralph R. Behnke, "Worry as a Function of Public Speaking State Anxiety Type," *Communication Reports*, 16, 2003, pp. 125-131.

6. Joe Ayres, "Perception of Speaking Ability: An Explanation for Speech Fright," *Communication Education*, July 1986, pp. 275-287.

7. See, e.g., Bernardo J. Carducci with Phillip G. Zimbardo, "Are You Shy?" *Psychology Today*, November/December 1995, pp. 34-41, 64-70, 78-82.

8. See D. W. Klopf, "Cross Cultural Apprehension Research: A Summary of Pacific Basin Studies," in J. A. Daly and J. A. McCroskey, eds., *Avoiding Communication: Shyness, Reticence, and Communication Apprehension.* Beverly Hills, CA: Sage, 1984, pp. 157-169; D. W. Klopf and R. E. Cambra, "Communication Apprehension Among College Students in America, Australia, Japan, and Korea,"

Journal of Psychology, 102, 1979, pp. 27-31; and S. M. Ralston, R. Ambler, and J. N. Scudder, "Reconsidering the Impact of Racial Differences in the College Public Speaking Classroom on Minority Student Communication Anxiety," *Communication Reports*, 4, 1991, pp. 43-50.

9. Elie Wiesel, *Souls on Fire.* New York: Summit, 1982.

10. Michael J. Lewis, "The Art of War," *New York Times Book Review*, September 17 2017, p. 21.

11. Michael Skapinker, "Chief Execs Should Learn the Art of Oratory," *Financial Times*, January 28, 2008, p. 11.

12. Wynton C. Hall, "Do Effective Speakers Make Effective Presidents?" *USA Today*, February 28, 2008, p. 11A.

13. Roger Ailes, *You Are the Message.* New York: Doubleday, 1989.

14. Ellen DeGeneres, Tulane commencement speech, 2009, www.goodnet.org/articles/1087.

15. Barbara Mueller, *Communicating With the Multicultural Consumer: Theoretical and Practical Perspectives.* New York: Peter Lang, 2008; Larry A. Samovar, Richard E. Porter, Edwin R. McDaniel, and Carolyn Roy, *Communication Between Cultures*, 9th ed., Belmont, CA: Wadsworth, 2016.

16. For a look at the topics treated recently in public speeches by political, organizational, and thought leaders, peruse Ted.com and see 2012 through 2017 issues of *Vital Speeches of the Day*.

17. Thomas Leech, *How to Prepare, Stage, and Deliver Winning Presentations.* New York: Amacom, 1982, p. 11.

Chapter 12

1. Randy Reddick and Elliot King, *The Online Student.* Fort Worth, TX: Harcourt Brace College, 1996, p. 3; information on conducting research, pp. 161-179, is particularly valuable. See also Wayne C. Booth, Gregory C. Colomb, and Joseph M. Williams, *The Craft of Research*, 2nd ed. Chicago: University of Chicago Press, 2003.

2. Russ Juskalian, "Video Search Engines Help Sort It All Out," *USA Today*, July 30, 2008, p. 3B.

3. For a more comprehensive treatment of supporting materials, see Teri Gamble and Michael Gamble, *The Public Speaking Playbook*, 2nd ed. Thousand Oaks, CA: Sage, 2018.

4. Megan Solan, "Serving Those Who Serve," in *Winning Orations.* Mankato, MN: Interstate Oratorical Association, 2005.

5. Ibid.

6. Susan E. Rice, "Why America Needs the U.N.," *Vital Speeches*, April 2011, pp. 147-150.

7. For a discussion of the power of examples in public speaking, see Gamble and Gamble; see also Scott Consigny, "The Rhetorical Example," *Southern Speech Communication Journal*, 41, 1976, pp. 121-134.

8. Solomon D. Trujillo, "Two Lives: The One We Make Defines Our Legacy," *Vital Speeches of the Day*, 66(6), January 1, 2000, p. 168.

9. Risa Lavizzo-Mourey, M.D., "Changing the Norms of Medicine and Health," *Vital Speeches of the Day*, June 2010, pp. 276-282.

10. Harvey Mackay, "Postgraduate Life," *Vital Speeches of the Day*, August 2008, p. 359.

11. William L. Laurence, "Eyewitness Account: Atomic Bomb Mission Over Nagasaki," *New York Times*, September 1945.

12. "I Have a Dream," by Martin Luther King, Jr. Reprinted by arrangement with the estate of Martin Luther King, Jr. c/o Writers House as agent for the proprietor, New York, NY: Copyright 1963 Dr. Martin Luther King, Jr., copyright renewed 1991 Coretta Scott King.

13. For decades, studies revealed how organization affects reception. For example, see Christopher Spicer and Ronald Bassett, "The Effect of Organization on Learning From an Informative Message," *Southern States Communication Journal*, 41, 1976, pp. 290-299; and John E. Baird Jr., "The Effects of Speech Summaries Upon Audience Comprehension of Expository Speech of Varying Quality and Complexity," *Central States Speech Journal*, 25, 1974, pp. 119-127.

14. Richard Nisbett, *The Geography of Thought: How Asians and Westerners Think Differently . . . and Why.* New York: Free Press, 2003.

15. National Public Radio, "Analysis: Geography of Thought," *Talk of the Nation.* Broadcast of interview of Richard Nisbett by Neal Conan, March 3, 2003. National Public Radio, Inc. Used with permission.

16. Ibid.

17. D. L. Thistlethwaite, H. DeHaan, and J. Kamenetzky suggested that a message is more easily understood and accepted if transitions are used; see "The Effect of Directive and Non-Directive Communication Procedures on Attitudes," *Journal of Abnormal and Social Psychology*, 51, 1955, pp. 107-118. Also of value on this aspect of speech organization is E. Thompson, "Some Effects of Message Structure on Listeners' Comprehension," *Speech Monographs*, 34, 1967, pp. 51-57.

18. See, e.g., Arran Gare, "Narratives and Culture: The Role of Stories in Self-Creation," *Telos*, Winter 2002; Jessica Lee Shumake, "Reconceptualizing Communication and Rhetoric From a Feminist Perspective," *Guidance and Counseling*, Summer 2002; and Janet Malcolm, "The Storyteller: How Rachel Maddow Constructs a Narrative," *New Yorker*, October 9, 2017, pp. 38-47.

19. Edward T. Hall. *The Hidden Dimension.* New York: Doubleday, 1966.

20. Myron W. Lustig, Jolene Koester, and Rona Halualani, *Intercultural Competence: Interpersonal Communication Across Cultures*, 8th ed. New York: Pearson, 2017.

21. See, e.g., R. S. Zaharna, "Rhetorical Ethnocentrism: Understanding the

Rhetorical Landscape of Arab–American Relations," paper presented at meeting of the Speech Communication Association, 1995, http://nw08.american.edu/~zaharna/rhetoric.htm.

22. For a more comprehensive treatment of introductions and conclusions, see Gamble and Gamble, *The Public Speaking Playbook*, 2nd ed. Thousand Oaks, CA: Sage, 2018.

23. David Petraeus, "The Surge of Ideas," *Vital Speeches of the Day*, July 2010, pp. 314-320.

24. Pink, "We Don't Change," *Vital Speeches of the Day*, October 2017, p. 307.

25. Adrienne Hallett, "Dying in Your Sleep," in *Winning Orations*. Northfield, MN: Interstate Oratorical Association, 2000, p. 99. Reprinted with permission.

26. Romaine Seguin, "Becoming Visible: Insights for Working Women From the Women of Hidden Figures," *Vital Speeches of the Day*, October 2017, pp. 304-306.

27. Marie S. Bilik, "Public Schools Must Thrive—Not Just Survive—in Troubled Times," *Vital Speeches of the Day*, July 2010, pp. 324-325.

28. Jessy Ohl, "Rising Sun, Rising Cancer," in *Winning Orations*. Mankato, MN: Interstate Oratorical Association, 2007, p. 31.

29. The quote from Robert Kennedy's speech has been attributed to George Bernard Shaw.

Chapter 13

1. Merrie Spaeth, "'Prop' Up Your Speaking Skills," *Wall Street Journal*, July 1, 1996, A14.

2. See Richard E. Mayer, ed., *Multimedia Learning*. New York: Cambridge University Press, 2009; Dale Cyphert, "PowerPoint and the Evolution of Electronic Evidence From the Contemporary Business Presentation," *American Communication Journal*, 11(2), Summer 2009, pp. 1-20.

3. See Garr Reynolds, *Presentation Zen*, 2nd ed. Berkeley CA: New Riders, 2012.

4. See Elena P. Zayas-Baya, "Instructional Media in the Total Language Picture," *International Journal of Instructional Media*, 5, 1977-1978, pp. 145-150.

5. Mary Panzer, "Photojournalism for the Web Generation," *Wall Street Journal*, July 8, 2008, p. D7.

6. Jae Yang and Kari Gelles, "USA Today Snapshots," *USA Today*, August 13, 2009, p. D7.

7. "America Incarcerated," *Time*, March 17, 2008, p. 14.

8. See, e.g., Drew Skau, "11 Infographics About Infographics," February 18, 2013, http://www.scribblelive.com/blog/2013/02/18/11-infographics-about-infographics.

9. See Richard B. Woodward, "Debatable 'Evidence,'" *Wall Street Journal*, May 4, 2011, p. D5, and David W. Dunlap, "Fake Bin Laden Death Photos Spread in Web and Fool Some Newspapers," *New York Times*, May 5, 2011, p. A17.

10. "College Faked Photo in Pitch for Diversity," *The Record*, September 21, 2000, p. A13; for more on this subject, see David D. Perlmutter and Nicole Smith Dahman, "(In)Visible Evidence in the Apollo Moon Landings," *Visual Communication*, 7(2), May 2008, pp. 229-251.

11. Pamela Grim, "Too Close to Ebola," *Discover*, June 2003, pp. 42-47.

12. Pinker, quoted in Ian Parker, "Absolute PowerPoint," *New Yorker*, May 28, 2001, pp, 76-87; also see Mark R. Stoner, "PowerPoint in a New Key," *Communication Education*, 56(3), July 2007, pp. 354-381.

13. L. Zuckerman, "Words Go Right to the Brain, But Can They Stir the Heart?" *New York Times*, April 17, 1999, pp. A17-A19.

14. Greg Jaffe, "What's Your Point, Lieutenant? Just Cut to the Pie Charts," *Wall Street Journal*, April 26, 2000, pp. A1, A6.

15. June Kronholz, "PowerPoint Goes to School," *Wall Street Journal*, November 12, 2002, pp. B1, B6.

16. Elizabeth Bumiller, "We Have Met the Enemy and He is PowerPoint," *New York Times*, April 27, 2010, pp. A1, A8.

17. Dean Dad, "PowerPoint Hates Freedom," April 28, 2010, https://www.insidehighered.com/blogs/confessions-community-college-dean/powerpoint-hates-freedom.

18. Ian Parker, "Absolute PowerPoint," *New Yorker*, May 28, 2001, pp. 76-87.

19. Frances Cole Jones, *How to WOW*. New York: Ballantine Books, 2008, p. 132; see also Dale Cyphert, "Presentation

Technology in the Age of Electronic Eloquence: From Visual Aid to Visual Rhetoric," *Communication Education*, 56(2), April 2007, pp. 168-192.

20. Roger Ailes, *You Are the Message*. New York: Doubleday, 1989, p. 17.

21. Ibid.

22. John Baldoni, "How to Speak in Soundbites," May 14, 2014, www.forbes.com/sites/johnbaldoni/2014/05/14/how-to-speak-in-sound-bites/#5f472d836599.

23. Ailes.

Chapter 14

1. See Francis Cairncross, "The Roots of Revolution and the Trendspotter's Guide to New Communications," in Erik P. Bucy, *Living in the Information Age: A New Media Reader*. Stamford, CT: Wadsworth/Thomson Learning, 2002, pp. 3-10.

2. Daniel Pink, *A Whole New Mind: Moving From the Information Age to the Conceptual Age*. New York: Riverhead Books, 2005; and Garr Reynolds, *Presentation Zen*. New York: New Ridges Press, 2008.

3. Richard Saul Wurman, *Information Anxiety 2*. Indianapolis: Que, 2000.

4. Although compiled several decades ago, a valuable source to consult is Charles Petrie, "Informative Speaking: A Summary and Bibliography of Related Research," *Speech Monographs*, 30, 1963, pp. 79-91.

5. See, e.g., Brendan Lemon, "Audiences Today Are

Getting in on the Act," *New York Times*, October 8, 2000, pp. AR5, AR22.

Chapter 15

1. See, e.g., Gerald R. Miller, "On Being Persuaded: Some Basic Distinctions," in James Price Dillard and Michael Pfau, eds., *The Persuasive Handbook: Developments in Theory and Practice*. Thousand Oaks, CA: Sage, 2002, pp. 3-16; and P. Brinol, D. D. Rucker, and R. E. Petty, "Naïve Theories About Persuasion: Implications for Information Processing and Consumer Attitude Change," *International Journal of Advertising: The Review of Marketing Communications*, 34, 2015, pp. 85-105.

2. Robert B. Cialdini, *Influence: Science and Practice*, 4th edition. Boston: Allyn & Bacon, 2001, p. 239. See also Cialdini, *Influence: The Psychology of Persuasion*, rev. ed. New York: Harper Business, 2006.

3. See Wallace Folderingham, *Perspectives on Persuasion*. Boston: Allyn & Bacon, 1966, p. 33; and James Price Dillard, "Persuasion Past and Present: Attitudes Aren't What They Used to Be," *Communication Monographs*, 60(1), March 1993, pp. 90-97.

4. Based on a speech by Amanda Taylor, "Drowsy Driving: A Deadly Epidemic," in *Winning Orations*. Mankato, MN: Interstate Oratorical Association, 2000, pp. 12-15.

5. Speakers can establish credibility early in a speech. For example, see R. Brooks and T. Scheidel, "Speech

as Process: A Case Study," *Speech Monographs*, 35, 1968, pp 1-7; and James M. Kouzes and Barry Z. Pozner, *Credibility: How Leaders Gain and Lose it, Why People Demand It*. New York: John Wiley & Sons, 2011.

6. Milton Rokeach, *The Open and Closed Mind*. New York: Basic Books, 1960.

7. Prominent theorists such as Leon Festinger, Fritz Heider, and Theodore Newcomb consider the desire for consistency a central motivator of behavior. For a more contemporary discussion of the topic, see Robert B. Cialdini, *Influence*, rev. ed. New York: Quill, 2000.

8. Cialdini, 2001, p. 116.

9. Ibid.

10. Abraham Maslow, *Motivation and Personality*. New York: Harper & Row, 1954, pp. 80-92.

11. See Buzz Bissinger, "Why College Football Should Be Banned," *Wall Street Journal*, May 5-6, 2012, p. C3.

12. See, e.g., Nancy M. Cavender and Howard Kahane, *Logic and Contemporary Rhetoric: The Use of Reason in Everyday Life*, 11th ed. Belmont, CA: Wadsworth, 2010.

Appendix

1. Eli Amdur, "How Workers Should Prepare for the World in 2050," *The Record*, May 23, 2008, pp. J1-J2.

2. Melinda Ligos, "Young Job Seekers Need New Clues," *New York Times*, August 8, 2001, p. G1; and Lois Einhorn report in "An Inner View of the Job Interview:

An Investigation of Successful Communicative Behavior," *Communication Education*, 30, pp. 217-228, that successful candidates were able to identify with the employer, support their arguments, organize their thoughts, clarify their ideas, and speak fluently.

3. Eli Amdur, "If It's Short Term, It's Not Really Networking," *The Record*, November 5, 2017, p. 1J.

4. John A. Challenger, "Internships Are Critical, But Difficult to Land," *The Record*, September 19, 2010, p. J1. See also Susan Adams, "10 Best Sites for Finding an Internship," *Forbes*, January 30, 2015.

5. John A. Challenger, "Social Networking Explodes as Job-Search Tool," *The Record*, February 27, 2011, p. J1.

6. Ibid.

7. Eli Amdur, "The Great All-American Cover Letter Challenge," *The Record*, September 12, 2010, pp. J1-J2.

8. Eli Amdur, "On a Résumé, There's Nothing Like a Good Opening," *The Record*, January 27, 2008, pp. J1, J2. See also "How to Write an Opening Statement for Your Résumé," www.gettinghired.com, January 26, 2012.

9. Rob Walker, "Résumés That Grab Digital Eyes," *New York Times*, July 10, 2016, p. BU7.

10. Barbara Kiviat, "Résumé? Check. Nice Suit? Check. Webcam," *Time*, November 9, 2009, pp. 89-90; Jonnelle Marte, "Nailing the Interview," *Wall Street Journal*, March 14, 2010, p. B4.

11. Jae Yang and Paul Trap, "Office Team Survey of 1,007 Workers," *USA Today*, October 4, 2017, p. 1B.

12. Adam Geller, "Problem Postings," *The Record*, March 17, 2003; and Kris Maher, "Résumé Rustling Threatens Online Job Sites," *Wall Street Journal*, February 25, 2003, pp. B1, B10.

13. See Mark L. Knapp, Roderick P. Hart, Gustav W. Friedrich, and Gary M Schulman, "The Rhetoric of Goodbye: Verbal and Nonverbal Correlates of Human Leave-Taking," *Speech Monographs*, 40, 1973, pp. 182-198.

14. David Koeppel, "On a Résumé, Don't Mention Moon Pies or Water Cannons," *New York Times*, November 24, 2001, Section 10, p. 1.

15. Charles J. Stewart and William B. Cash Jr., *Interviewing Principles and Practices*, 15th ed. New York: McGraw-Hill, 2017.

16. Arlene Hirsch, "Tell Me About Yourself Doesn't Mean 'Tell It All,'" *The Record*, November 28, 2004, pp. J1, J2; and Anthony DePalma, "Preparing for 'Tell Us About Yourself,'" *New York Times*, July 27, 2003, p. NJ1. See also Carole Martin, "Tell Me About Yourself—Ways to Answer This Question," www.monster.com.

17. Ibid.

18. Eli Amdur, "Train Yourself to Be a S.T.A.R. During Job Interviews," *The Record*, September 4, 2005, p. J1. See also Mike Simpson, "How to Master the S.T.A.R. Method for Interview Questions," 2017, https://theinterviewguys.com/star-method.

19. Eli Amdur, "An Interview Is a Two-Way Deal, So Ask Questions," *The Record*, September 4, 2005, p. J1.

20. Eli Amdur, "Be the Person Companies Will Want to Hire," *The Record*, October 24, 2004, pp. J1-J2.

21. Malcolm Gladwell, "What Do Job Interviews Really Tell Us?" *New Yorker*, May 29, 2000, pp. 68-86.

22. "Initial Minutes of Job Interview Are Critical," *USA Today*, January 2000, p. 8.

23. Eli Amdur, "The 10 General Rules to Help You Be a Good Interviewer," *The Record*, August 5, 2007, pp. J1, J2.

24. Einhorn.

25. Rachel Emma Silverman and Kemba Dunham, "Even in a Tight Market, Job Hunters Can Blunder," *Wall Street Journal*, June 20, 2000, p. B12.

26. See Gladwell, pp. 68-72, 84-86; and C. J. Stewart and W. B. Cash Jr., *Interviewing Principles and Practices*, 15th ed. New York: McGraw-Hill, 2017.

27. Marvin Walberg, "Interviewing: Expect the Unexpected," *The Record*, September 4, 2009, p. A9.

28. Joann Lublin, "Notes to Interviewers Should Go Beyond a Simple Thank You." *Wall Street Journal*, February 5, 2008, p. B1.

29. Ibid.

30. Sarah Skidore Sell, "Poll: Interview Questions Often Improper," *The Record*, November 3, 2017, p. 7L.

31. Paul Davidson, "'What's Your Salary?' A No-No in Interviews," *The Record*, May 1, 2017, p. 5A.

32. From David Kirby, "Selling Yourself: There Are

Questions You Shouldn't Answer," adapted from *New York Times*, January 30, 2001.

33. See, e.g., F. Mahoney, "Adjusting the Interview to Avoid Cultural Bias," *Journal of Career Planning and Employment*, 52, 1992, pp. 41-43.

34. Mary Williams Walsh, "Money Isn't Everything," *New York Times*, January 30, 2001, p. 10.

35. Claire Cain Miller, "Job Disconnect: Male Applicants, Feminine Language," *New York Times*, January 17, 2017, p. A3.

36. Ibid.

37. Marjorie Valbrun, "More Muslims Claim They Suffer Job Bias," *Wall Street Journal*, April 15, 2003, pp. B1, B8. See also Zak Adesina and Oana Marcico, "Is It Easier to Get a Job if You Are Adam or Mohammed? BBC World, February 20, 2017.

38. John Simons, "Hiring Bias Unchanged Over Time,

Study Says," *Wall Street Journal*, October 4, 2017, p. B9.

39. Alexandra Olson, "More Companies Seeking Diverse Advertising Teams," *The Record*, November 12, 2017, pp. 1B, 6B.

40. Sarah E. Needleman, "Job Seekers: Put Your Web Savvy to Work," *Wall Street Journal*, September 9, 2007, p. B3.

41. Kris Maher, "Blogs Catch on as Online Tool for Job Seekers and Recruiters, *Wall Street Journal*, September 28, 2004, p. B10. See also Superior Group, "The Top Ten HR and Recruiting Blogs," February, 2016.

42. For a discussion of online search techniques, see Cynthia Leshin, *Internet Investigations in Business Communication*. Saddle River, NJ: Prentice Hall, 1997.

43. See Zane K. Quible, "Electronic Résumés: Their Time Is Coming," *Business

Communication Quarterly*, 58, pp. 5-9. See also Sovren Group, *Tips for Electronic Résumés*, 2017, https://www.sovren.com/faq/TipsForElectronicResumes.pdf.

44. Wallace V. Schmidt and Roger N. Conaway, *Results Oriented Interviewing Principles, Practices and Procedures*. Boston: Allyn & Bacon, 1991, p. 11.

45. Kelsey Gee, "Radical Hiring Experiment: Résumés Are Out," *Wall Street Journal*, June 27, 2017, p. B4.

46. Mark Cedella, "Top 10 Blunders of Online Job Hunters," *The Record*, September 5, 2004, p. J1.

47. David Koeppel, "Web Can Help, but a Job Hunt Still Takes Lots of Hard Work," *New York Times*, September 12, 2004, pp. MB1, 3.

48. Sarah E. Needleman, "Thx for the Iview! I Wud (Heart) to Work 4 U!" *Wall Street Journal*, July 29, 2008, pp. D1, D4.

Index